2010
Poet's Market®

includes a 1-year online subscription to
Poet's Market on WritersMarket.com

W9-BJQ-971

WritersMarket.com
WHERE & HOW TO SELL WHAT YOU WRITE

THE ULTIMATE MARKET RESEARCH TOOL FOR WRITERS

To register your
2010 Poet's Market book and
START YOUR 1-YEAR ONLINE GENRE ONLY SUBSCRIPTION,
scratch off the block below to reveal your activation
code, then go to www.WritersMarket.com. Click on
"Sign Up Now" and enter your contact information
and activation code. It's that easy!

- UPDATED MARKET LISTINGS FOR YOUR INTEREST AREA
- EASY-TO-USE SEARCHABLE DATABASE
- DAILY UPDATES
- RECORD KEEPING TOOLS
- INDUSTRY NEWS
- PROFESSIONAL TIPS AND ADVICE

2010

23RD ANNUAL EDITION

POET'S
MARKET ®

Robert Lee Brewer, Editor

WRITER'S DIGEST BOOKS
CINCINNATI, OH

Publisher & Editorial Director, Writing Communities: Jane Friedman
Managing Editor, Writer's Digest Market Books: Alice Pope

Writer's Market Web site: www.writersmarket.com
Writer's Digest Web site: www.writersdigest.com

Distributed in Canada by Fraser Direct
100 Armstrong Avenue
Georgetown, ON, Canada L7G 5S4
Tel: (905) 877-4411

Distributed in the U.K. and Europe by David & Charles
Brunel House, Newton Abbot, Devon, TQ12 4PU, England
Tel: (+44) 1626 323200, Fax: (+44) 1626 323319
E-mail: postmaster@davidandcharles.co.uk

Distributed in Australia by Capricorn Link
P.O. Box 704, Windsor, NSW 2756 Australia
Tel: (02) 4577-3555

ISSN: 0883-5470
ISBN-13: 978-1-58297-582-5
ISBN-10: 1-58297-582-5

Cover design by Claudean Wheeler
Production coordinated by Greg Nock
Photographs © Frédéric Cirou/PhotoAlto

Contents

From the Editor

Poets are among the most passionate writers I know (and as the editor of Writer's Market I know quite a few). After all, poets learn very early in the process that there's just not any money in poetry unless they're already celebrities or have won every major literary prize available. Even then, they're probably supplementing their incomes with a "real" job. Yet, poets can't help but write poetry.

This edition of *Poet's Market* (my first as editor) has been designed to help poets share their passion with readers. The articles in the front of the book include helpful tips and information on how to deal with problem editors, avoid poetry cons, and submit your poems. These articles also cover such topics as how to have a successful poetry reading, an explanation of chapbooks, poetry translation, and how to handle the business of poetry.

Of course, there are hundreds of listings for publishers of books and chapbooks, magazines and journals, contests and awards, and conferences and workshops. Use these to narrow down where you submit your work, but always be sure (and here's an important tip) to check their websites (if available) for their most recent news and submission guidelines. It could make the difference between acceptance and rejection.

While creativity and the bending of rules can pay off when writing poetry, it's usually to a poet's benefit to follow the rules when submitting, whether online or via mail. If you devote the same time to submitting that you do to honing your poetic craft, you should find success getting published.

Until next time, keep poeming!

Robert Lee Brewer
Editor, *Poet's Market*
http://blog.writersdigest.com/poeticasides
robert.brewer@fwmedia.com

Getting Started

(and Using This Book)

Delving into the pages of *Poet's Market* indicates a commitment--you've decided to take that big step and begin submitting your poems for publication. How do you *really* begin, though? Here are eight quick tips to help make sense of the marketing/submission process:

1. Be an avid reader. The best way to hone your writing skills (besides writing) is to immerse yourself in poetry of all kinds. It's essential to study the masters; however, from a marketing standpoint, it's equally vital to read what your contemporaries are writing and publishing. Read journals and magazines, chapbooks and collections, anthologies for a variety of voices; scope out the many poetry sites on the Internet. Develop an eye for quality, and then use that eye to assess your own work. Don't rush to publish until you know you're writing the best poetry you're capable of producing.

2. Know what you like to write—and what you write best. Ideally, you should be experimenting with all kinds of poetic forms, from free verse to villanelles. However, there's sure to be a certain style with which you feel most comfortable, that conveys your true "voice." Whether you favor more formal, traditional verse or avant-garde poetry that breaks all the rules, you should identify which markets publish work similar to yours. Those are the magazines and presses you should target to give your submissions the best chance of being read favorably—and accepted. (See the Subject Index beginning on page 539 to observe how some magazines and presses specify their needs.)

3. Learn the "business" of poetry publishing. Poetry may not be a high-paying writing market, but there's still a right way to go about the "business" of submitting and publishing poems. Learn all you can by reading writing-related books and magazines. Read the articles and interviews in this book for plenty of helpful advice. Surf the Internet for a wealth of sites filled with writing advice, market news and informative links.

4. Research the markets. Study the listings in *Poet's Market* thoroughly; these present submission guidelines, editorial preferences and editors' comments as well as contact information (names, postal and e-mail addresses, Web site URLs). The Magazines/Journals section begins on page 59, the Book/Chapbook Publishers section on page 331, with the Contests & Awards section following on page 367. In addition, the indexes in the back of this book provide insights into what an editor or publisher may be looking for.

However, studying market listings alone won't cut it. The best way to gauge the kinds of poetry a market publishes is to read several issues of a magazine/journal or several of a press's books to get a feel for the style and content of each. If the market has a

Web site, log on and take a look. Web sites may include poetry samples, reviews, archives of past issues, exclusive content, and especially submission guidelines. (If the market is an online publication, the current issue will be available in its entirety.) If the market has no online presence, send for guidelines and sample copies (include a SASE—self-addressed stamped envelope—for guidelines; include appropriate cost for sample copy).

Submission guidelines are pure gold for the specific information they provide. However you acquire them—by SASE or e-mail, online, or in a magazine itself—make them an integral part of your market research.

5. Start slowly. It may be tempting to send your work directly to *The New Yorker* or *Poetry*, but try to adopt a more modest approach if you're just starting out. Most listings in this book display symbols that reflect the level of writing a magazine or publisher prefers to receive. The (○) symbol indicates a market that welcomes submissions from beginning or unpublished poets. As you gain confidence and experience (and increased skill in your writing), you can move on to markets coded with the (◑) symbol. Later, when you've built a publication history, submit to the more prestigious magazines and presses (the ● markets). Although it may tax your patience, slow and steady progress is a proven route to success.

6. Be professional. Professionalism is not something you should "work up to." Make it show in your first submission, from the way you prepare your manuscript to the attitude you project in your communications with editors.

Follow those guidelines. Submit a polished manuscript. (See "Frequently Asked Questions" on page 7 for details on manuscript formatting and preparation.) Choose poems carefully with the editor's needs in mind. *Always* include a SASE with any submission or inquiry. Such practices show respect for the editor, the publication and the process; and they reflect *your* self-respect and the fact that you take your work seriously. Editors love that; and even if your work is rejected, you've made a good first impression that could help your chances with your next submission.

2010 POET'S MARKET KEY TO SYMBOLS

N this market is recently established and appearing for the first time in *Poet's Market*

✖ this market did not appear in the previous edition of *Poet's Market*

◤ this market is located in Canada

◉ this market is located outside the U.S. and Canada

■ this market publishes primarily online

$ this market pays a monetary amount

○ this market welcomes submissions from beginning poets

◑ this market prefers submissions from skilled, experienced poets; will consider work from beginning poets

● this market prefers submissions from poets with a high degree of skill and experience

◎ this market has a specialized focus

⊘ this market does not consider unsolicited submissions

⊘ this market is currently closed to *all* submissions

● indicates market information of special note

ms, mss manuscript(s)

b&w black & white (art/photo)

SASE self-addressed, stamped envelope

IRC International Reply Coupon (replaces return postage when mailing to countries other than your own)

(For words and expressions relating specifically to poetry and submissions, see the Glossaries in the back of this book.)

Submission Tracker

Poem Title	Publication/ Contest	Editor/Contact	Date Sent	Date Returned	Date Accepted	Date Published	Pay Received	Comments

7. Keep track of your submissions. First, do *not* send out the only copies of your work. There are no guarantees your submission won't get lost in the mail, misplaced in a busy editorial office, or vanish into a black hole if the publication or press closes down. Create a special file folder for poems you're submitting. Even if you use a word processing program and store your manuscripts on disk, keep a hard copy file as well (and be sure to back up your electronic files).

Second, establish a tracking system so you always know which poems are where. This can be extremely simple: index cards, a chart created with word processing or database software, or even a simple notebook used as a log. (You can enlarge and photocopy the Submission Tracker on page 4 or use it as a model to design your own version.) Note the titles of the poems submitted (or the title of the collection if you're submitting a book/chapbook manuscript); the name of the publication, press, or contest; date sent; estimated response time; and date returned *or* date accepted. Additional information you may want to log: the name of the editor/contact, date the accepted piece is published and/or issue number of the magazine, type/amount of pay received, rights acquired by the publication or press, and any pertinent comments.

Without a tracking system, you risk forgetting where and when manuscripts were submitted. This is even more problematic if you simultaneously send the same manuscripts to different magazines, presses or contests. And if you learn of an acceptance by one magazine or publisher, you *must* notify the others that the poem or collection you sent them is no longer available. You run a bigger chance of overlooking someone without an organized approach. This causes hard feelings among editors you may have inconvenienced, hurting your chances with these markets in the future.

8. Don't fear rejection. Learn from it. No one enjoys rejection, but every writer faces it. The best way to turn a negative into a positive is to learn as much as you can from your rejections. Don't let them get you down. A rejection slip isn't a permission slip to doubt yourself, condemn your poetry or give up.

Look over the rejection. Did the editor provide any comments about your work or reasons why your poems were rejected? Probably he or she didn't. Editors are extremely busy and don't necessarily have time to comment on rejections. If that's the case, move on to the next magazine or publisher you've targeted and send your work out again.

If, however, the editor *has* commented on your work, pay attention. It counts for something that the editor took the time and trouble to say anything, however brief, good or bad. And consider any remark or suggestion with an open mind. You don't have to agree, but you shouldn't automatically disregard the feedback, either. Tell your ego to sit down and be quiet, then use the editor's comments to review your work from a new perspective. You might be surprised by how much you'll learn from a single scribbled word in the margin; or how encouraged you'll feel from a simple "Try again!" written on the rejection slip.

Keep these eight tips in mind as you prepare your poetry submissions, and keep *Poet's Market* at hand to help you along. Believe in yourself and don't give up! As the number of listings in this book shows, there are many opportunities for beginning poets to become published poets.

GUIDE TO LISTING FEATURES

On page 6 is an example of a Magazines/Journal listing (Book/Chapbook Publishers listings follow a similar format). Note the callouts that identify various format features of the listing. A key to the symbols displayed at the beginning of each listing is located on page 3, on the inside covers of this book and on a pull-out bookmark just inside the front cover.

EASY-TO-USE
REFERENCE
ICONS

WEB SITES

TYPES OF
POETRY
CONSIDERED

SPECIFIC
CONTACT
NAMES

DETAILED
SUBMISSION
GUIDELINES

EDITOR'S
COMMENTS

☑ SLANT: A JOURNAL OF POETRY

Box 5063, University of Central Arkansas, 201 Donaghey Ave., Conway AR 72035-5000. (501)450-5107. Web site: www. uca.edu/english/Slant/. Established 1987. **Contact:** James Fowler, editor.

Magazine Needs *Slant: A Journal of Poetry*, published annually in May, aims "to publish a journal of fine poetry from all regions of the United States and beyond." Wants "traditional and 'modern' poetry, even experimental; moderate length, any subject on approval of Board of Readers." Doesn't want "haiku, translations." Has published poetry by Susan H. Case, Philip Dacey, Elizabeth Howrd, Timothy Martin, Gilbert Wesley Purdy, and Nancy Scott. *Slant* is 120 pages, professionally printed on quality stock, flat-spined, with matte card cover. Receives about 1,400 poems/year, accepts 70-80. Press run is 175 (70-100 subscribers). Sample: $10.

How to Submit Submit up to 5 poems at a time. Lines/poem: poems should be of moderate length. No previously published poems or simultaneous submissions. Submissions should be typed; include SASE. "Put name, address (including e-mail if available), and phone number at the top of each page." Reads submissions September 1-November 15. Comments on rejected poems "on occasion." Guidelines available in magazine, for SASE, or on Web site. Responds in 3-4 months from November 15 deadline. Pays one contributor's copy. Poet retains rights.

Advice "We tend to publish those poems whose execution, line by line, does full justice to their conception. Often the decision to accept comes down to the matter of craft, language."

Frequently Asked Questions

The following FAQ (Frequently Asked Questions) section provides the expert knowledge you need to submit your poetry in a professional manner. Answers to most basic questions, such as "How many poems should I send?," "How long should I wait for a reply?" and "Are simultaneous submissions okay?" can be found by simply reading the listings in the Magazines/Journals and Book/Chapbook Publishers sections. See the introduction to each section for an explanation of the information contained in the listings. Also, see the Glossary of Listing terms on page 492.

Is it okay to submit handwritten poems?

Usually, no. Now and then a publisher or editor makes an exception and accepts handwritten manuscripts. However, check the preferences stated in each listing. If no mention is made of handwritten submissions, assume your poetry should be typed or computer-generated.

How should I format my poems for submission to magazines and journals?

If you're submitting poems by regular mail (also referred to as *land mail*, *postal mail* or *snail mail*), follow this format (also see sample on page 8):

   Poems should be typed or computer-printed on white 8½ × 11 paper of at least 20 lb. weight. Left, right and bottom margins should be at least one inch. Starting ½ inch from the top of the page, type your name, address, telephone number, e-mail address (if you have one) and number of lines in the poem in the *upper right* corner, in individual lines, single-spaced. Space down about six lines and type the poem title, either centered or flush left. The title may appear in all caps or in upper and lower case. Space down another two lines (at least) and begin to type your poem. Poems are usually single-spaced, although some magazines may request double-spaced submissions. (Be alert to each market's preferences.) Double-space between stanzas. Type one poem to a page. For poems longer than one page, type your name in the *upper left* corner; on the next line type a key word from the title of your poem, the page number, and indicate whether the stanza begins or is continued on the new page (i.e., MOTHMAN, Page 2, continue stanza *or* begin new stanza).

   If you're submitting poems by e-mail (also see sample on page 9):

   First, make sure the publication accepts e-mail submissions. This information, when available, is included in all *Poet's Market* listings. In most cases, editors will request that poems be pasted within the body of your e-mail, *not* sent as attachments. Many editors prefer this format because of the danger of viruses, the possibility of software

Articles & Information

Mailed Submission Format

DO leave ¹/₂" margin on top, at least 1" on sides and bottom.

DO list contact information and number of lines in upper right corner.

DO space down about 6 lines.

DO type title in all caps or upper/lower case. Center it or type flush with left margin.

DON'T type a byline but **DO** space down at least 2 lines.

DO double-space between stanzas.

DO type poems single-spaced unless guidelines specify double spacing.

For multi-page poems, **DO** show your name, key word(s) from title, page number, and "continue stanza" or "new stanza."

DO space down at least 3 lines before resuming poem.

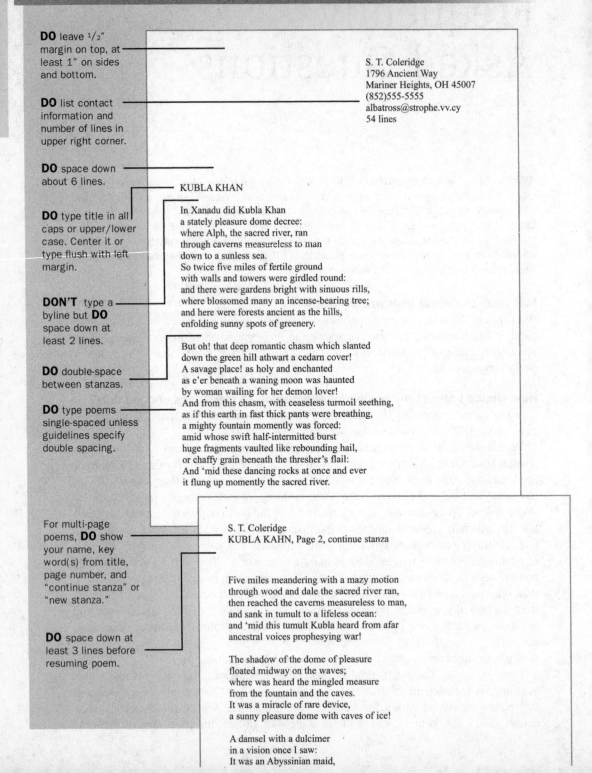

S. T. Coleridge
1796 Ancient Way
Mariner Heights, OH 45007
(852)555-5555
albatross@strophe.vv.cy
54 lines

KUBLA KHAN

In Xanadu did Kubla Khan
a stately pleasure dome decree:
where Alph, the sacred river, ran
through caverns measureless to man
down to a sunless sea.
So twice five miles of fertile ground
with walls and towers were girdled round:
and there were gardens bright with sinuous rills,
where blossomed many an incense-bearing tree;
and here were forests ancient as the hills,
enfolding sunny spots of greenery.

But oh! that deep romantic chasm which slanted
down the green hill athwart a cedarn cover!
A savage place! as holy and enchanted
as e'er beneath a waning moon was haunted
by woman wailing for her demon lover!
And from this chasm, with ceaseless turmoil seething,
as if this earth in fast thick pants were breathing,
a mighty fountain momently was forced:
amid whose swift half-intermitted burst
huge fragments vaulted like rebounding hail,
or chaffy grain beneath the thresher's flail:
And 'mid these dancing rocks at once and ever
it flung up momently the sacred river.

S. T. Coleridge
KUBLA KAHN, Page 2, continue stanza

Five miles meandering with a mazy motion
through wood and dale the sacred river ran,
then reached the caverns measureless to man,
and sank in tumult to a lifeless ocean:
and 'mid this tumult Kubla heard from afar
ancestral voices prophesying war!

The shadow of the dome of pleasure
floated midway on the waves;
where was heard the mingled measure
from the fountain and the caves.
It was a miracle of rare device,
a sunny pleasure dome with caves of ice!

A damsel with a dulcimer
in a vision once I saw:
It was an Abyssinian maid,

E-mail Submission Format

DO use a basic typeface and point size.

DO use the appropriate e-mail address.

DO consult guidelines for special instructions about formatting the subject line.

DO follow basic guidelines for a good cover letter.

DO provide contact information, including regular mail address.

DO be aware that formatting can become lost in an electronic submission. Keep it simple.

DO paste all poems within one message, one after the other, unless guidelines specify otherwise.

DON'T send submissions by e-mail unless editor says it's okay (in market listing or guidelines).

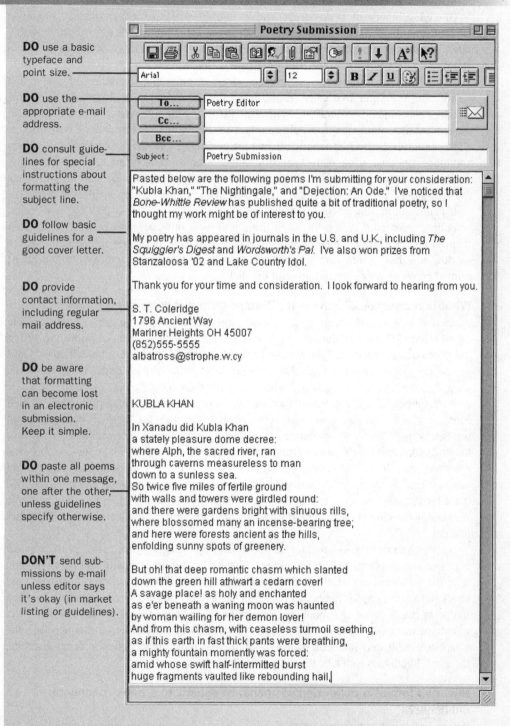

Poetry Submission

Arial   12   **B** *I* U

To...   Poetry Editor
Cc...
Bcc...
Subject: Poetry Submission

Pasted below are the following poems I'm submitting for your consideration: "Kubla Khan," "The Nightingale," and "Dejection: An Ode." I've noticed that *Bone-Whittle Review* has published quite a bit of traditional poetry, so I thought my work might be of interest to you.

My poetry has appeared in journals in the U.S. and U.K., including *The Squiggler's Digest* and *Wordsworth's Pal*. I've also won prizes from Stanzaloosa '02 and Lake Country Idol.

Thank you for your time and consideration. I look forward to hearing from you.

S. T. Coleridge
1796 Ancient Way
Mariner Heights OH 45007
(852)555-5555
albatross@strophe.w.cy

KUBLA KHAN

In Xanadu did Kubla Khan
a stately pleasure dome decree:
where Alph, the sacred river, ran
through caverns measureless to man
down to a sunless sea.
So twice five miles of fertile ground
with walls and towers were girdled round:
and there were gardens bright with sinuous rills,
where blossomed many an incense-bearing tree;
and here were forests ancient as the hills,
enfolding sunny spots of greenery.

But oh! that deep romantic chasm which slanted
down the green hill athwart a cedarn cover!
A savage place! as holy and enchanted
as e'er beneath a waning moon was haunted
by woman wailing for her demon lover!
And from this chasm, with ceaseless turmoil seething,
as if this earth in fast thick pants were breathing,
a mighty fountain momently was forced:
amid whose swift half-intermitted burst
huge fragments vaulted like rebounding hail,

incompatibility, and other concerns associated with e-mail attachments. Editors who consider e-mail attachments taboo may even delete the message without opening the attachment.

Of course, other editors do accept, and even prefer e-mail submissions as attachments. This information should be clearly stated in the market listing. If it's not, you're probably safer submitting your poems in the body of the e-mail. (All the more reason to pay close attention to details given in the listings.)

Note, too, the number of poems the editor recommends including in the e-mail submission. If no quantity is given specifically for e-mails, go with the number of poems an editor recommends submitting in general. Identify your submission with a notation in the subject line. While some editors simply want the words "Poetry Submission," others want poem titles. Check the market listing for preferences. **Note:** Because of spam, filters and other concerns, some editors are strict about what must be printed in the subject line and how. If you're uncertain about any aspect of e-mail submission formats, double-check the Web site (if available) for information or contact the publication for directions.

If you're submitting poems on disk:

Submit poems on disk *only* when the publication indicates this is acceptable. Even then, if no formatting preferences are given, contact the publisher for specifics before sending the disk. Make sure your disk is virus-free. Always include a hard copy (i.e., printed copy) of your submission with the disk.

What is a chapbook? How is it different from a regular poetry book?

A chapbook is a booklet, averaging 24-50 pages in length (some are shorter), usually digest-sized (5½ × 8½, although chapbooks can come in all sizes, even published within the pages of a magazine). Typically, a chapbook is saddle-stapled with a soft cover (card or special paper); chapbooks can also be produced with a plain paper cover the same weight as the pages, especially if the booklet is photocopied.

A chapbook is a much smaller collection of poetry than a full-length book (which runs anywhere from 50 pages to well over 100 pages, longer for "best of" collections and retrospectives). There are probably more poetry chapbooks being published than full-length books, and that's an important point to consider. Don't think of the chapbook as a poor relation to the full-length collection. While it's true a chapbook won't attract big reviews, qualify for major prizes or find national distribution through chain bookstores, it's a terrific way for a poet to build an audience (and reputation) in increments, while developing the kind of publishing history that may attract the attention of a book publisher one day.

Although some presses consider chapbooks through a regular submission process, many choose manuscripts through competitions. Check each publisher's listing for requirements, send for guidelines or visit the Web site (absolutely vital if a competition is involved), and check out some sample chapbooks the press has already produced (usually available from the press itself). Most chapbook publishers are as choosy as book publishers about the quality of work they accept. Submit your best poems in a professional manner. (See the Chapbook Publishers Index on page 498 for markets that consider chapbook manuscripts; the Book Publishers Index begins on page 501.)

How do I format a collection of poems to submit to a book/chapbook publisher?

Before you send a manuscript to a book/chapbook publisher, request guidelines (or consult the publisher's Web site, if available). Requirements vary regarding formatting, query letters and samples, length, and other considerations. Usually you will use 8½ × 11, 20 lb. white paper; set left, right and bottom margins of at least one inch; put your name and title of your collection in the top left corner of every page; limit poems to one per page (although poems certainly may run longer than one page); and number pages consecutively. Individual publisher requirements might include a title page, table of contents, credits page (indicating where previously published poems originally appeared) and biographical note.

If you're submitting your poetry book or chapbook manuscript to a competition, you *must* read and follow the guidelines. Failure to do so could disqualify your manuscript. Guidelines for a competition might call for an official entry form to accompany the submission, a special title page, a minimum and maximum number of pages, and specific formatting instructions (such as paginating the manuscript and not putting the poet's name on any of the manuscript pages).

What is a cover letter? Do I have to send one? What should it say?

A cover letter is your introduction to the editor, telling him a little about yourself and your work. Most editors indicate their cover letter preferences in their listings. If an editor states a cover letter is "required," absolutely send one! It's also better to send one if a cover letter is "preferred." Experts disagree on the necessity and appropriateness of cover letters, so use your own judgment when preferences aren't clear in the listing.

A cover letter should be professional but also allow you to present your work in a personal manner. (See the fictional cover letter on page 12 as an example.) Keep your letter brief, no more than one page. Address your letter to the correct contact person. (Use "Poetry Editor" if no contact name appears in the listing.) Include your name, address, phone number and e-mail address (if available). If a biographical note is requested, include 2-3 lines about your background, interests, why you write poetry, etc. Avoid praising yourself or your poems in your letter (your submission should speak for itself). Include titles (or first lines) of the poems you're submitting. You may list a few of your most recent publishing credits, but no more than five; and keep in mind that some editors find publishing credits tiresome—they're more interested in the quality of the work you're submitting to *them*.

Show your familiarity with the magazine to which you're submitting: comment on a poem the magazine published, tell the editor why you chose to submit to her magazine, mention poets the magazine has published. Use a business-style format for a professional appearance, and proofread carefully; typos, misspellings and other errors make a poor first impression. Remember that editors are people, too. Respect, professionalism and kindness go a long way in poet/editor relationships.

What is a SASE? An IRC (with SAE)?

A SASE is a self-addressed, stamped envelope—and you should never send a submission by regular mail without one. Also include a SASE if you send an inquiry to an editor. If your submission is too large for an envelope (for instance, a bulky book-length collection of poems), use a box and include a self-addressed mailing label with adequate return postage paper-clipped to it.

An IRC is an International Reply Coupon, enclosed with a self-addressed envelope for manuscripts submitted to foreign markets. Each coupon is equivalent in value to the minimum postage rate for an unregistered airmail letter. IRCs may be exchanged for

Articles & Information

Preparing Your Cover Letter

DO type on one side of 8¹/₂ x 11 20 lb. paper.

DO proofread carefully.

DO use a standard 12-point typeface (like Times New Roman).

DO list the poems you're submitting for consideration.

DO mention something about the magazine and about yourself.

DO be brief!

Perry Lineskanner
1954 Eastern Blvd.
Pentameter, OH 45007
(852) 555-5555
soneteer@trochee.vv.cy

April 24, 2009

Spack Saddlestaple, Editor
The Squiggler's Digest
Double-Toe Press
P.O. Box 54X
Submission Junction, AZ 85009

Dear Mr. Saddlestaple:

Enclosed are three poems for your consideration for *The Squiggler's Digest*: "The Diamond Queen," "The Boy Who Was Gromit," and "The Maker of Everything."

Although this is my first submission to your journal, I'm a long-time reader of *The Squiggler's Digest* and enjoy the scope of narrative poetry you feature. I especially enjoyed Sydney Dogwood's poetry cycle in Issue 4.

My own poetry has appeared recently in *The Bone-Whittle Review*, *Bumper-Car Reverie*, and *Stock Still*.

Thank you for considering my manuscript. I look forward to hearing from you.

Sincerely,

Perry Lineskanner

Note: The names used in this letter are intended to be fictional; any resemblance to real people, publications or presses is purely coincidental.

postage stamps at post offices in all foreign countries that are members of the Universal Postal Union (UPU). When you provide the adequate number of IRCs and a self-addressed envelope (SAE), you give a foreign editor financial means to return your submission (U.S. postage stamps cannot be used to send mail *to* the United States from outside the country). Purchase price is $2 per coupon. Call your local post office to check for availability (sometimes only larger post offices sell them).

Important

Important note about IRCs: Foreign editors sometimes find the IRCs have been stamped incorrectly by the U.S. post office when purchased. This voids the IRCs and makes it impossible for the foreign editor to exchange the coupons for return postage for your manuscript. When buying IRCs, make sure yours have been stamped correctly before you leave the counter. (The Postal Service clerk must place a postmark in the block with the heading *control stamp of the country of origin*.) More information about International Reply Coupons is available on the USPS website (www.usps.com).

To save time and money, poets sometimes send disposable manuscripts to foreign markets and inform the editor to discard the manuscript after it's been read. Some enclose an IRC and SAE for reply only; others establish a deadline after which they will withdraw the manuscript from consideration and market it elsewhere.

How much postage does my submission need?

As much as it takes—you do *not* want your manuscript to arrive postage due. Purchase a postage scale or take your manuscript to the post office for weighing. Remember, you'll need postage on two envelopes: the one containing your submission and SASE, and the return envelope itself. Submissions without SASEs usually will not be returned (and possibly may not even be read).

Note: New postage rates went into effect in May, 2009. There is now a new fee structure for First-Class Postage. For letters and cards (including business-size envelopes), the First-Class rate is 44 cents for the first ounce, and 17 cents per additional ounce up to and including 3.5 ounces. **Letter-sized mail that weighs more than 3.5 ounces is charged the "flats" rate** ("flats" include any envelope large enough to mail an 8½ × 11 manuscript page unfolded) of 88 cents for the first ounce, and 17 cents for each additional ounce up to and including 13 ounces. This means if you send a large envelope that weighs only one ounce, it costs 88 cents at the First-Class flats rate instead of the 44 cents charged for First-Class letters and cards. (See the charts on page 14 for First-Class rates for letters and flats, or go to www.usps.com for complete information on all rates questions.)

The USPS also offers its Click-N-Ship® program, which allows a customer to print domestic and international shipping labels with postage, buy insurance and pay for postage by credit card. See the USPS Web site for a one-time software download, to check system requirements and to register for an account.

The website is also your source for ordering supplies (such as postage scale and labels), reviewing postal regulations, calculating postage and more. Canada Post information and services are available at www.canadapost.com.

What does it mean when an editor says "no previously published" poems? Does this include poems that have appeared in anthologies? What if one of my poems appeared online through a group or forum?

If your poem appears *anywhere* in print for a public audience, it's considered "previously" published. That includes magazines, anthologies, Web sites and online journals, and even printed programs (say for a church service, wedding, etc.). See the explanation for rights

Postage Information

First-Class Mail Rates: Letters & Cards

1 ounce	$0.44	3 ounces 0.78	
2 ounces	$0.61	3.5 ounces	0.95
		Postcard	0.28

First-Class Mail Rates: Flats

Weight not over (ounces)	Rate	Weight not over (ounces)	Rate
1	$0.88	8	2.07
2	1.05	9	2.24
3	1.22	10	2.41
4	1.39	11	2.58
5	1.56	12	2.75
6	1.73	13	2.92
7	1.90		

Source: Web site of the United States Postal Service (www.usps.com)

U.S. and Canadian Postal Codes

AL	Alabama	MN	Minnesota	VA	Virginia
AK	Alaska	MS	Mississippi	WA	Washington
AZ	Arizona	MO	Missouri	WV	West Virginia
AR	Arkansas	MT	Montana	WI	Wisconsin
CA	California	NE	Nebraska	WY	Wyoming
CO	Colorado	NV	Nevada		
CT	Connecticut	NH	New Hampsire	**Canada**	
DE	Delaware	NJ	New Jersey	AB	Alberta
DC	District of	NM	New Mexico	BC	British Columbia
	Columbia	NY	New York	MB	Manitoba
FL	Florida	NC	North Carolina	NB	New Brunswick
GA	Georgia	ND	North Dakota	NL	Newfoundland &
GU	Guam	OH	Ohio		Labrador
HI	Hawaii	OK	Oklahoma	NS	Nova Scotia
ID	Idaho	OR	Oregon	NT	Northwest
IL	Illinois	PA	Pennsylvania		Territories
IN	Indiana	PR	Puerto Rico	NU	Nunavut
IA	Iowa	RI	Rhode Island	ON	Ontario
KS	Kansas	SC	South Carolina	PE	Prince Edward
KY	Kentucky	SD	South Dakota		Island
LA	Louisiana	TN	Tennessee	QC	Quebec
ME	Maine	TX	Texas	SK	Saskatchewan
MD	Maryland	UT	Utah	YT	Yukon
MA	Massachusetts	VT	Vermont		
MI	Michigan	VI	Virgin Islands		

below, especially *second serial (reprint) rights* and *all rights* for additional concerns about previously published material.

One exception to the above guidelines is if your poem appears online in a *private* poetry forum, critique group, etc. As long as the site is private (i.e., a password is required to view and participate), your poem isn't considered "published." However, if your poem is printed on an online forum or bulletin board that's available for public viewing, even if you must use a password to post the poem or to comment, then your poem is considered "published" as far as rights are concerned.

What rights should I offer for my poems? What do these different rights mean?

Editors usually indicate in their listings what rights they acquire. Most journals and magazines license *first rights* (a.k.a. *first serial rights*), which means the poet offers the right to publish the poem for the first time in any periodical. All other rights to the material remain with the poet. (Note that some editors state that rights to poems "revert to poets upon publication" when first rights are acquired.) When poems are excerpted from a book prior to publication and printed in a magazine/journal, this is also called *first serial rights*. The addition of *North American* indicates the editor is the first to publish a poem in a U.S. or Canadian periodical. The poem may still be submitted to editors outside of North America or to those who acquire reprint rights.

When a magazine/journal licenses *one-time rights* to a poem (also known as *simultaneous rights*), the editor has *nonexclusive* rights to publish the poem once. The poet may submit that same poem to other publications at the same time (usually markets that don't have overlapping audiences).

Editors/publishers open to submission of work already published elsewhere seek *second serial (reprint) rights*. The poet is obliged to inform them where and when the poem previously appeared so they can give proper credit to the original publication. In essence, chapbook or book collections license reprint rights, listing the magazines in which poems previously appeared somewhere in the book (usually on the copyright page or separate credits page).

If a publisher or editor requires you to relinquish *all rights*, be aware that you're giving up ownership of that poem or group of poems. You cannot resubmit the work elsewhere, nor can you include it in a poetry collection without permission or by negotiating for reprint rights to be returned to you. Before you agree to this type of arrangement, ask the editor first if he or she is willing to acquire first rights instead of all rights. If you receive a refusal and you don't want to relinquish all rights, simply write a letter withdrawing your work from consideration. Some editors will reassign rights to a writer after a given amount of time, such as one year.

With the growth in Internet publishing opportunities, *electronic rights* have become very important. These cover a broad range of electronic media, including online magazines, CD recordings of poetry readings and CD-ROM editions of magazines. When submitting to an electronic market of any kind, find out what rights the market acquires upfront (many online magazines also stipulate the right to archive poetry they've published so it's continually available on their websites).

What is a copyright? Should I have my poems copyrighted before I submit them for publication?

Copyright is a proprietary right that gives you the power to control your work's reproduction, distribution and public display or performance, as well as its adaptation to other forms. In other words, you have the legal right to the exclusive publication, sale or distribution of your poetry. What's more, your "original works of authorship" are protected as soon as they are "fixed in a tangible form of expression," i.e., written down or recorded. Since March 1989, copyright notices are no longer required to secure protection, so it's not necessary to include them on your poetry manuscript. Also, in many editors' minds, copyright notices signal the work of amateurs who are distrustful and paranoid about having work stolen.

If you still want to indicate copyright, use the © symbol or the word *copyright*, your name and the year. If you wish, you can register your copyright with the Copyright Office for a $45 fee, using Form TX (directions and form available for download from www.copyright. gov). Since paying $45 per poem is costly and impractical, you may prefer to copyright a group of unpublished poems for that single fee. Further information is available from the U.S. Copyright Office, Library of Congress, 101 Independence Ave. S.E., Washington DC 20559-6000; by download from www.copyright.gov; or by calling (202)707-3000 between 8:30 a.m. and 5:00 p.m. (EST) weekdays.

Special note regarding Copyright Office mail delivery: The "effective date of registration" for copyright applications is usually the day the Copyright Office actually receives all elements of an application (application form, fee and copies of work being registered). Because of security concerns, all USPS and private-carrier mail is screened off-site prior to arrival at the Copyright Office. This can add 3-5 days to delivery time and could, therefore, impact the effective date of registration. See the Web site for details about proper packaging, special handling and other related information.

Publishing Poetry

A Reality Check

by Nancy Breen

As the former editor of *Poet's Market*, I got a lot of questions about the whole process of writing and submitting poetry. Often similar questions were forwarded to me from *Writer's Market*. Regardless of the source, I tried to treat all such queries with respect and genuine concern for passing along what I hoped was valued information.

There were certain questions, though, that I dreaded receiving--because my answer invariably lead to disillusionment and disappointment as I splashed cold reality into the faces of unsuspecting (and uninformed) poets. Read further if you're curious about these questions, and especially if you're an aspiring poet yourself.

Is there any money in poetry?

It really hurts to tell ambitious writers that their efforts will result in little monetary gain. However, that's the brutal truth about poetry: There's no money in it, at least not for the average hard-working (and even widely published) poet.

Most poetry appears in little magazines and literary journals. These markets are unlikely to pay cash for the poetry they print, offering instead a copy or two of the issue in which the poet's work appears (called a *contributor's copy*). Online literary magazines usually don't pay at all, although many poets see the worldwide exposure of Internet publication as a type of compensation. While there are a few larger literary magazines that do pay, they're quite prestigious and receive thousands of submissions per year while choosing a small percentage for publication. That means intense competition and high rates of rejection. The same is true of the few commercial magazines that publish poetry, such as *The New Yorker* and *The Atlantic Monthly*.

In truth, if you had a poem accepted by every paying magazine and journal, you probably still wouldn't make a decent income.

The situation in poetry book publishing is just as financially grim. Few of the "major" publishers put out many volumes of poetry; and those volumes usually are by our best known, established poets, talented up-and-comers, and major prizewinners. (A few celebrity poetry books may be in the mix; but, obviously, you have to become a celebrity first for publishers to take interest in your poetry.)

NANCY BREEN is the former editor of *Poet's Market* (www.poetsmarket.com). Her chapbooks include: *Rites and Observances* (Finishing Line Press) and *How Time Got Away* (Pudding House Publications). She blogs at www.salmagundiexpress. wordpress.com.

Most poetry publishers are literary presses, often run through universities and colleges; or they're independent smaller presses. In either case, they don't have large sums of money to throw around for advances and royalties.

If you're disappointed, and even depressed by the low financial rewards of poetry publishing, ask yourself: When was the last time you bought a literary magazine or book of poetry? Few readers in America spend their dollars on poetry (and too often that includes the poets themselves).

Can you recommend a publisher for my 300-poem book manuscript?

First, reread the preceding section, especially the paragraphs about book publishers.

Next, if you haven't looked at the poetry shelves of your local bookstore lately, do a little market research. How many 300-poem books do you see? If you find one, is it by a single poet or is it an anthology? If the book is the work of one poet, review the biographical note for the poet's age, publishing history, academic background, awards won and hints about his or her standing in the literary community. If you don't have a similar biography as a poet, don't even think about trying to get such a massive collection of poems published.

Also, if you've never published any of your poems in literary magazines, don't start shopping for a book publisher just yet. The established route poets follow is to publish individual poems in magazines and journals (in print and online) before assembling a collection of any length. By publishing in magazines first, you establish some necessary credentials:

- You demonstrate you're familiar with the world of poetry publishing because you've been an active participant--publishers appreciate that.
- You prove that someone else has read and appreciated your work besides you, your friends and your family.
- You establish a track record of having worked successfully with editors.

There are occasional exceptions to the publish-in-magazines-first approach. The aforementioned celebrity poetry books are one example. And every few years there's a publishing phenomenon like Mattie Stepanek, the young boy with muscular dystrophy who sold millions of copies of his poetry books before his death at 14 in 2004. Such situations are unique unto themselves and represent exceptions, rather than the rule.

Keep in mind, too, that most poets progress from publishing in magazines to assembling a chapbook, rather than book manuscript. What is a chapbook? It's a soft cover publication of about 24-32 pages. Although bookstores don't stock chapbooks (even independent stores don't favor chapbooks because there's no spine showing the title--chapbooks are usually folded and saddle-stapled), chapbooks have become a very popular format. Production values range from simple to extravagant (depending on paper and cover stock), they can be produced and sold economically, and they're easy to offer for sale at readings. No, they don't make money for the poet *or* the press; but as I said earlier, money should never be a primary concern if you're serious about poetry.

Can you recommend an agent who can represent my poetry book?

As I said, there's little money in poetry. Agents work on commission, i.e., a percentage of what the poet is paid. Consequently, 15% of nothing doesn't make poetry attractive to agents.

As always, there may be exceptions. A highly successful poet may have an agent, especially if the poet does other writing that *does* benefit from representation. A beginning poet, though—especially beginning poet with a manuscript of 300 previously unpublished poems—probably is not going to find an agent. In fact, any poet who comes across an agent who does express interest should be wary. Ask questions, do your homework, don't sign anything until you've thoroughly researched the agent. And *never* pay for representation.

How can I get my self-published book of poetry into bookstores?

Whether your book is truly self-published or printed by a vanity publisher or print-on-demand publisher (known as POD, wherein a publisher stores your book digitally and prints out copies as they're purchased), distribution is going to be a challenge. Bookstores usually work with professional distributors to stock their shelves, an avenue that may be closed to poets who self-publish. Similarly, vanity publishers can't get your books into bookstores without a distributor, no matter what they may claim. POD publishers may rely more on their own online bookstores and author Web sites than working with a distributor.

In most bookstores, a limited amount of shelf space is devoted to poetry. Sometimes independent bookstores (i.e., not owned by national chains) are more open to stocking small press and self-published books; this is especially true if the poet is a local author.

Poets shouldn't focus on bookstores as a sole source of sales. Other methods of selling include offering books through a personal Web site; scheduling readings at coffeehouses, bookstores or even your own church or community center (where you can offer your book for sale to the audience); and sending promotional postcards to potential customers with information about how to order by mail. To learn more, and to brainstorm additional ideas for selling and promotion, try your library for books on self-publishing; or enter "selling self-published books" or similar phrases into a search engine for a range of information and perspectives on the Web.

And about those anthologies . . .

No reality check for poets would be complete without a mention of those poetry operations that sponsor contests and Web sites, the ones that publish huge anthologies of "winning" poems. If you choose to participate, that's your decision, but be aware of these points:

- *Everyone* who submits a poem to such contests is "chosen" to appear in an anthology, so there's no quality standard.
- Having a poem published in such an anthology is *not* a legitimate publishing credit (that is, serious publishers don't take such publishing credits seriously).
- If your poem(s) appear in such an anthology, or on an associated public Web site, your work is considered "published" and cannot be submitted to any magazine or contest that does not accept previously published work.

Some poets appreciate the sense of community they find at such Web sites. They simply enjoy seeing their work in print and online, and they don't mind spending huge sums for copies of the anthologies (or for the plaques, coffee mugs and other merchandise that may be available). And that's their prerogative, as long as those poets aren't deceiving themselves about what such publication means. If they use their anthology appearances as selling points to prospective editors and publishers, though, they may find that they and their poetry are not going to be taken seriously.

What are your objectives?

Be realistic about what the world of poetry publishing has to offer and what you hope to achieve. If writing good poetry is more important to you than money, recognition and the other trappings of high stakes publication, then you're on the right path. If, on the other hand, you hope to achieve fame and fortune through your poetry, well--you need a reality check.

The Age of the E-Poet

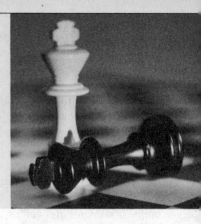

by Larina Warnock

Digital poetry is electronic literature that cannot exist on paper. It can move (an early online journal specializing in digital poetry was called *Poems That Go*) or include multimedia components, and it is often interactive and/or collaborative.

In 1992 William Gibson (author of the science fiction novel *Neuromancer*) released a precursor to today's net-based digital poetry: "Agrippa (A Book of the Dead)," a self-destructing poem on a floppy disk. As readers used the disk, it erased itself. (You can experience the poem now in the form of a screen-capture at www.boingboing. net/2008/12/09/gibsons-selfdetructi.html.)

Digital poetry is about as old as the Internet—which means, of course, that it's still quite young. One of the earliest examples of digital poetry is Peter Howard's 1997 work "Midwinter Fair" (www.hphoward.demon.co.uk/midwin/midwintr.htm), which operates on the same principle as the Choose Your Own Adventure books popular in the 1980s. "Midwinter Fair" contains hyperlinked words, and the reader chooses which of these to follow and in what order. Each reader therefore experiences the poem differently. Like much of the digital poetry that would follow, "Midwinter Fair" is interactive and nonlinear. It is also community-oriented: it has multiple authors, and is not static; even now it changes. Howard invites readers of the poem to participate by linking up their own work. He continues to make digital poems, and says that what appeals to him is that "digital poetry is still very much a new medium, so there aren't any rules, and pretty much everything is up for grabs."

Jason Nelson is currently one of the top artists in digital poetry; his works "game, game, game and again game" and "i made this. you play this. we are enemies" are available at www.secrettechnology.com. These are games, texts, and works of art. You don't just read them, play them, or view them; you experience them. They combine screen shots of the mundane web (Yahoo, Google, etc.), doodle-like artwork, and arcade game tropes, and they reveal poetry at odd moments. For Nelson, as for Howard, the appeal of digital poetry is its lack of history or tradition: "Digital poetry is conventionless. It's a lovely messy space, where poets can create whatever-the-hell they want, truly exploratory/adventurous, with all the fear and unease unknown directions bring."

There's an inherent irony in writing an article on digital poetry for a paper publication.

LARINA WARNOCK is a site administrator for The Academy of American Poets discussion forum. She is also the editor and founder of *The Externalist: A Journal of Perspectives* and has published her poetry in several publications.

It's such a fast-changing medium that by the time this article appears it will be out of date. But most, perhaps all, of these examples will still be available on the Internet. You should be able to go to the archives of Poems That Go, watch poetry videos at *Shape of a Box* or *HERE EXPLODES MY GIANT FACE*, and visit academic sites like the Electronic Literature Organization (eliterature.org) or the Electronic Poetry Center (epc.buffalo.edu/e-poetry). Turbulence is also a site to watch: founded in 1996, its mission is to commission and support net art. Among its projects is Tumbaramba, a conceptual artwork in the form of a Firefox extension. It's a sort of stealth literary magazine—you download the extension and, over time, 12 stories appear embedded in your browser. Projects like these show the unusual and surprising possibilities of digital poetry.

Speculative Poetry Markets

Are They Right for What You Write?

by Jeannine Hall Gailey

Have you ever heard of speculative fiction? Writers like Kelly Link or Haruki Murakami? Hopefully. But, have you heard of its less-well-known counterpart: speculative poetry?

Ironically, it wasn't until I published my first book of poetry, all about video game heroines, comic book characters, and ancient myths and folk tales, that I discovered a brave new world of publications with friendly editors, many avid readers, and actual pay—speculative magazines!

WHAT IS SPECULATIVE POETRY?

While defining "speculative" can be a slippery, "slipstream" venture, it entails some combination of reality, sci-fi, and possibly fantasy elements. If you've ever written a poem about scientific phenomena, a robot, a fairy tale, mythology, comic book characters, or any combination of those, then you've written a poem that would be welcome at a speculative poetry market. If you're a poet who has laughed at *Mystery Science Theater 3000*, sought out books about futuristic dystopias, or struck up a conversation about how contemporary manga has been influenced by Norse mythology, then you've probably written a speculative poem. Some examples of writers of speculative poetry include Edgar Allen Poe, Margaret Atwood, Ursula K. Le Guin, and Neil Gaiman.

Mike Allen, editor of *Mythic Delirium*, defines speculative poetry this way: "A speculative poem asks the reader to assume that superheroes exist, that ghosts walk the Earth, that life on other planets will make itself known, that magic works. Then, the poem proceeds with the understanding that it is rooted in a reality different from ours; that when a god steps through the front door or a dragon menaces the second-person narrator, the event is intended to be taken as something that's actually happening in that world, not just metaphor—though no doubt there is metaphoric meaning intended, too. There is no hard edge that divides it from all other poetry. Sometimes a poem can achieve an effect of ancient mystery or futuristic alienation through sheer use of language."

Award-winning novelist and poet Catherynne M. Valente says that "speculative poetry

JEANNINE HALL GAILEY is a San Diego writer whose first book of poetry, Becoming the Villainess, was published by Steel Toe Books. She was awarded a 2007 Dorothy Sargent Rosenberg Prize for Poetry and a 2007 Washington State Artist Trust GAP grant. Her poems have appeared in several publications, including The Iowa Review, The Columbia Poetry Review, and Smartish Pace. She currently teaches at the MFA program at National University.

deals with things that could never, haven't yet, or never once but might have happened in the real world. It's a huge box to play in, the one most poetry dealt with until very recently, when the worship of poetry verite took over.

The world of speculative poetry embraced me and allowed me, in this world where poetry is so hard to get out there, to publish five collections in four years. I've connected with my audience through cons, workshops, readings, and my blog—it's a new world, and there is literally no big poetry publishing industry to fight against."

There are many markets for speculative poetry—some of which you may have seen on the shelf at the local Barnes & Nobles, some of which you may never have heard of. Most of them are outside of what might be termed "the poetry mainstream."

SPECULATIVE POETRY MARKETS

Markets for speculative poetry include *The Magazine of Speculative Poetry, Mythic Delirium, Lady Churchhill's Rosebud Wristlet, Strange Horizons, Star*Line, Asimov's...* your copy of P*oet's Market* contains many listings that are open to this kind of poetry. There are also Internet journals such as *Goblin Fruit* and, may-it-rest-in-peace-or-be-raised-zombie-like-from-the-grave, *The Endicott Studio's Journal of Mythic Arts*. And there are anthologies that poems published in speculative-focused literary journals are eligible for; your speculative poems might be included in anthologies like *The Year's Best Fantasy and Horror* or the *Rhysling Award Anthology*. Compared to the usual literary magazine, some of these journals and anthologies have huge circulations and readerships; genre readers tend to be enthusiastic and loyal. Did I mention that a lot of them pay?

Mike Allen described *Mythic Delirium* as "a biannual poetry journal with a ten-year history. We publish around 20 poems in each issue, some with commissioned illustrations. We've published established authors like Ursula K. Le Guin, Jane Yolen and Catherynne M. Valente, but we've also given a number of beginning writers their first publications. Our website, www.mythicdelirium.com, features poems from recent issues and "classic" reprints, complete with art and audio readings. There's nobody around quite like us." In terms of what they're looking to publish, he says: *"Mythic Delirium* seeks poems that have an "otherworldly feel." This can mean they make use of science fictional settings and situations, or world mythologies and folk tales, or that they're simply strange and dream-like. Most of what we use is free verse, though formal verse is certainly welcome."

Roger Dutcher started *The Magazine of Speculative Poetry* with Mark Rich in 1984. "At the time we hoped to not only provide a market for SF/F/H poetry but to try, through the magazine and the poems we published, to define a "speculative poetry". He is "looking for poems that use science, fantasy and horror, to provoke new ways of seeing the human condition. Or the everyday viewed from another perspective."

Ordering and reading copies of different magazines that publish speculative poetry will help give you an idea of the variety of tastes of editors and the diversity in contemporary speculative writing. Some magazines, like *Asimov's*, lean more heavily towards science fiction, while *Goblin Fruit* leans towards fantasy and folklore. Like any market, researching a magazine will help you know if your work would be a good fit.

Discovering new markets for your work is like opening the door to another world. The world of speculative poetry seems welcoming, warmer than your usual literary enclave, and just a bit offbeat. And wouldn't it be nice to publish in a magazine your sci-fi-loving little brother might actually read?

Labor Poetics

On the Fringes

by Allison Hedge Coke

L abor Poetry renders a glimpse of humanity from its most common contemporary experience—the work life. Constructed of words meant to gift greater humanitarian empathy with the experience of fellow human example, it is made of, as Sandburg wrote, "Poems for the People" and as June Jordan conceived, "Poetry for the People." At its best, the actual worklife (craft) lends its sustaining ethic to thoroughly crafted poetry resulting from the impression. An introspective and transformative writing engagement, wherein one might truly parlay the labor of droll, or mundane, worklife into rich, meaningful poetic publication that reaps benefits far beyond the actuality of pay from the originating job. This subgenre is a people moving force in poetry. Delivering experiences of commonality and uniqueness, it is a necessary and highly publishable effort.

Labor Poetics conceptualize a socio-literary dignity and authenticity in working-class life. Poetics of personal, individual, and group experience in economic depression, worker organized labor, and/or labor movement events and history are ripe with fodder for the gleaning in this ever-expanding area of poetry. Worker-poets and poets with working-class background bring the life-drama dichotomies of restrictive and expansive working culture to the literary page. Most non-executive work-related subjects are suitable to this subgenre. Special attention is given to manual labor and blue-collar work. Recently, as a result of organizing to address education and clerical workers' conditions, and in consideration of the impact of technology on industry, the contemporary idea of labor has extended into non-administrative white-collar duty. This includes teaching, office support, and computing positions, especially those that were once industrial, e.g.: printing.

Much as Labor Day (or International Workers' Day) commemorates workers' struggle and celebrates workers' achievements, Labor Poetics provide a place in literature for raw and refined experiential witnessing, communication, concern for, and celebration of skill, ability and achievement of fair socio-economic treatment.

When union rank & file members unite to negotiate through collective bargaining, including fair treatment, fair pay, expected work procedures, benefit packages, guaranteed job safety measures, and management/administrative practice in hiring, promotion, lay-off, and termination, their efforts benefit all that follow in their footsteps and, in

ALLISON HEDGE COKE holds the Distinguished Paul W. Reynolds and Clarice Kingston Reynolds Endowed Chair of Poetry and Writing at the University of Nebraska, Kearney. Her books include the American Book Award winning volume Dog Road Woman and the Wordcraft Writer of the Year for Poetry volume Off-Season City Pipe (both from Coffee House Press), in addition to Rock Ghost, Willow, Deer, and Blood Run.

some ways, balances injustices they and their predecessors have endured. Political and community organizing play a great role in the purpose and language of Labor Poetry. Tribute and remembrance poetry, regarding notable and forgotten workers, organizers, and union martyrs, plays a significant role in truthfully developing a national literary history, serving a worker consciousness and notion of shared struggle and joint success. Suffering, endurance, and loss (love, limb, life) are common poetic accompaniments with highly relatable interests. Diaspora movement, relocation, and migrant camp experience are significantly underrepresented in literature, thus in demand.

Professionals in administration, law, and medicine may also write poetry regarding their paid and legitimate worklife, though categorically this would not be considered labor ethic inclusive, nor read as Labor Poetry. Cultural class conditions typically outweigh the intensity of the actual labor in this case. Crossover variables may exist in the case of volunteer, pro-bono, community service work in these areas (Doctors Without Borders, Peace Core, grassroots administration).

Labor poetry may include nature, landscape, and environmental theme, typically due to work directly related to the natural area and/or the need to find balance in an industrialized work-world. A worker poet's labor may also directly influence the stability and greenness of the surrounding environment. Detrimental environmental effects of labor are lauded as worthy considerations and a current hot topic in the sense of shaping a functional literary world beyond the poet's own hand.

Thought on Labor Poetry

"In his book co-authored with Grace Lee Boggs, *Facing Reality*, CLR James wrote that '…people all over the world, and particularly ordinary working people in factories, mines, fields, and offices, are rebelling every day in ways of their own invention…Their strivings, their struggles, their methods have few chroniclers.' Contemporary labor poetry speaks of and from these everyday acts of workplace resistance. Twenty-first century labor poets— at once transnational, social movement, and social justice unionism-based—chronicle the strife, struggles, and just rewards of the working majority across the globe."
—Mark Nowak, editor of XCP: *Cross-Cultural Poetics*.

"Working Class poetry and literature is the sustenance that defines us as Americans and connects us to the majority people of the rest of the world. This literature is the work and the feeds our souls and gives us hope in the struggle. It is what connects us to our humanity in a vicious world and declining economy. The stories we tell through poems, fiction and creative nonfiction remind us of whom we are, and these memories help us build upon our futures and our successes to become as meaningful and as important as the few who have the most. Working Class literature is the expression that unites the workers of the world and keeps us relevant in a fast paced global society that might otherwise forget us."
—M.L. Libeler, Wayne State University, editor of *Working Words*.

"Labor and poetry. The two are joined like those intricate knots you see on Celtic rings. When you're engaged in physical labor or mental labor unexpected moments pop up of selflessness and relief. You're a cog in the wheel, you're serving something beyond yourself. To labor at writing brings the same absence. You're a ghost on ice skates gliding toward something hidden in the distance. To labor at poetry is to be subsumed by the subject, the desire to get it as clear as you can, to investigate the inner petals without damaging the rose. There's a freedom in work that comes no other way."
—Janine Pommy Vega, poet

Nontraditional Journals

Unbound, Linked, Graphic, Moving, Noisy

by Elizabeth Bradfield

The conventional literary journal is a gorgeous thing: a conversation of aesthetics, a portable sampler. However, there is always room for improvement, experimentation, and innovation. Many publishers are reaching out into new fields for sharing, presenting, and conceptualizing poetry and poets have a chance to see their work participate in a different literary landscape. All publications listed here hold one thing in common that makes them "journals": they have an open submission policy.

Journals don't have to be paper-based, in fact, they don't even need to rely on letters. Sound poetry, a genre that explores the borders or music, recitation, and noise, has blossomed on the web. Anna Vitale, founder and co-editor of text*sound*, says, "We hope to encourage poets not working with sound to play and send us their experiments. We hope to connect musicians, thinking through language as sound and vice-versa, with each other and poets. We hope to create an expansive community of listeners and makers." James Sanders, editor of *a s l o n g a s i t t a k e s,* finds inspiration in sound poetry: "I'm always looking for different compositional methods and thought sound poetry might present new ways of thinking about composition."

Born Magazine and New River, both online publications, illustrate the dynamism of literature and visual art working together—not as illustration, but as something altogether different. *At New River*, the editors look for submissions of "digital writing." *Born Magazine* started as a traditional literary journal, but, editor Anmarie Trimble says, "the project became more collaborative as designers were most interested in interpreting the poetry and fiction" rather than making a page for it to rest on. Now at *Born* artists and writers are paired up for web-based collaborations.

Some publishers say the desire for new audiences led them away from the traditional model. Bronwyn Mauldin's site, GuerillaReads.com, features videos of poets reading their work in public spaces: "we have to reach out to people who don't think of themselves as readers.... If people are too busy to come to our readings, or don't know what a "reading" is, then we must take our readings to them." *Broadsided*'s tag line is "putting literature and art on the streets." Each month, *Broadsided* releases a letter-sized, printable PDF broadside on its Web site, then a network of volunteer "vectors" around the globe post it

ELIZABETH BRADFIELD is the author of Interpretive Work (Arktoi Books/Red Hen Press, 2008) and the founder of Broadsided (www.broadsidedpress.org), a grassroots-distributed publication that puts original literary/visual collaborations on the street. Her second collection, Approaching Ice, is due out in 2010 and her poems have appeared in The Atlantic Monthly, Poetry, Orion, and elsewhere. For more information, visit www.ebradfield.com .

locally. (See Poetry Northwest Style for more on *Broadsided*.)

Jennifer Flescher, a long-time postcard-lover and editor of *Tuesday; An Art Project*, wanted to produce printed work, but to step away from bound pages. Twice yearly, Tuesday releases a collection of letterpress postcards. "I want people to keep and share and throw away," she says.

How are these alternate ideas of publication received? *Drunken Boat* has been featured in the Whitney Biennial as well as honored by the Academy of American Poets. Ravi Shankar, *Drunken Boat*'s founding editor, has a big vision: "the web is changing consciousness in ways that are in their infancy, and part of that change manifests itself in the creation of new genres of art and spectatorship. We want to publish work where the medium of the web is constitutive of the meaning that's made. We don't want to replicate the paradigm of the page but rather utilize the added dimensions of the medium – sound, moving image, linking, interaction, globalization – to present an alternate vision of the possible future of literature."

The furor over poetry's "mattering" that Dana Gioia began might be one spark for these nontraditional publishers. Or it might be the restlessness of art itself, always seeking new conversations and new ways to participate in the world.

Nontraditional Publications Roundup

Born Magazine, www.bornmagazine.org
Creative collaborations of artists and writers that marry literary arts and interactive media

Broadsided, www.broadsidedpress.org
Monthly publications of original literary/visual collaborations to be downloaded, printed, and posted locally.

Drunken Boat, www.drunkenboat.com
Traditional poetry as well as web-based art forms such as hypertext, sound, video, etc.

Guerilla Reads, www.guerrillareads.com
Video performances of poets reading in public spaces

New River, www.cddc.vt.edu/journals/newriver/
Video performances of poets reading in public spaces

textsound, www.textsound.org
Sound poetry, both solo pieces and collaborations

Tuesday; An Art Project, www.tuesdayjournal.org
Poems, photographs, and prints on postcards

Poetry Northwest Style

A Publishers' Roundtable

by Susan Rich

As a young poet, I fantasized that someday I would find a publisher of my own. I imagined our first meeting in innocent detail. We would shake hands in New York in his corner office overlooking the Hudson; his bookshelves filled floor-to-ceiling with first editions of the press's Pulitzer prize-winning authors. Fifteen years ago, I could only conjure a "his" and a Northeast geography.

We would then hail a taxi for an elegant lunch at his private club. I would be initiated into the world of cigar smoke and sherry. After that, my ideas become hazy. The truth is, I had little to go on other than movies and the fragmented stories of a past professor or two.

If the cigar smoking, sherry drinking, poetry publisher ever did exist, he is almost certainly now extinct. Today, a publisher is more likely to be publishing poetry as a side business than as a sole endeavor. The "business" is more likely a non-profit organization, and that glass of sherry? Replaced by a double-shot latte, at least in the Pacific Northwest.

Not many people think of the Northwest as the poetry Mecca that it is. Poetry publishing is flourishing in Oregon, Washington, and even Alaska, in ever more creative ways. Whit Press connects fine writing with focused activism and has partnered with a farm conservation fund in order to make supporting poetry and buying local farmland one and the same. Broadsided Press while regional in its vision of an expansive landscape, actually exists primarily in the ether of the worldwide web. Seattle's, Floating Bridge Press not only publishes new and established poets, but also runs several reading series. And Copper Canyon Press, while the most established and oldest press here—over 35 years publishing only poetry—operates out of Fort Worden State Park in a white clapperboard building that looks more like a barn than an internationally renowned publishing house.

These five publishers from across the Pacific Northwest agreed to participate in this roundtable. They represent a cross-section of men and women, established and entrepreneurial who believe in bringing more poetry into the world. Two participants earn their living exclusively in the publishing industry, the remaining three work as a naturalist, teacher, and warehouse worker, volunteering their time and imaginations to create a space for contemporary poetry in our world.

SUSAN RICH teaches in the Humanities Division at Highline Community College outside Seattle, WA. She is the author of three books of poems, The Cartographer's Tongue, Cures Include Travel, and The Alchemist's Kitchen, all from White Pine Press.

Joseph Bednarik is the Marketing Director of Copper Canyon Press. Since 1972, **Copper Canyon Press** has fostered the work of emerging, established, and world-renowned poets. Books published by the Press have earned numerous awards, including the Pulitzer Prize, the National Book Award, and the National Book Critics Circle Award. Information about the poets and books published by Copper Canyon can be found at www.coppercanyonpress. org.

Elizabeth Bradfield is the author of *Interpretive Work* (Arktoi Books/Red Hen Press, 2008) and the founder of Broadsided (www.broadsidedpress.org). Her poems have been published in *The Atlantic Monthly, Poetry, Field* and are forthcoming in *The Believer and Orion*. Bradfield's second collection, Approaching Ice, will be published in late 2009. Currently a Stegner Fellow at Stanford University, when not writing, she works as a naturalist. More at www.ebradfield.com. Inspired by street art and traditional broadsides, **Broadsided Press** (www.broadsidedpress.org) publishes an original, literary/visual collaboration every month. The letter-sized PDF is designed to be downloaded from Broadsided's Web site and printed from any computer. "Vectors" around the country and abroad post Broadsided publications in their local coffee shops, bulletin boards, office doors, etc. "Our goal? To put literature and art on the streets. To create something gorgeous and cheap. To find an audience for literature and art beyond bookstores and galleries."

Kathleen Flenniken is one of four editors of Floating Bridge Press, and its board president. Her first book of poems is *Famous (University of Nebraska Press, 2006), winner of the Prairie Schooner Prize and an ALA Notable Book for 2007. For more information about Kathleen, please visit* www.KathleenFlenniken.com. Floating Bridge Press is a 501(c) (3) non-profit literary arts organization, founded in 1994. "Our mission is to recognize and promote the work of Washington State poets, through an annual Poetry Chapbook Award; the production of archival-quality chapbooks, anthologies, and broadsides; as well as community poetry readings." Authors published by the press include Nance Van Winckel, Molly Tenenbaum, Chris Forhan, Timothy Kelly and many others. For more information, please visit http://www.scn.org/floatingbridge/ .

Claudia Mauro is publisher and founder of Whit Press. She has published two collections of poetry, *Stealing Fire* (Whiteaker, 1996) and *Reading the River* (Whiteaker, 1999). Both collections were nominated for Lambda Book Awards. Her work appears in various journals throughout the Northwest, King County's Poetry on the Buses project, and as a permanent installation at The Seattle Public Library, Beacon Hill Branch. **Whit Press** is a nonprofit publishing organization dedicated to the transformational power of the written word. "Whit Press exists as an oasis to nurture and promote the rich diversity of literary work from women writers, writers from ethnic, social, and economic minorities, young writers, and first-time authors. We also create books that use literature as a tool in support of other nonprofit organizations working towards environmental and social justice. We are dedicated to producing beautiful books that combine outstanding literary content with design excellence."

Rodger Moody is the founding editor of Silverfish Review Press. His poems have appeared in *ZYZZYVA, Caliban, upstreet, Shankpainter,* and online in *The Northern Agrarian Monthly* and *Poets Against War*. A chapbook, *Unbending Intent*, was published by 26 Books (Portland, Oregon, 1997). He has made his living as a warehouse worker for the last 23 years. **Silverfish Review Press** (www.silverfishreviewpress.com) is a non-profit independent literary press that sponsors the annual Gerald Cable Book Award and other book projects; distributed by Small Press Distribution; member, Council of Literary Magazines and Presses.

What is the most unique or quirky aspect of your press?

Joseph Bednarik: We publish poetry exclusively, and have done so for over 35 years.

Elizabeth Bradfield: I suppose it's Broadsided Press's distribution method: total serendipity. We post our monthly broadsides online, which is not so strange, but the "true" publication comes when people download, print, and post them locally in cafes, offices, bus stops, etc. We want to get work out onto the streets where it can find people who might not seek out a literary journal. Our hope is that Broadsided can help public spaces become more complex, richer, more reflective of the inner life rather than the consumer life.

Some people have stepped forward and pledged to post one or two Broadsideds a month, and we call these volunteers Vectors. They are the heart of Broadsided. There are Vectors in almost every U.S. state and in several countries abroad—all Vector sites that we know of are listed on our Web site. However, even with this system, there's an element of chance. We don't really know precisely where Broadsided publications are posted, although some Vectors have shared their sites. One, for example, keeps a sheaf of Broadsided publications in her bag and puts them up on the inside of bathroom stalls—which I love. A Vector might be gone for a few months or otherwise unable to post, and that's fine. There might be secret or sporadic Vectors we don't know of. I have to say, as a person who likes spreadsheets and who alphabetizes her library, this letting go of the end result is a challenge, but a good one.

Claudia Mauro: Poet Muriel Rukyser said "The universe is made up of stories, not atoms." We take this idea seriously, and it is at the core of the Whit Press Mission. The poems and stories we're surrounded by matter, and they have a profound impact on our lives.

A nonprofit, independent literary press is a crucial component of true democracy. At a time when the mainstream mass media is promoting an increasingly cynical and divisive public discourse, Whit Press provides a forum for the truth of our collective experience through books. Nowadays, to respect the power and potential of the literary arts in this way is unfortunately unique—if not down right quirky.

Rodger Moody: Silverfish only publishes books of poetry. Which isn't all that quirky in and of itself. Maybe the most unique aspect is the name of the press. Though some have thought the press is named for a kind of fish, it actually is named after the insect, the silverfish, that we sometimes find in our books when we pull them off the library or bookstore shelf, or shelf at home. Silverfish eat paper. Librarians dislike them. What can I say? I was young and just out of grad school when I started out. I was trying to be clever and deep thinking. A mistake of youth.

Collaborative efforts between poetry publishers and the greater arts community seems to be on the rise. Could you talk a little bit about how you combine efforts with other arts communities?

Bradfield: Broadsided *is* collaboration: Each publication brings together original literary and visual work into a singular piece. The writing is selected from open submissions, and the visual work is created by a pool of artists who have agreed to be part of Broadsided. We've been lucky to receive work from amazing writers—both established and emerging—and to have a range of talented artists from different aesthetics engaged with the press. We feel that conversations of visual and written art enrich each field and create different ways for readers and viewers to engage with what we publish.

All the artists in our pool are people whose work we admire and respect, and we do not offer suggestions or ask for changes to the work submitted. Once we've chosen a piece of writing that we think will work for Broadsided, we email it out to the artists. Whoever responds first to "dibs" the writing is in charge of creating a visual response to the work. The artists is given free reign.

Kathleen Flenniken: Floating Bridge Press has always involved artists in our publications, hiring letterpress artists to design and print our chapbook covers, and using images of local artists' work on the covers of our *Pontoon* anthologies and *Floating Bridge Review*. Lately we have turned to the local community of artists asking for help with our fundraising event *The Great Art Party*. We receive donations of artwork in the $100 to $500 range. Arts patrons then purchase a $100 to $300 ticket allowing them to take the artwork of their choice in a lottery-style gala evening.

Of course, the press is very grateful to the local arts organizations which have generously provided funding to us year after year, including the Washington State Arts Commission, the City of Seattle Mayor's Office of Arts & Culture, and 4Culture.

Floating Bridge Press is also partnering with a major Seattle hotel looking to become more involved in the local arts scene. They are using our books as corporate gifts and commissioning 1,000 copies of a "family-friendly" anthology of Washington State poets to put in each hotel room in 2009.

Mauro: Our intention at Whit Press is to create books that reach beyond the page to become direct, positive community action tools. To be considered for publication, any project we release must have a very strong community service, collaborate component at its heart.

We create books that use literature as a tool in support of other nonprofit organizations working towards environmental and social justice. This is a key part of our mission. For example, we recently put together an anthology in collaboration with the PCC Farmland Fund Trust titled *In Praise of Fertile Land*. We collected work from our finest poets and storytellers, combined them with poems written specifically for this book by Seattle schoolchildren and sold the book through Puget Sound Consumers Coop stores. All the proceeds from the sale of the book went to purchasing and protecting farmland from development. *In Praise of Fertile Land* has already been a key component in saving one farm, hopefully it will help to save many more. Poetry saves farm! I love this book and this project model.

I addition to organization-based projects we have also initiated an annual publication series with Hedgebrook Retreat for Women Writers. Our first book in this series was a collection of poetry from Nigerian-American writer, Uchechi Kalu. We are about to release Ruth Forman's *Prayers Like Shoes* for this year. Next year, we'll publish a collection by Suhier Hammad. I am very excited about this series!

One of the ways that publishing has changed recently is the use of the Internet to expand outreach to a community of writers and of readers. Could you talk a little about how you've used Web sites, blogs, or other online opportunities? Do you think this has had an impact on your readership in terms of an expanding demographic? How can you tell?

Bednarik: This is a complicated question to unpack, because publishing hasn't been "changed" by the Internet—it's been revolutionized. The availability of poetry on the Internet can be vast beyond reason: Just now I put the word "poetry" into a web search engine and came up with over 203,000,000 sites and citations. What could this number possibly mean? If you invested one second per entry it would take nearly six and a half years *just to read the list.*

One underlying principle at Copper Canyon is that the word "publish" is rooted in "to make public," and for us, "making public" is producing high-quality books and working hard to promote them to readers. With that in mind, our most consistent use of the Internet has been to promote poetry books. But our use of the Internet is maturing and expanding. In late 2008 we successfully published out first "e-broadside"—a marriage of old and new technologies, letterpress and Internet.

Bradfield: Broadsided resides online and only has a physical component when people out there create one. I have a background in web design and online community sites. One of my first jobs out of college was as an editor for an Internet site in the early 1990s that was dedicated to creating a place for mothers to connect with one another (as a twist of fate, the offices were located in Port Townsend, Washington, home of Copper Canyon Press), and I was amazed by the strength of the connections and networks that online communities could forge.

When I started thinking about starting my own press, that experience definitely came to mind. I was living up in Alaska, and many of the discussions I had with fellow writers revolved around how distant we felt from the literary world. Yet all of us had friends "outside" that we stayed in touch with, and it seemed to me that there could be a way to start breaking down such geographic barriers. The web allows access to communities without bookstores or even roads. It taps into a more private mode of communication/community. As one friend who has been traveling a lot lately says, "Home is where the hard drive is." So, from the outset, the web was the site for Broadsided.

Flenniken: We have a Web site and blog, but neither is as high on our priority list as it might be. We use our most precious resource—our editors' volunteer hours—reading manuscripts, overseeing the publication of our books, writing grants and fundraising first. But we do use the blog to showcase our poets and events, and our Web site functions as a catalog of our publications and a repository for our mission statement and competition guidelines. Certainly the online catalog makes it easier for out-of-state readers to find us and buy our books. And, based on our PayPal figures, they have.

The goal is always to find readers, and the internet is pure potential. It's tantalizing to think of attracting a national audience to our regional press online—it may take just one whiz intern or highly motivated new editor to pull us into the deep end. I can't help observing, though, that even the poetry lions struggle to find new readers.

In what way, if any, do you see geography as being important to your press? Do you think there is such a thing as a northwest sensibility in terms of literature?

Bednarik: In the early days, Copper Canyon made it a point to publish northwest poets. Today, however, we look to the entire world for our poets, though we do publish our fair share from the northwest. As for a "northwest sensibility": If someone wanted to write a doctoral dissertation on the subject they probably could. There are no doubt certain images and themes that consistently appear in poets from this region. Our editor, for example, long ago grew weary of seeing the word combination "blue heron."

Flenniken: Floating Bridge is a regional press—until very recently a Washington State press—so geography is central to our identity. But I want to be clear: our books are of national caliber. There are certainly poets that embody the Northwest landscape (Richard Hugo comes immediately to mind), but they not of any particular school. I've observed a shared sensibility among a certain set of young Seattle poets, but that's attributable (and a tribute) to the abiding influence of Richard Kenney and Heather McHugh at the University of Washington, not a matter of geography.

We have a broad range of tastes on our editorial board, and our publications reflect it. Our anthologies may be limited to Washington State poets, but every sort of sensibility is represented. I resist the idea of a Northwest style of writing. It's too easy for the uninitiated to suppose we are provincial simply because we're regional.

Bradfield: Although the idea of Broadsided is to exist everywhere and anywhere, I don't think that I would have begun Broadsided if I hadn't lived in Alaska. I'd had ideas of bringing poetry into public spaces before, but they were more local ideas—billboards, maybe, or kiosks. There was something about the sprawl of Anchorage, the sense of a wide and loose net of writers in the state that made me want to start a press that could reach all of them, even those out in communities off the road system. And, too, I wanted to build a bridge between poets in Alaska and the rest of the U.S., because often it seemed that we were thought of and thought of ourselves as a bit "exotic" and thus not really part of serious poetic conversations going on "outside."

When I moved east to Cape Cod in my mid-twenties and then back west to Alaska in my thirties, I was struck by the different poets' voices that are known and visible in each place. Writers that I grew up loving and feeling close to—Linda Bierds, Tess Gallagher, Robert Wrigley—were not on the radar out east, not in the way that, say, Jean Valentine, Marie Howe, and Nick Flynn were. The regionalism surprised me. There are poets who operate on a national level, but there are plenty of amazing writers who are little-known outside their own corner of the country.

Mauro: I worked as an ocean/environmental science technician in Alaska for nearly 20 years. I also worked up there as a back-country pilot.

Over time what I saw was that we would do an environmental study, make management recommendations, then watch the environment degrade as those recommendations were ignored. Then we would do another study, and watch the environment degrade further, and on and on it seemed to go.

I realized that study after study could document exactly *how* the destruction of the natural world was effecting us, but if there was going to be any kind of lasting solution— we'd have to change our *hearts*, not just our laws. This inspired me to create Whit Press.

Poetry and storytelling work on consciousness itself, and the northwest—from Alaska to the Northern Rockies—has a profound influence. Even in the inner-city, from the streets to the internet cafes, the crows and ravens are still watching. The Wildness of our place is always very close.

As both a practicing poet and publisher, what do you view as the central challenge to this dual identity? How do you balance these somewhat opposing roles?

Flenniken: In my role as one of four editors, I validate my peers by publishing their work and helping them find an audience, and by paying them for their work, which in turn makes me feel useful and integral to the poetry community. My circle has widened considerably since I joined the press. When my first book came out, I had many more contacts, many more options for local readings and book sales, because of my association with Floating Bridge.

The challenge is finding enough time for both my own writing and the press. When there are press deadlines, or manuscripts to be read, or editorial duties calling, the press wins. Most other times, my writing wins. There's never enough time for the press. There's always some task calling.

What are you excited about? Any new projects (books, broadsides, collaborations) for the coming year? Can you tell us about one?

Bednarik: We're always excited about our new books, and we'll have 17 of them in 2009, including an anticipated debut, two bilingual Chinese translations, and a new book by Lucia Perillo.

Bradfield: This year, for example, we hope to launch a new feature for Broadsided that, in essence, allows the web visitor to become the designer/editor. We're calling it the "Mix-n-Match." Our plan is to have both writers and artists—anyone—submit work on a single topic/idea that Broadsided assigns. We will choose three pieces of writing and three pieces of art, and then they'll be put into a fancy web interface so that visitors to the site can put together the various pieces and make their own Broadsided publications. They will be able to move things around, resize images, and print their designs. We want people to play and participate and see how different pieces of writing and art interact to create something unique and utterly singular.

Flenniken: Our new annual magazine, *Floating Bridge Review*, includes a section that we reinvent with each issue. In the inaugural issue we solicited work from six Washington poets with forthcoming books. In the second issue we invited guest editor John Olson to curate. The third issue is still up in the air. We are inspired by this new flexibility.

Moody: I just finished prepress, with the help of a typesetter and cover designer, for the 2007 GCBA winner. I'll receive proofs tomorrow. The poet, Joel Friederich, is currently living with his wife, Lee Evans, and two sons, in Toyko, Japan. Which reminds me of how happy I am for e-mail as I use email for editing with the poet and for communicating with the typesetter, cover designer, and out-of-state printer. I like to think of a book as an art object. And I enjoy looking for ways to show care for the appearance or presentation of the work, both in regard to the inside text, and the cover.

What advice do you have for someone interested in starting an independent poetry press—someone who does not have much money, but does possess buckets of energy?

Mauro: Well, there's the old joke—

Q: "How do you make a small fortune in publishing?

A: "Start with a large fortune."

I think the thing that most writers and would-be publishers don't realize, is how difficult it is to distribute the work after it is produced. Distribution and access channels bottleneck through a very small number of mega-corporations. Thank goodness for librarians and the few independent booksellers that remain. Along with the nonprofit independent publishers, they are the superheroes of the literary arts.

I would advise anyone interested in starting a poetry press to realize that creating quality work is only the first step. The learning curve is near vertical, but it is vital to learn as much about the industry as possible *before* you start writing checks. And publishing itself must be a genuine passion, because one thing is certain—you're bound to make a "small fortune" in no time.

Bradfield: This is a tough one. If you've got web design skills, that, of course, is a way to avoid a lot of publication expenses. If you've got grant writing skills, the field opens. Two things I thought a great deal about in developing the idea of Broadsided that, in hindsight, I'm very glad of: first, I wanted to feel that I was offering something to the world that was truly unique. I didn't want to start a new publishing venture without considering how it could be distinct and perhaps expand the conversation of poetry in the world.

Second, I set up the pace of Broadsided (we publish one collaboration every month) so that I could do it even if I had a full-time job, even if things got crazy. I want Broadsided to have a long history. I suppose my final piece of advice would be to talk. Talk to everyone. Get ideas. Find a group of people you can bounce ideas off of, advisors who can challenge you and suggest routes and ideas you'd never have come up with alone. One of the surprising benefits of beginning Broadsided has been the people I've met through the press—I didn't expect it to become a community, but it has, and I feel very lucky for that.

Bednarik: Do your research. Read *So Many Books*, by Gabriel Zaid, and make lots of margin notes. Do an internship at a publisher you admire and ask every question you can think of. Create a list of all the poetry publishers in the country and see what books they've published over the past few years. Visit Poets House in New York City when they present their annual showcase of all the poetry books published in the previous year. Contact CLMP (Council of Literary Magazines and Presses) and see what services they offer a fledgling publisher. If, after all this preparation, some book or publisher or poet seizes your attention, work to figure out why. Then, if you haven't psyched yourself out, dive in. And keep reading, researching, and asking questions.

Flenniken: Floating Bridge Press started when seven folks in a writing group in Seattle ponied up $50 each and decided to publish a chapbook. I think Floating Bridge has been successful for 15 years now because we've kept our scope manageable, we operate on a strict budget, we're excellent grant writers, and we love the beautiful books we make. None of us is too important to do menial tasks. And we enjoy our work because we enjoy each other. I advise wine at every board meeting.

The Art of Failure

Poetry in Translation

by Okla Elliott

Translators are the shadow heroes of literature, the often forgotten instruments that make it possible for different cultures to talk to one another.

—Paul Auster

The historical importance of translation for English language poetry is undeniable. Henry Howard, the Earl of Surrey, invented blank verse in order to translate Virgil's *Æneid* in 1554, because the Latin original was unrhymed yet metered, and no equivalent existed in English. Blank verse, brought to us by a translator's ingenuity, allowed for Shakespeare's plays to be written as we know them. The sonnet (*sonetto* or "little song" in Italian) was created by Giacomo da Lentini and enjoyed a boom among Italian poets such as Calvalcanti, Dante, and Petrarch in the mid-13th and early 14th centuries. It was not until the 16th century that sonnets began appearing in English, in translations from Italian and from French. And the list of gifts translators have brought English poetry goes on—couplets, villanelles, sestinas, and, some have argued, even free verse via attempts to translate Chinese poetry. The question now is: What is the cultural and artistic place of translation in the age of globalization?

According to a Center for Book Culture study on the number of books translated into English between 2000-2006, it's a pretty dismal place. Most countries had fewer than one book per year translated into English, and literary heavyweights such as France, Italy, and Germany had fewer than ten books per year translated into English—and this includes novels and nonfiction as well as poetry. The percentage of books in translation tends to be estimated, by such organizations as the NEA and PEN, at about three percent of the total published in America. (Incidentally, there is an excellent blog about translation, out of the University of Rochester, called Three Percent, www.rochester.edu/College/translation/threepercent.) Does this mean the effort of translation is hopeless or unimportant? Not necessarily.

Translation is very complex; the process, the need, and the market for it are not so easily summed up. To understand the landscape, we have to look at the differences

OKLA ELLIOTT is an Assistant Professor at Ohio Wesleyan University. His nonfiction, poetry, short fiction, and translations have appeared or are forthcoming in A Public Space, Cold Mountain Review, Indiana Review, New Letters, Pedestal Magazine, and other publications. He is the author of The Mutable Wheel and Lucid Bodies and Other Poems. He is also co-editor, with Kyle Minor, of The Other Chekhov.

between publishing translation as books or in journals, translating contemporary or older work, working alone or collaboratively. Likewise, the politics and ethics of translation play a role. And perhaps most importantly, the process and joys of translation need to be understood.

THE PROCESS OF TRANSLATION

The primary goal of translation is to recreate the effect of the original poem in the target language (the language into which you are translating). The problem, of course, is that if the poet did her work properly in the original (or source) language, then she made use of every available trick and tactic, thus making the job of recreating the poem almost impossible. This is why Umberto Eco calls translation "the art of failure." But while perfection is perhaps not possible, there are thousands of excellent translations in existence. So, how were they done?

You have to determine whether you want to transport the source text into the target language or transport the reader of your translation to the source culture. If you are translating, for example, a contemporary Mexican poet, and the word *buñuelo* appears, you have to decide whether to replace this very specific Mexican sweet bun made with orange juice with some American equivalent (a honeybun perhaps) or to simply leave the Spanish word in the English translation and hope the reader knows what a *buñuelo* is. A third option is to retain the Spanish word and footnote it, though footnotes can ruin the effect of a poem if there are too many of them. The general rule is to avoid them when possible. Of course, the problem with replacing a Mexican pastry with a traditional American pastry is that—forgive the pun—you damage the original flavor of the poem, though you do not run the risk of losing or confusing your reader. But both tactics lead to problems, as nearly everything in translation does. I don't mean to suggest that a translation can't do both. In fact, most good translations do, but each successful translation, in order to have its singular effect as the original had *its* singular effect, ought to privilege one effort over the other.

Depending on the source text, your level of mastery of the source language, and whether there are pre-existing translations, the first stages of working on a new translation of a poem will differ wildly. When translating Latin and Greek literature, David Slavitt uses pre-existing literal prose translations of the poems as well as his personal knowledge of Latin and Greek "to turn the prose translations back into poems." Slavitt says, "When you translate prose, you are the original author's clerk, but when you translate poetry, you are his partner."

Frequently, translation is also done collaboratively. Likely the most famous contemporary duo is Richard Pevear and Larissa Volokhonsky, who have redone many of the Russian prose masterpieces. A notable team in poetry translation is Peter Burian and Alan Shapiro, who collaborate on translations of ancient literature. The make-up of the team is frequently a scholar of the source language/text and a poet who knows the tricks of English verse and who might have some knowledge of the source language.

But no matter your tactics or whether you work alone or with a collaborator, tough choices will have to be made. My translation of Jürgen Becker's poem "Oderbruch," which appeared in the *Indiana Review*, offers a simple example of the issues a translator runs into in nearly every line. I had translated "[g]elb graue Dämmerung" as "[g]old gray twilight" which caused the faculty member consulted about the accuracy of my translation to suggest that I change it to the more literal "[y]ellow gray twilight." In one sense, he was right—"gelb" means "yellow." But I felt that "gold" was close enough to the literal meaning, but it had the added poetic benefit of retaining the consonance and the number of syllables in the original. Ultimately, the poetry editors at *Indiana Review* agreed with me, but not because I was unquestionably right. We were both right about how to translate the line. It was simply that I was willing to make a small sacrifice in literalness to retain the music, whereas he was willing to make a small sacrifice of the music to retain a more exact meaning. Every poem will present a dozen or more moments where the translator must sacrifice one thing for another. Only rarely does a poem submit easily to transfer into a new language/culture. That, however, is also part of the joy. Nearly every translator speaks of the joy of finding an elegant solution to a seemingly insoluble problem.

Slavitt says, "I didn't take a Hippocratic Oath when I signed on to be a writer. I feel no obligation to the literal meaning of the text whatsoever." It's the pleasure of the original he is after. Does that mean Twinkies show up in Ovid? Well, fine, let it be so. Or so Slavitt says. But the business of translation is a highly contentious one, and one where opinions are unusually strong and criticisms often bitter.

One of the joys of translation is what you can learn by doing it. Slavitt went to the Eclogues and Georgics of Virgil in order to learn how to make a paragraph work in verse. Matthew Zapruder, author of *The Pajamaist* and translator of the Romanian poet Eugen Jebeleanu, reports, "I also had a sense right away that it would be a good thing for me, a poet just starting to find his way, to be inside the seriousness of the voice and the directness and implacable structure of the poems."

PUBLISHING TRANSLATIONS

The report on the market for poetry in translation is mixed. A recent *New York Review of Books* article points out that Iran publishes more literature in translation than the United States does—as do all European countries and most Latin American ones. That said, however, it has been my experience that original poetry and fiction are comparably hard to place in journals, whereas translation and nonfiction are much easier to place. This has, predictably, to do with the volume and quality of submissions in each genre, as well as current demand. Brett Fletcher Lauer, a poetry editor at *A Public Space* and an advisor editor at Columbia University's *Circumference*, a journal dedicated entirely to poetry in translation, offers the following theory on why translations tend to be better and therefore more likely to be accepted: "*A Public Space* receives a relatively small number of submissions of poetry in translation compared with the thousands of submissions of English-language poetry. That being said, the overall quality of translations submitted is very high. I'm not sure how to account for this fact." He goes on to speculate, "The process of translating and the dedication it requires makes it so that it cannot be casual work, but, instead, a sort of over-time, and what we receive reflects this."

"Generally journals were happy to publish the poems," says Zapruder of his translations of Jebeleanu. "I had more difficulty publishing the book; in fact, I finished the translations in 1998, and it took almost 10 years for the book to eventually come out with Coffee House Press."

Slavitt says, "If you translate a standard classic and are lucky enough to get it adopted as a text in enough courses, it will do much better than original poetry." But he adds, "If you translate someone who needs translating—Ausonius for instance—it's about even [with sales of original collections of poetry]." Given the generally poor sales of poetry collections, this might not be very heartening, but it ought to be. Either a book of translation will sell about the same as an original collection or considerably better, especially if you can recast a classic poet in a new translation.

Some of the journals most supportive of poetry in translation are *Absinthe, The Bitter Oleander, Circumference, Indiana Review, International Poetry Review, The Literary Review, Natural Bridge, New Letters, Poetry International,* and *A Public Space.* There are others, of course, but these are journals that are dedicated to translation solely or that publish some translation in nearly every issue. And presses that publish translation regularly include Northwestern University Press, Red Hen Press, Sheep Meadow Press, and Ugly Duckling Presse. If a new translator wants to discover what is happening in translation today, he or she would do well to peruse these publications.

ADVICE FOR GETTING STARTED

If you're a first-time translator, it is unlikely that you'll get the rights to translate and publish the work of a major author whose work is still under copyright—e.g., Günter Grass or Pablo Neruda. Mark Smith-Soto, the editor of *International Poetry Review* and a poet/translator in his own right, advises that a new translator find an author who enjoys a good reputation in his/her home country but who hasn't yet been translated into English. "If you ask a poet whether he'd like to be translated, the answer is generally going to be yes," Smith-Soto says. And here is where the unfortunate state of literature in translation can actually be a plus. Since there is so much excellent literature that has yet to be translated, you'll have plenty to choose from. But since you'll be spending many hours living in the poet's work, it's important to find work you admire. Otherwise, what should be a joy will become a chore. Once you've established yourself, then the larger gigs will come.

It's also worthwhile to have a working knowledge of translation theory, which sounds daunting but which in fact can be attained by reading two excellent books out from University of Chicago Press, *The Craft of Translation* and *Theories of Translation,* both edited by John Biguenet and Rainer Schulte. These two reasonably sized volumes will bring you from Dryden's thinking on translation through Goethe's and up to Gregory Rabassa's with excellent stops at Nietzsche's, Benjamin's, and others'.

So, read these books, read the journals that publish translations, read these two seminal texts on the theory and craft of translation, find poetry you admire, and get to work. It's rewarding for both the translator and for the literary culture as a whole.

Why Publishing a Chapbook Makes Sense

by Jeannine Hall Gailey

Maybe you've published some poems in good literary journals, you've started giving readings around town, and you're ready for the next step. You have a lot of poems in your repertoire, but aren't sure exactly how to get your work into the hands of the public. Now is the time to consider putting together a chapbook. This article describes the benefits of publishing chapbooks and how to go about it, including advice from chapbook publishers and writers with successful chapbooks.

What is a poetry chapbook?

Definitions abound (one is even included in the FAQ section at the beginning *of Poet's Market*), but today's chapbooks are primarily defined by length (usually less than 30 pages) and production (usually limited edition, sometimes handmade.) While some are beautiful book-arts products, perfect bound with high-quality covers, like those published by Washington State Chapbook Press Floating Bridge or Tupelo Press, a chapbook can also be a stapled-together affair produced at the local copy shop.

As for the means of production, there are many chapbook presses out there (New Michigan Press, Concrete Wolf, Floating Bridge, Finishing Line Press, Pudding House Press...). But you can also self-publish a chapbook to sell at readings.

Chapbooks used to be mainly an emerging poet's way of getting their work out to the public, but these days, presses like Sarabande Press have created in-demand chapbooks for well-known authors such as Louise Glück and James Tate as well. Dorianne Laux, for instance, recently published a chapbook, *Superman*, with Red Dragonfly Press.

Why a Poetry Chapbook?

The benefits are multiple. First, the task of putting together a chapbook collection of poems—thinking about organization, which poems to include or exclude, polishing up poems you meant to revise but never got around to—is great training for putting together a full-length book. Second, learning to market and sell your own work—getting over the embarrassment of asking bookstores to carry your chapbook, or telling friends about your

---

JEANNINE HALL GAILEY is a San Diego writer whose first book of poetry, Becoming the Villainess, was published by Steel Toe Books. She was awarded a 2007 Dorothy Sargent Rosenberg Prize for Poetry and a 2007 Washington State Artist Trust GAP grant. Her poems have appeared in several publications, including The Iowa Review, The Columbia Poetry Review, and Smartish Pace. She currently teaches at the MFA program at National University.

chapbook publication—is essential for any poet, because the usual marketing machinery of publishing (talk shows, end-caps at Barnes & Nobles, advertising campaigns) doesn't really exist in the poetry publishing world, which is run on slim margins by a very few overworked but dedicated people.

Kelli Russell Agodon, whose sold-out chapbook, *Geography*, was one of Floating Bridge Press' best sellers, talked about how the experience of having a chapbook had benefited her. "Having a chapbook has helped me by opening new doors. It has allowed me to have opportunities such as teaching or reading at poetry festivals and conferences that may not have been open to me if I didn't have a book. It also helped me understand the publishing process a little better before my full length collection. Also, crafting the chapbook really allowed me to focus on one particular subject."

Lana Ayers, editor and publisher at Concrete Wolf, a chapbook publisher, details further benefits. "Chapbooks provide an opportunity for authors to produce tightly woven or themed collections. And since most chapbooks, are less expensive than full-length collections, it is easier to convince a reader to take the plunge. Also, the shorter length of the collection can be less intimidating for readers new to poetry. So chapbooks are an all-around great opportunity for both poets and readers to get acquainted."

Kristy Bowen, editor and publisher at Dancing Girl Press, talks about why she started publishing chapbooks. "I also have a love for the chapbook itself as form, a small morsel of poetry that can be devoured in one sitting. Also, they are an affordable way to get new work into the hands of readers with very little fuss. I'm interested as well in how to expand the traditional notion of chapbooks further into the realm of book arts."

Writers have different motivations for publishing chapbooks—fascination with the form, building a relationship with an audience, or finding a home for a particular set of poems. Dorianne Laux described her decision to publish a chapbook after several highly successful full-length collections.

"I met Scott King, of Red Dragonfly Press while I was at the Anderson Center for the Arts for a writing residency and he was producing letterpress broadsides. He later asked if I'd like to do a chapbook. At the time, I wasn't sure if I had enough poems on a theme to make a book, but said yes anyway, not wanting to miss a chance to work with Scott. It took me about a year to come up with the poems in *Superman* which are all loosely based around pop culture figures, icons and objects of the 20th century. I wasn't yet ready for a fifth book of poems and so a chapbook seemed a great way to have something in the interim," she says.

"But more important was my desire to have a beautiful book, hand set on gorgeous paper and sewn together, something that would be a small, elegant gift I could give to friends," Laux continues. "It was also a way to bring attention to this small press and its poet/editor, Scott King, who had taught me so much about the quality of labor that went into reproducing a page of words before the invention of carbon paper, mimeo and Xerox machines, computers and desktop printers. It was exacting, dangerous and dirty work, performed amidst smoke, sparks and fire by some anonymous typesetter bent over in a greasy smock, delicately choosing the next stately letter with the deafening clatter of the molten lead foundry pounding against the drums in his ears. It's also wonderfully ironic to have a book about 20th century characters like Cher and The Beatles produced using a 16th century technology!"

So now you're intrigued. But how, exactly, do you put together a chapbook?

What does putting together a chapbook entail?

The good news is that it's a lot like putting together a book, but a more compact, and perhaps, more tightly-themed collection. Usually, writers have obsessions, and those obsessions manifest themselves over time. You'll find twenty poems on superheroes, for instance, or on abandoned gas stations in the Midwest. Or you'll find twenty poems that tell their own story.

Kelli Russell Agodon's advice for someone putting together a chapbook for the first time? "My advice would be to focus your chapbook on one subject, theme, or story. The best chapbooks look deeply at a topic, but also make new discoveries in their poems throughout the book. I suggest choosing only your strongest poems for your chapbook, then determine if there are certain poems you need to write to make the chapbook stronger and more complete."

Kristy Bowen adds that "sometimes, especially poets at the beginning of their career see a chapbook as a stepping stone to the first book, which it usually is, but I suspect they sometimes see the chapbook merely as a shorter volume sort of tossed together without any real feel of cohesion in the chapbook itself. So what you get is an odd mismatch of the poems they consider best, but without any sort of thematic or formal binding." So what is Dancing Girl Press' editor looking for? "We particularly look for work that has a strong sense of image and music, cohesiveness as a manuscript, interesting and surprising, sometimes unusual, use of language. We love humor when done well, strangeness, wackiness. Hybridity, collage, intertextuality. Manuscripts that create their own worlds."

This brings us to the next subject—how to get your chapbook published.

How Are Chapbooks Published?

You've got your manuscript of 15-30 pages of thematically-engaged, tightly edited poetry together, so now what? Well, many chapbook publishers, just like poetry book publishers, decide what they are going to publish through a contest system. Presses like this include Tupelo Press, Concrete Wolf, Pudding House, and New Michigan Press. If you go this route, you should research the publisher by obtaining at least one of their previous publications, checking out the production and writing quality, and decide if it's a good fit for you. If it is, then you send off your manuscript with a cover letter, a check (usually $10-15), and a SASE, and hope for the best. Some presses publish runners-up and finalists as well as winners. Be sure to read the guidelines thoroughly, and follow them to the letter.

Some chapbook publishers, like Sarabande Press, only publish through solicitation—that is, they contact the person they want to publish directly - so unless you get a call, you won't be getting your chapbook published through them. Some chapbook publishers will read "open submissions," for a few months a year, like Dancing Girl Press, but these are few and far between.

Of course, there's always self-publishing, and this is an easier (and more affordable) feat if you're attempting a saddle-stitched chapbook than a perfect bound book. You could even put it all up—your poems, the cover art, your table of contents and acknowledgements - on your own computer, using basic publishing software, print it out on your own laser printer, and staple it at your kitchen table. If you google "make your own saddle-stitched chapbook" you can find a couple of sets of instructions, or if you're lucky enough to have a book arts center near you, sign up for a class.

Marketing a Poetry Chapbook

Marketing a chapbook is, admittedly, more difficult to market than a poetry book. Many bookstores won't carry them because they are difficult to store and display. Your best bet is to talk an independent bookstore into carrying a copy or two on consignment. Most review outlets don't take chapbook reviews, and chapbooks are not usually eligible for major book awards.

But chapbooks are by nature ephemeral, and that can be an advantage. A limited run means an especially beautiful or well-written chapbook might later become a collector's item, and no writer keeps too many chapbooks on hand—and, unlike books, they don't take up too much space to store. Many people see chapbooks as a more intimate way to get to know a poet's work, and value the fact that the chapbooks may only be around for a short amount of time. Chapbooks are easy to sell at poetry readings, where the buyer is more likely to want a souvenir of that experience, and on poet's web sites, where the buyers are already familiar with the poet and their work. If you have friends with blogs, send them a review copy of your chapbook and ask them to say a few words.

So, remember this—give readings. Be an interesting, enthusiastic reader who has actually organized their work and practiced it a few times. This will increase the odds that audience members might want to buy your chapbook! And, make sure you have a personal web site or blog that your fans can come to and find out how to buy your chapbook— whether it's directly from you or from a link to your publisher or even Amazon. Don't make them hunt for it!

Why Should You Consider Publishing a Chapbook?

A chapbook gives you a way to connect with your reader. It gives your reader a physical reminder of your work, and sometimes it's a beautiful artifact, sometimes a humble set of copies, folded over and stapled. Creating a chapbook helps you practice organizing your work into a coherent collection. Selling your chapbook orients you in the world of marketing poetry, and, if you do it yourself or watch it being produced, a way to understand the physical work of book publishing.

Because of these benefits, it's more than just a step towards a full-length poetry collection—it's a way for you to build an audience, to put your work out into the world in a considered, deliberate way. Take a look at the chapbook publishers listed in Poet's Market, and order some samples to get an idea of the diversity of the production and content of chapbooks available as well as figure out which publisher might be right for you. Before you know it, you'll have something in hand to share at readings and with friends and family.

Finding Readers

How to Get Your Poetry into Their Hands

by Diane Lockward

Poets who are fortunate enough to have a full-length collection from a large publishing house receive the services of a marketing department with a budget that covers advertising and a book tour. But if you, like most of us, get your book from a small press, you will find that your publisher has little or no budget for promotion. There are a number of benefits to working with a small press publisher, for example, more involvement in the design of the book and a personal relationship with your publisher. However, if you want your book to find its way into the hands of readers, you are going to have to work to make that happen.

Spreading the Word

The work of promoting your book begins before the book is even out. Most small press publishers have found that ads are not cost effective, but they will design a press release and do a snail mailing for you. While you wait for your book to get published, compile an up-to-date snail mail list. Since mailings are expensive, include only your best prospects, not everyone you've ever met. Many publishers also do an email blitz, so prepare a list of email addresses. Your publisher will most likely send the press release and a review copy to journals that have published your work. Assemble a list of the names and addresses of those journals, but only the ones that run reviews.

After your book is published, supplement your publisher's mailings with your own. Many publishers provide postcards for this purpose, but if yours doesn't, you can design your own inexpensively at an online service such as vistaprint.com. Upload your cover image onto one side and add ordering information on the other, leaving space for name and address of the recipient. In your email notes include your cover image, but do not add an attachment as many people will not open it. It doesn't matter if people receive more than one notice about your book. Janet Holmes, publisher of Ahsahta Books, says, "Sometimes a reader needs to see the title of a book multiple times before it sinks in as something to acquire." Many recipients will appreciate—and act upon—the reminder.

Ask your publisher to provide you with the press release via attachment. Save it on your computer and include it with any additional review copies you mail out. Send the

DIANE LOCKWARD's second collection, *What Feeds Us* (Wind Publications), received the 2006 Quentin R. Howard Poetry Prize. Her poems appear in Garrison Keillor's *Good Poems for Hard Times* and in such journals as *Harvard Review, Spoon River Poetry Review,* and *Prairie Schooner.* (www.dianelockward.com)

press release to your college alumni newsletter. Put one up on the bulletin board where you work. Fire off some to local libraries and bookstores. Send another with a fact sheet to your local newspaper. Request an article and offer to go in for an interview. My local paper interviewed me and ran an article for each of my books. That would not have happened if I hadn't asked.

Lining Up Readings

Tom Hunley, director of Steel Toe Books, says, "Readings are far and away the #1 way for poets to sell books." Let your first reading be a book launch party. Invite your relatives, friends, and poet pals. Have food. This reading may well be your best sales event. If you have a friend with a book coming out around the same time, consider joining forces. Publisher Joan Cusack Handler celebrates each new CavanKerry Press book with a literary salon held in someone's home. Poet Claire Keyes (*The Question of Rapture*, Mayapple Press, 2008) had house readings held by friends. She and her hosts collaborated on the guest list and shared expenses.

After the initial round of readings, you need to get proactive. Poet Kate Greenstreet (*case sensitive*, Ahsahta Books, 2006) warns that "if you won't ask—and people aren't already inviting you—obviously, you won't be reading." To get readings, you need to compose a query letter. Keep it informative and succinct. I send most of mine by email with links to my website and online sites where my work is available. Make a list of venues in your area. Try bookstores, libraries, art galleries, coffeehouses—all the usual places. Then get creative. I have friends who've read in chocolate stores, wine bars, and hip jewelry stores. Contact local book clubs and suggest that your book be a selection. Offer to present a reading and discussion for the group. Senior citizens' residences and nursing homes are often looking for social programs. Offer your services for a reading. If you have friends who teach, offer to do a reading, a Q & A, and a workshop. Apply to conferences, festivals, and book fairs.

Target audiences that might likely have an interest in your work and in poetry. For example, I'm a former high school English teacher. One of my most successful readings was for a district-wide English department meeting. I read ten poems and offered ten teaching tips. The supervisor purchased a copy of my book for each department member—all forty of them. That presentation led to an offer to teach a six-hour workshop for a small group of teachers.

Also target groups that don't ordinarily attend readings but are somehow connected to your subject matter. Are your poems about flowers? Query nearby garden clubs and suggest a reading at one of their upcoming meetings. Do your poems deal with woman-related topics? Contact area women's clubs. Marion Haddad (*Somewhere Between Mexico and a River Called Home*, Pecan Grove Press, 2004) is the American-born daughter of Syrian immigrants and for 35 years lived a few minutes from the Mexican border, so she often seeks readings at Arab-American gatherings and border studies events. Richard Jeffrey Newman, whose *The Silence of Men* (CavanKerry, 2006) deals with gender, sexuality, and recovery from child sexual abuse, solicited and received an invitation to read at the 2008 Wellness and Writing Connections Conference. One of my favorite readings was at New York Life Investment Management, certainly an unlikely place for poetry, but the woman who heads Human Resources runs special programs for women employees. I proposed a reading entitled "Poetry and the Lives of Women." My host pre-ordered six of my books and had a drawing for them, a great alternative when reading at an event where selling books might not be appropriate.

Eventually you will need to seek readings outside of your own area. Remember that the farther you cast your net, the fewer responses you're likely to get. Cast it anyhow because you will get some responses. To find out where readings are held, map out the distance you're willing to travel. Then do a Google search, for example, "poetry venues in New Jersey" or "poetry readings in Boston." That should bring up some listings. If there's contact information, send off your query letter. Check out reading schedules on other poets' websites. Visit online calendars, for example, those at The Academy of American Poets' and Poets & Writers' websites. Use these to suggest possible venues to query. When you get readings, publicize them as widely as possible. List them in online calendars and send out email notices to people you know in the area of the reading. Do not rely solely on the venue host to drum up an audience for you.

Regardless of where you're reading, remember that you're promoting your book, so be prepared to read poems from the book. Greg Kosmicki, of The Backwaters Press, advises poets that while they may get tired of reading the same poems, the audience will be hearing them for the first time. Your listeners will be more inclined to buy your book if you hold it and read from it. Remember, too, that not everyone who attends your reading will buy your book. My own publisher, Charlie Hughes of Wind Publications, suggests that often the "value in a reading or personal appearance is not in the number of books sold at the event, but in getting the writer's name in the newspaper announcing the event—building name recognition." I usually bring along oversized postcards with my cover image on one side and a poem and ordering information on the other. I give these away and like to think that some of the recipients might make a later purchase. I also always carry some business cards with me, cover image on one side, contact information on the other.

Using the Internet

The internet is one of your best resources for promoting your book. If you don't already have a website, get one. Even if your publisher has a page for your book at the press' website, you should have your own website. You can get a domain name very inexpensively. Since this is your website's address, use your own name so people can easily locate your website. If you design your own website, you will pay only for the hosting. If you use a free hosting site, be sure it's ad-free. A website with ads looks awful and unprofessional. If you use a web designer's services, you will, of course, pay more, but don't go wild. Your site should include a bio, an image of your book cover, purchase information, sample poems, links to other poems, links to online reviews and interviews, a calendar of your readings, and contact information. Be sure your website is attractive and up to date. A website that is not maintained does not make a good impression.

Consider keeping a blog. There's a big community now of poet bloggers. A blog takes some time, but it's a great place to establish contacts with other poets and another place to display your book cover and list readings. You can add podcasts and videos, thus creating long-distance readings for potential fans who might not otherwise be able to get to a reading. Kate Greenstreet kept a blog for two years. She used it to do a series of more than 100 first-book interviews and undoubtedly earned many friends. As much as she gave to the poetry community, she got back in support when her own book came out.

Join an internet social network such as Facebook, MySpace, or Red Room. These are hot gathering places for poets, and all are free. I'm on Facebook where I create event listings for my readings and send out invitations to "friends" who live in the area of an upcoming reading. Without this resource, I would not know these people's names or how to contact them. I've learned about venues and booked readings through Facebook contacts, gotten an online interview, and participated in a college student's poetry course project. Richard Jeffrey Newman received an invitation from a Facebook contact to go to Chile as part of Chile Poesia, an international poetry festival. A poetry listserv will also put you among poets and offer opportunities for sales and readings.

A final suggestion for your internet use, this one fast and easy. Use your email signature to good advantage. Set your email program to automatically add a link to your website at the bottom of each new message you write. If you like, you can add a link to your blog or anything special you have online such as a poem feature. Think of the signature area as free billboard space. You'll be amazed how many people will click on those links and go visiting.

Keeping Expectations Realistic

Promoting your book is the business of poetry, but don't expect to make money. As Kate Greenstreet says, "When we're talking about selling poetry books, we're talking about doing business, but it isn't conventional business even if you work really hard at it." Richard Jeffrey Newman reminds us that books of poetry "find their audience one reader at a time, slowly, over time." If you want your book to find those readers, you need to be industrious, adventurous, persistent and patient.

10 Tips for the Perfect Poetry Reading

by Taylor Mali

The extent of the advice given to poets for how to present their work aloud at poetry readings usually boils down to reading slower, louder, and clearer. And while those are important improvements to almost anyone's style of recitation (albeit extremely difficult to *make yourself* do, especially at the same time), there are several other factors to keep in mind if you want your audience to appreciate your skills as a writer and perhaps even buy your book after the reading.

1. Try to make the first thing out of your mouth poetry. What else could be more important than immediately giving the audience an example of what they came to the reading to hear? Insipid chatter between poems is bad enough, but *introductory* insipid chatter is even worse and tends to go on and on. Sometimes it will be five minutes before a poet even gets to the first poem! Everything you think you need to say—thank yous, shout outs, announcements about journals in which your poetry will be forthcoming, or plugs for your books and next appearances—all of this can be mentioned after the first poem. Or maybe not at all (except for the thank yous).

2. Know what poems you will read and have them close at hand. Don't burden the audience with having to watch you flip through your own book or resort to looking at the table of contents while you make a self-deprecating joke only to realize finally that the poem you wanted to read is actually in your *other* book. Have your poems picked out in advance as well as the order in which you will read them. All of your fussing between poems counts toward the time you have been given to read

3. Don't be the poet who reads forever! Time limits do not only apply to bad poets; they apply to brilliant poets like you as well. Unfortunately, it's usually the bad poets who have no concept of time. Before the reading, rehearse your set (with a stopwatch if possible) and do not go over the time you've been allotted. Losing track of how long you've been reading is no excuse for going over. Don't ask the organizer to give you a signal when you have five minutes left or periodically look up and ask, "How am I doing on time?" It's your responsibility to know how you are "doing on time." If anything, be a little *under* time and leave your audience wanting more.

TAYLOR MALI is a teacher and voiceover artist. A classically trained Shakespearian actor, Mali was one of the original poets to appear on the HBO series Russell Simmons Presents Def Poetry. He is a veteran of the poetry slam and the author of What Learning Leaves and several spoken word CDs and DVDs. He lives and writes in New York City. For more information, visit www.taylormali.com

4. Keep your chatter between poems to a minimum. Most of what poets say between poems comes from nervousness and not any real need to explicate the poem.

5. Perform one poem by someone else. Depending on how much time you have been given, it's a nice idea to celebrate the work of someone else beside yourself. Introduce your audience to one of your favorite poems by one of your favorite poets. Tell them where they can find this particular poem and two things you love about it. Then, at the end of your reading of the poem, say the author's name one last time.

6. Perform at least one of your poems from memory. Once you experience the freedom of being able to make constant eye contact while having your hands completely free to gesture or hang naturally at your sides (which doesn't *feel* natural at all but looks perfectly normal), you will want to memorize more of your work. And you should! The roots of poetry are bardic, not literary, so it is entirely fitting to work on making the recitation of your poem a better performance. Work at memorizing more and more poetry every day. The mind is a muscle; the more you use it, the stronger it gets.

7. Let the audience clap if they want to clap. If one definition of a "performance" poem is that after it's over, the audience not only *wants* to applaud but *knows that applause is appropriate*, then you could say that one definition of an "academic" poem is that after it's over—assuming you know when that is—the audience doesn't even know if they are supposed to clap. Poets with limited performance skills will often request that audiences *not* applaud between poems because they are uncomfortable with the awkward silence that fills the room when they finish each poem. In fact, sometimes the only clue that such poets *have* finished a poem is when they say, "The next poem I'd like to read." Certainly don't telegraph the end of your poem by speeding up or trailing off or both. Rather build toward it, perhaps nodding your head ever so slightly at the end.

8. Make eye contact. Real eye contact. Look at different parts of the room as you glance up from your text every now and then. Poets who look at the exact same spot as they methodically lift their heads every seven seconds to pretend they are looking at the same person (whose chair is apparently attached to one of the lighting fixtures) aren't fooling anyone. It is better never to look up at all than to do so perfunctorily to mask your nervousness.

9. If there is a microphone, use it. Granted, when the microphone is attached to a podium, you won't have much choice but to use it. But faced with a solitary mic stand and the possibly awkward task of having to adjust it for your height while somehow also managing a bottle of water and the text from which you are about to read, you might decide you don't need a microphone at all. Not a good decision, even if you have a big, boomy voice. Without a microphone, you cannot get quiet when the poem invites it, or else no one will hear you when you do. Unless the system sounds like crap and has for the whole night, use the microphone, even if it takes a few extra seconds at the outset to adjust it.

10. Enjoy yourself. This seems obvious, but audiences love to see people who love what they do, especially when they do it well. Smile a lot. Try reciting an entire poem *while* smiling. Let people suspect you are having the time of your life. And whatever you do, don't ever suggest that your reading is a kind of torture you are inflicting on the audience ("Don't worry. You only have to listen to three more!"). You are a genius, and your words are the proof. Knock 'em dead!

Mistakes Poets Make

In putting together listings for *Poet's Market*, we ask editors for any words of advice they want to share with our readers. Often the editors' responses include comments about what poets should and shouldn't do when submitting work—the same comments, over and over. That means a lot of poets are repeating similar mistakes when they send out their poems for consideration.

The following list includes the most common of those mistakes—the ones poets should work hardest to avoid.

Not reading a publication before submitting work

Researching a publication is essential before submitting your poetry. Try to buy a sample copy of a magazine (by mail, if necessary) or at least see if an issue is available at the library. It may not be economically feasible for poets to purchase a copy of every magazine they target, especially if they send out a lot of poems. However, there are additional ways to familiarize yourself with a publication.

Read the market listing thoroughly. If guidelines are available, send for them by e-mail or regular mail, or check for them online. A publication's website often presents valuable information, including sample poems, magazine covers--and guidelines.

Submitting inappropriate work

Make good use of your research so you're sure you understand what a magazine publishes. Don't rationalize that a journal favoring free verse might jump at the chance to consider your long epic poem in heroic couplets. Don't convince yourself your experimental style will be a good fit for the traditional journal filled with rhyming poetry. Don't go into denial about whether a certain journal and your poetry are made for each other. It's counterproductive and ultimately wastes postage (not to mention time—yours and the editor's).

Submitting an unreasonable number of poems

If an editor recommends sending three to five poems (a typical range), don't send six. Don't send a dozen poems and tell the editor to pick the five she wants to consider. If the editor doesn't specify a number (or the listing says "no limit"), don't take that as an invitation to mail off 20 poems. The editors and staff of literary magazines are busy enough as it is, and they may decide they don't have time to cope with you. (When submitting book or chapbook manuscripts to publishers, make sure your page count falls within the range they state.)

Don't go to the other extreme and send only one poem, unless an editor says it's okay (which is rare). One poem doesn't give an editor much of a perspective on your work, and it doesn't give you very good odds on getting the piece accepted.

Ignoring the editor's preferences regarding formats

If an editor makes a point of describing a preferred manuscript format, follow it, even if that format seems to contradict the standard. (Standard format includes using $8\frac{1}{2} \times 11$ white paper and conventional typeface and point size; avoid special graphics, colors or type flourishes; put your name and address on every page.) Don't devise your own format to make your submission stand out. Keep everything clean, crisp and easy to read (and professional).

Be alert to e-mail submission formats. Follow directions regarding what the editor wants printed in the subject line, how many poems to include in a single e-mail, whether to use attachments or paste work in the body of the message, and other elements. Editors have good reasons for outlining their preferences; ignoring them could mean having your e-mail deleted before your poems are even read.

Omitting a self-addressed stamped envelope (SASE)

Why do editors continuously say "include a SASE with your submission?" Because so many poets don't do it. Here's a simple rule: Unless the editor gives alternate instructions, include a #10 SASE, whether submitting poems or sending an inquiry.

Writing bad cover letters (or omitting them completely)

Cover letters have become an established part of the submission process. There are editors who remain indifferent about the necessity of a cover letter, but many consider it rude to be sent a submission without any other communication from the poet.

Unless the editor says otherwise, send a cover letter. Keep it short and direct, a polite introduction of you and your work. (See "Frequently Asked Questions" on page 7 for more tips on cover letters, and an example.) Here are a few important Don'ts:

- **Don't** list all the magazines where your work has appeared; limit yourself to five magazine titles. The work you're submitting has to stand on its own.
- **Don't** tell the editor what a good poet you are—or how good someone else thinks you are.
- **Don't** tell the editor how to edit, lay out or print your poem. Some of those decisions are up to the editor, assuming she decides to accept your poem in the first place.
- **Don't** point out the poem is copyrighted in your name or include the copyright symbol. All poems are automatically copyrighted in the poet's name as soon as they're "fixed" (i.e., written down), and editors know this.

Not maintaining good editor/poet relations

Most editors are hard-working poetry lovers dedicated to finding and promoting good work. They aspire to turn submissions around as quickly as possible and to treat all poets with respect. They don't want to steal your work. Often they aren't paid for their labor and may even have to dip into their own pockets just to keep their magazines going.

Poets should finesse their communications with editors regarding problems, especially in initial letters and e-mail. Editors (and their magazines and presses) aren't service-oriented businesses, like the phone company. Getting huffy with an editor as if arguing with your cable provider about an overcharge is inappropriate. Attitude isn't going to get

Articles & Information

you anywhere; in fact, it could create additional obstacles.

That's not to say poets shouldn't feel exasperated when they're inconvenienced or ill treated. None of us likes to see our creations vanish, or to pay good money for something we're never going to receive (like a subscription or sample copy). However, exasperated is one thing; outraged is another. Too often poets go on the offensive with editors and make matters worse. Experts on how to complain effectively recommend you keep your cool and stay professional, no matter what kind of problem you're trying to work out.

For additional advice on editor/poet relations, see "Dealing With Problem Editors" on page 53.

Dealing With Problem Editors

There *are* problem editors out there, and we've all encountered them at one time or another. Some rip people off, prey on poets' desires to be published, or treat poets and their work with flagrant disregard. Fortunately, such editors are very much in the minority.

Now and then you may discover the disorganized editor or the overwhelmed editor; these two cause heartache (and heartburn) by closing up shop without returning manuscripts, or failing to honor paid requests for subscriptions and sample copies. More often than not, their transgressions are rooted in chaos and irresponsibility, not malicious intent. Frustrating as such editors are, they're not out to get you.

There are many instances, too, where larger circumstances are beyond an editor's control. For example, a college-oriented journal may be student-staffed, with editors changing each academic year. Funds for the journal may be cut unexpectedly by administration belt-tightening, or a grant could be cancelled. The editorial office may be moved to another part of the university. An exam schedule could impact a publishing schedule. All of these things cause problems and delays.

Then again, a literary journal may be a one-person, home-based operation. The editor may get sick or have an illness in the family. Her regular job may suddenly demand lots of overtime. There may be divorce or death with which the editor has to cope. A computer could crash. Or the editor may need to scramble for money before the magazine can go to the printer. Emergencies happen, and they take their toll on deadlines. The last thing the editor wants is to inconvenience poets and readers, but sometimes life gets in the way.

Usually, difficul ties with these kinds of "problem" editors can be resolved satisfactorily through communication and patience. There are always exceptions, though. Here are a few typical situations with problem editors and how to handle them:

An editor is rude. If it's a matter of bad attitude, take it with a grain of salt. Maybe he's having a rotten day. If there's abusive language and excessive profanity involved, let us know about it. (See the complaint procedure on page 55.)

An editor harshly criticizes your poem. If an editor takes time to comment on your poetry, even if the feedback seems overly critical, consider the suggestions with an open mind and try to find something valid and useful in them. If, after you've given the matter fair consideration, you think the editor was out of line, don't rush to defend your poetry or wave your bruised ego in the editor's face. Allow that the editor has a right to her opinion (which you're not obligated to take as the final word on the quality of your work), forget about it and move on.

An editor is slow to respond to a submission. As explained above, there may be many reasons why an editor's response takes longer than the time stated in the market listing or guidelines. Allow a few more weeks to pass beyond the deadline, then write a polite inquiry to the editor about the status of your manuscript. (Include a SASE if sending by regular mail.) Understand an editor may not be able to read your letter right away if deadlines are pressing or if he's embroiled in a personal crisis. Try to be patient. If you haven't received a reply to your inquiry after a month or so, however, it's time for further action.

An editor won't return your manuscript. Decide whether you want to invest any more time in this journal or publisher. If you conclude you've been patient long enough, write a firm but professional letter to the editor withdrawing your manuscript from consideration. Request that the manuscript be returned; but know, too, a truly indifferent editor probably won't bother to send it back or reply in any way. Keep a copy of your withdrawal letter for your files, make a new copy of your manuscript and look for a better market.

Also, contact *Poet's Market* by letter or e-mail with details of your experience. We always look into problems with editors, although we don't withdraw a listing on the basis of a single complaint unless we discover further evidence of consistent misbehavior. We do, however, keep complaints on file and watch for patterns of unacceptable behavior from any specific market.

An editor takes your money. If you sent a check for a subscription or sample copy and you haven't received anything, review your bank statement to see if the check has been cashed. If it has, send the editor a query. Politely point out the editor has cashed your check, but you haven't yet received the material you were expecting. Give the editor the benefit of the doubt: An upcoming issue of a magazine could be running late, your subscription could have been overlooked by mistake, or your copy could have been lost in transit or sent in error to the wrong address.

If your check has *not* been cashed, query the editor to see if your order was ever received. It may have been lost (in the mail or on the editor's desk), the editor may be holding several checks to cash at one time, or the editor may be waiting to cash checks until a tardy issue is finally published.

If you get an unsatisfactory response from the editor (or no response at all), wait a few weeks and try again. If the matter still isn't resolved, let us know about it. We're especially interested in publishers who take money from poets but don't deliver the goods. Be sure to send us all the details of the transaction, plus copies of any correspondence (yours and the editor's). We can't pursue your situation in any legal way or act as mediator, but we can ban an unscrupulous publisher from *Poet's Market* and keep the information as a resource in case we get later complaints.

Should you continue trying to get your money back from such editors? That's your decision. If your loss is under $10 (say, for a subscription or sample copy), it might cost you less in the long run to let the matter go. And the fee for a "stop payment" order on a check can be hefty—possibly more than the amount you sent the editor in the first place. Yes, it's infuriating to be cheated, but sometimes fighting on principle costs more than it's worth.

If your monetary loss is significant (for instance, you shelled out a couple hundred dollars in a subsidy publishing agreement), consider contacting your state attorney general's office for advice about small claims court, filing a complaint and other actions you can take.

Complaint Procedure

Important

If you feel you have not been treated fairly by a market listed in Poet's Market, we advise you to take the following steps:

- First, try to contact the market. Sometimes one phone call, letter, or e-mail can quickly clear up the matter. Document all your communications with the market.
- When you contact us with a complaint, provide the details of your submission, the date of your first contact with the market and the nature of your subsequent communication.
- We will file a record of your complaint and further investigate the market.
- The number and severity of complaints will be considered when deciding whether or not to delete a market from the next edition of *Poet's Market*.

Is It a 'Con'?

Think Before You Trust

What is a "con?" Con is short for "confidence," an adjective defined by Webster's as "of, relating to, or adept at swindling by false promise," as in "confidence man" or "confidence game." While the publishing world is full of legitimate opportunities for poets to gain honor and exposure for their work, there are also plenty of "cons." How can you tell the difference? The following are some of the most common situations that cost poets disappointment, frustration—and cash. Learn to spot them before submitting your work, and don't let your vanity be your guide.

ANTHOLOGIES

Has this happened to you? You see an ad in a perfectly respectable publication announcing a poetry contest with big cash prizes. You enter, and later you receive a glowing letter congratulating you on your exceptional poem, which the contest sponsor wants to include in his deluxe hardbound anthology of the best poetry submitted to the contest. The anthology costs only, say, $65. You don't have to buy it—they'll still publish your poem— but wouldn't you be proud to own one? And wouldn't it be nice to buy additional copies to give to family and friends? And for an extra charge you can include a biographical note. And so on . . .

Of course, when the anthology arrives, the quality of the poetry may not be what you were expecting, with several poems crammed unattractively onto a page. Apparently everyone who entered the contest was invited to be published; you basically paid cash to see your poem appear in a phone book-like volume with no literary merit whatsoever.

Were you conned? Depends on how you look at it. If you bought into the flattery and believed you were being published in an exclusive, high-quality publication, no doubt you feel duped. On the other hand, if all you were after was seeing your poem in print, even knowing you'd have to pay for the privilege, then you got what you wanted. (Unless you've deceived yourself into believing you've truly won an honor and now have a worthy publishing credit; you don't.)

If you don't want to add insult to injury, resist additional spiels, like having your poem printed on coffee mugs and t-shirts (you can do this yourself through print shops or online services like www.cafepress.com) or spending large sums on awards banquets and conferences. And, before you submit a single line of poetry, find out what rights the contest sponsor acquires. You may be relinquishing all rights to your poem simply by mailing it in or submitting it through a Web site. If the poem no longer belongs to you, the publisher can do whatever he wishes with it. Don't let your vanity propel you into a situation you'll always regret.

READING AND CONTEST FEES

Suppose you notice a promising market for your poetry, but the editor requires a set fee just to consider your work. Or you see a contest that interests you, but you have to pay the sponsor a fee just to enter. Are you being conned?

In the case of reading fees, keep these points in mind: Is the market so exceptional that you feel it's worth risking the cost of the reading fee to have your work considered? What makes it so much better than markets that do not charge fees? Has the market been around awhile, with an established publishing schedule? What are you paid if your work is accepted? Are reasonably priced samples available so you can judge the production values and quality of the writing?

Reading fees don't necessarily signal a suspicious market. In fact, they're increasingly popular as editors struggle with the costs of publishing books and magazines, including the man-hours required to read loads of (often bad) submissions. However, fees represent an additional financial burden on poets, who often don't receive any monetary reward for their poems to begin with. It's really up to individual poets to decide whether paying a fee is beneficial to their publishing efforts. Think long and hard about fee-charging markets that are new and untried, don't pay poets for their work (at the very least a print publication should offer a contributor's copy), charge high prices for sample copies or set fees that seem unreasonable.

Entry fees for contests often fund prizes, judges' fees, honorariums and expenses of running and promoting the contest (including publishing a "prize" collection or issue of a magazine). Other kinds of contests charge entry fees, from Irish dancing competitions to bake-offs at a county fair. Why not poetry contests?

That's not to say you shouldn't be cautious. Watch out for contests that charge higher-than-average fees, especially if the fees are out of proportion to the amount of prize money being given. (Look through the Contests & Awards section beginning on page 367 to get a sense of what most competitions charge; you'll also find contests in other sections of this book by consulting the Additional Contests & Awards index on page 438.) Find out how long the contest has been around, and verify whether prizes have been awarded each year and to whom. In the case of book and chapbook contests, send for one of the winning publications to confirm that the publisher puts out a quality product. Regard with skepticism any contest that tells you you've won something, then demands payment for an anthology, trophy or other item. (It's okay if a group offers an anthology for a modest price without providing winners with free copies. Most state poetry societies have to do this; but they also present cash awards in each category of the contest, and their entry fees are low.)

SUBSIDY PUBLISHERS, PRINT-ON-DEMAND

Poetry books are a hard sell to the book-buying public. Few of the big publishers handle these books, and those that do feature the "name" poets (i.e., the major prize winners and contemporary masters with breathtaking reputations). Even the small presses publish only so many books per year—far less than the number of poets writing.

No wonder so many poets decide to pay to have their poetry collections published. While some may self-publish (i.e., take full control of their book, working directly with a printer), others turn to subsidy publishers (also called "vanity publishers") and print-on-demand (POD) publishers.

There are many differences between subsidy publishing and POD publishing, as well as similarities (having to pay to get published is a big one). Whether or not you get conned is entirely up to you. You have to take responsibility for asking questions, doing research on presses, and reading the fine print on the contract to make sure you know exactly what you're paying for. There are landmines in dealing with subsidy and POD publishers, and you have to investigate thoroughly and intelligently to avoid damage.

Some questions to keep in mind: Are fees inflated compared to the product and services you'll be receiving? Will you still own the rights to your book? Does the publisher put out a quality product that's attractive and cleanly printed? (Get a sample copy and find out.) How many copies of the book will you receive? How much will you have to pay for additional copies? How will your book be sold and distributed? (Don't count on seeing your volume in bookstores.)

Will you receive royalties? How much? Does the publisher offer any kind of promotional assistance or is it all up to you? Will those promotion efforts be realistic and results-oriented? (Sometimes "promotion" means sending out review copies, which is a waste—such volumes are rarely reviewed.) Don't wait until *after* you've signed a contract (and a check) to raise these issues. Do your homework first.

Obviously, poets who don't stay on their toes may find themselves preyed upon. And a questionable publishing opportunity doesn't have to be an out-and-out rip-off for you to feel cheated. In every situation, you have a choice *not* to participate. Exercise that choice, or at least develop a healthy sense of skepticism before you fling yourself and your poetry at the first smooth talker who compliments your work. Poets get burned because they're much too impatient to see their work in print. Calm your ego, slow down and devote that time, energy and money toward reading other poets and improving your own writing. You'll find that getting published will eventually take care of itself.

Magazines/ Journals

L iterary magazines and journals usually provide a poet's first publishing success. In fact, you shouldn't be thinking about book/chapbook publication until your poems have appeared in a variety of magazines, journals and zines (both print and online). This is the preferred way to develop an audience, build publishing credits and learn the ins and outs of the publishing process.

In this section you'll find hundreds of magazines and journals that publish poetry. They range from small black-and-white booklets produced on home computers to major periodicals with high production values and important reputations. To help you sort through these markets and direct your submissions most effectively, we've organized information in each listing according to a basic format.

HOW LISTINGS ARE FORMATTED

Content of each market listing was provided or verified by a representative of the publication (editor, poetry editor, managing editor, etc.). Here is how that content is arranged within the listing:

Symbols. Icons at the beginning of each listing offer visual signposts to specific information about the publication: (🆕) this market is recently established and new to *Poet's Market*; (⊠) this market did not appear in the 2008 edition; (▣) this market publishes primarily online (although it may also produce an annual print version or a "best of" anthology); (⬛) this market is located in Canada or (▦) outside the U.S. and Canada; (**$**) this market pays a monetary amount (as opposed to contributor's copies); (☐) this market welcomes submissions from beginning poets; (◨) this market prefers submissions from skilled, experienced poets, will consider work from beginning poets; (◪) this market prefers submissions from poets with a high degree of skill and experience; (◎) this market has a specialized focus (listed in parentheses after magazine/journal title); (☑) this market does not consider unsolicited submissions; and (⊘) this market is closed to *all* submissions. (Keys to these symbols are listed on the inside covers of this book and on page 3.)

Contact information. Depending on what was provided by each editor, contact information includes: magazine/journal title (in bold) with areas of specialization noted in parentheses where appropriate; regular mail address; telephone number; fax number; e-mail address; Web site address; year the publication was established; the name of the person to contact (or an editorial title); and membership in small press/publishing organizations. (Note: If a magazine/journal publishes only online and/or wants submissions by e-mail exclusively, no street address may be given.)

Magazine Needs. It's important to study this section as you research potential markets. Here you'll find such helpful information as the editor's overview of the publication, with individual poetry needs and preferences; a list of recently published poets; production information (number of pages, printing/binding details, type of cover); the number of poetry submissions the publication receives vs. the number accepted; and press run, distribution and price information.

How to Submit. This section focuses on the specific details of submitting work: how many poems to send; minimum/maximum number of lines per poem; whether previously published poems or simultaneous submissions are considered; submission format preferences (including whether to submit by e-mail, and how); response times; payment; rights acquired and more.

Additional Information. Editors may use this section to explain other publishing activities, elaborate on some aspect of the magazine/journal, suggest future plans--anything beyond the basic details that readers may find of interest.

Contest/Award Offerings. This section discusses prizes and competitions associated with the publication, with either brief guidelines or a cross-reference to a separate listing in the Contests & Awards section.

Also Offers. Describes additional offerings associated with this publication (i.e., sponsored readings, Web site activities such as blogs and forums, related poetry groups, etc.).

Advice. Provides direct quotes from editors about everything from pet peeves to tips on writing to perspectives on the state of poetry today.

GETTING STARTED, FINDING MARKETS

If you don't have a certain magazine or journal in mind, read randomly through the listings, making notes as you go. (Don't hesitate to write in the margins, underline, use highlighters; it also helps to flag markets that interest you with Post-It Notes). Browsing the listings is an effective way to familiarize yourself with the kind of information presented and the publishing opportunities that are available at various skill levels.

If you have a specific market in mind, however, begin with the General Index. Here all the book's listings are alphabetized along with additional references that may be buried within a listing (such as a press name or competition title). Also, markets from the 2008 edition that don't appear in this book are included in the General Index, accompanied by a two-letter code explaining the market's absence (a key to these codes appears at the beginning of the General Index). Furthermore, publications that have changed names since the 2008 edition are listed in the General Index, cross-referenced to the new titles.

REFINE YOUR SEARCH

To supplement the General Index, we provide the following indexes to help you refine your marketing plan for submitting your poems to publications. Not every listing appears in one of these indexes, so use them only to reinforce your other research efforts:

Openness to Submissions Index categorizes markets according to the icons (☐ ☑ ☑ ◎) that appear at the beginning of each listing--signposts that indicate the level of writing an editor prefers to see. (For an explanation of these symbols, see page 3, the inside covers of this book or the handy tear-out bookmark just inside the front cover.)

Geographical Index sorts magazines and journals by state or by countries outside the U.S. Some markets are more open to poets from their respective regions, so this index is helpful when pinpointing local opportunities.

Subject Index groups markets according to areas of special focus. These include all specialized markets (appearing with the ◉ symbol) as well as broader categories such as online markets, poetry for children, markets that consider translations and others. When you want to submit a poem that features a certain topic or theme, is written in a specific form or style or addresses a unique audience, check this index first.

THE NEXT STEP

Once you know how to interpret the listings in this section and identify markets for your work, the next step is to start submitting your poems. See "Getting Started (and Using This Book)" on page 2 and "Frequently Asked Questions" on page 7 for advice, guidelines for preparing your manuscript and proper submissions procedures.

N E Z 2RIVER VIEW

7474 Drexel Dr., University City MO 63130. E-mail: long@2River.org. Website: www.2River.org.
Contact: Richard Long.

Magazines Needs *2River View*, published quarterly online, restricts each issue to ten poets.
"We prefer poems with these qualities: image, subtlety, and point of view; a surface of worldly
exactitude, as well as a depth of semantic ambiguity; and a voice that negotiates with its body of
predecessors." Robert Creeley, R. Virgil Davis, Tony Colella, David Appelbaum, Michelle Askin,
Rebecca Givens. Accepts 1-5% of unsolicited submissions.

How to Contact Submit up to 5 poems once per reading period. No previously published poems
or simultaneous submissions. Accepts e-mail submissions pasted into the body of the e-mail; no
fax or disk submissions. Reads submissions year round (see Web site for reading period for each
issue). Time between acceptance and publication is 3 months. Guidelines on Web site.

E Z 10TH MUSE

33 Hartington Rd., Southampton, Hants SO14 0EW England. E-mail: a.jordan@surfree.co.uk.
Established 1990. **Contact:** Andrew Jordan, editor.

Magazines Needs *10th Muse* "includes poetry and reviews, as well as short prose and graphics."
Has published poetry by Richard Caddel, Stephen M. Dickey, Andrew Duncan, Carrie Etter,
Becky Gould Gibson, and Bill Griffiths. *10th Muse* is 48-72 pages, A5, photocopied, saddle-
stapled, with card cover. Press run is 200. Single copy: £3.50 (UK); subscription: £9 for 3 issues
(UK). Make checks payable to *10th Muse*. "U.S. subscribers: Send $10 in bills for single copy
(including postage)."

How to Contact Submit up to 6 poems at a time. No e-mail submissions. Include SASE (or SAE
with IRCs). Responds in 3 months. Pays one contributor's copy. Staff reviews books of poetry.
Send materials for review consideration.

Tips "Poets should read a copy of the magazine first."

E Z THE 13TH WARRIOR REVIEW

Asterius Press, P.O. Box 5122, Seabrook NJ 08302-3511. E-mail: theeditor@asteriusonline.com.
Website: www.13thwr.org. Established 1997. **Contact:** John C. Erianne, editor.

Magazines Needs *The 13th Warrior Review*, published irregularly online, seeks "excellent literary-
quality poetry as well as fiction, essays, and reviews. All excellent poetry will be given serious
consideration." Has published poetry by P.Q. Perron, Cindy Rosmus, B.Z Niditch, Genine Hanns,
John Sweet, and Corey Ginsberg.

How to Contact Submit no more than 5 poems at a time. Considers simultaneous submissions,
but "not encouraged"; no previously published poems. Accepts e-mail submissions (encouraged;
pasted as text into body of message—no attachments). "Use 'submission' as the subject header.
Any submission that comes as a file attachment will be deleted without reply." Cover letter
is preferred; "should be brief and to the point." Include SASE for postal submissions. Time
between acceptance and publication is up to one year. Seldom comments on rejected poems.
Guidelines available on website. No payment. Acquires first rights, first electronic rights, and
non-exclusive anthology rights.

Tips "Write from love; don't expect love in return, don't take rejection personally, and don't let
anyone stop you."

N E Z 34TH PARALLEL

P.O. Box 4823, Irvine CA 92623. E-mail: tracesheridan@34thParallel.net. Website:
www.34thparallel.net/submit.html. **Contact:** Trace Sheridan Martin Chipperfield, Editor.

Member: CLMP

Magazines Needs *34th Parallel*, published quarterly in print and online, seeks "to promote and publish the exceptional writing of new and emerging writers overlooked by large commercial publishing houses and mainstream presses. "Wants "work that experiments with and tests boundaries. Anything that communicates a sense of wonder, reality, tragedy, fantasy, and/or brilliance." Does not want "historical romance, science fiction, erotica, Gothic horror, book reviews, or nonfiction." Single copy: $11; subscription: $36.

How to Contact Submit 1 poem only in an e-mail with a subject header containing the word "submission," the title of your work, and your name. Considers simultaneous submissions; no previously published poems. Accepts electronic submissions. Cover letter is required, containing a short bio about "your life, your writing, and where we can see some of your other work online. "Reads submissions year round. Often comments on rejected poems. Guidelines on Web site. Pays one contributor's copy in PDF format. "Magazine is copyrighted but the rights to all contributions remain with the owners."

☑ ◎ THE AARDVARK ADVENTURER

(Specialized: light verse; humor; subscribers given preference), Pickle Gas Press, 19 Abbotswood Crescent, Penfield NY 14526. (585)381-1003. E-mail: thearmchairaesthete@yahoo.com or bypaul@frontiernet.net. Established 1996. **Contact:** Paul Agosto, editor.

Magazines Needs *The Aardvark Adventurer*, published 2-3 times/year, is "a family-fun digest-style zine of humor, thought, and verse. Very short stories (less than 500 words) are sometimes included." Wants "light, brief humorous verse; any style; any 'family-acceptable' subject matter." Does not want anything "obscene, overly forboding; no graphic gore or violence." Submission MUST be accompanied by a SASE (#10 envelope). Has published poetry by Chris Brown, Laverne and Carol Frith, Lydia Williams, Andrew Bynom, and Douglas Empringham. *The Aardvark Adventurer* is 12 pages, digest-sized, photocopied, saddle-stapled. Receives about 500 poems/year, accepts about 40%. Press run is 150. Single copy: $5 postpaid and 2 First-Class stamps; subscription: $8/3 issues. Make checks payable to Paul Agosto. **"Subscription not required, but subscribers given preference."How to Submit** Lines/poem: 16 maximum. Considers previously published poems and simultaneous submissions, if indicated. Accepts e-mail submissions (pasted into body of message). Cover letter is preferred. Time between acceptance and publication is up to 12 months. Seldom comments on rejected poems. Guidelines available for SASE. Responds in 2 months. Pays 1 contributor's copy. Acquires one-time rights.

Tips "*The Aardvark Adventurer*, a digest-style publication with a very playful format, is a perfect opportunity for the aspiring poet."

☑ ABBEY

5360 Fallriver Row Court, Columbia MD 21044. E-mail: greisman@aol.com. Established 1970. **Contact:** David Greisman, editor.

Magazines Needs *Abbey* is "a more-or-less informal zine looking for poetry that does for the mind what the first sip of Molson Ale does for the palate." Does not want "pornography or politics." Has published poetry by Richard Peabody, Ruth Moon Kempher, Carol Hamilton, Harry Calhoun, Wayne Hogan, and Edmund Conti. *Abbey* is usually 20-26 pages, magazine-sized, photocopied, and held together with 1 low-alloy metal staple in the top left corner. Receives about 1,000 poems/year, accepts about 150. Press run is 200. Subscription: $2. Sample: 50¢.

How to Contact Responds in 1 month "except during baseball season." Pays 1-2 contributor's copies.

Additional Information Abbey Cheapochapbooks come out once or twice every 5 years,

averaging 10-15 pages. For chapbook consideration, query with 4-6 sample poems, bio, and list of publications. Responds in 2 months "including baseball season." Pays 25-50 author's copies.
Tips "I'm definitely seeing poetry from 2 schools—the nit'n'grit school and the textured/reflective school. I much prefer the latter."

◩ ◎ ABLE MUSE

(Specialized: form/style), 467 Saratoga Ave., #602, San Jose CA 95129-1326. Phone/fax: (267)224-7478. E-mail: submission@ablemuse.com. Website: www.ablemuse.com. Established 1999. **Contact:** Alex Pepple, editor.

Magazines Needs *Able Muse: a review of metrical poetry*, published 3 times/year, "spotlights formal poetry via an online presentation, in the supportive environment of art, photography, essays, interviews, book reviews, fiction, and a literary forum. Also includes electronic books of poetry. *Able Muse* exclusively publishes formal poetry. We are looking for well-crafted poems of any length or subject that employ skillful and imaginative use of meter, or meter and rhyme, executed in contemporary idiom, that reads as naturally as your free-verse poems." Does not want "free-verse, greeting card verse, or poems in forms with no regard to meter (such as a free verse pantoum, sestina, etc.)." Considers poetry by teens. "High levels of craft still required even for teen writers." Has published poetry by Mark Jarman, A.E. Stallings, Annie Finch, Rhina P. Espaillat, Rachel Hadas, and R.S. Gwynn. Receives about 1,500 poems/year, accepts about 5%.

How to Contact Submit 1-5 poems at a time. No previously published poems or simultaneous submissions. Accepts fax, e-mail, and disk submissions. "E-mail is the preferred medium of submission, but we also welcome snail mail, or submit directly from the Web site with the automated online submission form." Cover letter preferred. Time between acceptance and publication is 6-12 weeks. Sometimes comments on rejected poems. Sometimes publishes theme issues. Guidelines available for SASE, by e-mail, or on Web site. Responds in 4 months. Sometimes sends prepublication galleys. Acquires first rights. Reviews books of poetry. Send materials for review consideration.

Also Offers "Able Muse will provide a print version, currently in the works, in the near future. We are also planning a CD anthology of the best poems, stories, articles from previous issues, along with an accompanying audio CD of the poets and writers reading their works." Contest/Award Offerings Sponsors the semiannual Tipsy Muse Poetry Contest "is a light verse competition" with prize offerings of $200. Check Web site at http://eratosphere.ablemuse.com for contest dates. Entry Fee: $5/poem. Guidelines available for SASE, by e-mail, and on Web site.

Tips "Despite the rush to publish everything online, most of web-published poetry has been free verse. This is surprising given formal poetry's recent rise in popularity in the number of print journals that exclusively publish formal poetry. *Able Muse* attempts to fill this void bringing the best contemporary formalists online. Remember, content is just as important as form."

▣ ◩ ABRAMELIN, THE JOURNAL OF POETRY AND MAGICK

P.O. Box 337, Brookhaven NY 11719. E-mail: nessaralindaran@aol.com. Website: www. abramelin.net. Established 2006. **Contact:** Vanessa Kittle, editor.

Magazines Needs *Abramelin, the Journal of Poetry and Magick*, published biannually online and a yearly best of edition each December, offers "literary poetry and essays concerning the western esoteric traditions." Wants "poetry that shows rather than tells. Poems that make me jealous of the writer. Poems that are inspired with wonderful language and imagery. In short—literature. Poetry submissions needn't be about magick at all. I feel that real poetry is magick. In fact, poetry that is literally magickal in theme has to be twice as good." Does not want "rhyming poems. Very short fiction. But beware, I learned from the best." Considers poetry by teens. Has published poetry by Simon Perchik, Rich Kostelanetz, and Lyn Lifshin. *Abramelin* receives about 1,000 poems/year, accepts about 5%. Distributed free online. Number of unique visitors: 3,000/issue.

How to Contact Submit 1-5 poems at a time. Lines/poem: no minimum/maximum. Considers previously published poems and simultaneous submissions (with notification). Accepts e-mail (pasted into body of message) and disk submissions. Cover letter is preferred. Reads submissions year round. Submit seasonal poems 2 months in advance. Time between acceptance and publication is 1-3 months. Often comments on rejected poems. Sometimes publishes theme issues. Upcoming themes available in magazine or on Web site. Guidelines available by e-mail or on Web site. Responds in 1 month. Pays 1 contributor's copy. Acquires one-time rights, with option to include in a yearly print anthology. Rights revert to poets upon publication.

Additional Information Publishes an annual print anthology—40 pages, digest-sized, professionally printed, perfect-bound, with glossy full color cover. Single copy: $9.50. Make checks payable to Vanessa Kittle.

Tips "Bring the reader into the moment. Be as specific as possible."

☑ ◎ ABRAXAS

(Specialized: contemporary lyric; experimental), P.O. Box 260113, Madison WI 53726-0113. (608)238-0175. E-mail: abraxaspress@hotmail.com. Website: www.geocities.com/abraxaspress/. Established 1968. **Contact:** Ingrid Swanberg, editor/publisher.•ABRAXAS **does not consider unsolicited material, except as announced on its Web site as projects arise.**

Magazines Needs *ABRAXAS*, published "irregularly; 9- to 12-month intervals or much longer," is interested in poetry that's "contemporary lyric, experimental, and poetry in translation. When submitting translations, please include poems in the original language. *ABRAXAS'* new format features longer selections of fewer contributors." Does not want "political posing; academic regurgitations." Has published poetry by Ivan Argüelles, Denise Levertov, César Vallejo, d.a. levy, T.L. Kryss, and Andrea Moorhead. *ABRAXAS* is up to 80 pages, digest-sized, litho-offset-printed, flat-spined (saddle-stapled for smaller issues), with matte card cover with original art. Press run is 600. Subscription: $16 USD foreign (4 issues). Sample: $4 USD ($9 shipping for foreign orders).

How to Contact *ABRAXAS* will announce submission guidelines as projects arise. "Please check Web site for reading periods." Pays 1 contributor's copy, 40% discount on additional copies.

▣ ☑ (A BRILLIANT) RECORD MAGAZINE

E-mail: recordmag@hotmail.com. Website: www.recordblog.blogspot.com. Established 2007. **Contact:** Godfrey Logan.

Magazines Needs *(A Brilliant) Record Magazine*, published 4 times/year online, wants "quality poetry and short stories outside the box. If another magazine says it's not what they're looking for, then it's likely that I want it." *(A Brilliant) Record Magazine* (e-mail version) is about 20 pages. "Will accept 50% of what I receive." Press run is 200; "copies of the magazine are sent via e-mail; but if print copies are requested, they go first to those who have been accepted more than once on blog/site, and after that to those who request copies from what is left of run (4 copies at are sent out in that case)."

How to Contact Submit 6 poems at a time. Lines/poem: 5-10. Fiction or non-fction, 200-1,000; political commentary/rant; satire; restaurant and wine reviews. Considers simultaneous submissions; no previously published poems (does not consider poems posted on a public Web site/blog/forum or on a private, password-protected forum to be previously published). Accepts e-mail submissions (pasted into body of message); no disk submissions. Cover letter is preferred. "Just a few words about publishing history or inspiration for work. Will be included in publication." Reads submissions year round. Time between acceptance and publication is 1 day to 1 week. Never comments on rejected poems. "Please see previous work on blog/site to know what I'm looking for." Sometimes publishes theme issues. Upcoming themes available by e-mail ('Romance Language' issue in October with poetry that is more risqué and erotic; about love lost and found). Guidelines available by e-mail or on Web site. Responds in 1 week. Pays 1 contributor's copy via e-mail. Acquires one-time rights. Rights revert to poets upon publication. "Will not accept books for review but will accept well written reviews no more than 500 words."

Tips "Never give up on your dream of writing! Be patient! I have published at several different online publications, and it doesn't get any easier. Always support your literary magazines!"

N ABZ

PRESS P.O. Box 2746, Huntington WV 25727. E-mail: editorial@abzpress.com. Website: www. abzpress.com.

Magazines Needs *ABZ*, published annually, wants poetry using interesting and exciting language. Sample copies and subscriptions: $8.

How to Contact Submit 1 to 6 poems at a time. Reading period is September 1-December 1. Guidelines on Web site. "Contributors receive a small stipend and two copies of the magazine."

Additional Information Offers the ABZ First Book Poetry Prize for original poetry manuscripts between 48-80 pages. See Contests and Awards for additional information.

☐ ACM (ANOTHER CHICAGO MAGAZINE)

Left Field Press, 3709 N. Kenmore, Chicago IL 60613. E-mail: anotherchicagomagazine@yahoo. com. Website: www.anotherchicagomag.com. Established 1977. **Contact:** Michael Meinhardt, managing/poetry editor.

- Work published in *ACM* has been included frequently in *The Best American Poetry* and *The Pushcart Prize*.

Magazines Needs *ACM (Another Chicago Magazine)*, published semiannually in May and November, prints work "with emphasis on quality, experimental, politically aware prose, fiction, poetry, reviews, cross-genre work, and essays." Wants "traditional to experimental verse with an emphasis on message, especially poems with strong voices articulating social or political concerns." Does not want "religious verse." Has published poetry by Albert Goldbarth, Maureen Seaton, Sharon Darrow, Simon Perchik, Alice George, and R.T. Castleberry. *ACM* is 220 pages, digest-sized, offset-printed, includes ads. Press run is 2,000. Single copy: $8.

How to Contact Submit 3-4 typed poems at a time. Considers simultaneous submissions with notification; no previously published poems. Reads submissions February 1-August 31. Guidelines available on website; however, "The best way to know what we publish is to read what we publish. If you haven't read *ACM* before, order a sample copy to know if your work is appropriate." Responds in 3 months. Sends prepublication galleys. Pays monetary amount "if funds permit," and/or one contributor's copy and one-year subscription. Acquires first serial rights. Reviews books of poetry in 250-800 words. Send materials for review consideration.

Contest/Award Offerings Sponsors the annual Chicago Literary Awards. Prize: $1,000 and publication in *ACM*. **Entry fee:** $12 for 3 poems (300 total lines), $5 for each additional poem (up to 100 lines). **Deadline:** December 15th. Guidelines available on website.

⊞ ☑ ACUMEN MAGAZINE

Ember Press, 6 The Mount, Higher Furzeham, Brixham, South Devon TQ5 8QY England. E-mail: patricia@acumen-poetry.co.uk. Website: www.acumen-poetry.co.uk. Established 1971 (press), 1984 (Acumen). **Contact:** Patricia Oxley, poetry editor.

Magazines Needs *Acumen*, published 3 times/year in January, May, and September, is "a general literary magazine with emphasis on good poetry." Wants "well-crafted, high-quality, imaginative poems showing a sense of form." Does not want "experimental verse of an obscene type." Has published poetry by Ruth Padel, William Oxley, Hugo Williams, Peter Porter, Danielle Hope, and Leah Fritz. *Acumen* is 120 pages, A5, perfect-bound. Receives about 12,000 poems, accepts about 120. Press run is 650. Subscription: $45 surface/$50 air. Sample: $15.

How to Contact Submit 5-6 poems at a time. Considers simultaneous submissions (if not submitted to UK magazines); no previously published poems. "If a reply is required, please send IRCs. One IRC for a decision, 3 IRCs if work is to be returned." Willing to reply by e-mail to save IRCs. Responds in 3 months. Pays "by negotiation" and 1 contributor's copy. Staff reviews books of poetry in up to 300 words (single-book format) or 600 words (multi-book format). Send materials for review consideration to Glyn Pursglove, 25 St. Albans Rd., Brynmill, Swansea, West Glamorgan SA2 0BP Wales.

Tips "Read *Acumen* carefully to see what kind of poetry we publish. Also, read widely in many poetry magazines, and don't forget the poets of the past—they can still teach us a great deal."

▣ ☑ THE ADIRONDACK REVIEW

8405 Bay Parkway, Apt C8, Brooklyn NY 11214. E-mail: diane@blacklawrencepress.com (inquiries); tarpoetry@blacklawrencepress.com (submissions). Website: www.adirondackreview. homestead.com. Established 2000. **Contact:** Diane Goettel, editor.

Magazines Needs *The Adirondack Review*, published quarterly online, is a literary journal dedicated to quality free verse poetry and short fiction as well as book and film reviews, art, photography, and interviews. "We are open to both new and established writers. Our only requirement is excellence. We would like to publish more French and German poetry translations as well as original poems in these languages. We publish an eclectic mix of voices and styles, but all poems should show attention to craft. We are open to beginners who demonstrate talent, as well as established voices. The work should speak for itself." Wants "well-crafted, thoughtful writing full of imagery." Does not want "religious, overly sentimental, horror/gothic, rhyming, greeting card, pet-related, humor, or science fiction poetry." Has published poetry by Bob Hicok, Timothy Liu, Lola Haskins, D.C. Berry, David Rigsbee, and Paul Guest. Accepts about 3-5% of poems submitted.

How to Contact Submit 2-7 poems at a time. Considers simultaneous submissions (with notification); no previously published poems. Accepts e-mail submissions only. "All submissions should be pasted into the body of an e-mail (no attached files, please). We no longer accept postal submissions. All postal submissions will be discarded unread." Cover letter is preferred. Reads submissions year round. Submit seasonal poems 3 months in advance. Time between acceptance and publication is 1-3 months. Seldom comments on rejected poems. Guidelines available on Web site. Responds in 1 week to 4 months. Acquires first or one-time rights. Rights revert to poet upon publication. "We reserve the right to reprint the work in the event of a print-based anthology at a later date." Reviews books of poetry. Send materials for review consideration.

Contest/Award Offerings With Black Lawrence Press, offers The 46th Prize for Poetry (see separate listing in Contests & Awards).

Tips "Get your hands on all the good writing you can, including international, past, contemporary, Web-based, and print. Read much, write well, and send us what you love."

☐ ADVOCATE, PKA'S PUBLICATION

1881 Little West Kill Rd., Prattsville NY 12468. (518)299-3103. Established 1987.

Magazines Needs *Advocate, PKA's Publication*, published bimonthly, is an advertiser-supported tabloid using "original, previously unpublished works, such as feature stories, essays, 'think' pieces, letters to the editor, profiles, humor, fiction, poetry, puzzles, cartoons, or line drawings." Wants "nearly any kind of poetry, any length. Poetry ought to speak to people and not be so oblique as to have meaning only to the poet. If I had to be there to understand the poem, don't send it. Also looking for horse-related poems, stories, drawings, and photos." Does not want "religious or pornographic poetry." Considers poetry by children and teens (when included with release form signed by adult). Accepts about 25% of poems received. Circulation is 10,000; all distributed free. Subscription: $16.50 (6 issues). Sample: $5 (includes guidelines).

How to Contact Submit any number of poems at a time. Lines/poem: open. No previously published poems or simultaneous submissions. "Please, no work that has appeared on the Internet." Submissions may be typed or legibly handwritten. "Send a SASE with your submission; no postcards, please." Time between acceptance and publication is up to 6 months. Occasionally comments on rejected poems. Responds in 2 months. Guidelines available with sample copy ($4). Pays 2 contributor's copies. Acquires first rights only.

Tips "Always looking for horse/equine-oriented works."

☑ ◎ AFRICAN VOICES

(Specialized: ethnic, people of color)270 W. 96th St., New York NY 10025. (212)865-2982. Fax: (212)316-3335. E-mail: general@africanvoices.com or africanvoices@aol.com. Website: www.africanvoices.com. Established 1992. **Contact:** Layding Kaliba, poetry editor.

Magazines Needs *African Voices*, published quarterly, is an "art and literary magazine that highlights the work of people of color. We publish ethnic literature and poetry on any subject. We also consider all themes and styles: avant-garde, free verse, haiku, light verse, and traditional. We do not wish to limit the reader or author." Considers poetry written by children. Has published poetry by Reg E. Gaines, Maya Angelou, Jessica Care Moore, Asha Bandele, Tony Medina, and Louis Reyes Rivera. *African Voices* is about 48 pages, magazine-sized, professionally printed, saddle-stapled, with paper cover. Receives about 100 submissions/year, accepts about 30%. Press run is 20,000. Single copy: $4; subscription: $12. Sample: $5.

How to Contact Submit no more than 2 poems at any one time. Accepts previously published poems and simultaneous submissions. Accepts submissions by e-mail (in text box), by fax, and by postal mail. Cover letter and SASE required. Seldom comments on rejected poems. Guidelines available for SASE or on website. Responds in 3 months. Pays 2 copies. Acquires first or one-time rights. Reviews books of poetry in 500-1,000 words. Send materials for review consideration, attn. Layding Kaliba.

Also Offers Sponsors periodic poetry contests and readings. Send SASE for details.

Tips "We strongly encourage new writers/poets to send in their work. Accepted contributors are encouraged to subscribe."

$ ☑ AGNI

Boston University, 236 Bay State Rd., Boston MA 02215. (617)353-7135. Fax: (617)353-7134. E-mail: agni@bu.edu. Website: www.agnimagazine.org. Established 1972. **Contact:** Sven Birkerts, editor.

•Work published in *AGNI* has been included regularly in *The Best American Poetry* and *The Pushcart Prize*.

Magazines Needs *AGNI*, published semiannually, prints poetry, fiction, and essays "by both emerging and established writers. We publish quite a bit of poetry in forms as well as 'language' poetry, but we don't begin to try and place parameters on the 'kind of work' that *AGNI* selects." Wants readable, intelligent poetry—mostly lyric free verse (with some narrative and dramatic)— that somehow communicates tension or risk. Has published poetry by Patricia Goedicke, Stephen Dunn, Kim Addonizio, Kate Northrop, Matt Donovan, and Seamus Heaney. *AGNI* is typeset, offset-printed, perfect-bound. Circulation is 3,000 for subscriptions, mail orders, and bookstore sales. Subscription: $20. Sample: $10 ($12 for *30th Anniversary Poetry Anthology*).

How to Contact Submit no more than 5 poems at a time. Considers simultaneous submissions; no previously published poems. No e-mail submissions. Cover letter is required ("brief, sincere"). "No fancy fonts, gimmicks. Include SASE or e-mail address; no preformatted reply cards." Reads submissions September 1-May 31. Pays $20/page ($150 maximum), a 1 year subscription, and for print publication: 2 contributor's copies and 4 gift copies. Acquires first serial rights.

☐ ☑ AGNIESZKA'S DOWRY (AGD)

A Small Garlic Press (ASGP), 5445 N. Sheridan Rd., #3003, Chicago IL 60640. E-mail: marek@enteract.com and ketzle@ketzle.net (send submissions to both e-mail addresses simultaneously). Website: http://asgp.org. Established 1995. **Contact:** Marek Lugowski and Katrina Grace Craig, co-editors.

Magazines Needs *Agnieszka's Dowry (AgD)* is "a magazine published both in print and as a permanent Internet installation of poems and graphics, letters to Agnieszka. The print version consists of professionally crafted chapbooks. The online version comprises fast-loading pages employing an intuitive, if uncanny, navigation in an interesting space, all conducive to fast and comfortable reading. No restrictions on form or type. We use contextual and juxtapositional tie-ins with other material in making choices, so visiting the online AgD or reading a chapbook of an AgD issue is required of anyone making a submission." Single copy: $3 plus $3 shipping, if ordered from Web site by an individual. Make checks payable to A Small Garlic Press.

How to Contact Submit 5-10 poems at a time. Accepts e-mail submissions only (NOTE: pasted into body of message in plain text, sent to both editors simultaneously; no attachments). "Prisoners may make submissions by regular mail, and we will waive the requirement that they read a print issue." Sometimes comments on rejected poems. Guidelines and annotated catalog available on Web site only. Responds by e-mail or SASE, usually within 2 months. Pays 1 contributor's copy. Acquires one-time rights where applicable.

Additional Information A Small Garlic Press (ASGP) publishes up to 3 chapbooks of poetry/year. Query with a full online ms, ASCII (plain text) only.

☐ THE AGUILAR EXPRESSION

1329 Gilmore Ave., Donora PA 15033. (724)379-8019. E-mail: xyz0@access995.com (inquiries only). Website: www.wordrunner.com/xfaguilar. Established 1986. **Contact:** Xavier F. Aguilar, editor/publisher.

Magazines Needs *The Aguilar Expression*, published semiannually in summer and winter, encourages "poetics that deal with now, which our readers can relate to. In publishing poetry, I try to exhibit the unique reality that we too often take for granted and acquaint as mediocre." Has published poetry by Martin Kich and Gail Ghai. *The Aguilar Expression* is 4-20 pages, 5x7, typeset, printed on 20 lb. paper. Receives about 10-15 poems/month, accepts about 10-15/year. Circulation is 200. Sample: $8. Make checks payable to Xavier Aguilar.

How to Contact Submit up to 3 poems at a time. Lines/poem: 30 maximum. No e-mail submissions. Cover letter is required (include writing background). SASE (for contact purposes) is required. Manuscripts should be submitted in clear, camera-ready copy. Submit copies, not originals; mss will not be returned. "We encourage all writers to send a SASE for writer's guidelines before submitting." Responds in 2 months. Pays 2 contributor's copies.

$ ☑ ◎ AIM MAGAZINE

(Specialized: racial harmony & peace), P.O. Box 390, Milton WA 90354-0390. E-mail: apiladoone@ aol.com. Website: www.aimmagazine.org. Established 1974. **Contact:** Ruth Apilado, poetry editor.

Magazines Needs *Aim Magazine*, published quarterly, is "dedicated to racial harmony and peace." Uses 3-4 poems ("poetry with social significance mainly") in each issue. Considers poetry by high school students. Has published poetry by J. Douglas Studer, Wayne Dowdy, Ned Pendergast, and Maria DeGuzman. *Aim* is magazine-sized with glossy cover. Receives about 30 submissions/year, accepts about half. Press run is 10,000. Single copy: $5; subscription: $20.

How to Contact Considers simultaneous submissions. Lines/poem: 32 average. Publishes theme issues. Upcoming themes available for SASE. Guidelines available on Web site. Responds in 6 weeks. Pays $10/poem and 1 contributor's copy. Does not send an acceptance notice: "We simply send payment and magazine copy."

Tips "Read the work of published poets."

☑ ALASKA QUARTERLY REVIEW

University of Alaska Anchorage, 3211 Providence Dr., Anchorage AK 99508. Phone/fax: (907)786-6916. E-mail: ayaqr@uaa.alaska.edu. Website: www.uaa.alaska.edu/aqr. Established 1981. **Contact:** Ronald Spatz, executive editor.

•Poetry published in *Alaska Quarterly Review* has been selected for inclusion in *The Best American Poetry*, *The Pushcart Prize*, and *Beacon's Best* anthologies.

Magazines Needs *Alaska Quarterly Review*, published in 2 double issues/year, is "devoted to contemporary literary art. We publish both traditional and experimental fiction, poetry, literary nonfiction, and short plays." Wants all styles and forms of poetry, "with the most emphasis perhaps on voice and content that displays 'risk,' or intriguing ideas or situations." Has published poetry by Maxine Kumin, Jane Hirshfield, David Lehman, Pattiann Rogers, Albert Goldbarth, and Billy Collins. *Alaska Quarterly Review* is 224-300 pages, digest-sized, professionally printed, perfect-bound, with card cover with color or b&w photo. Receives up to 5,000 submissions/year, accepts 40-90. Press run is 2,800. Subscription: $18. Sample: $6.

How to Contact No fax or e-mail submissions. Reads submissions mid-August to mid-May; manuscripts are *not* read May 15-August 15. Responds in up to 5 months, "sometimes longer during peak periods in late winter." Pay depends on funding. Acquires first North American serial rights.

Additional Information Guest poetry editors have included Stuart Dybek, Jane Hirshfield, Stuart Dischell, Maxine Kumin, Pattiann Rogers, Dorianne Laux, Peggy Shumaker, Olena Kalytiak Davis, Nancy Eimers, Michael Ryan, and Billy Collins.

☑ ◎ ALBATROSS

(Specialized: environmental & nature poetry), The Anabiosis Press, 2 South New St., Bradford MA 01835. (978) 469-7085. E-mail: rsmyth@anabiosispress.org. Website: www.anabiosispress. org. **Contact:** Richard Smyth, editor.

Magazines Needs *Albatross*, published "as soon as we have accepted enough quality poems to publish an issue—about 1 per year," considers the albatross "to be a metaphor for the environment. The journal's title is drawn from Coleridge's *The Rime of the Ancient Mariner* and is intended to invoke the allegorical implications of that poem. This is not to say that we publish only environmental or nature poetry, but that we are biased toward such subject matter. We publish mostly free verse, and we prefer a narrative style." Wants "poetry written in a strong, mature voice that conveys a deeply felt experience or makes a powerful statement." Does not want "rhyming poetry, prose poetry, or haiku." Has published poetry by John Grey, Kathleen Kirk, Matthew J. Spireng, Marcia L. Hurlow, and Gabriel Welsch. *Albatross* is 28 pages, digest-sized, laser-typeset, with linen cover. Subscription: $8 for 2 issues. Sample: $5.

How to Contact Submit 3-5 poems at a time. Lines/poem: 200 maximum. No simultaneous submissions. Accepts e-mail submissions if included in body of message (but is "often quicker at returning mailed submissions"). Name and address must accompany e-mail submissions. Cover letter is not required. "We do, however, need bio notes and SASE for return or response. Poems should be typed single-spaced, with name, address, and phone number in upper left corner." Time between acceptance and publication is up to 6 months to a year. Guidelines available for SASE or on Web site. Responds in 1-2 months. Pays 1 contributor's copy. Acquires all rights. Returns rights provided that "previous publication in *Albatross* is mentioned in all subsequent reprintings."

Contest/Award Offerings The Anabiosis Press Chapbook Contest (see separate listing Contests & Awards).

Tips "We expect a poet to read as much contemporary poetry as possible. We want to be moved. When you read our poetry, we hope that it moves you in the same way that it moves us. We try to publish the kind of poetry that you would want to read again and again."

☑ ◎ ALIMENTUM, THE LITERATURE OF FOOD

(Specialized: poems about/referencing food; menupoems; recipe poems), P.O. Box 210028, Nashville TN 37221. E-mail: submissions@alimentumjournal.com (inquiries only). Website: www.alimentumjournal.com. Established 2005. **Contact:** Cortney Davis, poetry editor.

Magazines Needs *Alimentum, The Literature of Food*, published semiannually in winter and summer, is "the only literary journal all about food." Wants "fiction, creative nonfiction, and poetry all around the subject of food." Has published poetry by Dick Allen, Stephen Gibson, Carly Sachs, Jen Karetnik, Virginia Chase Sutton. *Alimentum* is 128 pages, 6x7½, perfect-bound, with matte coated cover with 4-color art, interior b&w illustration includes ads. Receives about 2,000 poems/year, accepts about 30-40. Press run is 2,000. Single copy: $10 ($18 Canada/foreign); subscription: $18 for 1 year ($30 Canada/foreign). Make checks payable to *Alimentum* (payment available online through credit card or PayPal).

How to Contact Submit no more than 5 poems at a time. Lines/poem: no minimum or maximum. Considers simultaneous submissions; no previously published poems. No e-mail submissions; postal submissions only. Include SASE. Check Web site for reading periods which vary from year to year. Guidelines available on Web site. Responds 1-3 months. Pays contributor's copy. Acquires First North American Serial rights. Rights revert to poets upon publication.

Also Offers Publishes an annual broadside of "menupoems" for restaurants during National Poetry Month in April.

Advice "While food is our subject, we like poems to be about more than just the food. As in the stories we publish, the poems should also carry a personal element, even a story, not just a list of ingredients. Some special poem categories that we look for are menupoems and recipe poems."

$ ☑ ◎ ALIVE NOW

(Specialized: sacred way of living; theme-driven issues), 1908 Grand Ave., P.O. Box 340004, Nashville TN 37203-0004. E-mail: AliveNow@upperroom.org. Website: www.alivenow.org or www.upperroom.org. **Contact:** Melissa Tidwell, editor.

Magazines Needs *Alive Now*, published bimonthly, is a devotional magazine that invites readers to enter an ever-deepening relationship with God. "*Alive Now* seeks to nourish people who are hungry for a sacred way of living. Submissions should invite readers to see God in the midst of daily life by exploring how contemporary issues impact their faith lives. Each word must be vivid and dynamic and contribute to the whole. We make selections based on a list of upcoming themes. Manuscripts which do not fit a theme will be returned." Considers avant-garde and free verse. *Alive Now* is 64 pages. Accepts 20 poems/year. Circulation is 70,000. Subscription: $17.95/ year (6 issues); $26.95 for 2 years (12 issues). Additional subscription information, including foreign rates, available on website.

How to Contact Submit up to 5 poems/theme at a time. Lines/poem: 10 minimum, 45 maximum. Accepts e-mail submissions (pasted into body of message). "Send up to 5 poems per theme in single e-mail, single-spaced, plain text. Put theme in subject line." Postal submissions should be typed, double-spaced, on 8½x11 paper; include SASE. "If you're submitting material for more than one theme, send a SASE for each theme represented. On each page you submit, include your name, address, and the theme for which the piece is being sent." Always publishes theme issues; all poems must relate to themes. Upcoming themes and guidelines available for SASE or on website. "We will notify contributors of manuscript status when we make final decisions for a theme, 3 months before the issue date. We place manuscripts on hold for specific issues; authors are free to request their manuscripts be returned to them at any time." Pays $40 or more on acceptance. Purchases newspaper, periodical, and electronic rights; may purchase one-time use.

Tips "*Alive Now* is ecumenical, including both lay persons and church professionals. Our readers are primarily adults, from young adults to older adults, and include persons of many cultures and ethnic backgrounds."

$ ☑ ◎ AMAZE: THE CINQUAIN JOURNAL

(Specialized: American cinquain), 10529 Olive St., Temple City CA 91780. E-mail: cinquains@ hotmail.com. Website: www.amaze-cinquain.com. Established 2002. **Contact:** Deborah P. Kolodji, editor. Webmaster: Lisa Janice Cohen.

Magazines Needs *AMAZE: The Cinquain Journal*, published quarterly (February, May, August, November) online, is a literary Webzine devoted to the cinquain poetry form. Wants American cinquains as invented by Adelaide Crapsey (5 lines with a 2-4-6-8-2 syllable pattern) and cinquain variations (mirror cinquains, crown cinquains, cinquain sequences, etc.). Does not want any poetry not based upon the American cinquain, nor "grammar-lesson" cinquains based upon parts of speech; nothing hateful, racist, or sexually explicit. Considers poetry by teens (16 and older). Has published poetry by an'ya, Ann K. Schwader, Michael McClintock, naia, and Denis Garrison. Receives about 1,500 poems/year, accepts about 100.

How to Contact Submit 1-5 poems at a time. Lines/poem: 5. Considers previously published poems; no simultaneous submissions. Accepts e-mail submissions; no disk submissioins. "E-mail submissions preferred, with poems in the body of the e-mail. Do not send attachments." Include SASE with postal mail submissions. Issue deadlines are the 15th of January, April, July, and October. Time between acceptance and publication is 3 weeks. "Poems are evaluated on quality, form, and content." Often comments on rejected poems. Guidelines available for SASE or on Web site. Responds in up to 6 weeks. Pays $1/poem on acceptance. Acquires one-time rights and reprint rights for annual print anthology.

▦ $ ☑ AMBIT

17 Priory Gardens, Highgate, London N6 5QY England. (44)(208)340-3566. E-mail: info@ambitmagazine.co.uk (inquiries only). Website: www.ambitmagazine.co.uk. **Contact:** Martin Bax, Carol Ann Duffy, and Henry Graham, poetry editors.

Magazines Needs *Ambit*, published quarterly, is a 96-page quarterly of avant-garde, contemporary, and experimental work. *Ambit* is perfect-bound, with 2-color cover with artwork. Accepts about 3% of submissions received. Subscription: £28 UK, £30/€44 rest of Europe, £32/$64 everywhere else. Sample: £6.50 UK, £7/€15 rest of Europe, £8/$18 overseas.

How to Contact Submit up to 6 poems at a time. No previously published poems or simultaneous submissions. No e-mail submissions. "SAE vital for reply;" include IRCs when submitting from outside of UK. Poems should be typed, double-spaced. Never comments on rejected poems. Guidelines available in magazine or on Web site. Responds in 3-4 months. Pays small token plus 2 contributor's copies. Staff reviews books of poetry. Send materials for review consideration to review editor.

Tips "Read a copy of the magazine before submitting!"

☑ ◎ THE AMERICAN DISSIDENT

(Specialized: engaged writing; poetry in English, French, Spanish), 1837 Main St., Concord MA 01742. E-mail: todslone@yahoo.com. Website: www.TheAmericanDissident.org. Established 1998. **Contact:** G. Tod Slone, editor.

Magazines Needs *The American Dissident*, published 2 times/year, provides "a forum for examining the dark side of the academic/literary established order, which not only seems to have been discouraging vigorous debate, cornerstone of democracy, but also outright censoring voices and ideas from the literary agora to the detriment of American Literature." Wants "poetry, reviews, and short (1,000 words) essays in English, French, or Spanish, written on the edge with a dash of personal risk and stemming from personal experience, conflict with power, and/or involvement." Submissions should be "iconoclastic and parrhesiastic in nature." *The American Dissident* is 56-64 pages, digest-sized, offset-printed, perfect-bound, with card cover. Press run is 200. Single copy: $8; subscription: $16.

How to Contact Submit 3 poems at a time. Considers simultaneous submissions; no previously published poems. No e-mail submissions. "Far too many poets submit without even reading the guidelines. Include SASE and cover letter containing not credits, but rather personal dissident information and specific events that may have pushed you to reject indoctrination and 'go upright and vital, and speak the rude truth in all ways' (Emerson)." Time between acceptance and publication is up to 2 months. Almost always comments on rejected poems. Guidelines available for SASE. Responds in 1 month. Pays 1 contributor's copy. Acquires first North American serial rights. Reviews books/chapbooks of poetry and other magazines in 250 words, single-book format. Send materials for review consideration.

Tips "For the sake of democracy, poetry needs to be much more than safe, comfortable, diversionary intellectual entertainment, and poets much more than public court jesters. If only the latter endeavored to be more than just working the poem and filling out applications for grants, fellowships, and contests. If only they questioned and challenged, rather than accepted. If only they heeded Villon ('*Estoit-il lors temps de moy taire*'), Thoreau ('Let your life be a counter friction to stop the machine'), Wole Soyinka ('Criticism, like charity, starts at home'), Sinclair Lewis ('Every Compulsion is put upon writers to become safe, polite, obedient, and sterile'), Yevtushenko ('A Poet is always in danger when he lives too safely'), Hemingway ('Writers are forged in injustice as a sword is forged') and James Baldwin ('The peculiar nature of this [the writer's] responsibility is that he must never cease warring with it [society], for its sake and for his own'). Do not be afraid to name names!"

AMERICAN LITERARY REVIEW

Dept. of English, University of North Texas, 1155 Union Circle #311307, Denton TX 76203-1307. (940)565-2755. E-mail: americanliteraryreview@yahoo.com. Website: www.engl.unt.edu/alr. **Contact:** Bruce Bond and Corey Marks, poetry editors.

Magazines Needs *American Literary Review*, published semiannually, considers all forms and modes of poetry, nonfiction, and fiction. "We are especially interested in originality, substance, imaginative power, and lyric intensity." Has published poetry by Kathleen Pierce, Mark Irwin, Stephen Dunn, William Olsen, Dave St. John, and Cate Marvin. *American Literary Review* is about 120 pages, digest-sized, attractively printed, perfect-bound, with color card cover with photo. Subscription: $10/year, $18 for 2 years. Sample: $6.

How to Contact Submit up to 5 typewritten poems at a time. Considers simultaneous submissions. No fax or e-mail submissions. Cover letter is required. Include author's name, address, phone number, and poem titles. Reads mss September 1-May 1. Guidelines available on Web site. Responds in up to 3 months. Pays 2 contributor's copies.

Contest/Award Offerings Send SASE for details.

THE AMERICAN POETRY JOURNAL

P.O. Box 2080 Aptos CA 95001-2080. E-mail: editor@americanpoetryjournal.com. Website: www.americanpoetryjournal.com. Established 2004. **Contact:** J.P. Dancing Bear, editor.

Magazines Needs *The American Poetry Journal*, published annually (July), seeks "to publish work using poetic device, favoring image, metaphor, and good sound. We like alliteration, extended metaphors, image, movement, and poems that can pass the 'so what' test. *The American Poetry Journal* has in mind the reader who delights in discovering what a poem can do to the tongue and what the poem paints on the cave of the mind." Wants poems "that exhibit strong, fresh imagery, metaphor, and good sound." Does not want "narratives about family, simplistic verse, annoying word hodge-podges." Has published poetry by C.J. Sage, Natasha Sage, Lola Haskins, Dorianne Laux, and Jennifer Juneau. *The American Poetry Journal* is 100 pages, 6X9, perfect-bound. Accepts about 1% of poems submitted. Single copy: $12; subscription: $12. Make checks payable to J.P. Dancing Bear.

How to Contact Submit 3-5 poems at a time. Considers simultaneous submissions; no previously published poems. E-mail submissions only. Cover letter is preferred. Considers unsolicited submissions October 1-April 30 (poets may submit no more than twice during the reading period). "We consider submissions from subscribers year round." Time between acceptance and publication is 8 months. "Poems are read first for clarity and technique, then read aloud for sound quality." Seldom comments on rejected poems. Guidelines available on Web site. Responds in 3 months. Pays one contributor's copy. Acquires first rights.

Contest/Award Offerings Offers The American Poet Prize and *The American Poetry Journal* Book Prize (see separate listings in Contests & Awards).

Tips "Know the magazine you are submitting to, before you commit your work and yourself. It's not that difficult, but it helps your odds when the editor can tell that you get what the magazine is about. Reading an issue is the easiest way to do this."

AMERICAN TANKA

(Specialized: English-language tanka), 4906 W. State Route 55, Troy OH 45373. E-mail: atanka@ earthlink.net. Website: www.americantanka.com. Established 1996. **Contact:** Tim W. Younce, executive director; Michael McClintock, editor.

Magazines Needs *American Tanka*, published annually, is devoted to single English-language tanka. Wants "concise and vivid language, good crafting, and echo of the original Japanese form, but with unique and contemporary content." Does not want "anything that's not tanka. No sequences or titled groupings." Has published poetry by Sanford Goldstein, Marianne Bluger, Jeanne Emrich, Tom Hartman, Larry Kimmel, Pamela Miller Ness, and George Swede. *American Tanka* is 95-120 pages, digest-sized, perfect-bound, with glossy cover. Single copy: $12; subscription: $20 for 2 issues, $28 for 3 issues. Make checks/money orders payable to *American Tanka* and send to Tim Younce, 4906 W. State Route 55, Troy OH 45373. All checks and money orders must be issued from a US bank.

How to Contact Submit up to 5 poems at a time (1 submission/reading period). No previously published poems or simultaneous submissions. Accepts submissions by e-mail (pasted into body of message) to MchlMcClintock@aol.com with "Submissions to AT" in the subject line, or by mail to Michael McClintock, Editor, 9230 N. Stoneridge Dr., Fresno CA 93720. Include SASE Guidelines available for SASE, by e-mail, or on Web site. Responds in up to 4 months. Acquires first North American serial rights.

Tips "Become familiar with the tanka form by reading both translations and English-language tanka. In your own tanka, be natural and concrete and vivid. Avoid clichés, overcrowded imagery, or attempting to imitate Japanese poems."

$ ☑ ◎ ANCIENT PATHS

(Specialized: Christian), P.O. Box 7505, Fairfax Station VA 22039. E-mail: SSBurris@cox.net. Website: www.editorskylar.com. Established 1998. **Contact:** Skylar H. Burris, editor.

Magazines Needs *Ancient Paths*, published biennially in odd-numbered years, provides "a forum for quality Christian literature and contains poetry, short stories, and art." Wants "traditional rhymed/metrical forms and free verse; subtle Christian themes. I seek poetry that makes the reader both think and feel." Does not want "'preachy' poetry, inconsistent meter, or forced rhyme; no stream of conscious or avant-garde work; no esoteric academic poetry." Has published poetry by Giovanni Malito, Ida Fasel, Diane Glancy, Walt McDonald, and Donna Farley. *Ancient Paths* is 80+ pages, digest-sized, photocopied, perfect-bound, with cardstock cover. Receives about 600 poems/year, accepts about 7%. Press run is 175; 90 distributed free to churches, libraries, and authors. Single copy: $12. Make checks payable to Skylar Burris.

How to Contact Submit up to 5 poems at a time. Lines/poem: 60 maximum. Considers previously published poems and simultaneous submissions. Accepts e-mail submissions "only if you reside outside the U.S.; submissions should be pasted directly into the message, single-spaced, 1 poem per message, using a small or normal font size, with name and address at the top of each submission. Use subject heading: ANCIENT PATHS SUBMISSION, followed by your title." For postal submissions, poems should be single-spaced; "always include name, address, and line count on first page of all submissions, and note if the poem is previously published and what rights (if any) were purchased." Check Web site for reading period for Issue 15. Time between acceptance and publication is up to one year. Often comments on rejected poems. Guidelines available for SASE or on Web site. Responds in 3-4 weeks "if rejected, longer if being seriously considered." Pays $10/poem and discount on reserved copies. No contributor's copy. Acquires one-time or reprint rights.

Tips "Read the great religious poets: John Donne, George Herbert, T.S. Eliot, Lord Tennyson. Remember not to preach. This is a literary magazine, not a pulpit. This does not mean you do not communicate morals or celebrate God. It means you are not overbearing or simplistic when you do so."

▦ ☑ THE ANTIGONISH REVIEW

P.O. Box 5000, Antigonish NS B2G 2W5 Canada. (902)867-3962. Fax: (902)867-5563. E-mail: TAR@stfx.ca. Website: www.antigonishreview.com. Established 1970. **Contact:** Jeanette Lynes, co-editor or Bonnie McIsaac, office manager.

Magazines Needs *The Antigonish Review*, published quarterly, tries "to produce the kind of literary and visual mosaic that the modern sensibility requires or would respond to. Subject matter can be anything; the style is traditional, modern, or post-modern limited by typographic resources. Purpose is not an issue." Does not want "erotica, scatalogical verse, excessive propaganda toward a certain subject." Has published poetry by Andy Wainwright, W.J. Keith, Michael Hulse, Jean McNeil, M. Travis Lane, and Douglas Lochhead. *The Antigonish Review* is 144 pages, digest-sized, offset-printed, flat-spined, with glossy card cover with art. Receives 2,500 submissions/year, accepts about 10%. Press run is 1,000. Subscription: $24 CAD, $30 CAD elsewhere. Sample: $7 CAD.

How to Contact Submit 5-10 poems at a time. Lines/poem: "not over 80, i.e., 2 pages." No previously published poems or simultaneous submissions. Accepts fax submissions; e-mail submissions accepted from overseas only. Include SASE (SAE and IRCs if outside Canada; "we cannot use U.S. postage") or we can respond by e-mail. Time between acceptance and publication is up to 8 months. Sometimes comments on rejected poems. Guidelines available for SASE, by e-mail, or on Web site. Responds in up to 6 months. Pays $30 CAD per page and 2 contributor's copies. Acquires first North American serial rights.

$ ☑ THE ANTIOCH REVIEW

P.O. Box 148, Yellow Springs OH 45387. (937)769-1365. Website: www.review.antioch.edu. Established 1941. **Contact:** Judith Hall, poetry editor.

• Work published in *The Antioch Review* has been included frequently in *The Best American Poetry, The Best New Poets,* and *The Pushcart Prize.*

Magazines Needs *The Antioch Review* "is an independent quarterly of critical and creative thought. For well over 50 years, creative authors, poets, and thinkers have found a friendly reception—regardless of formal reputation. We get far more poetry than we can possibly accept, and the competition is keen. Here, where form and content are so inseparable and reaction is so personal, it is difficult to state requirements or limitations. Studying recent issues of *The Antioch Review* should be helpful." Does not want "'light' or inspirational verse." Has published poetry by Richard Kenney, Eric Pankey, Dana Roeser, and others. Receives about 3,000 submissions/year. Circulation is 4,000; 70% distributed through bookstores and newsstands. Subscription: $40. Sample: $7.

How to Contact Submit 3-6 poems at a time. No previously published poems or simultaneous submissions. Include SASE with all submissions. Reads submissions September 1-May 1 only. Guidelines available on Web site. Responds in 8-10 weeks. Pays $15/published page plus 2 contributor's copies; additional copies available at 40% discount.

▣ $ ▢ ◎ AOIFE'S KISS

(Specialized: fantasy; science fiction), P.O. Box 782, Cedar Rapids IA 52406-0782. E-mail: aoifeskiss@yahoo.com. Website: www.samsdotpublishing.com. Established 2002. **Contact:** Tyree Campbell, managing editor. Member: The Speculative Literature Foundation (http://SpeculativeLiterature.org).

Magazines Needs *Aoife's Kiss*, published quarterly in print and online (the 2 versions are different), prints "fantasy, science fiction, sword and sorcery, alternate history, horror short stories, poems, illustrations, and movie and book reviews." Wants "fantasy, science fiction, spooky horror, and speculative poetry with minimal angst." Does not want "horror with excessive blood and gore." Considers poetry by children and teens. Has published poetry by Bruce Boston, Karen A. Romanko, Mike Allen, Corrine De Winter, Julie Shiel, and Marge B. Simon. *Aoife's Kiss* (print version) is 54 pages, magazine-sized, offset-printed, saddle-stapled, perfect-bound, with color paper cover, includes ads. Receives about 300 poems/year, accepts about 50 (17%). Press run is 150; 5 distributed free to reviewers. Single copy: $7; subscription: $22/year, $40 for 2 years. Make checks payable to Tyree Campbell/Sam's Dot Publishing.

How to Contact Submit up to 5 poems at a time. Lines/poem: prefers less than 100. Considers previously published poems; no simultaneous submissions. Accepts e-mail submissions (pasted into body of message); no disk submissions. "Submission should include snail mail address and a short (1-2 lines) bio." Reads submissions year round. Submit seasonal poems 6 months in advance. Time between acceptance and publication is 2-5 months. Often comments on rejected poems. Guidelines available on Web site. Responds in 4-6 weeks. Pays $5/poem, $3/reprint, $1 for scifaiku and related forms, and 1 contributor's copy. Acquires first North American serial rights. Reviews books/chapbooks of poetry. Send materials for review consideration to Tyree Campbell.

Tips "It's up to the writer to take the first step and submit work. Some of our best poems have come from poets who weren't sure if they were good enough. Horror poetry is a difficult sell with us."

☑ APALACHEE REVIEW

Apalachee Press, P.O. Box 10469, Tallahassee FL 32302. Website: www.apalacheereview.org. Established 1971. **Contact:** Michael Trammell, editor; Laura Newton and Dominika Wrozynski, poetry editors. Member: CLMP, AAP.

Magazines Needs *Apalachee Review*, published about twice/year, appears "as soon as we have enough good material." Has published poetry by Rita Mae Reese and Charles Harper Webb. *Apalachee Review* is 120 pages, digest-sized, professionally printed, perfect-bound, with card cover. Press run is 700. Subscription: $15 for 2 issues ($30 foreign). Sample: $5.

How to Contact Submit 3-5 poems at a time. Considers simulaneous submissions. Accepts submissions by postal mail only. "Submit clear copies, with name and address on each." SASE required. Reads submissions year round. Sometimes comments on rejected poems. Guidelines available for SASE or on Web site. Responds in 4 months, "but sometimes we get bogged down." Pays 2 contributor's copies. Poet retains rights. Staff reviews books of poetry. Send materials for review consideration.

☑ ▣ ☑ APPLE VALLEY REVIEW: A JOURNAL OF CONTEMPORARY LITERATURE

E-mail: editor@leahbrowning.net. Website: www.applevalleyreview.com. Established 2005. **Contact:** Leah Browning, editor. Member: Council of Literary Magazines and Presses (CLMP).

Magazines Needs *Apple Valley Review: A Journal of Contemporary Literature*, published semiannually online, features "beautifully crafted poetry, short fiction, and essays." Wants "work that has both mainstream and literary appeal. All work must be original, previously unpublished, and in English. Translations are welcome if permission has been granted. Preference is given to short (under 2 pages), non-rhyming poetry." Does not want "erotica, work containing explicit language or violence, or work that is scholarly, critical, inspirational, or intended for children." Considers poetry by children and teens; "all work is considered regardless of the author's age." Has published poetry by Anna Evans, Rob Hardy, Ona Gritz, Rosa Salazar, Karen Schubert, and David Cazden. Receives about 5,000+ poems/year, accepts less than 1%.

How to Contact Submit 2-6 poems at a time. Lines/poem: "no limit, though we prefer short poems (under 2 pages). No previously published poems or simultaneous submissions. Accepts e-mail submissions (pasted into body of message, with "poetry" in subject line); no disk submissions. Cover letter is preferred. "Include name, address, phone number, e-mail address, and a short biography (maximum 150 words)." Reads submissions year round. Submit seasonal poems 6 months in advance, "though our interest in seasonal poems is very limited." Time between acceptance and publication is 1-6 months. Sometimes comments on rejected poems. Guidelines available by e-mail or on Web site. Responds in 1 week to 3 months. Sometimes sends prepublication galleys. "This is not a paying market. However, all work published in the *Apple Valley Review* during a given calendar year will be considered for the annual *Apple Valley Review* Editor's Prize [see below]." Acquires first rights and first serial rights and retains the right to archive the work online for an indefinite period of time. "As appropriate, we may also choose to nominate published work for awards or recognition. Author retains all other rights."

Contest/Award Offerings Offers the annual *Apple Valley Review* Editor's Prize. Award varies. "In 2008, the prize was $100 and a book of short stories." Submit 2-6 poems. **Entry fee:** none. **Deadline:** rolling; all submissions to the *Apple Valley Review*, and all work published during a given calendar year will be considered for the prize.

Tips "Try to read as much as possible, and submit to markets that are publishing work that you enjoy. They are more likely to be a good fit."

N A PUBLIC SPACE

323 Dean St., Brooklyn NY 11217. (718)858-8067. E-mail: general@apublicspace.com. Website: www.apublicspace.org. **Contact:** Brigid Hughes, editor.

Magazines Needs *A Public Space*, published quarterly, "is an independent magazine of literature and culture. In an era that has relegated literature to the margins, we plan to make fiction and poetry the stars of a new conversation. We believe that stories are how we make sense of our lives and how we learn about other lives. We believe that stories matter." Single copy: $15; subscription: $36/year or $60/2 years.

How to Contact Submit up to 4 poems at a time. Considers simultaneous submissions; no previously published poems. Prefers submissions through online process; accepts mail. Include SASE. See Web site for submission dates and guidelines.

AQUARIUS

Flat 4, Room B, 116 Sutherland Ave., London W9 2QP England. Website: www.geocities.com/eddielinden. **Contact:** Eddie Linden, editor.

Magazines Needs *Aquarius*, published irregularly, prints poetry, fictional prose, essays, interviews, and reviews. Single copy: $10; subscription: $50 (U.S.). Special issue on the poets/writers George Barker and W.S. Graham available for £6 plus £1.25 p&p in United Kingdom.

How to Contact "Please note the magazine will not accept work unless writers have bought the magazine and studied the style/form of the work published." Payment is by arrangement.

$ ARC POETRY MAGAZINE

P.O. Box 81060, Ottawa ON K1P 1B1 Canada. E-mail: arc@arcpoetry.ca. Website: www.arcpoetry.ca. Established 1978. **Contact:** Pauline Conley, managing editor.

Magazines Needs *Arc Poetry Magazine*, published semiannually, prints poetry, poetry-related articles, interviews, and book reviews. "Tastes are eclectic. International submissions are welcome and encouraged." Has published poetry by Evelyn Lau, Michael Crummey, Erin Mouré, Patricia Young, and Joelene Heathcote. *Arc Poetry Magazine* is 130-160 pages, perfect-bound, printed on matte white stock "with a crisp, engaging design and a striking visual art portfolio in each issue." Receives about 1,000 submissions/year, accepts about 40-50 poems. Press run is 1,500. Single copy: $12.50 CAD, $18 CAD (U.S.), $20 CAD (overseas); subscription: 2 issues/1 year—$17.95 CAD (in Canada); 4 issues/2 years—$34.95 CAD (in Canada), $42.95 USD, $45.95 USD (overseas). Online ordering available for subscriptions and single copies (with occasional promotions).

How to Contact Submit 4-8 poems at a time. No previously published poems or simultaneous submissions. No e-mail submissions. Cover letter is required. Submissions should be single-spaced, with name and address on each page. Guidelines available for SAE and IRC or on Web site. Responds in 4-6 months. Pays $40 CAD/page plus 2 contributor's copies. Acquires first Canadian serial rights.

Contest/Award Offerings The Confederation Poets Prize is an annual award of $250 for the best poem published in *Arc* that year. *Arc* also sponsors an international Poem of the Year Contest: 1st Prize: $1,500 CAD; 2nd Prize: $1,000 CAD; 3rd Prize: $750 CAD. Guidelines available on website. **Entry fee:** $23 CAD for 4 poems. **Deadline:** June 30. Other awards include the Lampman-Scott Award for Poetry, Critic's Desk Award, and the Diana Brebner Prize for Poetry.

ARDENT!

Poetry in the Arts, 1909 Hollow Ridge Dr, Cedar Park, TX 78613. (512)699-8821. E-mail:rimer777@ gmail.co. Website: www.ardent.poetryinarts.org. Established 1985. **Contact**: Dillon McKinsey, editor.

Magazines Needs *Ardent!*, published semiannually, is a journal of poetry and art. All forms and styles are considered. *Ardent!* is perfect-bound.

How to Contact Accepts e-mail submissions, "but must adhere to the guidelines. See the *Ardent!* Web site for details." Submission by postal mail should be sent c/o *Ardent!* editors to the address listed above. Pays contributor's copies.

Contest/Award Offerings An annual award will be given for the best published submission of both poetry and art.

☑ ARIES: A JOURNAL OF CREATIVE EXPRESSION

Dept. of Languages and Literature, Texas Wesleyan University, 1201 Wesleyan St., Fort Worth TX 76105-1536. (817)531-4907. Fax: (817)531-6503. E-mail: sneeley@txwes.edu (inquiries only; no submissions). Website: www.department.txwes.edu/aries. Established 1985. **Contact:** Stacia Dunn Neeley, general editor.

Magazines Needs *Aries: A Journal of Creative Expression*, published annually in August, prints quality poetry, b&w photography/art, fiction, creative non-fiction, essays, and short plays. Poetry 3 to 50 lines. Original poetry in languages other than English welcome if submitted with English translation as companion. Has published poetry by Virgil Suárez, Richard Robbins, Susan Smith Nash, Gerald Zipper, and Lynn Veach Sadler. *Aries* is 70-90 pages, digest-sized, offset-printed, perfect-bound, with heavy cardstock cover and b&w art (1,500 dpi scans). Receives about 800 poems/year, accepts about 10%. Press run is 300. Single copy: $7; subscription: $7. Make checks payable to Aries @ Texas Wesleyan University.

How to Contact Send 5 submissions maximum per year. Lines/poem: 3 minimum, 50 maximum. Considers simultaneous submissions with notification; no previously published poems. Cover letter required. Include titles of submissions and 100-word bio required; no names allowed on submissions themselves. Accepts submissions September 1-January 31 only. Submit electronically to aries@txwes.edu or to mailing address above. Notification April/May; publication July/ August. "At least 3 reviewers read every submission via blind review. Personal response to every submission accompanied by a SASE or functioning e-mail address." Always comments on rejected poems. Guidelines available in magazine, for SASE, by e-mail, or on Web site. Responds in up to 6 months (notification of acceptance in April). Offers 50% off 2 contributor's copies. Acquires first rights.

Tips "Write in the voice that speaks from your unique position in the world. Our editors tend to choose works that show 'there's something at stake.'"

❏ ◎ ARKANSAS REVIEW: A JOURNAL OF DELTA STUDIES

(Specialized: work that evokes 7-state Mississippi River Delta region), P.O. Box 1890, State University AR 72467-1890. (870)972-3043. Fax: (870)972-3045. E-mail: jcollins@astate.edu. Website: www.clt.astate.edu/arkreview. Established 1968 (as Kansas Quarterly). **Contact:** Janelle Collins, general editor.

Magazines Needs *Arkansas Review: A Journal of Delta Studies*, published 3 times/year, is "a regional studies journal devoted to the 7-state Mississippi River Delta. Interdisciplinary in scope, we publish academic articles, relevant creative material, interviews, and reviews. Material must respond to or evoke the experiences and landscapes of the 7-state Mississippi River Delta (St. Louis to New Orleans)." Has published poetry by Greg Fraser, Jo McDougall, and Catherine Savage Brosman. *Arkansas Review* is 92 pages, magazine-sized, photo offset-printed, saddle-stapled, with 4-color cover. Receives about 500 poems/year, accepts about 5%. Press run is 600; 50 distributed free to contributors. Subscription: $20. Sample: $7.50. Make checks payable to ASU Foundation.

How to Contact Submit any number of poems at a time. No previously published poems or simultaneous submissions. Accepts e-mail and disk submissions. Cover letter is preferred. Include SASE. Time between acceptance and publication is about 6 months. Occasionally publishes theme issues. Guidelines available for SASE or by e-mail. Responds in 4 months. Pays 3 contributor's copies. Acquires first rights. Staff reviews books/chapbooks of poetry "that are relevant to the Delta" in 500 words, single- and multi-book format. Send materials for review consideration to Janelle Collins ("inquire in advance").

❏ THE ARMCHAIR AESTHETE

Pickle Gas Press, 19 Abbotswood Crescent, Penfield NY 14526. (585)381-1003. E-mail: thearmchairaesthete@yahoo.com or bypaul@frontiernet.net. Established 1996. **Contact:** Paul Agosto, editor.

Magazines Needs *The Armchair Aesthete*, published 2-3 times/year, is a zine of "thoughtful, well-crafted, concise fiction and poetry. Interested in both fiction and poetry." *The Armchair Aesthete* is 140-170 pages, digest-sized, desktop-published, photocopied, with card cover and plastic spiral bound. Receives about 300 poems/year, accepts about 25-30%. Submission must be accompanied by a SASE (#10 envelope). Recently published work by Chris Brown, Laverne and Carol Frith, Lydia Williams, Andrew Bynom, and Douglas Empringham. Subscription: $18/3 issues. Sample: $6.95 postpaid and 5 First-Class stamps. Make checks payable to Paul Agosto.

How to Contact Lines/poem: 60 maximum. Fiction: 4,500 words maximum. Considers previously published poems and simultaneous submissions, if indicated. Accepts e-mail submissions (pasted into body of message or attached MS Word file). Cover letter is preferred. Time between acceptance and publication is up to 12 months. Seldom comments on rejected poems. Guidelines available for SASE. Responds in 4-7 months. Pays 1 contributor's copy. Acquires one-time rights.

$ ❏ ARTFUL DODGE

Dept. of English, College of Wooster, Wooster OH 44691. E-mail: dbourne@wooster.edu. Website:

www.wooster.edu/artfuldodge/. Established 1979. **Contact:** Daniel Bourne, poetry editor.

Magazines Needs *Artful Dodge*, published annually, takes "a strong interest in poets who are continually testing what they can get away with successfully in regard to subject, perspective, language, etc.—but who also show mastery of current American poetic techniques, its varied textures and its achievement in the illumination of the particular. We require high craftsmanship as well as a vision that goes beyond one's own storm windows, grandmothers, or sexual fantasies (to paraphrase Hayden Carruth). Poems can be on any subject, of any length, from any perspective, in any voice." Wants poems "that utilize stylistic persuasions both old and new to good effect. We're not afraid of poems that try to deal with large social, political, historical, and even philosophical questions—especially if the poem emerges from one's own life experience and is not the result of armchair pontificating." Does not want "anything that doesn't connect with both the human and the aesthetic. No cute, rococo surrealism, someone's warmed-up, left-over notion of an avant-garde that existed 10-100 years ago, or any last bastions of rhymed verse in the civilized world." Encourages translations, "but we ask for original text and statement from translator that he/she has copyright clearance and permission of author." Has published poetry by Gregory Orr, Julia Kasdorf, Denise Duhamel, Tess Gallagher, and William Heyen. *Artful Dodge* is digest-sized, professionally printed, perfect-bound, with glossy cover, includes ads. Receives at least 2,000 poems/year, accepts about 60. Press run is 1,000. Single copy: $7; subscription: $7/year, $14 for 2 years, $25 for 4 years. Sample: $5 (back issue).

How to Contact Submit 6 poems at a time. Lines/poem: long poems may be of any length, but send only one at a time. Considers simultaneous submissions "if we are informed of acceptance elsewhere." Responds in up to one year. Pays 2 contributor's copies, "plus (currently) $5/page honorarium because of grants from the Ohio Arts Council." Send materials for review consideration; however, "there is no guarantee we can review them or respond! In fact, our reviews almost invariably involve books published by past contributors to the magazine."

Tips "We often offer encouragement to writers whose work we find promising, but *Artful Dodge* is more a journal for the already emerging writer than for the beginner looking for an easy place to publish. We have a sustained commitment to translation, especially from Polish and other East European literatures, and we feel the interchange between the American and foreign works on our pages is of great interest to our readers."

☑ ART TIMES: A LITERARY JOURNAL AND RESOURCE FOR ALL THE ARTS

P.O. Box 730, Mt. Marion NY 12456. Phone/fax: (845)246-6944. E-mail: info@arttimesjournal.com (inquiries only). Website: www.arttimesjournal.com. Established 1984. **Contact:** Raymond J. Steiner, poetry editor.

Magazines Needs *Art Times*, published monthly (combining Jan/Feb and July/Aug), is a tabloid newspaper devoted to the fine and performing arts. Focuses on cultural and creative articles and essays, but also publishes some poetry and fiction. Wants "poetry that strives to express genuine observation in unique language. All topics, all forms." *Art Times* is 20-26 pages, newsprint, includes ads. Receives 300-500 poems/month, accepts about 40-50/year. Circulation is 27,000; most distribution is free through galleries, performing arts centers, schools, museums, theatres, etc., in the Northeast Corridor of the U.S. Subscription: $15/year. Sample: $1 with 9x12 SAE and 3 First-Class stamps.

How to Contact Submit 4-5 typed poems at a time. Lines/poem: up to 20. No e-mail submissions. Include SASE with all submissions. Has an 18-month backlog. Guidelines available for SASE. Responds in 6 months. Pays 6 contributor's copies plus one-year subscription.

⬡ ▣ ☑ ASCENT ASPIRATIONS MAGAZINE

1560 Arbutus Dr., Nanoose Bay BC V9P 9C8 Canada. (250)468-7313. E-mail: ascentaspirations@ shaw.ca. Website: www.ascentaspirations.ca. Established 1997. **Contact:** David Fraser, editor.

Magazines Needs *Ascent Aspirations Magazine*, published quarterly online (February, May, August, November) and semiannually in print (late fall and late spring), specializes in poetry, short fiction, essays, and visual art. "A quality electronic and print publication, *Ascent* is dedicated to encouraging aspiring poets and fiction writers. We accept all forms of poetry on any theme. Poetry needs to be unique and touch the reader emotionally with relevant human, social, and philosophical imagery." Does not want poetry "that focuses on mainstream overtly religious verse." Considers poetry by children and teens. Has published poetry by Janet Buck and Taylor Graham. Work is considered for the print editions of *Ascent* through contests (see below). Receives about 1,500 poems/year, accepts about 15%.

How to Contact Submit 1-5 poems at a time. Considers previously published poems and simultaneous submissions. Prefers e-mail submissions (pasted into body of message or as attachment in Word); no disk submissions. "If you must submit by postal mail because it is your only avenue, provide a SASE with IRCs or Canadian stamps." Reads submissions on a quarterly basis year round. Time between acceptance and publication is 3 months. Editor makes decisions on all poems. Seldom comments on rejected poems. Occasionally publishes theme issues. Upcoming themes available on Web site. Responds in 3 months. Acquires one-time rights.

Contest/Award Offerings To fund the printing of the 2 semiannual anthologies, *Ascent* offers a contest for poetry and fiction. 1st Prize: $100 CAD; 2nd Prize: $75 CAD; 3rd Prize: $50 CAD; 4th Prize: $25 CAD; 5 Honorable Mentions: $10 CAD each. All winners and honorable mentions receive 1-2 copies of anthology; all other entrants published in anthology receive 1 free copy. Guidelines available for SASE, by e-mail, or on Web site. **Entry fee:** $5 CAD/poem or $10 CAD/3 poems. **Deadlines:** "these vary for each contest." **NOTE: "Fee, awards, and the number of copies for winners of contests can change. Refer always to the Web site for the most up-to-date information."**

Tips "Write with passion for your material. In terms of editing, always proofread to the point where what you submit is the best it can possibly be. Never be discouraged if your work is not accepted; it may be just not the right fit for the current publication."

☑ ASHEVILLE POETRY REVIEW

P.O. Box 7086, Asheville NC 28802. (828)649-0217. E-mail: editor@ashevillereview.com. Website: www.ashevillereview.com. Established 1994. **Contact:** Keith Flynn, founder/managing editor.

Magazines Needs *Asheville Poetry Review*, published annually, prints "the best regional, national, and international poems we can find. We publish translations, interviews, essays, historical perspectives, and book reviews as well." Wants "quality work with well-crafted ideas married to a dynamic style. Any subject matter is fit to be considered so long as the language is vivid with a clear sense of rhythm. We subscribe to the Borges dictum that great poetry is a combination of 'algebra and fire.'" Has published poetry by Sherman Alexie, Eavan Boland, Gary Snyder, Colette Inez, Robert Bly, and Fred Chappell. *Asheville Poetry Review* is 160-200 pages, digest-sized, perfect-bound, laminated, with full-color cover. Receives about 8,000 submissions/year, accepts about 5%. Press run is 2,000. Subscription: $22.50 for 2 years, $43.50 for 4 years. Sample: $13. **"We prefer poets purchase a sample copy prior to submitting."How to Submit** Submit 3-5 poems at a time. No previously published poems or simultaneous submissions. No e-mail submissions. Cover letter is required. Include comprehensive bio, recent publishing credits, and SASE. Reads submissions January 15-July 15. Time between acceptance and publication is up to one year. Poems are circulated to an editorial board. Seldom comments on rejected poems. Occasionally publishes theme issues. Guidelines available for SASE or on Web site. Responds in up to 7 months. Pays 1 contributor's copy. Rights revert back to author upon publication. Reviews books/chapbooks of poetry. Send materials for review consideration.

▣ ☑ ◎ ASININE POETRY

(Specialized: humor, satire), Mongrel Publications, P.O. Box 1349, New York NY 10276. E-mail: editor@asininepoetry.com. Website: www.asininepoetry.com. Established 1998 (print), 2001 (online). **Contact:** R. Narvaez, editor.

Magazines Needs *asinine poetry*, published monthly online, "features 10-12 new poems each month. We specialize in poetry that does not take itself too seriously." Wants "any form of poetry, but for us the poetry must be in a humorous, parodic, or satirical style. Many submissions to our site are slapdash, too broad, or funny on just one snickering level. We prefer well-crafted poems that may contain serious elements or cover serious subjects—but which are also amusing, absurd, or hilarious. We also love topical and occasional poems." Does not want serious, straightforward poems. Has published poetry by Hal Sirowitz, William Trowbridge, Elizabeth Swados, Daniel Thomas Moran, and Colonel Drunky Bob. Receives about 800 poems/year, accepts about 10%.

How to Contact Submit 3-4 poems at a time. Lines/poem: 50 maximum. Considers previously published poems and simultaneous submissions. Accepts e-mail (pasted into body of message) and disk submissions.

Contest/Award Offerings Sponsors 1 contest/year. Guidelines available on Web site.

☑ ATLANTA REVIEW

P.O. Box 8248, Atlanta GA 31106. E-mail: atlrev@yahoo.com (inquiries only). Website: www.atlantareview.com. Established 1994. **Contact:** Dan Veach, editor/publisher.

•Work published in *Atlanta Review* has been included in *The Best American Poetry* and *The Pushcart Prize*.

Magazines Needs *Atlanta Review*, published semiannually, is devoted primarily to poetry, but occasionally features interviews and b&w artwork. Wants "quality poetry of genuine human appeal." Has published poetry by Seamus Heaney, Billy Collins, Derek Walcott, Maxine Kumin, Alicia Stallings, and Thomas Lux. *Atlanta Review* is 128 pages, digest-sized, professionally printed on acid-free paper, flat-spined, with glossy color cover. Receives about 10,000 poems/year, accepts about 1%. Press run is 2,500. Single copy: $6; subscription: $10. Sample: $5.

How to Contact Submit no more than 5 poems at a time. No previously published poems. No e-mail submissions from within the U.S.; postal submissions only. Include SASE for reply. "Authors living outside the United States and Canada may submit work via e-mail." Cover letter is preferred. Include brief bio. Put name and address on each poem. Reads submissions according to the following deadlines: June 1 for Fall; December 1 for Spring. "While we do read year round, response time may be slower during summer and the winter holidays." Time between acceptance and publication is 6 months. Seldom comments on rejected poems. Guidelines available for SASE, by e-mail, or on Web site. Responds in 1 month. Pays 2 contributor's copies, author's discounts on additional copies. Acquires first North American serial rights.

Contest/Award Offerings *Atlanta Review* sponsors the Poetry 2010 International Poetry Competition (see separate listing in Contests & Awards).

$ ☑ THE ATLANTIC MONTHLY

P.O. Box 130149, Boston MA 02113. Website: www.theatlantic.com. Established 1857. **Contact:** David Barber, poetry editor.

Magazines Needs *The Atlantic Monthly* publishes some of the most distinguished poetry in

American literature. "We read with interest and attention every poem submitted to the magazine and, quite simply, we publish those that seem to us to be the best." Wants "the broadest possible range of work: traditional forms and free verse, the meditative lyric and the 'light' or comic poem, the work of the famous and the work of the unknown." Has published poetry by Maxine Kumin, Stanley Plumly, Linda Gregerson, Philip Levine, Ellen Bryant Voigt, and W.S. Merwin. Has a circulation of 500,000. Receives about 60,000 poems/year, accepts about 30-35. Subscription: $24.50 for 10 issues. Sample: $7.50 (back issue).

How to Contact Submit 2-6 poems at a time. No previously published poems or simultaneous submissions. No e-mail or disk submissions; postal submissions only. SASE required. Responds in 2-6 weeks. Always sends prepublication galleys. Pays about $4/line. Acquires first North American serial rights only.

Tips "We have long been committed to the discovery of new poets. Our one limitation is length; we are unable to publish very long poems, and authors should consult back issues of the magazine for precedents."

☒ ☐ ATLANTIC PACIFIC PRESS

279 Golf Rd., South Dartmouth MA 02748. (508)994-7869. E-mail: abcworks@att.net. **Contact:** Christine Leimbach Walen, editor. Established 2008.

Magazines Needs *Atlantic Pacific Press*, published quarterly, "is a journal of fiction, sci-fi, fantasy, nonfiction, drama, veterans/military, romance, mystery, horror, westerns, family life, children's stories, poetry, prose poetry, flash fiction, lyrics, cartoons, art, and photography." Does not want porn. Has published poetry by Deborah Valient, Robert Ludlow, George Hayden, Ted Richer, and Charles Rammelkamp. *Atlantic Pacific Press* is 75 pages, digest-sized, saddle-stapled, with cover art and photography welcome; includes ads. Accepts about 80% of poems/year. Single copy: $10; subscription: $30/year (4 copies). Make checks payable to *Atlantic Pacific Press*.

How to Contact Submit 3-6 poems at a time, maximum 10 pages. Considers previously published poems; no simultaneous submissions. Accepts e-mail submissions pasted into body of e-mail passage (no ms word attachments). Cover letter is required. "Include 50 word count bio." Reads submissions year round. Submit seasonal poems 3 months in advance. Time between acceptance and publication is 1-3 months. Sometimes comments on rejected poems. Guidelines available in magazine, for SASE, and by e-mail. Responds in 4 weeks. Pays $10 per accepted submission and 1 contributor's copy "if and when funds are available." Acquires first North American serial rights, first rights. All rights revert to poet upon publication. Reviews books, chapbooks of poetry, and other magazines and journals in 200 words.

Additional Information "Will consider publishing books and chapbooks under The Whale Inn Publishing House, publisher fo *Atlantic Pacific Press*."

Also Offers "Workshops and mentoring in poetry and fiction arranged by request."

Tips "Read poetry and fiction written by others. Join a writer's group and learn how to prepare a manuscript."

☑ ◎ THE AUROREAN

(Specialized: seasonal focus), Encircle Publications LLC, P.O. Box 187, Farmington ME 04938. (207)778-0467. E-mail: Aurorean@encirclepub.com (inquiries only). Website: www.encirclepub. com. Established 1992 (Encircle Publications); 1995 (The Aurorean). **Contact:** Cynthia Brackett-Vincent, editor.

Magazines Needs *The Aurorean*, published semiannually (spring/summer, fall/winter), uses "well crafted upbeat poetry. Seasonal/New England theme, but open to other subjects." Wants "short poems (4-6 lines). Publishes haiku section each issue. "Mostly free verse and occasional rhyme. We publish newer poets alongside the biggest names in the small press." Does not want "anything hateful, overly religious." Has published poetry by Patrick Carrington, Alan Catlin, Holly Guran, and Beth Paulson. *The Aurorean* is digest-sized, professionally printed, perfect-bound. Press run is 500-550. Single copy: $11 U.S., $12 international; subscription: $21 U.S. (2 issues), $25 international. Sample: back issues from previous quarterly format, $3 each; back issues of current semiannual format, $7 each. Make checks payable to Encircle Publications, LLC.

How to Contact Submit 1-5 poems at a time in a $10 envelope. Lines/poem: 40 maximum. Considers previously published poems. "Discourages simultaneous submissions "as we always reply in 3 months maximum. If you must submit simultaneously, be aware that none can be withdrawn once we have typeset/mailed a proof." Cover letter with brief introduction is preferred. "Fold cover letter separately and fold poems together. Poems folded individually cannot be reviewed." Include SASE with sufficient postage for return/reply; International submissions, include SAE and IRC. Manuscripts are acknowledged with a postcard or by e-mail upon receipt (e-mail address appreciated). Reads submissions August 16 - February 15 for spring/summer; February 15 - August 15 for fall/winter. Sends proofs with instructions on how to submit bios for each issue. Pays 2 contributor's copies per poem published (maximum 4 copies/issue). Acquires one-time rights. Appreciates credit if later published elsewhere. Two featured poets each issue (superb execution of poetic craft; in some way seasonally/New England reflective) receive publication of up to 3 poems with 100-word bio; 10 copies of magazine and 1-year subscription.

Additional Information Editor recommends 1 chapbook/issue ("small blurb and ordering information; we do not publish reviews"). Chapbook must have been published within the last 6 months; cannot be acknowledged or returned. Query via e-mail for more information.

Contest/Award Offerings Open Submissions "cannot be acknowledged or returned;" same deadlines as above: 1) Seasonal Poetic Quote: send 4 seasonal lines maximum from not-too-obscure poet; source MUST be cited to verify. Winner receives 2 free issues. 2) Editor's Chapbook Choice: send poetry chapbooks; editor recommends 1/issue ("small blurb and ordering information; not a review; do not send books for review"). Must have been published within the previous year. Specialized/Other: 1) Creative Writing Program Students. Winner receives publication of his/ her haiku, 3 copies of magazine, $10, and award certificate. Submissions MUST be sent per guidelines on contest page of Web site. 2) Best Poem of Last Issue: Independent Judge picks "Best Poem" from previous issue; winner receives $30.

Also Offers *The Unrorean* broadsheet, appears twice/year beginning of January and July for poems too long, experimental, or dark for magazine. "Still, nothing hateful." 2-4 11x17 pages, laser-printed. Sample: $2 postpaid. Include SASE for return/reply. No proofs, bios; open submission dates. Pays 1 contributor's copy/poem, 1 "editor's pick" receives 2. "Poets may submit for the magazine or broadsheet individually (work submitted individually for broadsheet is not acknowledged by postcard or e-mail). Work sent to the magazine will also be considered for the broadsheet, unless otherwise requested in cover letter."

Tips "Be familiar with your markets; don't submit blindly. Keep writing. Support the markets that support poets. *Poet's Market* is your best friend."

▣ ▢ ◎ AUTUMN LEAVES

(Specialized: poems from Native Americans), E-mail: sjball@mindspring.com. Website: www. sondra.net/al. Established 1996. **Contact:** Sondra Ball, publisher.

Magazines Needs *Autumn Leaves*, published twice/month, is a "magazine of original poetry, mostly by Native American authors, although I accept and publish poems by other people also." Wants "poetry of all styles." Does not want "anti-Indian poetry; seldom publish pro-war poetry."

Considers poetry written by children "under 14 for my 'kids' section. I want to be told the age of the child." Has published poetry by Johnny Rustywire, Larry Kibby, Harvest McCampbell, Richard Vallance, Shigeki Matsumura, and John Christain Hopkins. Receives about 7,000 poems/year, accepts about 15%.

How to Contact Submit 1-4 poems at a time. Lines/poem: no limit, "although I probably would not publish a book-length poem." Considers previously published poems and simultaneous submissions. Accepts e-mail submissions (pasted into body of message); no disk submissions. Cover letter is preferred. "If a person is a Native American (or First Nations) person, I would like to be told that, and also told what nation they are affiliated with." Reads submissions year round. Submit seasonal poems 2 months in advance. Time between acceptance and publication "anywhere from 2 months to a year." Sometimes comments on rejected poems. Sometimes publishes theme issues. "I publish theme issues on unexpected current events (such as Katrina) if I receive enough submissions on that issue; but I don't usually plan it beforehand." Guidelines available by e-mail. Responds in 2-3 months. No payment, "but I do send the author the URL of the individual poems." Acquires one-time rights. Rights revert to poet upon publication.

☑ ◎ AVOCET, A JOURNAL OF NATURE POEMS

(Specialized: nature; spirituality), P.O. Box 1717, Southold NY 11971. Website: www.avocetreview.com. Established 1997. **Contact:** Peter C. Leverich, editor.

Magazines Needs *Avocet, A Journal of Nature Poems*, published quarterly, is "devoted to poets who find meaning in their lives from the natural world in which they live." Wants "imagist poetry that explores the beauty and divinity in nature." Does not want "poems that have rhyme, cliché, abstraction, or sexual overtones." Has published poetry by Beth Beasley, David Chorlton, Martha Christina, Charles H. Harper, Michael Keshigian, Dennis Saleh, and Lisa D. Schmidt. *Avocet* is 56 pages, 414x512, professionally printed, saddle-stapled, with card cover. Single copy: $6; subscription: $24. Make checks payable to Peter C. Leverich.

How to Contact Submit 3-5 poems at a time. Considers previously published poems, if acknowledged. Cover letter with e-mail address is helpful. Include SASE for reply only; mss will not be returned. Time between acceptance and publication is up to 3 months. Responds in up to 2 months. Pays 1 contributor's copy.

◎ THE AWAKENINGS REVIEW

(Specialized: people living with mental illness), P.O. Box 177, Wheaton, IL 60187. E-mail: info@awakeningsproject.org. Website: www.awakeningsproject.org. Established 1999. **Contact:** Robert Lundin, editor.

Magazines Needs *The Awakenings Review*, published annually, prints works by people living with mental illness. Poet "must live with mental illness: consumer, survivor, family member, ex-patient." Wants "meaningful work, good use of the language. Need not be *about* mental illness." Has published poetry by Joan Rizzo, Wanda Washko, Ben Beyerlein, and Trish Evers. *The Awakenings Review* is 150 pages, digest-sized, perfect-bound, with glossy b&w cover. Receives about 800 poems/year, accepts about 10%. Press run is 1,000; 300 distributed free to contributors, friends. Single copy: $12 postpaid; subscription: $35. Make checks payable to *The Awakenings Review*.

How to Contact Submit 5 poems at a time. No previously published poems or simultaneous submissions. No e-mail submissions. Cover letter is preferred. Include SASE and short bio. Submit seasonal poems 6 months in advance. Time between acceptance and publication is 8 months. Poems are read by a board of editors. Often comments on rejected poems. Occasionally publishes theme issues. Guidelines available in magazine, for SASE, by e-mail, or on Web site.

Responds in one month. Pays 1 contributor's copy, plus discount on additional copies. Acquires first rights. Send materials for review consideration.

Tips "Write a cover letter outlining your relationship to mental illness: consumer, survivor, ex-patient, family member, therapist."

AXE FACTORY REVIEW

Cynic Press, P.O. Box 40691, Philadelphia PA 19107. E-mail: cynicpress@yahoo.com. Established 1986 (Axe Factory Review), 1996 (Cynic Press). **Contact:** Joseph Farley, editor/publisher.

Magazines Needs *Axe Factory Review*, published 1-4 times/year, spreads "the disease known as literature. The content is mostly poetry and essays, but we use short stories, too." Wants "eclectic work. Will look at anything but suggest potential contributors purchase a copy of the magazine first to see what we're like." Does not want "greeting card verse." Has published poetry by Taylor Graham, A.D. Winans, Normal, and John Sweet. *Axe Factory Review* is 20-40 pages, magazine-sized, neatly printed, saddle-stapled, with light card cover. Press run is 200. Single copy: $9 (current issue); subscription: $24 for 4 issues. Sample: $8 (back issue). Make checks payable to Cynic Press or Joseph Farley.

How to Contact Submit up to 10 poems at a time. Considers previously published poems ("sometimes, but let me know up front") and simultaneous submissions. Cover letter is preferred, "but not a form letter; tell me about yourself." Often comments on rejected poems. Pays 1-2 contributor's copies; "'featured poet' receives more." Reserves right to anthologize poems under Cynic Press; all other rights returned. Reviews books of poetry in 10-1,000 words. Send materials for review consideration.

Additional Information Cynic Press occasionally publishes chapbooks. Has published *Childhood* by B.Z. Niditch, *Rule of Thumb* by Kelley Jean White, M.D., *Yellow Flower Girl* by Xu Juan, *Under the Dogwoods* by Joseph Banford, *Ceiling of Mirrors* by Shane Allison, and *13 Ways of Looking at Godzilla* by Michael Hafer. **Reading fee:** $20. Make checks payable to Cynic Press. **No guarantee of publication.** Several anthologies planned; upcoming themes available in magazine, for SASE, or by e-mail.

Contest/Award Offerings Contest information available by e-mail.

Tips "Writing is a form of mental illness, spread by books, teachers, and the desire to communicate."

BABEL: THE MULTILINGUAL, MULTICULTURAL ONLINE JOURNAL AND COMMUNITY OF ARTS AND IDEAS

(Specialized: bilingual/foreign language), E-mail: submissions@towerofbabel.com. Website: www.towerofbabel.com. Established 1995. **Contact:** Malcolm Lawrence, editor-in-chief.

Magazines Needs "*Babel* is an electronic zine recognized by the UN as one of the most important social and human sciences online periodicals. Publishes regional reports from international stringers all over the planet, as well as features, round table discussions, fiction, columns, poetry, erotica, travelogues, and reviews of all the arts and editorials. We want to see poetry from all over the world, including multicultural or multilingual work, as well as poetry that has been translated from or into another language, as long as it is also in English. We also appreciate gay/lesbian and bisexual poetry. Writers whose work discriminates against the opposite sex, different cultures, or belief systems will not be considered."

How to Contact Submit no more than 10 poems at a time. Considers previously published poems and simultaneous submissions. Accepts e-mail submissions only. Cover letter is required. "Please send submissions with a résumé or bio as a Microsoft Word or RTF document attached to e-mail." Time between acceptance and publication varies; "usually no more than a month or 2 depending on how busy we are." Seldom comments on rejected poems. Guidelines available on Web site. Responds in 2-4 weeks. Reviews books/chapbooks of poetry and other magazines, single- and multi-book format. Open to unsolicited reviews. Send materials for review consideration.

Tips "We would like to see more poetry with first person male characters written by female authors as well as more poetry with first person female characters written by male authors. We would also like to see that dynamic in action when it comes to other languages, cultures, races, classes, sexual orientations, and ages. The best advice we could give to writers wanting to be published in our publication is simply to know what you're writing about and to write passionately about it."

$ ☐ ◎ BABYBUG MAGAZINE

(Specialized: children ages 6 months-2 years), Carus Publishing, 70 E. Lake St., Suite 300, Chicago IL 60601. Website: www.cricketmag.com. Established 1994. **Contact:** Submissions Editor.

Magazines Needs *BABYBUG Magazine*, published 9 times/year, is a read-aloud magazine for ages 6 months to 2 years. Wants "rhythmic, rhyming" short poems. *BABYBUG* is 24 pages, 6¼x7, printed on cardstock with nontoxic glued spine. Receives more than 1,200 submissions/month, accepts 25-30. Circulation is 48,000. Subscription: $33.95/year (9 issues). Sample: $5; sample pages available on Web site.

How to Submit Submit no more than 5 poems at a time. Lines/poem: 8 lines maximum. Considers previously published poems. Include SASE. Guidelines available for SASE or on Web site. Responds in 6 months. Pays $25 minimum on publication. Acquires North American publication rights for previously published poems; rights vary for unpublished poems.

Tips "Before attempting to write for *BABYBUG*, be sure to familiarize yourself with this age child and with the magazine itself."

☐ BABYSUE®

P.O. Box 15749, Chattanooga, TN 37415. Website: www.babysue.com and www.LMNOP.com. **Contact:** Don W. Seven, editor/publisher.

Magazines Needs *babysue*®, published twice/year, offers obtuse humor for the extremely open-minded. "We are open to all styles, but prefer short poems." No restrictions. Has published poetry by Edward Mycue, Susan Andrews, and Barry Bishop. *babysue*® is 32 pages, offset-printed. "We print prose, poems, and cartoons. We usually accept about 5% of what we receive." Sample: $5. Payment may be made in either cash, check, or money order payable to M. Fievet.

How to Contact Considers previously published poems and simultaneous submissions. Deadlines are March 30 and September 30 of each year. Seldom comments on rejected poems. Responds "immediately, if we are interested." Pays 1 contributor's copy. "We do occasionally review other magazines."

◖ BACKSTREET

P.O. Box 1377, Berthoud CO 80513. E-mail: backstreetqtrly@earthlink.net. Established 2004. **Contact:** Ray Foreman, editor.

Magazines Needs *Backstreet*, published 6 times/year, wants "strong, clear narrative poems relevant to the times and the human condition, and appropriate for a readership of experienced poets. We are a 'poet's magazine for poets' whose purpose is keeping them writing by providing an easy and regular publishing outlet. We are privately subsidized, never run contests, and offer subscriptions at minimal cost to poets who read other poets' work." Does not want "poems that are obscure in any way or poems that have meaning only to the writer." Has published poetry by Anselm Brocki, Charles Ries, Laurel Speer, Arthur Gotlieb, and Steven Levi. *Backstreet* "has a special layout that has the equivalent content of a 36-page magazine," laser-printed, stapled, with paper cover. Receives about 600 poems/year, accepts about 200. Press run is 150. Single copy: $2; subscription: $10 for 10 issues. Make checks payable to R. Foreman.

How to Contact Submit 3 poems at a time. Lines/poem: 15 minimum, 50 maximum. "Maximum width is 65 characters per line." Considers previously published poems and simultaneous submissions. No e-mail or disk submissions. "SASE for first submission only. No cover letter, bio, or credits list. No graphic layout. Flush left, preferably in Times Roman or Garamond. No long skinnys. Disposable sharp hard copies. Your work speaks for you." Reads submissions year round. Time between acceptance and publication is 3 months. Sometimes comments on rejected poems. Responds in one week to one month. Acquires one-time rights. Rights revert to poet upon publication.

Tips "To write better poems, read poems in current anthologies to get a feel for what is good. It almost never happens at most poetry readings. Poetry is essentially an abbreviated short story literary art on the page."

☑ THE BALTIMORE REVIEW

P.O. Box 36418, Towson MD 21286. Website: www.baltimorereview.org. Established 1996. Contact: Susan Muaddi Darraj, editor.

Magazines Needs *The Baltimore Review*, published twice/year (winter and summer), is "an eclectic collection of writing from Baltimore and beyond," showcasing creative nonfiction, short fiction, poetry, and book reviews. "We invite submissions from writers in the Baltimore region as well as nationally and internationally." Does not want "sentimental-mushy, loud, or very abstract poetry; corny humor; poorly crafted or preachy poetry." *The Baltimore Review* is 144 pages, 6x9, offset-lithograph-printed, perfect-bound, with 10-pt. CS1 cover. Subscription: $15/year, $28 for 2 years. Sample: $10 (includes $2 p&h). Make checks payable to *The Baltimore Review*.

How to Contact Submit 1-4 poems at a time. Considers simultaneous submissions, "but notify us immediately if your work is accepted elsewhere"; no previously published poems. Accepts submissions only via online submissions system at Web site. Cover letter is preferred. Reads submissions year round. Time between acceptance and publication is up to 4-6 months. "Poems are circulated to at least two reviewers." Sometimes comments on rejected poems. Guidelines available on website. Responds in up to 4 months. Pays 2 contributor's copies, reduced rate for additional copies.

Contest/Award Offerings Sponsors an annual poetry contest. Offers 1st Prize: $300 plus publication in *The Baltimore Review*; 2nd Prize: $150; 3rd Prize: $50. Submit 1-4 poems (no more than 5 pages total). All forms and styles accepted, including prose poems. Guidelines available on website. **Entry fee:** $12 (includes copy of issue in which 1st-Prize winner is published) or $20 (includes one-year subscription).

☐ BARBARIC YAWP

Boneworld Publishing, 3700 County Rt. 24, Russell NY 13684. (315)347-2609. Established 1996. Contact: John and Nancy Berbrich, editors.

Magazines Needs *Barbaric Yawp*, published quarterly, prints "the best fiction, poetry, and essays available." Encourages beginning writers. "We are not preachers of any particular poetic or literary school. We publish any type of quality material appropriate for our intelligent and wide-awake audience; all types considered: blank, free, found, concrete, traditional rhymed and metered forms." Does not want "any pornography, gratuitous violence, or any whining, pissing, or moaning." Considers poetry by teens. Has published poetry by Nancy Henry, Mark Spitzer, and Jeff Grimshaw. *Barbaric Yawp* is a 60-page booklet, stapled, with 67 lb. cover. Receives 2,000 poems/year, accepts about 5%. Press run is 150. Single copy: $4; subscription: $15/year (4 issues). Make checks payable to John Berbrich.

How to Contact Submit up to 5 poems at a time. Lines/poem: 50 maximum. Considers previously published poems and simultaneous submissions. Cover letter is preferred (1 page). Include a short publication history (if available) and a brief bio. Include SASE. Reads submissions year round. Time between acceptance and publication is up to 6 months. Often comments on rejected poems. Guidelines available for SASE. Responds in up to 2 months. Pays 1 contributor's copy. Acquires one-time rights.

Tips "Read a lot—Dead White Males and Living Black Females—and everyone in-between. Write often, summon the Muse, and don't fear rejection!"

▣ ▢ ◎ THE BAREFOOT MUSE

(Specialized: formal/metrical verse only), P.O. Box 115, Hainesport NJ 08036. E-mail: submissions@barefootmuse.com. Website: www.barefootmuse.com. Established 2005. **Contact:** Anna Evans, editor.

Magazines Needs *The Barefoot Muse*, published semiannually online, prints "only formal/metrical poetry (rhyme is optional). Poems in formal structures are most welcome. These include (but are not limited to) sonnets, villanelles, sestinas, triolets, pantoums, and rondeaus." Does not want "free verse; also, please do not send me rhyming poetry without first finding out what meter is." Has published poetry by Denise Duhamel, Jared Carter, Gail White, X.J. Kennedy, and Annie Finch. Receives about 1600 poems/year, accepts about 3%.

How to Contact Submit up to 5 poems at a time. Lines/poem: less than 40 preferred. Considers previously published poems ("by invitation only") and simultaneous submissions ("with notification"). Accepts e-mail submissions (pasted into body of message). Reads submissions year round. Time between acceptance and publication is up to 6 months. Sometimes comments on rejected poems. Guidelines available on Web site. Responds in 2 months. Always sends prepublications galleys. Acquires one-time rights. Rights revert to poet upon publication.

▣ $ ▢ BARNWOOD

4604 47th Ave. S., Seattle WA 98118-1824. (206)225-6887. E-mail: barnwoodpress@earthlink.net. Website: www.barnwoodpress.org. Established 1975. **Contact:** Tom Koontz, editor.

Magazines Needs *Barnwood*, published online, "serves poets and readers by publishing excellent poems." Does not want "expressions of prejudice such as racism, sexism." Has published poetry by Bly, Goedicke, Friman, and Stafford. Receives about 3,000 poems/year, accepts about 1%.

How to Contact Submit 1-3 poems at a time. Considers simultaneous submissions; no previously published poems. "

Tips "Emphasize imagination, passion, engagement, artistry."

▢ BARROW STREET

P.O. Box 1831, New York NY 10156. E-mail: infobarrow@gmail.com. Website: www.barrowstreet.org. Established 1998. **Contact:** Lorna Blake, Patricia Carlin, Peter Covino, and Melissa Hotchkiss, editors.

•Poetry published in *Barrow Street* is often selected for *The Best American Poetry*.

Magazines Needs *Barrow Street*, published semiannually, "is dedicated to publishing new and established poets." Wants "poetry of the highest quality; open to all styles and forms." Has published poetry by Molly Peacock, Lyn Hejinian, Carl Phillips, Marie Ponsot, Charles Bernstein, and Stephen Burt. *Barrow Street* is 96-120 pages, digest-sized, professionally printed, perfect-bound, with glossy cardstock cover with color or b&w photography. Receives about 3,000 poems/year, accepts about 3%. Press run is 1,000. Subscription: $15/year, $28 for 2 years, $42 for 3 years. Sample: $8.

How to Contact Submit up to 5 poems at a time. Considers simultaneous submissions (when notified); no previously published poems. Cover letter is preferred. Include brief bio. Must have name, address, e-mail, and phone on each page submitted or submission will not be considered. Reads submissions September 1 - May 31. Poems are circulated to an editorial board. Sometimes comments on rejected poems. Occasionally publishes theme issues. Guidelines available for SASE or on Web site. Responds in up to 9 months. Always sends prepublication galleys. Pays 2 contributor's copies. Acquires first rights.

Contest/Award Offerings The Barrow Street Press Book Contest (see separate listing in Contests & Awards).

Tips "Submit your strongest work."

☐ BATHTUB GIN

Pathwise Press, 2311 Broadway St., New Orleans LA 70125. E-mail: pathwisepress@hotmail.com. Website: www.pathwisepress.com. Established 1997. **Contact:** Christopher Harter, editor.

•**PLEASE NOTE:** "*Bathtub Gin*/Pathwise Press are on hiatus through 2009; interested parties should contact the magazine to check on status."

Magazines Needs *Bathtub Gin*, published semiannually in April and October, has "an eclectic aesthetic—we want to keep you guessing what is on the next page." Wants poetry that "takes a chance with language or paints a vivid picture with its imagery, has the kick of bathtub gin, which can be experimental or a sonnet." Does not want "trite rhymes, Bukowski wannabes (let the man rest), or confessionals." Has published poetry by Kell Robertson, Tom Kryss, Mike James, and Richard Krech. *Bathtub Gin* is about 60 pages, digest-sized, laser-printed, saddle-stapled, with 80 lb. coverstock cover. Receives about 1,200 poems/year, accepts about 5%. Press run is 300-350; 10 distributed free to reviewers, other editors, and libraries. Single copy: $5; subscription: $8. Sample: $3.50 (back issue). Foreign orders add $2. Make checks payable to Christopher Harter.

How to Contact Submit 4-6 poems at a time. Considers previously published poems and simultaneous submissions. Accepts e-mail submissions (pasted into body of message). Cover letter is required. "Three- to five-line bio required if you are accepted for publication; if none provided, we make one up." Include SASE. Reads submissions June 1-September 15 only, but accepts contributions for 2 issues. Time between acceptance and publication is up to 8 months. Sometimes comments on rejected poems. Guidelines available in magazine, for SASE, by e-mail, or on Web site. Responds in up to 2 months. Pays 2 contributor's copies. "We also sell extra copies to contributors at a discount, which they can give away or sell at full price."

Additional Information Pathwise Press's goal is to publish chapbooks, broadsides, and "whatever else tickles us." Has published *The Levelling Wind* by Kell Robertson, *Nothing But Love* by Mike James, *The United Colors of Death* by Mark Terrill, and *Living Room, Earth* by Carmen Germain. Guidelines available for SASE or on Web site.

Also Offers "We feature a 'News' section where people can list their books, presses, events, etc."

☑ BAYOU

c/o Genre editor, English Dept., University of New Orleans, 2000 Lakeshore Dr., New Orleans, LA 70148. E-mail: bayou@uno.edu. Established 1975 as The Panhandler (University of West Florida); 2002 as Bayou (co-published by University of West Florida and University of New

Orleans). Bayou is now solely published by the University of New Orleans. **Contact:** Joanna Leake, editor (University of New Orleans, Lakefront). Member: CLMP (Council of Literary Magazines and Presses).

Magazines Needs *Bayou Magazine*, published biannually, is "a young publication with an old soul. Each issue contains stunningly beautiful fiction, nonfiction, and poetry. One issue a year contains an award-winning play from the annual Tennessee Williams/New Orleans Literary Festival One-Act Play competition. From quirky shorts to more traditional stories, we are committed to publishing solid work. Regardless of style, at *Bayou* we are always interested first in a well-told tale. Our poetry and prose are filled with memorable characters observing their world, acknowledging both the mundane and the sublime, often at once, and always with an eye toward beauty. Contains a range of material from established, award-winning authors as well as new voices on the rise." Has published poetry by Eric Trethewey, Virgil Súaréz, Marilyn Hacker, Sean Beaudoin, Tom Whalen, and Mark Doty. *Bayou* is 130 pages, digest-sized, professionally printed, perfect-bound, with matte cardstock cover (artwork varies). Receives "hundreds of submissions," accepts "very few." Press run is 500; distributed free to students and faculty of University of West Florida and University of New Orleans. Single copy: $8; subscription: $15. Make checks payable to the UNO Foundation.

How to Contact Submit no more than 5 poems at a time. Lines/poem: "We have no strict length restrictions, though obviously it is harder to fit in very long poems." Considers simultaneous submissions; no previously published poems. No e-mail or disk submissions. "A brief cover letter is necessary, but don't tell us your life story, explain your poems, or tell us how wonderful your poems are. Do give us your contact information." Reads submissions year round, "but we tend to slow down in the summer months." Time between acceptance and publication varies "but we give the author a general idea when the work is accepted." Poems are circulated to an editorial board. Never comments on rejected poems. Guidelines available in magazine, for SASE, or by e-mail. Responds in 4 months. Pays 2 contributor's copies. Acquires first North American serial rights.

$ ◙ THE BEAR DELUXE

(Specialized: nature/ecology), P.O. Box 10342, Portland OR 97296-0342. (503)242-1047. E-mail: bear@orlo.org. Website: www.orlo.org. Established 1993. **Contact:** Casey Bush, poetry editor. Editor: Tom Webb. • The Bear Deluxe is published by Orlo, a nonprofit organization exploring environmental issues through the creative arts.

Magazines Needs *The Bear Deluxe*, published quarterly, provides "a fresh voice amid often strident and polarized environmental discourse. Street-level, non-dogmatic, and solution-oriented, *The Bear Deluxe* presents lively creative discussion to a diverse readership." Wants poetry "with innovative environmental perspectives." Has published poetry by Judith Barrington, Robert Michael Pyle, Mary Winters, Stephen Babcock, Carl Hanni, and Derek Sheffield. *The Bear Deluxe* is 48 pages, 9x12, newsprint, saddle-stapled, with brown Kraft paper cover. Receives about 1,200 poems/year, accepts about 20-30. Press run is 20,000; 18,000 distributed free on the streets of the western U.S. and beyond. Subscription: $20. Sample: $5. Make checks payable to Orlo.

How to Contact Submit 3-5 poems at a time. Lines/poem: 50 maximum. Considers previously published poems and simultaneous submissions "so long as noted." Accepts e-mail submissions (pasted into body of message). "We can't respond to e-mail submissions but do look at them." Poems are reviewed by a committee of 3-5 people. Publishes 1 theme issue/year. Guidelines available for SASE. Responds in 6 months. Pays $20/poem, 1 contributor's copy (more if willing to distribute), and subscription. Acquires first or one-time rights.

▦ ◪ ◎ THE BEATNIK COWBOY

(Specialized: Beat-influenced poetry), Ruamchoke Condoview 2, 37/447 Moo 2, Khao Pratumnak Rd., Nongprue, Banglamung, Chonburi 20150 Thailand, or c/o David S. Pointer, 803 West Main St., Apt. M, Murfreesboro TN 37129. E-mail: beatnik_cowboy@yahoo.com.au. Established 2004. **Contact:** Mr. Randall Rogers.

Magazines Needs *The Beatnik Cowboy*, published quarterly, wants " Beat-influenced poetry from all poets. We are a young and vibrant magazine, seeking to publish the best of the best poets of the world." Have published poetry by Steve Dalchinsky, David Pointer, Susan Maurer, Randall Rogers, and Joe Speer. *The Beatnik Cowboy* is 32 pages, magazine-sized, computer-generated, side-stapled (will be bound in the future), includes ads. Receives about 200 poems/year. Press run is 70; 25 distributed free. Single copy: $8 USD. Make checks payable to Randall Rogers. Subscription: $30.

How to Contact Submit 5 poems at a time. Shorter poems preferred. Considers previously published poems and simultaneous submissions. Accepts e-mail (as attachment) and disk submissions. Either post poems in the body of the text or as Word attachment. "Considering a 'worst poem submission but we love you for trying' special page. Winning poem gets a free annual subscription and maybe an eight by ten glossy of me, your humble editor. Also interested in some of the more self indulgent poems we have to plow through. But try to keep them short. Try for little blasts or bundles of electric truth, like a Jimi Hendrix extended solo." SAE with IRCs required for return of poems. Reads submissions year round. Submit seasonal poems 2 months in advance. Time between acceptance and publication is 3 months. "At times if we like your stuff we will encourage you to send in more." Sometimes comments on rejected poems. Guidelines available in the magazine, by SASE, or by e-mail request. Responds in 2 months. Acquires one-time rights.

◪ ◎ BELLEVUE LITERARY REVIEW

(Specialized: humanity, health, and healing), New York University School of Medicine, OBV-A612, 550 First Ave., New York NY 10016. (212)263-3973. E-mail: info@BLReview.org. Website: www. BLReview.org. Established 2001. **Contact:** Stacy Bodziak, managing editor. Member: CLMP.

•Work published in *Bellevue Literary Review* has appeared in *The Pushcart Prize.*

Magazines Needs *Bellevue Literary Review*, published semiannually, prints "works of fiction, nonfiction, and poetry that touch upon relationships to the human body, illness, health, and healing." Has published poetry by Rafael Campo, Sharon Olds, James Tate, David Wagoner, John Stone, and Floyd Skloot. *Bellevue Literary Review* is 160 pages, digest-sized, perfect-bound, includes ads. Receives about 1,800 poems/year, accepts about 3%. Press run is 5,000; distributed free to lit mag conferences, promotions, and other contacts. Single copy: $9; subscription: $15/ year, $35 for 3 years (plus $5/year postage to Canada, $8/year postage foreign). Make checks payable to *Bellevue Literary Review.*

How to Contact Submit up to 3 poems at a time. Lines/poem: prefers poems of one page or less. Considers simultaneous submissions. No previously published poems; work published on personal blogs or Web sites will be considered on a case-by-case basis. No e-mail or disk submissions. "We accept poems via regular mail and through our Web site; when submitting via regular mail, please include SASE." Cover letter is preferred. Reads submissions year round. Time between acceptance and publication is about 6-7 months. "Poems are reviewed by two independent readers, then sent to an editor." Sometimes comments on rejected poems. Sometimes publishes theme issues. Upcoming themes available on Web site. Guidelines available for SASE or on Web site. Responds in 3-5 months. Always sends prepublication galleys. Pays 2 contributor's copies and one-year subscription for author, plus one-year gift subscription for

friend. Acquires first North American serial rights. Rights revert to poet upon publication.
Contest/Award Offerings The annual Bellevue Literary Review Prize for Poetry (see separate listing in Contests & Awards).

☑ BELLINGHAM REVIEW

Western Washington University, Mail Stop 9053, Bellingham WA 98225. (360)650-4863. E-mail: bhreview@cc.wwu.edu. Website: www.wwu.edu/~bhreview. Established 1975. **Contact:** Poetry Editor. Editor-in-Chief: Brenda Miller.

Magazines Needs *Bellingham Review*, published twice/year, has no specific preferences as to form. Wants "well-crafted poetry, but are open to all styles." Has published poetry by David Shields, Tess Gallagher, Gary Soto, Jane Hirshfield, Albert Goldbarth, and Rebecca McClanahan. *Bellingham Review* is digest-sized, perfect-bound, with matte cover. Circulation is 1,600. Subscription: $12/year, $20 for 2 years, $20/year for libraries and institutions. Sample: $12. Make checks payable to *Bellingham Review*.

How to Contact Submit 3-5 poems at a time. Considers simultaneous submissions with notification. No e-mail submissions; accepts submissions by postal mail only. Include SASE. Reads submissions September 15-February 1 only (submissions must be postmarked within this reading period). Guidelines available for SASE or on website. Responds in 2 months. Pays 2 contributor's copies, a year's subscription, plus monetary payment (if funding allows). Acquires first North American serial rights.

Contest/Award Offerings The 49th Parallel Poetry Award (see separate listing in Contests & Awards).

☑ BELLOWING ARK

Bellowing Ark Press, P.O. Box 55564, Shoreline WA 98155. (206)440-0791. E-mail: bellowingark@bellowingark.org. Website: www.bellowingark.org. Established 1984. **Contact:** Robert R. Ward, editor.

Magazines Needs *Bellowing Ark*, published bimonthly, is a literary tabloid that prints "only poetry which demonstrates in some way the proposition that existence has meaning or, to put it another way, that life is worth living. We have no strictures as to length, form, or style; only that the work we publish is, to our judgment, life-affirming." Does not want "academic poetry, in any of its manifold forms." Has published poetry by Jerry Austin, Robert King, Tobi Cogswell, Esther Cameron, Mary Jo Balistrieri, Dolores Stewart, and Colleen Harris. Beginning in 2008 two cash awards, The Lois and Marine Robert Warden (poetry) and The Michael L. Newell (black and white line art), will be given. *Bellowing Ark* is 32 pages, tabloid-sized, printed on electrobright stock. Press run is 1,000. Subscription: $20/year. Sample: $4.

How to Contact Submit 3-6 poems at a time. "Absolutely no simultaneous submissions." No e-mail submissions; accepts postal submissions only. Guidelines available for SASE or on Web site. Responds in up to 3 months; publishes accepted work within the next 2 issues. Occasionally comments on rejected poems if they "seem to display potential to become the kind of work we want." Sometimes sends prepublication galleys. Pays 2 contributor's copies. Reviews books of poetry. Send materials for review consideration.

Additional Information Bellowing Ark Press publishes collections of poetry by **invitation only**.

☑ ◎ BELL'S LETTERS POET

(Specialized: subscribers preferred), P.O. Box 2187, Gulfport MS 39505-2187. E-mail: jimbelpoet@aol.com. Established 1956. **Contact:** Jim Bell, editor/publisher.

Magazines Needs *Bell's Letters Poet*, published quarterly, **must be purchased by contributors**

before they can be published. "Many say they stop everything the day [the magazine] arrives." Wants "clean writing in good taste; no vulgarity, no artsy vulgarity." Has published poetry by Betty Wallace, Paul Pross, Carrie Quick, and Kalman Gayler. *Bell's Letters Poet* is about 60 pages, digest-sized, photocopied on plain bond paper (including cover), saddle-stapled. Single copy: $7; subscription: $28. Sample: $5. "Send a poem (20 lines or under, in good taste) with your sample order, and we will publish it in our next issue."

How to Contact Submit 4 poems at a time. Lines/poem: 4-20. Considers previously published poems "if cleared by author with prior publisher"; no simultaneous submissions. No e-mail submissions; accepts submissions by postal mail only. Submission deadline is 2 months prior to publication. Accepted poems by subscribers are published immediately in the next issue. Guidelines available in magazine or for SASE. No payment for accepted poetry, but "many patrons send cash awards to the poets whose work they especially like." Reviews books of poetry by subscribers.

Contest/Award Offerings "The Ratings" is a competition in each issue. Readers are asked to vote on their favorite poems, and the "Top 40" are announced in the next issue, along with awards sent to the poets by patrons. News releases are then sent to subscriber's hometown newspaper.

Also Offers *Bell's Letters Poet* also features a telephone and e-mail exchange among poets, a birth-date listing, and a profile of its poets.

Tips "Tired of seeing no bylines this year? Subscription guarantees a byline in each issue."

☑ BELOIT POETRY JOURNAL

P.O. Box 151, Farmington ME 04938. (207)778-0020. E-mail: bpj@bpj.org (inquiries only). Website: www.bpj.org. Established 1950. **Contact:** John Rosenwald and Lee Sharkey, editors.

• Poetry published in the *Beloit Poetry Journal* has been included in *The Best American Poetry, Best New Poets*, and *The Pushcart Prize*.

Magazines Needs *Beloit Poetry Journal*, published quarterly, prints "the most outstanding poems we receive, without bias as to length, school, subject, or form. For more than 59 years of continuous publication, we have been distinguished for the extraordinary range of our poetry and our discovery of strong new poets." Wants "visions broader than the merely personal; language that makes us laugh and weep, recoil, resist—and pay attention. We're drawn to poetry that grabs hold of the whole body, not just the head." Has published poetry by Mark Doty, Albert Goldbarth, Patricia Goedicke, Karl Elder, John Haines, Sonia Sanchez, and Susan Tichy. *Beloit Poetry Journal* is about 48 pages, digest-sized, saddle-stapled, attractively printed, with "beautiful" 4-color covers. Circulation is 1,250. Subscription: $18/year, $48 for 3 years (individuals); $23/year, $65 for 3 years (institutions). Sample: $5.

How to Contact No previously published poems or simultaneous submissions. No e-mail submissions. "Submit any time, without query, in any legible form; no bio necessary. Unless it's a long poem, send what will go in a business envelope for 1 stamp. Don't send your life's work. We respond to most submissions within 2 weeks. Manuscripts under active consideration we keep for up to 4 months, circulating them among our readers, and continuing to winnow. At the quarterly meetings of the Editorial Board, we read aloud all the surviving poems and put together an issue of the best we have." Complete guidelines available on Web site. Pays 3 contributor's copies. Acquires first serial rights. Editor for Reviews and Exchanges reviews books by and about poets. Send books for review consideration to Marion Stocking, 24 Berry Cove Rd., Lamoine ME 04605.

Additional Information "To diversify our offerings, we occasionally publish chapbooks (most recently, the *Split This Rock* Chapbook of political poetry); these are almost never the work of a single poet."

Contest/Award Offerings Awards the Chad Walsh Poetry Prize ($2,500 in 2008) to a poem or group of poems published in the calendar year. "Every poem we publish in 2009 will be considered for the 2009 prize."

Tips "We are always watching for fresh music, live forms and language."

▣ $ ◎ BELTWAY POETRY QUARTERLY

(Specialized: Washington, D.C.-area poets), E-mail: beltway.poetry@juno.com. Website: www.beltwaypoetry.com. Established 2000. **Contact:** Kim Roberts, editor.

Magazines Needs *Beltway Poetry Quarterly*, published online, "features poets who live or work in the greater Washington, D.C., metro region. *Beltway* showcases the richness and diversity of Washington, D.C., authors, with poets from different backgrounds, races, ethnicities, ages, and sexual orientations represented. We have included Pulitzer Prize-winners and those who have never previously published. We publish academic, spoken word, and experimental authors—and those whose work defies categorization." Takes unsolicited submissions only for special themed issues. Themes change annually; check Web site for details. Has published poetry by Cornelius Eady, Anthony Hecht, E. Ethelbert Miller, Jane Shore, Sharan Strange, and Hilary Tham.

How to Contact *Other than annual themed issue, we consider poems by invitation only.* Theme issues have included poetic responses to Walt Whitman, the war in Iraq, and D.C. Places. 2 issues per year feature 5 poets from the greater-D.C. region, and these issues are open only by invitation. 1 issue per year is guest-edited." Never comments on rejected poems. Guidelines available on Web site.

Also Offers "Monthly Poetry News section has information on new publications, calls for entries, workshops, readings, and performances. Extensive links also include the most complete listing anywhere of artist residency programs in the U.S."

$ ▢ ◎ BEYOND CENTAURI

(Specialized: fantasy, science fiction, & mild horror for older children and teens), P.O. Box 782, Cedar Rapids IA 52406-0782. E-mail: beyondcentauri@yahoo.com. Website: www.samsdotpublishing.com. Established 2003. **Contact:** Tyree Campbell, managing editor. Member: The Speculative Literature Foundation.

Magazines Needs *Beyond Centauri*, published quarterly, contains "fantasy, science fiction, sword and sorcery, very mild horror short stories, poetry, and illustrations for readers ages 9-18." Wants "fantasy, science fiction, spooky horror, and speculative poetry for younger readers." Does not want "horror with excessive blood and gore." Considers poetry by children and teens. Has published poetry by Bruce Boston, Bobbi Sinha-Morey, Debbie Feo, Dorothy Imm, Cythera, and Terrie Leigh Relf. *Beyond Centauri* is 44 pages, magazine-sized, offset printed, perfect bound, with paper cover for color art, includes ads. Receives about 200 poems/year, accepts about 50 (25%). Press run is 100; 5 distributed free to reviewers. Single copy: $6; subscription: $20/year, $37 for 2 years. Make checks payable to Tyree Campbell/Sam's Dot Publishing.

How to Contact Submit up to 5 poems at a time. Lines/poem: prefers less than 100. Considers previously published poems; no simultaneous submissions. Accepts e-mail submissions (pasted into body of message); no disk submissions. "Submission should include snail mail address and a short (1-2 lines) bio." Reads submissions year round. Submit seasonal poems 6 months in advance. Time between acceptance and publication is 1-2 months. Often comments on rejected poems. Guidelines available on Web site. Responds in 4-6 weeks. Pays $2/original poem, plus 1 contributor's copy. Acquires first North American serial rights. Reviews books/chapbooks of poetry. Send materials for review consideration to Tyree Campbell.

Tips "We like to see submissions from younger writers."

$ ☑ ◎ BIBLE ADVOCATE

(Specialized: Christian), P.O. Box 33677, Denver CO 80233. E-mail: bibleadvocate@cog7.org. Website: www.cog7.org/BA. Established 1863. **Contact:** Sherri Langton, associate editor.

Magazines Needs *Bible Advocate*, published 8 times/year, features "Christian content—to be a voice for the Bible and for the church." Wants "free verse, some traditional, with Christian/Bible themes." Does not want "avant-garde poetry." *Bible Advocate* is 32 pages, magazine-sized. Receives about 30-50 poems/year, accepts about 10-20. Press run varies; all distributed free.

How to Contact Submit no more than 5 poems at a time. Lines/poem: 5 minimum, 20 maximum. Considers previously published poems (with notification) and simultaneous submissions. Prefers e-mail submissions. Cover letter is preferred. "No handwritten submissions, please." Time between acceptance and publication is up to 1 year. "I read them first and reject those that won't work for us. I send good ones to editor for approval." Seldom comments on rejected poems. Publishes theme issues. Guidelines available for SASE or on Web site. Responds in 2 months. Pays $20 and 2 contributor's copies. Acquires first, reprint, electronic, and one-time rights.

Tips "Avoid trite or forced rhyming. Be aware of the magazine's doctrinal views (send for doctrinal beliefs booklet)."

☑ BIG TOE REVIEW

E-mail: submissions@bigtoereview.com. Website: www.bigtoereview.com. Established 2004. **Contact:** Joshua Michael Stewart, editor.

Magazines Needs *Big Toe Review*, published online ("a new issue goes up when there are enough strong poems to warrant a new issue"), considers "all types of poems, but we really, really want prose poems. If you write in traditional forms, you better be doing something new with them." Does not want "anything trite." Has published poetry by Ellen Doré Watson, Ryan G. Van Cleave, David Dodd Lee, and Mary Koncel.

How to Contact Submit 3-5 poems at a time. "The shorter the poem, the better your chances." Considers previously published poems and simultaneous submissions. Accepts e-mail submissions only (pasted into body of message; "never, never attach document"); no disk submissions. Cover letter is required. Reads submissions year round. Sometimes comments on rejected poems. Guidelines available by e-mail or on Web site. Responds "as soon as possible." No payment. Acquires first North American serial rights.

Also Offers "There's a page dedicated to giving free advertisement for the books/chapbooks of poets who are contributors to the magazine, with links to where to buy the book in question."

Tips "Buy and read as much poetry as you write."

▣ ☑ ◎ THE BIG UGLY REVIEW

(Specialized: theme-driven issues), 490 Second St., Suite 200, San Fransisco CA 94107. E-mail: info@biguglyreview.com (inquiries); poetry@biguglyreview.com (submissions). Website: www. biguglyreview.com. Established 2004. **Contact:** Miriam Pirone, poetry editor.

Magazines Needs *The Big Ugly Review*, published 2 times/year online, showcases "emerging and established writers, photographers, filmmakers, and musicians. Each issue includes fiction (short stories and flash fiction), creative nonfiction, poetry, photo-essays, short films of 5 minutes or less, and downloadable songs, all related to that issue's theme." Wants "vivid and accurate poetry of any style, form, or length." Has published poetry by Edward Smallfield, Jennifer C. Chapis, Valerie Coulton, Stephen Hemenway, Diana Der-Hovanessian, and James Cihlar. Receives about 750-1,000 poems/year, accepts about 20.

How to Contact Submit no more than 6 poems at a time. Considers previously published poems and simultaneous submissions. Accepts e-mail submissions (pasted into body of message and as attachment); no disk submissions. "Send documents in Word or Word-readable attachments. Also paste the poems into the body of the e-mail text. Include your name, address, phone number, and e-mail on the first page." Cover letter is preferred. Reads submissions year round. Time between acceptance and publication is 1-2 months. Sometimes comments on rejected poems. Regularly publishes theme issues. Guidelines available on Web site. Responds "approximately 1 month after close of the issue's submission deadline." No payment. Author retains all rights.

☑ THE BITTER OLEANDER

4983 Tall Oaks Dr., Fayetteville NY 13066-9776. (315)637-3047. Fax: (315)637-5056. E-mail: info@bitteroleander.com. Website: www.bitteroleander.com. Established 1974. **Contact:** Paul B. Roth, editor/publisher.

•Poetry published in *The Bitter Oleander* has been included in *The Best American Poetry*; recognized by Public Radio's *Excellence In Print* award for best literary journal of 2005.

Magazines Needs *The Bitter Oleander*, published semiannually in April and October, seeks "highly imaginative poetry whose language is serious. Particularly interested in translations." Has published poetry by Alan Britt, George Kalamaras, Duane Locke, Silvia Scheibli, Shawn Fawson, Anthony Seidman, and Christine Boyka Kluge. *The Bitter Oleander* is 128 pages, digest-sized, offset-printed, perfect-bound, with glossy 4-color cover with art, includes ads. Receives about 12,000 poems/year, accepts less than 1%. Press run is 1,200. Single copy: $10; subscription: $18. Make checks payable to Bitter Oleander Press.

How to Contact Submit up to 8 poems at a time. Lines/poem: 30 maximum. No previously published poems. Allows simultaneous submissions. No e-mail submissions unless outside U.S. Cover letter is preferred. Include name and address on each page of ms. Does not read mss during July. Time between acceptance and publication is 6 months. "All poems are read by the editor only, and all decisions are made by this editor." Often comments on rejected poems. Guidelines available for SASE or on Web site. Responds within 1 month. Pays 1 contributor's copy.

Contest/Award Offerings Sponsors the Frances Locke Memorial Poetry Award (see separate listing in Contests & Awards).

Tips "We simply want poetry that is imaginative and serious in its delivery of language. So much flat-line poetry is written today that anyone reading one magazine after another cannot tell the difference."

☐ BLACK BOOK PRESS

1608 Wilmette Ave., Wilmette IL 60091. (847)302-9547. E-mail: blackbookpress1984@yahoo. com. Website: myspace.com/blackbookpress and www.blackbookpressmag.com. Established 2004. **Contact:** Kyle Van Heck, founder/editor.

Magazines Needs *Black Book Press*, published monthly, "is an independent poetry zine, aiming to give small and unpublished authors and artists a place to call home." Wants "non-rhyming free verse poetry, anything daring, out of the ordinary, or offbeat." Does not want "anything sounding like Robert Frost; no nature poetry, no greeting card verse. Do not prefer rhyming poetry." *Black Book Press* is about 28 pages, magazine-sized, photocopied, center stapled, with colored paper cover with b&w artwork. Receives about 500 submissions/year, accepts about 70%. Press run is 60; 20 distributed free to possible contributors and interested writers. Single copy: $2; subscription: $15 ("pays for stamps and paper only!"). Sample: $2 plus 6x9 SASE with 63¢ postage. Make any and all checks payable to Kyle Van Heck.

How to Contact Submit up to 5 poems at a time. Lines/poem: 4 minimum, up to 1 page maximum. Considers previously published poems and simultaneous submissions. Regular mail submissions strongly preferred; e-mail submissions accepted. Cover letter is required. "Always include short (3 lines) bio and SASE. Please type poems and include name, address, phone number, and e-mail on each page." Reads submissions year round. Submit seasonal poems 2 months in advance. Time between acceptance and publication is 1-4 months. "I am the editor (and a struggling writer). If the work is good and/or if I like it, I'll publish it. If it's interesting, strange, original, or different, I'll publish it." Often comments on rejected poems. **Prefers (but doesn't require) that contributors purchase a copy for $2 or a subscription for $15.** Guidelines available in magazine, for SASE, by e-mail, or on website. Responds "once a month by sending copy with published work (if accepted) or a reason for not publishing." Contrubutor's copy available for $1. Acquires one-time rights.

Additional Information Promotional stickers are available, 2 for $1; pins, $1 (large) and $1 (small). Make any and all checks payable to Kyle Van Heck. Send music for review consideration to Chris Kulawik or Scott Tomes.

Tips "Getting published can be tough and frustrating, but it will never happen if you don't try. Just send your work!"

$ ☑ BLACK WARRIOR REVIEW

P.O. Box 862936, Tuscaloosa AL 35486-0027. (205)348-4518. E-mail: bwr@ua.edu. Website: www.bwr.ua.edu. Established 1974. **Contact:** Whitney Holmes, poetry editor.

• Poetry published in *Black Warrior Review* has been included in *The Best American Poetry* and *The Pushcart Prize*.

Magazines Needs *Black Warrior Review*, published semiannually in February and October, prints poetry, fiction, nonfiction, art and comics by up-and-coming as well as accomplished writers. Has published poetry by Aimee Nezhukumatathil, Bob Hicok, Rachel Zucker, Tony Tost, Joshua Beckman, Alex Lemon, Beth Ann Fennelly, and Carol Guess. *Black Warrior Review* is 180 pages, digest-sized. Press run is 2,000. Subscription: $16/year, $28 for 2 years, $40 for 3 years. Sample: $10. Make checks payable to the University of Alabama.

How to Contact Submit up to 7 poems at a time. Considers simultaneous submissions if noted. No e-mail or disk submissions. Responds in up to 5 months. Pays up to $75 and one-year subscription. Acquires first rights. Reviews books of poetry in single- or multi-book format. Send materials for review consideration.

Tips "Subscribe or purchase a sample copy to see what we're after. For 33 years, we've published new voices alongside Pulitzer Prize winners. Freshness and attention to craft, rather than credits, impress us most."

ℕ ▣ ☑ BLOOD LOTUS

A JOURNAL OF POETRY AND ART, The Blind Press, P.O. Box 1190, Troy MT 59935. E-mail: editor@theblindpress.com (inquiries only). Website: www.theblindpress.com. Established 1993. **Contact:** Melody Sherosky, editor. E-mail: blootlotusjournal@gmail.com; bloodlotuspoetry@gmail.com. Website: www.bloodlotus.org. **Contact:** Stacia Fleegal, managing editor.

Magazines Needs *Blood Lotus*, published quarterly online, publishes "poetry, fiction, and anything in between!" Wants "fresh language, memorable characters, and beautiful artwork." Accepts 50% of submissions received.

How to Contact Submit 3-5 poems of free or formal verse to bloodlotuspoetry@gmail.com. Considers simultaneous submissions; no previously published poems. Reads submissions year round. Guidelines on Web site. Acquires first North American rights, electronic archival rights.

☑ ◎ BLUE COLLAR REVIEW

(Specialized: social, political, & working class issues), Partisan Press, P.O. Box 11417, Norfolk VA 23517. E-mail: red-ink@earthlink.net (inquiries only). Website: www.partisanpress.org. Established 1997 (Blue Collar Review); 1993 (Partisan Press). **Contact:** A. Markowitz, editor. Co-Editor: Mary Franke.

Magazines Needs *Blue Collar Review (Journal of Progressive Working Class Literature)*, published quarterly, contains poetry, short stories, and illustrations "reflecting the working class experience—a broad range from the personal to the societal. Our purpose is to promote and expand working class literature and an awareness of the connections between workers of all occupations and the social context in which we live. Also to inspire the creativity and latent talent in 'common' working people." Wants "writing of high quality that reflects the working class experience from delicate internal awareness to the militant. We accept a broad range of style and focus—but are generally progressive, political/social." Does not want anything "racist, sexist-misogynist, right wing, or overly religious. No 'bubba' poetry, nothing overly introspective or confessional, no academic/abstract or 'Vogon' poetry. No simple beginners rhyme or verse." Has published poetry by Simon Perchik, Jim Daniels, Kathryn Kirkpatrick, Marge Piercy, Alan Catlin, and Rob Whitbeck. *Blue Collar Review* is 60 pages, digest-sized, offset-printed, saddle-stapled, with colored card cover, includes ads. Receives hundreds of poems/year, accepts about 15%. Press run is 500. Subscription: $15/year, $25 for 2 years. Sample: $5. Make checks payable to Partisan Press.

How to Contact Submit up to 4 poems at a time; "no complete manuscripts, please." Considers previously published poems; no simultaneous submissions. No e-mail submissions; postal submissions only. Cover letter is preferred. Include full-size SASE for response. "Poems should be typed as they are to appear upon publication. Author's name and address should appear on every page. Overly long lines reduce chances of acceptance as line may have to be broken to fit the page size and format of the journal." Time between acceptance and publication is 3 months to a year. Poems are reviewed by editor and co-editor. Seldom comments on rejected poems. Guidelines available on Web site. Responds in 3 months. Sends prepublication galleys only upon request. Pays 1-3 contributor's copies. Considers reviews of chapbooks and journals.

Additional Information Partisan Press looks for "poetry of power that reflects a working class consciousness and moves us forward as a society. Must be good writing reflecting social realism including but not limited to political issues." Publishes about 3 chapbooks/year; not presently open to unsolicited submissions. "Submissions are requested from among the poets published in the *Blue Collar Review*." Has published *A Possible Explanation* by Peggy Safire and *American Sounds* by Robert Edwards. Chapbooks are usually 20-60 pages, digest-sized, offset-printed, saddle-stapled or flat-spined, with card or glossy covers. Sample chapbooks are $7 and listed on Web site.

Contest/Award Offerings Sponsors the annual Working People's Poetry Competition (see separate listing in Contests & Awards).

Tips "Don't be afraid to try. Read a variety of poetry and find your own voice. Write about reality, your own experience, and what moves you."

◎ BLUELINE

(Specialized: poems about the Adirondacks & similar regions), 125 Morey Hall, Dept. of English and Communication, SUNY Potsdam, Potsdam NY 13676. Fax: (315)267-2043. E-mail: blueline@ potsdam.edu. Established 1979. **Contact:** Rick Henry, editor-in-chief. Poetry Editor: Stephanie Coyne DeGhett. Member: CLMP.

Magazines Needs *Blueline*, published annually in May, is "dedicated to prose and poetry about the Adirondacks and other regions similar in geography and spirit." Wants "clear, concrete poetry that goes beyond mere description. We prefer a realistic to a romantic view." Does not want "sentimental or extremely experimental poetry." Uses poems on "nature in general, Adirondack Mountains in particular. Form may vary, can be traditional or contemporary." Has published poetry by L.M. Rosenberg, John Unterecker, Lloyd Van Brunt, Laurence Josephs, Maurice Kenny, and Nancy L. Nielsen. *Blueline* is 200 pages, digest-sized. Press run is 600. Sample: $7 (back issue).

How to Contact Submit 3 poems at a time. Lines/poem: 75 maximum; "occasionally we publish longer poems." No simultaneous submissions. Submit September 1-November 30 only. Include short bio. Poems are circulated to an editorial board. Sometimes comments on rejected poems. Guidelines available for SASE or by e-mail. Responds in up to 3 months. "Decisions in early February." Pays 1 contributor's copy. Acquires first North American serial rights. Reviews books of poetry in 500-750 words, single- or multi-book format.

Tips "We are interested in both beginning and established poets whose poems evoke universal themes in nature and show human interaction with the natural world. We look for thoughtful craftsmanship rather than stylistic trickery."

☑ BOMBAY GIN

Writing and Poetics Dept., Naropa University, 2130 Arapahoe Ave., Boulder CO 80302. (303)546-3540. Fax: (303)546-5297. E-mail: bgin@naropa.edu. Website: www.naropa.edu/writingandpoetics/bombaygin.html. Established 1974. **Contact:** Amy Catanzano.

Magazines Needs *Bombay Gin*, published annually in Fall and Spring, is the literary journal of the Jack Kerouac School of Disembodied Poetics at Naropa University. "Produced and edited by MFA students, *Bombay Gin* publishes established writers alongside unpublished and emerging writers. It has a special interest in works that push conventional literary boundaries. Submissions of poetry, prose, visual art, translation, and works involving hybrid forms and cross-genre exploration are encouraged. Translations are also considered. Guidelines are the same as for original work. Translators are responsible for obtaining any necessary permissions." Has published poetry by Amiri Baraka, Joanne Kyger, Jerome Rothenberg, Lawrence Ferlinghetti, Edwin Torres, and Edward Sanders. *Bombay Gin* is 150-200 pages, digest-sized, professionally printed, perfect-bound, with color card cover. Receives about 300 poems/year, accepts about 5%. Press run is 250; 100 distributed free to contributors. Single copy: $12.

How to Contact Submit up to 8 pages of poetry at a time. No previously published poems or simultaneous submissions. Accepts e-mail (as attachment) and disk (PC format) submissions. Cover letter is preferred. **Contact info should not appear anywhere on the ms (only on cover letter).** Poems should be typed/computer-generated in 12-pt. Times New Roman. SASE required for reply. Submissions are accepted September 1-March 1 only. Notification of acceptance/rejection: March 15. Guidelines available for SASE, by e-mail, or on Web site. Pays 2 contributor's copies. Acquires one-time rights.

☑ ◎ BORDERLANDS: TEXAS POETRY REVIEW

(Specialized: TX & Southwest writers; bilingual), P.O. Box 33096, Austin TX 78764. E-mail: borderlandspoetry@sbcglobal.net. Website: www.borderlands.org. Established 1992. **Contact:** Editor.

Magazines Needs *Borderlands: Texas Poetry Review*, published semiannually, prints "high-quality, outward-looking poetry by new and established poets, as well as brief reviews of poetry books and critical essays. Cosmopolitan in content, but particularly welcomes Texas and Southwest writers." Wants "outward-looking poems that exhibit social, political, geographical, historical, feminist, or spiritual awareness coupled with concise artistry. We also seek poems in 2 languages (one of which must be English), where the poet has written both versions." Does not want "introspective work about the speaker's psyche, childhood, or intimate relationships." Has published poetry by Walter McDonald, Naomi Shihab Nye, Mario Susko, Wendy Barker, Larry D. Thomas, and Reza Shirazi, and Scott Hightower. *Borderlands* is 100-150 pages, digest-sized, offset-printed, perfect-bound, with 4-color cover. Receives about 2,000 poems/year, accepts about 120. Press run is 1,000. Subscription: $20/year, $34 for 2 years. Sample: $12.

How to Contact Submit 4 typed poems at a time. No previously published poems or simultaneous submissions. No e-mail submissions. Include SASE (or SAE and IRCs) with sufficient return postage. Seldom comments on rejected poems. Guidelines available for SASE or on Web site. Responds in 6-8 months. Pays 1 contributor's copy. Acquires first rights. Reviews books of poetry in 1 page. Send materials for review consideration to Editors, *Borderlands*.

▣ ◘ BORN MAGAZINE

E-mail: editors@bornmagazine.org. Website: www.bornmagazine.org. Established 1996. **Contact:** Anmarie Trimble, editor. Contributing Editors: David J. Daniels, Tenaya Darlington, Jennifer Grotz, Michael Robins, Bruce Smith.

Magazines Needs *Born Magazine*, published online, is "an experimental venue that marries literary arts and interactive media. We publish multimedia 'interpretations' of poetry and prose, created by interactive artists in collaboration with poets and writers." Wants poems suited to "interpretation into a visual or interactive form. Due to the unusual, collaborative nature of our publication, we represent a variety of styles and forms of poetry." Has published poetry by Victorian Chang, Bob Hicok, Timothy Liu, Edward Hirsch, Marvin Bell, Michele Glazer, Major Jackson, Ander Monson, and Joyelle McSweeney.

How to Contact Submit 2-5 poems at a time. Considers previously published poems; no simultaneous submissions. Accepts e-mail submissions only (as Word documents or .txt files). Reads submissions year round. Submit seasonal poems 6 months in advance. Time between acceptance and publication is 3-6 months. "Poems must be accepted by the editor and 1 contributing editor. Selected works are forwarded to our art department, which chooses an artist partner to work with the writer. Artist and writer collaborate on a concept, to be realized by the artist. We also accept proposals for collaborating with an artist to create a piece from scratch." Never comments on rejected poems. Guidelines available on Web site. Responds in "a few months" to e-mail queries. Always sends prepublication galleys. No payment. "We can offer only the experience of participating in a collaborative community, as well as a broad audience (we average 40,000 readers to our site per month)." Acquires one-time rights.

Tips "We accept new and previously published work. *Born*'s mission is to nurture creativity and co-development of new literary art forms on the Web."

$ ◘ BOSTON REVIEW

35 Medford St., Suite 302, Somerville MA 02143. (617)591-0505. Fax: (617)591-0440. E-mail: review@bostonreview.net (inquiries only). Website: www.bostonreview.net. Established 1975. **Contact:** Timothy Donnelly, poetry editor. • Poetry submitted to Boston Review has been included in The Best American Poetry Anthology.

Magazines Needs *Boston Review*, published bimonthly, is a tabloid-format magazine of arts, culture, and politics. "We are open to both traditional and experimental forms. What we value most is originality and a strong sense of voice." Has published poetry by Frank Bidart, Lucie Brock-Broido, Peter Gizzi, Jorie Graham, Allen Grossman, John Koethe, and Karen Volkman. Receives about 5,000 submissions/year, accepts about 30 poems/year. Circulation is 15,000 nationally. Single copy: $5; subscription: $25. Sample: $5.

How to Contact Submit 5-6 poems at a time through online submissions system. Does not accept faxed or e-mailed submissions. Include brief bio. Time between acceptance and publication is 6 months to one year. Reads submissions September 15-May 15. Responds in 2-4 months. Payment varies. Acquires first serial rights. Reviews books of poetry, solicited reviews only. Send materials for review consideration.

Contest/Award Offerings The *Boston Review* Annual Poetry Contest (see separate listing in Contests & Awards).

☒ ◎ THE BREAD OF LIFE MAGAZINE

(Specialized: Catholic), 5100 South Service Road, Burlington ON L7L 6A5 Canada. (905)634-5433. Fax: (905)634-1495. E-mail: info@thebreadoflife.ca. Website: www.thebreadoflife.ca. Established 1977. **Contact:** Fr. Peter Coughlin, editor.

Magazines Needs *The Bread of Life*, published semimonthly, is "a Catholic charismatic magazine designed to encourage spiritual growth in areas of renewal in the Catholic Church today." Includes articles, poetry, and artwork. "It's good if contributors are members of The Bread of Life Renewal Centre, a nonprofit, charitable organization." *The Bread of Life* is 34 pages, magazine-sized, professionally printed, saddle-stapled, with glossy paper cover. Receives about 50-60 poems/year, accepts about 25%. Press run is 2,500 (subscribers only). Membership: $35/year (includes magazine subscription).

How to Contact Considers previously published poems and simultaneous submissions. Cover letter is preferred. Publishes theme issues. Guidelines available for SAE with IRC.

☑ ◎ THE BRIAR CLIFF REVIEW

Briar Cliff College, 3303 Rebecca St., Sioux City IA 51104-2340. E-mail: jeanne.emmons@briarcliff. edu (inquiries only). Website: www.briarcliff.edu/bcreview. Established 1989. **Contact:** Jeanne Emmons, poetry editor. Managing Editor: Tricia Currans-Sheehan. Member: CLMP; American Humanities Index; EBSCO/Humanities International Complete.

Magazines Needs *The Briar Cliff Review*, published annually in April, is "an attractive, eclectic literary and cultural magazine." Wants "quality poetry with strong imagery; especially interested in regional, Midwestern content with tight, direct, well-wrought language." Has published poetry by Sam Witt, Tana Jean Welch, and Julie Marie Wade. *The Briar Cliff Review* is 100 pages, magazine-sized, professionally printed on 100 lb. Altima Satin text paper, perfect-bound, with 4-color cover on dull stock. Receives about 1,000 poems/year, accepts about 30. Press run is 1,000. Sample: $15.

How to Contact Considers simultaneous submissions, but expects prompt notification of acceptance elsewhere; no previously published poems. No e-mail submissions; postal submissions only. Cover letter is required. "Include short bio. Submissions should be typewritten or letter quality, with author's name and address on each page. No manuscripts returned without SASE." Reads submissions August 1-November 1 only. Time between acceptance and publication is up to 6 months. Seldom comments on rejected poems. Guidelines available on Web site. Responds in 6-8 months. Pays 2 contributor's copies. Acquires first serial rights.

Contest/Award Offerings The *Briar Cliff Review* Annual Fiction, Poetry and Creative Nonfiction Contest (see separate listing in Contests & Awards).

▣ ☑ BRICK & MORTAR REVIEW

E-mail: brick.mortar.review@gmail.com. Website: www.bmreview.com. Established 2003. **Contact:** Jack Stull, senior editor.

Magazines/Journals

Magazines Needs *Brick & Mortar Review*, published quarterly online, seeks poetry "that is grounded in concrete language, i.e., that uses images. Avoid the use of empty, fluffy language such as 'beautiful,' 'freedom,' 'amazed,' 'spectacular,' 'love,' etc. Of course, these words can be used in the right context, but sparingly. We don't mind an occasional rhyme, but we don't want poetry that is forced into rhyme schemes."

How to Contact Submit 3 or more (up to 10) poems at a time. Considers simultaneous submissions if notified when poetry is accepted elsewhere; no previously published poems. Accepts e-mail submissions only (pasted into body of message); no disk submissions. "We accept and respond only via e-mail." Please include a brief bio (a few sentences about yourself). Reads submissions year round. Time between acceptance and publication can be months. "The editors independently review the submissions and then meet to discuss and vote." Seldom comments on rejected poems. Guidelines available on Web site. Responds in 2 months. No payment. Acquires one-time rights.

Contest/Award Offerings Offers annual award of 1st Prize: $1,000; 2nd Prize: $250; 3rd Prize: $100; plus possible Honorable Mentions. All winning poetry is published on the Web site. Considers simultaneous submissions (with notification of acceptance elsewhere). Submit 3 or more poems of any length. "If submitting by e-mail, make sure it's clear where each poem begins and ends; also write 'contest' in the subject box (see Web site for more details on submitting)." Guidelines available on Web site. **Entry fee:** $5/poem. **Deadline:** "We accept entries year round. Awards are given at the beginning of Fall." Judges: the editors.

⬛ ◎ BRILLIANT CORNERS: A JOURNAL OF JAZZ & LITERATURE

A JOURNAL FOR JEWISH FEMINISTS AND OUR FRIENDS, (Specialized: ethnic; women/feminism; social issues), P.O. Box 1206, Ann Arbor MI 48106. (888) 359-9188. E-mail: clare@bridgesjournal.org. Website: www.bridgesjournal.org. Established 1990. **Contact:** Clare Kinberg, managing editor. (Specialized: jazz-related literature)Lycoming College, Williamsport PA 17701. (570)321-4279. Fax: (570)321-4090. E-mail: feinstein@lycoming.edu. Website: www.lycoming.edu/BrilliantCorners. Established 1996. **Contact:** Sascha Feinstein, editor.

Magazines Needs *Brilliant Corners*, published semiannually, features jazz-related poetry, fiction, and nonfiction. "We are open as to length and form." Wants "work that is both passionate and well crafted—work worthy of our recent contributors." Does not want "sloppy hipster jargon or improvisatory nonsense." Has published poetry by Amiri Baraka, Jayne Cortez, Yusef Komunyakaa, Philip Levine, Sonia Sanchez, and Al Young. *Brilliant Corners* is 90 pages, digest-sized, commercially printed, perfect-bound, with color card cover with original artwork, includes ads. Accepts about 5% of work received. Press run is 350. Subscription: $12. Sample: $7.

How to Contact Submit 3-5 poems at a time. No previously published poems or simultaneous submissions. No e-mail or fax submissions. Cover letter is preferred. Reads submissions September 1-May 15 only. Seldom comments on rejected poems. Responds in 2 months. Pays 2 contributor's copies. Acquires first North American serial rights. Staff reviews books of poetry. Send materials for review consideration.

⬛ BRYANT LITERARY REVIEW

Faculty Suite F, Bryant University, 1150 Douglas Pike, Smithfield RI 02917. E-mail: blr@bryant.edu. Website: http://web.bryant.edu/~blr. Established 2000. **Contact:** Tom Chandler, editor. Member: CLMP.

Magazines Needs Bryant Literary Review, published annually in May, features poetry, fiction, photography, and art. "Our only standard is quality." Has published poetry by Michael S. Harper, Mary Crow, Denise Duhamel, and Baron Wormser. Bryant Literary Review is 125 pages, digest-sized, offset-printed, perfect-bound, with 4-color cover with art or photo. Receives about 3,000 poems/year, accepts about 1%. Press run is 2,500. Single copy: $8; subscription: $8.

How to Contact Submit 3-5 poems at a time. Cover letter is required. "Include SASE; please submit only once each reading period." Reads submissions September 1-December 31. Time between acceptance and publication is 5 months. Seldom comments on rejected poems. Guidelines available in magazine or on Web site. Responds in 3 months. Pays 2 contributor's copies. Acquires one-time rights.

Tips "No abstract expressionist poems, please. We prefer accessible work of depth and quality."

☑ BUFFALO CARP

1715 Second Ave., Rock Island IL 61201. (309)793-1213. Fax: (309)793-1265. E-mail: rcollins@quadcityarts.com. Website: www.quadcityarts.com. Established 1998. **Contact:** Ryan Collins, managing editor.

Magazines Needs *Buffalo Carp* is "a national literary journal featuring the best unpublished poetry and prose we can find." Wants "any style of poetry as long as it is well crafted, vivid, and accessible." Has published poetry by Ryan Van Cleave, Erin M. Bertram, Dorothea Lasky, Kristine Ong Muslim, and Arielle Greenberg. *Buffalo Carp* is 80-180 pages, digest-sized, offset-printed, perfect-bound, with coated, full-color cover with jury-selected, original artwork solicited by the editorial staff. Press run is 350; distributed free to selected libraries and schools. Single copy: $10. Sample: $7. Make checks payable to Quad City Arts.

How to Contact Submit up to 5 poems or 5 pages at a time between August 1 and April 1. Lines/poem: any. Considers simultaneous submissions "if notified immediately of other acceptance"; no previously published poems. Accepts e-mail submissions; no fax or disk submissions. Cover letter is preferred. Include SASE for acknowledgment only; "we do not return work." Reads submissions September-May. "We respond in July/August with acceptance or rejection." Time between acceptance and publication is about 6 months. Poems are circulated to an editorial board. Sometimes comments on rejected poems. "Although we can't comment on all submissions, we do offer advice to writers whose work shows promise." Guidelines available on Web site. Pays 2 contributor's copies. Acquires first North American serial rights.

Tips "Send us your best, most interesting work. Worry less about how you would classify the work and more about it being high-quality and stand-out. We are looking to go in new directions with upcoming issues, so send us what you think best represents you and not who your influences are. *Buffalo Carp* is not interested in blending in, and has no interest in homogenized work. Blow us away!"

☑ BURNSIDE REVIEW

P.O. Box 1782, Portland OR 97207. E-mail: sid@burnsidereview.org. Website: www.burnsidereview.org. Established 2004. **Contact:** Sid Miller, editor.

Magazines Needs *Burnside Review*, published every 9 months, prints "the best poetry we can get our hands on." Each issue includes 1 featured poet with an interview and new poems. "We tend to publish poetry that finds beauty in truly unexpected places; that combines urban and natural imagery; that breaks the heart." Open to all forms. Translations are encouraged. "Would like to see more lyric poetry." Has published poetry by Linda Bierds, Dorianne Laux, Christopher Howell, Kim Addonizio, Paul Guest, and Larissa Szporluk. *Burnside Review* is 80 pages, 6x6, professionally printed, perfect-bound. Receives about 2,500 poems/year, accepts about 50. Press run is 500. Single copy: $8; subscription: $13. Make checks payable to *Burnside Review* or order online.

How to Contact Submit 3-5 poems at a time. Considers simultaneous submissions; no previously published poems. Accepts e-mail only. "E-mailed submissions should include all poems and cover letter in 1 Word or RTF file sent as an attachment. The subject line should read 'Poetry Submission.' Send to submissions@burnsidereview.org. Check Web site for complete details. Please put name and address on each poem." Reads submissions year round. Submit seasonal poems 3-6 months in advance. Time between acceptance and publication is up to 9 months. "Editors read all poems." Seldom comments on rejected poems. Guidelines available on Web site. Responds in 2-4 months. Pays 1 contributor's copy. Acquires first rights.

Contest/Award Offerings The *Burnside Review* Chapbook Competition (see separate listing in Contests & Awards).

$ ☑ BUTTON MAGAZINE

P.O. Box 77, Westminster MA 01473. E-mail: sally@moonsigns.net. Website: http://moonsigns. net. Established 1993. **Contact:** Maude Piper, poetry editor.

Magazines Needs *Button*, published annually, is "New England's tiniest magazine of fiction, poetry, and gracious living." Wants "poetry that incises a perfect figure eight on the ice, but also cuts beneath that mirrored surface. Minimal use of vertical pronoun." Does not want "sentiment; no 'musing' on who or what done ya wrong." Has published poetry by Amanda Powell, Brendan Galvin, Jean Monahan, Mary Campbell, Kevin McGrath, and Ed Conti. *Button* is 30 pages, 414x512, saddle-stapled, with cardstock offset cover with illustrations that incorporate 1 or more buttons. Press run is 1,200. Subscription: $10/6 issues. "Sorry, no overseas subscriptions." Sample: $2, plus $2 S/H and 1 First-Class stamp.

How to Contact Submit no more than 2 poems at a time. "Do not submit more than twice in one year." No previously published poems. Cover letter is required. Time between acceptance and publication is up to 6 months. "Our reading period is April 1-September 30. Work sent at other times will be discarded." Poems are circulated to an editorial board. Often comments on rejected poems. Guidelines available by e-mail. Responds within 4 months. Pays honorarium and at least 2 contributor's copies. Acquires first North American serial rights.

Tips "Writing as therapy is fine. Publishing as therapy is not. Take the vertical pronoun (I) and write your poem without it. Still got something to say? Also, *Button* tries to reflect a world one would want to live in—this does not mean we make the space for various uncatalogued human vices (self-pity, navel gazing). If you can be really amusing about those, that's another story. Finally, writers who need to say they've published 1,200 poems in various magazines and then name all of the magazines—well, we don't really need to know. Aim high, write often, but re-fine, refine, refine. If you feel your work is ready to stand alongside poems by people who have also published in prominent national journals, please send, but bear in mind we are very exact-ing about what we publish. Occasionally we respond personally on ms."

$ ☑ ◎ BYLINE MAGAZINE

(Specialized: writers & writing), P.O. Box 111, Albion NY 14411. (585)355-3290. E-mail: bylinepoetry@gmail.com. Website: www.bylinemag.com. Established 1981. **Contact:** Donna M. Marbach, poetry editor.

Magazines Needs *ByLine*, published bimonthly, is a magazine for the encouragement of writers and poets. Uses 6-10 poems/issue. Wants "any subject, any style; must be well-crafted." Has published poetry by Patricia Fargnoli, Kathryn Howd Machan, Dee Shapiro, Allen Britt, C.E. Chaffin, and Thomas Holmes. *ByLine* is magazine-sized, professionally printed, includes ads. Receives about 2,500 poetry submissions/year, accepts about 100. Subscription: $29. Sample: $6.

How to Contact Submit up to 3 poems at a time. Lines/poem: less than 30 preferred. No previously published poems. Accepts e-mail submissions (preferred). Guidelines available for SASE or on web site. Pays $5 for On the Lighter Side. Acquires first North American serial rights. Reviews books about the writing or marketing of poetry in 250-500 words. Pays $25/review.

Additional Information Also seeking poetry-related how-to articles. Pays $35/article (500-700 words) and $50/article (1,500-1,800 words).

Contest/Award Offerings Sponsors up to 20 poetry contests and a biennial chapbook contest. Guidelines available for #10 SASE or on Web site.

Tips "Because our primary goal is to assist writers in improving and growing their craft, we are looking for poetry that is top-quality and shows skillful knowledge of poetic devices, techniques, and forms. Articles and book reviews should focus on poetic craft and the submission process. While we encourge new writers and are happy to work with them, we are seeking poetry that is concise, original, and a positive model for other poets."

⃟ CAKETRAIN

P.O. Box 82588, Pittsburgh PA 15218. E-mail: caketrainjournal@hotmail.com. Website: www. caketrain.org. Established 2003. **Contact:** Amanda Raczkowski and Joseph Reed, editors.

Magazines Needs "*Caketrain*is a literary journal and press based in Pittsburgh, Pennsylvania. Our interest is in bringing you, reader, the very best in contemporary creative writing, full stop. Our goals are for each issue of our journal to submerge you in a birthing tank for gelatinous language monsters, young masses of tentacular foci undulating as directed (in all, at once) by our eclectic stable of contributors; for each new book to seduce and ensnare you, sometimes intangibly, always undeniably; and for you, reader, to be able to draw at least one passage from our banks that prods your mind with a precision and power that feels as if it was written for your eyes alone." *Caketrain* journals and chapbooks are digest-sized, printed on 60 lb. acid-free, off-white stock, perfect-bound by a ten-point high-gloss cover stock. Price: $8.

How to Contact Submit up to 7 poems, works of fiction or creative nonfiction (no book reviews), works of visual art, or any combination. Considers simultaneous submissions; no previously published poems. Notify immediately if a piece is chosen for publication elsewhere. Accepts submissions by mail or e-mail (attached DOC, RTF or PDF preferred over pasted-in-the-body for text). Cover letter is required. Include SASE. "All unused print submissions will be recycled upon rejection. Please include a brief, press-ready biographical statement and any relevant contact information. Print name and title on the top of each poetry page." Guidelines available on Web site. Response time up to 6 months. Pays 1 contributor's copy. Rights revert to poet upon publication.

Contest/Award Offerings See Contests and Awards section for Caketrain Chapbook competition.

⃟ ⃟ CALLALOO: A JOURNAL OF AFRICAN DIASPORA ARTS & LETTERS

(Specialized: poetry dealing with African Diaspora), Dept. of English, Texas A&M University, 4212 TAMU, College Station TX 77843-4227. (979)458-3108. Fax: (979)458-3275. E-mail: callaloo@tamu.edu. Website: http://callaloo.tamu.edu. Established 1976. **Contact:** Charles H. Rowell, editor. • Poetry published in Callaloo has been included frequently in volumes of The Best American Poetry.

Magazines Needs *Callaloo: A Journal of African Diaspora Arts & Letters*, published quarterly, is devoted to poetry dealing with the African Diaspora, including North America, Europe, Africa, Latin and Central America, South America, and the Caribbean. Has published poetry by Aimé Césaire, Lucille Clifton, Rita Dove, Yusef Komunyakaa, Natasha Tretheway, and Carl

Phillips. Features about 15-20 poems (all forms and styles) in each issue along with short fiction, interviews, literary criticism, and concise critical book reviews. Circulation is 1,600 subscribers of which half are libraries. Subscription: $39, $107 for institutions.

How to Contact Submit complete ms in triplicate. No fax or e-mail submissions. Include cover letter with name, mailing address, e-mail address if available, and SASE. Responds in 6 months. Pays copies.

☐ ◎ CALYX, A JOURNAL OF ART AND LITERATURE BY WOMEN

(Specialized: poetry by & about women; multicultural), Calyx Books, P.O. Box B, Corvallis OR 97339-0539. (541)753-9384. Fax: (541)753-0515. E-mail: calyx@proaxis.com. Website: www. calyxpress.org. Established 1976. **Contact:** Beverly McFarland, senior editor.

Magazines Needs *CALYX, A Journal of Art and Literature by Women*, published 3 times every 18 months, contains poetry, prose, art, book reviews, essays, and interviews by and about women. Wants "excellently crafted poetry that also has excellent content." Has published poetry by Maurya Simon, Diane Averill, Carole Boston Weatherford, and Eleanor Wilner. *CALYX* is 6x8, handsomely printed on heavy paper, flat-spined, with glossy color cover. Single copy: $10 plus $4 shipping; subscription: $23/volume (3 issues), $41 for 2 volumes (6 issues). Sample: $14. See Web site for foreign and institutional rates.

How to Contact Send up to 6 poems at a time. Considers previously published poems "occasionally" and simultaneous submissions "if kept up-to-date on publication." No fax or e-mail submissions. Include SASE and short bio. "We accept copies in good condition and clearly readable. *CALYX* is edited by a collective editorial board." Reads submissions postmarked October 1-December 31 only. **Manuscripts received outside of reading period will be returned unread.** Guidelines available for SASE, by e-mail, or on Web site. Responds in 9 months. Pays one contributor's copy/poem, plus subscription. Send materials for review consideration.

Additional Information CALYX Books publishes one book of poetry/year. All work published is by women. Has published *Storytelling in Cambodia* by Willa Schneberg and *Black Candle: Poems about Women from India, Pakistan, and Bangladesh* by Chitra Banerjee Divakaruni. **Closed to submissions until further notice.**

Contest/Award Offerings The annual Lois Cranston Memorial Poetry Prize and the new Sarah Lantz Memorial Poetry Book Prize (see separate listing in Contests & Awards).

Tips "Read the publication and be familiar with what we have published."

◩ $ ☑ ◎ CANADIAN WRITER'S JOURNAL

(Specialized: writing), White Mountain Publications, Box 1178, New Liskeard ON P0J 1P0 Canada. (705)647-5424. Fax: (705)647-8366. E-mail: cwj@cwj.ca. Website: www.cwj.ca. **Contact:** Deborah Ranchuk, editor.

Magazines Needs *Canadian Writer's Journal*, published bimonthly, uses a few "short poems or portions thereof as part of 'how-to' articles relating to the writing of poetry, and occasional short poems with tie-in to the writing theme. We try for 100% Canadian content." *Canadian Writer's Journal* is digest-sized. Subscription "prices are under review as publishing schedule is changing." Sample: $9.

How to Contact Submit up to 5 poems at a time. No previously published poems. Accepts e-mail submissions (pasted into body of message, with 'Submission' in the subject line). Include SASE with postal submissions. "U.S. postage accepted; do not affix to envelope. Poems should be titled. Hard copy and SASE required if accepted." Responds in 3-6 months. Pays $2-5/poem and 1 contributor's copy.

⚄ $ ☑ THE CAPILANO REVIEW

(Specialized: avant-garde, experimental), 2055 Purcell Way, North Vancouver BC V7J 3H5 Canada. (604)984-1712. E-mail: tcr@capilanou.ca. Website: www.thecapilanoreview.ca. Established 1972. **Contact:** Submissions.

Magazines Needs *The Capilano Review*, published 3 times/year, is a literary and visual arts review. Wants "avant-garde, experimental, previously unpublished poetry. *The Capilano Review* is 100-120 pages, digest-sized, finely printed, perfect-bound, with glossy full-color card cover. Circulation is 800. Sample: $14.70 CAD prepaid.

How to Contact Submit 5-6 poems. No simultaneous submissions. No e-mail or disk submissions. Cover letter is required. Include SAE with IRCs; "submissions with U.S. postage will not be considered." Responds in up to 4 months. Pays $50-200 CAD, subscription, and 2 contributor's copies. Acquires first North American serial rights.

Tips "Read the magazine and web site before you submit. *The Capilano Review* receives dozens of manuscripts each week; unfortunately, the majority of them are simply inappropriate for the magazine."

☐ ◎ THE CARIBBEAN WRITER

(Specialized: Caribbean focus), University of the Virgin Islands, RR 1, P.O. Box 10,000, Kingshill, St. Croix USVI 00850. (340)692-4152. Fax: (340)692-4026. E-mail: info@thecaribbeanwriter.org. Website: www.thecaribbeanwriter.org. Established 1987. **Contact:** Ms. Quilin Mars.

•Poetry published in *The Caribbean Writer* has appeared in The Pushcart Prize.

Magazines Needs *The Caribbean Writer*, published annually, is a literary anthology with a Caribbean focus (Caribbean must be central to the literary work, or the work must reflect a Caribbean heritage, experience, or perspective). Has published poetry by Opal Palmer Adisa, Geoffrey Philp, and Thomas Reiter. *The Caribbean Writer* is 300 + pages, digest-sized, handsomely printed on heavy stock, perfect-bound, with glossy card cover. Press run is 1,200. Single copy: $15 plus $5 postage; subscription: $25. Sample: $7 plus $5 postage. (Note: postage to and from the Virgin Islands is the same as within the US.)

How to Contact Submit up to 5 poems at a time. Considers simultaneous submissions; no previously published poems. Accepts e-mail as attachment; no fax submissions. Blind submissions only: name, address, phone number, e-mail address, and title of ms should appear in cover letter along with brief bio. Title only on ms. Reads submissions by November 30 annual deadline. Guidelines available in magazine, for SASE, by e-mail, or on Web site. Pays 2 contributor's copies. Acquires first North American serial rights. Reviews books of poetry and fiction in 1,000 words. Send materials for review consideration.

Contest/Award Offerings All submissions are eligible for the Daily News Prize ($300) for the best poem or poems, The Marguerite Cobb McKay Prize to a Virgin Island author ($200), the David Hough Literary Prize to a Caribbean author ($500), the Canute A. Brodhurst Prize for Fiction ($400), and the Charlotte and Isidor Paiewonsky Prize ($200) for first-time publication.

$ ☐ ◎ CAT TALES: FANTASTIC FELINE FICTION

(Specialized: fantasy, crime, and science fiction involving cats), 9710 Traville Gateway Dr. #234, Rockville MD 20850.E-mail: cattales@wildsidepress.com. Website: www.weirdtalesmagazine. com. Established 2008. **Contact:** George H. Scithers, editor.

Magazines Needs *Cat Tales: Fantastic Feline Fiction*, published twice per year, is a trade paperback anthology which prints "fantasy, crime, and science fiction involving cats, with some poetry on those subjects." Wants "poetry touching on fantasy, crime, or science fiction involving cats. Both serious and humor accepted, inlucing limericks and double dactyls." Accepts poetry by children and teens. *Cat Tales: Fantastic Feline Fiction* is 176 pages, trade paperback sized, offset-printed, perfect-bound with a process color cover. Accepts about 3 poems per issue. Press run is 5,000.

How to Contact Submit up to 5 poems at a time. E-mail preferred. Include author address on every poem. Time between acceptance and publication varies. Poems are circulated to an editorial board. Seldom comments on rejected poems. Never publishes theme issues. Guidelines available for SASE or by e-mail. Responds in 1 month. Pays $1 or less/line and 2 contributor's copies. Acquires one-time rights.

Tips "Follow standard manuscript format."

☑ CAVEAT LECTOR

400 Hyde St., Apt. 606, San Francisco CA 94109-7445. Phone/fax: (415)928-7431. E-mail: editors@caveat-lector.org. Website: www.caveat-lector.org. Established 1989. **Contact:** Christopher Bernard and Ho Lin, principals.

Magazines Needs *Caveat Lector*, published 2 times/year, "is devoted to the arts and cultural and philosophical commentary. We publish visual art and music as well as literary and theoretical texts. Our Web site includes an art gallery and a multimedia section offering video and audio." Wants poems "on any subject, in any style, as long as the work is authentic in feeling and appropriately crafted. We are looking for accomplished poems, something that resonates in the mind long after the reader has laid the poem aside. We want work that has authenticity of emotion and high craft; poems that, whether raw or polished, ring true—and if humorous, are actually funny, or at least witty. Classical to experimental. Note: We sometimes request authors for audio of work we publish to post on our Web site." Has published poetry by Joanne Lowery, Simon Perchik, Les Murray, Alfred Robinson, and Ernest Hilbert. *Caveat Lector* is 32-48 pages, 11X414, photocopied, saddle-stapled, with b&w cover. Receives 200-600 poems/year, accepts about 2%. Press run is 250. Single copy: $3.50; subscription: $15 for 4 issues. Sample: $3.

How to Contact Submit up to 6 short poems, 3 medium-length poems, or 1 long poem at a time. Lines/poem:short, up to 50 each; medium, 51-100; long, up to 500. Considers simultaneous submissions, "but please inform us." Cover letter is not required, but appreciated. "Place name, address, and (optional) telephone number on each page. Include SASE and brief bio (100 words or less)." Reads submissions January-June. Time between acceptance and publication is 1 year. Sometimes comments on rejected poems. Guidelines available for SASE. Responds in 1 month. Pays 2 contributor's copies. Acquires first publication rights.

Tips "The 2 rules of writing are: 1) Revise it again. 2) Revise it again. The writing level of most of our submissions is pleasingly high. A rejection by us is not always a criticism of the work, and we try to provide comments to our more promising submitters."

☐ CC&D/CHILDREN, CHURCHES AND DADDIES

(formerly Children, Churches and Daddies), Scars Publications, 829 Brian Court, Gurnee IL 60031. E-mail: ccandd96@scars.tv. Website: http://scars.tv. Established 1993. **Contact:** Janet Kuypers, editor/publisher.

Magazines Needs *CC&D/Children, Churches and Daddies (The Unreligious, Non-Family-Oriented Literary Magazine)*, published monthly, contains poetry, prose, art, and essays. "Also run electronic issues and collection books. We accept poetry of almost any genre, but no rhyme or religious poems (look at our current issue for a better idea of what we're like). We are okay with gay/lesbian/bisexual, nature/rural/ecology, political/social issues, women/feminism." Does not want "racist, sexist (therefore we're not into pornography, either), or homophobic stuff." Has published poetry by Mel Waldman, Pat Dixon, Angeline Hawkes-Craig, Cheryl Townsend, Kenneth DiMaggio. *CC&D/Children, Churches and Daddies* (print) has ranged from 30 to 100 pages, been both digest-sized and standard-sized, photocopied, saddle-stapled; currently 40 pages, saddle-stitched and laser-printed. Receives hundreds of poems/year, accepts about 40%. Sample: $6 (print); free electronic sample online. Make checks payable to Janet Kuypers.

How to Contact Lines/poem: accepts longer works, "within 2 pages for an individual poem is appreciated." Considers previously published poems and simultaneous submissions. Accepts e-mail submissions (preferred, pasted into body of message or as attachment in Microsoft Word .doc file) or disk submissions. "When submitting via e-mail in body of message, explain in preceding paragraph that it is a submission; for disk submissions, mail floppy disk with ASCII text, or Macintosh disk." Comments on rejected poems "if asked." Guidelines available for SASE, by e-mail, or on Web site. Responds in 2 weeks.

Contest/Award Offerings Scars Publications sometimes sponsors a contest "where writing appears in an annual book." Write or e-mail (editor@scars.tv) for information.

Also Offers Also able to publish electronic chapbooks. Additional information available by e-mail or on Web site.

Tips "The Web site is a more comprehensive view of what *CC&D/Children, Churches and Daddies* does. All the information is there."

❍ CEREMONY, A JOURNAL OF POETRY AND OTHER ARTS

Dance of My Hands Publishing, 120 Vista Dr., Warminster PA 18974. E-mail: danceofmyhands@aol.com. Website: www.danceofmyhands.com. **Contact:** Melanie M. Eyth, editor.

Magazines Needs *Ceremony, a Journal of Poetry and Other Arts*, published biannually, encourages "all expression and articism. Beginning poets are especially encouraged." Wants poetry, short pieces of prose, photography and other printable arts. Considers poetry by teens. *Ceremony* is small, home-printed on 20 lb. recycled paper, and single staple-bound. Receives about 200 submissions/year, accepts 50%. Single copy: $3.

How to Contact Submit up to 6 poems at a time. Considers previously published poems and simultaneous submissions. Accepts e-mail submissions only. Reads submissions year round. Time between acceptance and publication is 1-2 years. Sometimes comments on rejected poems. Sometimes publishes theme issues. Guidelines available on Web site under 'Contact.' Pays 1 contributor's copy. Rights revert to poet upon publication.

ℕ ▣ ☑ CERISE PRESS

c/0 Sally Molini, P.O. Box 241187, Omaha NE 68124. E-mail: editors@cerisepress.com; submissions@cerisepress.com. Website: www.cerisepress.com. Established 2009. **Contact:** Karen Rigby, fiona Sze-Lorrain, Sally Molini, editors.

Magazines Needs *Cerise Press*, published 3 times/year, is an "online (with forthcoming print) journal of literature, arts, and culture based in the US and France, offering poetry, nonfiction, translations, fiction, artwork, and photography." Has published Victoria Chang, Ray Gonzalez, Eleanor Wilner, Tess Gallagher, Robert Kelly, Karen An-Hwei Lee.

How to Contact Submit 3-5 poems at a time. Considers simultaneous submissions. Accepts e-mail submissions. Cover letter is required. "Please let us know if work is accepted elsewhere. Do not query until three months from the date of submission." Reads submissions year round. Never comments on rejected poems. Guidelines on Web site. Responds in 2-3 months. Acquires first North American serial rights. Rights revert to poet upon publication. Reviews books and chapbooks of poetry, fiction, critical essays, biographies, photography, and more.

ℕ ▦ ▣ ◎ CHA: AN ASIAN LITERARY JOURNAL

E-mail: submissions@asiancha.com. Website: http://www.asiancha.com/index.php. **Contact:**

Tammy Ho Lai-ming and Jeff Zroback, editors. Online magazine. "Cha is the first and currently the only Hong Kong-based online literary quarterly journal dedicated to publishing creative works from and about Asia, primarily in English."

Magazines Needs List of upcoming themes available on Web site. Length: 100 words (min)-3,000 words (max). Publishes short shorts. Also publishes poetry.

How to Contact Accepts submissions by e-mail. Responds to queries in 3 months. Considers simultaneous submissions. Guidelines available on Web site.

☑ THE CHAFFIN JOURNAL

Dept. of English, Case Annex 467, Eastern Kentucky University, Richmond KY 40475-3102. (859)622-3080. Website: www.english.eku.edu/chaffin_journal. Established 1998. **Contact:** Robert W. Witt, editor.

Magazines Needs *The Chaffin Journal*, published annually in December, prints quality short fiction and poetry by new and established writers/poets. Wants any form, subject matter, or style. Does not want "poor quality." Has published poetry by Taylor Graham, Diane Glancy, Judith Montgomery, Simon Perchik, Philip St. Clair, and Virgil Suárez. *The Chaffin Journal* is 120 pages, digest-sized, offset-printed, perfect-bound, with plain cover with title only. Receives about 500 poems/year, accepts about 10%. Press run is 300; 40-50 distributed free to contributors. Single copy: $6; subscription: $6/year. Sample (back issue): $5. Make checks payable to *The Chaffin Journal*.

How to Contact Submit 5 poems per submission period. Considers simultaneous submissions (although not preferred); no previously published poems. No e-mail or disk submissions. Cover letter is preferred. "Submit typed pages with only one poem per page. Enclose SASE." Reads submissions June 1-October 1. Time between acceptance and publication is 6 months. Poems are reviewed by the general editor and 2 poetry editors. Never comments on rejected poems. Guidelines available in magazine or on Web site. Responds in 3 months. Pays 1 contributor's copy. Acquires one-time rights.

Tips "Submit quality work during our reading period; include cover letter and SASE."

☒ ☐ ◎ CHALLENGER INTERNATIONAL

(Specialized: poetry for/by teens), (250)991-5567. E-mail: danlukiv@sd28.bc.ca. Website: http://challengerinternational.20m.com/index.html. Established 1978. **Contact:** Dan Lukiv, editor.

Magazines Needs *Challenger international*, published annually, contains "poetry and (on occasion) short fiction." Wants "any type of work, especially by teenagers (our mandate: to encourage young writers, and to publish their work alongside established writers), providing it is not pornographic, profane, or overly abstract." Has published poetry from Canada, the continental U.S., Hawaii, Switzerland, Russia, Malta, Italy, Slovenia, Ireland, England, Korea, Pakistan, Australia, Zimbabwe, Argentina, and Columbia. *Challenger international* is generally 20-50 pages, magazine-sized, laser-printed, side-stapled. Press run is 50. *Challenger international* is distributed free to McNaughton Centre Secondary Alternate School sudents.

How to Contact Considers previously published poems and simultaneous submissions. Cover letter is required. Include list of credits, if any. Accepts e-mail submissions only; no postal submissions. "Sometimes we edit to save the poet rejection." Responds in 6 months. Payment is 1 e-copy (sent as an e-mail attachment) of the issue in which the author's work appears. Poet retains rights.

Additional Information Island Scholastic Press publishes chapbooks by authors featured in *Challenger international*. Pays 3 author's copies. Copyright remains with author. Distribution of free copies through McNaughton Centre.

Tips "We like imagistic poetry that makes sense."

$ ☑ ◎ CHAMPAGNE SHIVERS

(Specialized: horror poetry only), E-mail: ChampagneShivers@hotmail.com (accepts submissions by e-mail only). Website: http://samsdotpublishing.com/vineyard/Champagne%20Shivers.htm. Established 2002. **Contact:** Cathy Buburuz, editor.

Magazines Needs *Champagne Shivers* is "a classy horror magazine. This is not the place to submit offensive language. We prefer poetic, well-written horror." Wants "horror poetry only. We prefer poems that do not rhyme, but all verse will be considered. Poems 20-30 lines stand the best chance for acceptance, especially if they're scary and entertaining." Does not want "anything that isn't horror related, and always proof and edit before you send your submission. If your work does not have high entertainment or high impact, do not send it here." Has published poetry by Lee Clark Zumpe, Nancy Bennett, Steve Vernon, Kurt Newton, W.B. Vogel III, and Keith W. Sikora. *Champagne Shivers* is more than 60 pages, 8 1/2x11, professionally printed and perfect-bound, with full color cover art depicting a chilling, yet beautiful female. Receives about 1,000 poems/year, accepts 15 poems/issue. Press run and subscriber base vary; the only free copies go to reviewers and contributors. Single copy: $12 U.S. and Canada. Sample: $10 U.S. and Canada. ("Foreign countries, please inquire about costs.") Make checks payable to Tyree Campbell, Sam's Dot Publishing, P.O. Box 782, Cedar Rapids IA 52406-0782 (for subscriptions and sample copies only; DO NOT SEND SUBMISSIONS TO THIS ADDRESS).

How to Contact Submit 1 poem at a time. Lines/poem: 20-30. Considers previously published poems; no simultaneous submissions. Accepts e-mail submissions only (pasted into body of message; DO NOT SEND ATTACHMENTS) to ChampagneShivers@hotmail.com. Does not accept snail mail submissions. Cover letter is preferred. "Submit 1 poem with a bio written in the third person, your mailing address, and your e-mail address." Reads submissions year round. Submit seasonal poems 4 months in advance. Time between acceptance and publication is less than 6 months. Always comments on rejected poems. Guidelines available by e-mail or on Web site. Pays 10¢/line for unpublished poems; 5¢/line for previously published poems (let the editor know where and when the poem appeared), plus 1 contributor's copy. Acquires first North American serial rights to unpublished poems, one-time rights to previously published poems. All rights revert back to the writer upon publication.

Contest/Award Offerings Sam's Dot Publishing offers The James Award (Trophy) annually. The editor selects one poem per year from the pages of Champagne Shivers to nominate for the award. **Entry fee:** "None—it's free." **Deadline:** August. Guidelines available on Web site. "Never send snail mail submissions; always submit in the body of an e-mail after reading the information under How to Submit above."

Also Offers *Expressions (A Newsletter for Creative People Worldwide)*, edited by Cathy Buburuz (visit the Web site at www.samsdotpublishing.com/expressions.htm); the *Potter's Field* anthologies (a yearly collection of short horror stories focussing on unmarked graves, and stories that focus on cemeteries.

Tips "Submit horror poems only. I love psychological horror poetry, horror poetry about the Old West, horror poems about asylums, or anything that's just plain scary. I do not want poems about werewolves, vampires, ghosts, or traditional monsters. I want to read poetry that's fresh and exciting. Most of all, send me something that's high in entertainment, that's never been done before. Send poems that will give me and my audience the shivers."

▣ ◻ CHANTARELLE'S NOTEBOOK

E-mail: chantarellesnotebook@yahoo.com. Website: www.chantarellesnotebook.com. Established

2005. **Contact:** Kendall A. Bell and Christinia Bell, editors.

Magazines Needs *Chantarelle's Notebook*, published quarterly online, seeks "quality work from undiscovered poets. We enjoy poems that speak to us—poems with great sonics and visuals." Wants "all styles of poetry, as long as it's quality work." Does not want "infantile rants, juvenile confessionals, greeting card-styled verse, political posturing, or religious outpourings." Considers poetry by children and teens. "There are no age restrictions, but submissions from younger people will be held to the same guidelines and standards as those from adults." Has published poetry by Donna Vorreyer, Patricia Carragon, Corrine DeWinter, Taylor Graham, Corey Mesler, and Simon Perchik. Receives about 500 poems/year, accepts about 20%. Sample: see Web site for latest issue.

How to Contact Submit 3-5 poems at a time. Lines/poem: "shorter poems have a better chance, but long poems are fine." Considers previously published poems; no simultaneous submissions. Accepts e-mail submissions (pasted into body of message; "we will not open any attachments—they will be deleted"). Cover letter is required. "Please include a short bio of no more than 75 words, should we decide to accept your work." Reads submissions year round. Submit seasonal poems 2-3 months in advance. "The editors will review all submissions and make a decision within a week's time." Never comments on rejected poems. Guidelines available on Web site. "Please follow the guidelines—all the information is there!" Responds in 2-3 weeks. Acquires one-time rights. Rights revert to poets upon publication. "*Chantarelle's Notebook* is also accepting photo submissions. Please visit the Web site for guidelines on how to submit your photos to us."

Also Offers "*Chantarelle's Notebook* will publish a 'best of' print journal that will cull poems from each of the previous 4 quarterly issues in the past year. The authors of the poems chosen will receive 1 contributor's copy and can buy additional copies at half price."

Tips "Read as much poetry as you can. Immerse yourself in work other than your own. Turn off your television. Write from the pit of your stomach. Revise. Edit. Rewrite. Do not let rejections keep you off your path. The only way to become a great poet is to learn from all experiences, good and bad."

$ ☑ THE CHATTAHOOCHEE REVIEW

Georgia Perimeter College, 2101 Womack Rd., Dunwoody GA 30338. (770)274-5145. E-mail: gpccr@gpc.edu. Website: www.chattahoochee-review.org. Established 1980. **Contact:** Marc Fitten, editor-in-chief.

Magazines Needs *The Chattahoochee Review*, published quarterly, prints poetry, short fiction, essays, reviews, and interviews. "We publish a number of Southern writers, but *The Chattahoochee Review* is not by design a regional magazine. All themes, forms, and styles are considered as long as they impact the whole person: heart, mind, intuition, and imagination." Has recently published work by George Garrett, Jim Daniels, Jack Pendarvis, Ignacio Padilla, and Kevin Canty. *The Chattahoochee Review* is 160 pages, digest-sized, professionally printed, flat-spined, with four-color silk-matte card cover. Press run is 1,250; 300 are complimentary copies sent to editors and "miscellaneous VIPs." Subscription: $20/year. Sample: $6.

How to Contact Submit 3-5 poems at a time. No previously published poems or simultaneous submissions. No e-mail or disk submissions. Cover letter is "encouraged, but not required." Include bio material when sending cover letter. Poems should be typed on one side of page with poet's name clearly visible. No reply without SASE. Time between acceptance and publication is up to 4 months. Publishes theme issues. Guidelines available for SASE or on Web site. Responds in 1 week to 6 months. Pays $50/poem and 2 contributor's copies. Acquires first rights. Staff reviews books of poetry and short fiction in 1,500 words, single- or multi-book format. Send materials for review consideration.

☑ CHAUTAUQUA LITERARY JOURNAL

P.O. Box 613, Chautauqua NY 14722. E-mail: clj@uncw.edu. Website: http://writers.ciweb.org. Established 2003. **Contact:** Richard Foerster, editor.

- •Poetry published in *Chautauqua Literary Journal* has been included in *The Pushcart Prize* anthology.

Magazines Needs *Chautauqua Literary Journal*, published annually in June, prints poetry, short fiction, creative nonfiction, and book reviews. "We welcome poems that exhibit the writer's craft and attention to language, employ striking images and metaphors, engage the mind as well as the emotions, and reveal insights into the larger world of human concerns. The editor invites traditional as well as experimental work." Does not want "hackneyed inspirational versifying; poems typed in all capitals or on pastel paper." Has published poetry by Patricia Smith, Karl Shapiro, Douglas Goetsch, William Heyen, Robert Cording, and Randall Watson. *Chautauqua Literary Journal* is 178 pages, digest-sized, offset-printed, with notch adhesive binding and glossy cover with original artwork, includes ads. Receives about 4,000 poems/year, accepts about 40. Press run is 2,000; 300 distributed free to contributors and others. Single copy: $10; subscription: $18. Make checks payable to *Chautauqua Literary Journal*.

How to Contact Submit 4 poems maximum at a time. Considers simultaneous submissions (if notified); no previously published poems. No e-mail or disk submissions. Cover letter is preferred. "We prefer single-spaced manuscripts in 12 pt. font. Cover letters should be brief and mention recent publications (if any). SASE is mandatory." Reads submissions February 15-April 15 and August 15-November 15. Time between acceptance and publication is up to 1 year. "The editor is the sole arbiter, but we do have advisory editors who periodically make recommendations." Sometimes comments on rejected poems. Guidelines available on Web site. Responds in 3 months or less. Always sends prepublication galleys. Pays 2 contributor's copies. Acquires first rights "plus one-time non-exclusive rights to reprint accepted work in an anniversary issue." Reviews books/chapbooks of poetry in 750-1,000 words, single- and multi-book format. Send materials for review consideration to *Chautauqua Literary Journal*/Reviews, P.O. Box 2039, York Beach ME 03910.

Tips "Poets who are not avid readers of contemporary poetry will most likely not be writing anything of interest to us."

☑ CHERRY BLOSSOM REVIEW, THE

E-mail: thecherryblossomreview@yahoo.com. Website: http://www.geocities.com/ thecherryblossomreview/. Established 2007. **Contact:** Jennifer LeBlanc, editor

Magazine Needs The Cherry Blossom Review, published twice per year in print and online, is dedicated to haiku and short poems (fourteen lines maximum). The Cherry Blossom Review is approximately 28-32 pages, digest-sized and online, photocopied, saddle-stapled, with stock cover. Press run is 30; 25 distributed free to contributors and friends. Single copy: $4.50; subscription: $9. Make checks payable to Jennifer LeBlanc. Send e-mail asking for postal address.

How to Contact Submit 1-5 poems at a time. Considers simultaneous submissions. Does not consider previously published work (Considers poetry posted on a public Web site/blog/ forum and poetry posted on a private, password-protected forum as published). Accepts e-mail submissions (as attachment); no fax or disk submissions. Cover letter is required. "Send poetry submissions to thecherryblossomreview@yahoo.com. Do *not* send submissions to postal address. They will not be read. Please include a short, third person biography to be published with accepted poems." Reads submissions mid-May-midsummer. Check Web site for dates. Time between acceptance and publication is up to 10 months. Seldom comments on rejected poems. Never publishes theme issues. Guidelines available on Web site. Responds in 2 weeks.

Pays 1 contributor's copy. Acquires one-time publishing rights, "which includes publication on the Web site and in the corresponding print issue. Poetry will remain on the Web site for up to 8 months. Rights revert to poets upon publication.

Tips "Read contemporary poetry, write often, and proofread your work!"

☑ ◎ CHEST

(Specialized: Medical themes), 3300 Dundee Rd, Northbrook IL 60062.800-343-2222. E-mail: poetrychest@aol.com. Website: www.chestjournal.org. Established 1937. **Contact**: Michael Zack, M.D., poetry editor.

Magazines Needs *Chest*, published monthly, "is the official medical journal of the American College of Chest Physicians, the world's largest medical journal for pulmonologists, sleep, and critical care specialists, with over 22,000 subscribers." Wants "poetry with themes of medical relevance." *Chest* is approximately 300 pages, magazine-sized, perfect-bound, with a glossy cover, and includes ads. Press run is 22,000. Number of unique visitors: 900,000 to Web site. Subscription: $192. Make checks payable to American College Chest Physicians.

How to Contact Submit up to 3 poems at a time, between 10 and 80 lines. Only accepts e-mail submissions (as attachment or in body of e-mail); no fax or disk submissions. Brief cover letter preferred. Reads submissions year round. Poems are circulated to an editorial board. Sometimes comments on rejected poems. Never publishes theme issues. Guidelines available in magazine and on Web site. Responds in 2 months; always sends prepublication galleys. Retains all rights.

$ ◎ CHILDREN'S DIGEST

(Specialized: children ages 10-12), Children's Better Health Institute, 1100 Waterway Blvd., Indianapolis IN 46202. Website: www.cbhi.org or www.childrensdigestmag.org.

Magazines Needs *Children's Digest*, published bimonthly for The Children's Better Health Network, is a magazine for ages 10-12. "Prepares kids for the teen years." Wants light-hearted poetry appropriate for the age group. Reviews submissions for possible use in all Children's Better Health Institute publications.

How to Contact Manuscripts must be typewritten with poet's contact information in upper right-hand corner of each poem's page. SASE required. Submit seasonal material at least 8 months in advance. Guidelines available for SASE or on Web site. Responds in about 3 months. Pays $25 minimum for poetry. Acquires all rights.

Tips "We receive too many poetry submissions that are about kids, not for kids. Or, the subject matter is one that adults think children would or should like. Reading our guidelines is not enough. Careful study of current issues will acquaint writers with each title's 'personality.'"

$ ◎ CHILDREN'S PLAYMATE

(Specialized: children ages 6-8), Children's Better Health Institute, 1100 Waterway Blvd., Indianapolis IN 46202. Website: www.cbhi.org or www.childrensplaymatemag.org.

Magazines Needs *Children's Playmate*, published bimonthly by The Children's Better Health Institute, is a magazine for ages 6-8. "Strives to make learning fun." Wants light-hearted poetry appropriate for the age group. Reviews submissions for possible use in all Children's Better Health Institute publications.

How to Contact Manuscripts must be typewritten with poet's contact information in upper right-hand corner of each poem's page. SASE required. Submit seasonal material at least 8 months in advance. Guidelines available for SASE or on Web site. Responds in about 3 months. Pays $25 minimum for poetry. Acquires all rights.

Tips "We receive too many poetry submissions that are about kids, not for kids. Or, the subject matter is one that adults think children would or should like. Reading our guidelines is not enough. Careful study of current issues will acquaint writers with each title's 'personality.'"

✪ CHIRON REVIEW

522 E. South Ave., St. John KS 67576-2212. (620)786-4955. E-mail: ChironSubmissions@hotmail.com. Website: http://chironreview.com. Established 1982 as The Kindred Spirit. **Contact:** Gerald and Zachary Locklin, poetry editors.

Magazines Needs *Chiron Review*, published quarterly, is a tabloid using photographs of featured writers. No taboos. Has published poetry by Quentin Crisp, Felice Picano, Edward Field, Wanda Coleman, and Marge Piercy. Press run is about 1,000. Subscription: $17/year (4 issues).

How to Contact Submit up to 5 poems at a time. No longer accepts e-mail submissions. Guidelines available for SASE or on Web site. Responds in 2-6 weeks. Pays 1 contributor's copy, discount on additional copies. Acquires first-time rights. Reviews books of poetry in 500-700 words.

Additional Information Will also publish occasional chapbooks; see Web site for details.

✪ ◎ CHRISTIANITY AND LITERATURE

(Specialized: Christian; spirituality/inspirational), Humanities Division, Pepperdine University, 24255 Pacific Coast Highway, Malibu CA 90263. Website: www.pepperdine.edu/sponsored/ccl/journal. **Contact:** Julia S. Kasdorf, poetry editor (Pennsylvania State University, English Dept., 114 Burrows Bldg, University Park, PA 16802).

Magazines Needs *Christianity and Literature*, a quarterly scholarly journal, publishes about 4-6 poems/issue. Press run is 1,100. Single copy: $10; subscription: $25/year, $45 for 2 years. Make checks payable to CCL.

How to Contact Submit 1-6 poems at a time. No previously published poems or simultaneous submissions. Accepts submissions by surface mail only. Cover letter is required. Submissions must be accompanied by SASE. Time between acceptance and publication is 6-12 months. "Poems are chosen by our poetry editor." Guidelines available on Web site. Responds within 4 months. Pays 2 contributor's copies "and a dozen offprints to poets whose work we publish." Rights revert to poets upon written request. Reviews collections of literary, Christian poetry occasionally in some issues (no chapbooks).

Tips "We look for poems that are clear and surprising. They should have a compelling sense of voice, formal sophistication (though not necessarily rhyme and meter), and the ability to reveal the spiritual through concrete images. We cannot return submissions that are not accompanied by SASE."

$ ✪ THE CHRISTIAN SCIENCE MONITOR

The Home Forum Page, 210 Massachussetts Ave., P02-30, Boston MA 02115. E-mail: homeforum@csmonitor.com. Website: www.csmonitor.com. Established 1908. **Contact:** Judy Lowe, Home Forum editor.

Magazines Needs *The Christian Science Monitor*, an international daily newspaper, regularly features poetry in The Home Forum section. Wants "finely crafted poems that explore and celebrate daily life; that provide a respite from daily news and from the bleakness that appears in so much contemporary verse." Does not want "work that presents people in helpless or hopeless states; poetry about death, aging, or illness; or dark, violent, sensual poems. No poems that are overtly religious or falsely sweet." Considers free verse and fixed forms. Has published poetry by Diana Der-Hovanessian, Marilyn Krysl, and Michael Glaser. Publishes 1-4 poems/week.

How to Contact Submit up to 5 poems at a time. Lines/poem: Prefers poems under 20 lines. No previously published poems or simultaneous submissions. Accepts e-mail submissions only (by attachment in MS Word, 1 poem/e-mail). Pays $20/haiku; $40/poem.

$ ☑ ◎ CHRYSALIS READER

(Specialized: spirituality; themes), 1745 Gravel Hill Rd., Dillwyn VA 23936. Fax: (434)983-1074. E-mail: chrysalis@hovac.com. Website: www.swedenborg.com/chrysalis. Established 1985. **Contact:** Robert F. Lawson, poetry editor. Editor: Carol S. Lawson.

Magazines Needs *Chrysalis Reader*, published annually in September by the Swedenborg Foundation, is a "contribution to the search for spiritual wisdom, a book series that challenges inquiring minds through the use of literate and scholarly fiction, essays, and poetry." Wants "poetry that surprises, that pushes the language, gets our attention." Does not want anything "overly religious or sophomoric." Has published work by Robert Bly, Linda Pastan, Wesley McNair, Wyn Cooper, William Kloefkorn, and Virgil Suárez. *Chrysalis Reader* is 208 pages, 7x10, professionally printed on archival paper, perfect-bound, with coated coverstock. Receives about 1,000 submissions/year, accepts about 16 poems. Press run is 3,500. Sample: $10. (Sample poems available on Web site.)

How to Contact Submit no more than 5-6 poems at a time. Considers simultaneous submissions "if notified immediately when work is accepted elsewhere"; no previously published poems. Include SASE. Reads submissions year round. Time between acceptance and publication is typically 18 months. Regularly publishes theme issues (the 2010 issue theme is "Bridges"). Themes and guidelines available with SASE or on Web site. Responds in 3 months. Always sends prepublication galleys. Pays $25 and 3 contributor's copies. Acquires first-time rights. "We expect to be credited for reprints after permission is given."

Contest/Award Offerings The Bailey Prize (see separate listing in Contests & Awards).

Tips "Purchase a back issue, go online, or request your bookstore to order a reading copy so that you can better gauge what to submit."

☑ CIDER PRESS REVIEW

777 Braddock Lane, Halifax PA 17032. E-mail: editor@ciderpressreview.com (inquiries only). Website: http://ciderpressreview.com. Established 1999. **Contact:** Caron Andregg and Robert Wynne, co-editors.

Magazines Needs *Cider Press Review*, published annually, features "the best new work from contemporary poets." Wants "thoughtful, well-crafted poems with vivid language and strong images. We prefer poems that have something to say. We would like to see more well-written humor. We also encourage translations." Does not want "didactic, inspirational, greeting card verse, empty word play, therapy, or religious doggerel." Also welcomes reviews in not more than 500 words of current full-length books of poetry. Has published poetry by Robert Arroyo, Jr., Virgil Suárez, Linda Pastan, Kathleen Flenniken, Tim Seibles, Joanne Lowery, Thomas Lux, and Mark Cox. *Cider Press Review* is 128 pages, digest-sized, offset-printed, perfect-bound, with 4-color coated card cover. Receives about 2,500 poems/year, accepts about 3%. Press run is 750. Single copy: $12; subscription: $20 for 2 issues (1 journal, 1 book from the *Cider Press Review* Book Award). Sample: $10 (journal).

How to Contact Submit up to 5 poems at a time. No previously published poems or simultaneous submissions. Submit by postal mail or through online submission form at Web site. "International authors or special needs, please query via e-mail. Do not send unsolicited disk or e-mail submissions." Cover letter is preferred. Include short bio (50 words maximum). SASE required for reply. Reads submissions April 1-August 31 only. Time between acceptance and publication is 6-9 months. Poems are circulated to an editorial board. Guidelines available for SASE or on

Web site. Responds in 1-4 months. Always sends prepublication galleys. Pays 1 contributor's copy. Acquires first North American serial rights.

Contest/Award Offerings *The Cider Press Review* Book Award (see separate listing in Contests & Awards).

☑ CIMARRON REVIEW

205 Morrill Hall, Oklahoma State University, Stillwater OK 74078-0135. E-mail: cimarronreview@ yahoo.com. Website: http://cimarronreview.okstate.edu. Established 1967. **Contact:** Lisa Lewis, Alfred Corn, and Ai, poetry editors.

Magazines Needs *Cimarron Review*, published quarterly, is a literary journal "that takes pride in our eclecticism. We like evocative poetry (lyric or narrative) controlled by a strong voice. No restrictions as to subject matter." Wants "poems whose surfaces and structures risk uncertainty and which display energy, texture, intelligence, and intense investment." Has published poetry by William Stafford, John Ashbery, Grace Schulman, Barbara Hamby, Patricia Fargnoli, Phillip Dacey, Holly Prado, and Kim Addonizio. *Cimarron Review* is 100-150 pages, digest-sized, perfect-bound, with color cover. Press run is 600. Single copy: $7; subscription: $24/year ($28 Canada), $42 for 2 years ($48 Canada), $65 for 3 years ($72 Canada).

How to Contact Submit 3-5 poems at a time. Considers simultaneous submissions, "but please note in cover letter." No e-mail submissions; accepts postal submissions only. "Writers outside North America may query by e-mail." No response without SASE. Guidelines available on Web site. Responds in up to 6 months. Pays 2 contributor's copies. Acquires first North American serial rights only. Reviews books of poetry in 500-900 words, single-book format, occasionally multi-book.

$ ☑ THE CINCINNATI REVIEW

P.O. Box 210069, Cincinnati OH 45221-0069. (513)556-3954. E-mail: editors@cincinnatireview. com. Website: www.cincinnatireview.com. Established 2003. **Contact:** Don Bogen, poetry editor.

Magazines Needs *The Cincinnati Review*, published semiannually, is devoted "to publishing the best new poetry and literary fiction, as well as book reviews, essays, and interviews. Open to any schools, styles, forms—as long as the poem is well made and sophisticated in its language use and subject matter." *The Cincinnati Review* is 180-200 pages, digest-sized, perfect-bound, with matte paperback cover with full-color art, includes ads. Press run is 1,000. Single copy: $9 (current issue); subscription: $15. Sample: $7 (back issue).

How to Contact Submit up to 10 pages of poetry at a time. Considers simultaneous submissions with notification; no previously published poems. No e-mail or disk submissions. Cover letter is preferred. SASE required. Reads submissions September 1-May 31. Time between acceptance and publication is 6 months. "First-round reading by small, trained staff. Final decisions made by genre editors." Seldom comments on rejected poems. Guidelines available for SASE or on Web site. Responds in 6 weeks. Always sends prepublication galleys. Pays $30/page and 2 contributor's copies. Acquires first North American serial rights. Reviews books of poetry in 1,500 words, single-book format.

☑ ◎ CLARK STREET REVIEW

(Specialized: narrative and prose poetry), P.O. Box 1377, Berthoud CO 80513. E-mail: clarkreview@earthlink.net. Established 1998. **Contact:** Ray Foreman, editor.

Magazines Needs *Clark Street Review*, published 6 times/year, uses narrative poetry and short shorts. Tries "to give writers and poets cause to keep writing by publishing their best work."

Wants "narrative poetry under 100 lines that reaches readers who are mostly published poets and writers. Subjects are open." Does not want "obscure or formalist work." Has published poetry by Charles Ries, Anselm Brocki, Ed Galling, Ellaraine Lockie, and J. Glenn Evans. *Clark Street Review* is 20 pages, digest-sized, photocopied, saddle-stapled, with paper cover. Receives about 1,000 poems/year, accepts about 10%. Press run is 200. Single copy: $2; subscription: $10 for 10 issues postpaid for writers only. Make checks payable to R. Foreman.

How to Contact Submit 1-5 poems at a time. Lines/poem: 20 minimum, 75 maximum. Considers previously published poems and simultaneous submissions. Send "disposable sharp copies. Maximum width—65 characters. Include SASE for reply. No cover letter." Time between acceptance and publication is 4 months. "Editor reads everything with a critical eye of 30 years of experience in writing and publishing small press work." Often comments on rejected poems. Guidelines available for SASE or by e-mail. Responds in 3 weeks. Acquires one-time rights.

Tips "*Clark Street Review* is geared to the more experienced poet and writer deeply involved in the writer's life. There are tips and quotes throughout each issue that writers appreciate. As always, the work we print speaks for the writer and the magazine. Publishing excellence and giving writers a reason to write is our only aim. Well-crafted, interesting, and accessible human narrative poems will see ink in *CSR*."

☑ COAL CITY REVIEW

English Dept., University of Kansas, Lawrence KS 66045. E-mail: briandal@ku.edu. Established 1989. **Contact:** Brian Daldorph, editor.

Magazines Needs *Coal City Review*, published annually in the fall, prints poetry, short stories, reviews, and interviews—"the best material I can find. As Pound said, 'Make it new.'" Does not want "experimental poetry, doggerel, five-finger exercises, or beginner's verse." Has published poetry by Gary Lechliter, Phil Miller, Cheela Chilala, Maggie Sawkins, and Denise Low. *Coal City Review* is 100 pages, digest-sized, professionally printed on recycled paper, perfect-bound, with colored card cover. Accepts about 5% of material received. Press run is 200. Subscription: $10. Sample: $6.

How to Contact Submit 6 poems at a time. Considers previously published poems "occasionally"; no simultaneous submissions. No e-mail submissions. "Please do not send list of prior publications." Include name and address on each page. Seldom comments on rejected poems. Guidelines available for SASE. Responds in up to 3 months. Pays 1 contributor's copy. Reviews books of poetry in 300-1,000 words, mostly single-book format. Send materials for review consideration.

Additional Information *Coal City Review* also publishes occasional books and chapbooks as issues of the magazine, but **does not accept unsolicited book/chapbook submissions**. Most recent book is *Bird's Horn* by Kevin Rabas.

Tips "Care more (much more) about writing than publication. If you're good enough, you'll publish."

$ ◎ COBBLESTONE MAGAZINE

(Specialized: American history; children/teens ages 9-14), Editorial Dept., Cobblestone Publishing, 30 Grove St., Suite C, Peterborough NH 03458. Website: www.cricketmag.com. **Contact:** Meg Chorlian.

Magazines Needs COBBLESTONE *Magazine*, published 9 times/year, is a magazine of American history for children ages 9-14. "All material must relate to the theme of a specific upcoming issue in order to be considered." Wants "clear, objective imagery. Serious and light verse considered. Must relate to theme." Subscription: $33.95/year (9 issues). Sample: $5.95 plus $2.00 s&h

(include 10x13 SASE); sample pages available on Web site.

How to Contact Query first. Lines/poem: up to 100. No e-mail submissions or queries. Include SASE. Reads submissions according to deadlines for queries (see Web site for schedule and details). Always publishes theme issue. Guidelines available on Web site. Pays varied rates. Acquires all rights.

Tips "Writers are encouraged to study recent back issues for content and style."

$ ☑ COLORADO REVIEW

Center for Literary Publishing, Dept. of English, 9105 Campus Delivery, Colorado State University, Fort Collins CO 80523. (970)491-5449. E-mail: creview@colostate.edu. Website: http://coloradoreview.colostate.edu. Established 1956 (as Colorado Review), 1966 (resurrected as Colorado State Review), 1985 (renamed Colorado Review). **Contact:** Donald Revell, Sasha Steensen, and Matthew Cooperman, poetry editors. General Editor; Stephanie G'Schwind. Dan Beachy-Quick, Book Review Editor.

•Poetry published in *Colorado Review* has been included in *The Best American Poetry* and *Pushcart Prize Anthology*.

Magazines Needs *Colorado Review*, published 3 times/year, prints short fiction, poetry, and personal essays. Has published poetry by Alice Notley, Rae Armantrout, Tomaz Salamun, Kazim Ali, Rusty Morrison, Joseph Campana, Paul Hoover, and Fanny Howe. *Colorado Review* is about 224 pages, digest-sized, professionally printed, notch-bound, with glossy card cover. Press run is 1,300. Receives about 10,000 submissions/year, accepts about 2%. Subscription: $24/year. Sample: $10.

How to Contact Submit no more than 5 poems at a time. Considers simultaneous submissions, "but you must notify *Colorado Review* immediately if accepted elsewhere"; no previously published poems. No e-mail submissions. SASE required for response. Reads submissions September 1-May 1 only. Responds in 2 months, "often sooner." Pays $5/printed page. Acquires first North American serial rights. Reviews books of poetry, fiction, and nonfiction. "Most book reviews are solicited, but feel free to query." Send materials for review consideration.

Contest/Award Offerings Colorado Prize for Poetry (see separate listing in Contests & Awards).

☑ COLUMBIA: A JOURNAL OF LITERATURE AND ART

(212)854-4216. Fax: (212)854-7704. E-mail: info@columbiajournal.org. Website: www. columbiajournal.org. Established 1977. **Contact:** Dawn Marie Knopf, editor.

Magazines Needs *Columbia: A Journal of Literature and Art*, published annually, will consider "any poem that is eclectic and spans from traditional to experimental genres." Has published poetry by Louise Gluck, James Tate, Eamon Grennan, Mary Jo Salter, and Yuse Komunyakaa. *Columbia* is 176 pages, digest-sized, offset-printed, notch-bound, with glossy cover, includes ads. Receives about 2,000 poems/year, accepts about 2%. Press run is 2,000. Subscription: $10/year, $15 for 2 years. Sample: $8; back issue: $10.

How to Contact Submit up to 5 poems at a time. Considers simultaneous submissions when noted; no previously published poems. Accepts submissions through Web site only. Cover letter is preferred. Reads submissions year round. Poems are circulated to an editorial board. Seldom comments on rejected poems. Guidelines available in magazine or on Web site. Responds in 3-4 months. Pays 2 contributor's copies. Acquires first North American serial rights.

Contest/Award Offerings Sponsors annual contest with an award of $500. Submit no more than 5 poems/entry or 20 double-spaced pages for fiction and nonfiction submissions. **Entry fee:** $12. **Deadline:** see Web site or recent journal issue. All entrants receive a copy of the issue publishing the winners.

☑ COMMON GROUND REVIEW

40 Prospect St. Unit C1, Westfield, MA 01085. Website: www.cgreview.org. Established 1999. **Contact:** Larry O'Brien, editor.• Common Ground Review is affiliated with Western New England College.

Magazines Needs *Common Ground Review*, published semiannually, prints poetry and original artwork by the art editor Alice Ahrens Williams. Wants poetry with strong imagery; well-written free or traditional forms. Does not want greeting card verse, overly sentimental or political poetry. Has published poetry by James Doyle, Martin Galvin, Lyn Lifshin, Virgil Suárez, and Rennie McQuilken. *Common Ground Review* is 60+ pages, digest-sized, perfect-bound, with 4-color cover. Receives about 1,000 poems/year, accepts less than 10%. Press run is 125-150. Single copy: $12.50 (includes S&H). Orders: Make checks payable to *Common Ground Review* and send to 43 Winton Rd., East Windsor CT 06088.

How to Contact Submit 1-3 poems at a time. Lines/poem: 60 maximum. No previously published poems. Simultaneous submissions are allowed; see Web site for details. E-mail submissions are allowed. Cover letter is required, as is biography. "Poems should be single-spaced; include name, address, phone number, e-mail address, brief biography, and SASE (submissions without SASE will not be notified)." Reads submissions year round, but deadline for non-contest submissions is August 31. Submit seasonal poems 6 months in advance. Time between acceptance and publication is 4-6 months. "Editor reads and culls submissions. Final decisions made by editorial board." Seldom comments on rejected poems. Guidelines available in magazine or on Web site. Responds in 2 months. Pays 1 contributor's copy. Acquires one-time rights.

Contest/Award Offerings Sponsors an annual poetry contest. Offers 1st Prize: $150; 2nd Prize: $75; 3rd Prize: $50; Honorable Mentions. **Entry fee:** $10 for 1-3 unpublished poems. **Deadline:** February 28 for contest submissions only. All contest submissions are considered for publication in *Common Ground Review*.

Tips "Read journal before submitting. Beginning poets need to read what's out there, get into workshops, and work on revising. Attend writers' conferences. Listen and learn."

Ⓝ ▣ ☑ ◎ COMMON SENSE 2

(specialized: Pennsylvania, politics), E-mail: slatsboss@gmail.com. Website: www.commonsense2. com. Established 2007 **Contact:** Jack Ranig, poetry editor.

Magazines Needs *CommonSense 2*, published monthly online, is "a magazine of progressive political thought with a broad interest in the arts." Wants"any form and styles." Jack Lindeman, Richard O'Connell, Jack Conway, Eliza Kelley, and Belle Randall. Receives approximately 1200 poems/year, accepts about 50%. Number of unique visitors: 3,500-5,000.

How to Contact Submit 3-5 poems at a time. Considers previously published poetry and simultaneous submissions. Accepts e-mail submissions; no fax or dis. Cover letter is unnecessary. "We require bio information (a paragraph) and request a head shot photo file." Reads submissions year round. Submit seasonal poems 2 months in advance. Time between acceptance and publication is 2-8 weeks. Never comments on rejected poems. Guidelines available by e-mail. Responds in 6 months. Acquires first rights. Rights revert to poet upon publication.

Tips "We're open to excellent poetry on any subject though we're politically oriented."

$ ☑ ◎ COMMONWEAL

(Specialized: Catholic), 475 Riverside Dr., Room 405, New York NY 10115. E-mail: editors@ commonwealmagazine.org. Website: www.commonwealmagazine.org. **Contact:** Rosemary Deen, poetry editor.

Magazines Needs *Commonweal*, published every 2 weeks, is a Catholic general interest magazine for college-educated readers. Wants serious, witty, well-written poems. Does not publish inspirational poems. Circulation is 20,000. Subscription: $55.

How to Contact Lines/poem: 75 maximum. No simultaneous submissions. Only accepts hardcopy submissions with an SASE. Reads submissions September 1-June 30 only. Pays 50¢/line plus 2 contributor's copies. Acquires all rights. Returns rights when requested by the author. Reviews books of poetry in 750-1,000 words, single- or multi-book format.

☑ THE COMSTOCK REVIEW

4956 St. John Dr., Syracuse NY 13215. (315)488-8077. E-mail: poetry@comstockreview.org (inquiries only). Website: www.comstockreview.org. Established 1987 (as Poetpourri). **Contact:** John M. Bellinger, managing editor.

Magazines Needs Soon entering its 23rd year of publication, *The Comstock Review* is proud of its long-established reputation of publishing the finest known and unknown poets throughout North America. We choose our poems solely on the basis of what we consider to be their artistic merits. We are not swayed by long publishing histories. We are not afraid of the avant-garde, but shy from the overly obscure, the patently religious and the needlessly graphic. *The Comstock Review* is approximately 100 pages, digest-sized, professionally printed, perfect-bound. Press run is 500. Subscription: $20/year, $36/2 years. Samples issues available for $12.

How to Contact Submit 3-6 poems, one submission per reading period. No previously published poems; simultaneous submissions accepted, but discouraged. No poem must exceed 40 lines, beginning with the first line of text below the title. DO NOT count blank lines. Please also consider our 65 character line width when submitting. Postal submissions only. Cover letter is preferred. Include three line bio. Put name, address, phone number, and e-mail address on each page. Reads submissions January 1-April 1st only (at present; check Web site). Acceptances mailed out 8-12 weeks after close of reading period. Editorial comments and suggestions sometimes given. Guidelines available in magazine, for SASE, or on Web site. Pays 1 contributor's copy. Acquires first North American serial rights.

Contest/Award Offerings The annual Muriel Craft Bailey Memorial Award and the Jesse Bryce Niles Memorial Chapbook Award (see separate listings in Contests & Awards).

☑ CONCHO RIVER REVIEW

P.O. Box 10894, Angelo State University, San Angelo TX 76909. (915)942-2273. Fax: (915)942-2155. E-mail: jerry.bradley@lamar.edu. Website: www.angelo.edu/dept/english/publications/concho_river_review.htm. Established 1984. **Contact:** Jerry Bradley, poetry editor. Editor: Mary Ellen Hartje.

Magazines Needs *Concho River Review*, published twice/year, is a literary journal "particularly looking for poems with distinctive imagery and imaginative forms and rhythms. The first test of a poem will be its imagery. We prefer shorter poems; few long poems accepted." Has published poetry by Walt McDonald, Robert Cooperman, Mary Winters, William Wenthe, and William Jolliff. *Concho River Review* is 120-138 pages, digest-sized, professionally printed, flat-spined, with matte card cover. Receives 1,000 poems/year, accepts 60. Press run is 300 (200 subscribers, 10 libraries). Subscription: $14. Sample: $5.

How to Contact Submit 3-5 poems at a time. No simultaneous submissions. Accepts e-mail submissions (as attachment in Word). "No reply without SASE or e-mail address. No handwritten manuscripts accepted." Responds in 2-3 months. Pays 1 contributor's copy. Acquires first rights.

Tips "We're always looking for good, strong work—from well-known poets and those who have never been published before."

$ ✍ CONFRONTATION MAGAZINE

English Dept., C.W. Post Campus, Long Island University, 720 Northern Blvd., Brookville NY 11548-1300. (516)299-2720. Fax: (516)299-2735. E-mail: martin.tucker@liu.edu (inquiries only). Website: www.liu.edu/confrontation. Established 1968. **Contact:** Belinda Kremer, poetry editor. Editor-in-Chief: Martin Tucker.

Magazines Needs *Confrontation Magazine*, published semiannually, is interested "in all forms. Our only criterion is high literary merit. We think of our audience as an educated, lay group of intelligent readers. We prefer lyric poems." Does not want "sentimental verse." Considers poetry by children and teens. Has published poetry by David Ray, T. Alan Broughton, David Ignatow, Philip Appleman, Jane Mayhall, and Joseph Brodsky. *Confrontation* is about 300 pages, digest-sized, professionally printed, flat-spined. Receives about 1,200 submissions/year, accepts about 150. Circulation is 2,000. Subscription: $10/year. Sample: $3.

How to Contact Submit no more than 10 pages of poetry at a time. Lines/poem: "length generally should be kept to 2 pages." No previously published poems. "Prefer single submissions. Clear copy." No e-mail submissions; postal submissions only. Reads submissions September-May. "Do not submit mss June through August." Publishes theme issues. Upcoming themes available for SASE. Guidelines available on Web site. Responds in 2 months. Sometimes sends prepublication galleys. Pays $5-50 and 1 contributor's copy with discount available on additional copies. Staff reviews books of poetry. Send materials for review consideration.

Additional Information Occasionally publishes "book" issues or "anthologies." Most recent book is *Plenty of Exits: New and Selected Poems* by Martin Tucker, a collection of narrative, lyrical, and humorous poems.

Tips "We want serious poetry, which may be humorous and light-hearted on the surface."

✍ CONNECTICUT REVIEW

Southern Connecticut State University, 501 Crescent St., New Haven CT 06515. (203)392-6737. Fax: (203)392-5748. E-mail: ctreview@southernct.edu (inquiries only). Established 1968. **Contact:** Vivian Shipley, editor.

•Poetry published in *Connecticut Review* has been included in *The Best American Poetry* and *The Pushcart Prize* anthologies; has received special recognition for Literary Excellence from Public Radio's series *The Poet and the Poem*; and has won the Phoenix Award for Significant Editorial Achievement from the Council of Editors of Learned Journals (CELJ).

Magazines Needs *Connecticut Review*, published semiannually, contains essays, poetry, articles, fiction, b&w photographs, and color artwork. Has published poetry by Jack Bedell, Colette Inez, Maxine Kumin, Tony Fusco, Dana Gioia, and Marilyn Nelson. *Connecticut Review* is 208 pages, digest-sized, offset-printed, perfect-bound, with glossy 4-color cover. Receives about 2,500 poems/year, accepts about 5%. Press run is 3,000; 1,000 distributed free to Connecticut State libraries and high schools. Sample: $8. Make checks payable to Connecticut State University.

How to Contact Submit 3-5 typed poems at a time. Accepts submissions by postal mail only. Name, address, and phone number in the upper left corner of each page. Include SASE for reply only. Guidelines available for SASE. Pays 2 contributor's copies. Acquires first or one-time rights.

✍ CONNECTICUT RIVER REVIEW

53 Pearl Street, New Haven, CT 06511. Website: http://ct-poetry-society.org/publications.htm. Established 1978. **Contact:** Tony Fusco, editor.

Magazines Needs *Connecticut River Review*, published annually in July or August by the Connecticut Poetry Society, prints "original, honest, diverse, vital, well-crafted poetry." Wants "any form, any subject. Translations and long poems welcome." Has published poetry by Marilyn Nelson, Jack Bedell, Maria Mazziotti Gillan, and Vivian Shipley. *Connecticut River Review* is digest-sized, attractively printed, perfect-bound. Receives about 2,000 submissions/year, accepts about 100. Press run is about 300. Membership: $25 per year; includes *Connecticut River Review* and *Long River Run*, a members-only magazine.

How to Contact Submit no more than 3-5 poems at a time. Considers simultaneous submissions if notified of acceptance elsewhere; no previously published poems. Cover letter is preferred. Include bio. "Complete contact information typed in upper right corner; SASE required." Reads submissions October 1-April 15. Guidelines available for SASE or on Web site. Responds in up to 8 weeks. Pays 1 contributor's copy. "Poet retains copyright."

Tips "Read as much good poetry as you can before you write."

▣ ◪ CONTE, AN ONLINE JOURNAL OF NARRATIVE WRITING

E-mail: poetry@conteonline.net. Website: http://www.conteonline.net. Established 2005. **Contact:** Adam Tavel, poetry editor.

Magazines Needs *Conte, an Online Journal of Narrative Writing*, published semiannually online, prints "narrative writing of the highest quality. Writing that displays some degree of familiarity with our journal is likely to attract our attention, so make sure your work has a narrative bent." Has published poetry by Laura McCullough, R.T. Castleberry, Ann Iverson, Paul Hostovsky, Robin Greene, and Lyn Lifshin. Receives about 1,500 poems/year, accepts about 24. Number of unique visitors: approximately 1,000/month.

How to Contact Submit up to 3 poems at a time. "Query before sending poems over 100 lines in length." Considers simultaneous submissions ("please state clearly in your cover letter that your work is under consideration elsewhere and notify us immediately if it is accepted by another publication"); does not accept previously published poems (considers poetry posted on a public Web site/blog/forum and poetry posted on a private, password-protected forum as published). Accepts e-mail submissions (pasted into body of message); no fax or disk submissions. Cover letter is preferred. "Here at *Conte*, it is obvious when a writer is unfamiliar with our narrative mission, because he/she will rave about our 'avant-garde style' or 'embrace of the experimental.' Be aware of your own aesthetic leanings and send work to publications that are a snug fit. Cover letters are optional for some magazines, but we like to know a little about our submitters. The type of things you should probably include are: 1) how you learned about our journal; 2) a few places you have been published previously, if at all; and 3) whether or not you are sending a simultaneous submission." Reads submissions year round. Time between acceptance and publication is typically 2-4 months. "Since *Conte* is a small journal, it is truly a labor of love for our 2 editors. While we occasionally share work with one another during the screening process, primarily we rely on our respective expertise in poetry and prose when making editorial selections. Ultimately, a good poem is fresh and engaging from its very first line, so the chief responsibility for any poetry editor is to sift through cliché and mediocrity to share the best submitted work with the world." Sometimes comments on rejected poems. Sometimes publishes theme issues. Upcoming themes and guidelines available on Web site. Responds in 3 months. Sometimes sends prepublication galleys. Acquires one-time rights. Rights revert to poets upon publication.

$ ◪ ◎ CONTEMPORARY HAIBUN

(Specialized: haibun, haiga), P.O. Box 2461, Winchester VA 22604-1661. (540)722-2156. E-mail: jim.kacian@redmoonpress.com (inquires only). Website: www.redmoonpress.com. Established 1999 (as American Haibun & Haiga). **Contact:** Jim Kacian, editor/publisher.

Magazines Needs *contemporary haibun*, published annually in April, is the first Western journal dedicated to haibun and haiga. Considers poetry by children and teens. Has published poetry by Hortensia Anderson, Judson Evans, Bob Lucky, and Jeffery Woodward. *contemporary haibun* is 128 pages, digest-sized, offset-printed on quality paper, with 4-color heavy-stock cover. Receives several hundred submissions/year, accepts about 5%. Print run is 1,000. Subscription: $16.95 plus $4 p&h. Sample available for SASE or by e-mail.

How to Contact Submit up to 3 haibun or haiga at a time. Considers previously published poems. Accepts submissions online at www.poetrylives.com/cho/ as well as disk and postal submissions. Include SASE for postal submissions. Time between acceptance and publication varies according to time of submission. Poems are circulated to an editorial board. "Only haibun and haiga will be considered. If you are unfamiliar with the form, consult *Journey to the Interior*, edited by Bruce Ross, *contemporary haibun online* (at www.redmoonpress.com), or previous issues of *contemporary haibun*, for samples and some discussion." Guidelines available in magazine, for SASE, by e-mail, or on Web site. Pays $1/page. Acquires first North American serial rights.

Also Offers Publishes *The Red Moon Anthology*, "an annual volume of the finest English-language haiku and related work published anywhere in the world." (See separate listing in this section.)

Tips "It is best if you familiarize yourself with what is happening in the genre (and its close relatives) today before submitting. We strive to give all the work we publish plenty of space in which to resonate, and to provide a forum where the best of today's practitioners can be published with dignity and prestige."

⋈ ▣ $ ☯ CONTRARY

3114 S. Wallace St., Suite 2, Chicago IL 60616-3299. E-mail: chicago@contrarymagazine.com. Website: www.contrarymagazine.com. **Contact:** Jeff McMahon, editor Member: CLMP.

Magazines Needs *Contrary*, published quarterly online, contains "fiction, poetry, literary commentary, and prefers work that combines the virtues of all those categories. Founded at the University of Chicago, it now operates independently and not-for-profit on the South Side of Chicago. We like work that is not only contrary in content, but contrary in its evasion of the expectations established by its genre. Our fiction defies traditional story form. For example, a story may bring us to closure without ever delivering an ending. We don't insist on the ending, but we do insiste on the closure. And we value fiction as poetic as any poem. We look especially for plurality or meaning, for dual reverberation or beauty and concern. *Contrary's* poetry in particular often mimics the effects of fiction or commentary. We find ourselves enamored of prose poems because they are naturally ambiguous about form — they tug overtly on the forces of narrative — but prose poems remain the minority of all the poetic forms we publish."

How to Contact Submit no more than 3 poems per issue. Considers simultaneous submissions; no previously published poems. Accepts submissions through online form only. Reads submissions year round. See Web site for submission deadlines per issue. Often comments on rejected poems. Guidelines on Web site. $20 per byline, $60 for featured work. "Upon acceptance, *Contrary* acquires the following rights: 1) exclusive rights for the three-month period that the accepted work appears in the current issue of *Contrary* magazine, 2) the right to permanent inclusion of the work in *Contrary's* electronic archive, and 3) the right to reproduce the work in print and electronic collections of our content. After the current issue expires, the author is free to seek republication elsewhere, but *Contrary* must be credited upon republication."

☑ CONVERGENCE

E-mail: clinville@csus.edu. Website: www.convergence-journal.com. Established 2003. **Contact:** Cynthia Linville, managing editor.

Magazines Needs *Convergence*, published quarterly online, seeks "to unify the literary and visual arts and draw new interpretations of the written word by pairing poems and flash fiction with complementary art. We are open to many different styles, but we do not often publish formal verse. Read a couple of issues to get a sense of what we like; namely, well-crafted work with fresh images and a strong voice." Does not want "poetry with trite, unoriginal language or unfinished work." Has published poetry by Lola Haskins, Grace Cavalieri, Molly Fisk, and Renato Rosaldo. Receives about 800 poems/year, accepts about 10 per issue plus monthly selections for "Editor's Choice." Has about 200 online subscribers.

How to Contact Submit up to 5 poems at a time. Lines/poem: 60 maximum. No simultaneous submissions. Accepts e-mail submissions only. Reads submissions year round. Time between acceptance and publication is 1-2 months. Poems are circulated to an editorial board. Sometimes comments on rejected poems. Guidelines available on website. Responds in 6 months. No payment. Acquires first rights.

ℕ ▣ ☑ THE CORTLAND REVIEW

A LITERARY JOURNAL, (Specialized: poetry from prisoners only), P.O. Box 1234, New York NY 10276. Established 2001. Editor: K. Adams. 55 W. 26 St. Apt 32G, New York NY 10010. (678)428-1323. Fax: (770)956-0850. E-mail: tcr@cortlandreview.com. Website: www.cortlandreview.com. Established 1997 **Contact:** Ginger Murchison, editor.

• Poem published in the *Best American Poetry* in 2007.

Magazines Needs *The Cortland Review*, published 6 times/year, is "an online magazine publishing both established and up-and-coming writers from the print and online worlds. Using audio paired with text to complete the link between reader and poet, TCR provides regular and feature issues with poems and short fiction selected by staff as well as illustrious guest editors." Wants "free verse, formal, avant-garde." Does not want "inspirational, religious, political." Has published poetry by Billy Collins, Stephen Dunn, Seamus Heaney, Tony Hoagland, Sharon Olds, and Gerald Stern. Receives about 500 poems/year, accepts about 80-100. Receives about 82,000 unique visitors per month.

How to Contact Submit 3-5 poems at a time, up to 100 lines. No previously published poems or simultaneous submissions ("Previously published" work includes poetry posted on public Web sites/blogs/forums, and on private, password-protected forums). Poems should be submitted via online form accessible by menu on home page. Cover letter is required. "All work should be single-spaced. Do not use all caps, even for titles. Make sure entire submission is submitted in one online submission form." Submissions are closed June, July, and August. Poems are circulated to an editorial board or guest editor. Sometimes comments on rejected poems. Sometimes publishes theme issues by solicited contributors only. Guidelines available on Web site. Responds in 6-12 months. Prepublication galleys are available online. "TCR acquires the rights to publish and reproduce the author's material (text and audio) in Online, cassette, and CD/CD-ROM multimedia format." Reviews books of poetry. Book reviews should be queried.

☑ COTTONWOOD

(Specialized: Midwest emphasis), Cottonwood Magazine and Press, 1301 Jayhawk Blvd., Room 400, Kansas Union, University of Kansas, Lawrence KS 66045. (785)864-3777. E-mail: pwedge@ku.edu. Established 1965. **Contact:** Philip Wedge, poetry editor.

Magazines Needs *Cottonwood*, published semiannually, emphasizes the Midwest "but publishes the best poetry received regardless of region." Wants poems "on daily experience, perception; strong narrative or sensory impact, non-derivative." Does not want "'literary,' not 'academic.'" Has published poetry by Rita Dove, Virgil Suárez, Walt McDonald, and Luci Tapahonso. *Cottonwood* is 112 pages, digest-sized, printed from computer offset, flat-spined. Receives about 3,000 submissions/year, accepts about 20. Press run is 500-600. Single copy: $8.00. Sample: $5.

How to Contact Submit up to 5 pages of poetry at a time with SASE. Lines/poem: 60 maximum. No simultaneous or e-mailed submissions. Sometimes comments on rejected poems. Responds in up to 5 months. Pays 1 contributor's copy.

Additional Information Cottonwood Press "is auxiliary to *Cottonwood Magazine* and publishes material by authors in the region. **Material is usually solicited.**" Has published *Violence and Grace* by Michael L. Johnson and *Midwestern Buildings* by Victor Contoski.

Tips "Read the little magazines and send to ones you like."

Ⓝ ☑ THE COUNTRY DOG REVIEW

E-mail: countrydogreview@gmail.com. Website: www.countrydogreview.org. Established 2009. **Contact:** Danielle Sellers, editor.

Magazines Needs *The Country Dog Review*, published quarterly online, publishes "poetry, book reviews, and interviews with poets."Wants "poetry of the highest quality, not limited to style or region. Also accepts book reviews and interviews. Query first." Does not want "translations, fiction, nonfiction." Receives about 400 poems/year, accepts about 10%.

How to Contact Submit 3-5 poems at a time. No previously published poems or simultaneous submissions. Accepts e-mail submissions with attachment; no fax or disk submissions. Cover letter is required. Reads submissions year round. Submit seasonal poems 6 months in advance. Time between acceptance and publication is 1-4 months. Never comments on rejected poems. Sometimes publishes theme issues. Upcoming themes and guidelines available by e-mail and on Web site. Responds in 1-2 months. Sometimes sends prepublication galleys. Acquires first North American serial rights. Reviews books of poetry in 500 words, single-book format.

☑ CRAB CREEK REVIEW

7315 34th Ave NW, Seattle WA 98117. E-mail: editors@crabcreekreview.org. Website: www. crabcreekreview.org. Established 1983. **Contact:** Editors.

Magazines Needs *Crab Creek Review*, published biannually. Send us poetry, short fiction, and creative non-fiction that takes us somewhere unexpected, keeps us engaged, and stays with us beyond the initial reading. We appreciate lyrical and narrative forms of poetry, with a slight bias toward free verse. Translations are welcome—please submit with a copy of the poem in its original language, if possible." Has published poetry by Oliver de la Paz, Dorianne Laux, Greg Nicholl, and translations by Ilya Kaminsky and Matthew Zapruder. Fiction by karen Heuler and Daniel Homan. *Crab Creek Review* is an 80- to 120-page, perfect-bound paperback. Subscription: $15/year, $28/2 year. Sample: $6.

How to Contact "Please refer to our Web site as our contest/open submission periods have changed significantly." No e-mail submissions. Cover letter is preferred. Include SASE; "without one we will not consider your work." Responds in up to 6 months. Pays 2 contributor's copies.

$ ☑ CRAB ORCHARD REVIEW

Dept. of English, Mail Code 4503, Faner Hall 2380, Southern Illinois University Carbondale, 1000 Faner Dr., Carbondale IL 62901. Website: www.siu.edu/~crborchd. Established 1995. **Contact:** Allison Joseph, editor and poetry editor.

•*Crab Orchard Review* received a 2008 Literary Award and a 2008 Operating Grant from the Illinois Arts Council; poetry published in *Crab Orchard Review* has appeared in *The Best American Poetry* and *Beacon's Best of 1999* and *2000*.

Magazines Needs *Crab Orchard Review*, published semiannually in March and September, prints poetry, fiction, creative nonfiction, interviews, book reviews, and novel excerpts. Wants all styles and forms from traditional to experimental. Does not want greeting card verse; literary poetry only. Has published poetry by Luisa A. Igloria, Erinn Batykefer, Jim Daniels, Bryan Tso Jones. *Crab Orchard Review* is 280-300 pages, digest-sized, professionally printed, perfect-bound, with (usually) glossy card cover with color photos. Receives about 12,000 poems/year, accepts about 1%. Press run is 3,500; 100 exchanged with other journals; remainder in shelf sales. Subscription: $20. Sample: $12.

How to Contact Submit up to 5 poems at a time. Considers simultaneous submissions with notification; no previously published poems. Postal submissions only. Cover letter is preferred. "Indicate stanza breaks on poems of more than 1 page." Reads submissions April-November for Summer/Fall special theme issue, February-April for regular, non-thematic Winter/Spring issue. Time between acceptance and publication is 6 months to a year. "Poems that are under serious consideration are discussed and decided on by the managing editor and poetry editor." Seldom comments on rejected poems. Publishes theme issues. Upcoming themes available in magazine, for SASE, or on Web site. Guidelines available for SASE or on Web site. Responds in up to 9 months. Pays $20/page ($50 minimum), 2 contributor's copies, and 1 year's subscription. Acquires first North American serial rights. Staff reviews books of poetry in 500-700 words, single-book format. Send materials for review consideration to Jon C. Tribble, Managing Editor.

Contest/Award Offerings The Crab Orchard Series in Poetry Open Competition Awards, The Crab Orchard Series in Poetry First Book Award, and The Richard Peterson Poetry Prize (see separate listings in Contests & Awards).

Tips "Do not send any submissions via e-mail! Include SASE (#10 or larger) with all submissions and all queries—no postcards or small envelopes. Before you send work, check the Web site to see what issue we are currently reading submissions for. Being familiar with our reading schedule will help you submit appropriate work at the right time."

$ ☑ CRAZYHORSE

Dept. of English, College of Charleston, 66 George St., Charleston SC 29424. (843)953-7740. E-mail: crazyhorse@cofc.edu. Website: http://crazyhorse.cofc.edu. Established 1960. **Contact:** Garrett Doherty and Carol Ann Davis, poetry editors.

•Poetry published in *Crazyhorse* has appeared in *The Best American Poetry 2008* and *The Pushcart Prize*.

Magazines Needs *Crazyhorse*, published semiannually, prints fine fiction, poetry, and essays. "Send your best words our way. We like to print a mix of writing regardless of its form, genre, school, or politics. We're especially on the lookout for writing that doesn't fit the categories. Before sending, ask 'What's reckoned with that's important for other people to read?'" Has published poetry by David Wojahn, Mary Ruefle, Nance Van Winkle, Dean Young, Marvin Bell, and A.V. Christie. *Crazyhorse* is 160 pages, 8¾x8½, perfect-bound, with 4-color glossy cover. Receives about 15,000 poems/year. Circulation is 2,000. Single copy: $9; subscription: $16/year, $27 for 2 years, $36 for 3 years. Sample: $6. Make checks payable to *Crazyhorse*.

How to Contact Submit 3-5 poems at a time. Considers simultaneous submissions; no previously published poems. No fax, e-mail, or disk submissions. Cover letter is preferred. Reads submissions year round. "We read slower in summer." Time between acceptance and publication is 6 months. Seldom comments on rejected poems. Guidelines available in magazine, for SASE, by e-mail, or on Web site. Responds in 3 months. Sometimes sends prepublication galleys. Pays $20/page, 2 contributor's copies, and one-year subscription (2 issues). Acquires first North American serial rights.

Contest/Award Offerings The annual Lynda Hull Memorial Poetry Prize (see separate listing in Contests & Awards).

Tips "Feel strongly; then write."

$ □ ◎ CRICKET MAGAZINE

(Specialized: for young reades ages 9-14), Carus Publishing, 70 E. Lake St., Suite 300, Chicago IL 60601. Website: www.cricketmag.com. Established 1973. **Contact:** Submissions Editor.

Magazines Needs *CRICKET Magazine*, published monthly, is a literary magazine for young readers ages 9-14. Wants "serious and humorous poetry, nonsense rhymes." Does not want "forced or trite rhyming or imagery that doesn't hang together to create a unified whole." *CRICKET* is 64 pages, 8x10, saddle-stapled, with color cover. Circulation is 73,000. Subscription: $35.97/year (12 issues). Sample: $5; sample pages available on Web site.

How to Contact Submit no more than 5 poems at a time. Lines/poem: 50 (2 pages) maximum. Considers previously published poems. Put line count on each poem submitted. Include SASE. Guidelines available for SASE or on Web site. Responds in 6 months. Payment is up to $3/line on publication. Acquires North American publication rights for previously published poems; rights vary for unpublished poems.

Contest/Award Offerings Sponsors poetry contests for readers.

Tips "Our standards are very high, and we will accept only top-quality material. Before attempting to write for *CRICKET*, be sure to familiarize yourself with this age child and with the magazine itself."

☑ CRUCIBLE

Barton College, College Station, Wilson NC 27893. (252)399-6344. E-mail: tgrimes@barton.edu. Established 1964. **Contact:** Terrence L. Grimes, editor.

Magazines Needs *Crucible*, published annually in November, uses "poetry that demonstrates originality and integrity of craftsmanship as well as thought. Traditional metrical and rhyming poems are difficult to bring off in modern poetry. The best poetry is written out of deeply felt experience which has been crafted into pleasing form." Wants "free verse with attention paid particularly to image, line, stanza, and voice." Does not want "very long narratives, poetry that is forced." Has published poetry by Robert Grey, R.T. Smith, and Anthony S. Abbott. *Crucible* is 100 pages, digest-sized, professionally printed on high-quality paper, with matte card cover. Press run is 500. Sample: $7.

How to Contact Submit 5 poems at a time. No previously published poems or simultaneous submissions. "We require 3 unsigned copies of the manuscript and a short biography including a list of publications, in case we decide to publish the work." Reads submissions between Christmas and mid-April only. Responds in up to 4 months. Pays in contributor's copies.

Contest/Award Offerings The Sam Ragan Prize ($150), in honor of the former Poet Laureate of North Carolina, and other contests (prizes of $150 and $100). Guidelines available for SASE.

▦ ☑ CURRENT ACCOUNTS

16-18 Mill Lane, Horwich, Bolton BL6 6AT England. Phone/fax: (44)(120 4)669858. E-mail: bswscribe@aol.com. Website: http://www.freewebs.com/bankstreetwriters/currentaccounts. htm. Established 1994. **Contact:** Rod Riesco, editor.

Magazines Needs *Current Accounts*, published semiannually, prints poetry, fiction, and nonfiction by members of Bank Street Writers, and other contributors. Open to all types of poetry. "No requirements, although some space is reserved for members." Considers poetry by children and teens. Has published poetry by Pat Winslow, M.R. Peacocke, and Gerald England. *Current Accounts* is 52 pages, A5, photocopied, saddle-stapled, with card cover with b&w or color photo or artwork. Receives about 300 poems/year, accepts about 5%. Press run is 80; 8 distributed free to competition winners. Subscription: £6. Sample: £3. Make checks payable to Bank Street Writers (sterling checks only).

How to Contact Submit up to 6 poems at a time. Lines/poem: 100 maximum. No previously published poems (unpublished poems preferred) or simultaneous submissions. Prefers e-mail submissions (pasted into body of message). Cover letter is required. SAE or IRC essential for postal submissions. Time between acceptance and publication is 6 months. Seldom comments on rejected poems. Guidelines available for SASE, by fax, e-mail, or on Web site. Responds in 3 months. Pays 1 contributor's copy. Acquires first rights.

Also Offers Bank Street Writers meets once/month and offers workshops, guest speakers, and other activities. Write for details.

Tips "We like originality of ideas, images, and use of language. No inspirational or religious verse unless it's also good in poetic terms."

☐ CURRICULUM VITAE

Simpson Publications, P.O. Box 1082, Franklin PA 16323. E-mail: simpub@hotmail.com. Established 1995. **Contact:** Amy Dittman, managing editor.

Magazines Needs *Curriculum Vitae*, published semiannually in January and July, is "a zine where quality work is always welcome. We'd like to see more metrical work, especially more translations, and well-crafted narrative free verse is always welcome. We do not want to see rambling Bukowski-esque free verse or poetry that overly relies on sentimentality." *Curriculum Vitae* is 40 pages, digest-sized, photocopied, saddle-stapled, with 2-color cardstock cover. Receives about 500 poems/year, accepts about 75. Press run is 1,000. Subscription: $6 for 4 issues. Sample: $4.

How to Contact Submit 3 poems at a time. Considers previously published poems and simultaneous submissions. Cover letter is preferred ("to give us an idea of who you are"). "Submissions without a SASE cannot be acknowledged due to postage costs." Time between acceptance and publication is 8 months. Poetry is circulated among 3 board members. Often comments on rejected poems. Publishes theme issues. Guidelines available for SASE or by e-mail. Responds within 1 month. Pays 2 contributor's copies plus one-year subscription.

Additional Information "We're also interested in expanding our list of innovative side projects, books, graphic novels, chapbooks like *The Iowa Monster*, and the CV Poetry Postcard Project." Simpson Publications publishes about 5 chapbooks/year. Query with full manuscripts or well-thought-out plans with clips. Include SASE.

Also Offers "We are currently looking for poets who would like to be part of our Poetry Postcard series."

☑ CUTBANK

English Dept., University of Montana, Missoula MT 59812. (406)243-6156. E-mail: cutbank@ umontana.edu. Website: www.cutbankonline.org. Established 1973. **Contact:** Poetry Editor.

Magazines Needs *CutBank*, published semiannually, prints regional, national, and international poetry, prose, interviews, and artwork. Has published poetry by Richard Hugo, Carl Phillips, Sandra Alcosser, and Virgil Suarez. Press run is 1000. Single copy: $10; subscription: $12/2 issues. Sample: $4.

How to Contact Submit up to 5 poems at a time. Considers simultaneous submissions ("discouraged, but accepted with notification"). Poems should be single-spaced; include SASE. Reads submissions October 1-February 28 only. Accepts submissions December 1-February 28 for Patricia Goedicke Prize in Poetry, guest-judged Contest, $500 award plus publication. Guidelines available for SASE or on Web site. Responds in up to 4 months. Pays 2 contributor's copies. All rights return to author upon publication.

⬙ ☑ DALHOUSIE REVIEW

Dalhousie University, Halifax NS B3H 4R2 Canada. (902)494-2541. Fax: (902)494-3561. E-mail: dalhousie.review@dal.ca. Website: http://dalhousiereview.dal.ca. Established 1921. **Contact:** Anthony Stewart, editor.

Magazines Needs *Dalhousie Review*, published 3 times/year, is a journal of criticism publishing poetry and fiction. Considers poetry from both new and established writers. *Dalhousie Review* is 144 pages, digest-sized. Accepts about 5% of poems received. Press run is 500. Single copy: $15 CAD; subscription: $22.50 CAD, $28 USD. Make checks payable to *Dalhousie Review*.

How to Contact Lines/poem: 40. No previously published poems. No e-mail submissions except from outside North American (all other initial submissions are by means of hard copy only). "Submissions should be typed on plain white paper, double-spaced throughout. Spelling preferences are those of *The Canadian Oxford Dictionary*: catalogue, colour, program, travelling, theatre, and so on. Beyond this, writers of fiction and poetry are encouraged to follow whatever canons of usage might govern the particular story or poem in question, and to be inventive with language, ideas, and form. Please enclose a SASE (or SAE and IRC) for response." Reads submissions year round. Seldom comments on rejected poems. Occasionally publishes theme issues. Guidelines available for SAE and IRC or on Web site. Pays 2 contributor's copies and 10 off-prints.

◎ DARKLING MAGAZINE

(Specialized: poetry of a dark nature), Darkling Publications, 28780 318th Avenue, Colome SD 57528. (605)842-1402. E-mail: darkling@mitchelltelecom.net. Established 2005. **Contact:** James C. Van Oort, editor-in-chief.

Magazines Needs *Darkling Magazine*, published annually in June, is "primarily interested in poetry. All submissions should be dark in nature. Horror poetry is acceptable but not a requisite. All poetry submissions should help expose the darker side of man. Poetry of any form, style, etc., that is either dark or depressing will be strongly considered." Does not want "poetry aimed at making one feel good or experience the warm fuzzies. Such submissions will be trash-canned and will merit no response. 'Dark nature' does not mean whiny or overly murderous, and certainly being depressed does not make an artist's work dark. Pornography will not be considered and will merit no response. Profanity that is meritless or does not support the subject of any piece is unacceptable." Has published poems by Robert Cooperman, Kenneth DiMaggio, Cathy Porter and Simon Perchik, among others. Subscription: $15 with s&h. Make checks payable to Darkling Publications.

How to Contact Submit up to 8 poems at a time. Lines/poem: any length is acceptable, but "epic poems must be of exceptional quality." Considers previously published poems and simultaneous submissions. Will accept e-mail submissions; no disk submissions. Cover letter is required. Reads submissions October to April. Time between acceptance and publication is 2-3 months. Poems are circulated to an editorial board. Sometimes comments on rejected poems. Sometimes publishes theme issues. Guidelines available in magazine. Announces rejections and acceptance in April or May. Pays 1 contributor's copy. All rights revert to author upon publication.

Tips "We are always looking for new poets who have a voice we feel needs to be heard. Do not be afraid to ask questions. Our editorial staff will be very happy to communicate with you."

⋈ ▣ ☑ DEAD MULE SCHOOL OF SOUTHERN LITERATURE

E-mail: deadmule.poetry@gmail.com. Website: http://www.deadmule.com/. **Contact**: Helen Losse, poetry editor.

Magazines Needs "*The Dead Mule School of Southern Literature* wants stories. Good ones. Your writing? Hmmmmm. Write about sweat-dripping, Bible-thumping, pick-up driving, beer drinking rednecks. Chauvinistic, Mama-loving, hounddog-owning porch sitters - stereotypes we love to hate or hate to love. Heroes who drink sweet tea, eat Moon Pies, grits, and collards, frying in lard... lard pie, lard eggs, lard sandwiches. Lard. Mule skinners and mud runners. The esoteric, the strange, the truly captivating story will make it onto our pages. Be it about folks who are uncouth, semi-literate, tobacco chewing adolescents, or PhDs, Scholars, Scientists, Artists, Inventors, and Entrepreneurs. Write about brilliant, kind, thoughtful folks who will help you in your time of need or spit on your grandma. The South contains them all. There's no New South, there is only The South."

How to Contact Submit 1-4 Poems at a time. No previously published poems or simultaneous submissions. Submit by e-mail, "along with Southern Legitimacy Statement with your submission. *The Dead Mule* does not publish standard bios." Reads submissions year round. Guidelines found on Web site. "Submission to and acceptance by *Dead Mule* grants us first electronic and indefinite archive rights. All other rights revert to the author upon publication. Please credit *Dead Mule* as the first publisher if you reprint elsewhere; we like seeing our name in print, too."

☑ THE DERONDA REVIEW

P.O. Box 55164, Madison WI 53705. E-mail: derondareview@att.net (US), maber4kids@yahoo.com (Israel). Website: www.pointandcircumference.com. Established 1995. **Contact:** Esther Cameron, editor. Co-Editor for Israel: Mindy Aber Barad, P.O.B. 1299, Efrat 90435.

Magazines Needs *The Deronda Review*, published semiannually, seeks to "promote a literature of introspection, dialogue, and social concern." Wants "poetry of beauty and integrity with emotional and intellectual depth, commitment to subject matter as well as language, and the courage to ignore fashion. Welcome: well-crafted formal verse, social comment (including satire), love poems, philosophical/religious poems. *The Deronda Review* has a standing interest in work that sees Judaism as a source of values and/or reflects on the current situation of Israel and of Western civilization. Open, in principle, to writers of all ages." Has published poetry by Yakov Azriel, Ruth Blumert, Ida Fasel, Constance Rowell Mastores, Richard Moore, and Marc Widershien. *The Deronda Review* is 28-32 pages, magazine-sized, photocopied, saddle-stapled, with cardstock cover. Press run is 350. Single copy: $6; subscription: $12.

How to Contact Submit 3-5 poems at a time. Considers simultaneous submissions and previously published poems "on rare occasions." Cover letter is unnecessary. "Do include SASE with sufficient postage to return all manuscripts or with 'Reply Only" clearly indicated. First-time contributors in the U.S. are requested to submit by surface mail. Poets whose work is accepted will be asked for titles of books available, to be published in the magazine." Time between acceptance and publication is up to 1 year. Often comments on rejected poems. Does not offer guidelines because "the tradition is the only 'guideline.' We do encourage contributors to write for a sample." Responds in up to 4 months; "if longer, please query by e-mail." Pays 2 contributor's copies. Acquires first rights.

Additional Information *The Deronda Review* publishes the addresses of poets who would welcome correspondence. "Poets can also submit longer selections of work for publication on the 'Point and Circumference' Web site." Current projects include a blog that will post longer works, poems as they are accepted by the magazine, correspondence, etc. This should be launched by August 2009; check the website for updates.

Tips "The poem should speak to the ear and to the understanding, and it should be understood that understanding has social consequences. Like all our social functioning, poetry today suffers from a loss of community, which translates into a lack of real intimacy with the reader. Poets can work against this trend by remaining in touch with the poetry of past generations, by forming relationships in which poetry can be employed as the language of friendship, and by at least contemplating the concept of covenant. Publication should be an afterthought."

▣ ☑ DIAGRAM

c/o Ander Monson, Dept. of English, P.O. Box 210067, University of Arizona, Tucson AZ 85721-0067. E-mail: editor@thediagram.com. Website: www.thediagram.com. Established 2000. **Contact:** Ander Monson, editor. Member: CLMP.

- •Work appearing in *DIAGRAM* has been reprinted on the Poetry Daily and Verse Daily Web sites.

Magazines Needs *DIAGRAM*, published semimonthly online, prints "poetry, prose, and schematic (found or created), plus nonfiction, art, and sound. We're especially interested in unusual forms and structures, and work that blurs genre boundaries." Does not want light verse. Has published poetry by Arielle Greenberg, Jason Bredle, Lia Purpura, GC Waldrep, Lucy Corin, Kellie Wells, and Medbh McGuckian. Receives about 1,000 poems/year, accepts about 5%. Number of unique visitors:1,500/day.

How to Contact Submit 3-6 poems at a time. Lines/poem: no limit. Considers simultaneous submissions; no previously published poems. Electronic submissions accepted through submissions manager; no e-mail, disk, or fax submissions. Electronic submissions MUCH preferred; print submissions must include SASE." Cover letter is preferred. Reads submissions year round. Time between acceptance and publication is 1-10 months. Poems are circulated to an editorial board. Sometimes comments on rejected poems. Sometimes publishes theme issues. Guidelines available on website. Responds in 1-3 months. Always sends prepublication galleys. Acquires first rights and first North American serial rights. Rights revert to poet upon publication. Reviews books/chapbooks of poetry in 500-1,500 words, single- or multi-book format. Send materials for review consideration to Aaron Welborn, reviews editor.

Additional Information *DIAGRAM* also publishes periodic perfect-bound print anthologies.

Contest/Award Offerings Sponsors the annual *DIAGRAM*/Michigan Press Chapbook Contest (see separate listing in Contests & Awards).

☑ ◎ DIAL BOOKS FOR YOUNG READERS

(Specialized: poetry for children/teens), 345 Hudson St., New York NY 10014. Website: www. penguin.com. **Contact:** Submissions.

How to Contact "Submit entire picture book manuscripts, or the first 3 chapters of longer works. Please include a cover letter with brief bio and publication credits." Considers simultaneous submissions; no previously published poems. "Please note that, **unless interested in publishing them, Dial will not respond to unsolicited submissions.** Please do not include a self-addressed, stamped envelope with your submission. If Dial is interested, you can expect a reply from us within 4 months." Payment varies.

▣ ❑ ◎ DIAMOND DUST E-ZINE

(Specialized: poetry for/by teens; Christian; inspirational), E-mail: DiamondEditor@yahoo.com. Website: www.diamonddustmagazine.webs.com. Established 2005. **Contact:** Laura and Stephanie Rutlind, co-editors.

Magazines Needs *Diamond Dust E-zine*, published quarterly online, is "a magazine for teens and adults. Our goal is to inspire our readers in their Christian walk." Wants "poetry, short fiction, articles, book and music reviews, and fillers. Poetry of all types and all topics is considered. Submissions are not required to be religious, but we ask that they include good morals and clean content. 'Inspirational' is key." Does not want "to see anything that does not have clean content or high morals, or anything that is not inspirational." Considers poetry by teens. "Teens are encouraged to submit their work, but they must include their age and name or pen name." Accepts 20 poems/year. Available for free online.

How to Contact Submit 3 poems at a time. Lines/poem: less than 30. Considers previously published poems. Requires e-mail submissions (pasted into body of e-mail). Cover letter is required. "Tell us who you are and what you write. Include bio. If you're a teen, please include your age." Reads submissions year round. Submit seasonal poems 4 months in advance. Usually publishes theme issues. Guidelines and themes available by e-mail or on Web site. Responds within 2 months. No payment, but will include an author bio and contact links on Web site. "We acquire one-time electronic rights. All rights are given back to the author after publication. All pieces remain on our Web site for 2 issues and then they are deleted."

Tips "We love to work with beginning writers, so take a look at our current issue online. If you follow our guidelines and themes list, your submission has a good chance of achieving publication."

☑ ◎ JAMES DICKEY NEWSLETTER

(Specialized: life & works of James Dickey), Dept. of English, University of South Carolina, Columbia SC 29208. (803)777-4203. Fax: (803)777-9064. E-mail: tcompton@mailbox.sc.edu. Website: www.jamesdickey.org. Established 1984 (newsletter), 1990 (society). **Contact:** Thorne Compton, editor.

Magazines Needs *James Dickey Newsletter*, published semiannually in the spring and fall by the James Dickey Society, is "devoted to critical articles/studies of James Dickey's works/biography and bibliography." Publishes "a few poems of high quality. No poems lacking form, meter, or grammatical correctness." Has published poetry by Henry Taylor, Fred Chappell, George Garrett, and Dave Smith. *James Dickey Newsletter* is 50 pages, 8½X5½, neatly offset (back and front), saddle-stitched, with card back-cover. Single copy: $8; subscription: $12/year for individuals (includes membership in the James Dickey Society), $14 for U.S. institutions, $15.50 for foreign institutions.

How to Contact Accepts fax and e-mail (pasted into body of message/as attachment) submissions. "However, if poet wants written comments/suggestions line by line, send manuscript by postal mail with SASE." Cover letter is required. "Contributors should follow MLA style and standard manuscript format, sending one copy, double-spaced." Guidelines available in magazine or on Web site. Pays 2 contributor's copies. Acquires first rights. Reviews "only works on Dickey or that include Dickey."

Also Offers The James Dickey Society is devoted to discussions, dissemination, and interpretive scholarship and research concerning the works of James Dickey. Additional information available on Web site.

Tips "Consult issues [of newsletter] and guidelines [before submitting]."

▣ ☑ DIRTY NAPKIN, THE

E-mail: Jeremy@dirtynapkin.com. Website: www.dirtynapkin.com. Established 2007. **Contact:** Jeremy C. Ellis, managing director.

Magazines Needs "Have you ever felt the urgency to write while you were out, at a restaurant, say, and scribbled a thought down on a napkin or the closest thing you could find? Have you ever told your friends to 'hang on a sec' until you finished that thought? As writers, we do not know when the muse will slap us silly. Luckily, there are many napkins filling the world waiting for us to dirty them. The *Dirty Napkin*, published quarterly online, seeks to publish the best poetry, fiction, and letters in four issues a year. What are the best poems, stories, and letters, you ask? You tell us. The *Dirty Napkin* acknowledges that writing cannot be separate from the voice, breath, and the personality of the author; that should a piece of writing be separated from this literal voice, much power will be lost. Therefore, the *Dirty Napkin* seeks to include voice by having each author read their work online." Wants "any length and style, though the shorter amount of time it takes to cripple us with your brilliance, the better." Does not want "unfinished or undeveloped note taking." Has published poetry by Alicia Ostriker, Jane Mead, F.D. Reeve, Gerry LaFemina, Paula McLain, John Hoppenthaler. Single copy: $20 for print on demand, subscription $20 (includes access to all author recordings, discounts on special events, one free submission to Gerald Stern Poetry Prize, and much more).

How to Contact Submit 3 poems at a time. Accepts e-mail submissions (through online form); no fax or disk submissions. Cover letter is preferred. Reads submissions year round. Time between acceptance and publication is 2 months. Poems are circulated to an editorial board. Sometimes comments on rejected poems. Sometimes publishes theme issues. Upcoming themes and guidelines available on website. Responds in 1 month. Acquires first North American serial and electronic rights. Rights revert to poets upon publication.

Contest/Award Offerings The Gerald Stern Poetry Prize, offered annually, offers a 1st prize of $250 and a book chosen by Gerald Stern. Submit 4-8 poems. Wants "poems that show in Gerald's own words, 'courage, audacity, originality, humility, intelligence, and honesty.'" Guidelines available in magazine and on website. **Entry fee**: $5 and **Deadline**: March 1.

Also Offers "Each issue will feature one writer on its cover. The piece we like the best out of the pool of accepted writers wins the coveted cover. There are no entry fees or application materials other than the regular submission of your manuscript. If you win the *Cover Prize*, we will ask that you handwrite your piece on a napkin of your choosing. Your work will also appear typed inside."

☑ DI-VÊRSÉ-CITY

P.O. Box 41224, Austin TX 78704. E-mail: aipfdirector@gmail.com. Website: www.aipf.org. Established 1993. **Contact:** Susan Stockton.

Magazines Needs *di-veßrsé-city*, published annually in April, seeks "eclectic, well-crafted poems that touch not only the heart, but also the mind. Surprise us!" *di-veßrsé-city* is about 100 pages, digest-sized, professionally printed, perfect-bound, with glossy cardstock cover with original art. Receives about 600 poems/year, accepts about 15%. Make checks payable to Austin International Poetry Festival.

How to Contact Submit 3 poems at a time. Lines/poem: 48 maximum. No previously published poems or simultaneous submissions. Poets use the online submission form. "Follow Web site instructions carefully." Reads submissions December-February. Submit seasonal poems by February 1. Poems are circulated to an editorial board. Never comments on rejected poems. To submit, poets must register online at www.aipf.org and pay festival registration fee (see Web site). "You do not have to attend the festival to have a poem in *di-veßrsé-city*, but you must pay the fee." Guidelines available on Web site. Acquires first rights. Rights revert to poet upon publication.

Contest/Award Offerings Sponsors the annual Christina Sergeyevna Award. Offers cash prizes. **Entry fee:** all poems accepted for *di-veßrsé-city* are eligible. **Deadline:** February 1. Uses outside judge.

▣ ☑ DMQ REVIEW

E-mail: editors@dmqreview.com. Website: www.dmqreview.com. **Contact:** Sally Ashton, editor-in-chief.

Magazines Needs *DMQ Review*, published quarterly online, is "a quality magazine of poetry presented with visual art." Wants "finely crafted poetry that represents the diversity of contemporary poetry." Has published poetry by David Lehman, Ellen Bass, Amy Gerstler, Bob Hicok, Ilya Kaminsky, and Jane Hirshfield. Receives about 3,000-5,000 poems/year, accepts about 1%.

How to Contact Submit up to 3 poems at a time ("no more than once per quarter"). Considers simultaneous submissions (with notifications only); no previously published poems. Accepts e-mail submissions (pasted into body of message; no attachments will be read) only. "Please read and follow complete submission guidelines on our Web site." Reads submissions year round. Time between acceptance and publication is 1-3 months. Poems are circulated to an editorial board. Never comments on rejected poems. Responds within 3 months. Acquires first rights.

Additional Information Nominates for the Pushcart Prize. "We also consider submissions of visual art, which we publish with the poems in the magazine, with links to the artists' Web sites."

Tips "Read recent issues of *DMQ Review* before submitting, follow our guidelines, and send your best work."

☑ ◎ DOUBLE ROOM: A JOURNAL OF PROSE POETRY AND FLASH FICTION

E-mail: double_room@hotmail.com. Website: www.webdelsol.com/Double_Room. Established 2002. **Contact:** Mark Tursi and Peter Conners, co-editors. Web Designer and Associate Editor: Cactus May. Contributing Editors: Joyelle McSweeney and Jamey Dunham. Publisher: Michael Neff, Web del Sol.

Magazines Needs *Double Room: A Journal of Prose Poetry and Flash Fiction*, published semiannually online, is devoted entirely to the publication and discussion of prose poetry and flash fiction. Each issue also features contemporary artwork, reviews, interviews, and special features. Has published poetry by Cole Swensen, Rosmarie Waldrop, Ray Gonzalez, Sean Thomas Dougherty, Holly Iglesias, and Christopher Kennedy.

How to Contact Submit no more than 3 prose poems at a time. Considers simultaneous submissions ("but please notify us immediately if your work has been accepted elsewhere"). Accepts e-mail submissions (as attachment in MS Word or RTF; send all work as single attachment). "Write your last name in your subject line." Reads only during announced reading periods. Guidelines available on website. Acquires first North American serial rights and/or Electronic Rights. Reviews books/chapbooks of prose poetry and flash fiction. Query first by e-mail.

Tips "In addition to publishing the pp/ff forms, *Double Room* seeks to push them to the forefront of literary consideration by offering a Discussion On The Forms section in which contributors are asked to comment on a question related to the genre. For this reason we are looking for writers who, in addition to writing these forms, are interested in briefly discussing various aspects of them."

▣ ◻ DOWN IN THE DIRT

Scars Publications, 829 Brian Court, Gurnee IL 60031. E-mail: alexrand@scars.tv. Website: http://scars.tv. Established 2000. **Contact:** Alexandria Rand, editor.

Magazines Needs *Down in the Dirt*, published monthly online, prints "good work that makes you think, that makes you feel like you've lived through a scene instead of merely read it." Also can consider poems. Does not want smut, rhyming poetry, or religious writing. Has published work by I.B. Rad, Pat Dixon,Mel Waldman, and Ken Dean. *Down in the Dirt* is published "electronically as well as in print, either on the Web or in e-book form (PDF file)." Sample: available on Web site.

How to Contact Lines/poem: any length is appreciated. Considers previously published poems and simultaneous submissions. Accepts e-mail submissions (vastly preferred to snail mail; pasted into body of message or as Microsoft Word .doc file attachment) and disk submissions (formatted for Macintosh). Guidelines available for SASE, by e-mail, or on Web site. No payment. "Currently, accepted writings get their own web page in the "writings" section at http://scars.tv, and samples of accepted writings are placed into an annual collection book Scars Publications produces."

Additional Information Also able to publish electronic chapbooks. Write for more information.

Contest/Award Offerings Scars Publications sponsors a contest "where accepted writing appears in a collection book. Write or e-mail (editor@scars.tv) for information."

Tips "The Web site is a more comprehensive view of what *Down in the Dirt* does. All the information is there."

▣ ◿ DROWN IN MY OWN FEARS

E-mail: karinabowman@gmail.com. Website: http://drowninmyownfears.angelfire.com. Established 2007. **Contact:** Chantal Hejduk, editor.

Magazines Needs *Drown In My Own Fears*, published quarterly online, "is a poetry journal about the human condition, therefore, we want poems reflecting that. Poems submitted should be about love, hate, pain, sorrow, etc. We don't want maudlin sentimentality, we want the depths of your very being. We want well-written, deeply conceived pieces of work. Anything that isn't about the human condition really isn't for us." Wants "all styles of poetry, as long as it's your best work." Does not want "syrupy sweet, gooey nonsense, religious rants, political grandstandings." Considers poetry by teens. Has published poetry by Kendall A. Bell, MK Chavez, Taylor Graham, Natalie Lorenzo, Ray Succre, and Corey Mesler. Receives about 300 poems/year, accepts about 10%.

How to Contact Submit 3-5 poems at a time. "We prefer short poems, but long ones are ok." Considers previously published poems; no simultaneous submissions. Accepts e-mail submissions (pasted into body of e-mail message); no fax or disk submissions. Cover letter is rquired. Include a brief bio with your submission. Reads submissions year round. Submit seasonal poems 3 months in advance. Time between acceptance and publication is 1-2 months. Never comments on rejected poems. Sometimes publishes theme issues. Upcoming themes and guidelines available on Web site. Responds in 2-4 weeks. Acquires first rights. Rights revert to poets upon publication.

Tips "Try different writing styles and don't limit your poetic view to one way of thinking. Read lots of different poets. Write on little pieces of paper when an idea or a line comes. If you can't finish a poem in one sitting, come back to it later. You might find more inspiration in a day or two. Always rewrite and find avenues to workshop your poems. Several sets of eyes can certainly give you invaluable advice. True poets write because they must."

⬛ ⬛ ☑ DRUNKEN BOAT

119 Main Street, Chester CT 06412. (860)526-3318. E-mail: editor@drunkenboat.com. Website: www.drunkenboat.com. Established 1999. **Contact:** Ravi Shankar, founding editor. Member: CLMP.

Magazines Needs *Drunken Boat*, published annually online, is a multimedia publication reaching an international audience with an extremely broad aesthetic. Considers poetry by teens. "We judge by quality, not age. However, most poetry we publish is written by published poets with training in creative writing. "Has published more than 500 poets, including Heather McHugh, Jane Hirshfield, Alfred Corn, Alice Fulton, Ron Silliman, and Roseanna Warren. Received about 3,000 poems/year, accepts about 5%.

How to Contact Submit up to 3 poems at a time.Considers simultaneous submissions. Accepts e-mail submissions; no fax or disk. Cover letter is preferred. "Due to the high number of poetry submissions, we limit submissions to 3 poems, in Word or .rtf format. "Reads submissions year round. Time between acceptance and publication is 6-12 months. "Readers have MFAs in poetry, pass work to managing editor, who winnows further and passes to founding editor. "Sometimes comments on rejected poems. Sometimes publishes theme issues. Guidelines on Web site. Responds in 2-8 weeks. Always sends prepublication galleys. Acquires one-time rights. "Unless reprinted something already published, *Drunken Boat* has exclusive electronic rights of the work in question. Work that appears in print needs to acknowledge prior publication in *Drunken Boat*. Also, *Drunken Boat* reserves the right to republish work in print or DVD format with the permission of author/artist. "Reviews books, chapbooks of poetry. Will consider reviews of any length. Send materials for review consideration to editor@drunkenboat.com.

Additional Information Drunken Boat Media will begin in 2009 to publish two titles/year, whether in print or multimedia. Pursuant to that we will have a first-book contest and will solicit manuscripts on occasion."

Tips "*Drunken Boat* publishes the best of more traditional publication alongside works of art endemic to the medium of the web. We recommend you read the past issues of the magazine to get a sense of what we publish. We are open to a range of styles, from experimental to formal, and are open to collaborations and other non-traditional works."

⬛ ☑ EARTHSHINE

PO Box 245, Hummelstown PA 17036.E-mail: poetry@ruminations.us. Website: www. ruminations.us. Established 2007. **Contact:** Sally Zaino and Julie Moffitt, poetry editors.

Magazines Needs *Earthshine*, published irregularly in print, and online, features poetry and 1-2 pieces of cover art per volume. "When the online journal is full, a printed volume is produced and offered for sale. Subscriptions will be available as the publication becomes regular. The voice of *Earthshine* is one of illumination, compassion, humanity, and reason. Please see submission guidelines Web page for updated information. Poems are the ultimate rumination, and if the world is to be saved, the poets will be needed; they are who see the connections between all things, and the patterns shared. We seek poetry of high literary quality which will generate its own light for our readers." Has published poetry by Rachel Barroso, Fredrik Zydek, Steven Klepetar, Mario Susko.

How to Contact Submit no more than 6 poems at a time. Considers previously published poems; no simultaneous submissions. (Considers poetry posted on a public Web site/blog/forum and poetry posted on a private, password-protected forum as published.) "We prefer poems that have not been published elsewhere, but occasionally make exceptions. If a work has been published elsewhere, including on a personal Web site, please include the publication history." Accepts e-mail submissions (pasted into body of message); no fax or disk submissions. Cover letter is preferred. "Please let us know where you heard about *Earthshine*. If submitting by mail, please include a SASE for reply only. Please do not send the only copy of your work." Reads submissions year round. Submit seasonal poems 1 month in advance. Time between acceptance and publication is" online publication is almost immediate, printed publication TBD." Sometimes comments on rejected poems. Never publishes theme issues. Guidelines available in magazine, for SASE, and on Web site. Responds in 1-2 months. Pays 1 contributor copy. Acquires first rights, one-time rights, electronic rights (publication rights include online publication and publication in 1 printed volume. Request first rights if poem is previously unpublished; one-time rights if poem has appeared elsewhere. Archive rights negotiated separately." Rights revert to poets upon publication.

Also Offers "The parent of *Earthshine* is also at Ruminations.us, and offers full editing and review services for a fee."

N ⊞ ▣ ☑ ECLECTICA

E-mail: editors@eclectica.org. Website: www.eclectica.org. Online magazine. "Eclectica is a quarterly World Wide Web journal devoted to showcasing the best writing on the Web, regardless of genre. 'Literary' and 'genre' work appear side-by-side in each issue, along with pieces that blur the distinctions between such categories. Pushcart Prize, National Poetry Series, and Pulitzer Prize winners, as well as Nebula Award nominees, have shared issues with previously unpublished authors."

Magazines Needs High quality work in any genre.Also publishes poetry.

How to Contact Accepts submissions by e-mail. "While we will consider simultaneous submissions, please be sure to let us know that they are simultaneous and keep us updated on their publication status." Guidelines available on Web site. Acquires first North American serial rights, electronic rights.

⬚ ☑ THE ECLECTIC MUSE

(Specialized: rhyme; neo-classicist revival), Suite 307, 6311 Gilbert Rd., Richmond BC V7C 3V7 Canada. (604)277-3864. E-mail: jrmbooks@hotmail.com. Website: www.thehypertexts.com. Established 1989. **Contact:** Joe M. Ruggier, publisher.

Magazines Needs *The Eclectic Muse*, published annually at Christmas, is devoted "to publishing all kinds of poetry (eclectic in style and taste) but specializing in rhyme- and neo-classicist revival." Does not want "bad work (stylistically bad or thematically offensive)." Has published poetry by Mary Keelan Meisel, John Laycock, Philip Higson, Roy Harrison, Michael Burch, and Ralph O. Cunningham. *The Eclectic Muse* is magazine-sized, digitally copied, saddle-stapled, with paper cover. The number of pages varies from year to year (32 minimum to 56 maximum). Receives about 300 poems/year, accepts about 15%. Press run is 200; distributed free to all contributing authors plus selected gift subscription recipients. Single copy: $8; subscription: $25. Make checks payable to Joe M. Ruggier.

How to Contact Submit no more than 5 poems at a time. Lines/poem: 60 maximum; "please consult if longer." Considers previously published poems and simultaneous submissions. Accepts e-mail submissions (preferred, as a single .doc or .rtf attachment containing all 5 poems) and disk submissions. "Send your submission by regular mail only if you have no access to a computer or you are computer illiterate. Typeset everything in Times New Roman 12 point. If your poetry features indents and special line spacing, please make sure you reproduce these features yourself in your data entry since it will not be possible for the editor to determine your intentions." Cover letter is preferred. "Include brief bio (100 words maximum) with your name, credentials (degrees, etc.), occupation and marital status, your most major publication credits only, and any hobbies or interests." Provide SASE plus clear e-mail and postal addresses for communication and for sending contributor's copy. Reads submissions year round. Time between acceptance and publication is 1 year. Poems are circulated to an editorial board. Sometimes comments on rejected poems. **"If authors wish to have a manuscript carefully assessed and edited, the fee is $250 USD; will respond within 8 weeks."** Guidelines available in magazine or on Web site. Responds in 2 months. Pays 2 contributor's copies. Reviews books/chapbooks of poetry and other magazines/journals in 900 words. Send materials for review consideration to Joe M. Ruggier, managing editor.

Also Offers "Look us up on www.thehypertexts.com, where myself and my services are listed (featured) permanently. The host of this splendid poetry Web site is my U.S. associate, Mr. Michael Burch. He features, on this site, most of the leading names in contemporary North America."

Tips "An author's style is really the only thing which belongs to him as an artist to manipulate for his own purposes as he pleases. Truths and feelings do not belong to him exclusively and may not be bent or manipulated for his own purposes as he pleases. We do not want bad work where the poet feels that the message matters but the style is bad (not good workmanship), nor do we wish to publish work which seems to us to distort and bend truths and human feelings far too much."

☑ ◎ EKPHRASIS

(Specialized: ekphrastic verse), Frith Press, P.O. Box 161236, Sacramento CA 95816-1236. E-mail: frithpress@aol.com (inquiries only). Website: www.hometown.aol.com/ekphrasis1. Established 1995 (Frith Press) and 1997 (Ekphrasis). **Contact:** Laverne Frith and Carol Frith, editors.

•Poems from *Ekphrasis* have been featured on *Poetry Daily*.

Magazines Needs *Ekphrasis*, published semiannually in March and September, is an "outlet for the growing body of poetry focusing on individual works from any artistic genre." Wants "poetry whose main content is based on individual works from any artistic genre. Poetry should transcend mere description. Open to all forms." Does not want "poetry without ekphrastic focus. No poorly crafted work. No archaic language." Has published poetry by Jeffrey Levine, Peter Meinke, David Hamilton, Barbara Lefcowitz, Molly McQuade, and Annie Boutelle. *Ekphrasis* is 40-50 pages, digest-sized, photocopied, saddle-stapled. Subscription: $12/year. Sample: $6. Make checks payable, in U.S. funds, to Laverne Frith.

How to Contact Submit 3-5 poems at a time. Considers previously published poems "infrequently, must be credited"; no simultaneous submissions. Accepts submissions by postal mail only. Cover letter is required, including short bio with representative credits and phone number. Include SASE. Time between acceptance and publication is up to 1 year. Seldom comments on rejected poems. Guidelines available for SASE or on Web site. Responds in 4 months. Pays 1 contributor's copy. Nominates for Pushcart Prize. Acquires first North American serial or one-time rights.

Additional Information Until further notice, Frith Press will publish **occasional chapbooks by invitation only**.

Contest/Award Offerings The Ekphrasis Prize, which awards $500, "is now being presented to the best poem published in Ekphrasis in each calendar year, as determined by the editors of the journal. There will be no contest. No reading fees will be required. The 2008 contest prize was awarded to Steven Latermilch (*Parting of the Yang-Guan Gate*)."

Tips "With the focus on ekphrastic verse, we are bringing attention to the interconnections between various artistic genres and dramatizing the importance and universality of language. Study in the humanities is essential background preparation for the understanding of these interrelations."

$ ☑ ELLIPSIS

Westminster College of Salt Lake City, 1840 South 1300 East, Salt Lake City UT 84105. (801)832-2321. E-mail: ellipsis@westminstercollege.edu (inquiries only). Website: www.westminstercollege.edu/ellipsis. Established 1967. **Contact:** Poetry Editor (rotating editors). Faculty Advisor: Natasha Sajé.

Magazines Needs *Ellipsis*, published annually in April, needs "good literary poetry, fiction, essays, plays, and visual art." Has published poetry by Allison Joseph, Molly McQuade, Virgil Suárez, Maurice Kilwein-Guevara, Richard Cecil, and Ron Carlson. *Ellipsis* is 120 pages, digest-sized, perfect-bound, with color cover. Accepts about 5% of submissions received. Press run is 2,000; most distributed free through college. Sample: $7.

How to Contact Submit 3-5 poems at a time. Accepts e-mail submissions. Considers simultaneous submissions if notified of acceptance elsewhere; no previously published poems. No fax or e-mail submissions; postal submissions only. One poem per page, with name and contact information on every page. Include SASE and brief bio. Reads submissions August 1-November 1. Responds in up to 8 months. Pays $10/poem, plus two contributor's copies.

Contest/Award Offerings All accepted poems are eligible for the Ellipsis Award, which includes a $100 prize. Past judges have included Jorie Graham, Sandra Cisneros, Phillip Levine, and Stanley Plumly.

☑ EMRYS JOURNAL

P.O. Box 8813, Greenville SC 29604. E-mail: lydia.dishman@gmail.com. Website: www.emrys.org. Established 1982. **Contact:** Poetry Editor. Editor: L.B. Dishman.

• **Will begin reading submissions again August 1, 2009.**

Magazines Needs *Emrys Journal*, published annually in May, prints "literary or narrative poetry of less than 36 lines. Rhyming needs to be oustanding to be considered." Has published poetry by Kristin Berkey-Abbott, Adriano Scopino, John Popielaski, J. Morris, and Terri McCord. *Emrys Journal* is up to 120 pages, digest-sized, handsomely printed, flat-spined. Press run is 400 (250 subscribers, 10 libraries). Sample: $12 and 7 X 10 SASE with 4 First-Class stamps.

How to Contact *No mss will be read until August 1, 2009. Submit up to 5 poems at a time (per author). No previously published poems or simultaneous submissions. Accepts e-mail submissions (as attachment). Include SASE. Reads submissions August 1-November 1 only; no mss will be read outside the reading period. Time between acceptance and publication is up to 8 months. Guidelines available for SASE or on Web site. Responds "by the end of the reading period." Pays 5 contributor's copies.*

Contest/Award Offerings Sponsors the annual Nancy Dew Taylor Award for excellence in the art of poetry. Offers $250 prize to the author of the best poem published in *Emrys Journal* that year.

☑ ENGLISH JOURNAL

Interdisciplinary Studies in Curriculum & Instruction, National-Louis University, Tampa, FL 33609. (941)629-0541. Fax: (941)629-0541. E-mail: EJPoetry@nl.edu (submissions); asullivan@nl.edu (inquiries). **Contact:** Anne McCrary Sullivan, poetry editor.

Magazines Needs *English Journal*, established 1912, published 6 times annually by The National Council of Teachers of English, is a professional education journal, circulation over 20,000. "Poetry submissions that respond to announced themes, either implicitly or explicitly, are encouraged. Themes are announced in every issue and at the NCTE **http://www.englishjournal.colostate.edu/issuetopics.htm.**Poems may be in any form or style, serious or humorous." English Journal accepts fewer than 10% of submissions.

How to Contact Submissions are accepted electronically only. "Send by email attachment, for blind review, up to 5 poems with only phone number and initials on the page. In your e-mail message, include 50-60 word biographical statement. In e-mail subject line, include theme for which you are submitting." No previously published poems or simultaneous submissions. Seldom comments on rejected poems. Responds in 2-3 months after deadline. Pays 2 contributor's copies.

☑ ◎ EPITOME

(Specialized: northeastern OH women writers only), Implosion Press, 4975 Comanche Trail, Stow OH 44224-1217. (330)836-7808. E-mail: epitomepoetry@aol.com. Website: http://epitomemag. com. Established 1984. **Contact:** Cheryl Townsend, poetry editor.

Magazines Needs *epitome* is a regional publication for and by northeastern OH women. Wants "poetry that addresses the power of women to overcome social obstacles and injustices; poetry that is not subserviant to anyone. Poetry that celebrates being a woman. Material should be straight from the gut, uncensored and real. Any length as long as it works. All subjects OK, providing there are no 'isms.' We publish **ONLY** northeastern Ohio women in our Poetry and Featured Artist sections." Does not want rhymed verse. Sample: $5. Make checks payable to Implosion Press.

How to Contact Submit 3-8 poems at a time. Lines/poem: prefers "shorter, to-the-point work." Considers previously published poems if noted as such (include when and where each poem was originally published). Accepts e-mail submissions (pasted into body of message). Appreciates "a cover letter that tells how the poet found out about our magazine." Include name and address on each page; SASE for reply/return. Time between acceptance and publication is generally 5 months. Guidelines available for SASE, by e-mail, or on Web site. Responds within 4 months. Acquires one-time rights. Reviews books of poetry. Send materials for review consideration.

Additional Information In addition to *epitome*, Implosion Press publishes chapbooks by northeastern OH women writers.

Tips "Know your market. Request guidelines and/or a sample copy."

$ ☑ EPOCH

251 Goldwin Smith Hall, Cornell University, Ithaca NY 14853. (607)255-3385. Website: www. arts.cornell.edu/english/epoch.html. Established 1947. **Contact:** Nancy Vieira Couto, poetry editor.

Magazines Needs *Epoch*, published 3 times/year, has a distinguished and long record of publishing exceptionally fine poetry and fiction. Has published poetry by Kevin Prufer, Peter Dale Scott, Martin Walls, Maxine Kumin, Heather McHugh, and D. James Smith. *Epoch* is 128 pages, digest-sized, professionally printed, perfect-bound, with glossy color cover. Accepts less than 1% of the many submissions received each year. Has 1,000 subscribers. Subscription: $11/year domestic, $15/year foreign. Sample: $5.

How to Contact No simultaneous submissions. Manuscripts not accompanied by SASE will be discarded unread. Reads submissions September 15-April 15. Responds in up to 10 weeks. Occasionally provides criticism on mss. Pays 3 contributor's copies and at least $10/page. "We pay more when we have more!" Acquires first serial rights.

Tips "Read the magazine."

▦ ☑ ◎ EUROPEAN JUDAISM

(Specialized: emphasis on European Jewish theology/philosophy/literature/history), Leo Baeck College, The Sternberg Centre, 80 East End Rd., London N3 2SY England. Website: www. berghahnbooks.com/journals/ej. Established 1966. **Contact:** Ruth Fainlight, poetry editor.

Magazines Needs *European Judaism*, published twice/year, is a "glossy, elegant magazine with emphasis on European Jewish theology/philosophy/literature/history, with some poetry in every issue. Poems should (preferably) be short and have some relevance to matters of Jewish interest." Has published poetry by Linda Pastan, Elaine Feinstein, Daniel Weissbort, and Dannie Abse. *European Judaism* is 110 pages, digest-sized, flat-spined. Press run is 950 (about 500 subscribers, over 100 libraries). Subscription: $45 individual, $20 student, $162 institution.

How to Contact Submit 3-4 poems at a time. Lines/poem: short poems preferred. "I prefer unpublished poems, but poems from published books are acceptable." Cover letter is required. "No material is read or returned if not accompanied by SASE (or SAE with IRCs). We cannot use American stamps." Pays 1 contributor's copy.

$ ☑ ◎ EVANGEL

(Specialized: Christian), Light and Life Communications, P.O. Box 535002, Indianapolis IN 46253-5002. Established 1897. **Contact:** J. Innes, editor.

Magazines Needs *Evangel*, published quarterly, is an adult Sunday school paper. "Devotional in nature, it lifts up Christ as the source of salvation and hope. The mission of *Evangel* is to increase the reader's understanding of the nature and character of God and the nature of a life lived for Christ. Material that fits this mission and isn't longer than one page will be considered." Does not want rhyming work. *Evangel* is 8 pages, 5½ × 8½, printed in 4-color, unbound. Accepts about 5% of poetry received. Press run is about 10,000. Subscription: $2.49/quarter (13 weeks). Sample: free for #10 SASE.

How to Contact Submit no more than 5 poems at a time. Considers simultaneous submissions. Cover letter is preferred. "Poetry must be typed on 8½x11 white paper. In the upper left-hand corner of each page, include your name, address, phone number, and social security number. In the upper right-hand corner of cover page, specify what rights you are offering. One-eighth of the way down the page, give the title. All subsequent material must be double-spaced, with one-inch margins." Submit seasonal poems 1 year in advance. Seldom comments on rejected poems. Guidelines available for #10 SASE. "Write 'guidelines request' on your envelope so we can sort it from the submissions." Responds in up to 2 months. Pays $10 plus 2 contributor's copies. Acquires one-time rights.

Tips "Poetry is used primarily as filler. Send for sample and guidelines to better understand what and who the audience is."

☑ THE EVANSVILLE REVIEW

1800 Lincoln Ave., Evansville IN 47722. Phone/fax: (812)488-1042. E-mail: evansvillereview@evansville.edu. Website: http://english.evansville.edu/EvansvilleReview.htm. Established 1989. **Contact:** Dominic Huether or Preston Frasch, poetry editors.

•Poetry published in *The Evansville Review* has been included in *The Best American Poetry* and *The Pushcart Prize*.

Magazines Needs *The Evansville Review*, published annually in April, prints "prose, poems, and drama of literary merit." Wants "anything of quality." No excessively experimental work; no erotica. Has published poetry by Joseph Brodsky, J.L. Borges, John Updike, Willis Barnstone, Rita Dove, and Vivian Shipley. *The Evansville Review* is 140-200 pages, digest-sized, perfect-bound, with art on cover. Receives about 2,000 poems/year, accepts about 2%. Press run is 1,500. Sample: $5.

How to Contact Submit 3-5 poems at a time. Considers previously published poems and simultaneous submissions. No fax or e-mail submissions; postal submissions only. Cover letter is required. Include brief bio. Manuscripts not returned without SASE. Reads submissions

September 1-December 1 only. Time between acceptance and publication is 3 months. Poems are circulated to an editorial board. Seldom comments on rejected poems. Guidelines available for SASE or on website. Responds within 3 months of the deadline. Pays 2 contributor's copies. Rights remain with poet.

Contest/Award Offerings The Willis Barnstone Translation Prize (see separate listing in Contests & Awards).

◎ EXIT 13

(Specialized: geography/travel), P.O. Box 423, Fanwood NJ 07023-1162. (908)889-5298. E-mail: exit13magazine@yahoo.com. Established 1987. **Contact:** Tom Plante, editor.

Magazines Needs *Exit 13*, published annually, uses poetry that is "short, to the point, with a sense of geography." Has published poetry by Paul Brooke, Ruth Moon Kempher, Sandy McCord, Sander Zulauf, Paul Sohar, and Charles Rammelkamp. *Exit 13* is about 76 pages. Press run is 300. Sample: $8.

How to Contact Considers simultaneous submissions and previously published poems. Accepts e-mail submissions (no attachments). Guidelines available in magazine or for SASE. Responds in 4 months. Pays 1 contributor's copy. Acquires one-time and possible anthology rights.

Tips "*Exit 13* looks for adventure, a living record of places we've experienced. Every state, region, country, and ecosystem is welcome. Write about what you know and have seen. Send a snapshot of an 'Exit 13' road sign and receive a free copy of the issue in which it appears."

▣ ☑ FAILBETTER.COM

2022 Grove Ave., Richmond VA 23220. E-mail: submissions@failbetter.com. Website: www.failbetter.com. Established 2000. **Contact:** Mary Donnelly and Christina Kallery, poetry editors. Publishers: Thom Didato and Andrew Day. Member: CLMP.

•Works published in *failbetter* have received recognition in various award anthologies including *Best American Poetry*, *The Pushcart Prize* and *Best of the Net*.

Magazines Needs *failbetter.com*, published online, seeks "that which is at once original and personal. When choosing work to submit, be certain that what you have created could only have come from you." Publishes translations and interviews with such poets as Paul Muldoon, Marie Ponsot, Mary Jo Salter, and Billy Collins. Has published poetry by J. Allyn Rosser, Terrance Hayes, Mary Donnely, and Thaddeus Rutkowski. Receives about 2,000 poetry submissions/year, accepts about 9-12. Publishes 3-4 poets/issue.

How to Contact Submit 4-6 poems at a time. Lines/poem: "we're not concerned with length—one good sentence may find a home here, as the bulk of mediocrity will not." Considers simultaneous submissions; no previously published poems. Encourages e-mail submissions (pasted into body of message). "Send to submissions@failbetter.com only! Please read and follow submission guidelines posted on Web site. All e-mail submissions should include title in header. All poetry submissions must be included in the body of your e-mail. Please do not send attached files." Also accepts postal submissions; "please note, however, any materials accepted for publication must ultimately be submitted in electronic format in order to appear on our site." Cover letter is preferred. Reads submissions year round. Time between acceptance and publication is 4 months minimum and upward. Poems are circulated to an editorial board. Often comments on rejected poems. "It's not unusual to ask poets to re-submit, and their subsequent submissions have been accepted." Guidelines available on Web site. Responds in up to 4 months to e-mail submissions; up to 6 months by regular mail. "We will not respond to any e-mail inquiry regarding receipt confirmation or status of any work under consideration." No payment. Acquires exclusive first-time Internet rights; works will also be archived online. All other rights, including opportunity to publish in traditional print form, revert to the poet.

Tips "With a readership of more than 60,000 per issue, *failbetter* is one of the Web's widely read literary magazines, offering exposure of poets' works to a much broader, worldwide audience than the typical print journal. For both established and emerging poets our advice remains the same: We strongly recommend that you not only read the previous issue, but also sign up on our e-mail list (subscribe@failbetter.com) to be notified of future publications."

☑ FAT TUESDAY

560 Manada Gap Rd., Grantville PA 17028. E-mail: lionelstevroid@yahoo.com. Website: http://groups.yahoo.com/group/FatTuesday. Established 1981. **Contact:** Lionel Stevroid, editor.

Magazines Needs *Fat Tuesday*, published irregularly, is "a Mardi Gras of literary, visual, and audio treats featuring voices, singing, shouting, sighing, and shining, expressing the relevant to irreverent." Wants "prose poems, poems of irreverence, gems from the gut. Particularly interested in hard-hitting 'autofiction.'" Considers poetry by children and teens. Has published poetry by Chuck Taylor, Charles Bukowski, Mark Cramer, and Cotolo Patrick Kelly. *Fat Tuesday* is up to 60 pages, typeset (large type, heavy paper), saddle-stapled, usually chapbook-style (sometimes magazine-sized, unbound), with card cover, includes ads. Receives hundreds of submissions/year, accepts about 3-5%. Sample: $5, postage paid (all editions).

How to Contact Accepts e-mail submissions (pasted into body of message). Cover letter is "fine, the more amusing the better." Publishes theme issues. Responds in up to 3 months. Pays 2 contributor's copies if audio. Rights revert to author after publication. "Please join our web group (see website above) and submit all the material you want. Get read by other writers, non-writers, and wannabes."

Also Offers "In 1998, *Fat Tuesday* was presented in a different format with the production of a stereo audio cassette edition. *Fat Tuesday*'s Cool Noise features readings, music, collage, and songs, all in the spirit of *Fat*'s printed versions. *Fat Tuesday* has released other audio projects. In-print magazines will still be produced as planned when funds are available."

Tips "Support the magazine that publishes your work!"

☑ FAULTLINE

Dept. of English & Comparative Literature, University of California, Irvine, Irvine CA 92697-2650. (949)824-1573. E-mail: faultline@uci.edu. Website: www.humanities.uci.edu/faultline. Established 1991. **Contact:** Collier Nogues, poetry editor.

•Poetry published by *Faultline* has been included in *The Pushcart Prize*.

Magazines Needs *Faultline*, published annually each spring, features new poetry, fiction, and translation. Has published poetry by C.K. Williams, Larissa Szporluk, Yusef Komunyakaa, Amy Gerstler, and Killarney Clary. *Faultline* is about 200 pages, digest-sized, professionally printed on 60 lb. paper, perfect-bound, with 80 lb. coverstock. Receives about 5,000 poems/year, accepts less than 1%. Press run is 1,000. Single copy: $10. Sample: $5.

How to Contact Submit up to 5 poems at a time. Considers simultaneous submissions, "but please note in cover letter that the manuscript is being considered elsewhere." No fax or e-mail submissions. Cover letter is required. Include name, postal and e-mail addresses, and titles of work submitted; do not put name and address on ms pages themselves. SASE required. Reads submissions September 15-February 15 only. Poems are selected by a board of up to 6 readers. Seldom comments on rejected poems. Guidelines available for SASE or on Web site. Responds in 3 months. Pays 2 contributor's copies. Acquires first or one-time serial rights.

✔ FEELINGS OF THE HEART

3317 SE Emerson St., Topeka KS 66605. (785)969-0321. E-mail: apoetesswitch28@aol.com or allypoetesswitch@yahoo.com. Website: www.freewebs.com/feelingsoftheheartliteraryjournal. Established 1999. **Contact:** Alice M. Harnisch, editor/publisher/founder/poetess.

Magazines Needs *Feelings of the Heart*, published online, seeks "poetry from the heart." Considers poetry by children and teens. Has published poetry by Mark Hurley, Jerry S. Reynolds, and Sharon Kroenlein. *Feelings of the Heart* is 50 pages, newsletter format, magazine-sized, computer-printed, stapled, includes ads. Receives about 100 poems/year, accepts about 95%.

How to Contact Submit 5 poems at a time. Lines/poem: 20-40. Considers previously published poems and simultaneous submissions. Accepts e-mail (pasted into body of message or as attachment in Word). Cover letter is "important." Include name and address on every poem submitted. Time between acceptance and publication is less than 2 weeks with SASE or e-mail. Poems "are read by me, the editor, and decided by the poetic intent of poetry submitted." Often comments on rejected poems. "If asked why rejected, you will receive an answer."

Contest/Award Offerings Holds annual contests for cash prizes. Guidelines available on Web site.

Also Offers Prints poetry chapbooks for those interested **in being self-published**. E-mail for details.

Tips "Write poetry for yourself; publish for everyone else!"

✔ ◎ FEMINIST STUDIES

(Specialized: feminism), 0103 Taliaferro Hall, University of Maryland, College Park MD 207427726. (301)405-7415. Fax: (301)405-8395. E-mail: creative@feministstudies.org. Website: www.feministstudies.org. Established 1969. **Contact:** Minnie Bruce Pratt, creative writing editor.

Magazines Needs *Feminist Studies*, published 3 times/year, welcomes "all forms of written creative expression, which may include but is not limited to poetry and short fiction." Has published poetry by Dawn McDuffie, Liz Robbins, Maria Mazziotti Gillan, Mary Ann Wehler, Barbara Wiedemann, and Paola Corso. *Feminist Studies* is 250 pages, elegantly printed, flat-spined, paperback. Press run is 8,000. Sample: $17.

How to Contact No previously published poems ("we only consider original work that is not under review elsewhere") or simultaneous submissions. No fax submissions. Send 1 hard copy of submission as well as an electronic version (disk, CD, or e-mail). "We will not process creative submissions until we receive both a hard copy and electronic version." Retain a copy; work will not be returned. Reads submissions twice/year according to May 1 and December 1 deadlines. Responds by July 15 and February 15 with notice of board's decision. Regularly publishes theme issues. Guidelines available on Web site. Always sends prepublication galleys. Pays 2 contributor's copies.

▣ ✔ ◎ FICKLE MUSES

(Specialized: myth and legend), E-mail: editor@ficklemuses.com. Website: www.ficklemuses. com. Established 2006. **Contact:** Sari Krosinsky, editor.

Magazines Needs *Fickle Muses*, published weekly online, is a journal of myth and legend printing poetry, fiction, reviews, essays, and art. Open to all styles and forms. Has published poetry by Jeannine Hall Gailey, Robert Arthur Reeves, Carol L. MacKay, and Margarita Engle. Accepts about 10% of poems received. Number of unique visitors: 125/week.

How to Contact Submit up to 5 poems at a time. Lines/poem: no limits on length. Considers previously published poems and simultaneous submissions. Accepts e-mail submissions (pasted into body of message preferred, unless special formatting requires an attachment); no disk submissions. Cover letter is preferred. Reads submissions year round. Time between acceptance and publication is 3 months. Never comments on rejected poems. Guidelines available by e-mail or on Web site. Responds in up to 3 months. Acquires one-time rights. Rights revert to poets upon publication. Reviews books/chapbooks of poetry and other magazines/journals in 500 words, single-book format. For review consideration, query by e-mail.

$ ⊿ FIELD: CONTEMPORARY POETRY AND POETICS

Oberlin College, 50 N. Professor St., Oberlin OH 44074. (440)775-8408. E-mail: oc.press@ oberlin.edu (inquiries only). Website: www.oberlin.edu/ocpress. Established 1969. **Contact:** David Young.

• Work published in *FIELD* has been included frequently in *The Best American Poetry*.

Magazines Needs *FIELD: Contemporary Poetry and Poetics*, published semiannually in April and October, is a literary journal with "emphasis on poetry, translations, and essays by poets." Has published poetry by Michelle Glazer, Tom Lux, Carl Phillips, Betsy Sholl, Charles Simic, Jean Valentine and translations by Marilyn Hacker and Stuart Friebert. *FIELD* is 100 pages, digest-sized, printed on rag stock, flat-spined, with glossy color card cover. Subscription: $16/year, $28 for 2 years. Sample: $8 postpaid.

How to Contact Submit up to 5 poems at a time. No previously published poems or simultaneous submissions. No e-mail submissions. Include cover letter and SASE. Reads submissions year round. Seldom comments on rejected poems. Guidelines available for SASE, by e-mail, or on Web site. Responds in 4-6 weeks. Always sends prepublication galleys. Pays $15/page and 2 contributor's copies. Staff reviews books of poetry. Send materials for review consideration.

Additional Information Oberlin College Press publishes books of translations in the FIELD Translation Series. Books are usually flat-spined paperbacks averaging 150 pages. Query regarding translations. Also publishes books of poetry in the FIELD Poetry Series, **by invitation only**. Has published *Meaning a Cloud* by J.W. Marshall, *Lie Awake Lake* by Beckian Fritz Goldberg, *Chez Nous* by Angie Estes, *Stubborn* by Jean Gallagher, and *Red Studio* by Mary Cornish. Write for catalog or visit Web site to buy sample books.

Contest/Award Offerings Sponsors the annual FIELD Poetry Prize for a book-length collection of poems (see separate listing in Contests & Awards).

Tips "A sampling of 3-5 poems is desirable. Be sure to include enough postage on SASE if you want poems returned. We try to read promptly; please wait to submit poems elsewhere."

▣ $ ▢ ◎ THE FIFTH DI...

(Specialized: fantasy; science fiction), E-mail: fifth@samsdotpublishing.com. Website: www. samsdotpublishing.com. Established 1994. **Contact:** J. Alan Erwine, editor.

• Honored by Preditors & Editors as Best Fiction Zine.

Magazines Needs *The Fifth Di...*, published quarterly online, features fiction and poetry from the science fiction and fantasy genres. Open to most forms, but all poems must be science fiction or fantasy. Does not want horror, or anything that is not science fiction or fantasy. Considers poetry by children and teens. Has published poetry by Bruce Boston, Cathy Buburuz, Marge Simon, Aurelio Rico Lopez III, Terrie Relf, and John Bushore. Receives about 200 poems/year, accepts about 20.

How to Contact Submit 1 poem at a time. Lines/poem: no limit. No previously published poems or simultaneous submissions. Accepts e-mail submissions only (as attachment); no disk submissions. Cover letter is preferred. Reads submissions year round. Time between acceptance and publication is 1 month. Sometimes comments on rejected poems. Guidelines available on Web site. Responds in 1-3 months. Pays $5. Acquires first rights.

❂ ☑ FILLING STATION

P.O. Box 22135, Bankers Hall, Calgary AB T2P 4J5 Canada. (403)234-0336. E-mail: meditor. fs@gmail.com. Website: www.fillingstation.ca. Established 1993. **Contact:** Laurie Fuhr, general editor.

Magazines Needs *filling Station*, published 3 times/year, prints contemporary poetry, fiction, visual art, interviews, reviews, and articles. "We are looking for all forms of contemporary writing. but especially that which is original and/or experimental." Has published poetry by Fred Wah, Larissa Lai, Margaret Christakos, Robert Kroetsch, Ron Silliman, Susan Holbrook, and many more. *filling Station* is 80-100 pages, 8½ × 11, perfect-bound, with card cover, includes photos and artwork. Receives about 100 submissions for each issue, accepts approximately 10%. Press run is 700. Subscription: $22/year, $38 for 2 years. Sample: $8.

How to Contact E-mailed submissions for text is strongly encouraged. Submissions should include author's name, address, e-mail, and a short biography. Unaccepted submissions will not be returned unless suitable SASE is included. Considers simultaneous submissions, provided this is noted on submissions and they are withdrawn elsewhere if accepted by *filling Station*. No previously published material. Accepts submissions year round; deadlines vary. E-mail managing editor for next deadline. Guidelines available in magazine, for SASE, by e-mail, or on website. Responds in 4 months. Pays one-year subscription. Acquires first North American serial rights and non-exclusive rights to reprint and/or electronically publish material published in *filling Station*. All copyrights remain with that author or artist. "*filling Station* does not accept submissions that are racist, misogynist, and/or homophobic."

Tips "We favour work on the innovative cutting-edge. Please read our magazine before submitting."

☑ FIRST CLASS

Four-Sep Publications, P.O. Box 86, Friendship IN 47021. E-mail: christopherm@four-sep.com. Website: www.four-sep.com. Established 1994. **Contact:** Christopher M., editor.

Magazines Needs *First Class*, published in February and August, prints "excellent/odd writing for intelligent/creative readers." Wants "short postmodern poems." Does not want "traditional work." Has published poetry by Bennett, Locklin, Roden, Splake, Catlin, and Huffstickler. *First Class* is 48-56 pages, 414x11, printed, saddle-stapled, with colored cover. Receives about 1,500 poems/year, accepts about 30. Press run is 300-400. Sample: $6 (includes guidelines), or mini version $1. Make checks payable to Christopher M.

How to Contact Submit 5 poems at a time. Considers previously published poems and simultaneous submissions. No fax or e-mail submissions. Cover letter is preferred. "Manuscripts will not be returned." Time between acceptance and publication is 2-4 months. Often comments on rejected poems. Guidelines available in magazine, for SASE, or on Web site. Responds in 3 weeks. Pays 1 contributor's copy. Acquires one-time rights. Reviews books of poetry and fiction. Send materials for review consideration.

Additional Information Chapbook production available.

Tips "Belt out a good, short, thought-provoking, graphic, uncommon piece."

▦ FIRST OFFENSE

Sails Field, Mare Hill Road, Pulborough, West Sussex, RH 20 2 DS, England. E-mail: Tim@firstoffense.co.uk. Website: www.firstoffense.co.uk. Established 1985. **Contact:** Tim Fletcher, editor.

Magazines Needs *First Offense*, published 1-2 times/year, is "for contemporary poetry and is not traditional, but is received by most ground-breaking poets." Wants "contemporary, language, and experimental poetry and articles." *First Offense* is photocopied, "so we need well typed or word-processed manuscripts." Press run is 300. Subscription: £6.50 plus 75p for postage, or $9.50 plus $5 airmail, or equivalent in Euros. Make checks payable to Tim Fletcher.

How to Contact No previously published poems. "No reply without SAE."

Tips "Always buy a copy for research before submitting so as not to waste everyone's time."

$ ☑ FIVE POINTS

Georgia State University, P.O. Box 3999, Atlanta GA 30302-3999. (404)413-5833. Fax: (404)413-5877. Website: www.webdelsol.com/Five_Points. Established 1996. **Contact:** Megan Sexton, editor.

Magazines Needs *Five Points*, published 3 times/year, prints "quality poetry, fiction, nonfiction, interviews, and art by established and emerging writers." Wants "poetry of high quality that shows evidence of an original voice and imagination." Has published poetry by Charles Wright, Kim Addonizio, and Philip Levine. *Five Points* is about 200 pages, digest-sized, professionally printed, perfect-bound, with 4-color card cover, includes ads. Receives about 2,000 poems/year, accepts about 5%. Press run is 2,000. Single copy: $7 plus $1.50 shipping.

How to Contact Submit no more than 3 poems at a time (accepts 2 submissions/reading period). Lines/poem: 50 maximum. No previously published poems or simultaneous submissions. Cover letter is preferred. Reads submissions September 1-April 30 only. Time between acceptance and publication is 3 months. Poems are circulated to an editorial board. "First reader culls poems, then sends them to the final reader." Seldom comments on rejected poems. Guidelines available for SASE or on Web site. Responds in 3 months. Always sends prepublication galleys. Pays $50/poem, 2 contributor's copies, and one-year subscription. Acquires first North American serial rights.

Contest/Award Offerings The James Dickey Prize for Poetry (see separate listing).

☑ FLINT HILLS REVIEW

Dept. of English, Box 4019, Emporia State University, 1200 Commercial St., Emporia KS 66801. Fax: (620)341-5547. E-mail: krabas@emporia.edu. Website: www.emporia.edu/fhr/index.htm. Established 1995. **Contact:** The Editors.

Magazines Needs *Flint Hills Review*, published annually in late summer, is "a regionally focused journal presenting writers of national distinction alongside new authors." Wants all forms of poetry except rhyming. Does not want sentimental or gratuitous verse. Has published poetry by E. Ethelbert Miller, Elizabeth Dodd, Walt McDonald, and Gwendolyn Brooks. *Flint Hills Review* is about 100 pages, digest-sized, offset-printed, perfect-bound, with glossy card cover with b&w photo. Receives about 2,000 poems/year, accepts about 5%. Single copy: $7.

How to Contact Submit 3-5 poems at a time. Considers simultaneous submissions; no previously published poems. Accepts submissions by fax or e-mail (pasted into body of message). Cover letter is required. Include SASE. Reads submissions January-March only. Time between acceptance and publication is about one year. Seldom comments on rejected poems. Occasionally publishes theme issues. Guidelines available for SASE or on Web site. Pays 1 contributor's copy. Acquires first rights.

Contest/Award Offerings FHR hosts an annual nonfiction contest. **Entry Fee**: $10. **Deadline:** March 15.

Tips "Send writing with evidence of a strong sense of place."

☒ FLOYD COUNTY MOONSHINE

720 Christiansburg Pike, Floyd VA 24091. (850)241-3781. E-mail: floydshine@gmail.com.

Website: www.myspace.com/floydcountymoonshine. Established 2008 **Contact:** Aaron Moore, editor-in-chief

Magazines Needs *Floyd County Moonshine*, published 3 times/year, is a "literary and arts magazine in Floyd, Virginia and the New River Valley. We accept poetry, short stories, and essays addressing all manner of themes; however, preference is given to those works of a rural or Southern/Appalachian nature. We welcome cutting-edge and innovative fiction and poetry in particular." Wants "rustic innovation." Has published poetry by Steve Kistulentz, Louis Gallo, Ernie Wormwood, Rodney Smith, Chelsea Adams, and Justin Askins. *Floyd County Moonshine* is 70-100 pages, digest-sized, saddle-stitched, with a heavy glossy cover; includes ads. Receives 200 poems/year, accepts 25%. Press run is 200-500; subscribers 50-100, libraries, 5-10, 50-75 distributed free. Single copy: $7; subscription: $15/1 year, $25/2 years.

How to Contact Submit 3 poems at a time. No previously published poems or simultaneous submissions. Accepts e-mail submissions; no fax or disk. Cover letter is unnecessary. Reads submissions year round.

☑ FLYWAY, A JOURNAL OF WRITING AND ENVIRONMENT

206 Ross Hall, Iowa State University, Ames IA 50011-1201. Fax: (515)294-6814. E-mail: flyway@iastate.edu. Website: www.flyway.org. Established 1961. **Contact:** Stephen Pett, editor-in-chief.

Magazines Needs *Flyway, A Journal of Writing and Environment*, published 3 times/year, "is one of the best literary magazines for the money. It's packed with some of the most readable poems being published today—all styles, forms, lengths, and subjects." Does not want "elite-sounding free verse with obscure meanings, and pretty-sounding formal verse with obvious meanings." *Flyway* is 120 pages, digest-sized, professionally printed, perfect-bound, with matte card cover with color. Press run is 600. Subscription: $24. Sample: $8.

How to Contact Submit 4-6 poems at a time. Cover letter is preferred. "We do not read manuscripts between the first of May and the end of August." Responds in 6 weeks (often sooner). Pays 2 contributor's copies. Acquires first rights.

Contest/Award Offerings Sponsors an annual award for poetry, fiction, and nonfiction. Details available for SASE or on Web site.

▣ ☑ FOLIATE OAK ONLINE, THE

University of Arkansas, Arts and Humanities, Monticello AR 71656.870-460-1247. E-mail: foliateoak@uamont.edu. Website: www.foliateoak.uamont.edu. Established 1970. **Contact:** Diane Payne

•Association Collegiate Media Awards

Magazines Needs *The Foliate Oak Online*, published monthly online, prints prose, poetry, and artwork reviewed by college students, edited and added to the Web site. Wants "all genres and forms of poetry are accepted." Does not want: "we're not interested in homophobic, religious rants, or pornographic, violent stories. Please avoid using offensive language." Considers poetry by teens. Has published poetry by tony Hoagland, Richard Fein, and FJ Bergmann. Receives about 300 poems/year, accepts about 100. Number of unique visitors: 500 monthly.

How to Contact Submit no more than 5 poems at a time, maximum 30 lines. Does not accept previously published poems, no simultaneous submissions. (Considers poetry posted on a public website/blog/forum and poetry posted on a private, password-protected forum as published.) Accepts e-mail submissions as attachment); no fax or disk submissions. Cover letter is unnecessary. See Web site for guidelines; Word documents are preferred, submit a third person bio. Reads submissions year round. Submit seasonal poems 1 months in advance. Time between acceptance and publication is 2-3 weeks. Poems are circulated to an editorial board.

Always comments on rejected poems. Never publishes theme issues. Guidelines available on Web site. Responds in 1 week. Acquires one-time rights. Reviews other magazines/journals.

Additional Information "We are accepting submissions at this time! If accepted, the work will be posted in our monthly magazine for a minimum of 4 weeks. Send us what you have via e-mail."

Tips "Be original, have fun with it; if you are rejected, just keep sending us your work - we enjoy reading them!"

☑ FOLIO, A LITERARY JOURNAL AT AMERICAN UNIVERSITY

Dept. of Literature, American University, Washington DC 20016. (202)885-2990. Fax: (202)885-2938. E-mail: folio.editors@gmail.com. Website: www.foliojournal.org. Established 1984. **Contact:** Virginia Sheridan, poetry editor.

Magazines Needs *Folio*, published 2 times/year, is looking for work "that ignites and endures, is artful and natural, daring and elegant. Will accept formal and free verse." Does not want work of a sexually graphic or discriminatory nature. Has published poetry by Allison Joseph, CJ Sage, Denise Duhamel, Frannie Lindsay, Patrick Rosal, and Kathleen Kirk. *Folio* is 80 pages, digest-sized, with matte cover with graphic art. Receives about 1,000 poems/year, accepts about 25. Press run is 350; 50-60 distributed free to the American University community and contributors. Single copy: $6; subscription: $12/year. Make checks payable to "*Folio* at American University."

How to Contact Submit 4-6 poems at a time. Considers simultaneous submissions "with notice." No fax, e-mail, or disk submissions. Cover letter is preferred. "SASE required for notification only; manuscripts are not returned." Reads submissions September 1 -March 1. Time between acceptance and publication is 2 months. "Poems are reviewed by editorial staff and senior editors." Seldom comments on rejected poems. Occasionally publishes theme issues. Guidelines available on website. Pays 2 contributor's copies. Acquires first North American serial rights.

▣ ☑ FORPOETRY.COM

E-mail: poems@forpoetry.com. Website: www.forpoetry.com. Established 1999. **Contact:** Jackie Marcus, editor.

Magazines Needs *ForPoetry.Com*, published online with daily updates, seeks "to promote new and emerging poets, with or without MFAs. We will be publishing established poets, but our primary interest is in publishing excellent poetry, prose, and reviews." Wants "lyric poetry, vivid imagery, open form, natural landscape, philosophical themes—but not at the expense of honesty and passion." Does not want "city punk, corny sentimental fluff, or academic workshop imitations." Has published poetry by Sherod Santos, John Koethe, Robert Hass, Kim Addonizio, and Brenda Hillman.

How to Contact Submit no more than 2 poems at a time. Considers simultaneous submissions; no previously published poems. Accepts e-mail submissions only (pasted into body of message; no attachments). Cover letter is preferred. Reads submissions September-May only. Time between acceptance and publication is 2-3 weeks. "We'll read all submissions and then decide together on the poems we'll publish." Comments on rejected poems "as often as possible. We receive lots of submissions and are very selective about acceptances, but we will always try to send a note back on rejections." Guidelines available on Web site. Responds in 2 weeks. Reviews books/chapbooks of poetry and other magazines in 800 words.

Tips "As my friend Kevin Hull said, 'Get used to solitude and rejection.' Sit on your poems for several months or more. Time is your best critic."

☑ THE FOURTH RIVER

Chatham University, Woodland Rd., Pittsburgh PA 15232. E-mail: 4thriver@gmail.com. Website: http://fourthriver.chatham.edu. Established 2005. **Contact:** Christy Diulus, editor.

Magazines Needs *The Fourth River*, an annual publication of the MFA program at Chatham University, features "literature that engages and explores the relationship between humans and their environments." Wants "writings that are richly situated at the confluence of place, space, and identity, or that reflect upon or make use of landscape and place in new ways." *The Fourth River* is digest-sized, perfect-bound, with full-color cover by various artists. Accepts about 30-40 poems/year. Press run is 500. Single copy: $10; subscription: $18 for 2 years. Make checks payable to Chatham University.

How to Contact Submit 7 poems at a time. Lines/poem: submit 25 pages maximum. No previously published poems. No e-mail or disk submissions. Cover letter is preferred. "SASE is required for response." Reads submissions August 1-February 15. Time between acceptance and publication is 5-8 months. Poems are circulated to an editorial board. Sometimes comments on rejected poems. Sometimes publishes theme issues. Guidelines available on Web site. Responds in 3-5 months. Acquires first North American serial rights.

☒ $ ☑ FREEFALL MAGAZINE

Alexandra Writers' Centre Society, 922 Ninth Ave. SE, Calgary AB T2G 0S4 Canada. (403)264-4730. Website: www.freefallmagazine.ca. Established 1990. **Contact:** Member: AMPA and Magazines Canada.

Magazines Needs *FreeFall Magazine*, published in April and October, contains fiction, nonfiction, poetry, and interviews related to writers/writing, and artwork and photographs suitable for b&w reproduction. "*FreeFall*'s mandate is to encourage the voices of new, emerging, and experienced writers and provide an outlet for their work." Wants "poems in a variety of forms with a strong voice, effective language, and fresh images." Has published poetry by Christopher Wiseman, Sharon Drummond, Edna Alford, Joan Clarke, and Barry Butson. *FreeFall* is 100-120 pages, digest-sized, perfect-bound, glossy, with 60 lb. paper cover. Receives about 100 poems/year, accepts about 15%. Press run is 500; 30 distributed free to contributors, promotion. Single copy: $12.50 USD, $10 CAD; subscription: $25 USD, $20 CAD. Sample: $10 USD, $10 CAD.

How to Contact Submit up to 5 poems at a time. No previously published poems or simultaneous submissions. Accepts postal and disk submissions (ASCII, text format, must include hard copy); no e-mail submissions. Cover letter is required. Include 2-line bio and SASE. Reads submissions in January and July only. Time between acceptance and publication is 3 months. "All submissions are read by 8 editors." Seldom comments on rejected poems. Occasionally publishes theme issues. Guidelines available by mail request, for SAE and IRC, by e-mail, or on Web site. Responds in 3 months. Pays 1 contributor's copy and a nominal amount per page. Acquires first North American serial rights.

Additional Information See Web site for information about the Alexandra Writers' Centre Society activities and services, and for additional information about *FreeFall Magazine*.

Contest/Award Offerings Hosts an annual fiction and poetry contest. **Deadline:** December 31. Guidelines available by e-mail or on Web site.

☑ FREE LUNCH

P.O. Box 717, Glenview IL 60025-0717. Website: www.poetsfreelunch.org. Established 1988. **Contact:** Ron Offen, editor.

Magazines Needs *Free Lunch*, published 2 times/year, is "interested in publishing the whole spectrum of what is currently being produced by American poets. Features a 'Mentor Series,' in which an established poet introduces a new, unestablished poet. Mentor poets are selected by the editor and have included Maxine Kumin, Denise Duhamel, Billy Collins, Lucille Clifton, Donald Hall, Carolyn Forché, Wanda Coleman, Lyn Lifshin, Stephen Dunn, and Edward Hirsch. *Free Lunch* is especially interested in experimental work and work by unestablished poets." Wants "metaphors, similes, arresting images, and a sensitive and original use of language. We are interested in all genres—experimental poetry, protest poetry, formal poetry, etc. No restriction on form (except no haikus, please), length, style, purpose. No aversion to form, rhyme." Has published poetry by Jared Carter, Donald Hall, James Reiss, Stephen Dunn, Lisel Mueller, and Cathy Song. *Free Lunch* is 32-40 pages, digest-sized, attractively printed and designed, saddle-stapled. Press run is 1,200. Subscription: $12 ($15 foreign). Sample: $5 ($6 foreign). "*Free Lunch* seeks to provide all serious poets living in the U.S. with a free subscription. For details on free subscription, send SASE."

How to Contact Submit no more than 3 poems at a time. Considers simultaneous submissions; no previously published poems. Cover letter is preferred. "Although a cover letter is not mandatory, I like them. I especially want to know if a poet is previously unpublished, as I like to work with new poets." Reads submissions September 1-May 31. "Submissions sent at other times will be returned unread." Always comments on rejected poems. Responds in 2-3 months. Guidelines available for SASE or on Web site. Pays 1 contributor's copy plus subscription.

Contest/Award Offerings The Rosine Offen Memorial Award, a prize of $200, is awarded to 1 poem in each issue of *Free Lunch*. Winners are selected solely by the Board of Directors of Free Lunch Arts Alliance, and are announced in the following issue.

Tips "Archibald MacLeish said, 'A poem should not mean/But be.' I have become increasingly leery of the ego-centered lyric that revels in some past wrong, good-old-boy nostalgia, or unfocused ecstatic experience. Not receptive to art- or literature-referenced poems or poems about writing poems, other poems, poetry reading, etc. Poetry is concerned primarily with language, rhythm, and sound; fashions and trends are transitory and to be eschewed. Perfecting one's work is often more important than publishing it."

🌐 ☑ FREEXPRESSION

P.O. Box 4, West Hoxton, NSW 2171 Australia. (61)(2)9607-5559. E-mail: frexprsn@tpg.com.au. Website: www.freexpression.net. Established 1993. **Contact:** Peter F. Pike, managing editor.

Magazines Needs *FreeXpresSion*, published monthly, contains "creative writing, how-to articles, short stories, and poetry including cinquain, haiku, etc., and bush verse." Open to all forms. "Christian themes OK. Humorous material welcome. No gratuitous sex; bad language OK. We don't want to see anything degrading." Has published poetry by Ron Stevens, Ellis Campbell, John Ryan, and Ken Dean. *FreeXpresSion* is 28 pages, magazine-sized, offset-printed, saddle-stapled, with paper cover. Receives about 2,500 poems/year, accepts about 30%. Press run is 500. Single copy: $3.50 AUS; subscription: $42 AUS ($66 AUS overseas airmail). Sample: A4 SAE with $1 stamp (Australia) or 2 IRCs (overseas).

How to Contact Submit 3-4 poems at a time. Lines/poem: "very long poems are not desired but would be considered." Considers previously published poems and simultaneous submissions. Accepts e-mail (pasted into body of message) and disk submissions. Cover letter is preferred. Time between acceptance and publication is 2 months. Seldom comments on rejected poems. Publishes theme issues. Upcoming themes available in magazine, by e-mail, or on Web site. Guidelines available in magazine, for SAE and IRC, or by fax or e-mail. Responds in 2 months. Sometimes sends prepublication galleys. Pays 1 contributor's copy; additional copies available at half price. Acquires first Australian rights only. Reviews books of poetry in 500 words. Send materials for review consideration.

Additional Information *FreeXpresSion* also publishes books up to 200 pages **through subsidy**

arrangements with authors. "Some poems published throughout the year are used in *Yearbooks* (annual anthologies)."

Contest/Award Offerings Sponsors an annual contest with 3 categories for poetry: blank verse (up to 60 lines); traditional verse (up to 80 lines), and haiku. 1st Prize in blank verse: $200 AUS; 2nd Prize: $100 AUS; 1st Prize in traditional rhyming poetry: $250 AUS; 2nd Prize: $150 AUS; 3rd Prize: $100 AUS. Haiku, one prize $100 AUS. Guidelines and entry form available by e-mail.

Tips "Keep it short and simple."

⊠ ▣ FRINGE MAGAZINE

8 Willow Ave, #12, Arlington, MA 02144. (617)413-8674. E-mail: fringeeditors@gmail.com. Website: www.fringemagazine.org. Established 2006 Member: CLMP.

Magazines Needs "*Fringe*, pubished online quarterly, is dedicated to political and experimental literature, and was founded to fight the homogenization of culture and the loss of revolutionary writing at the high literary and popular levels. Our audience is diverse, garnering more than 16,000 page views each month from more than 40 countries. *Fringe* is a 501(c)3 public charity organized under the laws of Delaware whose nonprofit purpose is to diversify the existing literary aesthetic, publish genres that other magazines do not print, and to give crucial early publication credits to young writers, particularly to writers of color and women writers. In each issue, *Fringe* features one artist per genre."

How to Contact Submit a minimum of 4 but no more than 7 poems at a time in a single attachment. Longer poetry of 40 lines or more must be submitted separately, only one poem per submission. Please send in an attachment and include the words "Long Poem" in the subject heading of e-mail. Considers simultaneous submissions; no previously published poems. Considers poems posted to in journals, blogs, or other Web sites to be published. Cover letter required. Please include in e-mail a brief bio and your full name. Subject line should include your name, the title(s) of the works, and word and/or line counts for poetry. Can accept RTF attachments, as well as .doc, .jpg, .gif, or .png format. Cannot open .wps or .bin files. Do not include any personal information on attachment as submissions process is blind. Reads submissions year round. Guidelines available on Web site. Acquires first electronic publishing rights. Please note that accepted work remains part of *Fringe's* online archive system for reader access in the future.

◎ FROGPOND: JOURNAL OF THE HAIKU SOCIETY OF AMERICA

Haiku Society of America, P.O. Box 31, Nassau NY 12123. E-mail: gswede@ryerson.ca. Website: www.hsa-haiku.org. Established 1978. **Contact:** George Swede, editor.

Magazines Needs *Frogpond*, published triannually (February, June, October), is the international journal of the Haiku Society of America. Wants "contemporary English-language haiku, ranging from 1-4 lines or in a visual arrangement, focusing on a moment keenly perceived and crisply conveyed, using clear images and non-poetic language." Also considers "related forms: senryu, sequences, linked poems, and haibun. Has published poetry by all of the foremost haiku poets around the world. *Frogpond* is 96-100 pages, digest-sized, perfect-bound. Receives about 10,000 submissions/year, accepts about 500. *Frogpond* goes to 800 subscribers as well as to over a dozen foreign countries. Sample: $10 U.S. (back issue), $14 ROW. Make checks payable to Haiku Society of America.

How to Contact Submissions by e-mail preferred. No simultaneous submissions. Include SASE with postal submissions. Guidelines available for SASE or on Web site. Detailed instructions on Web site. Responds at the end of each submission period (June 1-August 1; September 15-November 15; February 15-April 15). Reviews books of poetry, usually in 1,000 words or less.

Contest/Award Offerings The "best of issue" prize is awarded to a poem from each issue of *Frogpond* through a gift from the Museum of Haiku Literature, located in Tokyo. The Haiku Society of America also sponsors The Harold G. Henderson Haiku Award Contest, the Gerald Brady Senryu Award Contest, the Bernard Lionel Einbond Memorial Renku Contest, the Nicholas A. Virgilio Memorial Haiku Competition for High School Students, the Mildred Kanterman Merit Book Awards for outstanding books in the haiku field. Guidelines available on Web site.

Tips "Submissions to *Frogpond* are accepted from both members and nonmembers, although familiarity with the journal will aid writers in discovering what it publishes."

$ ☑ FUGUE

200 Brink Hall, University of Idaho, P.O. Box 441102, Moscow ID 83844. E-mail: fugue@uidaho. edu. Website: www.uidaho.edu/fugue. Established 1990. **Contact:** Laura Powers, poetry editor.

Magazines Needs *Fugue*, published semiannually in summer and winter, is a literary magazine of the University of Idaho. "There are no limits on type of poetry; however, we are not interested in trite or quaint verse." Has published poetry by Sonia Sanchez, Simon Perchik, Denise Duhamel, Dean Young, and W.S. Merwin. *Fugue* is up to 200 pages, perfect-bound. Receives about 400 poems/semester, accepts only 15-20 poems/issue. Press run is 250. There is also an online version. Sample: $8.

How to Contact Submit 3-5 poems at a time (10 pages maximum). No previously published poems. Considers simultaneous submissions "with the explicit provision that the writer inform us immediately if the work is accepted for publication elsewhere." No e-mail submissions. Cover letter is required. "Include name, address, e-mail, phone number, poem titles, and a brief bio citing any awards/publications. Submissions without a #10 SASE will not be considered." Reads submissions September 1-May 1 only. Time between acceptance and publication is up to 1 year. "Submissions are reviewed by staff members and chosen with consensus by the editorial board. No major changes are made to a manuscript without authorial approval." Publishes theme issues. Guidelines available for SASE or on Web site. Responds in up to 5 months. Pays at least 1 contributor's copy plus an honorarium (up to $25 as funds allow). Acquires first North American serial rights.

Contest/Award Offerings "For information regarding our annual spring poetry contest, please visit our Web site."

Tips "We are looking for poetry that takes risks while demonstrating powerful voice and careful attention to language and craft. Proper manuscript format and submission etiquette are expected; submissions without proper SASE will not be read or held on file."

▣ ☑ FULLOSIA PRESS

The Rockaway Park Philosophical Society, P.O. Box 280, Ronkonkoma NY 11779. E-mail: deanofRPPS@aol.com. Website: http://rpps_fullosia_press.tripod.com. Established 1971. **Contact:** jd collins.

Magazines Needs *Fullosia Press*, published monthly online, presents news, information, satire, and right/conservative perspective. Wants any style of poetry. "If you have something to say, say it. We consider many different points of view." Does not want "anti-American, anti-Christian." Considers poetry by children with parental consent. Has published poetry by Awesome David Lawrence, Peter Vetrano, Michael Levy, Dr. Kelley White, and Taylor Graham. Receives about 50 poems/year, accepts about 40%. Single copy: $15 and SASE (free online); subscription: $25/year (free online). Make checks payable to RPPS-Fullosia Press.

How to Contact Accepts e-mail (pasted into body of message) and disk submissions. "E-mail preferred. Final submission by disk or e-mail only." Cover letter is required. Reads submissions when received. Submit seasonal poems 1 month in advance. Time between acceptance and publication varies. "I review all poems: 1) Do they say something?; 2) Is there some thought behind it?; 3) Is it more than words strung together?" Always comments on rejected poems. Publishes theme issues. Guidelines available for SASE, by e-mail, or on Web site. Responds in 1 month. Acquires one-time rights. Reviews books/chapbooks of poetry and other magazines/journals. Send materials for review consideration to RPPS-Fullosia Press.

Tips "Say what you have in mind without tripping over your own symbolism. We like poems that are clear, concise, to the point; American traditional heroes; Arthurian legend; American states. Everybody sings about Texas; has anyone written a poem to New Jersey?"

THE FURNACE REVIEW

E-mail: submissions@thefurnacereview.com. Website: www.thefurnacereview.com. Established 2004. **Contact:** Ciara LaVelle, editor.

Magazines Needs *The Furnace Review*, published quarterly online, is "dedicated to new writers and unique or groundbreaking work." Wants "all forms, from haiku to sonnets to free verse to totally experimental. Just make it interesting." Has published poetry by Carolynn Kingyens, Charles Geoghegan-Clements, Curtis Evans, and Richard Matthes. Receives about 1,500 pieces/year, accepts about 30.

How to Contact Submit up to 5 poems at a time. Lines/poem: 75 maximum. Considers simultaneous submissions; no previously published poems. Accepts e-mail submissions; no disk submissions. Cover letter is preferred. "Include a short biography with all submissions." Reads submissions year round. Time between acceptance and publication is 3 months. Poems are circulated to an editorial board. Sometimes comments on rejected poems. Guidelines available on Web site. Responds in 6 months. Acquires first North American serial rights.

GECKO

E-mail: geckogalpoet@hotmail.com. Established 1998. **Contact:** Rebecca Lu Kiernan, editor.

• "Due to the overwhelming response of Poet's Market readers and personal projects of the editor, we are currenly closed to unsolicited manuscripts. We hope to change this in the future when an assistant will assume some of the editor's duties."

GEORGETOWN REVIEW

Box 227, 400 E. College St., Georgetown KY 40324. (502)863-8308. Fax: (502)868-8888. E-mail: gtownreview@georgetowncollege.edu. Website: http://georgetownreview.georgetowncollege. edu. Established 1993. **Contact:** Steven Carter, editor. Member: CLMP.

Magazines Needs *Georgetown Review*, published annually in May, is a literary journal of poetry, fiction, and creative nonfiction. "We have no specific guidelines concerning form or content of poetry, but are always eager to see poetry that is insightful, rooted in reality, and human." Does not want "work that is merely sentimental, political, or inspirational." Considers poetry by children and teens. Has published poetry by Denise Duhamel, X.J. Kennedy, Fred Chappell, Frederick Smock, Mark Halperin, David Citino, William Greenway, James Harms, and Margarita Engle. *Georgetown Review* is 192 pages, digest-sized, offset-printed, perfect-bound, with 60 lb. glossy 4-color cover with art/graphics, includes ads. Receives about 1,000 poems/year, accepts about 50-60. Press run is 1,000. Single copy: $5; subscription: $5. Make checks payable to *Georgetown Review*.

How to Contact Submit 1-10 poems at a time. Lines/poem: open. Considers simultaneous submissions; no previously published poems. No fax, e-mail, or disk submissions. Cover letter is preferred. "In cover letter, please include short bio and a list of publications. Also, must include SASE for reply." Reads submissions September 1-March 15. Submit seasonal poems 1 year in advance. Time between acceptance and publication is 6-12 months. Poems are circulated to an editorial board. "The first reader passes the poem along to the poetry editor, and then a final decision is made by the poetry editor and the head editor." Seldom comments on rejected poems. Guidelines available for SASE, by e-mail, or on Web site. Responds in 1-3 months. Pays 2 contributor's copies. Acquires first North American serial rights. Reviews books/chapbooks of poetry in 1,000 words, multi-book format.

Contest/Award Offerings Sponsors annual contest, offering $1,000 prize and publication; runners-up also receive publication. Guidelines available for SASE, by e-mail, or on Web site. **Entry fee:** $10/poem, $5 for each additional poem.

$ ☑ THE GEORGIA REVIEW

The University of Georgia, 012 Gilbert Hall, Athens GA 30602-9009. (706)542-3481. E-mail: garev@uga.edu. Website: www.uga.edu/garev. Established 1947. **Contact:** The Editors.

Magazines Needs *The Georgia Review*, published quarterly, seeks "the very best work we can find, whether by Nobel laureates and Pulitzer Prize-winners or by little-known (or even previously unpublished) writers. All manuscripts receive serious, careful attention. We have featured first-ever publications by many new voices over the years, but encourage all potential contributors to become familiar with past offerings before submitting." Has published poetry by Rita Dove, Stephen Dunn, Margaret Gibson, Albert Goldbarth, and Lola Haskins. *The Georgia Review* is 200-232 pages, 7x10, professionally printed, flat-spined, with glossy card cover. Publishes 60-70 poems/year, less than .5% of those received. Press run is 4,500. Subscription: $30/year. Sample: $8.

How to Contact Submit 3-5 poems at a time. No simultaneous submissions. Reads year-round, but submissions postmarked May 15-August 15 will be returned unread. Guidelines available for SASE or on Web site. Responds in 2-3 months. Always sends prepublication galleys. Pays $3/line, one-year subscription, and 1 contributor's copy. Acquires first North American serial rights. Reviews books of poetry. "Our poetry reviews range from 500-word 'Book Briefs' on single volumes to 5,000-word essay reviews on multiple volumes."

Tips "Needless to say, competition is extremely tough. All styles and forms are welcome, but response times can be slower during peak periods in the fall and late spring."

☐ GERONIMO REVIEW

E-mail: geronimoreview@att.net. Website: www.sanjeronimofnd.org. Established 1998. Contact: S. Bass, editor. Secretary: g. bassetti.

Magazines Needs *geronimo review*, published online, will "publish on its Web site virtually everything submitted. Submit whatever strikes your fancy. Literally. Anything. Overt pornography, hate speech, etc., taken under editorial advisement." Has 2 submission categories: Open (these submissions are graded "mercilessly" by both editors and readers) and Amateur ("graded on an appropriate scale"). Wants "politics and political satire. Anything of unusual excellence, especially the short lyric." Has published poetry by Mark C. Peery, dada rambass, zeninubasho, geronimo bassetti, Élan B. Yergmoul, "and innumerable others."

How to Contact Submit 3 poems at a time. Lines/poem: 100 maximum (or the length demanded by the poem). Considers simultaneous submissions; no previously published poems. Accepts submissions by e-mail only (as Word attachment or pasted into body of message). Submissions in html will appear with poet's formatting. Reads submissions all year. Time between acceptance and publication is 2 weeks. Guidelines available on Web site. Responds in 3 weeks ("maybe").

Acquires all rights; returns to poet "on request." Send materials for review consideration.

Additional Information MaoMao Press will publish essays on and reviews of poetry in the future. **"Not presently accepting book submissions—watch our Web site.** *GR* will soon allow poets to post their work directly online, and will allow readers to comment on and vote, allowing superior material to float to the top." Artists will also be encouraged to post their art. Poets who have published a book may, on request, get their own page on the site.

Also Offers Plans anthology of *geronimo review* material.

Tips "Don't be Susan Wheeler. Be in the tradition of Yeats, Frost, Carroll, Stevens, and be really original and inspire strong reactions."

GERTRUDE

(Specialized: gay, lesbian, bisexual, transgendered, queer-identified & allied). P.O. Box 83948, Portland OR 97283. E-mail: poetry@gertrudepress.org. Website: www.gertrudepress.org. Established 1998. **Contact:** Steve Rydman, poetry editor. Founding Editor: Eric Delehoy.

Magazines Needs *Gertrude*, published semiannually, is the literary publication of Gertrude Press (see separate listing in Books/Chapbooks), "a nonprofit 501(c)(3) organization showcasing and developing the creative talents of lesbian, gay, bisexual, trans, queer-identified, and allied individuals." Has published poetry by Judith Barrington, Deanna Kern Ludwin, Casey Charles, Michael Montlack, Megan Kruse, and Noah Tysick. *Gertrude* is 64-112 pages, digest-sized, offset-printed, perfect-bound, with glossy 4-color cardstock cover with art. Receives about 500 poems/year, accepts about 6-8%. Press run is 300; 50 distributed free. Single copy: $8.25; subscription: $15/year, $27 for 2 years. Sample: $6.25. Make checks payable to Gertrude Press.

How to Contact Submit 6 poems at a time. Lines/poem: open. Considers simultaneous submissions; no previously published poems. Accepts e-mail submissions via the Web site only; no disk submissions. Cover letter is preferred. Include short bio and SASE. Reads submissions year round. Time between acceptance and publication is 3-6 months. Poems are circulated to an editorial board. Sometimes comments on rejected poems. Guidelines available in magazine, by e-mail, or on Web site. Responds in 3 months. Sometimes sends prepublication galleys. Pays 1 contributor's copy plus discount on additional copies/subscriptions. Acquires one-time rights. Rights revert to poets upon publication.

Contest/Award Offerings The Gertrude Press Poetry Chapbook Contest (see separate listing in Contests & Awards).

Tips "*Gertrude* publishes the best poetry that is received. While we are a queer publication, poetry need not be lesbigay-specific, and publication is open to all poets regardless of background."

$ THE GETTYSBURG REVIEW

Gettysburg College, Gettysburg PA 17325. (717)337-6770. Fax: (717)337-6775. E-mail: mdrew@gettysburg.edu. Website: www.gettysburgreview.com. Established 1988. **Contact:** Peter Stitt, editor.

- Work appearing in *The Gettysburg Review* has been included frequently in *The Best American Poetry* and *The Pushcart Prize*. Editor Peter Stitt won the first PEN/Nora Magid Award for Editorial Excellence.

Magazines Needs *The Gettysburg Review*, published quarterly, considers "well-written poems of all kinds." Has published poetry by Rita Dove, Alice Friman, Philip Schultz, Michelle, Boisseau, Bob Hicok, Linda Pastan, and G.C. Waldrep. Accepts 1-2% of submissions received. Press run is 4,500. Subscription: $28/year. Sample: $10.

How to Contact Submit 3-5 poems at a time. Considers simultaneous submissions; no previously published poems. Cover letter is preferred. Include SASE. Reads submissions September-May only. Occasionally publishes theme issues. "Response time can be slow during heavy submission periods, especially in the late fall." Pays $2.50/line, one-year subscription, and 1 contributor's copy. Essay-reviews are featured in most issues. Send materials for review consideration.

▣ ☑ GHOTI MAGAZINE

E-mail: editors@ghotimag.com. Website: www.ghotimag.com. Established 2005. **Contact:** CL Bledsoe, Donna Epler, and Jillian Meyer, editors.

Magazines Needs *Ghoti Magazine*, published quarterly online, prints "fiction, nonfiction, poetry, book reviews, and interviews with up-and-coming writers or those who have been ignored by the mainstream. *Ghoti Magazine* also publishes recipes by writers." Wants "fiction, poetry, nonfiction, and reviews of recent books. We are open to experimental and traditional styles, but our main criterion is quality. Is this piece of writing going to stay with a reader? In five years, will it be worth reading again? If so, *Ghoti Magazine* wants it." Does not want "self-absorbed work. If it's boring to you, it's boring to us." Has published poetry by Simon Perchik, Lyn Lifshin, Arlene Ang, Jo McDougall, Ace Boggess, and Barry Ballard. Receives about 1,000 poems/year, accepts about 40-50.

How to Contact Submit 3-5 poems at a time. Lines/poem: "there is no line limit, but longer poems must be able to sustain their length." Considers simultaneous submissions; no previously published poems. Accepts e-mail submissions only (pasted into body of message; "if the poems have complicated formatting, please paste them into the body of the e-mail and attach them to the e-mail as well"). Cover letter is preferred. Reads submissions year round. Submit seasonal poems 3 months in advance. Time between acceptance and publication is 3-6 months. "We have 3 editors. Generally at least 2 editors read each submission." Often comments on rejected poems. Guidelines available on Web site. Responds in 2 months. Acquires electronic rights. Rights revert to poet upon publication. Reviews books/chapbooks of poetry in 250-500 words, single-book format. "For review materials, contact the editors."

Tips "We are open to the prosaic, performance-oriented poetry that seems to mainly be written today, but we would much prefer to see poetry that experiments with language and sound, instead of just stating a case. Prosody is not a bad thing. We rarely publish political rants or anything that seems to be beating us over the heads with meaning. We judge each submission based on quality of the work, regardless of how many credits the author has."

⬚ $ ☑ GRAIN

P.O. Box 67, Saskatoon SK S7K 3K1 Canada. (306)244-2828. Fax: (306)244-0255. E-mail: grainmag@sasktel.net (inquiries only). Website: www.grainmagazine.ca. Established 1973. **Contact:** Gerry Hill, poetry editor.

Magazines Needs *Grain*, published quarterly, is "an internationally acclaimed literary journal that publishes engaging, surprising, eclectic, and challenging writing and images by Canadian and international writers and artists." Has published poetry by Lorna Crozier, Don Domanski, Cornelia Haeussler, Patrick Lane, Karen Solie, and Monty Reid. *Grain* is 128-144 pages, digest-sized, professionally printed. Press run is 1,100. Receives about 2,400 submissions/year. Subscription: $30 CAD/year, $46 CAD for 2 years. Sample: $13 CAD. (See Web site for U.S. and foreign postage fees.)

How to Contact Submit up to 12 pages of poetry, typed in readable font on one side only. No previously published poems or simultaneous submissions. No fax or e-mail submissions; postal submissions only. Cover letter with all contact information, title(s), and genre of work is required. "No staples. Your name and address must be on every page. Pieces of more than one page must be numbered. Please only submit work in one genre at one time." Reads submissions September-May only. "Manuscripts postmarked between June 1 and August 31 will be returned unread." Guidelines available in magazine, for SASE (or SAE and IRC), by fax, e-mail, or on Web site. Responds in 2-4 months. Pays $50-225 CAD (depending on number of pages) and 2 contributor's copies. Acquires first Canadian serial rights only. Copyright remains with the author.

Tips "Only work of the highest literary quality is accepted. Read several back issues."

☑ THE GREAT AMERICAN POETRY SHOW

The Muse Media, P.O. Box 69506, West Hollywood CA 90069. (323)656-6126. E-mail: info@ tgaps.net. Website: www.tgaps.net. Established 2002. **Contact:** Larry Ziman, editor/publisher.

Magazines Needs *The Great American Poetry Show*, published about every 3 years, is an 8½x11 hardcover serial poetry anthology. Wants poems on any subject, in any style, of any length. Has published poetry by Sara Berkeley, Alan Britt, Hector E. Estrada, Heidi Nye, Tom Smith, and Sarah Brown Weitzman. *The Great American Poetry Show* is 150 pages, sheet-fed offset-printed, perfect-bound, with cloth cover with art/graphics. "For our first volume, we read about 8,000 poems from about 1,400 poets and accepted only 113 poems from 83 poets." Press run is 1,000. Single copy: $35 (print), $7.50 (e-book, download only).

How to Contact Submit any number of poems at a time. Considers previously published poems and simultaneous submissions. Accepts e-mail submissions (as attachment). Cover letter is optional. Include SASE. "If we reject a submission of your work, please send us another group to go through. We have 3 editors who can handle a lot of submissions." Responds in 1-3 months ("depends on how busy we are"). Pays 1 contributor's copy.

Also Offers "Please visit our message boards where anyone can have us post poetry news, reviews, essays, articles, and recommended books."

Tips "We are very hard to please. But we are very easy to submit to. Do not get discouraged by rejections from us. Just keep sending us more poems to consider. Hopefully, we will find something we want to publish in your submissions. If we reject everything you send us, still do not get discouraged. Send your poems to other publishers until you find one who wants to publish your poetry."

▣ ☑ GREEN HILLS LITERARY LANTERN

McClain Hall, Truman State University, Kirksville MO 63501. (660)785-4513. E-mail: jbeneven@ truman.edu. Website: http://ll.truman.edu/ghllweb/. **Contact:** Joe Benevento, poetry editor.

Magazines Needs *Green Hills Literary Lantern*, published annually online in June, is "an open-access journal of short fiction and poetry of exceptional quality." Wants "the best poetry, in any style, preferably understandable. There are no restrictions on subject matter. Both free and formal verse forms are fine, though we publish more free verse overall." Does not want "haiku, limericks, or anything over 2 pages. Pornography and gratuitous violence will not be accepted. Obscurity for its own sake is also frowned upon." Has published poetry by Jim Thomas, Phillip Dacey, Susan Terris, Louis Philips, Francine Tolf, and Julie Lechevsky. Sample: $7 (back issue).

How to Contact Submit 3-7 poems at a time. Considers simultaneous submissions, "but not preferred"; no previously published poems. No e-mail submissions. Cover letter is preferred. Include list of publication credits. Type poems one/page. Often comments on rejected poems. Guidelines available for SASE, by e-mail, or on Web site. Responds within 4 months. Always sends prepublication galleys. Pays 2 contributor's copies. Acquires one-time rights.

Tips "Read the best poetry and be willing to learn from what you encounter. A genuine attempt is made to publish the best poems available, no matter who the writer. First-time poets, well-established poets, and those in between, all can and have found a place in the *Green Hills Literary Lantern*. We try to supply feedback, particularly to those we seek to encourage."

☑ GREEN MOUNTAINS REVIEW

Johnson State College, Johnson VT 05656. (802)635-1350. Fax: (802)635-1210. E-mail: gmr@ jsc.edu. Website: http://greenmountainsreview.jsc.vsc.edu. Established 1975. **Contact:** Neil Shepard, poetry editor.

•Poetry published in *Green Mountains Review* has been included in *The Best American Poetry* and *The Pushcart Prize* anthologies.

Magazines Needs *Green Mountains Review*, published twice/year, includes poetry (and other writing) by well-known authors and promising newcomers. Has published poetry by Carol Frost, Sharon Olds, Carl Phillips, David St. John, and David Wojahn. *Green Mountains Review* is 150-200 pages, digest-sized, flat-spined. Receives about 5,000 submissions/year, publishes 60 authors. Press run is 1,800. Single copy: $9.50 including postage; subscription: $15/year. Sample: $7 (back issue).

How to Contact Submit no more than 5 poems at a time. Considers simultaneous submissions. No e-mail submissions. Reads submissions September 1-March 1 only. Sometimes comments rejected poems. Publishes theme issues. Guidelines available for SASE. Responds in up to 6 months. Pays 2 contributor's copies plus one-year subscription. Acquires first North American serial rights. Send materials for review consideration.

☑ THE GREENSBORO REVIEW

MFA Writing Program, 3302 Hall for Humanities and Research Administration, University of North Carolina at Greensboro, P.O. Box 26170, Greensboro NC 27402. (336)334-5459. E-mail: anseay@uncg.edu. Website: www.greensbororeview.org. Established 1966. **Contact:** Jim Clark, editor.

•Work published in *The Greensboro Review* has been consistently anthologized or cited in *Best American Short Stories*, *New Stories from the South*, *The Pushcart Prize*, and *Prize Stories: The O. Henry Awards*.

Magazines Needs *The Greensboro Review*, published twice/year, showcases well-made verse in all styles and forms, though shorter poems (under 50 lines) are preferred. Has published poetry by Stephen Dobyns, Natasha Trethewey, Claudia Emerson, Thomas Lux, Stanley Plumly, and Alan Shapiro. *The Greensboro Review* is 144 pages, digest-sized, professionally printed, flat-spined, with colored matte cover. Subscription: $10/year, $25 for 3 years. Sample: $5.

How to Contact Submit no more than 5 poems at a time. Lines/poem: under 50 lines preferred. No previously published poems or simultaneous submissions. No fax or e-mail submissions. Cover letter is preferred. Include number of poems submitted. Provide SASE for reply; sufficient postage for return. Reads submissions according to the following deadlines: mss must arrive by September 15 to be considered for the Spring issue (acceptances in December), or February 15 to be considered for the Fall issue (acceptances in May). "Manuscripts arriving after those dates will be held for consideration for the next issue." Guidelines available in magazine, for SASE, or on Web site. Responds in 4 months. Always sends prepublication galleys. Pays 3 contributor's copies. Acquires first North American serial rights.

Tips "We want to see the best being written regardless of theme, subject, or style."

$ ☑ GULF COAST: A JOURNAL OF LITERATURE AND FINE ARTS

Dept. of English, University of Houston, Houston TX 77204-3013. (713)743-3223. Website: www.gulfcoastmag.org. Established 1986. **Contact:** Laurie Ann Cedilnik, managing editor; Sean

Bishop, associate editor; Lauren Berry, Anna Journey, Kent Shaw, poetry editors.

Magazines Needs *Gulf Coast: A Journal of Literature and Fine Arts*, published twice/year in April and October, includes poetry, fiction, essays, interviews, and color reproductions of work by artists from across the nation. While the journal features work by a number of established poets, editors are also interested in "providing a forum for new and emerging writers who are producing well-crafted work that takes risks." Has published poetry by Anne Carson, Carl Dennis, Terrance Hayes, Bob Hicok, Alice Notley, Srikanth Reddy, Karen Volkman, and Dean Young. *Gulf Coast* is 270 pages, 7x9, offset-printed, perfect-bound. Single copy: $10; subscription: $16/year, $28 for 2 years. Sample: $8.

How to Contact Submit up to 5 poems at a time. Considers simultaneous submissions with notification; no previously published poems. Cover letter is required. List previous publications and include a brief bio. Reads submissions September-April. Guidelines available for SASE or on Web site. Responds within 4-6 months. Pays $50/poem and 2 contributor's copies. Returns all rights (except electronic) upon publication.

Contest/Award Offerings Sponsors an annual poetry contest, awarding $1,000 and publication. **Entry fee:** $20 (includes one-year subscription). Make checks payable to *Gulf Coast*. Guidelines available on Web site.

☑ GULF STREAM MAGAZINE

English Dept., Florida International University, 3000 NE 151 St., North Miami Campus, North Miami FL 33181. (305)919-5599. E-mail: gulfstreamfiu@yahoo.com (inquiries only). Website: w3.fiu.edu/gulfstrm. Established 1989. **Contact:** Denise Sebesta Lanier, executive editor.

Magazines Needs *Gulf Stream*, published semiannually, is associated with the creative writing program at Florida International University. Wants "poetry of any style and subject matter as long as it's of high literary quality." Has published poetry by Gerald Costanzo, Naomi Shihab Nye, Jill Bialosky, and Catherine Bowman. *Gulf Stream* is 124 pages, digest-sized, flat-spined, printed on quality stock, with matte card cover. Accepts less than 10% of poetry received. Press run is 500. Subscription: $15. Sample: $5.

How to Contact Submit no more than 5 poems at a time. Considers simultaneous submissions with notification. Accepts electronic online submissions only; no snail mail/hard copy or e-mail submissions. "See Web site for details." Cover letter is required. Reads submissions September 1-March 1 only. Publishes theme issue every other issue. Guidelines available in magazine or on Web site. Responds in 3 weeks to 3 months. Pays 2 contributor's copies and 2 subscriptions. Acquires first North American serial rights.

☑ HAIGHT ASHBURY LITERARY JOURNAL

(Specialized: thematic issues), 558 Joost Ave., San Francisco CA 94127. (415)584-8264. E-mail: poetship@comcast.net (inquiries only). Established 1979-1980. **Contact:** Indigo Hotchkiss, Alice Rogoff, Gail Mitchell, and Cesar Love, editors.

Magazines Needs *Haight Ashbury Literary Journal*, published 1-2 times/year, is a newsprint tabloid that uses "all forms [of poetry]. Subject matter sometimes political, but open to all subjects. Poems of background—prison, multi-cultural experience—often published, as well as poems of protest. Few rhymes." Has published poetry by Dan O'Connell, Diane Frank, Dancing Bear, Lee Herrick, Al Young, and Laura Beausoleil. *Haight Ashbury* is 16 pages, includes ads. Press run is 2,500. Subscription: $16 for 4 issues; $40 for a lifetime subscription (all future and 9 back issues). Sample: $3.

How to Contact Submit up to 6 poems at a time. No e-mail submissions; postal submissions only (will accept e-mail submissions from overseas ONLY). "Please type 1 poem to a page, put name and address on every page, and include SASE. No bio." Sometimes publishes theme issues (each issue changes its theme and emphasis). Guidelines available for SASE. Responds in 4 months. Pays 3 contributor's copies, plus small monetary amount to featured writers. Rights revert to author.

Additional Information An anthology of past issues, *This Far Together*, is available for $15.

Tips "Do not send work that is longer than our magazine!"

$ ☑ HANGING LOOSE

Hanging Loose Press, 231 Wyckoff St., Brooklyn NY 11217. Website: www.hangingloosepress. com. Established 1966. **Contact:** Robert Hershon, Dick Lourie, and Mark Pawlak, poetry editors.

Magazines Needs *Hanging Loose*, published in April and October, "concentrates on the work of new writers." Wants "excellent, energetic" poems. Considers poetry by teens ("one section contains poems by high-school-age poets"). Has published poetry by Sherman Alexie, Paul Violi, Donna Brook, Kimiko Hahn, Harvey Shapiro, and Ha Jin. *Hanging Loose* is 120 pages, offset-printed on heavy stock, flat-spined, with 4-color glossy card cover. Sample: $12.

How to Contact Submit 4-6 poems at a time. No simultaneous submissions. "Would-be contributors should read the magazine first." Responds in 3 months. Pays small fee and 2 contributor's copies.

Additional Information Hanging Loose Press does not consider unsolicited book mss or artwork.

☑ HARPUR PALATE

Dept. of English, Binghamton University, P.O. Box 6000, Binghamton NY 13902-6000. E-mail: hppoetry@hotmail.com (queries only, no submissions). Website: http://harpurpalate. binghamton.edu. Established 2000. **Contact:** Joshua Keiter and Deborah Poe, poetry editors.

Magazines Needs *Harpur Palate*, published biannually, is "dedicated to publishing the best poetry and prose, regardless of style, form, or genre." Has published poetry by Marvin Bell, Ryan G. Van Cleave, Sascha Feinstein, Allison Joseph, Neil Shepard, and Ruth Stone. *Harpur Palate* is 180-200 pages, digest-sized, offset-printed, perfect-bound, with matte or glossy cover. Receives about 700 poems/year, accepts about 35. Press run is 1,000. Single copy: $10; subscription: $16/ year (2 issues). Sample: $5. Make checks payable to *Harpur Palate*.

How to Contact Submit 3-5 poems at a time. Lines/poem: "No restrictions; entire submission must be 10 pages or less." Considers simultaneous submissions, "but we must be notified immediately if the piece is taken somewhere else"; no previously published poems. No e-mail submissions. Cover letter is required. Reads submissions year round. Time between acceptance and publication is 2 months. Poems are circulated to an editorial board. Seldom comments on rejected poems. Guidelines available in magazine, for SASE, or on Web site. Responds in up to 6 months. Pays 2 contributor's copies. Acquires first North American serial rights.

Contest/Award Offerings The Milton Kessler Memorial Prize for Poetry (see separate listing).

Also Offers "We publish a Writing By Degrees supplement featuring fiction and poetry in the Winter issue. Writing By Degrees (http://writingbydegrees.binghamton.edu) is a creative writing conference run by graduate students in Binghamton's Creative Writing Program."

Tips "We have no restrictions on subject matter or form. Quite simply, send us your highest-quality poetry. Read through all of our submission instructions very carefully before sending your work (manuscripts that are not properly submitted will be discarded unread). Almost every literary magazine already says this, but it bears repeating: look at a copy of our publication (and other publications as well) to get an idea of the kind of writing published. Do an honest (perhaps even ruthless) assessment of your work to see if it's indeed ready to be submitted."

⧄ ☑ HARVARD REVIEW

Lamont Library, Harvard University, Cambridge MA 02138. (617)495-9775. Fax: (617)496-3692. E-mail: cathomps@fas.harvard.edu. Website: http://hcl.harvard.edu/harvardreview/. Established 1992 **Contact:** Major Jackson, poetry editor.

Magazines Needs Harvard Review, published semiannually, "has emerged as a major American literary journal with an eclectic mix of contributors in a wide variety of genres and styles."Does not want genre fiction. Seamus Heaney, John Ashbery, and Jorie Graham. Single: $13; Subscription: $16/year.

How to Contact Submit up to 5 poems.Considers simultaneous submissions. Accepts submissions by mail only (overseas only can submit by e-mail). Cover letter is required citing recent publications or awards. "Please include a SASE. Manuscripts must be paginated and clearly labeled with author's name on every page." Reads submissions year round. Guidelines available on Web site. Responds in up to 6 months. Pays 2 contributor's copies; additional copies $7. Acquires first North American serial rights.

Tips "We highly recommend that you familiarize yourself with Harvard Review before you submit your work. You can find both previous issues and subscription information online."

☑ HAWAI'I PACIFIC REVIEW

1060 Bishop St., Honolulu HI 96813. (808)544-1108. E-mail: pwilson@hpu.edu. Website: www.hpu.edu. Established 1987. **Contact:** Patrice M. Wilson, editor.

Magazines Needs *Hawai'i Pacific Review*, published annually in September by Hawai'i Pacific University, prints "quality poetry, short fiction, and personal essays from writers worldwide. Our journal seeks to promote a world view that celebrates a variety of cultural themes, beliefs, values, and viewpoints. We wish to further the growth of artistic vision and talent by encouraging sophisticated and innovative poetic and narrative techniques." Has published poetry by Wendy Bishop, Rick Bursky, Virgil Suárez, Bob Hikok, Daniel Gutstein, and Linda Bierds. *Hawai'i Pacific Review* is 80-120 pages, digest-sized, professionally printed on quality paper, perfect-bound, with coated card cover. Receives 800-1,000 poems/year, accepts up to 30-40. Press run is about 500 (100 shelf sales). Single copy: $8.95. Sample: $5.

How to Contact Submit up to 5 poems at a time. Lines/poem: 100 maximum. No previously published poems or simultaneous submissions. No fax or e-mail submissions. Cover letter is required. Include 5-line professional bio including prior publications. SASE required. "One submission per issue. No handwritten manuscripts. Include name on all pages." Reads submissions September 1-December 31 annually. Seldom comments on rejected poems. Guidelines available for SASE, by e-mail, or on Web site. Responds within 3 months. Pays 2 contributor's copies. Acquires first North American serial rights. Rights revert to poet upon publication. "Must acknowledge *Hawai'i Pacific Review* as first publisher."

Tips "We'd like to receive more experimental verse. Good poetry is eye-opening; it investigates the unfamiliar or reveals the spectacular in the ordinary. Good poetry does more than simply express the poet's feelings; it provides both insight and unexpected beauty. Send us your best work!"

▢ ◎ HEART: A JOURNAL OF SPIRITUAL WRITING

(Specialized: spiritual themes), c/o Mary H. Ber, 1481 W. Carmel Pointe Drive, Oro Valley AZ 85737. (520) 544-2832. E-mail: Maryhber@aol.com. Established 2008. **Contact:** Mary H. Ber, editor.

Magazines Needs *Heart: A Journal of Spiritual Writing*, published biannually, "is a non-denominational literary magazine dedicated to the affirmation of the meaning of life and to the qualities of the heart as a means of living life fully. People from many spiritual paths are now pointing at the human heart as the center of personal and global transformation." Wants "poems, stories, personal essays that promote these affirmations. We are hoping to get writing that mirrors many spiritual traditions and also writing from seekers involved in no specific tradition. Does not want proselytizing pieces or the conventional kind of inspirational writing. We will not accept writing that exhibits sentimentality or the simplification of complex issues." Considers poetry by children and teens. *Heart* is 36-48 pages, digest-sized, saddle-stitched, with glossy cover containing artwork or photography. Single copy: $8; subscription: $15. Make checks payable to Mary H. Ber.

How to Contact Submit up to 5 poems at a time. Considers previously published poems and simultaneous submissions. Accepts e-mail submissions (pasted into body of message); no fax or disk submissions. Cover letter is preferred. Reads submissions year round. Submit seasonal poems 6 months in advance. Time between acceptance and publication is 1 year. Poems are circulated to an editorial board. Always comments on rejected poems. Sometimes publishes theme issues. Guidelines available in magazine, for SASE, and by fax. Responds in 1 month. Pays 1 contributor's copy. Acquires one-time rights.

☑ HIDDEN OAK

402 S. 25th St., Philadelphia PA 19146. E-mail: hiddenoak@verizon.net. Established 1999. **Contact:** Louise Larkins, editor.

Magazines Needs *Hidden Oak*, published 2 or 3 times/year, seeks "well-crafted poems that make imaginative use of imagery to reach levels deeper than the immediate and personal. Both traditional forms and free verse are accepted. Especially welcome are poems which include time-honored poetic devices and reveal an ear for the music of language." *Hidden Oak* is 68-72 pages, digest-sized, photocopied, stapled, with original art/photograph on cover. Receives about 600 poems/year, accepts up to 40%. Press run is 100+. Single copy: $5; subscription: $12. Sample: $4. Make checks payable to Louise Larkins.

How to Contact Submit 3-6 poems at a time. Lines/poem: 30 maximum. Considers previously published poems (occasionally); no simultaneous submissions. Accepts e-mail submissions; no disk submissions. Cover letter is preferred. Include SASE. Submit seasonal poems 2-3 months in advance. Time between acceptance and publication is up to 3 months. Seldom comments on rejected poems. Might publish theme issues in the future. Guidelines available for SASE or by e-mail. Responds in 3 weeks. Pays 1 contributor's copy. Does not review books or chapbooks.

☑ HIRAM POETRY REVIEW

P.O. Box 162, Hiram OH 44234. (330)569-7512. Fax: (330)569-5166. E-mail: greenwoodwp@hiram.edu. Established 1966. **Contact:** Willard Greenwood, poetry editor.

Magazines Needs *Hiram Poetry Review*, published annually in spring, features "distinctive, beautiful, and heroic poetry." Wants "works of high and low art. We tend to favor poems that are pockets of resistance in the undeclared war against 'plain speech,' but we're interested in any work of high quality." Press run is 400 (300 subscribers, 150 libraries). Subscription: $9/year; $23/3 years.

How to Contact Send 3-5 poems at a time. Lines/poem: under 50 (3 single-spaced pages or less). Considers simultaneous submissions. No e-mail submissions. Cover letter is required. Include brief bio. Reads submissions year round. Responds in up to 6 months. Pays 2 contributor's copies. Acquires first North American serial rights. Rights return to poets upon publication. Reviews books of poetry in single- or multi-book format, no set length. Send materials for review consideration.

$ ☑ THE HOLLINS CRITIC

P.O. Box 9538, Hollins University, Roanoke VA 24020-1538. (540)362-6275. Website: www. hollins.edu/grad/eng_writing/critic/critic.htm. Established 1964. **Contact:** Cathryn Hankla, poetry editor.

Magazines Needs *The Hollins Critic*, published 5 times/year, prints critical essays, poetry, and book reviews. Uses a few short poems in each issue, interesting in form, content, or both. Has published poetry by William Miller, R.T. Smith, David Huddle, Margaret Gibson, and Julia Johnson. *The Hollins Critic* is 24 pages, magazine-sized. Press run is 500. Subscription: $9/year ($11 outside U.S.). Sample: $2.

How to Contact Submit up to 5 poems at a time using the online submission form at www. hollinscriticsubmissions.com, available from September 1-December 15. Submissions received at other times will be returned unread. Responds in 6 weeks. Pays $25/poem plus 5 contributor's copies.

Ⓝ Ⓟ ☑ ◎ HOLLY ROSE REVIEW

(Specialized: tattoos), E-mail: editor@hollyrosereview.com. Website: www.hollyrosereview. com. **Contact**: Theresa Edwards, MA, MFA; founder, editor, and publisher.

Magazines Needs *Holly Rose Review*, published quarterly online, publishes two themed issues and two non-themed issues per year in June, September, December, and March. "We are interested in poems and photos of tattoos that reach around the corner of life (or death) and grab. Both established and emerging artists from around the world are always welcome here."

How to Contact Submit four poems via e-mail. Considers simultaneous submissions; no previously published poems unless invited. See Web site for submission periods and themed issues. Regularly publishes theme issues. Guidelines on Web site. Acquires first North American electronic publication rights, archival rights. "All other rights remain the artist's at publication."

☑ HOME PLANET NEWS

P.O. Box 455, High Falls NY 12440. E-mail: homeplanetnews@yahoo.com. Website: www. homeplanetnews.org. Established 1979. **Contact:** Donald Lev, editor.

Magazines Needs *Home Planet News*, published 3 times/year, aims "to publish lively and eclectic poetry, from a wide range of sensibilities, and to provide news of the small press and poetry scenes, thereby fostering a sense of community among contributors and readers." Wants "honest, well-crafted poems, open or closed form, on any subject." Does not want "any work which seems to us to be racist, sexist, ageist, anti-Semitic, or imposes limitations on the human spirit." Considers poetry by children and teens. Has published poetry by Enid Dame, Antler, Lyn Lifshin, Gerald Locklin, Hal Sirowitz, and Janine Pommy Vega. *Home Planet News* is 24 pages, tabloid, Web offset-printed, includes ads. Receives about 1,000 poems/year, accepts up to 3%. Press run is 1,000 (300 subscribers). Single copy: $5; subscription: $12/3 issues, $18/6 issues.

How to Contact Submit 3-6 poems at a time. Lines/poem: no limit on length, "but shorter poems (under 30 lines) stand a better chance." No previously published poems or simultaneous submissions. Cover letter is preferred. "SASE is a must." Time between acceptance and publication is 1 year. Seldom comments on rejected poems. Occasionally publishes theme issues. Upcoming themes available in magazine. Guidelines available for SASE or on Web site; "however, it is usually best to simply send work." Responds in 4 months. Pays one-year gift subscription plus 3 contributor's copies. Acquires first rights. Rights revert to poet upon publication. Reviews books/chapbooks of poetry and other magazines in 1,200 words, single- and multi-book format. Send materials for review consideration to Donald Lev. "Note: we do have guidelines for book reviewers; please write for them or check Web site. Magazines are reviewed by a staff member."

Tips "Read many publications, attend readings, feel yourself part of a writing community, learn from others."

☑ HOMESTEAD REVIEW

Box A-5, 156 Homestead Ave., Hartnell College, Salinas CA 93901. (831)755-6943. Fax: (831)755-6751. E-mail: mteutsch@hartnell.edu. Website: www.hartnell.cc.ca.us/homestead_review. Established 1985. **Contact:** Maria Garcia Teutsch, editor.

Magazines Needs *Homestead Review*, published annually in April, seeks "avant-garde poetry as well as fixed form styles of remarkable quality and originality." Does not want "Hallmark-style writing or first drafts." Considers poetry written by children and teens. Has published poetry by Sally Van Doren, Kathryn Kirkpatrick, Laura Le Hew, Allison Joseph, and Hal Sirowitz. Receives about 1,000 poems/year, accepts about 15%. Press run is 500 (300 subscribers/libraries); 200 are distributed free to poets, writers, bookstores. Single copy: $10; subscription: $20/year. Make checks payable to *Homestead Review*.

How to Contact Submit 3 poems at a time. No previously published poems or simultaneous submissions. E-mail submissions preferred. Cover letter is required. "A brief bio should be included in the cover letter." Reads submissions year round. Deleted. Time between acceptance and publication is up to 6 months. "Manuscripts are read by the staff and discussed. Poems/fiction accepted by majority consensus." Often comments on rejected poems. Guidelines available for SASE. Responds in 5 months. Pays 1 contributor's copy. Acquires one-time rights.

Contest/Award Offerings Contest with categories for poetry and fiction. Offers 1st Prize: $250 plus publication in *Homestead Review*. All entries will be considered for publication in *Homestead Review*. Guidelines available on Web site. **Entry fee:** $15 for 3 poems. **Deadline:** see Web site for current dates.

Tips "Poetry is language distilled; do not send unpolished work. Join a workshop group if at all possible."

Ⓝ ▣ ▢ ◎ HOSPITAL DRIVE

(Specialized: Medical/Healthcare), Charlottesville VA 22908. (434)924-5856. Fax: (434)924-5986. E-mail: mhi-mag@virginia.edu. Website: http://hospitaldrive.med.virginia.edu. Established 2006. **Contact:** Dr. Daniel Becker, editor.

Magazines Needs *Hospital Drive*, published irregularly, "encourages original creative work that examines themes of health, illness, and healing. Submissions will be accepted from anyone, but preference is given to those involved in providing, teaching, studying, or researching patient care. All work will be judged anonymously by reviewers and the editorial board. Poems, short fiction, personal essays, reviews, photography, and visual art (painting, drawing, sculpture, mixed media) will be considered. Issues will be released at least once/year, and include invited work."

How to Contact Submit up to 5 poems at a time. Considers simultaneous submissions. Accepts e-mail submissions as attachment); no fax or disk submissions. Cover letter is unnecessary. "All works must be submitted by e-mail, accompanied by basic contact information and the titles of each piece. Attach each poem as a separate document to 1 e-mail. Put "poetry submission" in the e-mail subject line." Reads submissions year round. Time between acceptance and publication is 3-6 months. All submissions will be reviewed anonymously by the editorial board, "and only the highest quality work will be published." Never comments on rejected poems. Guidelines available on Web site.

$ ☑ THE HUDSON REVIEW

684 Park Ave., New York NY 10021. Website: www.hudsonreview.com. **Contact:** Julia Powers, assistant editor.

•Work published in *The Hudson Review* has been included in *The Best American Poetry*.

Magazines Needs *The Hudson Review*, published quarterly, is considered one of the most prestigious and influential journals in the nation. Editors welcome all styles and forms; however, competition is extraordinarily keen. Has published poetry by Marilyn Nelson, Hayden Carruth, Louis Simpson, and Dana Gioia. *The Hudson Review* is 176 pages, flat-spined. Subscription: $36/ year ($44 foreign), institutions $38/year ($42 foreign). Sample: $10.

How to Contact Submit no more than 10 poems at a time. No previously published poems or simultaneous submissions. Reads unsolicited mss. April 1-June 30 only. "Manuscripts submitted by subscribers who so identify themselves will be read throughout the year." Guidelines available in magazine, for SASE, or on Web site. Responds in 3 months. Always sends prepublication galleys. Pays 50¢/line and 2 contributor's copies.

Tips "Read the magazine to ascertain our style/sensibility."

$ ☑ HUNGER MOUNTAIN

The Vermont College Journal of Arts & LettersVermont College, 36 College St., Montpelier VT 05602. (802)828-8517. Fax: (802)828-8649. E-mail: hungermtn@vermontcollege.edu. Website: www.hungermtn.org. Established 2002. **Contact:** Miciah Bay Gault, managing editor. Member: CLMP.

Magazines Needs *Hunger Mountain, The Vermont College Journal of Arts & Letters*, published semiannually, prints "high-quality poetry, prose, and artwork selected by guest editors from the Vermont College MFA in Writing Program." Wants poems "ready for publication." Does not want entire mss, or children's or young adult poetry. Has published poetry by Hayden Carruth, Mark Doty, Carol Muske-Dukes, Maxine Kumin, Charles Simic, and Ruth Stone. *Hunger Mountain* is about 200 pages, 7x10, professionally printed, perfect-bound, with full-bleed color artwork on cover, includes ads (only in back). Receives about 600 poems/year, accepts about 5%. Press run is 1,500 (700 subscribers, 50 libraries, 200 shelf sales); 100 distributed free to writing centers, book fairs, and other journals. Single copy: $10; subscription: $17/year, $32 for 2 years, $60 for 4 years. Make checks payable to *Hunger Mountain*.

How to Contact Submit 3-10 poems at a time. Considers simultaneous submissions; no previously published poems. No fax, e-mail, or disk submissions. Cover letter is preferred. "**Include double copies of everything**, including cover letter." Reads submissions year round. Time between acceptance and publication is 6 months. Poems are circulated to an editorial board. Occasionally comments on rejected poems. Guidelines available for SASE, by fax, e-mail, or on Web site. Responds in 4 months. Always sends prepublication galleys. Pays $5/page (minimum $30) and 2 contributor's copies. Acquires first North American serial rights.

Contest/Award Offerings The annual Ruth Stone Prize in Poetry (see separate listing in Contests & Awards).

Tips "Always read submission guidelines and make sure your poems are appropriate for the magazine or journal!"

$ ▢ ◎ HUNGUR MAGAZINE

P.O. Box 782, Cedar Rapids IA 52406-0782. E-mail: hungurmagazine@yahoo.com. Website: www.samsdotpublishing.com. Established 2004. **Contact:** Terrie Leigh Relf. Member: The Speculative Literature Foundation (http://SpeculativeLiterature.org).

Magazines Needs *Hungur Magazine*, published biannually, features "stories and poems about vampires, and especially about vampires on other worlds." Prefers a "decadent literary style." Does not want "horror with excessive blood and gore." *Hungur Magazine* is 32 pages, magazine-sized, offset-printed, saddle-stapled, with paper cover with color art, includes ads. Receives about 200 poems/year, accepts about 20 (10%). Press run is 100/issue. Single copy: $8; subscription: $14/year. Make checks payable to Tyree Campbell/Sam's Dot Publishing.

How to Contact Submit up to 5 poems at a time. Lines/poem: prefers less than 200. No previously published poems or simultaneous submissions. Accepts e-mail submissions (pasted into body of message); no disk submissions. "Submission should include snail mail address and a short (1-2 lines) bio." Reads submissions year round. Submit seasonal poems 6 months in advance. Time between acceptance and publication is 3-4 months. Editor: Terrie Leigh Relf. Often comments on rejected poems. Guidelines available on Web site. Responds in 4-6 weeks. Pays $4/poem and 1 contributor's copy. Acquires first North American serial rights. Reviews books and chapbooks of poetry. Send materials for review consideration to Tyree Campbell.

Tips "It's up to the writer to take the first step and submit work. Some of our best poems have come from poets who weren't sure if they were good enough."

▣ THE HURRICANE REVIEW: A NATIONAL JOURNAL OF POETRY AND SHORT FICTION

English/Communications Dept., Pensacola Junior College, 1000 College Blvd., Pensacola FL 32504. (850)484-1424. Fax: (850)484-1149. E-mail: mwernicke@pjc.edu. Website: www.pjc.edu/academics/departments/english/hurricane.html. Established 1986. **Contact:** Marian Wernicke, faculty editor.

Magazines Needs *The Hurricane Review, A National Journal of Poetry and Short Fiction*, published annually in the fall, features poetry and short fiction. Wants poetry of "any style, any length. No biases other than quality." Does not want "inspirational or greeting card verse." Has published poetry by R.T. Smith, Sue Walker, Larry Rubin, Cornelius Eady, and Simon Perchik. *The Hurricane Review* is 100 pages, digest-sized, professionally printed, perfect-bound, with matte card cover. Receives about 1,000 poems/year, accepts about 50-60. Press run is 500. Subscription: $4. Sample: $4.

How to Contact Submit 3-5 poems at a time. No previously published poems or simultaneous submissions. Cover letter is preferred. Include bio and/or publication history. SASE required. Reads submissions August 1-May 15 only. Responds in 3 months, faster when possible. Pays 3 contributor's copies. Acquires first rights.

Tips "As David Kirby says, a poem should be well punctuated and give evidence of careful proof-reading. It should be understandable to a reader who is not the poet."

▣ ◎ THE HYCO REVIEW

an online arts and literary review (Specialized: work from NC resident/native poets)(formerly Reflections Literary Journal), P.O. Box 1197, Roxboro NC 27573. (336)599-1181, ext. 231. E-mail: reflect@piedmontcc.edu. Established 1999. **Contact:** Dawn Langley, editor.

Magazines Needs The *Hyco Review*, published annually in spring, prints poetry, short fiction, and creative nonfiction. Wants any styles and forms of poetry, including translations. Does not want material using obscenities, or culturally insensitive material. **Accepts submissions from NC authors only (residents or natives).** "If time and space permit, we'll consider submissions from southeastern U.S. authors and from authors we've previously published." Has published poetry by Robert Cooperman, Fredrick Zydek, Bruce Bennett, Fred Chappell, Shari O'Brien, and Daniel Green. The *Hyco Review* is 100-150 pages, digest-sized. Receives about 400 poems/year, accepts about 5%. Press run is 250 (20 subscribers, 4 libraries, 150 shelf sales); 75 distributed free to contributors, editors, advisors, local schools, and cultural sites. Single copy: $7; subscription: $7. Sample: $5 (back issue). Make checks payable to *Hyco Review*

How to Contact Submit 5 poems maximum at a time. Lines/poem: no longer than 1 page (single-spaced). Considers previously published poems and simultaneous submissions (if notified). Accepts e-mail submissions (pasted into body of message or as attachment in MS Word). "Include a 25-word bio with submission. Include 2 copies of each poem—1 with name and address, 1 without. Affix adequate postage to SAE for return of manuscript if desired, or use First-Class stamps on SAE for notification. Poems are read by an 8- to 12-member editorial board who rank submissions through 'blind' readings. Board members refrain from ranking their own submissions." Sometimes comments on rejected poems. Guidelines available in magazine, for SASE, or by e-mail. Responds in up to 9 months (in March or April). Pays 1 contributor's copy. Acquires first North American serial rights (if poem is unpublished) or one-time rights (if poem is previously published).

☑ IBBETSON ST. PRESS

25 School St., Somerville MA 02143-1721. (617)628-2313. E-mail: dougholder@post.harvard. edu. Website: http://homepage.mac.com/rconte. Established 1999. **Contact:** Doug Holder, editor; submissions editor: Irene Koronas; copy editor: Dorian Brooks.

Magazines Needs *Ibbetson St. Press*, published semiannually in June and November, prints "'down to earth' poetry that is well-written; has clean, crisp images; with a sense of irony and humor." Wants "mostly free verse, but are open to rhyme." Does not want "maudlin, trite, overly political, vulgar for vulgar's sake work." Has published poetry by Afaa Michael Weaver, Sarah Hannah, Gloria Mindock, Harris Gardner, Tracy Strauss, Robert K. Johnson, Gary Metras, and others. *Ibbetson St. Press* is 50 pages, magazine-sized, desktop-published, with glossy white cover, includes ads. Receives about 1,000 poems/year, accepts up to 30%. Press run is 200. Also archived at Harvard, Brown, University of Wisconsin, Poets House-NYC, and Buffalo University Libraries. Single copy: $7; subscription: $13. Make checks payable to *Ibbetson St. Press*.

How to Contact Submit 3-5 poems at a time. Considers previously published poems; no simultaneous submissions. No e-mail submissions; postal submissions only. Cover letter is required. Time between acceptance and publication is up to 5 months. "3 editors comment on submissions." Guidelines available for SASE. Responds in 2 months or more. Pays 1 contributor's copy. Acquires one-time rights. Reviews books/chapbooks of poetry and other magazines in 250-500 words. Send materials for review consideration.

Additional Information *Does not accept unsolicited chapbook mss.***Has published** *Promise Supermarket* **by Elizabeth Quinlan,** *Time Leaves,* **by Barbara Bialick,** *Manufacturing America,* **by Lisa Beatman,** *Awakenings,* **by Richard Wilhelm,** *From Mist to Shadow,* **by Robert K. Johnson, and** *Blood Soaked Dresses,* **by Gloria Mindock. Responds to queries in 1 month.**

Tips "Please buy a copy of the magazine you submit to—support the small press. In your work, be honest."

$ ☑ THE ICONOCLAST

1675 Amazon Rd., Mohegan Lake NY 10547-1804. Established 1992. **Contact:** Phil Wagner, editor/publisher.

Magazines Needs *The Iconoclast*, published 4 times/year, is a general interest literary journal. Wants "poems that have something to say—the more levels the better. Try for originality; if not in thought, then expression. Look for the unusual in the usual, parallels in opposites, the capturing of what is unique or often unnoticed in an ordinary, or extraordinary, moment; what makes us human—and the resultant glories and agonies. Our poetry is accessible to a thoughtful reading public." Does not want "greeting card verse or noble religious sentiments. Nothing sentimental, obscure, or self-absorbed." *The Iconoclast* is 64-96 pages, magazine-sized, photo offset-printed on 50 lb. white paper, includes ads. Receives about 2,000 poems/year, accepts up to 3%. Press run is 1,000-3,000. Subscription: $18 for 8 issues. Sample: $5.

How to Contact Submit 3-4 poems at a time. Time between acceptance and publication is 4 months to one year. Sometimes comments on rejected poems. Guidelines available for SASE. Responds in 1 month. Pays $2-5/poem for first North American rights (on publication), 1 contributor's copy per published page or poem, offers 40% discount on extras. Reviews books of poetry in 250 words, single-book format.

Tips "Poets merely collecting another credit need not apply. Show us you care about something other than self-mythologizing. And if we've already published you, it helps if you can indicate you actually read the work of anyone else in that issue."

▣ ▢ ILLOGICAL MUSE

313 Fulton St., Buchanan MI 49107. E-mail: illogicalmuse@yahoo.com. Website: www.geocities. com/illogicalmuse. Established 2004. **Contact:** Amber Rothrock, editor.

Magazines Needs *Illogical Muse*, an internet quarterly, welcomes "submissions of poetry, fiction, essays and artwork. Looks for well-crafted, intelligent verse in any form and on any subject." Does not want "anything overly graphic or explicit in content." Considers poetry written by children and teens. Has published poetry by Michael Lee Johnson, Sandra Hedin, B.Z. Niditch, Sara Crawford, and Marianne Lavalle-Vincent. Accepts 90% of the material received.

How to Contact Submit up to 6 poems at a time. Lines/poem: no more than 100. Considers previously published poems and simultaneous submissions. Absolutely no multiple submissions. Accepts e-mail submissions (pasted into body of message); no disk submissions. Cover letter is preferred. Include SASE, IRC's or valid e-mail for response. Work will be returned if proper postage is provided. Reads submissions year round. Submit seasonal poems 6 months in advance. Time between acceptance and publication is up to 1 year. Sometimes comments on rejected poems. "Current theme is Nature but there are special requirements for this issue so check guidelines before submitting. Guidelines available for SASE or on Web site. Responds in 6 months. Reviews books/chapbooks of poetry and fiction and other magazine/journals. Send materials for review consideration. Acquires one-time rights and electronic/archival rights for Web site. All rights remain with poet.

Also Offers Quarterly writing contest. More information available on the blog. Link from the Web site.

$ ▢ ◎ ILLUMEN

(Specialized: speculative poetry), P.O. Box 782, Cedar Rapids IA 52406-0782. E-mail: illumensdp@yahoo.com. Website: www.samsdotpublishing.com. Established 2004. **Contact:** Karen L. Newman, editor. Member: The Speculative Literature Foundation.

Magazines Needs *Illumen*, published biannually, contains speculative poetry and articles about speculative poetry. "Speculative poetry includes, but is not limited to, fantasy, science fiction, sword and sorcery, alternate history, and horror." Wants "fantasy, science fiction, spooky horror, and speculative poetry with minimal angst." Does not want "horror with excessive blood and gore." Considers poetry by children and teens. Has published poetry by Ian Watson, Bruce Boston, Sonya Taaffe, Mike Allen, Marge B. Simon, and David C. Kopaska-Merkel. *Illumen* is 50 pages, digest-sized, offset-printed, perfect-bound, with color cover with color art, includes ads. Receives about 200 poems/year, accepts about 50 (25%). Press run is 100/issue (20 subscribers, 50 shelf sales); 5 distributed free to reviewers. Single copy: $9; subscription: $15/year. Make checks payable to Tyree Campbell/Sam's Dot Publishing.

How to Contact Submit up to 5 poems at a time. Lines/poem: prefers less than 200. Considers previously published poems; no simultaneous submissions. Accepts e-mail submissions (pasted into body of message); no disk submissions. "Submission should include snail mail address and a short (1-2 lines) bio." Reads submissions year round. Submit seasonal poems 6 months in advance. Time between acceptance and publication is 1-2 months. Often comments on rejected poems. Guidelines available on Web site. Responds in 4-6 weeks. Pays 2 cents/word (minimum: $3) for original poems and 1 contributor's copy. Acquires first North American serial rights. Reviews books/chapbooks of poetry. Send materials for review consideration to Tyree Campbell.

Tips "It's up to the writer to take the first step and submit work. Some of our best poems have come from poets who weren't sure if they were good enough. Horror poetry is a difficult sell with us."

☑ ILLUMINATIONS

An International Magazine of Contemporary Writing Dept. of English, College of Charleston, 66 George St., Charleston SC 29424-0001. (843)953-1920. Fax: (843)953-3180. E-mail: lewiss@cofc. edu. Website: www.cofc.edu/Illuminations. Established 1982. **Contact:** Simon Lewis, editor.

Magazines Needs *Illuminations: An International Magazine of Contemporary Writing*, published annually, provides "a forum for new writers alongside already established ones." Open as to form and style, and to translations. Does not want to see anything "bland or formally clunky." Has published poetry by Brenda Marie Osbey, Geri Doran, Dennis Brutus, and Carole Satyamurti. *Illuminations* is 64-88 pages, digest-sized, offset-printed, perfect-bound, with 2-color card cover. Receives about 1,500 poems/year, accepts up to 5%. Press run is 400. Subscription: $15/2 issues. Sample: $10.

How to Contact Submit up to 6 poems at a time. No previously published poems or simultaneous submissions. Accepts fax, e-mail (pasted into body of message, no attachments), and disk submissions. Cover letter is preferred (brief). Time between acceptance and publication "depends on when received. Can be up to a year." Occasionally publishes theme issues. Guidelines available by e-mail or on Web site. Responds within 2 months. Pays 2 contributor's copies plus 1 subsequent issue. Acquires all rights. Returns rights on request.

$ ☑ ◎ IMAGE: ART, FAITH, MYSTERY

(Specialized: religious faith; Judeo-Christian), 3307 3rd Ave. W., Seattle WA 98119. E-mail: image@imagejournal.org. Website: www.imagejournal.org. Established 1989. **Contact:** Gregory Wolfe, publisher.

Magazines Needs *Image: Art, Faith, Mystery*, published quarterly, "explores and illustrates the relationship between faith and art through world-class fiction, poetry, essays, visual art, and other arts." Wants "poems that grapple with religious faith, usually Judeo-Christian." Has published poetry by Philip Levine, Scott Cairns, Annie Dillard, Mary Oliver, Mark Jarman, and Kathleen Norris. *Image* is 136 pages, 10x7, printed on acid-free paper, perfect-bound, with glossy 4-color cover, includes ads. Receives about 800 poems/year, accepts up to 2%. Has 4,200 subscribers (100 are libraries). Subscription: $39.95. Sample: $16 postpaid.

How to Contact Submit up to 4 poems at a time. No previously published poems. No e-mail submissions. Cover letter is preferred. Time between acceptance and publication is 1 year.

Guidelines available on Web site. Responds in 3 months. Always sends prepublication galleys. Pays 4 contributor's copies plus $2/line ($150 maximum). Acquires first North American serial rights. Reviews books of poetry in 2,000 words, single- or multi-book format. Send materials for review consideration.

☑ ◎ INDEFINITE SPACE

(Specialized: experimental, visual, minimalistic) P.O. Box 40101, Pasadena CA 91114. Established 1992. Website: www.indefinitespace.net. **Contact:** Marcia Arrieta, editor/publisher.

Magazines Needs *Indefinite Space*, published annually, prints experimental, visual, and minimalistic poetry. Does not want rhyming poetry. Has published poetry by Marthe Reed, Anne Blonstein, Kevin Magee, Petra Backonja, Peter Layton, and Jill Magi. *Indefinite Space* is 48 pages, digest-sized. Single copy: $7; subscription: $12 for 2 issues. Make checks payable to Marcia Arrieta.

How to Contact Considers simultaneous submissions; no previously published poems. Seldom comments on rejected poems. Guidelines available on Web site. Responds in up to 3 months. Poet retains copyright.

$ ☑ INDIANA REVIEW

Ballantine Hall 465, 1020 E. Kirkwood Ave., Bloomington IN 47405-7103. (812)855-3439. E-mail: inreview@indiana.edu. Website: www.indiana.edu/~inreview. Established 1976. **Contact:** Nina Mamikunian, editor.

- •Poetry published in *Indiana Review* has been included in *The Best American Poetry* and *The Pushcart Prize*.

Magazines Needs *Indiana Review*, published semiannually, includes prose, poetry, creative nonfiction, book reviews, and visual art. "We look for an intelligent sense of form and language, and admire poems of risk, ambition, and scope." Wants "all types of poems—free verse, traditional, experimental. Reading a sample issue is the best way to determine if *Indiana Review* is a potential home for your work. Any subject matter is acceptable if it is written well. Translations are welcome." Has published poetry by Denise Duhamel, Sherman Alexie, Marilyn Chin, Julianna Baggott, and Alberto Rios. *Indiana Review* is 160 pages, digest-sized, professionally printed, flat-spined, with color matte cover. Receives more than 9,000 submissions/year, accepts up to 60. Has 2,000 subscribers. Subscription: $17/year, $28 for 2 years. Sample: $9.

How to Contact Submit 4-6 poems at a time. Lines/poem: "do not send more than 10 pages of poetry per submission." Considers simultaneous submissions with notification; no previously published poems. Cover letter with brief bio is desired. SASE is mandatory for response. Guidelines available on Web site. "We try to respond to manuscripts in 3-4 months. Reading time is often slower during summer and holiday months." Pays $5/page ($10 minimum), 2 contributor's copies, and remainder of year's subscription. Acquires first North American serial rights only. Reviews books of poetry. Send materials for review consideration.

Contest/Award Offerings Holds yearly poetry and prose-poem contests. Guidelines available for SASE or on Web site.

$ ◻ INKWELL

Manhattanville College, 2900 Purchase St., Purchase NY 10577. (914)323-7239. Fax: (914)323-3122. E-mail: inkwell@mville.edu. Website: www.inkwelljournal.org. Established 1995. **Contact:** Poetry Editor. Member: CLMP.

- •*Inkwell* is produced in affiliation with the Master of Arts in Writing program at Manhattanville College, and is staffed by faculty and graduate students of the program.

Magazines Needs *Inkwell*, published semiannually, features "emerging writers, high quality poems and short stories, creative nonfiction, artwork, literary essays, memoir and interviews on writing by established figures, and yearly compeitions in poetry and fiction." Wants "serious work—very well made verse, any form, any genre." Does not want "doggerel, light or humorous verse." Has published poetry by Thomas Lux, Penelope Scambly Schott, Katherine Mosby, Jim Daniels, John Hoppenthaler, and Jennifer Perrine. *Inkwell* is 150 pages, digest-sized, press-printed, perfect-bound, with cover with illustration/photography. Receives about 2,500 poems/year, accepts about 40. Press run is 1,000. Single copy: $8; subscription: $16/year. Sample: $6 (back issue). Make checks payable to Manhattanville College—*Inkwell*.

How to Contact Submit up to 5 poems at a time. Lines/poem: 70 maximum. Considers simultaneous submissions; no previously published poems. ("Previously published" work includes poetry posted on a public Web site/blog/forum, but not on a private, password-protected forum.) No fax, e-mail, or disk submissions. Cover letter is required. "Omit name of author from text." Include SASE. Reads submissions August 1-November 30. Time between acceptance and publication is 5 months. Poems are circulated to an editorial board. Sometimes comments on rejected poems. Guidelines available for SASE or on Web site. Responds in 3 months. Pays $10/page and 2 contributor's copies. Acquires first North American serial rights. Rights revert to poets upon publication.

Contest/Award Offerings The Inkwell Annual Poetry Competition (see separate listing in Contests & Awards).

▣ ☑ IN OUR OWN WORDS

Burning Bush Publications, P.O. Box 4658, Santa Rosa CA 95402. Website: www.bbbooks.com. **Contact:** Abby Bogomolny, editor.

Magazines Needs *In Our Own Words*, published annually online, seeks poetry and prose poems for its literary e-zine. Wants "thought-provoking, creative, alternative writing. We choose work that inspires compassion, peace, and respect for diversity in original and unexpected ways." Does not want "manuscripts of full-length books." Sample: past issues available on Web site.

How to Contact Cover letter is required. "Send submissions to us by U.S. mail only. Include SASE. If you want us to reply via e-mail, include your e-mail address! We will ask you for a digital file via e-mail, if we want to publish your submission." Reads submissions according to the following deadline: Annual Edition, June 1st. Guidelines available on Web site. Rights revert to poet upon publication.

Contest/Award Offerings The Burning Bush Poetry Prize (see separate listing in Contests & Awards).

Tips "Our readers are interested in love, social and economic justice, liberation movements, spirituality and improving the quality of life in all communities."

▤ ☑ INTERPRETER'S HOUSE

19 The Paddox, Oxford OX2 7PN England. Website: www.interpretershouse.org.uk. Established 1996. **Contact:** Merryn Williams.

• Business correspondence (including subscriptions) should go to Matt Bright, Upper Flat, 251 Abingdon Rd., Oxford OX1 4TH England.

Magazines Needs *Interpreter's House*, published 3 times/year in February, June, and October, prints short stories and poetry. Wants "good poetry, not too long." Does not want "Christmas-card verse or incomprehensible poetry." Has published poetry by Dannie Abse, Tony Curtis, Pauline Stainer, Alan Brownjohn, Peter Redgrove, and R.S. Thomas. *Interpreter's House* is 74 pages, A5, with attractive cover design. Receives about 1,000 poems/year, accepts up to 5%.

Press run is 300 (200 subscribers). Single copy: £3 plus 55p. postage; subscription: £12 for 3 issues. Sample: £3.50.

How to Contact Submit 5 poems at a time. No previously published poems or simultaneous submissions. Cover letter is preferred. Time between acceptance and publication is 2 weeks to 3 months. Often comments on rejected poems. Guidelines available for SASE (or SAE and IRC). Responds "fast." Pays 1 contributor's copy.

Contest/Award Offerings Sponsors the Bedford Open Poetry Competition. Send SAE and IRC for details.

☑ ◎ IN THE GROVE

(Specialized: poetry by CA writers), P.O. Box 16195, Fresno CA 93755. (559)442-4600, ext. 8105. Fax: (559)265-5756. E-mail: leeherrick@hotmail.com. Website: www.inthegrove.net. Established 1996. **Contact:** Lee Herrick.

Magazines Needs *In the Grove*, published annually, publishes "short fiction, essays, and poetry by new and established writers currently living in the Central Valley and throughout California." Wants "poetry of all forms and subject matter. We seek the originality, distinct voice, and craft of a poem." Does not want "greeting card verse or forced rhyme. Be fresh. Take a risk." Has published poetry by Andres Montoya, Corrinne Clegg Hales, Daniel Chacon, Lawson Fusao Inada, Amy Uyematsu, and Charles Harper Webb. *In the Grove* is 80-100 pages, digest-sized, photocopied, perfect-bound, with heavy cardstock cover. Receives about 500 poems/year, accepts up to 10%. Press run is 200 (50 subscribers, 100 shelf sales); 50 distributed free to contributors, colleagues. Subscription: $12. Sample: $6.

How to Contact Submit 3-5 poems at a time. Considers previously published poems ("on occasion") and simultaneous submissions ("with notice"). Cover letter is preferred. Time between acceptance and publication is up to 6 months. "Poetry editor reads all submissions and makes recommendations to editor, who makes final decisions." Seldom comments on rejected poems. Guidelines available for SASE or on Web site. Responds in 3-6 months. Pays 1 contributor's copy. Acquires first or one-time rights as well as right to publish on Web site. Rights return to poets upon publication.

☑ ◎ INVERTED-A HORN

(Specialized: traditional poetry with meter and rhyme), Inverted-A, Inc., P.O. Box 267, Licking MO 65542. E-mail: amnfn@well.com. Established 1977. **Contact:** Nets Katz and Aya Katz, editors.

Magazines Needs *Inverted-A Horn*, published irregularly, welcomes political topics, social issues, and science fiction. Wants traditional poetry with meter and rhyme. Does not want to see anything "modern, formless, existentialist." *Inverted-A Horn* is usually 9 pages, magazine-sized, offset-printed. Press run is 300. Sample: SASE with postage for 2 ounces (subject to availability).

How to Contact Considers simultaneous submissions. Accepts e-mail submissions (as attachment, ASCII). Responds in 4 months. Pays 1 contributor's copy; offers 40% discount on additional copies.

Additional Information Inverted-A, Inc. is a very small press that evolved from publishing technical manuals for other products. "Our interests center on freedom, justice, and honor." Publishes 1 chapbook/year.

Tips "I strongly recommend that would-be contributors avail themselves of this opportunity to explore what we are looking for. Most of the submissions we receive do not come close."

☑ IODINE POETRY JOURNAL

P.O. Box 18548, Charlotte NC 28218-0548. (704)595-9526. E-mail: iodineopencut@aol.com. Website: www.iodinepoetryjournal.com. Established 2000. **Contact:** Jonathan K. Rice, editor/publisher.

- •Poetry published in *Iodine Poetry Journal* has been selected for inclusion in *The Best American Poetry*.

Magazines Needs *Iodine Poetry Journal*, published semiannually, provides "a venue for both emerging and established poets." Wants "good poetry of almost any style, including form (e.g., pantoum and sestina) and experimental." Does not want rhyme, religion, or pornography. Has published poetry by Fred Chappell, Peter Cooley, Colette Inez, Ron Koertge, and R.T. Smith. *Iodine Poetry Journal* is 78 pages, digest-sized, perfect-bound, with full-color laminated cover, includes ads. Receives about 2,000 poems/year, accepts about 60 poems/issue. Press run is 350. Single copy: $7; subscription: $12/year (2 issues) $22 for 2 years (4 issues). Sample: "Back issues vary in price." Make checks payable to *Iodine Poetry Journal*.

How to Contact Submit 3-5 poems at a time. Lines/poem: 40 or less preferred, "but not totally averse to longer poems." No previously published poems or simultaneous submissions. Accepts e-mail submissions from international poets only; no disk submissions. Cover letter is preferred. "Always include SASE, and specify if SASE is for return of manuscript or reply only. I like a brief introduction of yourself in the cover letter." Reads submissions year round. Submit seasonal poems 6 months in advance. Time between acceptance and publication is 6 months to 1 year. Poems are circulated to an editorial board. "I occasionally have other readers assist in the selection process, but editor makes the final decision." Sometimes comments on rejected poems. Guidelines available in magazine, for SASE, or on Web site. Responds in 2-3 months. Sometimes sends prepublication galleys. Pays 1 contributor's copy and discounts extra copies of the issue in which work appears. Acquires first North American serial rights.

Also Offers "Shorter work is published in *Open Cut*, the summer broadside. Payment is 3 copies of the broadside. The broadside is 11X17 folded to pamphlet size, which will fit into a #10 envelope. It's a free publication that appears between the Spring and Fall issues of *Iodine* and is distributed to subscribers and at poetry readings hosted by the editor. Sample copies can be obtained by sending a #10 SASE. *Open Cut* is archived in the Special Collections of some university libraries."

$ ☑ THE IOWA REVIEW

308 EPB, University of Iowa, Iowa City IA 52242. (319)335-0462. E-mail: iowa-review@uiowa.edu. Website: www.iowareview.org. Established 1970. **Contact:** David Hamilton, editor.

- •Poetry published in *The Iowa Review* has appeared often in *The Best American Poetry* and *The Pushcart Prize*.

Magazines Needs *The Iowa Review*, published 3 times/year, prints fiction, poetry, essays, reviews, and, occasionally, interviews. "We simply look for poems that, at the time we read and choose, we find we admire. No specifications as to form, length, style, subject matter, or purpose. Though we print work from established writers, we're always delighted when we discover new talent." *The Iowa Review* is 192 pages, professionally printed, flat-spined. Receives about 5,000 submissions/year, accepts up to 100. Press run is 2,900; 1,500 distributed to stores. Subscription: $25. Sample: $9.

How to Contact Submit 3-6 poems at a time. No e-mail submissions. Cover letter (with title of work and genre) is encouraged. SASE required. Reads submissions "only during the Fall semester, September through November, and then contest entries in the spring." Time between acceptance and publication is "around a year." Occasionally comments on rejected poems or offers suggestions on accepted poems. Responds in up to 4 months. Pays $25 for the first page and $15 for each subsequent page, 2 contributor's copies, and a one-year subscription. Acquires first North American serial rights, non-exclusive anthology rights, and non-exclusive electronic rights.

Contest/Award Offerings *The Iowa Review* Award in Poetry, Fiction, and Essay (see separate listing in Contests & Awards).

$ ☑ ◎ ISOTOPE: A JOURNAL OF LITERARY NATURE AND SCIENCE WRITING

Dept. of English, Utah State University, 3200 Old Main Hill, Logan UT 84322-3200. (435)797-3697. Fax: (435)797-3797. E-mail: leslie.brown@usu.edu. Website: http://isotope.usu.edu. Established 2003. **Contact:** Leslie Brown, managing editor. Member: CLMP.

Magazines Needs *Isotope*, published semianually, features literary nature and science writing. Has published poetry by Pattiann Rogers, Susan Maurer, Joanne Lowery, John Gilgun, Jim Fisher, and Thomas Joswick. *Isotope* is 56 pages, magazine-sized, offset-printed, saddle-stapled, perfect-bound, with coverstock cover with color artwork. Receives about 1,200 poems/year, accepts about 20. Press run is 1,500 (1,000 subscribers, 20 libraries, 200 shelf sales); 300 distributed free to contributors, funders, and reviewers. Single copy: $10; subscription: $15. Make checks payable to *Isotope*.

How to Contact Submit 5 poems at a time. Considers simultaneous submissions; no previously published poems. No fax, e-mail, or disk submissions. Cover letter is preferred. "Include SASE, brief bio in cover letter." Reads submissions July 1-October 15. Time between acceptance and publication is 6-18 months. "Decisions are made by Poetry Editor and Magazine Editor." Rarely comments on rejected poems. Sometimes publishes theme issues. Guidelines available for SASE or on Web site. Responds in 6-9 months. Sends prepublication galleys. Pays $50/poem, 4 contributor's copies, and one-year subscription. Acquires first North American serial rights. Rights revert to poet upon publication.

Contest/Award Offerings *Isotope* sponsors an Editors' Prize in poetry. Offers annual award of $300 and publication. Submit up to 5 poems totaling no more than 10 pages. All entries are considered for publication. Guidelines available for SASE or on Web site. **Entry fee:** $20 (includes 2 year magazine subscription). **Deadline:** submit July 1-October 15 (postmark).

$ ◎ JACK AND JILL

(Specialized: children ages 7-10), Children's Better Health Institute, 1100 Waterway Blvd., Indianapolis IN 46202. Website: www.cbhi.org or www.jackandjillmag.org. Established 1938.

Magazines Needs *Jack and Jill*, published bimonthly by The Children's Better Health Network, is a magazine for ages 7-10. Wants light-hearted poetry appropriate for the age group. Reviews submissions for possible use in all Children's Better Health Institute publications.

How to Contact Manuscripts must be typewritten with poet's contact information in upper right-hand corner of each poem's page. SASE required. Submit seasonal material at least 8 months in advance. Guidelines available for SASE or on Web site. Responds in about 3 months. Pays $25 minimum for poetry.

Tips "We receive too many poetry submissions that are about kids, not for kids. Or, the subject matter is one that adults think children would or should like. Reading our guidelines is not enough. Careful study of current issues will acquaint writers with each title's 'personality.'"

▣ ☑ ◎ JERRY JAZZ MUSICIAN

(Specialized: mid-20th century America), 2207 NE Broadway, Portland OR 97232. (503)287-5570. Fax: (801)749-9896. E-mail: jm@jerryjazz.com. Website: www.jerryjazz.com.

Magazines Needs *Jerry Jazz Musician*, published monthly online, "celebrates mid-20th century America, with an emphasis on jazz, film, literature, art, civil rights history, and politics of the era. Open to all topics and poetic forms." Considers poetry by children and teens. Has published poetry by Pablo Neruda, Jim Harrison, Kenneth Rexroth, Golda Soloman, and Bunny M. Receives about 300 poems/year, accepts about 50. Has 4,000 subscribers; distributed free to 150,000 unique Internet visitors/month.

How to Contact Submit 1-2 poems at a time. Lines/poem: 6-100. Considers previously published poems and simultaneous submissions. Accepts e-mail submissions. "Would prefer e-mail submissions pasted into message; however, if font and style are essential to the poem's success, will accept a Microsoft Word attachment." Cover letter is preferred. Reads submissions year round. Submit seasonal poems 4 months in advance. Time between acceptance and publication is 1 month. "Editor consults with a variety of readers, or may make choice on his own." Often comments on rejected poems. Guidelines available on Web site. Responds in 1 month. Poet retains all rights.

☑ ◎ JEWISH CURRENTS

(Specialized: translations of Yiddish & Hebrew; Jewish subjects)45 E. 33rd St., 4th Floor, New York NY 10016. (212)889-2523. E-mail: jewishcurrents@circle.org. Website: www.jewishcurrents. org. Established 1946. **Contact:** Lawrence Bush, editor.

Magazines Needs *Jewish Currents*, published 6 times/year, prints articles, reviews, fiction, and poetry "about Jewish subjects or presenting a Jewish point of view on an issue of interest, including translations from Yiddish and Hebrew (original texts should be submitted with translations)." *Jewish Currents* is 48 pages, magazine-sized, offset-printed, saddle-stapled. Press run is 12,500. Subscription: $30/year. Sample: $5.

How to Contact Submit 4 poems at a time. No previously published poems or simultaneous submissions. Cover letter is required. "Include brief bio with author's publishing history." Poems should be typed, double-spaced; include SASE. Time between acceptance and publication is up to 2 years. Often comments on rejected poems. Responds within 3 months. Always sends prepublication galleys. Pays 6 contributor's copies. Reviews books of poetry.

Tips "Be intelligent, original, unexpected, comprehensible."

☒ ☑ JONES AV.

OEL Press, 88 Dagmar Ave., Toronto ON M4M 1W1 Canada. (416)461-8739. E-mail: oel@ interlog.com. Website: www.interlog.com/~oel. Established 1994. **Contact:** Paul Schwartz, editor/publisher.

Magazines Needs *Jones Av.*, published quarterly, contains "poems from the lyric to the ash can; starting poets and award winners." Wants poems "concise in thought and image. Prose poems sometimes. Rhymed poetry is very difficult to do well these days; it better be good." Has published poetry by Bert Almon, Michael Estabrook, John Grey, Bernice Lever, B.Z. Niditch, and Elana Wolff. *Jones Av.* is 24 pages, digest-sized, photocopied, saddle-stapled, with card cover. Receives about 300 poems/year, accepts 30-40%. Press run is 100. Subscription: $12. Sample: $3. Make checks payable to Paul Schwartz.

How to Contact Submit 3-5 poems at a time. Lines/poem: up to 30. No previously published poems or simultaneous submissions. Accepts e-mail submissions (pasted into body of message). Cover letter is required. Include bio and SASE (or SAE with IRCs). "Remember, U.S. stamps cannot be used in Canada." Time between acceptance and publication is up to 1 year. Often comments on rejected poems. Occasionally publishes theme issues. Upcoming themes available in magazine. Guidelines available for SASE or on Web site. Responds in 3 months. Pays 1 contributor's copy.

Acquires first rights. Staff reviews books/chapbooks of poetry and other magazines/journals in 50-75 words, multi-book format. Send materials for review consideration.

Tips "Request and study a sample issue of the publication if you are not familiar with the editor's taste."

$ ☑ THE JOURNAL

Dept. of English, The Ohio State University, 164 W. 17th Ave., Columbus OH 43210. (614)292-4076. Fax: (614)292-7816. E-mail: thejournal@osu.edu. Website: http://english.osu.edu/research/journals/thejournal/. Established 1972. **Contact:** Kathy Fagan and Michelle Herman, co-editors.

Magazines Needs *The Journal*, published twice/year, includes reviews, quality fiction and nonfiction, and poetry. "We're open to all forms; we tend to favor work that gives evidence of a mature and sophisticated sense of the language." Has published poetry by Beckian Fritz Goldberg, Terrance Hayes, Bob Hicok, and Linda Bierds. *The Journal* is 128-144 pages, digest-sized, professionally printed on heavy stock. Receives about 4,000 submissions/year, accepts about 200. Press run is 1,900. Subscription: $12. Sample: $7.

How to Contact Considers simultaneous submissions, "but please notify us of this at time of submission." No fax or e-mail submissions. Occasionally comments on rejected poems. Occasionally publishes theme issues. Guidelines available on Web site. Responds in up to 3 months. Pays 2 contributor's copies "and an honorarium of $20-50 when funds are available." Acquires first North American rights and electronic rights. Returns rights on publication. Reviews books of poetry.

Contest/Award Offerings Chooses the winning ms in the Ohio State University Press/*The Journal Award* (see separate listing in Contests & Awards).

Tips "However else poets train or educate themselves, they must do what they can to know our language. Too much of the writing we see indicates poets do not, in many cases, develop a feel for the possibilities of language, and do not pay attention to craft. Poets should not be in a rush to publish—until they are ready."

▦ ☑ THE JOURNAL

Original Plus Press, 17 High St., Maryport, Cumbria CA15 6BQ England. E-mail: smithsssj@aol.com. Website: http://members.aol.com/smithsssj/index.html. Established 1994. **Contact:** Sam Smith.

Magazines Needs *The Journal*, published 3 times a year, features English poetry/translations, reviews, and articles. Wants "new poetry howsoever it comes; translations and original English-language poems." Does not want "staid, generalized, all form/no content." Has published poetry by David H. Grubb, Gary Allen, and Ozdemir Asaf. *The Journal* is 40 pages, A4, offset-printed, stapled. Receives about 1,000 poems/year, accepts about 5%. Press run is 100-150. Single copy: £3; subscription: £8 for 3 issues. Outside UK, single copy: £4; subscription: £11 for 3 issues. Make checks payable to Sam Smith or through PayPal. Back issues £2.

How to Contact Submit up to 6 poems at a time. Considers previously published poems and simultaneous submissions. Accepts e-mail submissions. Cover letter is preferred. "Please send 2 IRCs with hard-copy submissions." Time between acceptance and publication is up to 1 year. Often comments on rejected poems. Guidelines available for SASE (or SAE and IRC). Responds in 1 month. Always sends prepublication galleys. Pays 1 contributor's copy.

Additional Information Since 1997, Original Plus Press has been publishing collections of poetry. This last year alone has published books by Idris Caffrey, Chris Hardy, and Colin Shaddick. Send SASE (or SAE and IRC) or e-mail for details.

Tips "I prefer poetry that has been written with thought—both to what it is saying and how it is being said."

☑ ◎ JOURNAL OF NEW JERSEY POETS

(Specialized: of, by, for NJ poets), English Dept., County College of Morris, 214 Center Grove Rd., Randolph NJ 07869-2086. (973)328-5471. Fax: (973)328-5425. E-mail: szulauf@ccm.edu. Established 1976. **Contact:** Sander Zulauf, editor. Associate Editors: Debra DeMattio, Gina Serafin, Matt Ayres, and Philip Chase.

Magazines Needs *Journal of New Jersey Poets*, published annually in April, is "not necessarily about New Jersey—but of, by, and for poets from New Jersey." Wants "serious work that conveys the essential, real, whole emotional moment of the poem to the reader without sentimentality." Has published poetry by Joe Weil, X.J. Kennedy, Marvin Silbersher, Tina Kelley, Gerald Stern, Kenneth Burke, and Catherine Doty. *Journal of New Jersey Poets* is about 90 pages, perfect-bound, offset-printed on recycled stock. Press run is 600. Single copy: $10; subscription: $16 for 2 issues ($16/issue for institutions). Sample: $5.

How to Contact Poets who live or work in New Jersey (or who formerly lived or worked here) are invited to submit up to 3 poems with their New Jersey bio data mentioned in the cover letter. Accepts fax and e-mail submissions, "but they will not be acknowledged nor returned. Include SASE with sufficient postage for return of manuscript, or provide instructions to recycle." Annual deadline for submissions: September 1. Time between acceptance and publication is within 1 year. Guidelines available for SASE or by e-mail. Responds in up to 1 year. Pays 2 contributor's copies and a one-year subscription. Acquires first North American serial rights. All reviews are solicited. Send 2 copies of books for review consideration.

Tips "Read the *Journal* before submitting. Realize we vote on everything submitted, and rejection is mostly an indication of the quantity of submissions received and the enormous number of New Jersey poets submitting quality work."

☑ ◎ JOURNAL OF REGIONAL CRITICISM

(Specialized: surrealism; science fiction/fantasy; spirituality; symbols), Arjuna Library Press, 1025 Garner St., D, Space 18, Colorado Springs CO 80905-1774. E-mail: pfuphoff@earthlink. net. Website: http://home.earthlink.net/~pfuphoff/. Established 1963 (library), 1979 (press). **Contact:** Ct. Pf. Joseph A. Uphoff, Jr., executive director.

Magazines Needs *Journal of Regional Criticism*, published frequently in varied format, features "surrealist prose poetry, visual poetry, dreamlike, short and long works; no obscene, profane (will criticize but not publish), unpolished work." Has published work by Aliya Mehdi, Carlos Ponce-Melendez, James Livingston, Jane Stuart, Randall Brock, Janette Patterson-Schafer, and Ronald Orszag. *Journal of Regional Criticism* is published in JPG files (on CD-ROM) of collage, writing, mathematical, fine art theory, and criticism.

How to Contact Send 1 or 2 short poems at a time. "Upon request will treat material as submitted for reprint, one-time rights." Accepts submissions by postal mail only, including CD-ROM: PDF or JPG, ASF. Cover letter is required. Include SASE. Guidelines (on sample CD) available for SASE. Reviews books of poetry "occasionally." Send materials for review consideration.

Additional Information "The Arjuna Library Press is avant-garde, designed to endure the transient quarters and marginal funding of the literary phenomenon (as a tradition) while presenting a context for the development of current mathematical ideas in regard to theories of art, literature, and performance; publication is now by CD-ROM, JPG, and ASF files. Each disk is unique. The poet is sent a color Xerox hard copy, poems illustrated by photographic and artistic experiments in an irregular format. Photocopy printing allows for very limited editions and irregular format.

Quality is maintained as an artistic materialist practice." Publishes 6-12 disks/year, averaging 600 MB (50 pages) each. Sample: $10.

Also Offers "The Arjuna Library Digital Visual Dream Laboratory and Acoustic Studio is extending publication beyond photocopy printing while maintaining respect for artistic relics such as manuscript copies and original photographs or papers. The format will remain varied and irregular (poetic, stream of consciousness production). Poetry is published in writing and with video of poets reading their works. Austerity is due to limited resources and expense of equipment and supplies. Works are now illustrated in color. Development work is continuing of the publication of poetry by the writers listed (Mehdi, Ponce-Melendez, et. al.)."

Tips "Web site exhibition of visual poetics and literature has proceeded through the Mail Art phenomenon. This is an excellent means of contacting the public in an impersonal way; it remains true that there are other venues to develop the commercial profile. As a general rule, we should use principles of scientific observation (minimum interference) such that the proferred dimensions are not strained or reconfigured. If the membership grows too large, rather than excluding contributors by pyramidal elitism, more organization can be founded. In this way, an accurate assessment can be maintained as to how many individuals are requesting service. Instead of redesigned organization, the pyramidal elitism can be established by supplemental organization. It follows that acceptance then rises to the level of competency of the artist or writer within a system that provides continuing adequate support for newcomers and advancing practitioners. Thus, we do not need a surrender by vulgar insults: irony can be separated from the other reputable constructs. The audience can gravitate to protected interests. Some of the *Journal of Regional Criticism* will be published and exhibited by the internet including sites such as Artmajeur, eSnips, and Open Fluxus."

JOURNAL OF THE AMERICAN MEDICAL ASSOCIATION (JAMA)

(Specialized: poetry related to a medical experience), 515 N. State St., Chicago IL 60654. (312)464-2428. Fax: (312)464-5824. E-mail: jamams@jama-archives.org. Website: www.jama. com. Established 1883. **Contact:** Charlene Breedlove, associate editor.

Magazines Needs *Journal of the American Medical Association (JAMA)*, published weekly, includes a poetry and medicine column and publishes poetry "in some way related to a medical experience, whether from the point of view of a health care worker or patient, or simply an observer. No unskilled poetry." Has published poetry by Jack Coulehan, Floyd Skloot, and Walt McDonald. *JAMA* is magazine-sized, flat-spined, with glossy paper cover. Receives about 750 poems/year, accepts about 7%. Has 360,000 subscribers (369 libraries). Subscription: $66. Sample: free, "no SASE needed."

How to Contact No previously published poems or simultaneous submissions. Accepts submissions by fax or through *JAMA*'s Web-based submissions and review system at http://manuscripts.jama.com (or click the "Information for Authors/Reviewers" button on the www.jama.com home page). "I appreciate inclusion of a brief cover letter; mention of other publications and special biographical notes are always of interest." Publishes theme issues (i.e., in 2007: access to care; malaria; chronic diseases of children; violence/human rights; medical education; poverty and human development). "However, we would rather that poems relate obliquely to the theme." Guidelines available on Web site. Pays 1 contributor's copy, more by request. "We ask for a signed copyright release, but publication elsewhere is consistently granted."

KAIMANA: LITERARY ARTS HAWAI'I

(Specialized: HI, Pacific references). Hawai'i Literary Arts Council, P.O. Box 11213, Honolulu HI 96828. Website: www.hawaii.edu/hlac. Established 1974. **Contact:** Tony Quagliano, editor. •

Poets published in Kaimana have received the Pushcart Prize, the Hawaii Award for Literature, the Stefan Baciu Award, the Cades Award, and the John Unterecker Award.

Magazines Needs *Kaimana: Literary Arts Hawai'i*, published annually, is the magazine of the Hawai'i Literary Arts Council. Wants poems with "some Pacific reference—Asia, Polynesia, Hawai'i—but not exclusively." Has published poetry by Kathryn Takara, Howard Nemerov, Anne Waldman, Reuel Denney, Haunani-Kay Trask, and Simon Perchik. *Kaimana* is 64-76 pages, 7½x10, saddle-stapled, with high-quality printing. Press run is 1,000. Subscription: $15, includes membership in HLAC. Sample: $10.

How to Contact Cover letter is preferred. Sometimes comments on rejected poems. Guidelines available in magazine or on Web site. Responds with "reasonable dispatch." Pays 2 contributor's copies.

Tips "Hawai'i gets a lot of 'travelling regionalists,' visiting writers with inevitably superficial observations. We also get superb visiting observers who are careful craftsmen anywhere. *Kaimana* is interested in the latter, to complement our own best Hawai'i writers."

$ ⊚ KALEIDOSCOPE: EXPLORING THE EXPERIENCE OF DISABILITY THROUGH LITERATURE AND THE FINE ARTS

701 S. Main St., Akron OH 44311-1019. (330)762-9755. Fax: (330)762-0912. E-mail: mshiplett@udsakron.org. Website: www.udsakron.org/kaleidoscope.htm. Established 1979. **Contact:** Gail Willmott, editor-in-chief.

Magazines Needs *Kaleidoscope: Exploring the Experience of Disability through Literature and the Fine Arts*, published twice/year in January and July, is based at United Disability Services, a not-for-profit agency. Poetry should deal with the experience of disability, but is not limited to that experience when the writer has a disability. Wants high-quality poetry with vivid, believable images and evocative language. Does not want "stereotyping, patronizing, or offending language about disability." Has published poetry by Gerald Wheeler, Jeff Worley, Barbara Crooker, and Sheryl L. Nelms. *Kaleidoscope* is 64 pages, magazine-sized, professionally printed, saddle-stapled, with 4-color semigloss card cover. Press run is 1,500 (for libraries, social service agencies, health care professionals, universities, and individual subscribers). Single copy: $6; subscription: $10 individual, $15 agency.

How to Contact Submit up to 6 poems at a time. Considers previously published poems and simultaneous submissions "as long as we are notified in both instances." Accepts fax and e-mail submissions. Cover letter is required. Send photocopies with SASE for return of work. "All submissions must be accompanied by an autobiographical sketch and should be double-spaced, with pages numbered and author's name on each page." Reads submissions by March 1 and August 1 deadlines. Publishes theme issues. Upcoming themes available in magazine, for SASE, by fax, e-mail, or on Web site. Guidelines available for SASE, by fax, e-mail, and on Web site. Responds within 3 weeks; acceptance or rejection may take 6 months. Pays $10-25 plus 2 contributor's copies. Rights revert to author upon publication. Staff reviews books of poetry. Send materials for review consideration.

⊘ KARAMU

Dept. of English, Eastern Illinois University, Charleston IL 61920. Website: www.eiu.edu/~karamu. Established 1966. **Contact:** Olga Abella, editor.

- •*Karamu* has received grants from the Illinois Arts Council, and has won recognition and money awards in the IAC Literary Awards competition.

Magazines Needs *Karamu*, published annually in May or June, aims to "provide a forum for the best contemporary poetry and fiction that comes our way. We especially like to print the works of new writers. We like to see poetry that shows a good sense of what's being done with poetry currently." Wants "poetry that builds around real experiences, real images, and real characters, and that avoids abstraction, overt philosophizing, and fuzzy pontifications. We prefer well-structured free verse, poetry with an inner, sub-surface structure as opposed to, let's say, the surface structure of rhymed quatrains. We have definite preferences in terms of style and form, but no such preferences in terms of length or subject matter." Does not want "the openly didactic poem. We don't want poems that preach against or for some political or religious viewpoint. The poem should first be a poem." Has published poetry by Jackie Bartley, Philip Lee Williams, Brent Fisk, H.E. Wright, Doug Ramspeck, and Susan Case. *Karamu* is 150 pages, digest-sized, handsomely printed (narrow margins), with matte cover. Receives submissions from about 300 poets each year, accepts 40-50 poems. Press run is 500 (300 subscribers, 15 libraries). Single copy: $8. Sample: $6 for 2 back issues.

How to Contact Submit no more than 5 poems at a time. No previously published poems or simultaneous submissions. "Always include a SASE for reply and return of material. Sufficient postage is necessary for return of work." Reads submissions September 1-February 15 only; "for fastest decision, submit January through February 15." Critiques "a few of the better poems. We want the poet to consider our comments and then submit new work." Time between acceptance and publication is up to 1 year. Occasionally publishes theme issues. Guidelines available for SASE. Pays 1 contributor's copy. Acquires first serial rights.

Tips "Follow the standard advice: Know your market. Read contemporary poetry and the magazines you want to be published in. Be patient."

❏ ◎ KELSEY REVIEW

(Specialized: Mercer County, NJ writers only), Liberal Arts Division, Mercer County Community College, P.O. Box B, Trenton NJ 08690. E-mail: kelsey.review@mccc.edu. Website: www.mccc.edu/community_kelsey-review.shtml. Established 1988. **Contact:** Ed Carmien or Holly-Katharine Johnson, editors.

Magazines Needs *Kelsey Review*, published annually in September by Mercer County Community College, serves as "an outlet for literary talent of people living and working in Mercer County, New Jersey only." Has no specifications as to form, length, subject matter, or style. Fiction: 4,000 word limit. Poetry: Not more than 6 pages. Non-Fiction: 2,500 word limit. Black and White art. Does not want to see poetry "about kittens and puppies." Has published poetry by Vida Chu, Carolyn Foote Edelmann, and Mary Mallery. *Kelsey Review* is about 90 glossy pages, 7x11, with paper cover. Receives 100+ submissions/year, accepts 10. Press run is 2,000; all distributed free to contributors, area libraries, bookstores, and schools.

How to Contact Submit up to 6 poems at a time. No previously published poems or simultaneous submissions. No fax or e-mail submissions. Manuscripts must be typed. Submit poems by May 1 deadline. Guidelines available by e-mail. Responds in August of each year. Pays 3 contributor's copies. All rights revert to authors.

$ ☑ THE KENYON REVIEW

Walton House, Kenyon College, Gambier OH 43022. (740)427-5208. Fax: (740)427-5417. E-mail: kenyonreview@kenyon.edu. Website: www.KenyonReview.org. Established 1939. **Contact:** David Lynn, editor.

Magazines Needs *The Kenyon Review*, published quarterly, contains poetry, fiction, essays, criticism, reviews, and memoirs. Features all styles, forms, lengths, and subject matters. Considers translations. Has published poetry by Billy Collins, Diane Ackerman, John Kinsella, Carol Muske-Dukes, Diane di Prima, and Seamus Heaney. *The Kenyon Review* is 180 pages, digest-sized, flat-spined. Receives about 6,000 submissions/year. Press run is 6,000. Also now publishes *KR Online*, a separate and complementary literary magazine. Sample: $12 (includes postage).

How to Contact Submit up to 6 poems at a time. No previously published poems or simultaneous submissions. Accepts submissions **through online registration only** at www.kenyon-review.org/submissions (group poems in a single document; do not submit poems individually). Reads submissions September 15-January 15. Guidelines available on Web site. Responds in up to 4 months. Payment for accepted work is made upon publication. Author retains rights and will receive a contract upon acceptance. Does not consider unsolicited reviews.

Tips "Read recent issues of the *Review* to become familiar with the type and quality of writing being published before submitting your work."

☑ ◎ THE KERF

(Specialized: humanity; environmental consciousness)College of the Redwoods, 883 W. Washington Blvd., Crescent City CA 95531. Established 1995. **Contact:** Ken Letko, editor.

Magazines Needs *The Kerf*, published annually in fall, features "poetry that speaks to the environment and humanity." Wants "poetry that exhibits an environmental consciousness." Considers poetry by children and teens. Has published poetry by Ruth Daigon, Meg Files, James Grabill, and George Keithley. *The Kerf* is 54 pages, digest-sized, printed via Docutech, saddle-stapled, with CS2 coverstock. Receives about 2,000 poems/year, accepts up to 3%. Press run is 400 (150 shelf sales); 100 distributed free to contributors and writing centers. Sample: $5. Make checks payable to College of the Redwoods.

How to Contact Submit up to 5 poems (7 pages maximum) at a time. No previously published poems or simultaneous submissions. Reads submissions January 15-March 31 only. Time between acceptance and publication is 3 months. "Our editors debate (argue for or against) the inclusion of each manuscript." Seldom comments on rejected poems. Guidelines available for SASE. Responds in 2 months. Sometimes sends prepublication galleys. Pays one contributor's copy. Acquires first North American serial rights.

Tips "Provide insights."

$ ☑ THE KIT-CAT REVIEW

244 Halstead Ave., Harrison NY 10528-3611. (914)835-4833. E-mail: kitcatreview@gmail.com. Established 1998. **Contact:** Claudia Fletcher, editor.

Magazines Needs *The Kit-Cat Review*, published quarterly, is named "after the 18th-century Kit-Cat Club whose members included Addison, Steele, Congreve, Vanbrugh, and Garth. Its purpose is to promote/discover excellence and originality." Wants quality work—traditional, modern, experimental. Has published poetry by Coral Hull, Virgil Suárez, Margret J. Hoehn, Louis Phillips, Chayym Zeldis, and Marin Sorescu. *The Kit-Cat Review* is 75 pages, digest-sized, laser-printed/photocopied, saddle-stapled, with colored card cover. Receives about 1,000 poems/year. Press run is 500. "*The Kit-Cat Review* is part of the collections of the University of Wisconsin (Madison) and the State University of New York (Buffalo)." Subscription: $25. Sample: $7. Make checks payable to Claudia Fletcher.

How to Contact Submit any number of poems at a time. Considers previously published poems and simultaneous submissions. "Cover letter should contain any relevant bio." Time between acceptance and publication is 2 months. Responds within 6 months. Pays up to $100/poem plus 2 contributor's copies. Acquires first or one-time rights.

▣ ◻ ◎ KOTAPRESS LOSS JOURNAL

(Specialized: grief & healing in relation to death of a child), (206)251-6706. E-mail: editor@ kotapress.com. Website: www.kotapress.com. Established 1999. **Contact:** Kara L.C. Jones, editor.

Magazines Needs *KotaPress Loss Journal*, published monthly online, provides support "of the grief and healing process after the death of a child. We publish *only* non-fictional poetry that somehow relates to grief and healing in relation to the death of a child. Please do not make up poems about this kind of loss and send them just to get in the magazine; it is insulting to many of our readers who are living this reality. As always, our interest is more in the content and story rather than one's ability to write in form; more in the ideas of poetry therapy rather than the academic, critique, competitive ideas normally fostered in universities." Has published poetry by John Fox, Poppy Hullings, Patricia Wellingham-Jones, Carol Jo Horn, and Sarah Bain.

How to Contact "Please read current and some archived issues of the *Loss Journal* before sending anything. Then send a letter explaining your interest in contributing. We are interested in knowing how your personal experiences with death, dying, grief, and healing are playing out in the specific poems you are submitting. Include a bio if you wish to see one published with your poems after acceptance. Send your letter, poems, and bio as text all in one e-mail. Multiple e-mails will be ignored. File attachments will be deleted without ever being opened or acknowledged. Make sure the subject line of your e-mail says 'Loss Journal Submission'—we get over 600 e-mails a day, most of them spam, so we sort and read based on the subject line." Reads submissions year round on a rolling basis. Time between acceptance and publication is up to 2 months. Guidelines available on Web site. Responds in 2 months. Acquires one-time electronic rights and archive rights. "We do not remove works from our archives. Please see our Web site to find out more about us and about what we offer. We look forward to hearing from you and reading your poetry."

Tips "If you are interested in contributing to our *Loss Journal*, it is really important that you read the journal first. This will tell you a lot about the voice of the work we publish and how your poems might 'fit the bill' for us. Please understand that while we acknowledge that all losses are difficult, we do not equate pet loss with child loss—and we do not equate fictional ideas about loss with the reality of death and dying. Read the journal first. Then submit your poems if you feel they fit the mission of our journal."

$ ◻ ◎ LADYBUG MAGAZINE

(Specialized: children ages 2-6), Carus Publishing, 70 E. Lake St., Suite 300, Chicago IL 60601. Website: www.cricketmag.com. Established 1990. **Contact:** Submissions Editor.

Magazines Needs *LADYBUG Magazine*, published monthly, is a reading and listening magazine for young children (ages 2-6). Wants poetry that is "rhythmic, rhyming; serious, humorous, active." *LADYBUG* is 40 pages, 8x10, staple-bound, with full color cover. Receives more than 1,200 submissions/month, accepts 25-30. Circulation is 120,000. Subscription: $35.97/year (12 issues). Sample: $5; sample pages available on Web site.

How to Submit Submit no more than 5 poems at a time. Lines/poem: up to 20. Considers previously published poems. Include SASE. Responds in 6 months. Guidelines available for SASE or on Web site. Pays $3/line ($25 minimum) on publication. Acquires North American publication rights for previously published poems; rights vary for unpublished poems.

Tips "In evaluating manuscripts, we look for beauty of language and a sense of joy or wonder. Before attempting to write for *LADYBUG*, be sure to familiarize yourself with this age child and with the magazine itself."

☑ LAKE EFFECT: A JOURNAL OF THE LITERARY ARTS

School of Humanities & Social Sciences, Penn State Erie, 4951 College Dr., Erie PA 16563-1501. (814)898-6281. Fax: (814)898-6032. E-mail: gol1@psu.edu. Website: www.pserie.psu.edu/lakeeffect. Established 1978 (as Tempus ; renamed Lake Effect in 2001). **Contact:** George Looney, editor-in-chief. Member: CLMP.

Magazines Needs *Lake Effect*, published annually in March/April, provides "an aesthetic venue for writing that uses language precisely to forge a genuine and rewarding experience for our readers. *Lake Effect* wishes to publish writing that rewards more than 1 reading, and to present side-by-side the voices of established and emerging writers." Wants "poetry aware of, and wise about, issues of craft in forming language that is capable of generating a rich and rewarding reading experience." Does not want "sentimental verse reliant on clichés." Has published poetry by Norman Dubie, Beckian Fritz Goldberg, David Kirby, Susan Ludvigson, Harry Humes, and Chase Twichell. *Lake Effect* is 180 pages, digest-sized, offset-printed, perfect-bound, with gloss-by-flat film lamination cover. Receives about 3,000 poems/year, accepts about 1%. Press run is 800 (300 shelf sales); 300 distributed free to contributors and writing programs. Single copy: $6; subscription: $6. Make checks payable to The Pennsylvania State University.

How to Contact Submit 3-5 poems at a time. Considers simultaneous submissions; no previously published poems. No fax, e-mail, or disk submissions. Cover letter is required. Reads submissions year round. Time between acceptance and publication is up to 4 months. "The poetry staff reads the poems, meets and discusses them to come to a consensus. Poetry editor, along with editor-in-chief, makes final decisions." Occasionally comments on rejected poems. Guidelines available in magazine or on Web site. Responds in up to 4 months. Pays 2 contributor's copies. Acquires first North American serial rights.

Tips "*Lake Effect* strives to provide an attractive venue for the good work of both established and emerging writers. We care about the integrity of poetry, and care for the poems we accept."

▣ ☑ LANGUAGEANDCULTURE.NET

E-mail: review@languageandculture.net. Website: www.languageandculture.net. Established 2001. **Contact:** Liz Fortini, editor.

Magazines Needs *Languageandculture.net*, published twice/year online, prints contemporary poetry in English. Also accepts translations of Spanish, French, German, Italian, and Russian; "other languages under review." No restrictions on form. Considers poetry by teens. Publishes 20-40 poems/issue.

How to Contact Submit up to 5 poems at a time. Lines/poem: 70 maximum. Considers previously published poems and simultaneous submissions. Accepts e-mail submissions; no disk submissions. "Return e-mail address must be included." Cover letter is preferred. Include brief bio. Reads submissions "yearly." Time between acceptance and publication "varies; no longer than 6-8 months." Poems are circulated to an editorial board. Rarely comments on rejected poems. No payment. Acquires one-time electronic rights.

Tips "Enrich your lives with different perspectives and poetry styles."

$ ▢ ◎ LEADING EDGE

(Specialized: science fiction/fantasy only), 4087 JKB, Provo UT 84602. E-mail: fiction@leadingedgemagazine.com. Website: www.leadingedgemagazine.com. **Contact:** poetry director.

Magazines Needs *Leading Edge*, published biannually, is a journal of science fiction and fantasy. Wants "high-quality poetry reflecting both literary value and popular appeal. We accept traditional science fiction and fantasy poetry, but we like innovative stuff." Does not want "graphic sex, violence, or profanity." Considers poetry by children and teens. Has published poetry by Michael Collings, Tracy Ray, Susan Spilecki, and Bob Cook. *Leading Edge* is digest-sized. Receives about 60 poems/year, accepts about 6. Single copy: $5.95; subscription: $10 (2 issues), $20 (4 issues), $27.50 (6 issues).

How to Contact Submit 1 or more poems at a time. No simultaneous submissions or previously published poems. No e-mail submissions. Cover letter is preferred. "Include name, address, phone number, length of poem, title, and type of poem at the top of each page. Please include SASE with every submission." Guidelines available in magazine, for SASE, or on Web site. Responds in 2-4 months. Always sends prepublication galleys. Pays $10 for the first 4 typeset pages, $1.50 for each additional page, plus 2 contributor's copies. Acquires first North American serial rights.

Tips "Poetry is given equal standing with fiction; it is not treated as filler, but as art."

☑ LEAGUE OF LABORING POETS, THE

P.O. Box 1266, San Clemente CA 91724. (626)807-0697. E-mail: laboringpoets@yahoo.com. Established 2007. **Contact**: Tom Conroy, publisher/editor.

Magazines Needs *The League of Laboring Poets*, published quarterly, "includes chapbook reviews, interviews with poets, some photography." Wants "all types of poetry, favors free verse, haiku, and tanka." Does not want "religious, sentimental, defamatory or bigoted poems." *The League of Laboring Poets* is 28 pages, digest-sized, offset, stiched binding, with color photograph cover. Receives about 600 poems/year, accepts about 10%. Press run is 250; distributed free to 22. Single copy: $3.50; subscription: $10/year. Make checks payable to Tom Conroy.

How to Contact Submit 3-5 poems at a time, maximum 80 lines, though will go over for a great poem. Considers previously published poems and simultaneous submissions. Considers poetry posted on a public Web site/blog/forum and poetry posted on a private, password-protected forum as published. Accepts e-mail submissions; no fax or disk submissions. Cover letter is preferred. Reads submissions year round. Time between acceptance and publication is up to 8 weeks. Poems are circulated to an editorial board. Never comments on rejected poems. Guidelines available in magazine or for SASE. Responds in 2 weeks. Pays 2 contributor copies, 1 poem in the Best Of issue awarded $25. Acquires one-time rights. Rights revert to poets upon publication. Reviews books and chapbooks of poetry in 600-800 words.

Additional Information Also seeking submissions for a trifold insert included with each issue featuring haiku and tanka.

Contest/Award Offerings Best of Issue offered quarterly offers a $25 prize for best poem in each issue. All poems submitted are considered. No entry fee. Deadline: January 1, April 1, August 1, and October 1.

Tips "Strong imagery and well crafted words/sounds are appreciated. No gimmicky poetry accepted."

☑ THE LEDGE

40 Maple Ave., Bellport NY 11713. E-mail: tkmonaghan@aol.com. Website: www.theledgemagazine.com. Established 1988. **Contact:** Timothy Monaghan, editor-in-chief/publisher.

Magazines Needs *The Ledge* seeks "poignant poems that utilize language and imagery in a fresh, original fashion. We favor poems that speak to the human experience." Wants "inspired, imaginative, well-crafted verse, and we're open to all styles and schools of writing. Each issue of *The Ledge* features a wide and eclectic range of work by poets of all backgrounds and persuasions. Excellence is the ultimate criterion." Has published poetry by Michael Colonnese, Jennifer Gresham, Melody Lacina, Leslie Anne McIlroy, Jennifer Perrine, and Matthew Spireng.

The Ledge is 240 pages, 6x9, typeset, perfect-bound, with glossy cover. Accepts 3% of poetry received. Press run is 1,000. Single copy: $10; subscription: $20 for 2 issues, $36 for 4 issues, $48 for 6 issues.

How to Contact Submit 3-5 poems at a time. Considers simultaneous submissions; no previously published poems. Include SASE. Reads submissions September-May. Responds in 6-8 months. Pays 1 contributor's copy; $6 each additional copy. Acquires one-time rights.

Contest/Award Offerings *The Ledge* Poetry Awards Competition and *The Ledge* Poetry Chapbook Contest (see separate listings in Contests & Awards).

☑ LEFT BEHIND, A JOURNAL OF SHOCK LITERATURE

832 Shasta Dr., Colton CA 92324. E-mail: Jeffe@epicentermagazine.org. Website: www. myleftbehind.com. Established 2007. **Contact:** Jeff Green, editor.

Magazines Needs *Left Behind, A Journal of Shock Literature*, published semiannually, prints poetry, short stories, short plays, screenplays, and essays. Wants "the work you thought was too racy to ever admit you wrote. The blasphemous, erotic, misanthropic, political incorrectable, homoerotic, homophobic, homo-habilis, scatological—you know, the good stuff. Formal, free verse, experimental, visual/concrete are all welcome. Surprise us. The serious and dark are encouraged, but the humorous is prized. Make us blush and say, 'Jeez, did we print that?' Imagine Bukowski, but without the soft touch." Has published Arthur Gottlieb, Louis E. Bourgeois, Ed Galing, Mary Copeland, Nebucadnezzar Johnson, and Guy R. Beining. *Left Behind* is 100 pages, digest-sized, full-color laser-printed, perfect-bound, with color cover, includes ads. Press run is 1000. Single copy: $8. Make checks payable to Jeff Green.

How to Contact Submit 6 poems at a time. Lines/poem: "no range limit; but we are only 80 pages, so if it's long, it's got to be good." Considers previously published poems and simultaneous submissions. Accepts e-mail submissions (as attachment; "Left Behind" should be in subject line) and disk submissions; no fax. Cover letter is preferred. Reads submissions year round. Time between acceptance and publication is 8 months. Poems are circulated to an editorial board. Sometimes comments on rejected poems. Guidelines available in magazine or for SASE. Responds in 2 months. Pays 1 contributor's copy. Acquires one-time rights. Rights revert to poet upon publication. Reviews books/chapbooks of poetry and other magazines/journals in single-book format. Send materials for review consideration to Jeff Green.

Tips "For humorous work, read it to your friends and see if they laugh before submitting it to *Left Behind*. For poetry, attend an open mic and see how the audience responds. If there are no open mics in your area, start one."

☑ ◎ LEFT CURVE

(Specialized: political; social issues), P.O. Box 472, Oakland CA 94604-0472. (510)763-7193. E-mail: editor@leftcurve.org. Website: www.leftcurve.org. Established 1974. **Contact:** Csaba Polony, editor.

Magazines Needs *Left Curve*, published "irregularly, about every 10 months," addresses the "problem(s) of cultural forms, emerging from the crisis of modernity, that strives to be independent from the control of dominant institutions, and free from the shackles of instrumental rationality." Wants poetry that is "critical culture, social, political, 'post-modern.' We will look at any form of poetry, from experimental to traditional." Does not want "purely formal, too self-centered, poetry that doesn't address in sufficient depth today's problems." Has published poetry by John Berger, Vincent Ferrini, Devorah Major, Jack Hirschman, and Lawrence Ferllinghetti. *Left Curve* is 144 pages, magazine-sized, offset-printed, perfect-bound, with 4-color Durosheen cover, includes ads. Press run is 2,000 (250 subscribers, 100 libraries, 1,600 shelf sales). Subscription:

$35/3 issues (individuals), $50/3 issues (institutions). Sample: $12.

How to Contact Submit up to 5 poems at a time. Lines/poem: "most of our published poetry is 1 page in length, though we have published longer poems of up to 8 pages." Accepts e-mail or disk submissions. Cover letter is required. "Explain why you are submitting." Publishes theme issues. Guidelines available for SASE, by e-mail, or on Web site. Responds in up to 6 months. Pays 2-3 contributor's copies. Send materials for review consideration.

◎ LILITH MAGAZINE: INDEPENDENT, JEWISH & FRANKLY FEMINIST

250 W. 57th St., Suite 2432, New York NY 10107-0172. (212)757-0818. Fax: (212)757-5705. E-mail: info@lilith.org. Website: www.lilith.org. Established 1976. **Contact:** Poetry Editor.

Magazines Needs *Lilith Magazine: Independent, Jewish & Frankly Feminist*, published quarterly, is "an independent magazine with a Jewish feminist perspective" that uses poetry by Jewish women "about the Jewish woman's experience." Does not want poetry on other subjects. "Generally we use short rather than long poems." Has published poetry by Irena Klepfisz, Lyn Lifshin, Marcia Falk, Adrienne Rich, and Muriel Rukeyser. *Lilith Magazine* is 48 pages, magazine-sized, with glossy color cover. Publishes about 4 poems/year. Press run is about 10,000 (about 6,000 subscribers). Subscription: $26/year. Sample: $7.

How to Contact Send up to 3 poems at a time. No simultaneous submissions or e-mail submissions. "Please put name and contact info on each sheet submitted. Copy should be neatly typed and proofread for typos and spelling errors. Short cover letters only." Sometimes comments on rejected poems. Guidelines available for SASE or on Web site. Responds in up to 6 months.

Tips "Read a copy of the publication before you submit your work. Please be patient."

◙ LIPS

7002 Blvd. East, #2-26G, Guttenberg NJ 07093. (201)662-1303. E-mail: LBoss79270@aol.com. Established 1981. **Contact:** Laura Boss, poetry editor.

Magazines Needs *Lips*, published twice/year, takes pleasure "in publishing previously unpublished poets as well as the most established voices in contemporary poetry. We look for quality work: the strongest work of a poet; work that moves the reader; poems that take risks that work. We prefer clarity in the work rather than the abstract. Poems longer than 6 pages present a space problem." Has published poetry by Robert Bly, Allen Ginsberg, Michael Benedikt, Maria Gillan, Stanley Barkan, Lyn Lifshin, and Ishmael Reed. *Lips* is about 150 pages, digest-sized, flat-spined. Receives about 16,000 submissions/year, accepts about 1%. Press run is 1,000 (200 subscribers, 100 libraries). Sample: $10 plus $2 for postage.

How to Contact Submit 6 pages maximum at a time. Poems should be typed. Reads submissions September-March only. Guidelines available for SASE. Responds in 1 month (but has gotten backlogged at times). Sometimes sends prepublication galleys. Pays 1 contributor's copy. Acquires first rights.

Tips "Remember the 2 T's: Talent and Tenacity."

◙ THE LISTENING EYE

Kent State Geauga Campus, 14111 Claridon-Troy Rd., Burton OH 44021. (440)286-3840. E-mail: grace_butcher@msn.com. Website: www.geocities.com/Athens/3716. Established 1970 (for student work), 1990 (as national publication). **Contact:** Grace Butcher, editor.

Magazines Needs *The Listening Eye*, published annually in early fall, prints poetry, short fiction, creative nonfiction, and art. Wants "high literary-quality poetry. Any subject, any style." Does not want "trite images or predictable rhyme." Considers poetry by children and teens if high

Magazines/Journals

literary quality. Has published poetry by Alberta Turner, Virgil Suárez, Walter McDonald, and Simon Perchik. *The Listening Eye* is 52-60 pages, digest-sized, professionally printed, saddle-stapled, with card stock cover with b&w or color art. Receives about 200 poems/year, accepts about 5%. Press run is 200. Single copy: $4. Make checks payable to Grace Butcher.

How to Contact Submit up to 4 poems at a time. Lines/poem: "prefer shorter poems (less than 2 pages), but will consider longer if space allows." Accepts previously published poems "occasionally"; no simultaneous submissions. No e-mail submissions "unless from overseas." Cover letter is required. Poems should be typed, single-spaced, 1 poem/page—name, address, phone number, and e-mail address in upper left-hand corner of each page—with SASE for return of work. Reads submissions January 1-April 15 only. Time between acceptance and publication is up to 6 months. Poems are circulated to the editor and 2 assistant editors who read and evaluate work separately, then meet for final decisions. Occasionally comments on rejected poems. Guidelines available in magazine or for SASE. Responds in 1 month. Pays 2 contributor's copies. Acquires first or one-time rights.

Contest/Award Offerings Awards $30 to the best sports poem in each issue.

Tips "I look for tight lines that don't sound like prose; unexpected images or juxtapositions; the unusual use of language; noticeable relationships of sounds; a twist in viewpoint; an ordinary idea in extraordinary language; an amazing and complex idea simply stated; play on words and with words; an obvious love of language. Poets need to read the 'Big 3'—Cummings, Thomas, Hopkins—to see the limits to which language can be taken. Then read the 'Big 2'—Dickinson to see how simultaneously tight, terse, and universal a poem can be, and Whitman to see how sprawling, cosmic, and personal. Then read everything you can find that's being published in literary magazines today, and see how your work compares to all of the above."

▣ ☑ LITERAL LATTÉ

200 E. 10th St., Suite 240, New York NY 10003. (212)260-5532. E-mail: litlatte@aol.com. Website: www.literal-latte.com. Established 1994. **Contact:** Dorie Davidson, assistant editor.

Magazines Needs *Literal Latté*, published continually online, is a literary journal of "pure prose, poetry, and art. Open to all styles of poetry—quality is the determining factor." Has published poetry by Allen Ginsberg, Carol Muske, Amy Holman, and John Updike. Receives about 3,000 poems/year, accepts 1%.

How to Contact Considers simultaneous submissions; no previously published poems. No e-mail submissions; postal submissions only. Cover letter is required. Include bio and SASE (or e-mail for response only). Time between acceptance and publication is within 1 year. Often comments on rejected poems. Guidelines available by e-mail or on Web site. Responds in 5 months.

Additional Information "We will publish an anthology in book form at the end of each year, featuring the best of our Web magazine."

Contest/Award Offerings *Literal Latté* Poetry Awards and *Literal Latté* Food Verse Awards (see separate listings in Contests & Awards).

▣ ☑ ◎ LITERARY MAMA

(Specialized: writing by mothers about mothering), E-mail: poetry@literarymama.com (submissions) or info@literarymama.com (inquiries). Website: www.literarymama.com. Established 2003. **Contact:** Sharon Kraus, poetry editor.

Magazines Needs *Literary Mama*, published monthly online, prints fiction, poetry, and creative nonfiction by writers of all ages who are "self-identified" mothers. "We also publish literary criticism, book reviews, and profiles about mother writers. *Literary Mama* is doing something for mama-centric literature that no one else is doing. The poetry, fiction, and creative nonfiction that may be too long, too complex, too ambiguous, too deep, too raw, too irreverent, too ironic, too body-conscious, and too full of long words for the general reader will find a home with us. While there are plenty of online literary magazines that publish writing like this, none devote themselves exclusively to writing about motherhood." Wants poems of any form that are "extraordinary for their vision, craft, integrity, and originality; centered around parenting; written by writers who are also self-identified mothers: biological, non-biological, step, transgender, adoptive." Receives about 70 poems/month, accepts about 5%.

How to Contact Submit 4 poems maximum at a time. Considers previously published poems (if they are not otherwise available on the Web) and simultaneous submissions. Accepts e-mail submissions (pasted into body of message; no attachments); no disk submissions. Include full name plus the word "submission" in your subject line. Cover letter is required. "Please include name, brief bio, and contact information." Reads submissions year round except for December and June. Time between acceptance and publication is 2-16 weeks. "The final decision about all poetry submissions is made by the poetry editor." Sometimes comments on rejected poems. Guidelines available on Web site. Responds in 3-6 months. No payment. Acquires first rights for previously unpublished work, non-exclusive one-time rights for reprints. Reviews books/chapbooks of poetry. Query via e-mail prior to sending materials for review consideration.

☑ THE LITERARY REVIEW: AN INTERNATIONAL JOURNAL OF CONTEMPORARY WRITING

Fairleigh Dickinson University, 285 Madison Ave., Madison NJ 07940. (973)443-8564. Fax: (973)443-8364. E-mail: tlr@fdu.edu. Website: www.theliteraryreview.org. Established 1957. **Contact:** Minna Proctor, editor-in-chief.

Magazines Needs *The Literary Review*, published quarterly, seeks "work by new and established poets that reflects a sensitivity to literary standards and the poetic form." No specifications as to form, length, style, subject matter, or purpose. Has published poetry by David Citino, Rick Mulkey, Virgil Suárez, Gary Fincke, and Dale M. Kushner. *The Literary Review* is about 180 pages, digest-sized, professionally printed, flat-spined, with glossy color cover. Receives about 1,200 submissions/year, accepts 100-150. Press run is 2,000 (800 subscribers, one-third are overseas). Sample: $7 domestic, $8 outside U.S.; request a "general issue."

How to Contact Submit up to 5 typed poems at a time. Accepts only online submissions at www.theliteraryreview.org/submit.html. Considers simultaneous submissions. No fax or e-mail submissions. **Read-time September 1 through May 31**. Sometimes comments on rejected poems. Publishes theme issues. Responds in 4-6 months. Always sends prepublication galleys. Pays 2 contributor's copies. Acquires first rights. Reviews books of poetry in 500 words, single-book format. Send materials for review consideration.

Also Offers *TLR Online*, available on the Web site, features original work not published in the print edition. Has published poetry by Renée Ashley and Catherine Kasper.

Tips "Read a general issue of the magazine carefully before submitting."

▦ ▣ ◻ LIVING POETS MAGAZINE

Dragonheart Press, 11 Menin Rd., Allestree, Derby DE22 2NL England. E-mail: submissions@dragonheartpress.com. Website: www.dragonheartpress.com. Established 1995. **Contact:** Sean Woodward, executive editor.

Magazines Needs *Living Poets Magazine*, published irregularly online, provides a showcase for poetry. Wants "crafted poetry with strong imagery." Does not want "constrained rhyming structures." Receives about 400 poems/year, accepts about 20%. Digital sample: $10 (printable from PDF). Make checks payable to S. Woodward or via PayPal.

How to Contact Submit 3 poems at a time. Considers previously published poems and simultaneous submissions. Accepts e-mail submissions. Cover letter is preferred. Include bio and publication credits. Time between acceptance and publication is 1-2 months. Often comments on rejected poems. Publishes theme issues. Guidelines available for SASE, by e-mail, or on Web site. Responds in 3 months. Pays 1 contributor's copy. Reviews books/chapbooks of poetry or other magazines in single-book format. Send materials for review consideration to Review Editor, Dragonheart Press.

Contest/Award Offerings Sponsors Dragonheart Press Annual Poetry Competition. **Deadline:** December 31. Guidelines available for SASE (or SAE and IRC) or by e-mail (competition@ dragonheartpress.com).

☑ LONE STARS MAGAZINE

4219 Flint Hill St., San Antonio TX 78230-1619. E-mail: lonestarsmagazine@yahoo.com. Website: www.lonestarsmagazine.net. Established 1992. **Contact:** Milo Rosebud, editor/publisher.

Magazines Needs *Lone Stars*, published 3 times/year, features "contemporary poetry." Wants poetry "that holds a continuous line of thought." Does not want "profanity." Considers poetry by children and teens. Has published poetry by Bernie Bernstein, Crayton Moody, Eve J. Blohm, and Cecil Boyce. *Lone Stars* is 25 pages, magazine-sized, photocopied, saddle-stapled, bound with tape. Press run is 200. Single copy: $6; subscription: $20 for 4 issues. Sample: $5.50. Past issues: $2.

How to Contact Submit 3-5 poems at a time. Considers previously published poems and simultaneous submissions. Cover letter is preferred. Submit poems on any subject, formatted and "typed the way you want them in print." **Charges reading fee of $1 per poem.** Time between acceptance and publication is 3-6 months. Guidelines available for SASE. Responds within 3 months. Acquires one-time rights.

Contest/Award Offerings Sponsors annual "Songbook" Lyric Poetry Contest. Details available for SASE.

Tips "Submit poetry that expresses a reasonable train of thought."

▣ ◎ LONG ISLAND QUARTERLY

(Specialized: Long Island, NY poets), P.O. Box 114, Northport NY 11768. E-mail: Liquarterly@ aol.com. Website: www.poetrybay.com. Established 1990. **Contact:** George Wallace, editor/ publisher.

Magazines Needs *Long Island Quarterly*, published online, is a journal of poetry (mostly lyric free verse) by people on or from Long Island. "Surprise us with fresh language. No conventional imagery, self-indulgent confessionalism, compulsive article-droppers." Has published poetry by Edmund Pennant and David Ignatow.

How to Contact Submit 3 poems at a time. Accepts e-mail submissions (preferred; pasted into body of message; "no attachments will be opened"). Include name and address on each page for postal entries; submissions without SASE are not returned. Cover letter with brief bio stating connection to Long Island region is required. Responds in 3 months.

Tips "1) Go beyond yourself; 2) Don't be afraid to fictionalize; 3) Don't write your autobiography—if you're worth it, maybe someone else will."

☑ LONG STORY SHORT, AN E-ZINE FOR WRITERS

P.O. Box 475, Lewistown MT 59457. E-mail: dencassino@gmail.com. Website: www. alongstoryshort.net. Established 2003. **Contact:** Linda Barnett-Johnson, poetry editor.

Magazines Needs *Long Story Short, An E-zine for Writers*, published monthly online, is "eclectic—

open to all forms and styles" of poetry. Does not want "profanity; overly explicit sex." Considers poetry by children (ages 10 and up) and teens. Has published poetry by Carolyn Howard-Johnson, Patricia Wellingham-Jones, Floriana Hall, Russell Bittner, and Marie Delgado Travis. **How to Contact** Submit up to 3 poems at a time. Short, concise poems are preferred. Considers previously published poems and simultaneous submissions. Accepts e-mail submissions only ("paste poems in the body of your e-mail; no attachments will be opened"). Include a brief biography and permission to use e-mail address for reader contact. Reads submissions year round. Submit seasonal poems 4 months in advance. Time between acceptance and publication is up to 6 months, depending on theme. "Poems are reviewed and chosen by the poetry editor." Often comments on rejected poems. Guidelines available on Web site. ("Read them!") All rights reserved by author.

Also Offers Free newsletter with poetry of the month chosen by poetry editor; includes author's bio and Web page listed in the e-zine. Also provides resource page on Web site. Offers light critique of submissions upon request, and a free writing forum.

Tips "*Long Story Short* is an e-zine dedicated to the advancement of writers. It has been voted one of the 101 Best Web sites for Writers by the readers of *Writer's Digest Magazine*."

☑ LOUISIANA LITERATURE

SLU Box 10792, Southeastern Louisiana University, Hammond LA 70402. (504)549-5022. E-mail: lalit@selu.edu. Website: http://louisianaliterature.org. **Contact:** Jack Bedell, editor.

Magazines Needs *Louisiana Literature*, published twice/year, considers "creative work from anyone, though we strive to showcase our state's talent. We appreciate poetry that shows firm control and craft; is sophisticated yet accessible to a broad readership. We don't use highly experimental work." Has published poetry by Claire Bateman, Elton Glaser, Gray Jacobik, Vivian Shipley, D.C. Berry, and Judy Longley. *Louisiana Literature* is 150 pages, 634x934, handsomely printed on heavy matte stock, flat-spined, with matte card cover. Single copy: $8 for individuals; subscription: $12 for individuals, $12.50 for institutions.

How to Contact Submit 3-5 poems at a time. No simultaneous submissions. No fax or e-mail submissions. "Send cover letter, including bio to use in the event of acceptance. Enclose SASE and specify whether work is to be returned or discarded." Reads submissions year round, "although we work more slowly in summer." Publishes theme issues. Guidelines available for SASE or on website. Sometimes sends prepublication galleys. Pays 2 contributor's copies. Send materials for review consideration; include cover letter.

Contest/Award Offerings The *Louisiana Literature* Prize for Poetry (see separate listing in Contests & Awards).

Tips "It's important to us that the poets we publish be in control of their creations. Too much of what we see seems arbitrary."

☑ ◎ THE LOUISIANA REVIEW

(Specialized: LA poets, LA-related poetry), Division of Liberal Arts, Louisiana State University at Eunice, P.O. Box 1129, Eunice LA 70535. (337)550-1315. E-mail: malleman@lsue.edu. Website: www.lsue.edu/LA-Review/. Established 1999. **Contact:** Dr. Michael Alleman, poetry editor.

Magazines Needs *The Louisiana Review*, published annually during the fall or spring semester, offers "Louisiana poets, writers, and artists a place to showcase their most beautiful pieces. Others may submit Louisiana- or Southern-related poetry, stories, and b&w art, as well as interviews with Louisiana writers. We want to publish the highest-quality poetry, fiction, and art." Wants "strong imagery, metaphor, and evidence of craft." Does not want "sing-song rhymes, abstract, religious, or overly sentimental work." Has published poetry by Gary Snyder, Antler, David

Cope, and Catfish McDaris. *The Louisiana Review* is 100-200 pages, digest-sized, professionally printed, perfect-bound. Receives up to 2,000 poems/year, accepts 40-50. Press run is 300-600. Single copy: $5.

How to Contact Submit up to 5 poems at a time. No previously published poems. No fax or e-mail submissions. "Include cover letter indicating your association with Louisiana, if any. Name and address should appear on each page." Reads submissions year round. Time between acceptance and publication is up to 2 years. Pays one contributor's copy. Poets retain all rights.

Tips "Be true to your own voice and style."

☑ THE LOUISVILLE REVIEW

Spalding University, 851 S. Fourth St., Louisville KY 40203. (502)585-9911, ext. 2777. E-mail: louisvillereview@spalding.edu. Website: www.louisvillereview.org. Established 1976. **Contact:** Poetry Editor. Associate Editor: Kathleen Driskell.

Magazines Needs *The Louisville Review*, published twice/year, prints all kinds of poetry. Has a section devoted to children's poetry (grades K-12) called The Children's Corner. Considers poetry by children and teens. Has published poetry by Wendy Bishop, Gary Fincke, Michael Burkard, and Sandra Kohler. *The Louisville Review* is 150 pages, digest-sized, flat-spined. Receives about 700 submissions/year, accepts about 10%. Single copy: $8; subscription: $14/year, $27/2 years, $40/3 years (foreign subscribers add $6/year for s&h). Sample: $5.

How to Contact Considers simultaneous submissions; no previously published poems. No e-mail submissions. Include SASE for reply only. "Poetry by children must include permission of parent to publish if accepted. Address those submissions to The Children's Corner." Reads submissions year round. Time between acceptance and publication is up to 4 months. Submissions are read by 3 readers. Guidelines available on Web site. Responds in 4-6 months. Pays in contributor's copies.

Tips "We look for the striking metaphor, unusual imagery, and fresh language."

☑ LULLWATER REVIEW

Emory University, P.O. Box 122036, Atlanta GA 30322. (404)727-6184. E-mail: LullwaterReview@ yahoo.com. Established 1990. **Contact:** Amy Cheng and Erin Crews, editor-in-chief.

Magazines Needs *Lullwater Review*, published in May and December, prints poetry, short fiction, and artwork. Wants poetry of any genre with strong imagery, original voice, on any subject. Does not want profanity or pornographic material. Has published poetry by Amy Greenfield, Peter Serchuk, Katherine McCord, and Ha Jin. *Lullwater Review* is 60-80 pages, magazine-sized, with full-color cover, includes b&w and color pictures. Press run is 1,200. Subscription: $8 for individuals, $10 for institutions. Sample: $5.

How to Contact Submit 6 or fewer poems at a time. Considers simultaneous submissions; no previously published poems. Cover letter is preferred. Prefers poems single-spaced with name and contact info on each page. "Poems longer than 1 page should include page numbers. We must have a SASE with which to reply." Reads submissions September 1-May 15 only. Time between acceptance and publication is up to 6 months. Poems are circulated to an editorial board. Seldom comments on rejected poems. Guidelines available for SASE. Responds in 5 months maximum. Pays 3 contributor's copies. Acquires first North American serial rights.

Tips "Keep writing, find your voice, don't get frustrated. Please be patient with us regarding response time. We are an academic institution."

☑ LUNGFULL!MAGAZINE

316 23rd St., Brooklyn NY 11215. E-mail: lungfull@rcn.com. Website: http://lungfull.org.

Established 1994. **Contact:** Brendan Lorber, editor/publisher.

•*LUNGFULL!* was the recipient of a grant from the New York State Council for the Arts.

Magazines Needs *LUNGFULL!magazine*, published annually, prints "the rough draft of each poem, in addition to the final, so that the reader can see the creative process from start to finish. We recommend you get a copy before submitting." Wants "any style as long as it's urgent, immediate, playful, probing, showing great thought while remaining vivid and grounded. Poems should be as interesting as conversation." Does not want "empty poetic abstractions." Has published poetry by Alice Notley, Lorenzo Thomas, Tracie Morris, Hal Sirowitz, Eileen Myles, and John Ashbery. *LUNGFULL!* is 200 pages, 8½x7, offset-printed, desktop-published, perfect-bound, with glossy waterproof 2-color cover, includes ads. Receives about 1,000 poems/year, accepts 3%. Press run is 3,000 (600 subscribers, 2300 shelf sales); 100 distributed free to contributors. Single copy: $9.95; subscription: $39.80 for 4 issues, $19.90 for 2 issues. Sample: $12.95. Make checks payable to Brendan Lorber, or order online.

How to Contact Submit up to 6 poems at a time. Considers previously published poems and simultaneous submissions (with notification; "however, other material will be considered first and stands a much greater chance of publication"). Accepts e-mail submissions. "We prefer hard copy by USPS—but e-submissions can be made in the body of the e-mail itself; submissions with attachments will be deleted unread." Cover letter is preferred. Time between acceptance and publication is up to 8 months. "The editor looks at each piece for its own merit and for how well it will fit into the specific issue being planned based on other accepted work." Guidelines available by e-mail. Responds in 1 year. Pays 2 contributor's copies. "Read the magazine before submitting and mention why you want to be published in LUNGFULL! in your cover letter."

Also Offers "Each copy of *LUNGFULL!magazine* contains a Cultural Attache Sticker—they can be removed from the magazine and placed on any flat surface to make it a little less flat. Previous stickers contain statements like 'Together we can keep the poor poor' and 'You only live once—just not as long as in countries with free healthcare.'"

Tips "Failure demands a certain dedication. Practice makes imperfection, and imperfection makes room for the amazing. Only outside the bounds of acceptable conclusions can the astounding transpire, can writing contain anything beyond twittering snack food logic and the utilitarian pistons of mundane engineering."

☑ ◎ THE LUTHERAN DIGEST

(Specialized: Christian; inspirational; short poems), P.O. Box 4250, Hopkins MN 55343. (952)933-2820. Fax: (952)933-5708. E-mail: tldi@lutherandigest.com. Website: www.lutherandigest.com. Established 1953. **Contact:** David Tank, editor.

Magazines Needs *The Lutheran Digest,* published quarterly, aims to "entertain and encourage believers and to subtly persuade non-believers to embrace the Lutheran-Christian faith. We publish short poems that will fit in a single column of the magazine. Most are inspirational, but that doesn't necessarily mean religious." Does not want "avant-garde poetry." Considers poetry by children and teens. Has published poetry by Kathleen A. Cain, William Beyer, Margaret Peterson, Florence Berg, and Erma Boetkher. *The Lutheran Digest* is 64 pages, digest-sized, offset-printed, saddle-stapled, with 4-color paper cover, includes local ads. Receives about 200 poems/year, accepts 10-20%. Press run is 60,000-65,000; most distributed free to Lutheran churches. Subscription: $16/year, $22/2 years. Sample: $3.50.

How to Contact Submit 3 poems at a time. Lines/poem: 25 maximum. Considers previously published poems and simultaneous submissions. Accepts fax and e-mail (as attachment) submissions. Cover letter is preferred. "Include SASE if return is desired." Time between acceptance and publication is up to 9 months. "Poems are selected by editor and reviewed by publication panel." Guidelines available for SASE or on Web site. Responds in 3 months. Pays credit and 1 contributor's copy. Acquires one-time rights.

Tips "Poems should be short and appeal to senior citizens. We also look for poems that can be sung to traditional Lutheran hymns."

◲ ◎ THE LYRIC

(Specialized: rhymed poetry, traditional), P.O. Box 110, Jericho Corners VT 05465. Phone/fax: (802)899-3993. E-mail: Lyric@sover.net. Established 1921. **Contact:** Jean Mellichamp-Milliken, editor.

Magazines Needs *The Lyric*, published quarterly, is "the oldest magazine in North America in continuous publication devoted to traditional poetry." Prints about 55 poems/issue. Wants "rhymed verse in traditional forms, for the most part, with an occasional piece of blank or free verse. Our themes are varied, ranging from religious ecstasy to humor to raw grief, but we feel no compulsion to shock, embitter, or confound our readers. We also avoid poems about contemporary political or social problems—'grief but not grievances,' as Frost put it. Frost is helpful in other ways: If yours is more than a lover's quarrel with life, we are not your best market. And most of our poems are accessible on first or second reading. Frost again: 'Don't hide too far away.'" Has published poetry by Rhina P. Espaillat, Gail White, Joseph Awad, Alfred Dorn, Barbara Loots, and Glenna Holloway. *The Lyric* is 32 pages, digest-sized, professionally printed with varied typography, with matte card cover. Press run is 750 (600 subscribers, 40 libraries). Receives about 3,000 submissions/year, accepts 5%. Subscription: $15/year, $28/2 years, $38/3 years (U.S.), $17/year for Canada and other countries (in U.S. funds only). Sample: $4.

How to Contact Submit up to 6 poems at a time. Lines/poem: 40 maximum. Considers simultaneous submissions (although "not preferred"); no previously published poems. Cover letter is "often helpful, but not required. Subscription will not affect publication of submitted poetry." Guidelines available for SASE or by e-mail. Responds in 3 months ("average; inquire after 6 months"). Pays 1 contributor's copy.

Contest/Award Offerings All contributors are eligible for quarterly and annual prizes totaling $650. Also offers the Lyric College Contest, open to undergraduate students. Awards prize of $400. **Deadline:** December 15. Send entries to Tanya Cimonetti, 1393 Spear St., S., Burlington VT 05403.

Tips "Our *raison d'eßtre* has been the encouragement of form, music, rhyme, and accessibility in poetry. As we witness the growing tide of appreciation for traditional/lyric poetry, we are proud to have stayed the course for 89 years, helping keep the roots of poetry alive."

▣ ◲ LYRIC POETRY REVIEW

P.O. Box 2494, Bloomington IN 47402. E-mail: lyric@lyricreview.org. Website: www.lyricreview. org. Established 2001. **Contact:** Nathaniel Perry, editor. Member: CLMP.

•Poems published in *Lyric Poetry Review* have appeared in *The Best American Poetry* and *The Pushcart Prize* as well as on the Poetry Daily and Verse Daily Web sites.

Magazines Needs *Lyric Poetry Review*, published semiannually, presents "poetry by Americans and translations of both little-known and celebrated poets from around the world." Also publishes interviews and literary essays on poetry or poetics. Wants "poetry that has strong musicality and lyricism. We are open to all styles, including longer poems and lyrical narratives. We tend to publish more than 1 poem by any given author and try to find a group of poems that demonstrates both range and consistency of voice." Has published poetry by Marilyn Hacker, Maurice Manning, Czeslaw Milosz, Jean Valentine, Alicia Ostriker, and Gerald Stern. *Lyric Poetry Review* is 96 pages, digest-sized, perfect-bound, with full-color cover with original artwork. Receives about 2,500 poems/year, accepts about 5%. Press run is 1,000. Single copy: $9; subscription: $15/year (subscribers outside U.S. add $5 postage). Make checks payable to *Lyric Poetry Review*.

How to Contact Submit 3-6 poems at a time. Considers simultaneous submissions if notified; no previously published poems. No e-mail or disk submissions. Cover letter is required. Reads submissions year round. Response time may be considerably slower in the summer months. Time between acceptance and publication is up to 1 year. "We strongly advise that those submitting work read a recent issue first." Seldom comments on rejected poems. Occasionally publishes theme issues. Upcoming themes available by e-mail. Guidelines available in magazine, for SASE, or on Web site. Responds in up to 4 months. Always sends prepublication galleys. Pays 2 contributor's copies. Acquires first rights. Solicits reviews.

☑ THE MACGUFFIN

Schoolcraft College, 18600 Haggerty Rd., Livonia MI 48152-2696. (734)462-4400, ext. 5327. Fax: (734)462-4679. E-mail: macguffin@schoolcraft.edu. Website: www.schoolcraft.edu/macguffin. Established 1984. **Contact:** Carol Was, poetry editor.

Magazines Needs *The MacGuffin*, published 3 times/year, prints "the best poetry, fiction, nonfiction, and artwork we find. We have no thematic or stylistic biases. We look for well-crafted poetry." Does not want "pornography, triteness, and sloppy poetry. We do not publish haiku, concrete, or light verse." Has published poetry by Susan Terris, Gabriel Welsch, Linda Nemec Foster, Conrad Hilberry, and Laurence Lieberman. *The MacGuffin* is 160 pages, 6x9, perfect-bound, with color cover. Press run is 500; the rest are local sales, contributor copies, and distribution to college offices. Subscription: $22. Sample: $6.

How to Contact Submit no more than 5 poems at a time. Lines/poem: 400 maximum. Considers simultaneous submissions if informed; no previously published poems. Accepts fax, e-mail (as Word attachment only; do not paste into body of message), and disk/CD submissions. Cover letter is required. "List titles and brief bio in cover letter. Do not staple work." Poems should be typed, single-spaced, 1 per page. Poet's name, address, and e-mail should appear on each page. Include SASE. Guidelines available for SASE, by fax, e-mail, or on Web site. Responds in 4-6 months. Pays 2 contributor's copies plus discount on additional copies. Rights revert to poets upon publication.

Contest/Award Offerings The National Poet Hunt Contest (see separate listing in Contests & Awards).

☑ THE MADISON REVIEW

University of Wisconsin-Madison, Dept. of English, 6193 Helen C. White Hall, 600 N. Park St., Madison WI 53706. (608)263-2566. E-mail: madisonreview@yahoo.com. Website: www.madisonreview.org. Established 1978. **Contact:** Poetry Editor.

Magazines Needs *The Madison Review*, published semiannually in May and December, seeks poems that are "smart and tight, that fulfill their own propositions." Does not want "religious or patriotic dogma and light verse." Has published poetry by Simon Perchik, Amy Quan Barry, Mitch Raney, Erica Meitner, and Henry B. Stobbs. Selects 15-20 poems from a pool of 750. Subscription: $15/year, $25 for 2 years. Sample: $8.

How to Contact Submit up to 6 poems at a time. No simultaneous submissions. No e-mail submissions. Cover letter is preferred. Include SASE. Submissions must be typed. Guidelines available in magazine, for SASE, by e-mail, or on Web site. Usually responds in 9 months. Pays 2 contributor's copies.

Tips "Contributors: Know your market! Read before, during, and after writing. Treat your poems better than job applications!"

$ ☑ ◎ THE MAGAZINE OF FANTASY & SCIENCE FICTION

P.O. Box 3447, Hoboken NJ 07030. E-mail: FandSF@aol.com. Website: www.fsfmag.com. Established 1949. **Contact:** Gordon Van Gelder, editor.

- •*The Magazine of Fantasy & Science Fiction* is a past winner of the Hugo Award and World Fantasy Award.

Magazines Needs *The Magazine of Fantasy & Science Fiction*, published monthly 11 times/year, is "one of the longest-running magazines devoted to the literature of the fantastic." Wants only poetry that deals with the fantastic or the science-fictional. Has published poetry by Rebecca Kavaler, Elizabeth Bear, Sophie M. White, and Robert Frazier. *The Magazine of Fantasy & Science Fiction* is 160 pages, digest-sized, offset-printed, perfect-bound, with glossy cover, includes ads. Receives about 20-40 poems/year, accepts about 1%. Press run is 35,000 (20,000 subscribers). Single copy: $4.99; subscription: $34.97. Sample: $5. Make checks payable to *The Magazine of Fantasy & Science Fiction*.

How to Contact Submit 1-3 poems at a time. No previously published poems or simultaneous submissions. No e-mail or disk submissions. Time between acceptance and publication is up to 2 years, but usually about 9 months. "I buy poems very infrequently—just when one hits me right." Seldom comments on rejected poems. Guidelines available for SASE or on Web site. Responds in up to 1 month. Always sends prepublication galleys. Pays $50/poem and 2 contributor's copies. Acquires first North American serial rights.

⟳ ◻ MAGNAPOETS

13300 Tecumseh Rd. E. Suite 226, Tecumseh ON Canada N8N 4R8. E-mail: Magnapoets@gmail. com. Website: www.magnapoets.com. Established 2008 **Contact:** Aurora Antonovic, editor-in-chief.

Magazines Needs *Magnapoets*, published semiannually in January and July, prints "all forms of poetry, as well as short stories and articles." Wants all forms of poetry, including free verse, formal poetry, tanka, haiku, senryu. Does not want "anything hateful, racist, bigoted, or overtly partisan." Considers poetry by teens. Has published poetry by Robert Pinsky, Kirsty Karkow, Elisha Porat, Peggy Lyles Wills, Curtis Dunlap, an'ya. *Magnapoets* is 36-40 pages, magazine-sized, digital press print format, saddle-stitched, with a glossy cover with full-sized color photograph or art. Single copy: $5 CAN; subscription: $10 CAN. Make checks payable to Aurora Antonovic.

How to Contact Follow submissions guidelines properly and be sure to submit to the appropriate editor and include "Magnapoets" in the subject line.. Email submissions only. Submit up to 3 poems of free verse and formal poetry, maximum 48 lines including title, to Ursula Gibson at UrsulaTG1@aol.com ; for haiku and tanka, send up to 10 poems at a time, to Aurora Antonovic at Magnapoets@gmail.com ; for short stories, submit ONE prose piece, Word length: 250 - 2,500 words to Marie Lecrivain at marie@poeticdiversity.org. Cover letter is preferred. Include a 25-word (or less) bio. Reads submissions in the months of May and October. Time between acceptance and publication is 2-3months. "Each editor edits his/her own section separately. Send submissions to each individual editor as specified. Currently, we have 5 editors: Ursula T. Gibson (free verse and form), Marie Lecrivain (short stories), David Herrle (special features), Guest Editor(haiku and senryu), Aurora Antonovic (tanka). Never comments on rejected poems. Never publishes theme issues. Guidelines available in magazine and on Web site. Responds in 2 months. Pays 1 contributor's copy. Acquires first serial rights (magazine is distributed internationally). Rights revert to poets upon publication.

Additional Information "We publish themed anthologies twice a year. For information, see the Web site."

Tips "Send your best work. Follow the guidelines as detailed on the site."

☐ ◎ THE MAGNOLIA QUARTERLY

(Specialized: membership required to submit), P.O. Box 10294, Gulfport MS 39506. E-mail: writerpllevin@gmail.com. Website: www.gcwriters.org. Established 1999. **Contact:** Phil L. Levin, poetry editor. Publication of the Gulf Coast Writers Association.

Magazines Needs *The Magnolia Quarterly* publishes poetry, fiction, nonfiction, reviews, and photography. **Membership required to submit to magazine** (exception: each issue features a non-member poet chosen by the poetry editor). Will consider all styles of poetry. Does not want "pornography, racial or sexist bigotry, far-left or far-right political poems." Has published poetry by Leonard Cirino, Catharine Savage Brosman, Angela Ball, Jack Bedell, and Larry Johnson. *The Magnolia Quarterly* is 28 pages, magazine-sized, stapled, with paper cover, includes ads. Single copy: $5; subscription: included in $30 GCWA annual dues. Make checks payable to Gulf Coast Writers Assocation. Editing service offered on all prose.

How to Contact Submit 1-5 poems at a time. Lines/poem: open. Considers previously published poems and simultaneous submissions. Prefers e-mail submissions. Cover letter is preferred. Reads submissions year round. Time between acceptance and publication varies. Guidelines available in magazine, for SASE, by e-mail, or on Web site. No payment. Returns rights to poet upon publication.

Also Offers The Gulf Coast Writers Association, "a nationally recognized organization dedicated to encouraging all writers." **Contests/Award Offerings** "Let's Write" contest, with cash prizes for poetry and prose. Additional information available on Web site.

▦ ☑ MAGPIE'S NEST

176 Stoney Lane, Sparkhill, Birmingham B12 8AN England. E-mail: magpies-nest@tiscali.co.uk. Established 1979. **Contact:** Mr. Bal Saini, editor.

Magazines Needs *Magpie's Nest*, published quarterly, seeks "cutting-edge, modern poetry and fiction that deals with the human condition." Does not want "love poetry or self-obsessed work." *Magpie's Nest* receives about 200 poems/year, accepts about 25%. Press run is 200 (150 subscribers, 50 shelf sales). Single copy: $5; subscription: $20. Sample: $4.

How to Contact Submit 4 poems at a time. Lines/poem: 10 minimum, 40 maximum. Considers previously published poems and simultaneous submissions. Accepts e-mail submissions. Cover letter is preferred. "Keep copies of submitted poems as those not used are binned." Reads submissions September 1-June 30 only. Time between acceptance and publication is 3 months. Seldom comments on rejected poems. Occasionally publishes theme issues. Responds in 3 months. Pays 1 contributor's copy. Reviews books of poetry and other magazines in 200 words, single-book format. Send materials for review consideration.

Tips "Read past issues of the magazine to assess the editor's taste/preference."

☑ MAIN STREET RAG

P.O. Box 690100, Charlotte NC 28227-7001. (704)573-2516. E-mail: editor@mainstreetrag.com. Website: www.MainStreetRag.com. Established 1996. **Contact:** M. Scott Douglass, editor/publisher.

Magazines Needs *Main Street Rag*, published quarterly, prints "poetry, short fiction, essays, interviews, reviews, photos, art. We like publishing good material from people who are interested in more than notching another publishing credit, people who support small independent publishers like ourselves." Will consider "almost anything," but prefers "writing with an edge—either gritty or bitingly humorous. Contributors are advised to visit our Web site prior to submission to confirm current needs." Has published poetry by Silvia Curbelo, Sean Thomas Dougherty, Denise Duhamel, Cathy Essinger, Ishle Yi Park, and Dennis Must. *Main Street Rag* is about 120 pages, digest-sized, perfect-bound, with 12-pt laminated color cover. Receives about 5,000 submissions/year; publishes 35-50 poems and 2-4 short stories per issue. Press run is about 800 (300 subscribers, 15 libraries). Single copy: $8; subscription: $24/year, $45 for 2 years.

How to Contact Submit 6 pages of poetry at a time. No previously published poems or simultaneous submissions. **Accepts e-mail submissions from subscribers only**. Cover letter is preferred. "No bios or credits—let the work speak for itself." Time between acceptance and publication is up to 1 year. Guidelines available for SASE, by e-mail, or on Web site. Responds within 6 weeks. Pays 1 contributor's copy. Acquires first North American print rights.

Contest/Award Offerings Main Street Rag's Annual Poetry Book Award and Main Street Rag's Annual Chapbook Contest (see separate listings in Contests & Awards).

Tips "Small press independents exist by and for writers. Without their support (and the support of readers), we have no reason to exist. Sampling first is always appreciated."

🔲 $ ☑ THE MALAHAT REVIEW

University of Victoria, P.O. Box 1700, STN CSC, Victoria BC V8W 2Y2 Canada. (250)721-8524. Fax: (250)472-5051. E-mail: malahat@uvic.ca (inquiries only). Website: www.malahatreview. ca. Established 1967. **Contact:** John Barton, editor.

Magazines Needs *The Malahat Review*, published quarterly, is "a high-quality, visually appealing literary journal that has earned the praise of notable literary figures throughout North America. Its purpose is to publish and promote poetry and fiction of a very high standard, both Canadian and international." Wants "various styles, lengths, and themes. The criterion is excellence." Has published poetry by Steven Heighton and Jan Zwicky. Receives about 2,000 poems/year, accepts about 100. Subscription: $35 CAD for individuals, $50 CAD for institutions (or U.S. equivalent). Sample: $16.45 USD.

How to Contact Submit 5-10 poems at a time. No previously published poems or simultaneous submissions. No e-mail submmissions; postal submissions only. Include SASE with Canadian stamps or IRC with each submission. Guidelines available for SASE (or SAE and IRC). Responds usually within 3 months. Pays $40 CAD per printed page, 2 contributor's copies, and 1 year's subscription. Acquires first world serial rights. Reviews Canadian books of poetry.

Contest/Award Offerings Presents the P.K. Page Founders' Award for Poetry, a $1,000 prize to the author of the best poem or sequence of poems to be published in *The Malahat Review*'s quarterly issues during the previous calendar year. Also offers the biennial Long Poem Prize and Far Horizons Award for Poetry (see separate listings in Contests & Awards).

🔲 ☑ MANNEQUIN ENVY

E-mail: poetry@mannequinenvy.com. Website: www.mannequinenvy.com. Established 2004. **Contact:** Patrick Carrington, poetry editor.

Magazines Needs *Mannequin Envy*, published quarterly online, is a journal of visual and literary arts. Wants "distilled writing that gets to the point without just painting a pretty picture. Improvisational, imperfect, innovative, quirky, non-linear, raw, brave. There is no shortage of really nice poems out there. We do not want 'nice.' We want to feel a physical reaction to your work. Nausea. Embarrassment. Arousal. Something. Make the mannequin turn and notice." Has published poetry by John Sweet, Lynn Strongin, Kelley White, Tim Mayo, and Charles Fishman. Receives about 2,000 poems/year, accepts about 10%.

How to Contact Submit 3-5 poems at a time. Considers simultaneous submissions; no previously published poems. Accepts e-mail submissions (pasted into body of message); no disk submissions. Cover letter is preferred. "Please check guidelines online." Reads submissions as follows: March 1-30 (Spring), May 1-30 (Summer), July 1-30 (Fall), and October 1-30 (Winter). "**Summer issue not open to regular submissions**. Featuring collections of the combined visual art and poetry of individual artists. Submit to Jennifer VanBuren, Editor, at editor@mannequinevy.com. See Web site for more details." Time between acceptance and publication is 1 month. Rarely comments on rejected poems. Guidelines available on Web site. Responds in 10 weeks. Always sends prepublication galleys. No payment. Acquires first rights; "we request the right to publish work in 1 anthology, in print or otherwise." Rights revert to poet upon publication. "We will nominate poets for the Pushcart Prize."

$ ☑ MANOA

A Pacific Journal of International Writing 1733 Donaghho Rd., Honolulu HI 96822. Fax: (808)956-3083. E-mail: mjournal-l@hawaii.edu. Website: http://manoajournal.hawaii.edu. Established 1989. **Contact:** Frank Stewart, poetry editor.

•Poetry published in *Manoa* has also appeared in volumes of *The Best American Poetry*.

Magazines Needs *Manoa*, published twice/year, is a general interest literary magazine that considers work "in many forms and styles, regardless of the author's publishing history. However, we are not for the beginning writer. It is best to look at a sample copy of the journal before submitting." Has published poetry by Arthur Sze, Ai, Linda Gregg, Jane Hirshfield, and Ha Jin. *Manoa* is 240 pages, 7x10, offset-printed, flat-spined. Receives about 1,000 poems/year, accepts 1%. Press run is more than 2,500 (several hundred subscribers, 130 libraries, 400 shelf sales). "In addition, *Manoa* is available through Project Muse to about 900 institutional subscribers throughout the world." Subscription: $22/year. Sample: $10.

Tips "We are not a regional journal, but each issue features a particular part of Asia or the Pacific; these features, which include poetry, are assembled by guest editors. The rest of each issue features work by poets from the U.S. and elsewhere. We welcome the opportunity to read poetry from throughout the country, but we are not interested in genre or formalist writing for its own sake, or in casual impressions of the Asia-Pacific region."

☑ MANY MOUNTAINS MOVING

A Pacific Journal of International Writing 1733 Donaghho Rd., Honolulu HI 96822. Fax: (808)956-3083. E-mail: mjournal-l@hawaii.edu. Website: http://manoajournal.hawaii.edu. Established 1989. **Contact:** Frank Stewart, poetry editor. : a literary journal of diverse contemporary voices549 Rider Ridge Dr., Longmont CO 80501. (303)485-0800, ext. 2. E-mail: editors@mmminc.org. Website: www.mmminc.org. Established 1994. **Contact:** Poetry Editor.

•Poetry published in *Many Mountains Moving* has also been included in volumes of *The Best American Poetry* and *The Pushcart Prize*.

Magazines Needs *Many Mountains Moving: a literary journal of diverse contemporary voices*, published annually in the fall, welcomes "previously unpublished poetry, fiction, nonfiction, reviews, and art from writers and artists of all walks of life." Wants "all forms of poetry, welcoming writing with intelligence, wit, craft, and guile. We look for any form of excellent writing, and also appreciate work that reflects the diversity of our culture. Translations and book reviews are welcome." Has published Robert Bly, Lorna Dee Cervantes, Amiri Baraka, Allen Ginsberg, Yusef Komunyakaa, and Adrienne Rich. *Many Mountains Moving* is over 200 pages, digest-sized, with 4-color glossy cover. Receives 5,000 poems/year, accepts 1%. Press run is 600. Single copy: $12; subscription: $12/year.

How to Contact Submit 3-8 poems at a time. Considers simultaneous submissions; no previously published poems. Cover letter is encouraged. "See guidelines on the Web site for reading periods for paper submissions. Year-round online submissions **with a $2 reading fee** at www. mmm-submissions.org." Seldom comments on rejected poems. Guidelines available on Web site. Responds within 3 months; "if we are seriously considering a submission, we may take longer." Sends prepublication galleys (PDFs by e-mail). Pays 1 contributors copy; additional copies available at discount. Acquires first North American serial rights and "rights to publish in a future edition of the *Best of Many Mountains Moving Anthology*."

Contest/Award Offerings Many Mountains Moving Poetry Book Contest (see separate listing in Contests & Awards) and The Many Mountains Moving Poetry and Flash Fiction Contests. Guidelines available on Web site.

Tips "Although we feature many established poets, we also publish many new writers in every issue. We recommend that poets read through at least 1 issue to familiarize themselves with the type of work we generally publish."

☑ MARGIE/THE AMERICAN JOURNAL OF POETRY

P.O. Box 250, Chesterfield MO 63006-0250. Fax: (636)532-0539. E-mail: margiereview@aol.com. Website: www.margiereview.com. Established 2001. **Contact:** Robert Nazarene, founding editor.

•Multiple selections from *MARGIE* have appeared in *The Best American Poetry*.

Magazines Needs *MARGIE/The American Journal of Poetry*, published annually in the fall, features "superlative poetry. No limits as to school, form, or subject matter. Imaginative, risk-taking poetry which disturbs and/or consoles is of paramount interest. A distinctive voice is prized." Has published poetry by Billy Collins, Molly Peacock, Emmylou Harris, Charles Simic, Paul Muldoon, Ted Kooser, Maxine Kumin, Sally VanDoren, David Wagoner, and Robert Wrigley. *MARGIE* is about 450+ pages, digest-sized, professionally printed, perfect-bound, with glossy cover with art/graphics, includes ads. Receives about 40,000-50,000 poems/year, accepts less than 1%. **Available by subscription only.** Single copy: $19.95 for individuals (1 copy, shipping included), $24.95 for institutions and foreign

How to Contact Submit 3-5 poems at a time. Considers simultaneous submissions (notify in cover letter). Reads submissions according to the following schedule: open reading period is June 1-July 15 (one submission/poet during this time); **subscribers only** may submit up to 4 times annually, year round ("please mark 'Subscribe' on the outside of submission envelope"). Time between acceptance and publication is up to 1 year. Editor makes final decision. Sometimes comments on rejected poems. Guidelines available in magazine, for SASE, or on Web site. Responds in 1-3 weeks. Pays 1 contributor's copy. Acquires first rights. All rights revert to poet upon publication.

Tips "Read, read, read. Then: write. Be audacious, innovative, unafraid, distinctive. Finally, give generously to human and animal rights organizations."

▣ $ ☐ ◎ THE MARTIAN WAVE

(Specialized: science fiction related to exploration/settlement of the Solar System), P.O. Box 782, Cedar Rapids IA 52406-0782. E-mail: martianwave@samsdotpublishing.com. Website: www.samsdotpublishing.com. Established 1997. **Contact:** J. Alan Erwine, editor. Member: The Speculative Literature Foundation (http://SpeculativeLiterature.org).

Magazines Needs *The Martian Wave*, now a print zine, features "science fiction poetry and stories that are related in some way to the exploration and/or settlement of the Solar System." Does not want "anything other than science fiction." Considers poetry by children and teens. Has published poetry by Marge B. Simon, Kristine Ong Muslim, Christina Sng, Aurelio Rico Lopez III, s.c. virtes, and Tyree Campbell. Receives about 150 poems/year, accepts about 16 (12%).

How to Contact Submit up to 5 poems at a time. Lines/poem: prefers less than 100. No previously published poems or simultaneous submissions. Accepts e-mail submissions (pasted into body of message); no disk submissions. "Submission should include snail mail address and a short (1-2 lines) bio." Reads submissions year round. Submit seasonal poems 6 months in advance. Time between acceptance and publication is 1-2 months. Sometimes comments on rejected poems. Guidelines available on Web site. Responds in 4-6 weeks. Pays $5/poem. Acquires first North American serial rights.

Tips "It's up to the writer to take the first step and submit work. Some of our best poems have come from poets who weren't sure if they were good enough. Most important is our theme. The poem must be related to the exploration and/or settlement of the Solar System."

$ ☑ THE MASSACHUSETTS REVIEW

South College, University of Massachusetts, Amherst MA 01003. (413)545-2689. E-mail: massrev@external.umass.edu. Website: www.massreview.org. **Established 1959. Contact:** Deborah Gorlin and Ellen Watson, poetry editors.

•Work published in *The Massacusetts Review* has been included frequently in *The Best American Poetry*.

Magazines Needs *The Massachusetts Review*, published quarterly, prints "fiction, essays, artwork, and excellent poetry of all forms and styles." Has published poetry by Catherine Barnett, Billy Collins, and Dara Wier. *The Massachusetts Review* is digest-sized, offset-printed on bond paper, perfect-bound, with color card cover. Receives about 2,500 poems/year, accepts about 25. Press run is 1,600 (1,100-1,200 subscribers, 1,000 libraries, the rest for shelf sales). Subscription: $27/year U.S., $35 outside U.S., $37 for libraries. Sample: $9 U.S., $12 outside U.S.

How to Contact No previously published poems or simultaneous submissions. Reads submissions October 1-May 31 only. "Guidelines are available online at our Web site, as is our new online submission manager." Responds in 2 months. Pays $25 plus 2 contributor's copies.

$ ☑ ◎ MATURE YEARS

(Specialized: aging; Christian), P.O. Box 801, 201 Eighth Ave. S., Nashville TN 37202. (615)749-6292. Fax: (615)749-6512. E-mail: matureyears@umpublishing.org. **Established 1954. Contact:** Marvin W. Cropsey, editor.

Magazines Needs *Mature Years*, published quarterly, aims to "help persons understand and use the resources of Christian faith in dealing with specific opportunities and problems related to aging. Poems may or may not be overtly religious. Poems should not poke fun at older adults, but may take a humorous look at them." Does not want "sentimentality and saccharine. If using rhymes and meter, make sure they are accurate." *Mature Years* is 112 pages, magazine-sized, perfect-bound, with full-color glossy paper cover. Press run is 55,000. Sample: $5.75.

How to Contact Lines/poem: 16 lines of up to 50 characters maximum. Accepts fax and e-mail submissions (e-mail preferred). Submit seasonal and nature poems for spring from December through February; for summer, March through May; for fall, June through August; and for winter, September through November. Time between acceptance and publication is up to 1 year. Guidelines available for SASE or by e-mail. Responds in 2 months. Pays $1/line upon acceptance.

☑ ⊚ **MEASURE: A REVIEW OF FORMAL POETRY**

Dept. of English, The University of Evansville, 1800 Lincoln Ave., Evansville IN 47722. (812)488-2963. E-mail: pb28@evansville.edu. Website: http://measure.evansville.edu. Established 2005. **Contact:** The Editors.

Magazines Needs *Measure: A Review of Formal Poetry* is "dedicated to publishing the best metrical, English-language verse from both the United States and abroad. In each issue we strive to bring you the best new poetry from both established and emerging writers, and we also reprint a small sampling of poems from the best books of metrical poetry published the previous year. Likewise, each issue includes interviews with some of our most important contemporary poets and offers short critical essays on the poetry that has helped to shape the craft." Wants "English-language metrical poetry with no particular stanza preference. See our Web site or a back issue for examples. *Measure* also reprints poems from books; send copy for consideration." Does not want "fixed forms written in free verse; syllabics; quantitative." Has published poetry by Timothy Steele, R.S. Gwynn, Philip Dacey, X.J. Kennedy, Rachel Hadas, and Charles Rafferty. *Measure* is 180 pages, digest-sized, perfect-bound, with glossy cover with color artwork. Receives about 1,500 poems/year, accepts about 10%. Press run is 1,000. Single copy: $10; subscription: $18 for one year, $34 for 2 years, $50 for 3 years. Make checks payable to *Measure*.

How to Contact Submit 3-5 poems at a time. Lines/poem: no minimum or maximum. No previously published poems or simultaneous submissions. No e-mail or disk submissions. Cover letter is preferred. "All submissions should be typed. Each poem should include the poet's name and phone number. A self-addressed stamped envelope must accompany the submission." Reads submissions year round. Time between acceptance and publication "depends." Never comments on rejected poems. Guidelines available in magazine, for SASE, or on Web site. Responds in 2-3 months, longer in summer. Pays 2 contributor's copies. Acquires one-time rights. Rights revert to poet upon publication.

Additional Information Prints the winners of the annual Howard Nemerov Sonnet Award (see separate listing in Contests & Awards).

⊚ **THE MENNONITE**

(Specialized: Christian), P.O. Box 347, Newton KS 67114-0347. (316)283-5155, ext. 231. Fax: (316)283-0454. E-mail: gordonh@themennonite.org. Website: www.themennonite.org. Established 1885. **Contact:** Gordon Houser, associate editor.

Magazines Needs *The Mennonite*, published twice/month, seeks "Christian poetry—usually free verse, not too long, with multiple layers of meaning." Does not want "sing-song rhymes or poems that merely describe or try to teach a lesson." Has published poetry by Jean Janzen and Julia Kasdorf. *The Mennonite* is 32 pages, magazine-sized, with full-color cover, includes ads. Receives about 200 poems/year, accepts about 5%. Press run is 12,500 (11,000 subscribers). Single copy: $3; subscription: $43.95. Sample: $3.

How to Contact Submit up to 4 poems at a time. Considers previously published poems and simultaneous submissions. Accepts e-mail submissions (preferred). Cover letter is preferred. Time between acceptance and publication is up to 1 year. Seldom comments on rejected poems. Occasionally publishes theme issues. Guidelines available for SASE. Responds in 2 weeks. Pays 1 contributor copy. Acquires first or one-time rights.

☑ **MERIDIAN**

University of Virginia, P.O. Box 400145, Charlottesville VA 22904-4145. (434)982-5798. E-mail: MeridianUVA@yahoo.com or MeridianPoetry@gmail.com. Website: www.readmeridian.org. Established 1998. **Contact:** Poetry Editor.

- Work published in *Meridian* has appeared in *The Best American Poetry* and *The Pushcart Prize*.

Magazines Needs *Meridian*, published semiannually, prints poetry, fiction, nonfiction, interviews, and reviews. Has published poetry by Joelle Biele, David Kirby, Larissa Szporluk, and Charles Wright. *Meridian* is 190 pages, digest-sized, offset-printed, perfect-bound, with color cover. Receives about 2,500 poems/year, accepts about 30 (less than 1%). Press run is 1,000 (750 subscribers, 15 libraries, 200 shelf sales); 150 distributed free to writing programs. Single copy: $7; subscription: $12/year. Make checks payable to *Meridian*.

How to Contact Submit up to 4 poems at a time. Considers simultaneous submissions (with notification of acceptance elsewhere); no previously published poems. No e-mail or disk submissions; accepts postal and online submissions (**$2 upload fee for up to 4 poems**; no fee for postal submissions). Cover letter is preferred. Reads submissions September-May primarily (do not send submissions April 15-August 15; accepts online submissions year round). Time between acceptance and publication is 1-2 months. Seldom comments on rejected poems. Guidelines available on Web site. Responds in 1-4 months. Always sends prepublication galleys and author contracts. Pays 2 contributor's copies (additional copies available at discount). Reviews books of poetry.

Contest/Award Offerings *Meridian* Editors' Prize Contest offers annual $1,000 award. Submit online only; see Web site for formatting details. **Entry fee:** $16, includes one-year subscription to *Meridian* for all US entries or one copy of the prize issue for all international entries. **Deadline:** December or January; see Web site for current deadline.

❏ MERIDIAN ANTHOLOGY OF CONTEMPORARY POETRY

P.O. Box 970309, Boca Raton FL 33497. E-mail: LetarP@aol.com. Website: www. MeridianAnthology.com. Established 2002. **Contact:** Phyliss L. Geller, editor/publisher; Marilyn Krepf, literary editor.

Magazines Needs *Meridian Anthology of Contemporary Poetry*, next published in 2010, seeks "poetry that is contemporary, insightful, and illuminating; that touches the nerves. It should have color, content, and be deciphering of existence." Does not want vulgarity, clichés. Has published poetry by Elizabeth Swados, Ann McGovern, Gladys Justin Carr, Alan Britt, and Doug Ramspeck. Has reprinted poetry (with poet's permission) by Philip Levine and Jane Hirshfield, Dorianne Laux, Marie Howe. *Meridian Anthology of Contemporary Poetry* is 110-168 pages, digest-sized, offset-printed, perfect-bound, with soft cover. Press run is 500-1,000. Single copy: Volume 6 for $16 in late 2008; Volume 5 is $16, Volume 4 is $14, Volume 3 is $13, $9 for Volume 2, $7 for Volume 1. $1 and $3.50 S/H for each additional anthology. Make checks payable to *Meridian Anthology of Contemporary Poetry*.

How to Contact Submit 1-5 poems at a time. Lines/poem: 78 maximum. Considers previously published poems and simultaneous submissions. No e-mail or disk submissions. Cover letter is preferred. Must include SASE. Reads submissions March-December. Time between acceptance and publication is up to one year. Seldom comments on rejected poems. Guidelines available for SASE or on Web site. Responds in 2-6 months, "depending on backlog." Acquires one-time rights. Please include consent to publish, form is available on Web site.

Additional Information "Volume 5, anniversary issue featured reprinted poems by Dorianne Laux, Jane Hirshfield, and Marie Howe. Volume 4 featured Jane Hirshfield, Volume 3 featured Philip Levine). Editing services available: please go to our website for information."

Tips "A poem must have a reason for existence, some universal tendril."

$ ☑ MICHIGAN QUARTERLY REVIEW

University of Michigan, 0576 Rackham Bldg., 915 E. Washington St., Ann Arbor MI 48109. (734)764-9265. E-mail: mqr@umich.edu. Website: www.umich.edu/~mqr. Established 1962. **Contact:** Vicki Lawrence, managing editor.

• Poetry published in *Michigan Quarterly Review* is included frequently in volumes of *The Best American Poetry* and *The Pushcart Prize* anthologies.

Magazines Needs *Michigan Quarterly Review* is "an interdisciplinary, general interest academic journal that publishes mainly essays and reviews on subjects of cultural and literary interest." Wants all kinds of poetry except light verse. No specifications as to form, length, style, subject matter, or purpose. Has published poetry by Susan Hahn, Campbell McGrath, Carl Phillips, and Cathy Song. *Michigan Quarterly Review* is 160 pages, digest-sized, professionally printed, flat-spined, with glossy card cover. Receives about 1,400 submissions/year, accepts about 30. Press run is 2,000 (1,200 subscribers, half are libraries). Single copy: $7; subscription: $25. Sample: $4.

How to Contact No previously published poems or simultaneous submissions. No e-mail submissions. Cover letter is preferred. "It puts a human face on the manuscript. A few sentences of biography is all I want, nothing lengthy or defensive." Prefers typed mss. Publishes theme issues. Upcoming themes available in magazine and on Web site. Guidelines available for SASE or on Web site. Responds in 6 weeks. Always sends prepublication galleys. Pays $8-12/page. Acquires first rights only. Reviews books of poetry. "All reviews are commissioned."

Contest/Award Offerings The Laurence Goldstein Poetry Award, an annual cash prize of $1,000, is given to the author of the best poem to appear in *Michigan Quarterly* during the calendar year. "Established in 2002, the prize is sponsored by the Office of the President of the University of Michigan."

Tips "There is no substitute for omnivorous reading and careful study of poets past and present, as well as reading in new and old areas of knowledge. Attention to technique, especially to rhythm and patterns of imagery, is vital."

☑ THE MIDWEST QUARTERLY

Pittsburg State University, Pittsburg KS 66762. (620)235-4689. Fax: (620)235-4686. E-mail: smeats@pittstate.edu. Website: www.pittstate.edu/engl/mwq/MQindex.html. Established 1959. **Contact:** Stephen Meats, poetry editor.

Magazines Needs *The Midwest Quarterly* publishes "articles on any subject of contemporary interest, particularly literary criticism, political science, philosophy, education, biography, and sociology. Each issue contains a section of poetry usually 12 poems in length." Wants "well-crafted poems, traditional or untraditional, that use intense, vivid, concrete, and/or surrealistic images to explore the mysterious and surprising interactions of the natural and inner human worlds." Does not want "'nature poems,' per se, but if a poem doesn't engage nature in a significant way, as an integral part of the experience it is offering, I am unlikely to be interested in publishing it." Has published poetry by Peter Cooley, Jim Daniels, Naomi Shihab Nye, Jonathan Holden, William Kloefkorn, and Jeanne Murray Walker. *The Midwest Quarterly* is 130 pages, digest-sized, professionally printed, flat-spined, with matte cover. Press run is 650 (600 subscribers, 500 libraries). Receives about 4,000 poems/year, accepts about 50. Subscription: $15. Sample: $5.

How to Contact Submit no more than 5 poems at a time. Lines/poem: 60 maximum ("occasionally longer if exceptional"). Considers simultaneous submissions; no previously published poems. No fax or e-mail submissions. "Manuscripts should be typed with poet's name on each page. Submissions without SASE cannot be acknowledged." Comments on rejected poems "if the poet or poem seems particularly promising." Occasionally publishes theme issues or issues devoted to the work of a single poet. Guidelines available on Web site. Responds in 2 months. Pays 2 contributor's copies. Acquires first serial rights. Reviews books of poetry by *Midwest Quarterly*-published poets only.

Tips "Keep writing; read as much contemporary poetry as you can lay your hands on; don't let rejection discourage you from sending your work out to editors."

◎ MIDWIFERY TODAY

(Specialized: childbirth), P.O. Box 2672, Eugene OR 97402-0223. (541)344-7438. Fax: (541)344-1422. E-mail: editorial@midwiferytoday.com. Website: www.midwiferytoday.com. Established 1986. **Contact:** Cheryl K. Smith, editor.

Magazines Needs *Midwifery Today*, published quarterly, provides "a voice for midwives and childbirth educators. We are a midwifery magazine. Subject must be birth or birth profession related." Does not want poetry that is "off subject or puts down the subject." *Midwifery Today* is 75 pages, magazine-sized, offset-printed, saddle-stapled, with glossy card cover with b&w photos and b&w artwork, includes ads. Press run is 5,000 (3,000 subscribers, 1,000 shelf sales). Subscription: $50. Sample: $10.

How to Contact No previously published poems. Accepts e-mail submissions (pasted into body of message or as attachment). Cover letter is required. Time between acceptance and publication is 1-2 years. Seldom comments on rejected poems. Publishes theme issues. Upcoming themes and deadlines available on Web site. Guidelines available for SASE or on Web site. Responds in 6 months. Pays 2 contributor's copies. Acquires first rights.

Tips "With our publication, please stay on the subject."

$ ☑ MILLER'S POND

H&H Press (570)376-2821. Fax: (570)376-2674. E-mail: publisher@millerspondpoetry.com. Website: http://millerspondpoetry.com. Established 1987. **Contact:** C.J. Houghtaling, publisher.

Magazines Needs *miller's pond*, published online with an annual print version each January, features contemporary poetry, interviews, reviews, and markets. Wants "contemporary poetry that is fresh, accessible, energetic, vivid, and flows with language and rhythm." Does not want "religious, horror, pornographic, vulgar, rhymed, preachy, lofty, trite, or overly sentimental work." Has published poetry by Vivian Shipley, Barbara Crooker, Philip Memmer, and Shoshauna Shy.

How to Contact As of 2009 *miller's pond* will be exclusively an e-zine and will not publish in hard copy format. "All submissions must be sent electronically from our Web site. Mail sent through the post office will be returned. No payment for accepted poems or reviews. Current guidelines, updates, and changes are always available on our Web site. Check there first before submitting anything."

Additional Information Books are available for sale via Web site, phone, or fax.

Tips "Believe in yourself. Perseverance is a writer's best 'tool.' Study the contemporary masters: Vivian Shipley, Billy Collins, Maxine Kumin, Colette Inez, Hayden Carruth. Please check our Web site before submitting."

◎ MINAS TIRITH EVENING-STAR: JOURNAL OF THE AMERICAN TOLKIEN SOCIETY

(Specialized: fantasy; Middle-Earth, Tolkien), American Tolkien Society, P.O. Box 97, Highland MI 48357-0097. E-mail: editor@americantolkiensociety.org. Website: www.americantolkiensociety.org. Established 1967. **Contact:** Amalie A. Helms, editor.

Magazines Needs *Minas Tirith Evening-Star: Journal of the American Tolkien Society*, published quarterly, uses poetry of fantasy about Middle-Earth and Tolkien. Considers poetry by children and teens. Has published poetry by Thomas M. Egan, Anne Etkin, Nancy Pope, and Martha Benedict. *Minas Tirith Evening-Star* is digest-sized, offset-printed from typescript, with cartoon-like b&w graphics. Press run is 400. Single copy: $3.50; subscription: $12.50. Sample: $3. Make checks payable to American Tolkien Society.

How to Contact Considers previously published poems ("maybe"); no simultaneous submissions. Accepts e-mail and disk submissions. Cover letter is preferred. Sometimes comments on rejected poems. Occasionally publishes theme issues. Guidelines available for SASE or by e-mail. Responds in 2 weeks. Sometimes sends prepublication galleys. Pays 1 contributor's copy. Reviews related books of poetry; length depends on the volume ("a sentence to several pages"). Send materials for review consideration.

Additional Information Under the imprint of W.W. Publications, publishes collections of poetry of fantasy about Middle-Earth and Tolkien. Books/chapbooks are 50-100 pages. Publishes 2 chapbooks/year. For book or chapbook consideration, submit sample poems.

Also Offers Membership in the American Tolkien Society is open to all, regardless of country of residence, and entitles one to receive the quarterly journal. Dues are $12.50/year to addresses in U.S., $12.50 in Canada, and $15 elsewhere. Sometimes sponsors contests.

Tips "Adhere to the guidelines and show talent."

☑ ◎ THE MINNESOTA REVIEW

English Dept., Carnegie Mellon University, Baker Hall, Pittsburgh PA 15213. Fax: (412)268-7989. E-mail: editors@theminnesotareview.org (inquiries only). Website: www.theminnesotareview. org. Established 1960. **Contact:** Poetry Editor.

Magazines Needs *the minnesota review*, published biannually, seeks "poetry that explores some aspect of social or political issues and/or the nature of relationships." Does not want "nature poems, and no lyric poetry without the above focus." Has published poetry by Hollander and Fuentes Lemus. *the minnesota review* is about 200 pages, digest-sized, flat-spined, with b&w glossy card cover. Press run is 1,500 (800 subscribers). Subscription: $30/2 years for individuals, $45/year for institutions. Sample: $15.

How to Contact No fax or e-mail submissions. Cover letter is preferred. Include "brief intro with address." Address submissions to "Poetry Editor" (i.e., not to a specific editor by name). SASE with sufficient postage required for return of ms. Publishes theme issues. Upcoming themes available for SASE. Responds in up to 4 months. Pays 2 contributor's copies. "Rights revert to author at printing, though *the minnesota review* asks to be referenced whenever and wherever the poem is reprinted. Further, we reserve the right to post content on our Web site."

◎ MOBIUS: THE JOURNAL OF SOCIAL CHANGE

(Specialized: Socially and politically relevant poetry and fiction), 505 Christianson St, Madison WI 53714. 608-242-1009. E-mail: fmschep@charter.net. Website: mobiusmagazine.com. Established 1989 **Contact:** F.J. Bergmann, poetry editor or Fred Schepartz, general editor

Magazines Needs *Mobius: The Journal of Social Change*, published quarterly, prints socially and politically relevant poetry and fiction and "is distributed free in Madison, WI, and to libraries and subscribers." Wants any form of poetry on themes of social change. Does not want "heavy-handed, transparent didacticism." Considers poetry by teens; however, the publication is not directed at children. Has published poetry by Greg Markee, Tom Neale, Richard Roe, Dennis Trudell, John Tuschen. *Mobius* is 14-24 pages, magazine-sized, offset print, saddle-stapled with cardstock cover and black-and-white art, includes ads. Receives about 500 poems/year, accepts about 20. Press run is 1000; distributed free to local coffee shops and bookstores. Single copy:

$2.50; subscription: $10. Make checks payable to *Mobius*.

How to Contact Submit 5 poems at a time. Considers previously published poems and simultaneous submissions. Accepts e-mail submissions (pasted into body of message); no fax or disk submissions. Cover letter is unnecessary. Include short bio and mailing address; postal submissions must include e-mail address or SASE. Reads submissions year round. Time between acceptance and publication is up to 6 months. Sometimes comments on rejected poems. Never publishes theme issues. Guidelines available by e-mail and on Web site. Responds in 3 months. Pays 2 contributor's copies. Acquires one-time and electronic rights ("reserves right to publish on Web site also"). Rights revert to poets upon publication.

Tips "Prose with line breaks is not poetry. Predictable rants will disappoint us."

$ ☑ ◎ MODERN HAIKU

(Specialized: haiku/senryu/haibun only; translations), P.O. Box 7046, Evanston IL 60204-7046. Email: trumbullc@comcast.net. Website: www.modernhaiku.org. Established 1969. **Contact:** Charles Trumbull, editor.

Magazines Needs *Modern Haiku*, published 3 times/year in February, June, and October, is "the foremost international journal of English-language haiku and criticism. We are devoted to publishing only the very best haiku being written. We also publish articles on haiku and have the most complete review section of haiku books." Wants "haiku in English (including translations into English) that incorporate the traditional aesthetics of the haiku genre, but which may be innovative as to subject matter, mode of approach or angle of perception, and form of expression. Haiku, senryu, haibun, and haiga only; no tanka or renku. No special consideration given to work by children and teens." Has published haiku by Roberta Beary, Billy Collins, Lawrence Ferlinghetti, Carolyn Hall, Sharon Olds, Gary Snyder, John Stevenson, George Swede, and Cor van den Heuvel. *Modern Haiku* is 120 pages (average), digest-sized, printed on heavy quality stock, with full-color cover illustrations and frequent color sections. Receives about 15,000-14,000 submissions/year, accepts about 1,000. Press run is 650. Subscription: $26 ppd. Sample: $11 ppd in the U.S.

How to Contact Submit "a maximum of 20 haiku on one or two letter-sized sheets." No e-mail submissions from North America. No previously published haiku or simultaneous submissions. Put name and address on each sheet. Include SASE. Guidelines available for SASE or on Web site. Responds in 4-6 weeks. Pays $1/haiku; no contributor's copies. Acquires first international serial rights. Reviews of books of haiku by staff and freelancers by invitation in 350-1,000 words, usually single-book format. Send materials for review consideration with complete ordering information.

Contest/Award Offerings Sponsors the annual Robert Spiess Memorial Haiku Competition. Guidelines available for SASE or on Web site.

Tips "Take the time to find out what haiku really are. We do not want sentimentality, pretty-pretty, or pseudo-Japanese themes. Five-seven-five syllable count, rhyme, ego, and intellectualizations are viewed with suspicion."

◻ MUDFISH

Box Turtle Press, 184 Franklin St., New York NY 10013. (212)219-9278. E-mail: mudfishmag@aol.com. Established 1983. **Contact:** Jill Hoffman, editor.

Magazines Needs *Mudfish*, published annually by Box Turtle Press, is an annual journal of poetry and art. Wants "free verse with energy, intensity, and originality of voice, mastery of style, the presence of passion." Has published poetry by Charles Simic, Jennifer Belle, Stephanie Dickinson, Ronald Wardall, Doug Dorph, and John Ashbery. Press run is 1,200. Single copy: $12 plus $3.50 s subscription: $24 for 2 years (price includes s&h).

How to Contact Submit 4-6 poems at a time. No previously published poems or simultaneous submissions. No e-mail submissions; postal submissions only. Responds "immediately to three months." Pays one contributor's copy.

Contest/Award Offerings Sponsors the Mudfish Poetry Prize Award of $1,000. **Entry fee:** $15 for up to 3 poems, $3 for each additional poem. **Deadline:** varies. Guidelines available for SASE.

Tips "Send your best poems—those with heart and craft."

▣ ☑ MUDLARK: AN ELECTRONIC JOURNAL OF POETRY & POETICS

Dept. of English, University of North Florida, Jacksonville FL 32224-2645. (904)620-2273. Fax: (904)620-3940. E-mail: mudlark@unf.edu. Website: www.unf.edu/mudlark. Established 1995. **Contact:** William Slaughter, editor.

Magazines Needs *Mudlark: An Electronic Journal of Poetry & Poetics*, published online "irregularly, but frequently," offers 3 formats: issues of *Mudlark* "are the electronic equivalent of print chapbooks; posters are the electronic equivalent of print broadsides; and flash poems are poems that have news in them, poems that feel like current events. The poem is the thing at *Mudlark*, and the essay about it. As our full name suggests, we will consider accomplished work that locates itself anywhere on the spectrum of contemporary practice. We want poems, of course, but we want essays, too, that make us read poems (and write them?) differently somehow. Although we are not innocent, we do imagine ourselves capable of surprise. The work of hobbyists is not for *Mudlark*." Has published poetry by John Allman, Denise Duhamel, Taylor Graham, Susan Kelly-Dewitt, Frederick Pollack, and Peter Waldor. *Mudlark* is archived and permanently on view at www.unf.edu.

How to Contact Submit any number of poems at a time. Considers previously published poems ("inasmuch as issues of *Mudlark* are the electronic equivalent of print chapbooks, some of the individual poems in them might, or might not, have been previously published; if they have been, that previous publication must be acknowledged"); no simultaneous submissions ("because of our short turn-around time"). "Only poems that have not been previously published will be considered for *Mudlark* posters, the electronic equivalent of print broadsides, or for *Mudlark* flash poems." Accepts e-mail submissions; no fax submissions. Cover letter is optional. Time between acceptance and publication is up to 3 months. Seldom comments on rejected poems. Guidelines available for SASE, by e-mail, or on Web site. Responds in "1 day to 1 month, depending..." Always sends prepublication galleys "in the form of inviting the author to proof the work on a private Web site that *Mudlark* maintains for that purpose." No payment; however, "one of the things we can do at *Mudlark* to 'pay' our authors for their work is point to it here and there. We can tell our readers how to find it, how to subscribe to it, and how to buy it—if it is for sale. Toward that end, we maintain A-Notes (on the authors) we publish. We call attention to their work." Acquires one-time rights.

Tips "*Mudlark* has been reviewed well and often. At this point in its history, *Mudlark* has established itself, arguably, as one of the few serious rivals in the first generation of the electronic medium, to print versions of its kind. Look at *Mudlark*, visit the Web site, spend some time there. Then make your decision: to submit or not to submit."

☑ NASSAU REVIEW

English Dept., Nassau Community College, Garden City NY 11530-6793. (516)572-7792. Established 1964. **Contact:** Editorial Board.

Magazines Needs *Nassau Review*, published annually in September, is a "creative and research vehicle for Nassau College faculty and the faculty of other colleges." Wants "serious, intellectual poetry of any form or style. Submissions from adults only. No college students; graduate students acceptable. Want only poems of high quality." Does not want "light or satiric verse." Has published poetry by Patti Tana, Dick Allen, David Heyen, Joan Sevick, and Mario Susko. *Nassau Review* is about 190 pages, digest-sized, flat-spined. Receives up to 1,900 poems/year, accepts about 20-25. Press run is 1,100. Sample: free.

How to Contact Submit 3 poems at a time (only once per yearly issue). No previously published poems or simultaneous submissions. Submit 3 copies of each poem. SASE required for reply. "Manuscripts will not be returned unless SASE includes sufficient postage." Reads submissions November 1-March 1 only. Guidelines available for SASE. Responds in up to 4 months. Pays 2 contributor's copies.

Contest/Award Offerings Sponsors an annual poetry contest with $200 award. **Deadline:** March 31.

Tips "We want professional-level, high-quality work!"

☑ THE NATIONAL POETRY REVIEW

P.O. Box 2080, Aptos CA 95001-2080. Website: www.nationalpoetryreview.com. Established 2003. **Contact:** C.J. Sage, editor.

•Poetry appearing in *The National Poetry Review* has also appeared in *The Pushcart Prize.*

Magazines Needs *The National Poetry Review* seeks "the most stunning, memorable poems available. The editors celebrate Frost's declaration that the best poems begin in delight and end in wisdom. *TNPR* considers both experimental and 'mainstream' work." Does not want "overly self-centered or confessional poetry, simple autobiography, prose poems, or vulgarity." Has published poetry by Bob Hicok, Jennifer Michael Hecht, Larissa Szplorluk, Margot Schilpp, Nance Van Winkel, and Ted Kooser. *The National Poetry Review* is 64 pages, perfect-bound, with full-color cover. Accepts less than 1% of submissions received. Single copy: $10; subscription: $15/year. Make checks payable to C.J. Sage only.

How to Contact Submit 3-5 poems at a time. Considers simultaneous submissions "with notification only." Submissions are accepted through e-mail only between June 1 and August 31 unless you are a subscriber or benefactor. Put your name in the subject line of your e-mail and send to tnprsubmissions@yahoo.com." Cover letter with bio is preferred. Subscribers and benefactors may submit any time during the year (please write 'subscriber' or 'benefactor' in the subject line). Reading period for non-subscribers is June through August only. See Web site before submitting." Time between acceptance and publication is no more than 1 year. "The editor makes all publishing decisions." Seldom comments on rejected poems. Guidelines available in magazine or on Web site. Usually responds in about 8 weeks. Pays 1 contributor's copy "and small honorarium if funds are available." Acquires first rights.

Contest/Award Offerings The Annie Finch Prize for Poetry, The Laureate Prize for Poetry, and *The National Poetry Review* Book Prize (see separate listings in Contests & Awards).

Tips "Read an issue or 2 before submitting. Send only your very best work."

☑ NATURAL BRIDGE

Dept. of English, University of Missouri-St. Louis, One University Blvd., St. Louis MO 63121. E-mail: natural@umsl.edu. Website: www.umsl.edu/~natural. Established 1999. **Contact:** Jamie Nelson, managing editor. Member: CLMP.

Magazines Needs *Natural Bridge*, published biannually, seeks "fresh, innovative poetry, both free and formal, on any subject. We want poems that work on first and subsequent readings— poems that entertain and resonate and challenge our readers. *Natural Bridge* also publishes fiction, essays, and translations." Has published poetry by Ross Gay, Beckian Fritz Goldberg, Joy Harjo, Bob Hicok, Sandra Kohler, and Timothy Liu. *Natural Bridge* is 150-200 pages, digest-sized, printed on 60 lb. opaque recycled, acid-free paper, true binding, with 12 pt. coated glossy or matte cover. Receives about 1,200 poems/year, accepts about 1%. Press run is 1,000 (200 subscribers, 50 libraries). Single copy: $8; subscription: $15/year, $25/2 years. Make checks payable to *Natural Bridge*.

How to Contact Submit 4-6 poems at a time. Lines/poem: no limit. Considers simultaneous submissions; no previously published poems. No e-mail or disk submissions. "Submissions should be typewritten, with name and address on each page. Do not staple manuscripts. Send SASE." Reads submissions July 1-August 31 and November 1-December 31. Time between acceptance and publication is 9 months. "Work is read and selected by the guest-editor and editor, along with editorial assistants made up of graduate students in our MFA program. We publish work by both established and new writers." Sometimes comments on rejected poems. Sometimes publishes theme issues. Upcoming themes available on Web site. Guidelines available in magazine or on website. Responds in 5 months after the close of the submission period. Sometimes sends prepublication galleys. Pays 2 contributor's copies plus one-year subscription. Rights revert to author upon publication.

ⓝ NAUGATUCK RIVER REVIEW

E-mail: naugatuckriver@aol.com. Website: www.naugatuckriverreview.com. Established 2008 **Contact:** Lori Desrosiers, managing editor/publisher.

Magazines Needs The *Naugatuck River Review*, published semiannually, "is a literary journal for great narrative poetry looking for narrative poetry of high caliber, where the narrative is compressed with a strong emotional core." Considers poetry by teens. Has published poetry by Edward Byrne, Sheila Nickerson, Roderick Bates, Frederick Lord, Derek Sheffield, and Allen Braden. *Naugatuck River Review* is 77 pages, digest-sized, perfect-bound with paper and artwork cover. Receives about 500 poems/year, accepts about 55. Press run is print-on-demand. Single copy: $20; Subscription (starting with next issue): $20/year. Make checks payable to Lori Desrosiers.

How to Contact Submit 3 poems at a time. Lines/poem: 50. Considers previously published poems and simultaneous submissions. Accepts e-mail submissions; no fax or disk. Cover letter is preferred. Include a brief bio and mailing information. Reads submissions January 1-March 1 and July 1-September 1. Time between acceptance and publication is 2-3 months. "I use 3-4 guest editors each issue who blind-read submissions." Never comments on rejected poems. Sometimes publishes theme issues. Guidelines available in magazine and on Web site. Responds in 2-12 weeks. Always sends prepublication galleys. Pays 1 contributor's copy. Acquires first North American serial rights.

ⓩ NERVE COWBOY

P.O. Box 4973, Austin TX 78765. Website: www.jwhagins.com/nervecowboy.html. Established 1995. **Contact:** Joseph Shields and Jerry Hagins, co-editors.

Magazines Needs *Nerve Cowboy*, published semiannually, features contemporary poetry, short fiction, and b&w drawings. Editors will also consider color artwork for the front cover of an issue. "Open to all forms, styles, and subject matter, preferring writing that speaks directly and minimizes literary devices." Wants "poetry of experience and passion which can find that raw nerve and ride it. We are always looking for that rare writer who inherently knows what word comes next." Has published poetry by Mather Schneider, Suzanne Allen, Micki Myers, Charles Harper Webb, Karl Koweski, and David J. Thompson. *Nerve Cowboy* is 64 pages, 7x8½, attractively printed, saddle-stapled, with color artwork cover. Accepts about 5% of submissions received. Press run is 400. Subscription: $20 for 4 issues. Sample: $6.

How to Contact Submit 3-7 poems at a time. Considers previously published poems with notification; no simultaneous submissions. Cover letter is preferred. Include bio and credits. Put name and mailing address on each page of ms. Seldom comments on rejected poems. Guidelines available for SASE or on Web site. Responds in 3 months. Pays 1 contributor's copy. Acquires first or one-time rights.

Contest/Award Offerings The *Nerve Cowboy* Chapbook Contest (see separate listing Contests & Awards).

$ ☑ THE NEW CRITERION

The Foundation for Cultural Review, Inc., 900 Broadway, Suite 602, New York NY 10003. Website: www.newcriterion.com. **Contact:** David Yezzi, poetry editor.

Magazines Needs *The New Criterion*, published monthly (except July and August), is a review of ideas and the arts, printing poetry of high literary quality. Has published poetry by Donald Justice, Andrew Hudgins, Elizabeth Spires, and Herbert Morris. *The New Criterion* is 90 pages, 7x10, flat-spined. Sample: $7.

How to Contact Accepts submissions by postal mail only. Cover letter is required. Responds in 3 months. Pays $2.50/line ($75 minimum).

Tips "To have an idea of who we are or what we stand for, poets should consult back issues."

$ ☑ NEW ENGLAND REVIEW

Middlebury College, Middlebury VT 05753. (802)443-5075. E-mail: nereview@middlebury.edu (inquiries only). Website: www.nereview.com. Established 1978. **Contact:** Poetry Editor.

•Work published in *New England Review* is frequently included in *The Best American Poetry*.

Magazines Needs *New England Review*, published quarterly, is a prestigious, nationally distributed literary journal. Has published poetry by Carl Phillips, Lucia Perillo, Linda Gregerson, and Natasha Trethewey. *New England Review* is 200+ pages, 7x10, printed on heavy stock, flat-spined, with glossy cover with art. Receives 3,000-4,000 poetry submissions/year, accepts about 70-80 poems/year. Subscription: $30. Sample: $10. Overseas shipping fees add $25 for subscription, $12 for Canada; international shipping $5 for single issues.

How to Contact Submit up to 6 poems at a time. No previously published poems or simultaneous submissions. Accepts submissions by postal mail only; accepts questions by e-mail. "Cover letters are useful." Address submissions to "Poetry Editor." Reads submissions postmarked September 1-May 31 only. Time between acceptance and publication is 3-6 months. Responds in up to 3 months. Always sends prepublication galleys. Pays $10/page ($20 minimum) plus 2 contributor's copies. Send materials for review consideration.

Tips "Read a few copies of the magazine before submitting work. Our response time is reasonable, so please do not send simultaneous submissions."

☑ NEW LETTERS

University of Missouri-Kansas City, 5101 Rockhill Rd., Kansas City MO 64110. (816)235-1168. Fax: (816)235-2611. E-mail: newletters@umkc.edu. Website: www.newletters.org. Established 1934 (as University Review), 1971 (as New Letters). **Contact:** Robert Stewart, editor.

Magazines Needs *New Letters*, published quarterly, "is dedicated to publishing the best short fiction, contemporary poetry, literary articles, photography, and artwork by both established writers and new talents." Wants "fresh, new writing of all types. Short works are more likely to be accepted than very long ones." Has published poetry by Naomi Shihab Nye, Albert Goldbarth, Quincy Troupe, Ellen Bass, Joseph Millar, and Mia Leonin. *New Letters* is about 180 pages, digest-sized, professionally printed, flat-spined, with glossy 4-color cover with art. Press run is

3,600. Subscription: $22. Sample: $10.

How to Contact Submit no more than 6 poems at a time. No previously published poems. No e-mail submissions. Short cover letter is preferred. Guidelines available on website.

Contest/Award Offerings The annual *New Letters* Prize for Poetry (see separate listing in Contests & Awards).

Tips "Write with originality and freshness in language, content, and style. Avoid clichés in imagery and subject."

⊞ ☑ NEW MEXICO POETRY REVIEW

44 Via Punto Nuevo, Santa Fe NM 87508. E-mail: nmpr@live.com. Website: newmexicopoetryreview. com. Established 2009. **Contact:** Kathleen Johnson, editor.

Magazines Needs *New Mexico Poetry Review*, published semiannually in April and October, is dedicated to publishing strong, imaginative, well-crafted poems by both new talents and established writers. Wants "poems, prose poems, poetry-related essays, and interviews." Does not want "dull or pretentious writing." *New Mexico Poetry Review* is 60-80 pages, digest-sized, professionally printed, perfect-bound, with a full-color glossy card with art, includes ads. Press run is 500. Single copy: $8; subscription: $15/year. Make checks payable to Kathleen Johnson, editor.

How to Contact Submit up to 5 poems at a time of no more than 70 lines. Considers simultaneous submissions; no previously published poems. Accepts e-mail submissions pasted into body of e-mail message; no fax or disk submissions. Cover letter is not required. Reads submissions year round. Time between acceptance and publication is 4-6 months. Sometimes comments on rejected poems. Sometimes publishes theme issues. Guidelines available for SASE, by e-mail, or on Web site. Responds in 1-3 months. Sometimes sends prepublication galleys. Pays 1 contributor's copy. Acquires first North American serial rights. Reviews books and chapbooks of poetry in 500-700 words, single and multi-book format.

Additional Information Publishes occasional books and chapbooks, but does not accept unsolicited book/chapbook submissions.

Tips "Read as much good poetry as you can. Learn from the best. Take chances."

⊞ ☑ NEW OHIO REVIEW

English Dept., 360 Ellis Hall, Athens OH 45701. (740)597-1360. E-mail: noreditors@ohio.edu. Website: www.ohiou.edu/nor. Established 2007. Member: CLMP.

Magazines Needs *NOR*, published biannually in Spring and Fall, is publishes fiction, nonfiction, and poetry. Wants "literary submissions in any genre. Translations are welcome if permission has been granted." Billy Collins, Stephen Dunn, Marjorie Perloff, Kim Addonizio, William Olson. Single: $9; Subscription: $16.

How to Contact Submit up to 6 poems at a time. "Do not submit more than once every six months." Considers simultaneous submissions. Notify immediately if work is accepted elsewhere."Accepts mail only. Include SASE or IRC, or provide a valid e-mail address (international submissions only).Primary reading period is September through May, but will accept submissions year round.Guidelines available on Web site.

$ ☑ NEW ORLEANS REVIEW

Box 195, Loyola University, New Orleans LA 70118. (504)865-2295. Fax: (504)865-2294. Website: http://neworleansreview.org. Established 1968. **Contact:** Katie Ford, poetry editor.

Magazines Needs *New Orleans Review*, published twice/year, is an international journal of poetry, fiction, essays, book reviews, and interviews. Wants "dynamic writing that demonstrates attention to the language and a sense of the medium; writing that engages, surprises, moves us. We subscribe to the belief that in order to truly write well, one must first master the rudiments: grammar and syntax, punctuation, the sentence, the paragraph, the line, the stanza." Has published poetry by Chrisopher Howell, Martha Zweig, Lee Upton, Jeffrey Levine, Carlie Rosemurgy, and D.C. Berry. *New Orleans Review* is 120-200 pages, elegantly printed, perfect-bound, with glossy card cover. Receives about 3,000 mss/year. Press run is 1,500. Single copy: $10. Sample: $6.

How to Contact Submit 3-6 poems at a time "using our electronic submission system on our Web site. We no longer accept poetry submissions via air mail." Considers simultaneous submissions "if we're notified immediately upon acceptance elsewhere"; no previously published poems. No fax submissions. Brief cover letter is preferred. Guidelines available on Web site. Responds in 2-4 months. Pays 2 contributor's copies and honorarium. Acquires first North American serial rights.

$ ☑ THE NEW RENAISSANCE

26 Heath Rd. #11, Arlington MA 02474-3645. E-mail: marccreate@aol.com (inquiries only). Website: www.tnrlitmag.net. Established 1968. **Contact:** Frank Finale, poetry editor. Editor-in-Chief: Louise T. Reynolds.

Magazines Needs *the new renaissance*, published spring and fall ("resources permitting'), is "intended for the 'renaissance' person—the generalist, not the specialist. We publish the best new writing and translations and offer a forum for articles on political, sociological topics; feature established as well as emerging visual artists and writers; highlight reviews of small press; and offer essays on a variety of topics from visual arts and literature to science. Open to a variety of styles, including traditional." Has published poetry by Anita Susan Brenner, Anne Struthers, Marc Widershien, Miguel Torga (trans. Alexis Levetin), Stephen Todd Booker, and Rabindranath Togore (trans. Wendy Barker and S. Togore). *the new renaissance* is 144-182 pages, digest-sized, professionally printed on heavy stock, flat-spined, with glossy color cover. Receives about 650 poetry submissions/year, accepts about 40. Press run is 1,500 (760 subscribers, 132 libraries). Single copy: $12.50 (current), $11.50 (recent), $7.50 (back issue); subscription: $30 for 3 issues in U.S., $35 in Canada, $38 all others. "All checks in U.S. dollars. A 3-issue subscription covers 18-22 months."

How to Contact Submit 3-6 poems at a time, "unless a long poem—then 1." Considers simultaneous submissions, if notified; no previously published poems "unless magazine's circulation was under 250." Always include SASE or IRC. Accepts submissions by postal mail only; "when accepted, we ask if a disk is available, and we prefer accepted translations to be available in the original language on disk. **All poetry submissions are tied to our Awards Program for poetry published in a 3-issue volume; judged by independent judges.**" Entry fee: $16.50 for nonsubscribers, $11.50 for subscribers, "for which they receive 2 back issues or a recent issue or an extension of their subscription. Submissions without entry fee are returned unread." Reads submissions January 2-June 30. Guidelines available for SASE. Responds in 5 months. Pays $21-40 (more for the occasional longer poem), plus 1 contributor's copy/poem. Acquires all rights but returns rights provided *the new renaissance* retains rights for any *the new renaissance* collection. Reviews books of poetry.

Contest/Award Offerings The Awards Program offers 3 prizes of $250, $125, and $50, with 3-4 Honorable Mentions of $25 each; all submissions are tied to the Awards Program (see above for entry fee).

Tips "Read, read, read! And support the literary magazines that support serious writers and poets. In 2002, more than 350 separate submissions came in, all without the required fee. Since our Poetry Awards Program has been in effect since 1995, and since we've notified all markets about our guidelines and entry fee, this just shows an indifferent, careless reading of our magazine's requirements."

☑ NEW SOUTH

(formerly GSU Review), Campus Box 1894, Georgia State University, MSC 8R0322 Unit 8, Atlanta GA 30303-3083. E-mail: gsu_review@langate.gsu.edu. Website: www.review.gsu.edu. Established 1980. **Contact:** poetry editor.

Magazines Needs *New South*, published semiannually, prints fiction, poetry, nonfiction, and visual art. Wants "original voices searching to rise above the ordinary. No subject or form biases." Does not want pornography or Hallmark verse. *New South* is 160 + pages. Press run is 2,000; 500 distributed free to students. Single copy: $5; subscription: $8/year; $14 for 2 issues. Sample: $3 (back issue).

How to Contact Submit up to 3 poems at a time. Considers simultaneous submissions (with notification in cover letter); no previously published poems. No e-mail submissions. Name, address, and phone/e-mail must appear on each page of ms. Cover letter is required. Include "a 3-4 line bio, a list of the work(s) submitted in the order they appear, and your name, mailing address, phone number, and e-mail address." Include SASE for notification. Time between acceptance and publication is 3-5 months. Seldom comments on rejected poems. Guidelines available for SASE, by e-mail, or on Web site. Pays 2 copies. Rights revert to poets upon publication.

Contest/Award Offerings The *New South* Annual Writing Contest offers $1,000 for the best poem; copy of issue to all who submit. Submissions must be unpublished. Submit up to 3 poems on any subject or in any form. "Specify 'poetry' on outside envelope." Guidelines available for SASE, by e-mail, or on Web site. **Deadline:** March 4. Competition receives 200 entries. Past judges include Sharon Olds, Jane Hirschfield, Anthony Hecht, Phillip Levine and Jake Adam York. Winner will be announced in the Spring issue.

Tips "Avoid clichéd and sentimental writing but as all advice is filled with paradox—write from the heart. We look for a smooth union of form and content."

▦ ▣ ☑ ◉ THE NEW VERSE NEWS

(Specialized: current news, issues, & events), E-mail: editor@newversenews.com. Website: www.newversenews.com. Established 2005. **Contact:** James Penha, editor.

Magazines Needs *The New Verse News*, published online and updated "every day or 2," has "a clear liberal bias, but will consider various visions and views." Wants "poems, both serious and satirical, on current events and topical issues; will also consider prose poems and short-short stories and plays." Does not want "work unrelated to the news." Receives about 700 poems/year, accepts about 300.

How to Contact Submit 1-5 poems at a time. Lines/poem: no length restrictions. No previously published poems or simultaneous submissions. Accepts e-mail submissions (pasted into body of message); no disk submissions. Reads submissions year round. Submit seasonal poems 1 month in advance. "Normally, poems are published immediately upon acceptance." Poems are circulated to an editorial board. Sometimes comments on rejected poems. Guidelines available on Web site. Responds in 1-3 weeks. No payment. Acquires first rights. Rights revert to poet upon publication.

▦ $ ☑ THE NEW WRITER

P.O. Box 60, Cranbrook, Kent TN17 2ZR England. (44)(1580)212626. Fax: (44)(1580)212041. E-mail: admin@thenewwriter.com. Website: www.thenewwriter.com. Established 1996.

Contact: Catherine Smith, poetry editor.

Magazines Needs *The New Writer*, published 6 times/year, is "aimed at writers with a serious intent, who want to develop their writing to meet the high expectations of today's editors. The team at *The New Writer* is committed to working with its readers to increase the chances of publication through masses of useful information and plenty of feedback. More than that, we let you know about the current state of the market with the best in contemporary fiction and cutting-edge poetry, backed up by searching articles and in-depth features." Wants "short and long unpublished poems, provided they are original and undeniably brilliant. No problems with length/form, but anything over 2 pages (150 lines) needs to be brilliant. Cutting edge shouldn't mean inaccessible. No recent disasters—they date." Does not want "'my baby/doggie' poems, God poems that sound like hymns, dum-dum rhymes, or comic rhymes (best left at the pub)." *The New Writer* is 56 pages, A4, professionally printed, saddle-stapled, with paper cover. Press run is 1,500 (1,350 subscribers); 50 distributed free to publishers, agents. Single copy: £6.25 in U.S. (5 IRCs required); subscription: £37.50 in U.S. "We have a secure server for subscriptions and entry into the annual Prose and Poetry Prizes on the Web site. Monthly e-mail newsletter included free of charge in the subscription package."

How to Contact Submit up to 3 poems at a time. Lines/poem: 150 maximum. Does not consider previously published poems. Accepts e-mail submissions (pasted into body of message). Time between acceptance and publication is up to 6 months. Often comments on rejected poems. Guidelines available for SASE (or SAE with IRC) or on Web site. Pays £3 voucher plus 1 contributor's copy. Acquires first British serial rights.

Contest/Award Offerings Sponsors *The New Writer* Prose & Poetry Prizes annually. "All poets writing in the English language are invited to submit an original, previously unpublished poem or a collection of 6-10 poems. Up to 25 prizes will be presented, as well as publication for the prize-winning poets in an anthology, plus the chance for a further 10 shortlisted poets to see their work published in *The New Writer* during the year." Guidelines available by e-mail or on Web site.

$ ☑ THE NEW YORKER

4 Times Square, New York NY 10036. E-mail: poetry@newyorker.com. Website: www.newyorker.com. Established 1925. **Contact:** Paul Muldoon, poetry editor.

•Poems published in *The New Yorker* often have been included *The Best American Poetry*.

Magazines Needs *The New Yorker*, published weekly, prints poetry of the highest quality (including translations). Subscription: $47/year (47 issues), $77 for 2 years (94 issues).

How to Contact Submit no more than 6 poems at a time. No previously published poems or simultaneous submissions. Accepts e-mail submissions (pasted into body of message or as attachment). Include poet's name in the subject line and as the title of attached document. "We prefer to receive no more than two submissions per writer per year." Pays top rates.

☑ NEW YORK QUARTERLY

P.O. Box 2015, Old Chelsea Station, New York NY 10113. Website: www.nyquarterly.org. Established 1969. **Contact:** Raymond Hammond, editor.

Magazines Needs *New York Quarterly*, published 3 times/year, seeks to print "a most eclectic cross-section of contemporary American poetry." Has published poetry by Charles Bukowski, James Dickey, Lola Haskins, Lyn Lifshin, Elisavietta Ritchie, and W.D. Snodgrass. *New York Quarterly* is digest-sized, elegantly printed, flat-spined, with glossy color cover. Subscription: $28.

How to Contact Submit 3-5 poems at a time. No e-mail submissions, but accepts electronic submissions on Web site. Considers simultaneous submissions with notification. No previously published poems. Include your name and address on each page. "Include SASE; no international postage coupons." Guidelines available on Web site. Responds within 6 weeks. Pays in contributor's copies.

◙ NEW ZOO POETRY REVIEW

P.O. Box 36760, Richmond VA 23235. Website: http://members.aol.com/newzoopoet. Established 1997. **Contact:** Angela Vogel, editor.

Magazines Needs *New Zoo Poetry Review*, published annually in January, prints "free verse in well-crafted lyric and narrative forms. Our goal is to publish established poets alongside lesser-known poets of great promise." Wants "serious, intellectual poetry of any form, length, or style. Rhyming poetry only if exceptional." Does not want "light verse, song lyrics, or greeting card copy. If you're not reading the best of contemporary poetry, then *New Zoo Poetry Review* is not for you." Has published poetry by Heather McHugh, Leonard Gontarek, Frannie Lindsay, Marlys West, Natasha Sajé, and Martha Collins. *New Zoo Poetry Review* is 30-40 pages, digest-sized, photocopied, saddle-stapled, with card cover with with illustration or photo. Receives about 1,000 poems/year, accepts about 4%. Press run is 200. Single copy: $5.

How to Contact Submit 3-5 poems at a time. Considers simultaneous submissions; no previously published poems. Cover letter is required. Include SASE and brief bio. Seldom comments on rejected poems. Responds in 2 months. Pays 1 contributor's copy. Acquires first North American serial rights. "Poets are discouraged from submitting more than once in a 12-month period. Please do not write to us for these submission guidelines. We understand and encourage simultaneous submissions and think threatening to 'blacklist' poets who do so responsibly is unfortunate. *NZPR* responds to submissions in an appropriate timeframe and seeks thereby to gather the best work out there."

☐ NIBBLE

6507 Melville Dr., Oakland CA. E-mail: nibblepoems@gmail.com. Website: http://nibblepoems. wordpress.com. Established 1995 **Contact:** Jeff Fleming, editor.

Magazines Needs *nibble*, published bimonthly, is a journal of poetry "focusing on short poems (less than 20 lines)." Does not want "inaccessible, self-important poems." *nibble* is 24 pages, digest-sized, laser-printed, side-stapled, with a cardstock, imaged cover. Receives about 500 poems/year, accepts about 250. Press run is 250; 50 distributed free to schools. Single copy: $5; Subscription: $20/6 issues. Make checks payable to Jeff Fleming.

How to Contact Prefers e-mail submissions. Submit 3-5 poems at a time. SASE required for mail submissions; cover letter is required. Reads submissions year round. Time between acceptance and publication is 2 months. Often comments on rejected poems. Sometimes publishes theme issues. Upcoming themes available by e-mail. Guidelines available for SASE and by e-mail. Responds in 2-4 weeks. Pays 1 contributor's copy. Acquires one-time rights. Reviews books and chapbooks of poetry.

Additional Information Occasionally will publish chapbooks.

◙ NIMROD: INTERNATIONAL JOURNAL OF POETRY AND PROSE

University of Tulsa, 800 S. Tucker Dr., Tulsa OK 74104-3189. (918)631-3080. Fax: (918)631-3033. E-mail: nimrod@utulsa.edu. Website: www.utulsa.edu/nimrod. Established 1956. **Contact:** Manly Johnson, poetry editor.

•Poetry published in *Nimrod* has been included in *The Best American Poetry*.

Magazines Needs *Nimrod: International Journal of Poetry and Prose*, published 2 times/year, is "an active 'little magazine,' part of the movement in American letters which has been essential to the development of modern literature." Publishes an awards issue in the fall, featuring the prizewinners of its national competition, and a thematic issue each spring. "Poems in non-award issues range from formal to freestyle with several translations." Wants "vigorous writing that is neither wholly of the academy nor the streets; typed manuscripts." Has published poetry by Diane Glancy, Judith Strasser, Steve Lautermilch, Virgil Suárez, and Jen-Mark Sens. *Nimrod* is about 200 pages, digest-sized, professionally printed on coated stock, perfect-bound, with full-color glossy cover. Receives about 2,000 submissions/year, accepts 1%. Press run is 2,500. Subscription: $18.50/year U.S., $20 foreign. Sample: $11. "Specific back issues available. Please send check or money order."

How to Contact Submit 5-10 poems at a time. No fax or e-mail submissions. Publishes theme issues. Guidelines available for SASE, by e-mail, or on Web site. Responds in up to 3 months. "During the months that the *Nimrod* Literary Awards competition is being conducted, reporting time on non-contest manuscripts will be longer." Pays 2 contributor's copies, plus reduced cost on additional copies.

Contest/Award Offerings The annual *Nimrod*/Hardman Writing Awards, including The Pablo Neruda Prize for Poetry (see separate listing in Contests & Awards).

Also Offers Sponsors the *Nimrod*/Hardman Awards Workshop, a one-day workshop held annually in October. Cost is about $50. Send SASE for brochure and registration form.

$ ☑ NINTH LETTER

Dept. of English, University of Illinois, 608 S. Wright St., Urbana IL 61801.E-mail: info@ninthletter.com. Website: www.ninthletter.com. Established 2004. **Contact:** Jodee Stanley, editor. Member: CLMP; CELJ.

- *Ninth Letter* won Best New Literary Journal 2005 from the Council of Editors of Learned Journals (CELJ) and has had poetry selected for *The Pushcart Prize*, *Best New Poets*, and *The Year's Best Fantasy and Horror*.

Magazines Needs *Ninth Letter*, published semiannually, is "dedicated to the examination of literature as it intersects with various aspects of contemporary culture and intellectual life." Open to all forms of poetry. Wants "exceptional literary quality." Has published poetry by Cate Marvin, L.S. Asekoff, Patricia Smith, Bob Hicok, Sharmila Voorakkara, Geri Doran, and Angie Estes. *Ninth Letter* is 176 pages, 9x12, offset-printed, perfect-bound, with 4-color cover with graphics. Receives about 9,000 poems/year, accepts about 40. Press run is 2,500 (500 subscribers, 1,000 shelf sales); 500 distributed free, 500 to contributors, media, and fundraising efforts. Single copy: $14.95; subscription: $21.95/year. Sample: $8.95 (back issue). Make checks payable to *Ninth Letter*.

How to Contact Submit no more than 6 poems or 10 pages at a time. No previously published poems. Electronic submissions accepted through Web site. No e-mail or disk submissions. Cover letter is preferred. "SASE must be included for reply." Reads submissions September 1-April 30 (inclusive postmark dates). Time between acceptance and publication is 5-6 months. Poems are circulated to an editorial board. Sometimes comments on rejected poems. Guidelines available for SASE, by e-mail, or on Web site. Responds in 2 months. Always sends prepublications galleys. Pays $25/page and 2 contributor's copies. Acquires first North American serial rights. Rights revert to poet upon publication.

☑ ◎ THE NOCTURNAL LYRIC

Journal of the Bizarre, (Specialized: horror), P.O. Box 542, Astoria OR 97103. E-mail: nocturnallyric@melodymail.com. Website: www.angelfire.com/ca/nocturnallyric. Established

1987. **Contact:** Susan Moon, editor.

Magazines Needs *The Nocturnal Lyric, Journal of the Bizarre*, published annually, features "bizarre fiction and poetry, primarily by new writers." Wants "poems dealing with the bizarre: fantasy, death, morbidity, horror, gore, etc. Any length" Does not want "boring poetry." Has published poetry by Eric Martin, Michael J. Frey, David L. Paxton, Herbert Jerry Baker, Debbie Berk, and Kenneth C. Wickson. *The Nocturnal Lyric* is 40 pages, digest-sized, photocopied, saddle-stapled, includes ads. Receives about 200 poems/year, accepts about 35%. Press run is 400 (40 subscribers). Single copy: $3 U.S., $5 foreign. Make checks payable to Susan Moon.

How to Contact Submit up to 4 poems at a time. Considers previously published poems and simultaneous submissions. No e-mail submissions. Seldom comments on rejected poems. Guidelines available in magazine, for SASE, or on Web site. Responds in up to 6 months. Pays 50¢ "discount on subscription" coupons. Acquires one-time rights.

Tips "Don't follow the trends. We admire the unique."

$ ☑ NORTH AMERICAN REVIEW

University of Northern Iowa, 1222 West 27th St., Cedar Falls IA 50614-0516. (319)273-6455. Fax: (319)273-4326. E-mail: nar@uni.edu. Website: http://webdelsol.com/NorthAmReview/NAR. Established 1815. **Contact:** Vince Gotera, poetry editor.

Magazines Needs *North American Review*, published 5 times/year, is "the oldest literary magazine in America." Wants "poetry of the highest quality; poems that are passionate about subject, language, and image. Especially interested in work that addresses contemporary North American concerns and issues, particularly with the environment, race, ethnicity, gender, sexual orientation, and class." Has published poetry by Debra Marquart, Nick Carbó, Yusef Komunyakaa, Virgil Suárez, Nance Van Winckel, and Dara Wier. *North American Review* is about 48 pages, magazine-sized, professionally printed, saddle-stapled, with glossy full-color paper cover. Receives about 10,000 poems/year, accepts 100. Press run is 2,500 (1,500 subscribers, 1,000 libraries). Subscription: $22 in U.S., $29 in Canada, $32 foreign. Sample: $5.

How to Contact Submit 3-6 poems at a time. No previously published poems or simultaneous submissions. No fax, e-mail, or disk submissions. Cover letter is preferred. Include brief bio and list poem titles. Include SASE. Time between acceptance and publication is up to 1 year. Guidelines available in magazine, for SASE, by e-mail, or on Web site. Responds in 4 months. Always sends prepublication galleys. Pays $1/line ($20 minimum, $100 maximum) and 2 contributor's copies. Acquires first North American serial rights only. Rights revert to poets upon publication.

Contest/Award Offerings The annual James Hearst Poetry Prize (see separate listing in Contest & Awards).

$ ◎ NORTH CAROLINA LITERARY REVIEW

(Specialized: NC topics, work by NC authors), Dept. of English, East Carolina University, Greenville NC 27858-4353. (252)328-1537. E-mail: bauerm@mail.ecu.edu. Website: www.ecu.edu/nclr. Established 1992. **Contact:** Margaret Bauer, editor.

Magazines Needs *North Carolina Literary Review*, published annually in the summer, contains "articles and other works about North Carolina topics or by North Carolina authors." Wants "poetry by writers currently living in North Carolina, those who have lived in North Carolina, or those using North Carolina for subject matter." Has published poetry by Betty Adcock, James Applewhite, and A.R. Ammons. *North Carolina Literary Review* is 200 pages, magazine-sized. Receives about 100 submissions/year, accepts about 10%. Press run is 1,000 (350 subscribers, 100 libraries, 100 shelf sales); 100 distributed free to contributors. Subscription: $20 for 2 years,

$36 for 4 years. Sample: $15.

How to Contact Submit 3-5 poems at a time. No e-mail submissions. Cover letter is required. "Submit two copies and include SASE or e-mail address for response." Reads submissions August 1-April 30 only. Time between acceptance and publication is up to 1 year. Often comments on rejected poems. Guidelines available for SASE, by e-mail, or on Web site. Responds in 3 months within reading period. Sometimes sends prepublication galleys. Pays 2-year subscription plus 1-2 contributor's copies. Acquires first or one-time rights. Reviews books of poetry by North Carolina poets in up to 2,000 words, multi-book format. Poets from North Carolina may send books for review consideration. Rarely reviews chapbooks.

☐ ◎ NORTH CENTRAL REVIEW

(Specialized: undergraduate writers), North Central College, CM #235, 30 N. Brainard St., Naperville IL 60540. (630)637-5280. Fax: (630)637-5221. E-mail: nccreview@noctrl.edu. Website: http://orgs.northcentralcollege.edu/review. Established 1936. **Contact:** The Editors ("editors change year to year, but postal and e-mail addresses don't").

Magazines Needs *North Central Review*, published semiannually, considers "work in all literary genres, including occasional interviews, from undergraduate writers globally. The journal's goal is for college-level, emerging creative writers to share their work publicly and create a conversation with each other. ALL styles and forms are welcome as submissions. The readers tend to value attention to form (but not necessarily fixed form), voice, and detail. Very long poems or sequences (running more than 4 or 5 pages) may require particular excellence because of the journal's space and budget constraints." Does not want "overly sentimental language and hackneyed imagery. These are all-too-common weaknesses that readers see in submissions; we recommend revision and polishing before sending work." Considers poetry by teens (undergraduate writers only). *North Central Review* is 120 pages, digest-sized, perfect-bound, with cardstock cover with 4-color design. Press run is about 750, distributed free to contributors and publication reception attendees. Single copy: $5; subscription: $10. Make checks payable to North Central College.

How to Contact Submit up to 5 poems at a time. Lines/poem: "no limit, but poems running more than 4-5 pages may undergo particular scrutiny." No previously published poems or simultaneous submissions. Accepts e-mail submissions (as Word attachments only); no fax submissions. Cover letter is preferred. Include name, postal address, phone number, and e-mail address (.edu address as proof of student status). If necessary (i.e., .edu address not available), include a photocopy of student ID with number marked out as proof of undergraduate status. Reads submissions September-March, with deadlines of February 15 and October 15. Time between acceptance and publication is 1-4 months. Poems are circulated to an editorial board. "All submissions are read by at least 3 staff members, including an editor." Rarely comments on rejected poems. Guidelines available on Web site, in magazine, for SASE, or by e-mail. Responds in 1-4 months. Pays 2 contributor's copies. Acquires one-time rights. Rights revert to poet upon publication.

Tips "Don't send anything you just finished moments ago—rethink, revise, and polish. Avoid sentimentality and abstraction. That said, the *North Central Review* publishes beginners, so don't hesitate to submit and, if rejected, submit again."

◎ NORTH DAKOTA QUARTERLY

Merrifield Hall Room 110, 276 Centennial Dr. Stop 7209, Grand Forks ND 58202-7209. E-mail: ndq@und.nodak.edu. Website: www.und.nodak.edu/org/ndq. Established 1910. **Contact:** Robert Lewis, editor.

Magazines Needs *North Dakota Quarterly* is published by the University of North Dakota. Seeks material related to the arts and humanities—essays, fiction, interviews, poems, reviews, and visual art. Wants poetry "that reflects an understanding not only of the difficulties of the craft, but of the vitality and tact that each poem calls into play." Has published poetry by Maxine Kumin, Paul Muldoon, Robert Bagg, James Scully, Patricia Schneider, and Marianne Boruch. *North Dakota Quarterly* is about 200 pages, digest-sized, professionally designed and printed, perfect-bound, with full-color artwork on white card cover. Has 550 subscribers. Subscription: $25/year. Sample: $8.

How to Contact Submit 5 poems at a time. No previously published poems or simultaneous submissions. No e-mail submissions; accepts only typed hard-copy submissions by postal mail. Time between acceptance and publication varies. Responds in up to 6 weeks. Always sends prepublication galleys. Pays 2 contributor's copies. Acquires first serial rights.

Tips "We look to publish the best fiction, poetry, and essays that, in our estimation, we can. Our tastes and interests are best reflected in what we have been recently publishing, and we suggest that you look at some current numbers."

☑ NORTHWEST REVIEW

5243 University of Oregon, Eugene OR 97403. (541)346-3957. Fax: (541)346-0537. E-mail: nweditor@uoregon.edu (inquiries only). Website: http://nwr.uoregon.edu. Established 1957. **Contact:** Geri Doran, general editor.

•Poetry published by *Northwest Review* has been included in *The Best American Poetry*.

Magazines Needs *Northwest Review*, published 3 times/year is "looking for smart, crisp writing about poetry and poetics. The only criterion for acceptance of material for publication is that of excellence." Has published poetry by Ted Hughes, Olga Broumas, and William Stafford. *Northwest Review* is digest-sized, flat-spined. Receives about 3,500 submissions/year, accepts about 4%. Press run is 1,300. Single copy: $8; subscription: $22/year (3 issues). Sample: $4.

How to Contact *Is not currently accepting poetry submissions.*

$ ☑ NORTHWOODS JOURNAL

Northwoods Press, P.O. Box 298, Thomaston ME 04861-0298. (207)226-7528. E-mail: cal@americanletters.org. Website: www.americanletters.org. Established 1972 (Northwoods Press), 1993 (Northwoods Journal). **Contact:** Robert Olmsted, editor.

Magazines Needs *Northwoods Journal*, published quarterly, is a literary magazine for writers that publishes fiction, essays, reviews, nonfiction, and poetry. Interested in "all writers who feel they have something to say and who work to say it well. We have no interest in closet writers, vanity authors, or credit-seekers. All writers seeking an audience, working to improve their craft, and determined to 'get it right' are welcome here." *Northwoods Journal* is about 40 pages, digest-sized. Subscription: available only through membership in the Conservatory of American Letters (CAL) ($25/year). Sample: $6.50 and 6x9 SASE with $1.31 postage affixed.

How to Contact No previously published poems or simultaneous submissions. No e-mail submissions; submit by postal mail only. **Reading fee: $1 for 2 poems for CAL members, $1/poem for nonmembers.** "CAL offers 1 free read (up to 5 poems) per year if poetry is submitted simultaneously with membership or renewal." Make checks payable to CAL. Guidelines available for SASE or on Web site. "See guidelines before submitting anything." Pays 10¢ per line on average; "we do not provide free issues."

Additional Information Northwoods Press considers "books by working poets only. No subsidy permitted. No closet poets, vanity poets, or credit-seekers. All accepted books offer opportunity to include CD of author (or others) reading the book, or selections from the book. Original

CD to be produced by author as we have no recording studio. No reading fee for book-length works. We would like to publish up to 12 books per year, but never receive enough quality manuscripts." Requires a personal marketing plan of prospective buyers and **membership in the Conservatory of American Letters (CAL)**.

Also Offers Publishes *The Annual Northwoods Anthology*. Considers poetry and fiction. **Deadline:** December 31. Guidelines available for #10 SASE or on Web site. Pays cash on acceptance.

Tips "Reading fees hold submissions down to a level that someone with 'yes' authority can actually read. They limit competition in a big way. We never get enough of anything. Reading this blurb does not equal 'knowing your market.' Read a few issues. Anyone who submits to a magazine or anthology they've never seen deserves whatever happens."

$ ☑ NOTRE DAME REVIEW/ND[RE]VIEW

840 Flanner Hall, University of Notre Dame, Notre Dame IN 46556. (574)631-6952. Fax: (574)631-4795. E-mail: english.ndreview.1@nd.edu. Website: www.nd.edu/~ndr/review.htm. Established 1994. **Contact:** Managing Editor.

Magazines Needs *Notre Dame Review*, published semiannually, aims "to present a panoramic view of contemporary art and literature—no one style is advocated over another. We are especially interested in work that takes on big issues by making the invisible seen." Has published poetry by W.S. Merwin, R.T. Smith, Moira Egan, Michael Harper, Floyd Skloot, and Kevin Ducey. *Notre Dame Review* is 170 pages, magazine-sized, perfect-bound, with 4-color glossy cover, includes ads. Receives about 400 poems/year, accepts 10%. Press run is 2,000 (500 subscribers, 150 libraries, 1,000 shelf sales); 350 distributed free to contributors, assistants, etc. Single copy: $8; subscription: $15/year. Sample: $6 (back issue).

How to Contact Submit 3-5 poems at a time. Considers simultaneous submissions; no previously published poems. Cover letter is required. Reads submissions September-November and January-March only. Time between acceptance and publication is 3 months. Seldom comments on rejected poems. Publishes theme issues. Guidelines available on Web site. Responds in 3 months. Always sends prepublication galleys. Pays small gratuity on publication, plus 2 contributor's copies. Acquires first rights. Staff reviews books of poetry in 500 words, single- and multi-book format. Send materials for review consideration.

Additional Information *nd[re]view* is the online companion to *Notre Dame Review*, offering "interviews, critique, and commentary on authors and artists showcased within the pages of the print magazine." See Web site for more details.

Contest/Award Offerings The Ernest Sandeen Prize in Poetry (see separate listing in Contests & Awards).

Tips "Read magazine before submitting."

▦ ▣ ☑ NTHPOSITION

E-mail: toddswift@clara.co.uk. Website: www.nthposition.com. Established 2002. **Contact:** Todd Swift, poetry editor.

Magazines Needs *nthposition*, published monthly online, is an eclectic, London-based journal dedicated to poetry, fiction, and nonfiction "with a weird or innovative edge." Wants "all kinds of poetry—from spoken word to new formalist to linguistically innovative. We also publish political poetry." Does not want poetry from never-before-published authors. Has published poetry by Charles Bernstein, George Szirtes, Stephanie Bolster, and Mimi Khalvati. Receives about 2,000 poems/year, accepts about 10%.

How to Contact Submit 2-6 poems at a time. No previously published poems or simultaneous submissions. Accepts e-mail submissions only (pasted into body of message, no attachments).

Cover letter is required. "A brief author's bio is appreciated." Reads submissions throughout the year. Time between acceptance and publication is 4 months. "Poems are read and selected by the poetry editor, who uses his own sense of what makes a poem work online to select." Never comments on rejected poems. Occasionally publishes theme issues. Guidelines available by e-mail or on Web site. Responds in 6 weeks. No payment. Does not request rights but expects proper acknowledgement if poems reprinted later.

Also Offers Publishes special theme e-books from time to time, such as *100 Poets Against the War*.

Tips "Never give up; keep writing. Poetry is a life's work."

▦ ▢ OBSESSED WITH PIPEWORK

8 Abbot's Way, Pilton, Somerset BA4 4BN England. (44)(1749)890019. E-mail: cannula. dementia@virgin.net. Established 1995. **Contact:** Charles Johnson, editor.

Magazines Needs *Obsessed with Pipework*, published quarterly, is "very keen to publish strong new voices—'new poems to surprise and delight' with somewhat of a high-wire aspect." Wants "original, exploratory poems—positive, authentic, oblique maybe—delighting in image and in the dance of words on the page." Does not want "the predictable, the unfresh, the rhyme-led, the clever, the didactic, the sure-of-itself. No formless outpourings, please." Has published poetry by David Hart, Jennifer Compton, Susan Wicks, Carol Burns, Lucille Gang Shulklapper, and Maria Jastrzebska. *Obsessed with Pipework* is 49 pages, A5, stapled, with card cover. Receives about 1,500 poems/year, accepts about 10%. Press run is 70-100. Single copy: £3.50; subscription: £12. Sample: £2 if available. Make checks payable in pounds to Flarestack Publishing. Back issues are also available online at www.poetrymagazines.org.uk.

How to Contact Submit maximum of 6 poems at a time. No previously published poems or simultaneous submissions. Accepts e-mail submissions ("paste a maximum of 6 poems in the body of the message, as attached files may become lost or corrupted"). Cover letter is preferred. Often comments on rejected poems. Guidelines available for SASE or by e-mail. Responds in 2 months. Pays 1 contributor's copy. Acquires first rights.

Tips "Most beginning poets show little evidence of reading poetry before writing it! Join a poetry workshop.

ℕ ▢ ◎ OCEAN DIAMOND

8 Old Sawmill Road, Holliston MA 01746. (508)429-0928. E-mail: oceandiamondhaiku@yahoo. com. Website: www.geocities.com/oceandiamondhaiku/. Established 2008. **Contact:** Jennifer LeBlanc, editor.

Magazines Needs *Ocean Diamond*, published semiannually, is a print and online literary journal dedicated to haiku and short poems (fourteen lines or less). Wants haiku and short poems only. 28-32 pages, digest-sized, photocopied, saddle-stapled, with a stock cover. Single copy: $4.50; subscription: $9.

How to Contact Submit 1-5 poems at a time. 14 lines maximum. Considers simultaneous submissions; no previously published poems. Accepts e-mail submissions (pasted into body of e-mail). Cover letter is required. Reads submissions mid-May through midsummer. Check Web site for dates. Time between acceptance and publication is 7 months. Never comments on rejected poems. Guidelines on Web site. Responds in 2 weeks. Pays 1 contributor's copy. Acquires one-time publishing rights, "which includes publication on the Web site and in the corresponding print issue. Poetry will remain on the Web site for up to 8 months."

Tips "Read contemporary poetry, write often, and proofread your work!"

Magazines/Journals

☐ THE OLD RED KIMONO

Georgia Highlands College, 3175 Cedartown Highway SE, Rome GA 30161. E-mail: napplega@ highlands.edu. Website: www.highlands.edu/ork. Established 1972. **Contact:** Dr. Nancy Applegate, Sean Jepson, Amanda Stegall, and Spencer Musick, editors.

Magazines Needs *The Old Red Kimono*, published annually, prints original, high-quality poetry and fiction. Has published poetry by Walter McDonald, Peter Huggins, Ruth Moon Kempher, John Cantey Knight, Kirsten Fox, and Al Braselton. *The Old Red Kimono* is 72 pages, magazine-sized, professionally printed on heavy stock, with colored matte cover with art. Receives about 500 submissions/year, accepts about 60-70. Sample: $3.

How to Contact Submit 3-5 poems at a time. Accepts e-mail submissions (pasted into body of message). Reads submissions September 1-March 1 only. Guidelines available for SASE or on Web site. Responds in 3 months. Pays 2 contributor's copies. Acquires first publication rights.

☒ ◎ OPEN MINDS QUARTERLY

(Specialized: writing by those who have experienced mental illness), The Writer's Circle, 680 Kirkwood Dr., Building 1, Sudbury ON P3E 1X3 Canada. (705)675-9193, ext. 8286. E-mail: openminds@nisa. on.ca. Website: www.nisa.on.ca. Established 1997. **Contact:** Dinah Laprairie, editor.

Magazines Needs *Open Minds Quarterly* provides a "venue for individuals who have experienced mental illness to express themselves via poetry, short fiction, essays, first-person accounts of living with mental illness, book/movie reviews." Wants "unique, well-written, provocative poetry." Does not want overly graphic or sexual violence. Considers poetry by children and teens. Has published poetry by Pamela MacBean, Sophie Soil, Alice Parris, and Kurt Sass. *Open Minds Quarterly* is 24 pages, magazine-sized, saddle-stapled, with 100 lb. stock cover with original artwork, includes ads. Receives about 300 poems/year, accepts about 30%. Press run is 750; 400 distributed free to potential subscribers, published writers, advertisers, and conferences and events. Single copy: $5.40 CAD, $5 USD; subscription: $35 CAD, $28.25 USD (special rates also available). Make checks payable to NISA/Northern Initiative for Social Action.

How to Contact Submit 1-5 poems at a time. Considers previously published poems and simultaneous submissions. Accepts e-mail and disk submissions. Cover letter is required. "Info in cover letter: indication as to 'consumer/survivor' of the mental health system status." Reads submissions year round. Submit seasonal poems at least 8 months in advance. Time between acceptance and publication is 6-18 months. "Poems are first reviewed by poetry editor, then accepted/rejected by the editor. Sometimes, submissions are passed on to a third party for input or a third opinion." Seldom comments on rejected poems. Guidelines available for SASE, by fax, e-mail, or on Web site. Responds in up to 4 months. "Rarely" sends prepublication galleys. "All authors own their work—if another publisher seeks to reprint from our publication, we request they cite us as the source."

Contest/Award Offerings "The Brainstorm Poetry Contest runs in first 2 months of each year. Contact the editor for information."

Also Offers "All material not accepted for our journal will be considered for The Writer's Circle Online, our Internet publication forum. Same guidelines apply. Same contact person."

Tips "We are unique in that our outlets help to reduce the stigma surrounding mental illness by illustrating the creative talents of individuals suffering from mental illness."

▦ ☐ ORBIS: AN INTERNATIONAL QUARTERLY OF POETRY AND PROSE

17 Greenhow Ave., West Kirby, Wirral CH48 5EL England. E-mail: carolebaldock@hotmail.com. Established 1968. **Contact:** Carole Baldock, editor.

Magazines Needs *Orbis: An International Quarterly of Poetry and Prose* features "news, reviews,

views, letters, prose, and quite a lot of poetry." Wants "more work from young people (this includes 20-somethings) and women writers." *Orbis* is 84 pages, digest-sized, professionally printed, flat-spined, with full-color glossy card cover. Receives "thousands" of submissions/year. Single copy: £5 UK, £5 overseas (€10, $14 USD); subscription: £17 UK, £23 overseas (€30, $46 USD).

How to Contact Submit up to 4 poems at a time. Accepts e-mail submissions "from outside UK only; send no more than 2 poems, pasted into body of message (no attachments)." For postal submissions, "1 poem/page; enclose SASE (or SAE and 2 IRCs) with all correspondence." Responds in up to 1 month. Reviews books and other magazines. Send books for review consideration to Nessa O'Mahony, 5 Walnut View, Brookwood, Scholarstown Road, Rathfarnham, Dublin 16, Ireland. Send magazines for review consideration to Nathan Jones, Belvedere Rd., Princes Park, Liverpool L8 3TF England.

Contest/Award Offerings Prizes in each issue: £50 for featured writer (3-4 poems); £50 Readers' Award for piece receiving the most votes; £50 split among 4 (or more) runners-up.

☑ OVER THE TRANSOM

825 Bush St. #203, San Francisco CA 94108. (415)928-3965. E-mail: jsh619@earthlink.net. Established 1997. **Contact:** Jonathan Hayes, editor.

Magazines Needs *Over The Transom*, published 2 times/year, is a free publication of art and literature. Open to all styles of poetry. "We look for the highest quality poetry and art that best fits the issue." Considers poetry by children and teens. Has published poetry by Garrett Caples, Richard Lopez, Glen Chesnut, Daniel J. Langton. *Over The Transom* is 32 pages, magazine-sized, saddle-stapled, with cardstock cover. Receives about 1,000 poems/year, accepts about 5%. Press run is 300 (100 subscribers); 150 distributed free to cafes, bookstores, universities, and bars. Single copy: free. Sample: $3. Make checks payable to Jonathan Hayes.

How to Contact Submit 5 poems at a time. Considers previously published poems and simultaneous submissions. Accepts e-mail submissions; no disk submissions. Must include a SASE with postal submissions. Reads submissions year round. Time between acceptance and publication is 2-6 months. Never comments on rejected poems. Occasionally publishes theme issues. Guidelines available for SASE or by e-mail. Responds in 2 months. Sometimes sends prepublication galleys. Pays 1 contributor's copy. Acquires first rights.

Tips "Editors have differing tastes, so don't be upset by rejection. Always send a SASE for response."

☑ OYEZ REVIEW

Roosevelt University, Dept. of Literature and Languages, 430 S. Michigan Ave., Chicago IL 60605. (312)341-2157. Fax: (312)341-2156. E-mail: oyezreview@roosevelt.edu. Website: www.roosevelt.edu/oyezreview. Established 1965. **Contact:** Janet Wondra, editor.

Magazines Needs *Oyez Review*, published annually in January by Roosevelt University's MFA Program in Creative Writing, receives "submissions from across the nation and around the world. We're open to poetic sequences and longer poems provided they hold the reader's attention. We welcome skilled and polished work from newcomers as well as poems from established authors. The quality of the individual poem is key, not the poet's reputation." Has published poetry by Gary Fincke, Moira Egan, Gaylord Brewer, Barbara De Cesare, Prairie Markussen, Gary Held. *Oyez Review* is 90 pages, digest-sized. Accepts 5% of poems received. Press run is 800. Single copy: $5.

How to Contact Submit up to 5 poems, no more than 10 pages of poetry at a time. No simultaneous submissions. No fax, e-mail, or disk submissions. Cover letter is required. "Be sure to include a three- to five-sentence biography and complete contact information, including phone and e-mail." Reads submissions August 1-October 1 only. Time between acceptance and publication is 2 months. Guidelines available on Web site. Responds in 3 months. Pays 2 contributor's copies. Acquires first North American serial rights.

☑ PACIFIC COAST JOURNAL

P.O. Box 56, Carlsbad CA 92018. E-mail: pcj@frenchbreadpublications.com (inquiries only). Website: www.frenchbreadpublications.com/pcj. Established 1992. **Contact:** Stillson Graham, editor.

Magazines Needs *Pacific Coast Journal,* published quasi-quarterly, is an "unprofessional literary magazine. Whatever you think that means, go with it." Has published poetry by Michael Meinhoff, Guy R. Beining, and A.D. Winans. *Pacific Coast Journal* is 40 pages, digest-sized, photocopied, saddle-stapled, with cardstock cover. Receives 750 poems/year, accepts about 3%. Press run is 200. Single copy: $4; subscription: $14. Sample: $3.

How to Contact Submit up to 6 poems or 12 pages at a time. Considers simultaneous submissions; no previously published poems. No e-mail submissions. Cover letter is preferred. Encourages the inclusion of e-mail address in lieu of SASE for response. Time between acceptance and publication is 3-18 months. Sometimes comments on rejected poems. Guidelines available for SASE, by e-mail, or on Web site. Responds in 6-9 months (usually). Pays 1 contributor's copy. Acquires one-time rights.

Tips "We like experiments."

☑ PACKINGTOWN REVIEW

English Dept., UH 2027, University of Illinois at Chicago, 601 S. Morgan St., Chicago IL 60607. E-mail: editors@packingtownreview.com. Website: www.packingtownreview.com. Established 2007. **Contact:** Tasha Fouts or Snezana Zabic, editors-in-chief.

Magazines Needs *Packingtown Review,* published annually in November, prints poetry and imaginative and critical prose by emerging and established writers. "We welcome submissions of poetry, scholarly articles, drama, creative nonfiction, fiction, and literary translation, as well as genre-bending pieces." Wants "well crafted poetry. We are open to most styles and forms. We are also looking for poetry that takes risks and does so successfully. We will consider articles about poetry." Does not want "uninspired and unrevised work." *Packingtown Review* is 250 pages, magazine-sized. Press run is 500. Single copy: see Web site for prices.

How to Contact Submit 3-5 poems at a time. Considers simultaneous submissions (with notification); no previously published poems (considers poems posted on a public Web site/blog/forum previously published, but not those posted on a private, password-protected forum). No e-mail or disk submissions. Cover letter is required. "Please include a SASE. If you have simultaneously submitted these poems, please indicate in the cover letter and let us know ASAP if a poem is accepted elsewhere." Reads submissions year round. Poems are circulated to an editorial board. Sometimes comments on rejected poems. Sometimes publishes theme issues. Guidelines available on Web site. Responds in 3 months. Always sends prepublication galleys. Pays 2 contributor's copies. Acquires first North American serial rights. Rights revert to poets upon publication. Review books/chapbooks of poetry and other magazines/journals. Send materials for review consideration to Madeleine Monson-Rosen.

▣ $ ☑ PAINTED BRIDE QUARTERLY

Drexel University, Dept. of English and Philosophy, 3141 Chestnut St., Philadelphia PA 19104. E-mail: pbq@drexel.edu (inquiries only). Website: http://pbq.drexel.edu. Established 1973.

Contact: Poetry Editors.

Magazines Needs *Painted Bride Quarterly*, published online, "aims to be a leader among little magazines published by and for independent poets and writers nationally. We have no specifications or restrictions. We'll look at anything." Has published poetry by Robert Bly, Charles Bukowski, S.J. Marks, and James Hazen. *Painted Bride Quarterly* is printed as one hardcopy anthology annually. Single copy: $15.

How to Contact Submit up to 5 poems at a time. Lines/poem: any length. No previously published poems. No e-mail submissions. "Submissions must be original, typed, and should include a short bio." Time between acceptance and publication is 6-9 months. Seldom comments on rejected poems. Occasionally publishes theme issues. Guidelines available on website. Pays one-year subscription, one half-priced contributor's copy, and $5/accepted piece. Publishes reviews of poetry books.

Contest/Award Offerings Sponsors an annual poetry contest and a chapbook competition. **Entry fee:** required for both. Guidelines available for SASE or on website.

◎ PARADOXISM

A JOURNAL OF HAIKU (Specialized: form/style, haiku/tonka/haibun); SOCIAL ALTERNATIVES (Specialized: social issues); POST PRESSED14 Fig Tree Pocket Rd., Chapel Hill Q 4069. Australia. E-mail: ksamuelowicz@optusnet.com.au. Website: http://users.bigpond.net.au/ReportWright/PaperWasp/PaperWasp.html. Paper Wasp established 1972, Social Alternatives established 1971. **Contact:** Katherine Samuelowicz, manager. (Specialized: avant-garde, experimental) University of New Mexico, Gallup NM 87301. E-mail: smarand@unm.edu. Website: www.gallup.unm. edu/ ~ smarandache/a/Paradoxism.htm. Established 1990. **Contact:** Florentin Smarandache, editor.

Magazines Needs *Paradoxism*, published annually, prints "avant-garde poetry, experiments, poems without verses, literature beyond the words, anti-language, non-literature and its literature, as well as the sense of the non-sense; revolutionary forms of poetry. Paradoxism, a 1980s movement of anti-totalitarian protest, is based on excessive use of antitheses, antinomies, contradictions, paradoxes in creation." Wants "avant-garde poetry, 1-2 pages, any subject, any style (lyrical experiments)." Does not want "classical, fixed forms." Has published poetry by Paul Georgelin, Mircea Monu, Ion Rotaru, Michéle de LaPlante, and Claude LeRoy. *Paradoxism* is 52 pages, digest-sized, offset-printed, with soft cover. Press run is 500; distributed "to its collaborators, U.S. and Canadian university libraries, and the Library of Congress as well as European, Chinese, Indian, and Japanese libraries."

How to Contact No previously published poems or simultaneous submissions. Do not submit during the summer. "We do not return published or unpublished poems or notify the author of date of publication." Responds in up to 3 weeks. Pays 1 contributor's copy.

Additional Information Paradoxism Association also publishes 2 poetry paperbacks and 1-2 chapbooks/year, including translations. "The poems must be unpublished and must meet the requirements of the Paradoxism Association." Responds to queries in 2 months; to mss in up to 3 weeks. Pays 50 author's copies. Sample e-books available on Web site at www.gallup.unm. edu/ ~ smarandache/eBooksLiterature.htm.

Tips "We mostly receive traditional or modern verse, but not avant-garde (very different from any previously published verse). We want anti-literature and its literature, style of the non-style, poems without poems, non-words and non-sentence poems, very upset free verse, intelligible unintelligible language, impersonal texts personalized, transformation of the abnormal to the normal. Make literature from everything; make literature from nothing!"

☑ PASSAGES NORTH

English Dept., Northern Michigan University, 1401 Presque Isle Ave., Marquette MI 49855. (906)227-1203. E-mail: passages@nmu.edu. Website: http://myweb.nmu.edu/ ~ passages. Established 1979. **Contact:** Austin Hummell, poetry editor.

Magazines Needs *Passages North*, published annually in spring, prints poetry, short fiction, creative nonfiction, essays, and interviews. Publishes work by established and emerging writers. Has published poetry by Moira Egan, Frannie Lindsay, Ben Lerner, Bob Hicok, and Gabe Gudding. *Passages North* is 250 pages. Circulation is 1,500. Single copy: $13; subscription: $13/year, $23 for 2 years. Sample: $3 (back issue).

How to Contact Submit up to 6 poems at a time. Considers simultaneous submissions. Time between acceptance and publication is 6 months. Reads submissions September-May only. Responds in 2 months. Pays 2 contributor's copies.

Contest/Award Offerings Sponsors the Elinor Benedict Poetry Prize every other year. 1st Prize: $1,000, plus 2 Honorable Mentions. **Entry fee:** $10 for 1-3 poems (each entrant receives the contest issue of *Passages North*). Make checks payable to Northern Michigan University. **Deadline:** reads entries October 15-February 15. Guidelines available for SASE, by e-mail, or on Web site.

☑ PATERSON LITERARY REVIEW

Poetry Center, Passaic County Community College, Cultural Affairs Dept., One College Blvd., Paterson NJ 07505-1179. (973)684-6555. Fax: (973)523-6085. E-mail: mgillan@pccc.edu. Website: www.pccc.edu/poetry. Established 1979. **Contact:** Maria Mazziotti Gillan, editor/ executive director.

•The Poetry Center Library at Passaic County Community College has an extensive collection of contemporary poetry and seeks small press contributions to help keep it abreast.

Magazines Needs *Paterson Literary Review*, published annually, is produced by the The Poetry Center at Passaic County Community College. Wants poetry of "high quality; clear, direct, powerful work." Has published poetry by Diane di Prima, Ruth Stone, Marge Piercy, and Laura Boss. *Paterson Literary Review* is 300-400 pages, magazine-sized, professionally printed, saddle-stapled, with glossy 4-color card cover. Press run is 2,500. Sample: $13.

How to Contact Submit up to 5 poems at a time. Lines/poem: 100 maximum. Considers simultaneous submissions. Reads submissions December 1-March 31 only. Responds within 1 year. Pays 1 contributor's copy. Acquires first rights.

Contest/Award Offerings The Allen Ginsberg Poetry Awards and The Paterson Poetry Prize (see separate listings in Contests & Awards).

Also Offers Publishes *The New Jersey Poetry Resource Book* ($5 plus $1.50 p&h) and *The New Jersey Poetry Calendar*. The Distinguished Poets Series offers readings by poets of international, national, and regional reputation. Poetryworks/USA is a series of programs produced for UA Columbia-Cablevision. See Web site for details about these additional resources.

▦ ☐ PATTAYA POETRY REVIEW

Classic Village, 95/31 Moo 10 Nong Phrue, Banglamung, Chonburi 20150 Thailand. 6681 7177 941. E-mail: jsutta@yahoo.com. Established 2003. **Contact:** Jiraporn Sutta, editor.

Magazines Needs *Pattaya Poetry Review*, published quarterly, prints poetry. Wants "all types and styles, especially traditional forms." *Pattaya Poetry Review* is 16 pages, digest-sized, with cardstock cover. Receives about 200 poems/year, accepts about 20%. Press run is 70. Single copy: $9; subscription: $16.

How to Contact Submit no more than 3 poems at a time. Considers previously published poems and simultaneous submissions. Accepts e-mail submissions only. Reads submissions year round. Time between acceptance and publication is 3 months. Sometimes comments on rejected poems. Guidelines available. Responds in 3 months. Sometimes sends prepublication galleys. Pays 1 contributor's copy. Returns rights upon written request. Send materials for review consideration to Jiraporn Sutta.

☑ PAVEMENT SAW

Pavement Saw Press, 321 Empire Street, Montpelier OH 43543. E-mail: info@pavementsaw.org. Website: http://pavementsaw.org. Established 1992. **Contact:** David Baratier, editor.

Magazines Needs *Pavement Saw*, published annually in August, wants "letters and short fiction, and poetry on any subject, especially work." Does not want "poems that tell; no work by a deceased writer, and no translations." Dedicates 15-20 pages of each issue to a featured writer. Has published poetry by Simon Perchik, Sofia Starnes, Alan Catlin, Adrianne Kalfopoulou, Jim Daniels, and Mary Weems. *Pavement Saw* is 88 pages, digest-sized, perfect-bound. Receives about 9,000 poems/year, accepts less than 1%. Press run is 550. Single copy: $8; subscription: $14. Sample: $7. Make checks payable to Pavement Saw Press.

How to Contact Submit 5 poems at a time. Lines/poem: 1-2 pages. Considers simultaneous submissions, "as long as poet has not published a book with a press run of 1,000 or more"; no previously published poems. No e-mail submissions; postal submissions only. Cover letter is required. "No fancy typefaces." Seldom comments on rejected poems. Guidelines available in magazine or for SASE. Responds in 4 months. Sometimes sends prepublication galleys. Pays at least 2 contributor's copies. Acquires first rights.

Additional Information Pavement Saw Press also publishes books of poetry. "Most are by authors who have been published in the journal." Published "7 titles in 2005 and 7 titles in 2006; 5 were full-length books ranging from 80 to 240 pages."

Contest/Award Offerings Transcontinental Poetry Award and Pavement Saw Press Chapbook Award (see separate listings in Contests & Awards).

☑ PEARL

3030 E. Second St., Long Beach CA 90803-5163. (562)434-4523 or (714)968-7530. E-mail: pearlmag@aol.com (inquiries only). Website: www.pearlmag.com. Established 1974. **Contact:** Joan Jobe Smith, Marilyn Johnson, and Barbara Hauk, poetry editors.

Magazines Needs *Pearl*, published semiannually in May and November, is interested "in accessible, humanistic poetry that communicates and is related to real life. Humor and wit are welcome, along with the ironic and serious. No taboos, stylistically or subject-wise." Does not want "sentimental, obscure, predictable, abstract, or cliché-ridden poetry. Our purpose is to provide a forum for lively, readable poetry that reflects a wide variety of contemporary voices, viewpoints, and experiences—that speaks to real people about real life in direct, living language, profane or sublime. Our Spring/Summer issue is devoted exclusively to poetry, with a 12- to 15-page section featuring the work of a single poet." Has published poetry by Fred Voss, David Hernandez, Lisa Glatt, Jim Daniels, Nin Andrews, and Frank X. Gaspar. *Pearl* is 112-136 pages, digest-sized, offset-printed, perfect-bound, with glossy cover. Press run is 700. Subscription: $21/year (includes a copy of the Pearl Poetry Prize-winning book). Sample: $8.

How to Contact Submit 3-5 poems at a time. Lines/poem: no longer than 40 lines preferred, each line no more than 10-12 words, to accommodate page size and format. Considers simultaneous submissions ("must be acknowledged as such"); no previously published poems. No e-mail submissions; postal submissions only. Cover letter is appreciated. "Handwritten submissions and unreadable printouts are not acceptable." Reads submissions January-June only. Time between acceptance and publication is up to 1 year. Guidelines available for SASE or on Web site. Responds in 2 months. Sometimes sends prepublication galleys. Pays 1 contributor's copy. Acquires first serial rights.

Additional Information Pearl Editions publishes the winner of the Pearl Poetry Prize only (see separate listing in Contests & Awards). All other books and chapbooks are by invitation only.

Tips "Advice for beginning poets? Just write from your own experience, using images that are as concrete and sensory as possible. Keep these images fresh and objective. Always listen to the music."

☑ PEBBLE LAKE REVIEW

15318 Pebble Lake Dr., Houston TX 77095. E-mail: submissions@pebblelakereview.com. Website: www.pebblelakereview.com. Established 2002. **Contact:** Amanda Auchter, editor.

•Poems published in *Pebble Lake Review* appear regularly on Verse Daily (www.versedaily. org) and were included in *Pushcart Prize XXXI: Best of the Small Presses*.

Magazines Needs *Pebble Lake Review*, published 3 times/year in April, August, and December, seeks "high-quality, image-rich poetry that demonstrates attention to language, form, and craft. Looking for more experimental work." Does not want "anything cliché, Hallmark-style, racist, or erotic." Has published poetry by Kelli Russell Agodon, Denise Duhamel, Jeannine Hall Gailey, Ilya Kaminsky, Dzvinia Orlowsky, and Marge Piercy. *Pebble Lake Review* is 200 pages, digest-sized, perfect-bound, with color cover. Receives about 10,000 poems/year, accepts less than 5%. Single copy: $10; subscription: $24/year. Make checks payable to *Pebble Lake Review*.

How to Contact Submit 3-5 poems at a time. Considers simultaneous submissions with notification; no previously published poems. Accepts e-mail submissions (pasted into body of message; attachments accepted if Word documents); no disk submissions. Cover letter is required. Include SASE. Reads submissions year round. Time between acceptance and publication is 3-6 months. "Poems are circulated between the editors, and the decision is finalized by the editor-in-chief." Seldom comments on rejected poems. Guidelines available in magazine, for SASE, by e-mail, or on website. Sometimes sends prepublication galleys. Pays one contributor's copy. Acquires one-time rights; rights are returned to author upon publication. Reviews books/chapbooks of poetry in 500-1,000 words, single-book format. Send materials for review consideration.

Also Offers Selects poets to read work as part of the *Pebble Lake Review* Audio Project. E-mail the online editor at webmaster@pebblelakereview for details.

▣ $ ☑ THE PEDESTAL MAGAZINE

E-mail: pedmagazine@carolina.rr.com (inquiries only; make submissions through online submission form). Website: www.thepedestalmagazine.com. Established 2000. **Contact:** John Amen, editor-in-chief. Member: CLMP.

Magazines Needs *The Pedestal Magazine*, published bimonthly online, prints "12-15 poems per issue, as well as fiction, interviews, and book reviews. We are open to a wide variety of poetry, ranging from the highly experimental to the traditionally formal." Receives about 5,000 poems/year, accepts about 1%. "We have a readership of approximately 13,000 per month."

How to Contact Submit up to 6 poems at a time. Lines/poem: open. Considers simultaneous submissions; no previously published poems. No e-mail or disk submissions. "Submissions are accepted via a submission form provided in the 'Submit' section of the Web site. Our submissions schedule is posted in the guidelines section." Time between acceptance and publication is 2-4 weeks. Poems are circulated to an editorial board. Sometimes comments on rejected poems. Sometimes publishes theme issues. Guidelines available on Web site. Responds in 4-6 weeks. Always sends prepublication galleys (by e-mail). Pays $30/poem. Acquires first rights. Reviews books/chapbooks of poetry in 850-1,000 words. "Please query via e-mail prior to sending books or related materials."

☐ ◎ THE PEGASUS REVIEW

(Specialized: theme-driven issues), P.O. Box 88, Henderson MD 21640-0088. (410)482-6736. E-mail: bounds1@comcast.net (inquiries only). Established 1980. **Contact:** Art Bounds, editor.

Magazines Needs *The Pegasus Review*, now a quarterly, focuses on a specific theme for each issue and issued in calligraphic format. "Since themes might change it is advisable to contact editor about current themes. With us, brevity is the key. Themes may be submitted in the way of poetry, short-short fiction and essays." Has published work by Jane Stuart, Ed Galing, John Grey, and Burton R. Hoffman. Press run is 120 (100 subscribers, 2 libraries). Subscription: $12. Sample: $2.50, including shipping and handling.

How to Contact Submit 3-5 poems at a time. Lines/poem: 24 maximum. Considers previously published poems, "if there is no conflict or violation of rights agreement," and simultaneous submissions, "but author must notify proper parties once specific material is accepted." No e-mail submissions. "Brief cover letter with specifics as they relate to one's writing background are welcome." Include name and address on each page. "The usual SASE would be appreciated, unless told to recycle material." Responds within 1 month, often with a personal response. Pays 2 contributor's copies and an occasional book award. Themes for 2010: January - The Home; April - Humor; July - Youth and Age; and October - On Writing.

Tips "Write and circulate your work. Constantly strive to improve your writing craft through local writers' groups and/or writing conferences. Remember: writers need readers, so offer to read your work before a group (schools, senior citizen centers, libraries)."

▦ ☑ PENNINE INK

Mid Pennine Arts, The Gallery, Yorke St., Burnley BB11 1HD England. E-mail: sheridansdandl@yahoo.co.uk. Established 1983. **Contact:** Laura Sheridan, editor.

Magazines Needs *Pennine Ink*, published annually in January, prints poems and short prose pieces. *Pennine Ink* is 48 pages, A5, with b&w illustrated cover. Receives about 400 poems/year, accepts about 40. Press run is 200. "Contributors wishing to purchase a copy of *Pennine Ink* should enclose £3 ($6 USD) per copy."

How to Contact Submit up to 6 poems at a time. Lines/poem: 40 maximum; prose: no longer than 1,000 words. Considers previously published poems and simultaneous submissions. Accepts e-mail submissions. Seldom comments on rejected poems. Responds in 3 months. Pays 1 contributor's copy.

Tips "Submissions should be accompanied by a suitable SASE (or SAE with IRCs) for return of work."

▦ ☑ PENNINE PLATFORM

Frizingley Hall, Frizinghall Rd., Bradford, West Yorkshire BD9 4LD England. Website: www.pennineplatform.co.uk. Established 1973. **Contact:** Nicholas Bielby, poetry editor.

Magazines Needs *Pennine Platform*, published 2 times/year in May and November, seeks any kind of poetry but concrete. "All styles—things good of their kind." Has published poetry by Gerard Benson, Miklos Radnoti (trans. Thomas Land), Mike Shields, Sam Smith, William Connely, and Milner Place. *Pennine Platform* is 60 pages, A5, digitally printed, stapled, with matte card cover with graphics. Receives about 1,000 submissions/year, accepts about 100. Circulation is 300 including libraries and universities. Subscription: £8.50 UK, £10 rest of Europe, £12 ROW (all payable in sterling only). Sample: £4.50 UK, £6 ROW.

How to Contact Submit up to 6 poems at a time. Lines/poem: open, "but poems of fewer than 40 lines have a better chance." Submissions must be typed. Comments on all poems (if SAE or e-mail address is provided). Responds in up to 6 months. Pays 1 contributor's copy. Acquires first serial rights. Reviews books of poetry, multi-book format. Send materials for review consideration.

Tips "Pay attention to technique. Intelligent thoughtfulness and intelligent humor both appreciated. Religious poetry (but not religiosity) accepted."

☑ PENNSYLVANIA ENGLISH

Penn State DuBois, DuBois PA 15801-3199. (814)375-4814. E-mail: ajv2@psu.edu (inquiries only). Established 1988. **Contact:** Antonio Vallone, editor.

Magazines Needs *Pennsylvania English*, published annually, is "sponsored by the Pennsylvania College English Association." Wants poetry of "any length, any style." Has published poetry by Liz Rosenberg, Walt MacDonald, Amy Pence, Jennifer Richter, and Jeff Schiff. *Pennsylvania English* is up to 200 pages, digest-sized, perfect-bound, with full-color cover. Press run is 500. Subscription: $10/year.

How to Contact Submit 3 or more poems at a time. Considers simultaneous submissions; no previously published poems. No e-mail submissions. Submissions must be typed. Include SASE. Guidelines available for SASE. Responds in 6 months. Pays 2 contributor's copies.

Tips "Poetry does not express emotions; it evokes emotions. Therefore, it should rely less on statements and more on images."

☑ ◎ THE PENWOOD REVIEW

(Specialized: spirituality, the sacred), P.O. Box 862, Los Alamitos CA 90720-0862. E-mail: submissions@penwoodreview.com. Website: www.penwoodreview.com. Established 1997. **Contact:** Lori M. Cameron, editor.

Magazines Needs *The Penwood Review*, published semiannually, seeks "to explore the spiritual and sacred aspects of our existence and our relationship to God." Wants "disciplined, high-quality, well-crafted poetry on any subject. Rhyming poetry must be written in traditional forms (sonnets, tercets, villanelles, sestinas, etc.)." Does not want "light verse, doggerel, or greeting card-style poetry. Also, nothing racist, sexist, pornographic, or blasphemous." Has published poetry by Kathleen Spivack, Anne Babson, Hugh Fox, Anselm Brocki, Nina Tassi, and Gary Guinn. *The Penwood Review* is about 40 pages, magazine-sized, saddle-stapled, with heavy card cover. Press run is 50-100. Single copy: $6; subscription: $12.

How to Contact Submit 3-5 poems at a time. Lines/poem: less than 2 pages preferred. No previously published poems or simultaneous submissions. Accepts e-mail submissions (pasted into body of message). Cover letter is preferred. 1 poem to a page with the author's full name, address, and phone number in the upper right corner. Time between acceptance and publication is up to 1 year. "Submissions are circulated among an editorial staff for evaluations." Never comments on rejected poems. Responds in up to 4 months. Pays with subscription discount of $10 and, with subscription, 1 additional contributor's copy. Acquires one-time rights.

☑ PEREGRINE

Amherst Writers & Artists, P.O. Box 60111, Florence MA 01062. (413)253-3307. E-mail: peregrine@amherstwriters.com. Website: www.amherstwriters.com. Established 1983. **Contact:** Nancy Rose, editor.

Magazines Needs *Peregrine*, published annually, features poetry and fiction. Open to all styles, forms, and subjects except greeting card verse. "*Peregrine* has provided a forum for national and international writers since 1983, and is committed to finding excellent work by emerging as well as established authors. We publish what we love, knowing that all editorial decisions are subjective." Has published poetry by Willie James King, Virgil Suárez, Susan Terris, Myron Ernst, Pat Schneider, Edwina Trentham, Sacha Webley, Fred Yannantuono, and Ralph Hughes. *Peregrine* is 104 pages, digest-sized, professionally printed, perfect-bound, with glossy cover. Press run is 1,000. Single copy: $15. Sample: $12. Make checks payable to AWA Press.

How to Contact Submit 3-5 poems at a time. Lines/poem: 60 maximum (including spaces). Considers simultaneous submissions; no previously published poems. No e-mail submissions. Include cover letter with bio, 40 words maximum; indicate line count for each poem. Enclose sufficiently stamped SASE for return of mss; if disposable copy, enclose #10 SASE for response. Reads submissions January 15-April 15 (postmark) only. Each ms read by several readers; final decisions made by the editor. Guidelines available for #10 SASE or on Web site. Pays 2 contributor's copies. Acquires first rights.

Tips "Check guidelines before submitting your work. Familiarize yourself with *Peregrine*."

☑ PERMAFROST: A LITERARY JOURNAL

c/o English Dept., University of Alaska Fairbanks, P.O. Box 755720, Fairbanks AK 99775. E-mail: fbpfrost@uaf.edu. Website: www.uaf.edu/english/permafrost. Established 1977. **Contact:** Poetry Editor.

Magazines Needs *Permafrost: A Literary Journal*, published in May/June, contains poems, short stories, creative nonfiction, b&w drawings, photographs, and prints. "We survive on both new and established writers, hoping and expecting to see the best work out there. We publish any style of poetry provided it is conceived, written, and revised with care. While we encourage submissions about Alaska and by Alaskans, we also welcome poems about anywhere, from anywhere. We have published work by E. Ethelbert Miller, W. Loran Smith, Peter Orlovsky, Jim Wayne Miller, Allen Ginsberg, and Andy Warhol." *Permafrost* is about 200 pages, digest-sized, professionally printed, flat-spined. Subscription: $9/year, $16/2 years, $22/3 years. Back-issues $5.

How to Contact Submit up to 5 poems at a time. Considers simultaneous submissions. "Poems should be typed, with author's name, address, phone, and e-mail at the top of each page." Reads submissions September 1-March 15. Included SASE; "e-mail submissions will not be read." Sometimes comments on poems. Guidelines available on Web site. Responds in 2-3 months. Pays 1 contributor copy; reduced contributor rate on additional copies.

Contest/Award Offerings The Midnight Sun Poetry Chapbook Contest (formerly the Susan Blalock Contest; see separate listing).

☑ ◉ PERSPECTIVES

(Specialized: Christian), Dept. of English, Hope College, Holland MI 49422-9000. **Contact:** Rhoda Janzen, poetry editor.

Magazines Needs *Perspectives*, published 10 times/year, aims "to express the Reformed faith theologically; to engage in issues that Reformed Christians meet in personal, ecclesiastical, and societal life; and thus to contribute to the mission of the church of Jesus Christ." Wants "poems excellent in craft and significant in subject, both traditional and free in form. We publish 1-2 poems every other issue." Has published poetry by Ann Hostetler, Paul Willis, and Priscilla Atkins. *Perspectives* is 24 pages, magazine-sized, Web offset-printed, saddle-stapled, with paper cover containing b&w illustration. Receives about 300 poems/year, accepts 6-20. Press run is 3,300. Subscription: $30. Sample: $3.50.

How to Contact No previously published poems or simultaneous submissions. Cover letter is preferred. Include SASE. "Submissions without SASE will not be returned." Time between acceptance and publication is 3-12 months. Responds in 3-6 months. Pays 5 contributor's copies.

Acquires first rights.

☐ ◎ PHILADELPHIA STORIES

(Specialized: submissions from PA, NJ, DE resident poets), 93 Old York Road, Ste 1/#1-753 Jenkintown PA 19046. E-mail: info@philadelphiastories.org. Website: www.philadelphiastories. org. Established 2003. **Contact:** Conrad Weiser. Member: CLMP.

Magazines Needs *Philadelphia Stories*, published quarterly, publishes "literary fiction, poetry, and art from Pennsylvania, New Jersey, and Delaware—and provide it to the general public free of charge." Wants "polished, well crafted poems." Does not want "first drafts." Considers poetry by teens. Has published poetry by Daniel Abdal-Hayy Moore, Scott Edward Anderson, Sandy Crimmins, Liz Dolan, Alison Hicks, and Margaret A. Robinson. *Philadelphia Stories* is 24 pages, magazine-sized, saddle-stapled, with 4-color cover with original art, includes ads. Receives about 600 poems/year, accepts about 15%. Press run is 12,000 per quarter, distributed free. Subscription: "we offer $20 memberships that include home delivery." Make checks payable to *Philadelphia Stories*.

How to Contact Submit 3 poems at a time. Lines/poem: 36. Considers simultaneous submissions; no previously published poems. Accepts submissions through online submission form at www. philadelphiastories.org/submissions; no disk submissions. Cover letter is preferred. Reads submissions year round. Time between acceptance and publication is 3 months. Poems are circulated to an editorial board. "Each poem is reviewed by a preliminary board that decides on a final list; the entire board discusses this list and chooses the mutual favorites for print and Web." Guidelines available on Web site. Responds in 3 months. "We send a layout proof to check for print poems." Acquires one-time rights. Rights revert to poets upon publication. Reviews books of poetry.

☑ PHOEBE: A JOURNAL OF LITERATURE AND ART

MSN 2C5, George Mason University, 4400 University Dr., Fairfax VA 22030-4444. (703)993-2915. E-mail: phoebe@gmu.edu (inquiries only). Website: www.phoebejournal.com. Established 1970. **Contact:** Poetry Editor.

Magazines Needs *Phoebe: A Journal of Literature and Art*, published semiannually in September and February, is interested in the uncanny, the assured—solid poetry. Has published poetry by C.D. Wright, Russell Edson, Yusef Komunyakaa, Rosemarie Waldrop, Charles Bernstein, and The Pines. Press run is 3,000, with 35-40 pages of poetry in each issue. Receives 4,000 submissions/ year. Single copy: $6; subscription: $12/year.

How to Contact Submit up to 5 poems at a time. No simultaneous submissions. No e-mail submissions; postal submissions only. Include SASE and a short bio. Reads submissions September 1-April 15 (postmark); mss postmarked April 16-August 31 will not be read. Guidelines available for SASE or on Web site. Responds in up to 3 months. Pays 2 contributor's copies or one-year subscription.

Additional Information Check http://phoebejournal.blogspot.com for additional information and commentary about *Phoebe*.

Contest/Award Offerings The Greg Grummer Poetry Award (see separate listing in Contests & Awards).

☑ THE PINCH

Dept. of English, University of Memphis, Memphis TN 38152-6176. (901)678-4591. Fax: (901)678-2226. E-mail: thepinch@memphis.edu. Website: www.thepinchjournal.com or www. mfainmemphis.com. Established 1980. **Contact:** Kristen Iversen, editor-in-chief.

Magazines Needs *The Pinch* (previously *River City*), published semiannually (fall and spring), prints fiction, poetry, interviews, creative nonfiction, and visual art. Has published poetry by Albert Goldbarth, Maxine Kumin, Jane Hirshfield, Terrance Hayes, S. Beth Bishop, and Naomi Shahib Nye. *The Pinch* is 160 pages, 7x10, professionally printed, perfect-bound, with colorful glossy cover and color art and photography. Press run is 1,500. Sample: $10.

How to Contact Submit no more than 5 poems at a time. No e-mail submissions. Include SASE. "We do not read in the summer months." Reads submissions according to these deadlines only: August 15-November 1 (Spring issue) and January 15-March 15 (Fall issue). Guidelines available for SASE, by e-mail, or on Web site. Responds in up to 3 months. Pays 2 contributor's copies.

Contest/Award Offerings Offers an annual award in poetry. 1st Prize: $1,000 and publication; 2nd- and 3rd-Prize poems may also be published. Any previously unpublished poem of up to 2 pages is eligible. No simultaneous submissions. Poems should be typed and accompanied by a cover letter. Author's name should not appear anywhere on ms. Manuscripts will not be returned. Guidelines available for SASE, by e-mail, or on Web site. **Entry fee:** $15 for up to 3 poems (includes one-year subscription). **Deadline:** January 15-March 15 (inclusive postmark dates). Winners will be notified in July; published in subsequent issue.

▣ ▢ THE PINK CHAMELEON—ONLINE

E-mail: dpfreda@juno.com. Website: www.geocities.com/thepinkchameleon/index.html. Established 1985 (former print version), 1999 (online version). **Contact:** Mrs. Dorothy P. Freda, editor.

Magazines Needs *The Pink Chameleon—Online* published annually online, contains "family-oriented, upbeat poetry, any genre in good taste that gives hope for the future." Wants "poems about nature, loved ones, rare moments in time." Does not want "pornography, cursing, swearing; nothing evoking despair." Also considers poetry by children and teens. Receives about 50 poems/year, accepts about 50%.

How to Contact Submit 1-4 poems at a time. Lines/poem: 6 minimum, 24 maximum. Considers previously published poems; no simultaneous submissions. Accepts e-mail submissions only (pasted into body of message; "please, no attachments"). Use plain text and include a brief bio. Reads submissions January-April 30th and September-October 31st. Time between acceptance and publication is up to 1 year depending on date of acceptance. "As editor, I reserve the right to edit for grammar, spelling, sentence structure, flow; omit redundancy and any words or material I consider in bad taste." Often comments on rejected poems. Guidelines available by e-mail or on Web site. Responds in 1 month. No payment. Acquires one-time, one-year publication rights. All rights revert to poet in 6 months to a year, depending on date of acceptance.

Tips "Always keep a typed hard copy or a back-up disk of your work for your files. Mail can go astray. And I'm human, I can accidentally delete or lose the submission."

▨ PINYON

Dept. of Languages, Literature & Communications, Mesa State College, 1100 North Ave., Grand Junction CO 81051. E-mail: pinyonpoetry@hotmail.com. Established 1995. **Contact:** Randy Phillis, editor.

Magazines Needs *Pinyon*, published annually in June, prints "the best available contemporary American poetry and fiction. No restrictions other than excellence. We appreciate a strong voice." Does not want "inspirational, light verse, or sing-song poetry." Has published poetry by Mark Cox, Barry Spacks, Wendy Bishop, and Anne Ohman Youngs. *Pinyon* is about 120 pages, magazine-sized, perfect-bound. Receives about 4,000 poems/year, accepts 2%. Press run is 300; 100 distributed free to contributors, friends, etc. Subscription: $8/year. Sample: $4.50. Make checks payable to Pinyon, MSC.

How to Contact Submit 3-5 poems at a time. No previously published poems or simultaneous submissions. Cover letter is preferred. "Name, address, e-mail, and phone number on each page. SASE required." Reads submissions August 1-December 1. "3 groups of assistant editors, led by an associate editor, make recommendations to the editor." Seldom comments on rejected poems. Guidelines available for SASE. Responds in February. Pays 2 contributor's copies. Acquires one-time rights.

Tips "Send us your best work!"

☑ PIRENE'S FOUNTAIN

E-mail: pirenepublisher@gmail.com. Website: pirenesfountain.com. Established 2008. **Contact:** Oliver Lodge, Charles Morrison, Tony Walbran, submissions editors; magazine editor: Lark Vernon. Publisher: Ami Kaye.

Magazines Needs *Pirene's Fountain* is published online 3 times per year in January, May, and October. Does not want "blatantly religious/political themes, anything obscene, pornographic, or discriminatory in nature." Has published work by Lisel Mueller, Alison Croggan, Dorianne Laux, Rebecca Seiferle, Joseph Millar, Kim Addonizio, Dimitris Varos, Cynthia Bracket-Vincent, Aine MacAodha, and Marc Beaudin. Receives about 600 poems/year, accepts about 20%.

How to Contact Submit 3-8 poems at a time. Considers previously published poems and simultaneous submissions. Considers poetry posted on a public Web site/blog/forum and poetry posted on a private, password-protected forum as published. Accepts e-mail submissions pasted into body of message; no fax or disk submissions. Cover letter is unnecessary but 50-100 word bio is required. Reads submissions during the months of November, April, and September. Submit seasonal poems anytime. Time between acceptance and publication is 4 to 6 weeks. Poems are circulated to an editorial board. Never comments on rejected poems. Sometimes publishes theme issues. Guidelines available on Web site. Responds in 4 to 5 weeks. Poets retain copyright to their own work, rights revert to poets upon publication.

Also Offers "We offer a poetry discussion group on Facebook, entitled 'PF Poetry.' Membership on Facebook is free and approval from a PF officer is required. E-mail publisher for details if interested."

Tips "Please read submission guidelines carefully and send in *at least* 3 poems."

☑ ◎ PLAINSONGS

(Specialized: Great Plains poems encouraged), Dept. of English, Hastings College, Hastings NE 68902-0269. (402)461-7352. Fax: (402)461-7756. E-mail: plainsongs@hastings.edu (inquiries only). Established 1980. **Contact:** Laura Marvel Wunderlich, editor.

Magazines Needs *Plainsongs*, published 3 times/year, considers poems "on any subject, in any style, but free verse predominates. Plains region poems encouraged." *Plainsongs'* title suggests not only its location on the Great Plains, but its preference for the living language, whether in free or formal verse. "*Plainsongs* is committed to poems only, to make space without visual graphics, bios, reviews, or critical positions." Has published poetry by Judith Tate O'Brien, Andrew H. Oerke, Lyn Lifshin, Larsen Bowker, and Louis Daniel Brodsky. *Plainsongs* is 40 pages, digest-sized, laser-set, printed on thin paper, saddle-stapled, with one-color matte card cover with generic black logo. "Published by the English department of Hastings College, the magazine is partially financed by subscriptions. Although editors respond to as many submissions with personal attention as they have time for, the editor offers specific observations to all contributors who also subscribe." Subscription: $15 for 3 issues. Sample: $5.

How to Contact Submit up to 6 poems at a time, with name and address on each page. No fax, e-mail, or disk submissions; postal submissions only. Reads submissions according to the following deadlines: July 15 for Winter issue; November 15 for Spring issue; March 15 for Fall issue. Responds 7-8 weeks after deadline. Guidelines available for SASE. Pays 2 contributor's copies and one-year subscription. Acquires first rights.

Contest/Award Offerings 3 poems in each issue receive a $25 prize. "A short essay in appreciation accompanies each award poem."

Tips "We like poems that seem to be aware of modernist and post-modernist influences during the last hundred years, not necessarily by imitation or allusion, but by using the tools provided by that rich heritage. Poets need to read and absorb the work of other poets."

☑ PLAIN SPOKE

6199 Steubenville Road SE, Amsterdam OH 43903. (740)543-4333. E-mail: plainspoke@gmail. com. Website: www.plainspoke.net. Established 2007. **Contact:** Cindy Kelly, editor.

Magazines Needs *Plain Spoke*, published quarterly, publishes "poetry heavy in sense images and with a clear, plain-spoken voice." Wants "Americana, nostalgia, narrative." Does not want "esoteric, universal, cliché." Has published poetry by Claudia Burbank, Hannah Craig, Amy Sargent. *Plain Spoke* is 36-52 digest-sized, laser-printed, saddle-stitched, with a color art on cardstock cover. Receives about 2,500 poems/year, accepts about 5%. Press run is 300. Single copy: $6; subscription: $20. Make checks payable to Amsterdam Press.

How to Contact Submit up to 6 poems at a time, preferably under 40 lines. Considers simultaneous submissions, no previously published poems (considers poetry posted on a public Web site/blog/forum). Accepts e-mail submissions (pasted into body of message) and disk submissions; no fax submissions. Cover letter is required. Paper submissions require an SASE. Reads submissions year round. Submit seasonal poems 3 months in advance. Time between acceptance and publication is 1-4 months. Poems are circulated to an editorial board. Sometimes comments on rejected poems. Never publishes theme issues. Guidelines available for SASE, by e-mail, and on Web site. Responds in 1 week. Pays 1 contributor's copy. Acquires first North American serial rights. Rights revert to poets upon publication. Reviews books and chapbooks of poetry in single-book format. Send materials for review consideration to Reviews Editor, *Plain Spoke*.

$ ☑ PLEIADES

Pleiades Press, Dept.of English, University of Central Missouri, Warrensburg MO 64093. (660)543-8106. E-mail: pleiades@ucmo.edu. Website: http://www.ucmo.edu/englphil/ pleiades/. Established 1990. **Contact:** Kevin Prufer, editor.

•Poems published in *Pleiades* have appeared in *The Best American Poetry* and *The Pushcart Prize*.

Magazines Needs *Pleiades*, published semiannually in April and October, prints poetry, fiction, literary criticism, belles lettres (occasionally), and reviews. Open to all writers. Wants "avant-garde, free verse, and traditional poetry, and some quality light verse." Does not want anything "pretentious, didactic, or overly sentimental." Has published poetry by James Tate, Joyce Carol Oates, Brenda Hillman, Wislawa Szymborska, Carl Phillips, and Jean Valentine. *Pleiades* is 160 pages, digest-sized, perfect-bound, with heavy coated cover with color art. Receives about 9,000 poems/year, accepts fewer than 1%. Press run is 2,500-3,000; about 200 distributed free to educational institutions and libraries across the country. Single copy: $6; subscription: $12. Sample: $5. Make checks payable to Pleiades Press.

How to Contact Submit 3-5 poems at a time. Considers simultaneous submissions with notification; no previously published poems. Cover letter is preferred. Include brief bio. Time between acceptance and publication "can be up to 1 year. Each poem published must be accepted by 2 readers and approved by the poetry editor." Seldom comments on rejected poems. Guidelines available for SASE or on Web site. Responds in up to 3 months. Payment varies. Acquires first and second serial rights.

$ ◎ PLOUGHSHARES

Emerson College, 120 Boylston St., Dept. P, Boston MA 02116. (617)824-8753. Website: www. pshares.org. Established 1971. **Contact:** Poetry Editor.

•Work published in *Ploughshares* has been selected frequently for *The Best American Poetry*.

Magazines Needs *Ploughshares*, published 3 times/year, is "a journal of new writing guest-edited by prominent poets and writers to reflect different and contrasting points of view. Translations are welcome if permission has been granted." Editors have included Carolyn Forché, Gerald Stern, Rita Dove, Chase Twichell, and Marilyn Hacker. Has published poetry by Donald Hall, Li-Young Lee, Robert Pinsky, Brenda Hillman, and Thylias Moss. *Ploughshares* is 200 pages, digest-sized. Receives about 2,500 poetry submissions/year. Press run is 7,000. Subscription: $24 domestic, $36 foreign. Sample: $10.95 current issue, $8.50 back issue.

How to Contact Submit 1-3 poems at a time. Considers simultaneous submissions if indicated as such; no previously published poems. Postal submissions only, include SASE. Cover letter is preferred. Reads submissions August 1-March 31 (postmark); mss submitted April 1-July 31 will be returned unread. "We suggest you read a few issues (online or in print) before submitting. Check our website for any special guidelines." Responds in up to 5 months. Always sends prepublication galleys. Pays $25/printed page ($50 minimum, $250 maximum), plus 2 contributor's copies and a subscription.

$ ▢ ◎ POCKETS

(Specialized: Christian; poetry by/for children; thematic issues), P.O. Box 340004, Nashville TN 37203-0004. E-mail: pockets@upperroom.org. Website: www.pockets.org. **Contact:** Lynn W. Gilliam, editor.

Magazines Needs *Pockets*, published monthly (except February), is an interdenominational magazine for children ages 6-11. "Each issue is built around a specific theme, with material (including poetry) that can be used by children in a variety of ways. Submissions do not need to be overly religious; they should help children experience a Christian lifestyle that is not always a neatly wrapped moral package but is open to the continuing revelation of God's will." Considers poetry by children.

How to Contact Lines/poem: 24 maximum. Considers previously published poems (first reprint only). No fax or e-mail submissions. Submissions should be typed, double-spaced, on 8½x11 paper, accompanied by SASE for return. "Those who wish to save postage and are concerned about paper conservation may send a SASP for notification of accepted manuscripts. Please list the titles of the submissions on the postcards. We will recycle the paper the submission is printed on." Reads submissions year round. Publishes theme issues; themes are available each year the end of December. Guidelines available on Web site (under Adults/Writer's Corner). Pays $2/line ($25 minimum) for poems. Pays on acceptance. Places mss on long-term hold for specific issues. Acquires newspaper, periodical, and electronic rights.

◎ POEM

Huntsville Literary Association, P.O. Box 2006, Huntsville AL 35804. Website: www.hla-hsv.org. Established 1967. **Contact:** Rebecca Harbor, editor.

Magazines Needs *Poem*, published twice/year in May and November, consists entirely of poetry.

"We publish both traditional forms and free verse." Wants poems "characterized by compression, rich vocabulary, significant content, and evidence of 'a tuned ear and practiced pen.' We want coherent work that moves through the particulars of the poem to make a point. We equally welcome submissions from established poets as well as from less-known and beginning poets." Does not want translations. Has published poetry by Kathryn Kirkpatrick, Peter Serchuk, and Kim Bridgford. *Poem* is 90 pages, digest-sized, flat-spined, printed on good stock paper, with a clean design and a matte cover. Prints more than 60 poems/issue, generally featured 1 to a page. Press run is 500. Single copy: $10; subscription: $20. Sample: $7 (back issue).

How to Contact Send 3-5 poems at a time. No previously published poems or simultaneous submissions. Include SASE. Reads submissions year round. Guidelines available for SASE or on Web site. Responds in 1-2 months. Pays 2 contributor's copies. Acquires first serial rights.

☐ ☑ POEMELEON: A JOURNAL OF POETRY

E-mail: editor@poemeleon.org. Website: www.poemeleon.org.Established 2005. **Contact:** Cati Porter, editor Member: CLMP, Online Literary Association.

- •Poems from recent issues have been selected for inclusion in Verse Daily's Web Monthly Feature, NewPages'WordsMatter: A Selection of Poetry & Prose on the Web, and Best New Poets 2007.

Magazines Needs *Poemeleon: A Journal of Poetry*, published semiannually online, wants all forms and styles of poetry. Does not want "overly religious or sentimental, greeting card verse." Has published poetry by Tony Barnstone, Catherine Daly, Ann Fisher-Wirth, Richard Garcia, Eloise Klein Healy, Bob Hicok. Poemeleon receives about 1,000 poems/year, accepts about 150-200. Number of unique visitors: 25,000/year.

How to Contact Submit 3-5 poems at a time. Considers previously published poems (as long as they have not appeared online) and simultaneous submissions ("as long as we are notified promptly if a poem is taken elsewhere"). Considers poetry posted on a public Web site/blog/forum as published. Accepts e-mail submissions (pasted into body of message, as attachment, or by the upload form located on the guidelines page of the Web site.); no fax, paper, or disk submissions. Cover letter is preferred. "Each issue is devoted to a particular type of poetry (past issues include poems of place, ekphrastic poems, poems in form, and the prose poem). Please check the guidelines page for specifics before submitting." Reads submissions year round. Time between acceptance and publication is about 2 months. Poems are circulated to an editorial board. Sometimes comments on rejected poems. Regularly publishes them issues. Upcoming themes and guidelines available on Web site. Responds in 2-4 months. Always sends prepublication galleys. Acquires one-time rights. Rights revert to poets upon publication. Reviews books and chapbooks of poetry.

Contest/Award Offerings Mystery Box Contest offers a prize of the Mystery Box and publication on the Web site. Submit 1 poem. Guidelines available on Web site. **Entry fee:** none **Deadline:** none.

Tips "Please read our guidelines before submitting."

☑ POEMS & PLAYS

English Dept., Middle Tennessee State University, Murfreesboro TN 37132. (615)898-2712. Established 1993. **Contact:** Gaylord Brewer, editor.

Magazines Needs *Poems & Plays*, published annually in the spring, is an "eclectic publication for poems and short plays." No restrictions on style or content of poetry. Has published poetry by Naomi Wallace, Kate Gale, James Doyle, and Ron Koertge. *Poems & Plays* is 88 pages, digest-sized, professionally printed, perfect-bound, with coated color card cover. Receives 1,500 poems per issue, publishes 30-35 "typically." Press run is 800. Subscription: $10 for 2 issues. Sample: $6.

How to Contact No previously published poems or simultaneous submissions. Reads submissions October-November only. "Work is circulated among advisory editors for comments and preferences. All accepted material is published in the following issue." Sometimes comments on rejected poems. Responds in 2 months. Pays 1 contributor's copy. Acquires first publication rights only.

Contest/Award Offerings Considers chapbook mss (poems or short plays) of 20-24 pages for The Tennessee Chapbook Prize. "Any combination of poems or plays, or a single play, is eligible. The winning chapbook is printed within *Poems & Plays*." Winning author receives 50 copies of the issue. SASE required. **Entry fee:** $15 (includes 1 copy of the issue). **Deadline:** same as for the magazine (October-November). Past winners include Tammy Armstrong and Joanne Lowery. "The chapbook competition annually receives over 150 manuscripts from the U.S. and around the world."

$ ☑ POESIA

(Specialized: venue for Northwest AK poets), Indian Bay Press, One West Mountain St., Fayetteville AR 72701. (479)444-9323. Fax: (479)444-9326. E-mail: editor@indianbaypress.com. Website: www.indianbaypress.com. Established 2003. **Contact:** Jay Ross, editor.

Magazines Needs *Poesia*, published biannually, prints poetry and poetry reviews of all genres. "Although we accept manuscripts worldwide, our purpose is to offer a venue that currently does not exist for unpublished writers in Northwest Arkansas. We accept and encourage submissions of poetry and poetry review from foreign poets." *Poesia* is digest-sized, offset-printed, perfect-bound, includes ads. Receives about 1,000 poems/year, accepts about 30-40%. Press run is 2,000; 15% distributed free for promotions. Single copy: $9.95; subscription: $18/year, $32 for 2 years. Make checks payable to Indian Bay Press.

How to Contact Submit 3 poems at a time. No previously published poems or simultaneous submissions. Accepts e-mail (as attachment) submissions in word document format only or CD submissions. Cover letter is required. "Include name, address, SASE, and biographical information, as well as previous publishing credits." See Web site for reading periods. Time between acceptance and publication is 3 months. Never comments on rejected poems. Guidelines available on Web site. Responds in 1 week. Pays $10/poem and 2 contributor's copies. Acquires one-time rights. Rights revert to author upon publication. Reviews books and chapbooks of poetry in 250-500 words, single-book format. Send materials for review consideration to Attn: Editor, Indian Bay Press.

☑ ◎ POESY MAGAZINE

(Specialized: Boston, MA & Santa Cruz, CA), P.O. Box 7823, Santa Cruz CA 95061. (831)239-4419. E-mail: info@poesy.org. Website: www.poesy.org. Established 1991. **Contact:** Brian Morrisey, editor/publisher.

Magazines Needs *POESY Magazine*, published biannually, is "an anthology of American poetry. *POESY*'s main concentrations are Boston, Massachusetts and Santa Cruz, California, 2 thriving homesteads for poets, beats, and artists of nature. Our goal is to unite the 2 scenes, updating poets on what's happening across the country." Wants to see "original poems that express observational impacts with clear and concise imagery. Acceptence is based on creativity, composition, and relation to the format of *POESY*." Does not want "poetry with excessive profanity. We would like to endorse creativity beyond the likes of everyday babble." Has published poetry by Lawrence Ferlinghetti, Jack Hirschman, Edward Sanders, Todd Moore, Diane Di Prima, and Julia Vinograd.

POESY is 16 pages, magazine-sized, newsprint, glued/folded, includes ads. Receives about 1,000 poems/year, accepts about 10%. Press run is 1,000; most distributed free to local venues. Single copy: $1; subscription: $12/year. Sample: $2. Make checks payable to Brian Morrisey.

How to Contact Submit 3-5 poems at a time. Lines/poem: 32 maximum. No previously published poems or simultaneous submissions. Accepts e-mail (submissions@poesy.org) and disk submissions. "Snail mail submissions are preferred with a SASE." Cover letter is preferred. Reads submissions year round. Time between acceptance and publication is 1 month. "Poems are accepted by the Santa Cruz editor/publisher based on how well the poem stimulates our format." Guidelines available in magazine, for SASE, by e-mail, or on Web site. Responds in 1 month. Sometimes sends prepublication galleys. Pays 3 contributor's copies. Acquires one-time rights. Reviews books/chapbooks of poetry and other magazines/journals in 1,000 words, single-book format. Send materials for review consideration to *POESY*, c/o Brian Morrisey.

Tips "Stay away from typical notions of love and romance. Become one with your surroundings and discover a true sense of natural perspective."

☑ POETALK

P.O. Box 11435, Berkeley CA 94712-2435. E-mail: poetalk@aol.com. Website: www. bayareapoetscoalition.org. Established 1974. **Contact:** Maggie Morley, editor.

Magazines Needs *POETALK*, currently published 1-2 issues/year, is the poetry journal of the Bay Area Poets Coalition (BAPC) and publishes about 65 poets in each issue. "*POETALK* is open to all. No particular genre. Rhyme must be well done." *POETALK* is 36 pages, digest-sized, photocopied, saddle-stapled, with heavy card cover. Press run is 400. Subscription: $5/2 issues. Sample: $2.

How to Contact Submit 3-5 poems at a time, no more than twice/year. Lines/poem: under 35 preferred; longer poems of outstanding quality considered. Considers previously published poems and simultaneous submissions, but must be noted. Cover letter is preferred. Include SASE. "Manuscripts should be clearly typed, single-spaced, and include author's name and mailing address on every page. Include e-mail address if you have one." Usually responds in up to 6 months. Pays 1 contributor's copy. All rights revert to author upon publication.

Contest/Award Offerings Sponsors yearly contest. **Deadline:** submit October 1-November 15 (postmark). Guidelines available in early September for SASE, by e-mail, or see posting on Web site.

Also Offers Bay Area Poets Coalition holds monthly readings (in Berkeley, CA). BAPC has 150 members. BAPC Membership: $15/year (includes subscription to *POETALK* and other privileges); extra outside U.S.

Tips "If you don't want suggested revisions, you need to say so clearly in your cover letter or indicate on each poem submitted."

◎ POETICA MAGAZINE, REFLECTIONS OF JEWISH THOUGHT

P.O. Box 11014, Norfolk VA 23517. Fax: (757)399-3936. E-mail: poeticamag@aol.com. Website: www.poeticamagazine.com. Established 2002. **Contact:** Michal Mahgerefteh, publisher/editor.

Magazines Needs *Poetica Magazine, Reflections of Jewish Thought*, published 3 times/year, offers "an outlet for the many writers who draw from their Jewish backgrounds and experiences to create poetry/prose/short stories, giving both emerging and recognized writers the opportunity to share their work with the larger community." Does not want long pieces, haiku, rhyming poetry. Considers poetry by children and teens, grades 6-12. *Poetica* is 64 pages, digest-sized, desktop-published, saddle-stapled, with glossy cardstock cover with b&w art, includes some ads. Receives about 500 poems/year, accepts about 60%. Press run is 350. Single copy: $5;

subscription: $14.

How to Contact Submit 3 poems at a time. Lines/poem: 2 pages maximum. Considers simultaneous submissions. No e-mail or disk submissions. Cover letter is optional. Reads submissions year round. Time between acceptance and publication is 1 year. Seldom comments on rejected poems. Occasionally publishes theme issues. Guidelines available for SASE or on Web site. Responds in 1 month. Pays 1 contributor's copy. Poet retains all rights.

Contest/Award Offerings Offers annual poetry contest with up to $50 awarded for First Prize; up to 5 Honorable Mentions. Selected poems will be published in future issues of *Poetica*. Accepts simultaneous submissions. No limit on number of entries (3 poems constitute an entry). Submit 2 copies of each poem, single-spaced, no more than 1 poem/page. Include poet's name on all pages. No e-mail submissions. Include SASE for results only; mss will not be returned. Guidelines available on Web site. **Entry fee:** $12 for up to 3 poems. **Deadline:** March 31 annually. Judge: Jane Ellen Glasser. Notifies winners by June. Other contests include the Poet of the Month Award, Annual Chapbook Award, and Annual Ekphrastic Award.

⊕ ▢ ◎ POETIC HOURS

(Specialized: subscriptions encouraged; raises money for charity), 43 Willow Rd., Carlton, Nolts NG4 3BH England. E-mail: erranpublishing@hotmail.com. Website: www.poetichours. homestead.com. Established 1993. **Contact:** Nicholas Clark, editor.

Magazines Needs *Poetic Hours*, published semiannually, aims "to encourage and publish new poets, i.e., as a forum where good but little known poets can appear in print; and **to raise money for third world and other charities**. *Poetic Hours* features poetry by invited poets and others." Wants "any subject; rhyme preferred but not essential; suitable for wide-ranging readership." Does not want "gothic, horror, extremist, political, self-interested." *Poetic Hours* is an online publication. Receives about 500 poems/year, accepts about 40%. Free to read on magazines website but accepted poets asked to make a contrbution towards nominated charities if accepted.

How to Contact Submit 4-6 poems at a time. Lines/poem: 30 maximum. Considers previously published poems; no simultaneous submissions. Accepts e-mail (preferred; pasted into body of message) and disk (non-returnable) submissions. Time between acceptance and publication is 3 months. "Poems are read by editors and, if found suitable, are used." Always comments on rejected poems. Responds "within a week, whenever possible." Acquires one-time rights.

Additional Information *Poetic Hours* is non-profit-making; all proceeds go to various charities, particularly well-building and children's charities. A page of each issue is set aside for reporting how money is spent.

Tips "We welcome newcomers and invite those just starting out to have the courage to submit work. The art of poetry has moved from the hands of book publishers down the ladder to the new magazines. This is where all the best poetry is found."

▣ ◎ POETIC LOGIC

(Specialized: FL resident poets; renga; radio feature), E-mail: poeticlogic@earthlink.net. Website: www.wmfe.org Established 2002. **Contact:** Sara Schlossman, producer/editor; Charlene L. Edge and Jennifer Zamansky, associate readers.

Magazines Needs *Poetic Logic* is "in transition. We started as a broadcast segment on your local NPR radio affiliate as a way to feature Central Florida poets and poets of national reputation as they toured through our listening area. Since the radio station had to make some changes, our format, too, will change. Poetic Logic is gearing up for its Web launch and will broaden the reach to include poets from the entire state of Florida. We have featured the work of Teri Witek,

Ilyse Kusnetz, Terry Godbey, Philip F. Deave, and Billy Collins."

How to Contact Submit 5 poems at a time. Lines/poem: prefers no more than 40. Considers previously published poems and simultaneous submissions. E-mail submissions ONLY. Cover letter is preferred. Include short bio. Reads submissions year round "but slower in summer and in winter holiday season." Submit seasonal poems 2 months in advance. Time between acceptance and publication is 2-5 months. Responds in 3-6 months. Acquires electronic rights. All rights revert to author."

Also Offers "The *Poetic Logic* Renga Chain began in April of 2005 and will be revived and posted on the new Web site. Contributors sign up, are assigned a sequence number, and when their number is up, compose a tanka to link with the previous contributor's work. The Renga is open to all Florida residents and non-residents. Guidelines for joining this work-in-progress are on the Web site."

Tips "Read the work of the poets we have listed as it shows our broad spectrum of preferences."

▣ ☑ POETIC MATRIX, A PERIODIC LETTER

P.O. Box 1223, Madera CA 93639. (559)673-9402. E-mail: poeticmatrix@yahoo.com. Website: www.poeticmatrix.com and www.poeticmatrixpress.com. Established 1997 in Yosemite. **Contact:** John Peterson, editor/publisher.

Magazines Needs *Poetic Matrix, a periodic letteR*, published 2 times/year online, seeks poetry that "creates a 'place in which we can live' rather than telling us about the place; poetry that draws from the imaginal mind and is rich in the poetic experience—hence the poetic matrix." Does not want poetry that talks about the experience. Has published poetry by Lyn Lifshin, Tony White, Gail Entrekin, James Downs, Joan Michelson, and Brandon Cesmat.

How to Contact Accepts e-mail submissions (pasted into body of message, no attachments). Guidelines available by e-mail or on Web site. Acquires one-time rights.

Additional Information "*Poetic Matrix* has a call for manuscripts for the Slim Volume Series every 2 years. See Web site for when reading dates are set and for additional guidelines and awards. The Slim Volume Series is for manuscripts of 65-75 pages." **Charges reading fee of $17.**

Tips "We seek writing of quality, with passion and intelligence."

$ ☑ POETRY

444 N. Michigan Ave., Suite 1850, Chicago IL 60611. E-mail: poetry@poetrymagazine.org (send Letters to the Editor to editors@poetrymagazine.org). Website: www.poetrymagazine.org. Established 1912. **Contact:** The Editors. • Work published in Poetry is frequently included in The Best American Poetry and The Pushcart Prize: Best of the Small Presses.

Magazines Needs *Poetry*, published monthly by The Poetry Foundation (see separate listing in Organizations), "has no special manuscript needs and no special requirements as to form or genre: We examine in turn all work received and accept that which seems best." Has published poetry by the major voices of our time as well as new talent. *Poetry* is 5½x9, elegantly printed, flat-spined. Receives 90,000 submissions/year, accepts about 300-350. Press run is 16,000. Single copy: $3.75; subscription: $35 ($38 for institutions). Sample: $5.50.

How to Contact Submit no more than 4 poems at a time. No previously published poems or simultaneous submissions. Electronic submission preferred. When submitting by post put return address on outside of envelope; include SASE. Submissions must be typed, single-spaced, with poet's name and address on every page. Guidelines available for SASE. Responds in 1-2 months. Pays $10/line (with a minimum payment of $150). Reviews books of poetry in multi-book formats of varying lengths. Does not accept unsolicited reviews.

Contest/Award Offerings 7 prizes (Bess Hokin Prize, Levinson Prize, Frederick Bock Prize, J. Howard and Barbara M.J. Wood Prize, John Frederick Nims Memorial Prize, Friends of Literature Prize, Union League Civic and Arts Poetry Prize) ranging from $300 to $5,000 are awarded annually to poets whose work has appeared in the magazine that year. Only verse already published in *Poetry* is eligible for consideration; no formal application is necessary.

Also Offers *Poetry*'s Web site offers featured poems, letters, reviews, interviews, essays, and Web-exclusive features.

▣ ◕ POETRYBAY

P.O. Box 114, Northport NY 11768. (631)427-1950. Fax: (631)367-0038. E-mail: poetrybay@aol.com. Website: www.poetrybay.com. Established 2000. **Contact:** George Wallace, editor.

Magazines Needs *Poetrybay*, published semiannually online, seeks "to add to the body of great contemporary American poetry by presenting the work of established and emerging writers. Also, we consider essays and reviews." Has published poetry by Robert Bly, Yevgeny Yevtushenko, Marvin Bell, Diane Wakoski, Cornelius Eady, and William Heyen.

How to Contact Submit 5 poems at a time. Considers simultaneous submissions; no previously published poems. Accepts e-mail submissions (pasted into body of message); no disk submissions. Time between acceptance and publication is 2 months. Seldom comments on rejected poems. Occasionally publishes theme issues. Guidelines available on Web site. Sometimes sends prepublication galleys. Acquires first-time electronic rights. Reviews books/chapbooks of poetry and other magazines/journals. Send materials for review consideration.

▦ ▢ ◎ THE POETRY CHURCH MAGAZINE

(Specialized: subscribers only; Christian), Moorside Words and Music, Eldwick Crag Farm, High Eldwick, Otley Road, Bingley BD16 3BB United Kingdom. +44 (0)1274 563 078. E-mail: reavill@globalnet.co.uk. Website: www.waddysweb.freeuk.com. Established 1982 (Feather Books); 1996 (The Poetry Church Magazine). **Contact:** Tony Reavill, editor.

Magazines Needs *The Poetry Church Magazine*, published quarterly, contains Christian poetry, prayers, and hymns. Wants "Christian or good religious poetry." Does not want "unreadable blasphemy." **Publishes subscribers' work only.** Considers poetry by children over age 10. Has published poetry by Laurie Bates, Joan Sheridan Smith, Idris Caffrey, Isabella Strachan, Walter Nash, and Susan Glyn. *The Poetry Church Magazine* is 40 pages, digest-sized, photocopied, saddle-stapled, with illustrated cover. Receives about 1,000 poems/year, accepts about 500. Press run is 1,000. Single copy: free; subscription: £12 for 4 issues ($20 USD). Make checks payable in sterling to Feather Books. Payment can also be made through Web site.

How to Contact Submit 2 poems at a time. Lines/poem: usually around 20, "but will accept longer." Considers previously published poems and simultaneous submissions. Cover letter is preferred (with information about the poet). No e-mail submissions; postal submissions only. Include SASE, or SAE and IRC. Submissions must be typed. **Publishes "only subscribers' poems as they keep us solvent."** Time between acceptance and publication is 4 months. "The editor does a preliminary reading, then seeks the advice of colleagues about uncertain poems." Responds within 1 week. Poets retain copyright.

Additional Information Feather Books publishes the Feather Books Poetry Series, collections of around 20 Christian poems and prayers. Has recently published the Glyn family, Walter Nash, David Grieve, and Rosie Morgan Barry. "We have now published 300 poetry collections by individual Christian poets." Books are usually photocopied, saddle-stapled, with illustrated covers. "We do not insist, but **most poets pay for their work. Enquire for current costs.** If they can't afford it, but are good poets, we stand the cost. We expect poets to read *The Poetry Church*

Magazine to get some idea of our standards."

Also Offers Each winter and summer, selected poems appear in *The Poetry Church Collection*, the leading Christian poetry anthology used in churches and schools.

Tips "We find it better for poets to master rhyme and rhythm before trying free verse. Many poets seem to think that if they write 'down' a page they're writing poetry, when all they're doing is writing prose in a different format. But good free verse is accpted."

☑ POETRY INTERNATIONAL

Dept. of English & Comparative Literature, San Diego State University, 5500 Campanile Dr., San Diego CA 92182-8140. (619)594-1522. Fax: (619)594-4998. E-mail: poetryinternational@ rohan.sdsu.edu. Website: http://poetryinternational.sdsu.edu. Established 1996. **Contact:** Fred Moramarco, editor.

Magazines Needs *Poetry International*, published annually in November, is "an eclectic poetry magazine intended to reflect a wide range of poetry being written today." Wants "a wide range of styles and subject matter. We're particularly interested in translations." Does not want "cliché-ridden, derivative, or obscure poetry." Has published poetry by Adrienne Rich, Robert Bly, Hayden Carruth, Kim Addonizio, Maxine Kumin, and Gary Soto. *Poetry International* is 200 pages, perfect-bound, with coated cardstock cover. Press run is 1,500. Single copy: $12; subscription: $24/2 years (plus s&h).

How to Contact Submit up to 5 poems at a time. Considers simultaneous submissions, "but prefer not to"; no previously published poems. No fax or e-mail submissions. Reads submissions September 1-30 only. Time between acceptance and publication is 8 months. Poems are circulated to an editorial board. Seldom comments on rejected poems. Responds in up to 4 months. Pays 2 contributor's copies. Acquires all rights. Returns rights "50/50," meaning they split with the author any payment for reprinting the poem elsewhere. "We review anthologies regularly."

Tips "We're interested in new work by poets who are devoted to their art. We want poems that matter—that make a difference in people's lives. We're especially seeking good translations and prose by poets about poetry."

☷ ☑ POETRY KANTO

Kanto Gakuin University, Kamariya-cho 3-22-1, Kanazawa-ku, Yokohama 236-8502 Japan. E-mail: alan@kanto-gakuin.ac.jp. Website: http://home.kanto-gakuin.ac.jp/~kg061001/. Established 1984 by William I. Elliott. **Contact:** Alan Botsford, editor.

Magazines Needs *Poetry Kanto*, published annually in November by the Kanto Gakuin University, is a journal bridging east and west, featuring "outstanding poetry that navigates the divide of ocean and language from around the world. We seek exciting, well-crafted contemporary poetry in English, and also encourage and publish high-quality English translations of modern and emerging Japanese poets. All translations must be accompanied by the original poems." See Web site for sample poems. Has published poetry by Harryette Mullen, Ilya Kaminsky, Beth Ann Fennelly, Vijay Seshadri, Michael S. Collins, Mari L'Esperance, Michael Sowder, and Sarah Arvio. *Poetry Kanto* is 120 pages, 6x9, professionally printed on coated stock, perfect-bound, with glossy cover. Press run is 1,000; many are distributed free worldwide to schools, poets, and presses. The magazine is unpriced. Sample: send SAE with IRCs.

How to Contact Submit 5 poems at a time maximum. No previously published poems or simultaneous submissions. Prefers e-mail submissions (as attachment in Word). Cover letter is required. Include brief bio. All postal submissions require SAE and IRCs. Reads submissions December - April. Guidelines available on Web site. Pays 3-5 contributor's copies.

Tips "From forebears, learn; from the future, write; in the present, live."

▣ ☑ POETRY MIDWEST

(913)469-8500, ext. 4705. E-mail: submit@poetrymidwest.org (submissions); editors@ poetrymidwest.org (queries). Website: www.poetrymidwest.org. Established 2000. **Contact:** Matthew W. Schmeer, editor/publisher.

Magazines Needs *Poetry Midwest*, published 3 times/year online (winter, spring/summer, fall), features poetry, nongenre microfiction, and brief creative nonfiction from new and established writers. Wants free verse, traditional Western forms, traditional Asian forms other than haiku and senryu, prose poems, long poems, nongenre microfiction (up to 300 words), and brief creative nonfiction (up to 300 words). Does not want science fiction, fantasy, inspirational, religious, or children's verse or fiction; anything of an overtly political or religious nature; or spoken word poetry. Has published poetry by Philip Dacey, Cherryl Floyd-Miller, Rhoda Janzen, J. Patrick Lewis, Adrian Matejka, and Matt Rasmussen. *Poetry Midwest* is 20-100 pages, published online as a (free) downloadable Adobe Acrobat PDF file. Receives about 1,500 poems/year, accepts about 7%.

How to Contact Submit 3 poems at a time. Lines/poem: 3 minimum, 10 pages maximum. Considers simultaneous submissions; no previously published poems. "Submit via e-mail only. Submissions should be pasted into the body of an e-mail message with 'Poetry Midwest Submission' in subject line (omit quotation marks). Absolutely no e-mail file attachments. E-mail messages containing attachments will be deleted upon receipt. Do not send submissions via postal mail; they will be returned unread." Reads submissions year round. Submit seasonal poems 3-6 months in advance. Time between acceptance and publication is 3 months to one year. "I read submissions as they are received, deciding whether or not to use a piece based on its own literary merits and whether it fits in with other poems selected for an issue in progress." Seldom comments on rejected poems. Guidelines available by e-mail or on website. Responds in up to 6 months. Acquires first rights or first North American serial rights as well as first electronic rights, reprint rights, and electronic archival rights.

Tips "Submissions to online journals should reflect the same attention to detail that goes into submissions to traditional print journals. Fancy display fonts, distracting animated graphics, and pictures of you and/or your significant other and/or pets do not increase the likelihood of a piece being accepted; in fact, they almost ensure your piece will be automatically rejected. There are professional standards for submitting to literary journals which can be found on many websites and in most handbooks for creative writers. Follow those guidelines and any market-specific requests if you want your submission seriously considered."

☑ POETRY NORTHWEST

4232 SE Hawthorne Blvd., Portland OR 97215. (503)236-0615. E-mail: editors@poetrynw.org. Website: www.poetrynw.org. Established 1959. **Contact:** David Biespiel, editor.

Magazines Needs *Poetry Northwest* is published semiannually in March and October. "The mission of *Poetry Northwest* is to publish the best poetry written in English. In the words of founding editor Carolyn Kizer, we aim to 'encourage the young and the inexperienced, the neglected mature, and the rough major talents and the fragile minor ones.' All styles and aesthetics will find consideration." Has published poetry by Theodore Roethke, Czeslaw Milosz, Anne Sexton, Harold Pinter, Thom Gunn, and Philip Larkin. *Poetry Northwest* is 40+ pages, magazine-sized, Web press-printed, saddle-stapled, with 4-color cover, includes ads. Receives about 10,000 poems/year, accepts about 1%. Press run is 2,000. Single copy: $8. Sample: $9. Make checks payable to *Poetry Northwest*.

How to Contact Submit 4 poems at a time maximum. No previously published poems or simultaneous submissions. No e-mail or disk submissions. Cover letter is required. Time between acceptance and publication is 2 months. Sometimes comments on rejected poems. Sometimes publishes theme issues. Upcoming themes available in magazine or by e-mail. Guidelines available on Web site. Responds in 4-6 weeks ("except during July and August; submissions sent during these months will be considered in September"). Always sends prepublication galleys. Pays 2 contributor's copies. Acquires all rights. Returns rights to poets upon request. Reviews books of poetry in single- and multi-book format.

▦ ☑ POETRY NOTTINGHAM

11 Orkney Close, Stenson Fields, Derbyshire DE24 3LW England. Established 1946. Website: http://nottinghampoetrysociety.co.uk. **Contact:** Adrian Buckner, editor.

Magazines Needs *Poetry Nottingham*, published 3 times/year, features articles and reviews in addition to poetry. Open to submissions from UK and overseas. Has published poetry from Europe, Australasia, the U.S., and Japan. *Poetry Nottingham* is 6x8, perfect-bound, professionally printed. Receives about 2,000 submissions/year, accepts about 120. Press run is 250. Single copy: £4; subscription: £12 UK, £20 overseas. Checks payable to Poetry Nottingham Publications. Subscribers who wish to pay in U.S. dollars please send check for $25, payable to Karen Crosbie, to 1036 Menlo Avenue, Apt 103, Los Angeles, CA, 90006. Single copy $7.

How to Contact Submit up to 6 poems at a time. No previously published poems. Cover letter is required. "Send SAE and 3 IRCs for stamps. No need to query." Responds in 2 months. Pays 1 contributor's copy. Staff reviews books of poetry, usually confined to UK publications.

Contest/Award Offerings The Nottingham Open Poetry Competition offers cash prizes, annual subscriptions, and publication in *Poetry Nottingham*. Open to all. Guidelines available on Web site.

Tips "We seek to provide an uncluttered environment for poems of wit, poems of concise lyrical intensity, and poems that are bold enough to expand on a theme."

◻ POETRY OF THE PEOPLE

3341 SE 19th Ave., Gainesville FL 32641. (352)375-0244. E-mail: poetryforaquarter@yahoo.com. Website: poetryofthepeople.com. Established 1986. **Contact:** Paul Cohen, poetry editor.

Magazines Needs *Poetry of the People*, published semimonthly as a pamphlet, is open to all forms of poetry. Wants "humorous poetry, love poetry, nature poetry, and fantasy." Does not want "racist or highly ethnocentric poetry. We do not like poetry that lacks images or is too personal or contains rhyme to the point that the poem has been destroyed." Also considers poetry written in French and Spanish. Considers poetry by children and teens. Has published poetry by Laura Stamps, Dan Matthews, Jenica Deer, Shannon Dixon, Kristi Castro, and Peggy C. Hall. *Poetry of the People* is 4 pages, magazine-sized. Sample: $4 for 11 pamphlets.

How to Contact Submit "as many poems as you want" at a time. Accepts e-mail and disk submissions. Include SASE with postal submissions. Cover letter is required (often publishes the cover letter). Include bio. "Autobiographical information is important in understanding the poetry." Often comments on rejected poems. Guidelines available by e-mail or on website. Responds within 18 months. Pays 5 contributor's copies. Acquires first rights.

Tips "You should appeal to as broad an audience as possible. Nature makes people happy."

▦ ☑ POETRY SALZBURG REVIEW

University of Salzburg, Dept. of English, Akademiestrasse 24, Salzburg A-5020 Austria. (43) (662)8044-4422. Fax: (43)(662)8044-167. E-mail: editor@poetrysalzburg.com. Website: www.poetrysalzburg.com. Established 2001. **Contact:** Dr. Wolfgang Goertschacher, Mag. Andreas Schachermayr, editors; editorial board: Prof. Robert Dassanowsky, Dept. of Languages and

Cultures, University of Colorado, 1420 Austin Bluffs, Colorado Springs, CO 80933, USA, rvondass@uccs.edu; David Miller, 99 Mitre Road, London, SE1 8PT, GB katermurr@btinternet.com; William Bedford, The Croft, 3 Manor Farm Court, Purton Stoke, Wiltshire SN5 4LA, GB, w.bedford@btopenworld.com.

Magazines Needs *Poetry Salzburg Review*, published twice/year, contains "articles on poetry, mainly contemporary, and 60 percent poetry. Also includes essays on poetics, review-essays, interviews, artwork, and translations. We tend to publish selections by authors who have not been taken up by the big poetry publishers. Nothing of poor quality." Has published poetry by Paul Muldoon, Alice Notley, Samuel Menashe. *Poetry Salzburg Review* is about 200 pages, A5, professionally printed, perfect-bound, with illustrated card cover. Receives about 5,000 poems/year, accepts 5%. Press run is 500. Single copy: $12; subscription: $22 (cash preferred; subscribers can also pay with PayPal). Make checks payable to Wolfgang Goertschacher. "No requirements, but it's a good idea to subscribe to *Poetry Salzburg Review*."

How to Contact No previously published poems or simultaneous submissions. Accepts e-mail submissions (as attachment). Time between acceptance and publication is 6 months. Seldom comments on rejected poems. Occasionally publishes theme issues. Responds in 2 months. No payment. Acquires first rights. Reviews books/chapbooks of poetry as well as books on poetics. Send materials for review consideration.

☑ THE POET'S ART

(Specialized: family-friendly writing), 171 Silverleaf Lane, Islandia NY 11749. (631)439-0427. E-mail: davidirafox@yahoo.com (inquiries only). Established 2000. **Contact:** David Fox, editor.

Magazines Needs *The Poet's Art*, published quarterly, is "a family-style journal, accepting work from the unpublished to the well known and all levels in between." Wants "family-friendly, positive poetry; any form considered. Topics include humor, nature, inspirational, children's poetry, or anything else that fits the family-friendly genre." Does not want "violent, vulgar, or overly depressing work. Work is read and accepted by the mentally-ill population, but they should keep in mind this is a family-friendly journal." Considers poetry by children and teens, "any age, as long as it's good quality; if under 18, get parents' permission." Has published poetry by John Brummel, Pearl Clark, Janet Goven, Robert Donald Spector, and Jane Stuart. *The Poet's Art* is 40 or more pages, magazine-sized, photocopied, paper-clipped or stapled, with computer cover, includes ads. Receives about 100 poems a year, accepts about 50%. Press run is 30+. "Due to limited supplies, only those who submit or whose review is accepted receive a copy; foreign contributors must pay for a copy. (There are no samples or subscriptions offered by this magazine.)"

How to Contact Submit "as many poems that will fit on 1 page" at a time ("you can submit more, if compelled to do so; extra accepted pieces will be spread over a few issues"). Lines/poem: rarely accepts anything over 1 page. Considers simultaneous submissions ("list any other small press journals (if any) poems titles"). No e-mail or disk submissions; postal submissions only. Cover letter is preferred. "It's only polite. And include a SASE—a must! (I have been lax in this rule about SASEs, but I will now throw any submissions without a SASE away!)" Reads submissions year round, "but poets should be aware we are currently backlogged into December of 2009, as of this listing. I review all poems submitted and then decide what I wish to publish." Always comments on rejected poems. Reviews chapbooks of poetry and other magazines/journals, "but editors and authors must write reviews themselves. After all, who knows your magazine/journal or chapbook better than you? (Little-known/newer journals sent in by editors or contributors get first consideration for reviews)." Send to David Fox.

Tips "We enjoy and value loyalty, but remember to send your work out to as many magazines/journals as you can. Poetry is meant to be shared. Family-friendly poetry for this journal, please!

Also, I am NOT a book publisher, or an agent. Please do not send book-length mss to be published or to find a publisher. You may send chapbooks for review only."

◙ ☑ POET'S ESPRESSO

1426 Telegraph Ave., #4, Stockton CA 95204. E-mail: poetsespresso@gmail.com. Website: www. poetsespresso.com. Established 2005. **Contact:** Donald R. Anderson, editor (e-mail preferred).

Magazines Needs *Poet's Espresso*, published bimonthly online and in print, is "a small black and white publication of poetry, art, photography, recipes, and local events." Sponsored by the Writers' Guild, a club of San Joaquin Delta College. "We value variety, appropriateness for most age groups, and poetry that goes well with the season of the issue, visual and bilingual poetry (side by side with translation), and of length that will fit on our half-sheet pages." Does not want "profanity, racially prejudiced, otherwise offensive material, porn, submissions that are excessively long, illegible writing, nor your only copy of the poem." Considers poetry by all ages. "Please include contact info of parent if from a minor." Has published poetry by David Humphreys, Nikki Quismondo, Susan Richardson Harvey, and Allen Field Weitzel. *Poet's Espresso* (print edition) is 24-28 pages, digest-sized, printed "on College's industrial printers," stapled, with colored paper cover with b&w photograph/artwork, includes ads. Accepts about 100 poems/year. Press run is 750 and growing; 650+ distributed free in the Central Valley, Sacramento, and Bay Areas to coffee shops, colleges, bookstores, and restaurants. Number of unique visitors (online): "small count with rapid growth." Single copy: $2; subscription: $8/ year (6 issues). Sample: free in return for review or swap for a desired publication. Make checks payable to Donald Anderson.

How to Submit Submit "as many poems as you wish" at a time. Lines/poem: "from quote-size up to 80." Considers previously published poems and simultaneous submissions with notification. Accepts e-mail (as attachment in MS Word [.doc], MS Works [.wps], rich text [.rtf], InDesign Interchange [.inx], or notepad [.txt] formats) and disk submissions; no fax submissions.. "If postal submissions, submit copies, not originals of works, bio, optional photo. Pieces will not be returned, will respond if accepted with copy of publication. Text must be typed/printed without illegible markings." "In any submission except ads, 2 to 4 line biography about the poet/artist is required, written in third person. Biography photo is optional. You may include info for readers to contact you, if you wish." Reads submissions year round. "Deadline for submissions are on or before the 25th of the month prior to the issue." Jan. 25 deadline for Feb-Mar, Mar. 25 for Apr-May, May 25 for Jun-Jul, Jul. 25 for Aug-Sep, Sep. 25 for Oct-Nov, Nov. 25 for Dec-Jan. Submit seasonal poems at least 1 week in advance. Time between acceptance and publication is 1 to 12 months. "Include SASE with cover requesting response if want release from publishing consideration of works after submission. Otherwise may publish up to 12 months after submission. The editor bases acceptance upon space available, interest and meeting the guidelines." Sometimes comments on rejected poems. Regularly publishes (seasonal) theme issues. Guidelines available for SASE with cover letter request, or by e-mail, or on Web site. Responds in up to 2 months. Sometimes sends prepublication galleys (upon request). Pays 1 contributor's copy (extra copies at $2 postage per copy). Acquires one-time rights for print edition; acquires electronic rights "to keep an archived issue available online indefinitely in the future." "Rights remain with author to publish in any way; rights are given to *Poet's Espresso* for indefinite archive on Web site and 1 issue of the newsletter". Send materials for review consideration by e-mail or to Donald R. Anderson by postal mail with cover letter.**Additional Information** "We occasionally publish anthologies. For info on other works we have published, please visit the Web site for the book *Sun Shadow Mountain* and other projects linked on the project page at www.rainflowers.org."

Advice "Be definitive, stand out, and yet link to a common experience."

▣ ◻ THE POET'S HAVEN

Website: www.PoetsHaven.com. Established 1997. **Contact:** Vertigo Xi'an Xavier, publisher.

Magazines Needs *The Poet's Haven* is a website "featuring poetry, artwork, stories, reviews, essays, and much more." Wants work that's "emotional, personal, and intimate with the author or subject. Topics can cover just about anything." Does not publish religious material." Has published poetry by Dianne Borsenik, John Burroughs, T.M. Goöttl, Michael Lee Johnson, and Katherine Zaleski. Work published on *The Poet's Haven* is left on the site permanently. Receives about 1,000 poems/year, accepts about 70%.

How to Contact Considers previously published poems and simultaneous submissions. Accepts submissions through online form only. Time between acceptance and publication is about 2 weeks. Never comments on rejected poems. Guidelines available on Web site. No payment for online publication; pays 1 contributor's copy for print edition. Acquires rights to publish on the Web site permanently and in any future print publications. Poet retains rights to have poems published elsewhere, "provided the other publishers do not require first-time or exclusive rights."

Additional Information Publishes print editions of *The Poet's Haven Digest*. Check Web site for information or to order sample copies. Publishes audio podcast as Saturday Night with the Poet's Haven. Check Web site for submission information or to download sample episodes.

Also Offers Message forums, publisher's blog, and open-mic events.

▣ ◻ POET'S INK

E-mail: poet_Kelly@yahoo.com. Website: www.PoetsInk.com. Established 2005. **Contact:** Kelly Morris.

Magazines Needs *Poet's Ink*, published monthly online, seeks "poetry of all kinds. Work by new poets is published alongside that of more experienced poets." Does not want "bad rhyme, clichés, poetry riddled with abstractions." Considers poetry by teens. "Will be judged by the same standards as poetry by adults." Has published poetry by Alexandria Webb, David Waite, Colin Baker, Megan Arkenburg, and Robert Demaree. Receives about 300 poems/year, accepts about 15%.

How to Contact Submit 3-5 poems at a time. Lines/poem: 2 minimum, 100 maximum ("longer poems better not be long-winded!"). Considers previously published poems and simultaneous submissions. Accepts e-mail submissions (as attachment); no disk submissions. Cover letter is preferred. "No funky formatting of poems!" Reads submissions year round. Time between acceptance and publication is 1 month. Often comments on rejected poems. Sometimes publishes theme issues. Guidelines available by e-mail or on Web site. Responds in 1-2 weeks. Acquires one-time rights. Rights revert to poets upon publication.

Tips "Read guidelines carefully before submitting. Take advantage of all the advice you get, but also follow your heart."

▦ ▣ ◪ POETS ON THE LINE

P.O. Box 20292, Brooklyn NY 11202-0292. E-mail: llerner@mindspring.com. Website: www.echonyc.com/~poets. Established 1995 (founded by Andrew Gettler and Linda Lerner). **Contact:** Linda Lerner, editor.

•**Currently not accepting unsolicited work.**

◪ ◎ THE POET'S PEN

(Specialized: members/subscribers preferred), The Society of American Poets (SOAP), 387 N. Hall Street, Lyons, GA 30436. (912)526-6295. E-mail: DrRev@msn.com. Established 1984.

Contact: Dr. Charles E. Cravey, editor.

Magazines Needs *The Poet's Pen*, published quarterly by The Society of American Poets, is "open to all styles of poetry and prose—both religious and secular." Does not want "gross or 'X-rated' poetry without taste or character." Has published poetry by Najwa Salam Brax, Henry Goldman, Henry W. Gurley, William Heffner, Linda Metcalf, and Charles Russ. *The Poet's Pen* uses poetry **primarily by members and subscribers**, but outside submissions are also welcome. Subscription: included in membership, $30/year ($25 for students). Sample: $10.

How to Contact Submit 3 poems at a time/quarter. Considers simultaneous submissions and previously published poems, if permission from previous publisher is included. Include name and address on each page. "Submissions or inquiries will not be responded to without a #10 business-sized SASE. We do stress originality and have each new poet and/or subscriber sign a waiver form verifying originality." Publishes seasonal/theme issues. Guidelines available in magazine, for SASE, or by e-mail. Sometimes sends prepublication galleys. Always comments on rejected poems.

Contest/Award Offerings Sponsors several contests each quarter, with prizes totaling $100-250. Also offers Editor's Choice Awards each quarter. The President's Award for Excellence is a prize of $50. **Deadline:** November 1. Also publishes a quarterly anthology from poetry competitions in several categories with prizes of $25-100. Guidelines available for SASE or by e-mail.

Tips "Be honest with yourself above all else. Read the greats over and again and study styles, grammar, and what makes each unique. Meter, rhythm, and rhyme are still the guidelines that are most acceptable today."

🔲 ⬜ POETS' PODIUM

(Specialized: subscribers given priority)2-3265 Front Rd., E. Hawkesbury ON K6A 2R2 Canada. E-mail: kennyel@hotmail.com. Website: http://geocities.com/poetspodium/. Established 1993. **Contact:** Ken Elliott, Catherine Heaney Barrowcliffe, Robert Piquette, or Ron Barrowcliffe, associate editors.

Magazines Needs *Poets' Podium*, published quarterly, is a newsletter that aims "to promote the reading and writing of the poetic form, especially among those being published for the first time." Poetry specifications are open. **Priority is given to valued subscribers.** Nevertheless, when there is room in an issue, we will publish nonsubscribers." Does not want poetry that is "gothic, erotic/sexual, gory, bloody, or that depicts violence." Subscription: $15 USD. Sample: $3 USD.

How to Contact Submit 3 poems at a time. Lines/poem: 4 minimum, 25 maximum. Considers previously published poems and simultaneous submissions. Cover letter is required. Include SASE (or SAE and IRC), name, address, and telephone number; e-mail address if applicable. Time between acceptance and publication varies. Guidelines available for SASE (or SAE and IRC), or by fax or by e-mail. Pays 3 contributor's copies. All rights remain with the author.

Tips "Poetry is a wonderful literary form. Try your hand at it. Send us the fruit of your labours."

⬛ THE PORTLAND REVIEW

Portland State University, P.O. Box 347, Portland OR 97207-0347. (503)725-4533. Fax: (503)725-4534. Website: www.portlandreview.org. Established 1956. **Contact:** Chris Cottrell, editor.

Magazines Needs *The Portland Review*, published 3 times/year by Portland State University, seeks "submissions exhibiting a unique, compelling voice and content of substance. Experimental poetry welcomed." Has published poetry by Gaylord Brewer, Richard Bentley, Charles Jensen, Mary Biddinger, and Jerzy Gizella. *The Portland Review* is about 130 pages. Receives about

1,000 poems/year, accepts about 30. Press run is 1,000 for subscribers, libraries, and bookstores nationwide. Single copy: $9; subscription: $28/year, $54/2 years. Sample: $8.

How to Contact Submit up to 5 poems at a time. Considers simultaneous submissions; no previously published poems. Accepts postal submissions only. Include phone number, e-mail address, and other contact information on ms. Indicate whether you wish ms returned; if so, include SASE (otherwise mss will be recycled automatically). Reads submissions year round except during the months of June, July, and August. Guidelines available for SASE or on Web site. "Our Web site is a general introduction to our magazine, with samples of our poetry, fiction, and art." Responds in up to 4 months. Pays 1 contributor's copy. Acquires first North American rights.

Tips "Include a SASE and specify if submissions need to be returned. Otherwise, they will be recycled."

▣ ◩ THE POTOMAC

2020 Pennsylvania Ave. NW, Suite 443, Washington DC 20006. E-mail: charles.rammelkamp@ssa. gov. Website: http://thepotomacjournal.com. Established 2004. **Contact:** Charles Rammelkamp, editor. Member: Web del Sol.

Magazines Needs *The Potomac*, published quarterly online, features political commentary, cutting-edge poetry, flash fiction, and reviews. Open to all forms of poetry by new and established writers. Has published poetry and fiction by Robert Cooperman, Michael Salcman, Joanne Lowery, Pamela Painter, and L.D. Brodsky. Receives a "variable" number of poems/year, accepts about 50-60. Sample: free online.

How to Contact Submit any number of poems at a time. Considers simultaneous submissions; no previously published poems. Accepts e-mail submissions (as attachment) only; no postal or disk submissions. Cover letter is preferred. Reads submissions year round. Time between acceptance and publication is 3 months. Often comments on rejected poems. Guidelines available on website. Responds in 2 months. Sometimes sends prepublication galleys. No payment. Acquires one-time rights. Reviews books/chapbooks of poetry and other magazines/journals in up to 2,000 words, single- and multi-book format. Send materials for review consideration.

Tips "We welcome the opportunity to read work from new writers."

◩ POTOMAC REVIEW: A JOURNAL OF ARTS & HUMANITIES

Montgomery College, 51 Mannakee St., Rockville MD 20850. (240)567-4100. E-mail: potomacrevieweditor@montgomerycollege.edu. Website: www.montgomerycollege.edu/potomacreview. Established 1994. **Contact:** Julie Wakeman-Linn, editor.

Magazines Needs *Potomac Review: A Journal of Arts & Humanities*, published semiannually in November and May, wants "stories with unique setting and plots, as well as fiction that has a compelling voice. We welcome poetry, both free verse and in-form (translations accepted). Essays and creative nonfiction are also welcome." Has published work by David Wagoner, William Jollif, Mary Collins, Patricia Schultheis, Joan Siegal, and Paul Freidinger. *Potomac Review* is 150 pages, digest-sized, 50 lb paper; 65 lb cover stock. Receives about 2,500 poems/year, accepts 3%. Subscription: $18/year (includes 2 issues). Sample: $10.

How to Contact Submit up to 3 poems (5 pages maximum) at a time. Considers simultaneous submissions; no previously published poems. Cover letter is preferred. Include brief bio; enclose SASE. Time between acceptance and publication is up to 1 year. Poems are read "in house," then sent to poetry editor for comments and dialogue. Often comments on rejected poems. Does not publish theme issues. Guidelines available on Web site. Responds within 3 months. Pays 2 contributor's copies and offers 40% discount on additional copies.

Contest/Award Offerings Sponsors an annual poetry contest and annual fiction contest. Guidelines available in magazine (fall/winter issue), for SASE.

Tips "Read a current issue to see what kind of work delights us. We like a wide variety of subjects, and we especially love memorable characters and evocative imagery. Keep checking Web site for updates and changes."

⬚ $ ⬚ ◎ THE PRAIRIE JOURNAL

Prairie Journal Press, P.O. Box 61203, Brentwood Post Office, 217-3630 Brentwood Rd. NW, Calgary AB T2L 2K6 Canada. E-mail: prairiejournal@yahoo.com. Website: www.geocities.com/prairiejournal. Established 1983. **Contact:** A. Burke, editor.

Magazines Needs *The Prairie Journal*, published twice/year, seeks poetry "of any length; free verse, contemporary themes (feminist, nature, urban, non-political), aesthetic value, a poet's poetry." Does not want to see "most rhymed verse, sentimentality, egotistical ravings. No cowboys or sage brush." Has published poetry by Liliane Welch, Cornelia Hoogland, Sheila Hyland, Zoe Lendale, and Chad Norman. *The Prairie Journal* is 40-60 pages, digest-sized, offset-printed, saddle-stapled, with card cover, includes ads. Receives about 1,000 poems/year, accepts 10%. Press run is 600; the rest are sold on newsstands. Subscription: $10 for individuals, $18 for libraries. Sample: $8 ("use postal money order"). No U.S. stamps.

How to Contact No previously published poems or simultaneous submissions. No e-mail submissions. "We will not be reading submissions until such time as an issue is in preparation (twice yearly), so be patient and we will acknowledge, accept for publication, or return work at that time." Guidelines available for postage ("no U.S. stamps, please"; get IRCs from USPS) or on Web site. Sometimes sends prepublication galleys. Pays $10-50 and 1 contributor's copy. Acquires first North American serial rights. Reviews books of poetry, "but must be assigned by editor. Query first."

Additional Information For chapbook publication by Prairie Journal Press, **Canadian poets only** (preferably from the plains region). Has published *Voices From Earth*, selected poems by Ronald Kurt and Mark McCawley, and *In the Presence of Grace* by McCandless Callaghan. "We also publish anthologies on themes when material is available." Query first, with 5 sample poems and cover letter with brief bio and publication credits. Responds to queries in 2 months; to mss in 6 months. Payment in modest honoraria.

Also Offers Publishes "Poems of the Month" online. Submit up to 4 poems **with $1 reading fee** by postal mail.

Tips "Read recent poets! Experiment with line length, images, metaphors. Innovate."

⬚ PRAIRIE SCHOONER

201 Andrews Hall, P.O. Box 880334, University of Nebraska, Lincoln NE 68588-0334. (402)472-0911. Fax: (402)472-9771. E-mail: jengelhardt2@unl.edu. Website: http://prairieschooner.unl.edu. Established 1926. **Contact:** James Engelhardt, managing editor. • Poetry published in Prairie Schooner has been selected for inclusion in The Best American Poetry and The Pushcart Prize.

Magazines Needs *Prairie Schooner*, published quarterly, prints poetry, fiction, personal essays, interviews, and reviews. Wants "poems that fulfill the expectations they set up." No specifications as to form, length, style, subject matter, or purpose. Has published poetry by Alicia Ostriker, Marilyn Hacker, D.A. Powell, Stephen Dunn, and David Ignatow. *Prairie Schooner* is about 200 pages, digest-sized, flat-spined. Receives about 5,500 submissions/year, uses about 300 pages of poetry. Press run is 2,500. Single copy: $9; subscription: $28. Sample: $6.

How to Contact Submit 5-7 poems at a time. No simultaneous submissions. No fax or e-mail submissions; postal submissions only. Reads submissions September 1-May 1 (mss must be received during that period). Guidelines available for SASE or on Web site. Responds in 4 months, "sooner if possible." Always sends prepublication galleys. Pays 3 contributor's copies. Acquires all rights. Returns rights upon request without fee. Reviews books of poetry. Send materials for review consideration.

Contest/Award Offerings "All manuscripts published in *Prairie Schooner* automatically will be considered for our annual prizes." These include The Strousse Award for Poetry ($500), the Bernice Slote Prize for Beginning Writers ($500), the Hugh J. Luke Award ($250), the Edward Stanley Award for Poetry ($1,000), the Virginia Faulkner Award for Excellence in Writing ($1,000), the Glenna Luschei Prize for Excellence ($1,500), and the Jane Geske Award ($250). Also, each year 10 Glenna Luschei Awards ($250 each) are given for poetry, fiction, and nonfiction. All contests are open only to those writers whose work was published in the magazine the previous year. Editors serve as judges. Also sponsors The *Prairie Schooner* Book Prize (see separate listing Contests & Awards).

Also Offers Editor-in-Chief Hilda Raz also promotes poets whose work has appeared in her pages by listing their continued accomplishments in a special section (even when their work does not concurrently appear in the magazine).

☐ ◎ PRAYERWORKS

(Specialized: praying; the elderly), P.O. Box 301363, Portland OR 97294-9363. (503)761-2072. E-mail: jay4prayer@aol.com. Established 1988. **Contact:** V. Ann Mandeville, editor.

Magazines Needs *PrayerWorks*, published weekly, is a newsletter "encouraging elderly people to recognize their value to God as prayer warriors." Established as a ministry to people living in retirement centers, *PrayerWorks* features "prayers, ways to pray, stories of answered prayers, teaching on a Scripture portion, articles that build faith, and poems." *PrayerWorks* is 4 pages, digest-sized, desktop-published, photocopied, folded. Receives about 50 poems/year, accepts about 25%. Press run is 1,000. Subscription: free.

How to Contact Submit 5 poems at a time. Considers previously published poems and simultaneous submissions. Accepts e-mail submissions (WordPerfect or Microsoft Word attachments). Cover letter is preferred. 1 poem/page. Time between acceptance and publication is usually within 1 month. Seldom comments on rejected poems. Publishes theme issues relating to the holidays (submit holiday poetry 2 months in advance). Guidelines available for SASE. Responds in 3 weeks. Pays 5 or more contributor's copies.

◙ PRESA

P.O. Box 792, Rockford MI 49341. E-mail: presapress@aol.com. Website: www.presapress.com. Established 2003. **Contact:** Roseanne Ritzema, editor.

Magazines Needs *Presa*, published twice/year, prints poems, reviews, essays, photos, criticism, and prose. Wants "imagistic, surreal, experimental, and personal poetry. Dedicates 6-8 pages of each issue to a featured poet." Does not want "political or didactic poetry." Has published poetry by Antler, Eric Greinke, Richard Kostelanetz, Donald Lev, Lyn Lifshin, Simon Perchik, and Jared Smith. *Presa* is 48-64 pages, digest-sized laser printed on 20-24 lb. paper, saddle-stitch bound with a color cover artwork on card stock; includes ads. Receives about 2,500 poems/year, accepts about 5%. Press run is 500. Single copy: $8.50; subscription: $15. Make checks payable to Presa Press.

How to Contact Submit 3-5 poems at a time. Considers previously published poems. (Considers poetry posted on a public Web site/blog/forum and poetry posted on a private, password-protected forum as published.) Accepts postal submissions only. Cover letter is preferred. Reads submissions year round. Time between acceptance and publication is 8-12 weeks. Poems are circulated to an editorial board. Never comments on rejected poems. Never publishes theme issues. Guidelines available in magazine, for SASE, and by e-mail. Responds in 4-8 weeks. Pays 2 contributor's copies. Acquires first North American serial rights and the right to reprint in anthologies. Rights revert to poets upon publication. Reviews books and chapbooks of poetry. Send materials for review consideration to Roseanne Ritzema.

Tips "Read an issue or check our Web site."

⚓ $ ☑ PRISM INTERNATIONAL

Creative Writing Program, University of British Columbia, Buchanan E462, 1866 Main Mall, Vancouver BC V6T 1Z1 Canada. E-mail: prism@interchange.ubc.ca. Website: http://prism.arts.ubc.ca. Established 1959. **Contact:** Editor (rotating title).

•*PRISM international* is one of the top literary journals in Canada.

Magazines Needs *PRISM international*, published quarterly, prints poetry, drama, short fiction, creative nonfiction, and translation into English in all genres. "We have no thematic or stylistic allegiances: Excellence is our main criterion for acceptance of manuscripts." Wants "fresh, distinctive poetry that shows an awareness of traditions old and new. We read everything." Considers poetry by children and teens. "Excellence is the only criterion." Has published poetry by Margaret Avison, Elizabeth Bachinsky, John Pass, Warren Heiti, Don McKay, Bill Bissett, and Stephanie Bolster. *PRISM international* is 80 pages, digest-sized, elegantly printed, flat-spined, with original color artwork on a glossy card cover. Receives 1,000 submissions/year, accepts about 80. Circulation is for 1,200 subscribers. Subscription: $28/year, $46 for 2 years. Sample: $11. "Subscribers outside of Canada, please pay in U.S. dollars."

How to Contact Submit up to 6 poems at a time. No previously published poems or simultaneous submissions. No e-mail submissions. Cover letter is required. Include brief introduction and list of previous publications. Poems must be typed or computer-generated (font and point size open). Include SASE (or SAE with IRCs). "Note: American stamps are not valid postage in Canada. No SASEs with U.S. postage will be returned. Translations must be accompanied by a copy of the original." Guidelines available for SASE (or SAE with IRCs), by e-mail, or on Web site. Responds in up to 6 months. Pays $40/printed page (for poetry) and one-year subscription; plus an additional $10/printed page to selected authors for publication online. Editors sometimes comment on rejected poems. Acquires first North American serial rights.

Contest/Award Offerings Introducing the first annual Poetry Contest in 2009. First prize: $1,000; second prize: $300; third prize: $200. Entry fee: $28 for 3 poems; $7 per additional poem. Entry fee includes one-year subscription. Deadline: January 30. The editorial board also awards an annual $500 prize to an outstanding poetry contributor in each volume.

Tips "While we don't automatically discount any kind of poetry, we prefer to publish work that challenges the writer as much as it does the reader. We are particularly looking for poetry in translation."

$ ☑ ◎ PROVINCETOWN ARTS

(Specialized: Cape Cod & area art colony culture), P.O. Box 35, 650 Commercial St., Provincetown MA 02657. (508)487-3167. E-mail: cbusa@comcast.net. Website: www.provincetownarts.org. Established 1985. **Contact:** Christopher Busa, editor.

Magazines Needs *Provincetown Arts*, published annually in July, prints quality poetry, focusing "broadly on the artists and writers who inhabit or visit the tip of Cape Cod." Seeks to "stimulate creative activity and enhance public awareness of the cultural life of the nation's oldest continuous art colony. Drawing upon a century-long tradition rich in visual art, literature, and theater, *Provincetown Arts* publishes material with a view towards demonstrating that the artists' colony, functioning outside the urban centers, is a utopian dream with an ongoing vitality." Has published poetry by Bruce Smith, Franz Wright, Sandra McPherson, and Cyrus Cassells. *Provincetown Arts* is about 170 pages, magazine-sized, perfect-bound, with full-color glossy cover. Press run is 10,000. Sample: $10.

How to Contact Submit up to 3 poems at a time. No e-mail submissions; "all queries and submissions should be sent via postal mail." Submissions must be typed. Reads submissions October-February. Guidelines available for SASE. Responds in 3 months. Usually sends prepublication galleys. Pays $25-100/poem plus 2 contributor's copies. Acquires first rights. Reviews books of poetry in 500-3,000 words, single- or multi-book format. Send materials for review consideration.

Additional Information The Provincetown Arts Press has published 8 volumes of poetry. The Provincetown Poets Series includes *At the Gate* by Martha Rhodes, *Euphorbia* by Anne-Marie Levine (a finalist in the 1995 Paterson Poetry Prize), and *1990* by Michael Klein (co-winner of the 1993 Lambda Literary Award).

⊞ ☑ PULSAR POETRY MAGAZINE

Ligden Publishers, 34 Lineacre, Grange Park, Swindon, Wiltshire SN5 6DA England. (44) (01793)875941. E-mail: pulsar.ed@btopenworld.com. Website: www.pulsarpoetry.com. Established 1992. **Contact:** David Pike, editor.

Magazines Needs *Pulsar Poetry Magazine*, published every March and September, "encourages the writing of poetry from all walks of life. Contains poems, reviews, and editorial comments." Wants "hard-hitting, thought-provoking work; interesting and stimulating poetry." Does not want "racist material. Not keen on religious poetry." Has published poetry by A.C. Evans, Chris Hardy, Kate Edwards, Elizabeth Birchall, and Michael Newman. *Pulsar* is 40-44 pages, A5, professionally printed, saddle-stapled, with glossy full-color cover, includes ads. Press run is 300; several distributed free to newspapers, etc. Subscription: $18 (£8 UK). Sample: $9. Make checks payable to Ligden Publishers.

How to Contact Submit 3 poems at a time. No previously published poems or simultaneous submissions. Accepts e-mail submissions (pasted into body of message). "Send no more than 2 poems via e-mail; file attachments will not be read." Cover letter is preferred. Include SAE with adequate IRCs for a reply only (mss not returned if non-UK). Manuscripts should be typed. Time between acceptance and publication is about 1 month. "Poems can be published in next edition if it is what we are looking for. The editor and assistant read all poems." Seldom comments on rejected poems. Guidelines available for SASE (or SAE and IRC) or on Web site. Responds within 1 month. Pays 1 contributor's copy. Acquires first rights. "Originators retain copyright of their poems." Staff reviews poetry books and CDs (mainstream); word count varies. Send materials for review consideration.

Tips "Give explanatory notes if poems are open to interpretation. Be patient and enjoy what you are doing. Check grammar, spelling, etc. (should be obvious). Note: we are a nonprofit-making society."

☐ PULSE ONLINE LITERARY JOURNAL

12 Center St., Rockland ME 04841 (contest address only, all other submissions by e-mail). (760)243-8034. E-mail: mainepoet@mac.com. Website: www.heartsoundspressliterary.com. Established 1997. **Contact:** Carol Bachofner, poetry editor.

Magazines Needs *Pulse Online Literary Journal* is open to formal poetry as well as free verse. Wants "your best. Send only work revised and revised again! Translations welcome with submitted original language piece." Does not want "predictable, sentimental, greeting card verse. No gratuitous sexuality or violence. No religious verse or predictable rhyme." Has published poetry by Walt McDonald and Lyn Lifshin. Receives about 400 poems/year, accepts about 30-45%.

How to Contact Submit 3-5 poems at a time. Lines/poem: up to 120. Considers previously published poems. Only accepts e-mail submissions (pasted into body of e-mail); no disk submissions. Cover letter is required. "Send bio of 50-100 words with submission." Reads submissions year round. Submit seasonal poems 2 months in advance. Time between acceptance and publication is 3-4 weeks. Sometimes comments on rejected poems. Sometimes publishes theme issues. Themes for 2009 were April-September: Urban Landscape; September-December: Movements. Guidelines available on Web site. Responds in 3-4 weeks. Acquires first rights. Reviews books/chapbooks of poetry.

Contest/Award Offerings Sponsors the annual Pulse Poetry Prize. Offers 1st Prize: $90; 2nd Prize: $45; 3rd Prize: $20; plus 3 Honorable Mentions and publication to prizewinners. Submit 3 poems up to 120 lines each. **Entry fee:** $10/entry (multiple entries okay with additional fee for each). **Deadline:** August 2010. Guidelines available by e-mail or on Web site.

Also Offers Offers personal editing in prose and poetry. For prose, e-mail Liz Pinto at lpinto@sbcglobal.net; for poetry e-mail Carol Bachofner at mainepoet@mac.com.

Tips "Be relentless in the revision process. Read widely. Write *something* every day."

▦ ☑ PURPLE PATCH

25 Griffiths Rd., West Bromwich B7I 2EH England. E-mail: ppatch66@hotmail.com. Website: www.purplepatchpoetry.co.uk. Established 1975. **Contact:** Geoff Stevens, editor.

Magazines Needs *Purple Patch*, published quarterly, is a poetry and short prose magazine with reviews, coments, and illustrations. "All good examples of poetry considered." Does not want "poor rhyming verse, non-contributory swear words or obscenities, hackneyed themes." Has published poetry by Raymond K. Avery, Bryn Fortey, Bob Mee, B.Z. Niditch, and Steve Sneyd. *Purple Patch* is 24 pages, digest-sized, photocopied, side-stapled, with cover on the same stock with b&w drawing. Receives about 2,500 poems/year, accepts about 8%. Circulation varies. Subscription: £5 UK/3 issues; $20 USD (send dollars). Make checks (sterling only) payable to G. Stevens.

How to Contact Submit 2 or more poems at a time. Lines/poem: 40 maximum. No e-mail submissions; postal submissions only. Cover letter is preferred. Include self-introduction. Submissions must be sent return postage-paid. Reads submissions year round. Time between acceptance and publication is 4 months. Comments on rejected poems. Occasionally publishes theme issues. Upcoming themes available for SASE (or SAE and IRCs). Guidelines available in magazine or on Web site. Responds in one month to Great Britain; can be longer to U.S. Pays one contributor's copy "to European writers only; overseas contributors must purchase a copy to see their work in print." Acquires first British serial rights. Staff reviews poetry chapbooks, short stories, and tapes in 30-300 words. Send materials for review consideration.

Tips "Don't just send one poem. Send at least two, and I'll try to like them."

$ ◎ PURPOSE

(Specialized: Mennonite; poetry for young adults & adults), Mennonite Publishing Network, 616 Walnut Ave., Scottdale PA 15683-1999. (724)887-8500. E-mail: horsch@mpn.org. **Contact:** James E. Horsch, editor.

Magazines Needs *Purpose*, published by Mennonite Publishing Network (the official publisher for the Mennonite Church in the U.S. and Canada), is a "religious young adult/adult monthly." Focuses on "action-oriented, discipleship living." *Purpose* is digest-sized with 4-color printing throughout. Press run is 8,000. Receives about 2,000 poems/year, accepts 150. Sample: (with guidelines) $2 and 9x12 SAE.

How to Contact Lines/poem: up to 12. Considers simultaneous submissions. Prefers e-mail submissions. Postal submissions should be double-spaced, typed on one side of sheet only. Responds in 6 months. Guidelines available electronically or for SASE. Pays $7.50 to $20 per poem plus 2 contributor's copies.

☑ QUARTERLY WEST

Dept. of English/LNCO 3500, University of Utah, 255 S. Central Campus Dr., Salt Lake City UT 84112-9109. (801)581-3938. E-mail: quarterlywest@yahoo.com (inquiries only). Website: www. quarterlywest.utah.edu. Established 1976. **Contact:** Kathryn Cowles and Stacy Kidd, poetry editors; Paul Ketzle and Brenda Sieczkowski, editors.

•Poetry published in *Quarterly West* has appeared in *The Best American Poetry* and in numerous Pushcart Prize anthologies.

Magazines Needs *Quarterly West*, published semiannually, seeks "original and accomplished literary verse—free or formal." Also considers translations (include originals with submissions). No greeting card or sentimental poetry. Has published poetry by Quan Barry, Medbh McGuckian, Alice Notley, Brenda Shaughnessy, Bob Hicok, David Kirby, and Linh Dinh. *Quarterly West* is 160 pages, digest-sized, offset-printed, with 4-color cover art. Receives 2,500 submissions/year, accepts less than 1%. Press run is 1,500 (500 subscribers, 300-400 libraries). Subscription: $14/year, $25 for 2 years. Sample: $8.50.

How to Contact Submit 3-5 poems at a time. Online submissions only, guidelines available on Web site. Considers simultaneous submissions, with notification; no previously published poems. Reads submissions September 1-May 1. Seldom comments on rejected poems. Responds in up to 6 months. Pays 2 contributor's copies and money when possible. Acquires first North American serial rights. Returns rights with acknowledgment and right to reprint. Reviews books of poetry in 1,000-3,000 words.

$ ☐ ◎ ELLERY QUEEN'S MYSTERY MAGAZINE

(Specialized: mystery/suspense), 475 Park Ave. S., 11th Floor, New York NY 10016. E-mail: elleryqueenmm@dellmagazines.com (inquries only). Website: www.themysteryplace.com. Established 1941. **Contact:** Janet Hutchings.

Magazines Needs *Ellery Queen's Mystery Magazine*, published 10 times/year, uses primarily short stories of mystery, crime, or suspense—little poetry. *Ellery Queen's Mystery Magazine* is 112 pages (double-issue, published twice/year, is 240 pages), digest-sized, professionally printed on newsprint, flat-spined, with glossy paper cover. Single copy: $5.50 by check to publisher, available for $4.99 on newsstands; subscription: $55.90.

How to Contact Considers simultaneous submissions; no previously published poems. No e-mail submissions; postal submissions only. Include SASE with submissions. Guidelines available for SASE or on Web site. Responds in 3 months. Pays $15-65 and 3 contributor's copies.

☑ QUERCUS REVIEW

Quercus Review Press, Modesto Junior College, Division of Literature & Language Arts, 435 College Ave., Modesto CA 95350. (209)575-6183. E-mail: pierstorffs@mjc.edu. Website: www. quercusreview.com. Established 1999. **Contact:** Sam Pierstorff, editor.

Magazines Needs *Quercus Review*, published annually in May/June, prints high-quality poetry, fiction, and b&w art. "We publish numerous nationally recognized and award-winning writers from across the nation." Wants "writing with a pulse. Writing that reflects a unique voice." Does not want "rhyme, religious, or cliché writing." Considers poetry by children and teens. Has published poetry by X.J. Kennedy, Gerald Locklin, Naomi Shihab Nye, Amiri Baraka, Charles Harper Webb, and Dorianne Laux. *Quercus Review* is 112 pages, digest-sized, professionally printed, perfect-bound, with full-color cover. Receives about 3,500 poems/year, accepts less than 10%. Press run is 500; 100 distributed free to contributors and local bookstores. Single copy: $8; subscription: $20 for 2 years (includes 2 issues of *Quercus Review*, plus annual book award winner). Make checks payable to "MJC (QR)."

How to Contact Submit 3-5 poems at a time. Lines/poem: prefers 40 maximum, but will consider longer. No previously published poems or simultaneous submissions. No e-mail or disk submissions. Cover letter is required. Include brief bio and SASE. Reads submissions year round. Time between acceptance and publication is usually 3 weeks to 3 months. "Poems are selected by 5-person staff of editors, which rotates annually." Guidelines available on Web site. Sometimes sends prepublication galleys. Pays 1 contributor's copy, 30% discount on additional copies. Acquires first rights.

Contest/Award Offerings Quercus Review Press Poetry Series Book Award (see separate listing in Contests & Awards).

Tips "Avoid overusing the world 'soul,' but feel free to drown us in fresh imagery and bold language. We like poems with a pulse. Make us laugh or cry, but don't bore or try too hard to impress us."

☑ QUEST

Freiburger Hall, Lynn University, 3601 N. Military Trail, Boca Raton FL 33431. E-mail: jdaily@lynn.edu. Established 1997. **Contact:** John Daily, editor.

Magazines Needs *Quest*, published annually in April, is a literary and arts journal. Wants "poems with a clear voice that use careful diction to create poetry in which sound and sense work together, creating fresh perception." Does not want "poems that rely on profanity or shock value." Has published poetry by Jeff Morgan, John Daily, Eugene Martel, Andrea Best, Lizbeth Keiley, Fred Cichocki, Johanne Perron, and Brittany Barbarino. *Quest* is digest-sized, laser-printed, saddle-stapled, with 32 lb. bright white coverstock cover printed with 4-color process. Receives about 100 poems/year, accepts about 25. Press run is 200 (one library subscriber); 150 distributed free to Lynn University faculty, staff, and students. Single copy: $5. Make checks payable to Lynn University.

How to Contact Submit up to 3 poems at a time. No previously published poems or simultaneous submissions. No e-mail or disk submissions. Cover letter is preferred. "Include adequate SASE if you want work returned." Reads submissions mid-September to mid-January. Time between acceptance and publication is up to 7 months. "The Lynn English Department faculty and selected students form the Editorial Board to review submissions." Seldom comments on rejected poems. Responds in up to 4 months. Pays 1 contributor's copy. Acquires one-time rights.

Tips "Even the freest of verse has its roots in the formal elements."

Ⓝ ☑ QUIDDITY: INTERNATIONAL LITERARY JOURNAL AND PUBLIC-RADIO PROGRAM

1500 N. Fifth St., Springfield IL 62702. (217)525-1420. E-mail: quiddity@sci.edu. Website: www.sci.edu/quiddity. Established 2007. **Contact:** poetry editor. Member: CLMP, AWP.

Magazines Needs *Quiddity*, published semi-annually, is "a print journal and public-radio program featuring poetry, prose, and artwork by new, emerging, and established contributors from around the globe. Please visit the website for guidelines." Has published work by J.O.J. Nwachukwu-Agbada, Kevin Stein, Douglas Blackmon, and Adam Braver. *Quiddity* is 176 pages, 7X9, perfect-bound, with 60 lb. full color cover. Receives about 2,500 poems/year, accepts about 5%. Press run is 1,000. Single copy: $9; subscription: $15/year. Make checks payable to *Quiddity*.

How to Contact Submit up to 5 poems at a time, no more than 10 pages. Considers simultaneous submissions; no previously published poems (previously published includes work posted on a public Web site/blog/forum and on private, password-protected forums). Cover letter is preferred. "Address to poetry editor, SASE required (except international). See Web site for reading dates. Time between acceptance and publication is 6 months to 2 years. Poems are circulated to an editorial board. Never comments on rejected poems. Sometimes publishes theme issues. Upcoming themes and guidelines available on Web site. Responds in 6 months. Typically sends prepublication galleys. Pays 1 contributor's copy. Acquires first North American serial rights and electronic rights (reprint and broadcast). Rights revert to poet on publication. Considers reviews for books of poetry only when sent from publisher. Send materials for review consideration to poetry editor.

Contest/Award Offerings Sponsors the annual Teresa A. White Creative Writing Award. **Entry fee**: $15. "See Web site for guidelines, deadline, and prize information. All entries are considered for publication."

☑ ◎ RADIX MAGAZINE

(Specialized: poetry that expresses a Christian world-view), E-mail: RadixMag@aol.com. Website: www.radixmagazine.com. Established 1969. **Contact:** Luci Shaw, poetry editor. Editor: Sharon Gallagher.

Magazines Needs *Radix Magazine*, published quarterly, is named for the Latin word for "root" and "has its roots both in the 'real world' and in the truth of Christ's teachings." Wants poems "that reflect a Christian world-view, but aren't preachy." Has published poetry by John Leax, Czeslaw Milosz, Madeleine L'Engle, and Luci Shaw. *Radix* is 32 pages, magazine-sized, offset-printed, saddle-stapled, with 60-lb. self cover. Receives about 120 poems/year, accepts about 10%. Press run varies. Sample: $5. Make checks payable to *Radix Magazine*.

How to Contact Submit 1-4 poems at a time. No previously published poems or simultaneous submissions. Accepts e-mail submissions only. Submit seasonal poems 6 months in advance. Time between acceptance and publication is 3 months to 3 years. "We have a serious backlog. The poetry editor accepts or rejects poems and sends the accepted poems to the editor. The editor then publishes poems in appropriate issues. If more than one poem is accepted from any poet, there will probably be a long wait before another is published, because of our backlog of accepted poems." Seldom comments on rejected poems. Occasionally publishes theme issues. Responds in 2 months. Pays 2 contributor's copies. Acquires first rights. Returns rights upon request. Reviews books of poetry.

Tips "*Radix* has a distinctive voice and often receives submissions that are completely inappropriate. Familiarity with the magazine is recommended before sending any submissions."

☑ ◎ THE RAINTOWN REVIEW

(Specialized: formal/traditional poetry), E-mail: Oelfkej@aol.com. Website: www.centralavepress.com/html. Established 1996. **Contact:** John Oelfke, publisher.

Magazines Needs *The Raintown Review*, published 2 times/year in December and July, contains poetry "and the occasional literary criticism or review." Wants well-crafted poems. "We are primarily a venue for formal/traditional poetry." Has published poetry by William Baer, Joseph S. Salemi, Richard Moore, Annie Finch, Dana Gioia, Daniel Hoffman, A.E. Stallings, Richard Wilbur, and many others. *The Raintown Review* is 120 pages, perfect-bound. Receives about 1,500 poems/year, accepts 10-15%. Press run is 150 (most go to subscribers and contributors). Subscription: $24/year, $45 for 2 years, $65 for 3 years. Sample: $12. Make checks/money orders payable to Central Ave Press, 2132A Central SE #144, Albuquerque NM 87106.

How to Contact Submit 3-5 poems at a time. Lines/poem: no restrictions. Considers previously published poems (with acknowledgment of previous publication) and simultaneous submissions. Accepts e-mail submissions only (pasted into body of message); no postal submissions. Comments on rejected poems if requested at the time of submission. Guidelines available on Web site. Usually responds in 2 months, if possible. Pays 1 contributor's copy. Acquires one-time rights.

☑ ◎ RATTAPALLAX

(Specialized: the diversity of world cultures), 532 La Guardia Place, Suite 353, New York NY 10012. E-mail: info@rattapallax.com. Website: www.rattapallax.com. Established 1998. **Contact:** Poetry Editor.

Magazines Needs *Rattapallax*, published semiannually, is named for "Wallace Steven's word for "the sound of thunder. The magazine includes a DVD featuring poetry films and audio files. *Rattapallax* is looking for the extraordinary in modern poetry and prose that reflect the diversity of world cultures. Our goals are to create international dialogue using literature and focus on what is relevant to our society." Has published poetry by Anthony Hecht, Sharon Olds, Lou Reed, Marilyn Hacker, Billy Collins, and Glyn Maxwell. *Rattapallax* is 112 pages, magazine-sized, offset-printed, perfect-bound, with 12-pt. CS1 cover. Receives about 5,000 poems/year, accepts 2%. Press run is 2,000 (100 subscribers, 50 libraries, 1,200 shelf sales); 200 distributed free to contributors, reviews, and promos. Single copy: $7.95; no subscriptions. Make checks payable to *Rattapallax*.

How to Contact Submit 3-5 poems at a time. Considers simultaneous submissions; no previously published poems. Accepts e-mail submissions (sent as simple text) from outside the U.S. and Canada; all other submissions must be sent via postal mail (SASE required). Cover letter is preferred. Reads submissions year round; issue deadlines are June 1 and December 1. Time between acceptance and publication is 6 months. "The editor-in-chief, senior editor, and associate editor review all the submissions and then decide on which to accept every week. Near publication time, all accepted work is narrowed, and unused work is kept for the next issue." Often comments on rejected poems. Guidelines available by e-mail or on Web site. Responds in 2 months. Always sends prepublication galleys. Pays 2 contributor's copies. Acquires first rights.

☑ RATTLE

12411 Ventura Blvd., Studio City CA 91604. (818)505-6777. E-mail: timgreen@rattle.com. Website: www.rattle.com. Established 1994. **Contact:** Timothy Green, editor.

Magazines Needs *RATTLE*, published semiannually in June and December, includes poems, essays, reviews, interviews with poets, and a tribute section dedicated to a specific ethnic or vocational group. Wants "high-quality poetry of any form. Nothing unintelligible." Considers some poetry by children and teens (ages 10-18). Has published poetry by Lucille Clifton, Charles Simic, Mark Doty, Sharon Olds, Billy Collins, and Stephen Dunn. *RATTLE* is 196 pages, digest-sized, neatly printed, perfect-bound, with 4-color coated card cover. Receives about 8,000 submissions/year, accepts 200. Press run is 4,000. Subscription: $18/year, $30/2 years, $36/3 years. Sample: $10. Make checks payable to *RATTLE*.

How to Contact Submit up to 5 poems at a time. Considers simultaneous submissions "if notified immediately by e-mail or phone should they be taken elsewhere." Accepts e-mail submissions (pasted into body of message). Cover letter is required (with e-mail address, if possible). Include bio. For postal submissions, put name, address, and phone number on each page in upper right corner; include SASE. Reads submissions year round. Seldom comments on rejected poems (unless requested by the author). Guidelines available in magazine, by e-mail, or on Web site. Responds in up to 2 months. Pays 2 contributor's copies. Rights revert to poet upon publication. Publishes reviews of books of poetry online. Send materials for review consideration.

Additional Information Welcomes essays up to 2,000 words on poetry or the writing process. Publishes a biannual electronic issue in March and September, e-mailed as a PDF to 4,000 subscribers, featuring excerpts from poetry collections, chapbooks, reviews, and print issue previews.

Contest/Award Offerings The *RATTLE* Poetry Prize (see separate listing in Contests & Awards).

▣ $ ☑ ◎ RAVING DOVE

(Specialized: Anti-violence, anti-hate, human rights, social justice), P.O. Box 28, West Linn OR 97068.E-mail: ravingdove@gmail.com. Website: www.ravingdove.org. Established 2004. **Contact**: Jo-Ann Moss, editor.

•Nonprofit status granted by U.S. government.

Magazines Needs *Raving Dove*, published quarterly, "is an online literary journal that publishes original poetry, nonfiction, fiction, photography, and art with universal anti-violence, anti-hate, human rights, and social justice themes. We share sentiments that oppose physical and psychological violence in all its forms, including war, discrimination against sexual orientation, and every shade of bigotry." Wants free verse only, any length. Has published poetry by Howard Camner, Marguerite Bouvard, John Kay, Harry Youtt. Receives about 750 poems/year, accepts about 30. Number of visitors is "2,000/month and growing."

How to Contact Considers simultaneous submissions. Accepts e-mail submissions only; allows attachments. No fax, disk, or postal submissions. Cover letter is unnecessary. "Poetry Submission" must appear as the subject of the e-mail; all submissions must include full name, general geographic location, and a third-person bio of 100 words or less. Weblinks are permitted. Reads submissions year round. Time between acceptance and publication is no more than 3 months. Sometimes comments on rejected poems. Guidelines available on Web site. Always sends prepublication galleys ("the link to the poet's Web page at *Raving Dove* is sent prior to publication"). Responds in 3 months. Payment is based on funding. Acquires first North American and Internet serial rights, exclusive for the duration of the edition in which the poetry appears (see submission guidelines on Web site for further information). Rights revert to poets at the end of the issue.

Tips "*Raving Dove* is not a political journal. Material for or against one specific person or entity will not be considered, fictitious or otherwise. We are seeking intelligent reflections as a path to greater understanding. Please follow submission guidelines carefully. Guidelines can be found at http://www.ravingdove.org/submissions.

☑ REDIVIDER

Dept. of Writing, Literature, and Publishing, Emerson College, 120 Boylston St., Boston MA 02118. E-mail: redividerpoetry@gmail.com. Website: www.redividerjournal.org. Established 1990 (as Beacon Street Review). **Contact:** Poetry Editor (changes annually, see Web site). Member: CLMP.

Magazines Needs *Redivider*, published semiannually, prints high-quality poetry, art, fiction, and creative nonfiction. Wants "all styles of poetry. Most of all, we look for language that seems fresh and alive on the page, that tries to do something new. Read a sample copy for a good idea." Does not want "greeting card verse or inspirational verse." Has published poetry by Bob Hicok, Billy Collins, Paul Muldoon, Tao Lin, Claudia Emerson, and Bobby Byrd. *Redivider* is 100 + pages, digest-sized, offset-printed, perfect-bound, with 4-color artwork on cover. Receives about 1,000 poems/year, accepts about 30%. Press run is 1,000. Single copy: $6; subscription: $10. Make checks payable to *Redivider* at Emerson College.

How to Contact Submit 3-6 poems at a time. Considers simultaneous submissions, but requires notification if your work is taken elsewhere; no previously published poems. For online submissions, e-mail poems as a single file. Cover letter is required. Reads submissions year round. Seldom comments on rejected poems. Guidelines available in magazine, for SASE, by e-mail, or on Web site. Responds in 5 months. Pays 2 contributor's copies. Acquires first North American serial rights. Reviews books of poetry in 500 words, single-book format. Send materials for review consideration, Attn: Review Copies. "Book reviews and interviews are internally generated."

Tips "We want your finished product—don't send your experimental first draft!"

$ ◎ RED LIGHTS

2740 Andrea Drive, Allentown PA 18103-4602. (212)875-9342. E-mail: mhazelton@rcn.com. Established 2004. **Contact:** Marilyn Hazelton, editor.

Magazines Needs *red lights*, published semiannually in January and June, is devoted to English-language tanka and tanka sequences. Wants "print-only tanka, mainly 'free-form' but also strictly syllabic 5-7-5-7-7; will consider tanka sequences and tan-renga." Considers poetry by children and teens. Has published poetry by Sanford Goldstein, Michael McClintock, Laura Maffei, Linda Jeannette Ward, Jane Reichhold, and Michael Dylan Welch. *red lights* is 28-36 pages, 8½x3¾, offset-printed, saddle-stapled, with Japanese textured paper cover; copies are numbered. Receives about 1,200 poems/year, accepts about 20%. Press run is 150. Single copy: $7; subscription: $14 U.S., $15 USD Canada, $17 USD foreign. Make checks payable to Pamela Miller Ness.

How to Contact Submit 10 tanka or 2 sequences at a time (maximum). No previously published poems or simultaneous submissions. No e-mail or disk submissions. Include SASE. Reads submissions year round. Time between acceptance and publication "depends on submission time." Guidelines available for SASE. Acquires first rights.

Contest/Award Offerings "Each issue features a '*red lights* featured tanka' on the theme of 'red lights.' Poet whose poem is selected receives 1 contributor's copy."

$ ◹ ◎ THE RED MOON ANTHOLOGY OF ENGLISH LANGUAGE HAIKU

P.O. Box 2461, Winchester VA 22604-1661. (540)722-2156. E-mail: jim.kacian@redmoonpress. com. Website: www.redmoonpress.com. Established 1996. **Contact:** Jim Kacian, editor/publisher.

Magazines Needs *The Red Moon Anthology of English Language Haiku*, published annually in February, is "a collection of the best haiku published in English around the world." Considers poetry by children and teens. Has published haiku and related forms by John Barlow, Lee Gurga, Bill Pauly, and Cor van den Heuvel. *The Red Moon Anthology of English Language Haiku* is 184 pages, digest-sized, offset-printed on quality paper, with 4-color heavy-stock cover. Receives several thousand submissions/year, accepts less than 2%. Print run is 1,000 for subscribers and commercial distribution. Subscription: $16.95 plus $4 p&h. Sample available for SASE or by e-mail.

How to Contact "We do not accept direct submissions to the *Red Moon Anthology*. Rather, we employ an editorial board who are assigned journals and books from which they cull and nominate. Nominated poems are placed on a roster and judged anonymously by the entire editorial board twice a year." Guidelines available for SASE or by e-mail. Pays $1/page. Acquires North American serial rights.

Also Offers *contemporary haibun*, "an annual volume of the finest English-language haibun and haiga published anywhere in the world." (See separate listing in this section.)

Tips "Haiku is a burgeoning and truly international form. It is nothing like what your fourth-grade teacher taught you years ago, and so it is best if you familiarize yourself with what is happening in the genre (and its close relatives) today before submitting. We strive to give all the work we publish plenty of space in which to resonate, and to provide a forum where the best of today's practitioners can be published with dignity and prestige."

▣ ◪ ◎ THE REDNECK REVIEW

an online poetry journal, P.O. Box 8718, Atlanta GA 31106. E-mail: editor@redneckreview.com. Website: www.redneckreview.com. Established 2000. **Contact:** Penya Sandor, editor.

Magazines Needs *The Redneck Review*, published semiannually online, is "born out of the rich literary tradition of the South." Wants "writing that is interesting, has energy, and doesn't feel like homework." Considers poetry by children and teens. Has published poetry by Denise Duhamel, Marie Howe, Walt McDonald, Hal Sirowitz, Ben Satterfield, and Jean Trounstine. Publishes about 15-20 poems/issue.

How to Contact Submit no more than 5 poems at a time. Considers previously published poems and simultaneous submissions. Accepts e-mail and disk submissions. Cover letter is preferred. "If sending submissions by postal mail, include SASE unless you have an e-mail address. Poems won't be returned." Time between acceptance and publication "depends." Often comments on rejected poems. Guidelines available on Web site. Response time varies. Sometimes sends prepublication galleys. No payment. "Authors retain rights, but we ask that they mention our journal if they publish the poem again." Send materials for review consideration to *The Redneck Review*.

Tips "There are many respectable literary journals that publish well-written but dull writing. We would prefer to read literature that is electric, not just technically well crafted."

◪ RED ROCK REVIEW

English Dept. J2A, College of Southern Nevada, 3200 E. Cheyenne Ave., North Las Vegas NV 89030. (702)651-4094. Fax: (702)651-4639. E-mail: richard.logsdon@csn.edu. Website: http://sites.csn.edu/english/redrockreview/. Established 1994. **Contact:** Dr. Richard Logsdon, senior editor. Poetry Editor: Jeanie French. Associate Editor: Todd Moffett.

Magazines Needs *Red Rock Review*, published semiannually in May and December, prints "the best poetry available," as well as fiction, creative nonfiction, and book reviews. Has published poetry by Dorianne Laux, Kim Addonizio, Ellen Bass, Cynthia Hogue, and Dianne di Prima. *Red Rock Review* is about 130 pages, magazine-sized, professionally printed, perfect-bound, with 10-pt. CS1 cover. Accepts about 15% of poems received/year. Press run is 750. Sample: $5.50.

How to Contact Submit 2-3 poems at a time. Lines/poem: 80 maximum. Considers simultaneous submissions; no previously published poems. Accepts disk submissions. Cover letter and SASE are required. Submissions should be "mailed flat, not folded, into a letter-sized envelope." Reads submissions September-May. Time between acceptance and publication is 3-5 months. "Poems go to poetry editor, who then distributes them to 3 readers." Seldom comments on rejected poems. Guidelines available for SASE or on Web site. Responds in 3-5 months. Pays 2 contributor's copies. Acquires first North American serial rights. Reviews books/chapbooks of poetry in 500-1,000 words, multi-book format. Send materials for review consideration.

◪ RED WHEELBARROW

De Anza College, 21250 Stevens Creek Blvd., Cupertino CA 95014. E-mail: SplitterRandolph@

deanza.edu. Website: www.deanza.edu/redwheelbarrow. Established 1976 (as Bottomfish Magazine). **Contact:** Randy Splitter or Ken Weisner.

• **"Please note:** We are not affiliated with Red Wheelbarrow Press or any similarly named publication."

Magazines Needs *Red Wheelbarrow*, published annually in spring, is a college-produced, national magazine. Wants "diverse voices." Has published poetry by Mark Brazaitis, Arthur Gottlieb, Lyn Lifshin, Guadalupe Garcia McCall, Mario Susko, and Taylor Graham. *Red Wheelbarrow* is about 250 pages, book-sized, printed on heavy stock with b&w graphics, perfect-bound. Press run is on demand. Single copy: $10. Sample: $2.50 (for back issue).

How to Contact Submit up to 5 poems at a time. Accepts e-mail submissions. Include SASE or e-mail address for reply. Reads submissions September-January (January 31 deadline). Responds in 2-6 months, depending on backlog. Pays 1 contributor's copy.

Tips "We seek diverse voices from around the country and the world."

RENDITIONS: A CHINESE-ENGLISH TRANSLATION MAGAZINE

Research Centre for Translation, Chinese University of Hong Kong, Shatin, N.T., Hong Kong. (852)2609-7407. Fax: (852)2603-5110. E-mail: renditions@cuhk.edu.hk. Website: www.renditions.org. **Contact:** The Editor.

Magazines Needs *Renditions: A Chinese-English Translation Magazine*, published twice/year in May and November, uses "exclusively translations from Chinese, ancient and modern." Poems are printed with Chinese and English texts side by side. Has published translations of the poetry of Yang Lian, Gu Cheng, Shu Ting, Mang Ke, and Bei Dao. *Renditions* is about 150 pages, magazine-sized, elegantly printed, perfect-bound, with glossy card cover. Single copy: $19.90; subscription: $29.90/year, $49.90/2 years, $69.90/3 years.

How to Contact Submissions should be accompanied by Chinese originals. Accepts e-mail and fax submissions. "Submissions by postal mail should include two copies. Use British spelling." Sometimes comments on rejected translations. Publishes theme issues. Guidelines available on Web site. Responds in 2 months. Manuscripts usually not returned.

Additional Information Also publishes a hardback series (Renditions Books) and a paperback series (Renditions Paperbacks) of Chinese literature in English translation. "Will consider" book mss; query with sample translations.

RHINO

P.O. Box 591, Evanston IL 60204. Website: www.rhinopoetry.org. Established 1976. **Contact:** Deborah Nodler Rosen, Helen Degen Cohen, or Ralph Hamilton, co-editors.

• *RHINO* poems have been reprinted in *The Best American Poetry*, nominated for Pushcart Prizes, and won repeated Illinois Arts Council awards.

Magazines Needs *RHINO*, published annually in spring, prints poetry, short-shorts, and translations. Wants "work that reflects passion, originality, engagement with contemporary culture, and a love affair with language. We welcome free verse, formal poetry, innovation, and risk-taking." Has published poetry by Geoffrey Forsyth, Penelope Scambly Schott, F. Daniel Rzicznek, and Ricardo Pau-Llosa. *RHINO* is 150 pages, 7x10, printed on high-quality paper, with card cover with art. Receives 8,000-10,000 submissions/year, accepts 90-100, or 1%. Press run is 800. Single copy: $12. Sample: $5 (back issue).

How to Contact Submit 3-5 poems or 1-3 short-shorts once during reading period. Considers simultaneous submissions with notification; no previously published poems. Include SASE. Expects electronic copy upon acceptance. Reads submissions April 1-October 1. Guidelines available for SASE or on Web site. Responds in up to 6 months. Pays 2 contributor's copies.

Acquires first rights only.

◪ ☑ ◎ RHODE ISLAND ROADS

(Specialized: RI/New England themes), E-mail: asurkont@local.net. Website: www.riroads. com. Established 2000. **Contact:** Amanda Surkont, poetry editor.

Magazines Needs *Rhode Island Roads*, published monthly online, features work with Rhode Island and New England themes. Open to all forms and styles, although "rhyme will have difficulty finding a home here." Considers poetry by children and teens. Has published poetry by Audrey Friedman, Barbara Schweitzer, Michele F. Cooper, Pat Hagneur, Lauri Burke, and Peggy Conti. Receives about 150 poems/year, accepts 12-16/year. Has about 70,000 readers/month. Sample: can view sample pages for free online.

How to Contact Submit up to 5 poems at a time. Lines/poem: "We are flexible." Considers previously published poems and simultaneous submissions. Accepts e-mail submissions only (pasted into body of message). "We'll ask for a bio if we use your work." Reads submissions year round. Submit seasonal poems 3 months in advance. Time between acceptance and publication is 2 months "unless seasonal, then it could be several months." Sometimes comments on rejected poems. Sometimes publishes theme issues. Upcoming themes available by e-mail. Guidelines available by e-mail or on Web site. "I try to respond within a week or two." Pays free subscription. Acquires one-time rights and electronic rights. "We archive." Rights revert to poet upon publication. "Electronic rights returned to author if requested."

Tips "Know your market. Read the publication before submitting poems. Get a feel for what we like. We sometimes suggest an alternative market for work. We suggest poets make a commitment to subscribing to five lit mags per year; we have more writers of poetry than readers. This is not a good balance."

☑ ◎ RIBBONS: TANKA SOCIETY OF AMERICA JOURNAL

5921 Cayutaville Rd, Alpine NY 14805. E-mail: davidb@htva.net. Website: www. tankasocietyofamerica.com. Established 2000. **Contact:** Dave Bacharach, editor.

Magazines Needs *Ribbons: Tanka Society of America Journal*, published quarterly, seeks and regularly prints "the best tanka poetry being written in English, together with reviews, critical and historical essays, commentaries, and translations." Wants "poetry that exemplifies the very best in English-language tanka, which we regard as 'the queen of short form poetry,' having a significant contribution to make to the short poem in English. All schools and approaches are welcome." Tanka should "reflect contemporary life, issues, values, and experience, in descriptive, narrative, and lyrical modes." Does not want "work that merely imitates the Japanese masters." Considers poetry by children and teens. "We have no age restrictions." Has published poetry by Cherie Hunter Day, Marianne Bluger, Sanford Goldstein, Larry Kimmel, John Stevenson, and George Swede. *Ribbons* is 60-72 pages, 6x9 perfect-bound, with color cover and art. Receives about 2,000 poems/year, accepts about 20%. Press run is 275; 15 distributed free. Single copy: $10; subscription: $30. Make checks payable to Tanka Society of America and contact Carole MacRury, Secretary/Treasurer (e-mail: macrury@whidbey.com; 1636 Edwards Dr., Point Roberts, WA 98281).

How to Contact Submit 1-8 poems at a time. Lines/poem: 5 minimum; sequences of up to 50 total lines considered. No previously published poems or simultaneous submissions. Prefers e-mail submissions (pasted into body of message); no disk submissions. "Postal submissions must include SASE." Reads submissions year round. "See the publication or contact the editor for specific deadlines for each issue." Time between acceptance and publication is 2 months. Sometimes comments on rejected poems. Regularly publishes theme issues. Guidelines available in magazine or on Web site. Responds in 4-8 weeks. No payment. Acquires one-time rights. Rights revert to poet upon publication. Reviews books/chapbooks of poetry and other magazines/journals in 250-1,200 words, single- or multi-book format. Send materials for review consideration to the editor or to Michael McClintock, President, Tanka Society of America, 9230 N. Stoneridge Lane, Fresno CA 93720.

Additional Information "Features in each issue include 'Poet and Tanka' (various writers); 'Tanka Cafe' by Michael McClintock; 'Tanka Favorites,' essays by various writers, book reviews, and topical and historical essays and commentaries. About 200 new tanka appear in each issue. McClintock's 'Tanka Cafe' uses up to 45 poems per issue on a given theme, with critical commentary relating to contemporary tanka in English trends, styles, techniques, and subject matter."

Contest/Award Offerings The annual Tanka Society of America International English-Language Tanka Competition (see separate listing in Contests & Awards). "Additionally, a Members' Choice Award of $25 is given each quarter for a poem appearing in the 'Tanka Cafe' feature; non-cash Editor's Choice Awards are also featured in each issue."

Tips "Work by beginning as well as established English-language tanka poets is welcome; first-time contributors are encouraged to study the tanka form and contemporary examples before submitting. No particular school or style of tanka is preferred over another; our publications seek to showcase the full range of English-language tanka expression and subject matter through the work of new and established poets in the genre from around the world."

☑ RIVER OAK REVIEW

Elmhurst College, 190 Prospect Ave., Elmhurst IL 60126. (630)617-6483. Website: www.riveroakreview.org. Established 1993. **Contact:** Ann Frank Wake, poetry editor.

Magazines Needs *River Oak Review*, published annually with plans to go biannual, prints high-quality poetry, short fiction, and creative nonfiction. "We are a national journal striving to publish midwestern poets in each issue." Has published poetry by Wendy Bishop, Jim Elledge, James Doyle, Ken Meisel, and Robin Becker. *River Oak Review* is at least 128 pages, digest-sized, neatly printed, perfect-bound, with glossy color cover with art. Publishes about 5% of poetry received. Press run is 500. Single copy: $10; subscription: $10/year, $20/2 years. Sample: $5. Make checks payable to *River Oak Review*.

How to Contact Submit 4-6 poems at a time. No previously published poems or simultaneous submissions. SASE required. Reads submissions year round. Sometimes comments on rejected poems. Guidelines available for SASE or on Web site. Tries to respond in 3 months. Pays 2 contributor's copies. Acquires first North American serial rights.

Tips "Mary Oliver suggests that poets should read modern poetry for at least 2 hours for every hour they spend writing. Our experience as editors bears this out." We agree in principle with Stanley Kunitz, who told his poetry students to 'End on an image and don't explain it!' While we don't mean this literally, we do think that a 'less is more' philosophy usually results in better poems."

$ ☑ RIVER STYX MAGAZINE

3547 Olive St., Suite 107, St. Louis MO 63103-1014. Website: www.riverstyx.org. Established 1975. **Contact:** Richard Newman, editor.

•Poetry published in *River Styx* has been selected for inclusion in past volumes of *The Best American Poetry*, *Beacon's Best*, *Best New Poets* and *The Pushcart Prize*.

Magazines Needs *River Styx Magazine*, published 3 times/year in April, August, and December, is "an international, multicultural journal publishing both award-winning and previously undiscovered writers. We feature poetry, short fiction, essays, interviews, fine art, and photography." Wants "excellent poetry—original, energetic, musical, and accessible." Does not want "chopped prose or opaque poetry that isn't about anything." Has published poetry by Jennifer Perrine, Louis Simpson, Molly Peacock, Marilyn Hacker, Yusef Komunyakaa, Andrew Hudgins, and Catie Rosemurgy. *River Styx Magazine* is 100-120 pages, digest-sized, professionally printed on coated stock, perfect-bound, with color cover, includes ads. Receives about 8,000 poems/year, accepts 60-75. Press run is 2,500 (1,000 subscribers, 80 libraries). Subscription: $20/year, $35/2 years. Sample: $9.

How to Contact Submit 3-5 poems at a time. Manuscripts should be "legible copies with name and address on each page." Reads submissions May 1-November 30 only. No electronic submissions. Time between acceptance and publication is up to 1 year. Sometimes comments on rejected poems. Publishes 1 theme issue/year. Upcoming themes available in magazine or on Web site. Guidelines available for SASE or on Web site. Responds in up to 5 months. Pays 2 contributor's copies and one-year subscription, plus $15/page. Acquires one-time rights.

Contest/Award Offerings Sponsors an annual poetry contest. Past judges include Kim Addonizio, Alan Shapiro, Dorianne Laux, Ellen Bryant Voigt, Philip Levine, and Naomi Shihab Nye. **Deadline:** May 31. Guidelines available for SASE or on Web site.

▣ ▢ ◉ ROAD NOT TAKEN: THE JOURNAL OF FORMAL POETRY, THE

(Specialized: formal poetry), E-mail: jimatshs@yahoo.com. Website: www.journalofformalpoetry. com. Established 2007. **Contact:** Dr. Jim Prothero, co-editor.

Magazines Needs *The Road Not Taken: the Journal of Formal Poetry*, published quarterly online, prints formal poetry "in the tradition of Frost, Wordsworth, Tennyson, Hopkins, etc." Wants "formal poetry only. Nature and spiritual poetry always of interest but not required. Also essays/blogs on the topic of formal poetry would be of interest." Does not want free verse. Accepts poetry by children and teens; no age limitations, "it just has to be excellent."

How to Contact Submit 5 poems at a time. Considers previously published poems; no simultaneous submissions. (Considers poetry posted on a public Web site/blog/forum as published.) Accepts e-mail submissions (pasted into body of message); no fax or disk submissions. Cover letter is unnecessary. Reads submissions year round. Submit seasonal poems 3 months in advance. Time between acceptance and publication is 2 months. Poems are circulated to an editorial board. "There are 2 editors, Dr. Jim Prothero and Dr. Don Williams. Poems must meet both of our approval." Sometimes comments on rejected poems. Never publishes theme issues. Guidelines available by e-mail and on Web site. Responds in 1 month. Acquires one-time rights. Rights revert to poets upon publication.

Tips "Frost is really our patron here. We like skilled formal poetry and nature or spiritual topics are of interest."

▣ ☑ ◉ ROADRUNNER HAIKU JOURNAL

(Specialized: haiku, senryu, short haiku-like poetry), E-mail: scott@roadrunnerjournal.net or ztemttocs@gmail.com. Website: www.roadrunnerjournal.net. Established 2004. **Contact:** Scott Metz, editor.

Magazines Needs *Roadrunner Haiku Journal*, published quarterly online, is "an international Web journal that publishes the most innovative modern haiku written today." Wants haiku, senryu, and short haiku-like poetry. Does not want tanka, haiga, or haibun. Considers poetry by children and teens. Has published poetry by Fay Aoyagi, Richard Gilbert, Jim Kacian, Dhugal Lindsay, and Dietmar Tauchner. Receives about 5,000 poems/year, accepts about 5%. Distributed free online. Number of unique visitors: 25,000/year.

How to Contact Submit 5-15 poems at a time. Lines/poem: "less than 5 or so." No previously published poems or simultaneous submissions. Accepts e-mail submissions only (pasted into body of message, with "Roadrunner Submission" and poet's name in subject line); no disk submissions. Cover letter is unnecessary. "Please include a short bio." Reads submissions year round. Time between acceptance and publication is less than 3 months. Sometimes comments on rejected poems. Guidelines available on Web site. Responds in 2 weeks. Sometimes sends prepublication galleys. Acquires first rights. Rights revert to poets upon publication.

☑ ROANOKE REVIEW

English Dept., Roanoke College, 221 College Lane, Salem VA 24153. E-mail: review@roanoke. edu. Website: www.roanoke.edu/roanokereview/. Established 1967. **Contact:** Paul Hanstedt, poetry editor.

Magazines Needs *Roanoke Review*, published annually in June, uses poetry that is "grounded in strong images and unpretentious language." Has published poetry by Will Wells, Jeff Daniel Marion, and Charles Wright. *Roanoke Review* is 200 pages, digest-sized, professionally printed, with matte card cover with full-color art. Receives 400-500 submissions of poetry/year, accepts 20-40. Press run is 250-300 (150 subscribers, 50 libraries). Single copy: $8; subscription: $13/2 years. Sample: $5.

How to Contact Submit original typed mss, no photocopies. Guidelines available on Web site. Responds in 3 months. Pays 2 contributor's copies "plus cash when budget allows."

Tips "Be real. Know rhythm. Concentrate on strong images."

☑ THE ROCKFORD REVIEW

P.O. Box 858, Rockford IL 61105. E-mail: daveconnieross@aol.com. Website: http://writersguild1. tripod.com. Established 1971. **Contact:** David Ross, editor.

Magazines Needs *The Rockford Review*, published twice/year by the Rockford Writers' Guild, features poetry and prose by members and other contributors from across the country and abroad. Wants "experimental or traditional poetry that provides fresh insight into the human condition in a literal or satirical voice." Open to veterans and novices alike. "We delight in discovering new talent." Considers poetry by children and teens. *The Rockford Review* is about 100 pages, digest-sized, professionally printed, perfect-bound. Press run is 350.

How to Contact Submit up to 3 poems at a time. Lines/poem: 50 maximum. Considers simultaneous submissions; no previously published poems (including those published on the Internet). No e-mail submissions; accepts postal submissions only. Cover letter is required. "Include your name, address, phone number, e-mail address (if available), a 3-line bio, and an affirmation that the poems are unpublished electronically or in print." SASE required for return. Guidelines available for SASE or on Web site. Responds in 2 months. Pays 1 contributor's copy and an invitation to be a guest of honor at annual summer Gala Reading & Reception in July. Acquires first North American serial rights.

Contest/Award Offerings Editor's Choice Prizes of $25 are awarded each issue. Also sponsors an Ides of March Poetry and Prose Contest for adults and youth, with cash prizes and publication in the summer *Rockford Review*. Details available on Web site.

Also Offers Rockford Writers' Guild is a nonprofit corporation established 60 years ago "to promote good writing of all forms and to nurture literary artists of all stages." Monthly meetings and newsletters offer practical tips on writing/marketing from professional guest poets, and open mics for contests/works in progress. Levels of membership/dues: $35/year. Further information available for SASE, by e-mail, or on Web site.

Tips "If the heart/soul of your poetry raises/answers questions about coping with the human condition, try us first—we're on the same page."

$ ☑ ◎ ROCKY MOUNTAIN RIDER MAGAZINE

(Specialized: horses; cowboy poetry; Northern Rockies region), P.O. Box 1011, Hamilton MT 59840. (406)363-4085 or (800)509-1537. Fax: (406)363-1056. E-mail: info@rockymountainrider. com. Website: www.rockymountainrider.com. Established 1993. **Contact:** Natalie Riehl, editor.

Magazines Needs *Rocky Mountain Rider Magazine*, published monthly, is a regional all-breed horse magazine. Wants "cowboy poetry; western or horse-themed poetry." *Rocky Mountain Rider Magazine* is 68+ pages, magazine-sized, Web offset-printed on SuperCal, stapled. Publishes 0-2 poems/issue. Press run is 16,500; distributed free through 500+ locations in 11 states.

How to Contact Submit 1-10 poems at a time. Lines/poem: keep length to no more than 5 stanzas. Considers previously published poems and simultaneous submissions. No e-mail submissions; postal submissions only. Cover letter is preferred. Include SASE. Seldom comments on rejected poems. Occasionally publishes theme issues. Guidelines available for SASE. Pays $10/poem. Acquires one-time rights. Reviews books of poetry. Send materials for review consideration.

◻ ◎ RUAH: A JOURNAL OF SPIRITUAL POETRY

Power of Poetry, 1421 N. Causeway Blvd., #200, Metairie LA 70001. E-mail: ruahjournal@yahoo. com. Website: http://plumapictures.com. Established 1990. **Contact:** Armando P Ibáñez, O.P., general editor.

Magazines Needs *Ruah: A Journal of Spiritual Poetry*, published annually in September, provides "a 'non-combative forum' for poets who have had few or no opportunities to publish their work." Theme: spiritual poetry. Wants "poetry that is of a 'spiritual nature,' i.e., describes an experience of the Transcendent. No religious affiliation preferences; no style/format limitations." Does not want "Satanic verse." Has published poetry by Jean Valentine, Alberto Rios, Luci Shaw, and Wendell Berry. *Ruah* is 60-80 pages, digest-sized, photocopied, perfect-bound, with glossy cardstock cover with color photo. Receives about 350 poems/year, accepts 10-20%. Press run is 250 (about 100 subscribers, 7 libraries, 10 shelf sales); 50 distributed free to authors, reviewers, and inquiries. Subscription: donated cost of $10 plus $1.75 s&h. Sample: $5 plus $1.75 s&h. Make checks payable to Pluma Pictures/POP.

How to Contact Submit 3-5 poems at a time. Lines/poem: no more than 4 typed pages. Considers simultaneous submissions; no previously published poems. "Submitted manuscripts will not be returned. Be sure to keep a copy for yourself. We prefer e-mail submissions via attachments in MS Word 97. Submit poems January 1-March 31 only. Time between acceptance and publication is up to 6 months. "Poems are reviewed by writers and/or scholars in field of creative writing/ literature." Guidelines available for SASE or by e-mail. Responds in 2 weeks. Pays 1 contributor's copy/poem. Acquires first rights, including right to publish poems on Web site.

Tips "*Ruah* is a gathering place in which new poets can come to let their voices be heard alongside and in the context of 'more established' poets. The journal hopes to provide some breakthrough experiences of the Divine at work in our world."

☑ SALT HILL

English Dept., Syracuse University, Syracuse NY 13244. (315)443-1984. E-mail: salthilljournal@ gmail.com. Website: www.salthilljournal.net. Established 1994. **Contact:** Poetry Editor.

Magazines Needs *Salt Hill*, published semiannually, is "published by a group of writers affiliated with the Creative Writing Program at Syracuse University." Has published poetry by Campbell McGrath, Dean Young, Kim Addonizio, and James Tate. *Salt Hill* is 120-150 pages, digest-sized, perfect-bound, includes ads. Receives about 3,000 poems/year, accepts about 2%. Press run is 1,000. Subscription: $15/year. Sample: $8 domestic, $11 foreign.

How to Contact Submit 5 poems at a time. Considers simultaneous submissions; no previously published poems. Cover letter is preferred. Include a brief bio. Time between acceptance and publication is up to 8 months. Seldom comments on rejected poems. Guidelines available for SASE. Responds in up to 9 months. Pays 2 contributor's copies. Acquires one-time rights.

☑ THE SAME

P.O. Box 494, Mount Union PA 17066. E-mail: riverfrontreadings@yahoo.com. Website: http://tsmag.itgo.com. Established 2000. **Contact:** Philip Miller, editor.

Magazines Needs *The Same*, published semiannually, prints nonfiction (essays, reviews, literary criticism), poetry, and short fiction. Wants "eclectic poetry (formal to free verse,'mainstream' to experimental, all subject matter.)" Considers poetry by children and teens. Has published poetry by Phyllis Becker, Graham Duncan, Patricia Lawson, Holly Posner, Stephen Stepanchev, and Robert Weaver. *The Same* is 50-100 pages, desktop-published, perfect-bound, with cardstock cover. Receives about 2,000 poems/year, accepts about 5%. Press run is 250 (125 subscribers/shelf sales). Single copy: $5; subscription: $10 for 2 issues, $18 for 4 issues. Make checks payable to Philip Miller.

How to Contact Submit 1-7 poems at a time. Lines/poem: 120 maximum. No previously published poems or simultaneous submissions "without query." Prefers e-mail submissions (pasted into body of message). Cover letter is optional. "Include SASE if you want a snail mail response. If you don't want your manuscript returned, you may omit the SASE if we can respond by e-mail." Please query before submitting fiction and non-fiction. Reads submissions year round. Time between acceptance and publication can be up to 11 months. Sometimes comments on rejected poems. Guidelines available for SASE, by e-mail, or on Web site. Responds within 2 months. Pays one contributor's copy. Acquires first North American serial rights and online rights for up to 9 months; returns rights to poet.

Additional Information Publishes 1-3 chapbooks/year. **Solicited mss only.** Chapbooks are 24-32 pages, desktop-published, saddle-stapled, with cardstock covers. Pays 25 author's copies (out of a press run of 100).

Tips "Our motto is 'Everyone else is different, but we're the same!' We are eclectic and non-doctrinaire."

☐ ◎ SAMSARA: THE MAGAZINE OF SUFFERING

P.O. Box 467, Ashburn VA 20147. E-mail: rdfgoalie@gmail.com. Website: www.samsaramagazine.net. Established 1993. **Contact:** R. David Fulcher, editor.

Magazines Needs *Samsara, The Magazine of Suffering*, published biannually, prints poetry and fiction dealing with suffering and healing. "Both metered verse and free verse poetry are welcome if dealing with the theme of suffering/healing." Has published poetry by Michael Foster, Nicole Provencher, and Jeff Parsley. *Samsara* is 80 pages, magazine-sized, desktop-published, with color cardstock cover. Receives about 200 poems/year, accepts about 15%. Press run is 300 (200 subscribers). Single copy: $5.50; subscription: $10. Sample: $4.50. Make checks payable to R. David Fulcher.

How to Contact Submit up to 5 poems at a time. Lines/poem: 3 minimum, 100 maximum. Considers simultaneous submissions "if noted as such"; no previously published poems. Cover letter is preferred. No e-mail submissionis; accepts submissions by postal mail only. Time between acceptance and publication is 3 months. Seldom comments on rejected poems. Guidelines available for SASE or on Web site. Responds in 2 months. Pays 1 contributor's copy.

Acquires first North American serial rights. Reviews books/chapbooks of poetry in 500 words, single-book format. Send material for review consideration.

✑ THE SARANAC REVIEW

CVH, Plattsburgh State University, 101 Broad St., Plattsburgh NY 12901. (518)564-2241. E-mail: saranacreview@plattsburgh.edu. Website: http://research.plattsburgh.edu/saranacreview. Established 2004. **Contact:** Poetry Editor.

Magazines Needs *The Saranac Review*, published annually in the fall, wants poetry from both U.S. and Canadian writers. Does not want "amateurish or 'greeting card' poetry." Has published poetry by Jim Daniels, Rustin Larson, Diane Swan, T. Alan Broughton, Alexis Lathem, and Katia Grubisic. *The Saranac Review* is magazine-sized, with color photo or painting on cover, includes ads. Press run is 1,000. Single copy: $12/$14CA; subscription: $15/year, $20 for 2 years, $28 for 3 years, $45 for 5 years ($18/year for institutions—multi-year subscriptions receive 15% discount); all Canadian subscriptions add $3/year. Make checks payable to Subscriptions/*The Saranac Review*.

How to Contact Submit no more than 3 poems at a time. Considers simultaneous submissions if notified; no previously published poems. No e-mail or disk submissions. Cover letter is appreciated. Include phone and e-mail contact information (if possible) in cover letter. Manuscripts will not be returned without SASE. Reads submissions September 1-February 15 (firm). Poems are circulated to an editorial board. Sometimes comments on rejected poems. Guidelines available on Web site. Responds in 3-6 months. Pays 2 contributor's copies. Acquires first rights.

ℕ ◻ ◎ SCIENCE EDITOR

12100 Sunset Hills Road, Suite 130, Reston VA 20190. (703)437-4377. Fax: (703)435-4390. E-mail: mknatterud@surgery.arizona.edu. Website: www.CouncilScienceEditors.org. Established 2000 **Contact:** Mary E. Knatterud, PhD, editor. Member: Council of Science Editors (CSE).

Magazines Needs *Science Editor*, published bimonthly, is "a forum for the exchange of information and ideas among professionals concerned with publishing in the sciences." Wants "up to 90 typeset lines of poetry on the intersection of science (including but not limited to biomedicine) and communication. Geared toward adult scholars, writers, and editors in communication and the sciences." Has published poetry by Mary Knatterud, Judy Meiksin, David Goldblatt, Mary Donnelly, Nancy Overcott, Jyothirmai Gubili, Neil H. Segal, Michele Arduengo. *Science Editor* is approx. 32 pages, magazine-sized, 4-color process, saddle-stitched, with an 80 pd Dull Cover; includes ads. Press run is 1,500. Single copy: $12 US; $15 Int'l. "Journal is a membership benefit; dues are $164 per year; nonmember subscriptions: $55 US; $68 Int'l/year." Make checks payable to Council of Science Editors (CSE).

How to Contact Submit up to 3 poems at a time, maximum 90 lines. Does not consider previously published poems or simultaneous submissions. Accepts e-mail submissions (pasted into the body of message), no fax or disk. "Submit both cover letter and poetry by e-mail only in the body of the same e-mail message, with no attachments." Submit seasonal poems 9 months in advance. Time between acceptance and publication is 3-6 months. Sometimes comments on rejected poems. Guidelines available by e-mail. Responds in 3-6 weeks. Pays 3 contributor's copies. Acquires one-time rights, electronic rights. "Science Editor is posted online. Issues at least one year old are openly displayed accessible. Issues less than one year old can be accessed only by Council of Science Editors members." Rights revert to poet upon publication.

Tips "The cover letter (i.e., the e-mail message preceding the poetry, which must also be in the body of that same e-mail) should include the poet's phone number, current title and workplace, and complete US mail address, as well as a short paragraph about his or her educational and professional background, including whether he or she has had any poetry or other literary work published before; note that this material may be edited for inclusion in the column, if the poetry is accepted."

▣ $ ▢ ◎ SCIFAIKUEST

(Specialized: scifaiku, horror-ku, tanka, senryu, haibun, and other minimalist poetry forms), P.O. Box 782, Cedar Rapids IA 52406-0782. E-mail: gatrix65@yahoo.com. Website: www.samsdotpublishing.com. Established 2003. **Contact:** Tyree Campbell, managing editor. Member: The Speculative Literature Foundation.

• Scifaikuest was voted #1 poetry magazine in the 2004 Preditors & Editors poll.

Magazines Needs *Scifaikuest*, published quarterly both online and in print, features "science fiction/fantasy/horror minimalist poetry, especially scifaiku, and related forms. We also publish articles about various poetic forms and reviews of poetry collections. The online and print versions of *Scifaikuest* are different." Wants "artwork, scifaiku and speculative minimalist forms such as tanka, haibun, ghazals, senryu. No 'traditional' poetry." Has published poetry by Tom Brinck, Oino Sakai, Deborah P. Kolodji, Aurelio Rico Lopez III, Joanne Morcom, and John Dunphy. *Scifaikuest* (print edition) is 32 pages, digest-sized, offset-printed, perfect-bound, with color cardstock cover, includes ads. Receives about 500 poems/year, accepts about 160 (32%). Press run is 100/issue; 5 distributed free to reviewers. Single copy: $7; subscription: $20/year, $37 for 2 years. Make checks payable to Tyree Campbell/Sam's Dot Publishing.

How to Contact Submit 5 poems at a time. Lines/poem: varies, depending on poem type. No previously published poems or simultaneous submissions. Accepts e-mail submissions (pasted into body of message). No disk submissions; artwork as e-mail attachment or inserted body of e-mail. "Submission should include snail mail address and a short (1-2 lines) bio." Reads submissions year round. Submit seasonal poems 6 months in advance. Time between acceptance and publication is 1-2 months. "Editor Teri Santitoro makes all decisions regarding acceptances." Often comments on rejected poems. Guidelines available on Web site. Responds in 6-8 weeks. Pays $1/poem, $4/review or article, and 1 contributor's copy. Acquires first North American serial rights.

Tips "It's up to the writer to take the first step and submit work. Some of our best poems have come from poets who weren't sure if they were good enough. A basic knowledge of writing traditional haiku is helpful."

▦ ☑ SEAM

P.O. Box 1051, Sawston, Cambridge CB22 3WT England. E-mail: seam.magazine@googlemail.com (inquiries only). Website: www.seampoetry.co.uk. Established 1994. **Contact:** Anne Berkeley, editor.

Magazines Needs *Seam*, published twice/year in spring and autumn, is "international in outlook and open to experimental work and authorized translations." Wants "good contemporary poetry and "high-quality poems that engage the reader." Has published poetry by Mike Barlow, Jane Holland, Sheenagh Pugh, Julian Stannard, George Szirtes, and Tamar Yoseloff. *Seam* is 72 pages, A5, perfect-bound, with b&w cover. Receives about 2,000 poems/year, accepts about 5%. Press run is 300. Subscription: £8/year (£12 or $18 overseas). Sample: £4.50 (£5.50 or $9 overseas). Payments accepted through PayPal.

How to Contact Submit 5-6 poems at a time. No simultaneous submissions or previously published poems (if published in UK). No e-mail submissions. Type each poem on 1 sheet of paper (A4 size). Sometimes comments on rejected poems. Pays 1 contributor's copy. Can reply by e-mail to save postage and time standing in line at post office for International Reply Coupons.

☑ SEEMS

P.O. Box 359, Lakeland College, Sheboygan WI 53082-0359. (920)565-1276 or (920)565-3871. Fax: (920)565-1206. E-mail: elderk@lakeland.edu. Website: www.seems.lakeland.edu. Established 1971. **Contact:** Karl Elder, editor.

Magazines Needs *SEEMS*, published irregularly, prints poetry, fiction, and essays. 2 of the issues are considered chapbooks, and the editor suggests sampling *SEEMS* #14, "What Is The Future Of Poetry?" ($5), consisting of essays by 22 contemporary poets; "if you don't like it, return it, and we'll return your $5." "Explain That You Live: Mark Strand with Karl Elder" (*SEEMS* #29) is available for $3. Has published poetry by Philip Dacey, William Hathaway, William Heyen, Sapphire, and Frank Stanford. *SEEMS* is handsomely printed, nearly square (7x814), saddle-stapled. Publishes less than .5% of submissions received. Press run is 500 (more than 250 subscribers, 20 libraries). Single copy: $4; subscription: $16 for 4 issues.

How to Contact Lines/poem: open. No simultaneous submissions. No fax or e-mail submissions. Cover letter is optional. Include biographical information, SASE. Reads submissions year round. There is a 1- to 2-year backlog. "People may call or fax with virtually any question, understanding that the editor may have no answer." Guidelines available on Web site. Responds in up to 3 months (slower in summer). Pays 1 contributor's copy. Acquires first North American serial rights and permission to publish online. Returns rights upon publication.

Additional Information *Word of Mouth* (alias Seems) — with focus on work that integrates economy of language, "the musical phrase," forms of resemblance, and the sentient — will consider unpublished poetry, fiction, and creative nonfiction. Subsequent issues may include themes and will alternate with chapbooks from Word of Mouth Books (query for the no-fee, any-genre, chapbook contest: elderk@lakeland.edu). See the editor's Web site at www.karlelder. com. "Links to my work and an interview may provide insight for the potential contributor."

Tips "Visit the *SEEMS* Web site."

☑ SENECA REVIEW

Hobart and William Smith Colleges, Geneva NY 14456. (315)781-3392. Fax: (315)781-3348. E-mail: senecareview@hws.edu. Website: www.hws.edu/senecareview/. Established 1970. **Contact:** David Weiss, editor.

•Poetry published in *Seneca Review* has been included in *The Best American Poetry* and The Pushcart Prize anthologies.

Magazines Needs *Seneca Review*, published semiannually, seeks "serious poetry of any form, including translations. Also essays on contemporary poetry and lyrical nonfiction. You'll find plenty of free verse here—some accessible and some leaning toward experimental—with emphasis on voice, image, and diction. All in all, poems and translations complement each other and create a distinct editorial mood in each issue." Does not want "light verse." Has published poetry by Seamus Heaney, Rita Dove, Denise Levertov, Stephen Dunn, and Hayden Carruth. *Seneca Review* is 100 pages, digest-sized, professionally printed on quality stock, perfect-bound, with matte card cover. Receives 3,000-4,000 poems/year, accepts about 100. Press run is 1,000. Subscription: $11/year, $20 for 2 years, $28 for 3 years. Sample: $7.

How to Contact Submit 3-5 poems at a time. No previously published poems or simultaneous submissions. No e-mail submissions; postal submissions only. SASE required. Reads submissions September 1-May 1 only. "Submit only once during the annual reading period." Guidelines available on Web site. Responds in up to 3 months. Pays 2 contributor's copies and a 2-year subscription.

$ ☑ THE SEWANEE REVIEW

University of the South, 735 University Ave., Sewanee TN 37383-1000. (931)598-1246. E-mail: lcouch@sewanee.edu. Website: www.sewanee.edu/sewanee_review. Established 1892 ("thus being our nation's oldest continuously published literary quarterly"). **Contact:** George Core, editor.

Magazines Needs *Sewanee Review*, published quarterly, is open "to all styles and forms: formal sequences, metered verse, structured free verse, sonnets, and lyric and narrative forms—all accessible and intelligent. Fiction, criticism, and poetry are invariably of the highest establishment standards. Many of our major poets appear here from time to time." Has published poetry by Wendell Berry, George Bilgere, Catherine Savage Brosman, David Mason, Leslie Norris, and Christian Wiman. *The Sewanee Review* is nearly 200 pages, conservatively bound in matte paper, always of the same typography. Press run is 2,600. Subscription: $25/year for individuals, $45/year for institutions. Sample: $8.50 U.S., $9.50 foreign.

How to Contact Submit up to 6 poems at a time. Lines/poem: 40 maximum. No simultaneous submissions. No e-mail submissions; postal submissions only. "Unsolicited works should not be submitted between June 1 and August 31. A response to any submission received during that period will be greatly delayed." Guidelines available in magazine or on Web site. Responds in 2 months. Pays per line, plus 2 contributor's copies (and reduced price for additional copies). Solicits brief, standard, and essay-reviews.

Contest/Award Offerings Winners of the Allen Tate Prize and the Aiken Taylor Award for Modern American Poetry are determined by the editorial board and a prize committee; poets cannot apply for these awards.

Tips "Please keep in mind that for each poem published in *The Sewanee Review*, approximately 250 poems are considered."

☐ ◎ SHEMOM

(Specialized: parenting), 2486 Montgomery Ave., Cardiff CA 92007. E-mail: pdfrench@cox.net. Established 1997. **Contact:** Peggy French, editor.

Magazines Needs *Shemom*, published 3 times/year, is a zine that "celebrates parenting and the joys and struggles that present themselves on that journey." Includes poetry, essays, book and CD reviews, recipes, art, and children's poetry. Open to any style, but prefers free verse. "We showcase writers of all ages that reflect on life's varied experiences. We often feature hiaku." *Shemom* is 10-20 pages. Receives about 100 poems/year, accepts 50%. Press run is 60 (30 subscribers). Single copy: $3.50; subscription: $12/4 issues. Make checks payable to Peggy French.

How to Contact Submit 3 poems at a time. Considers previously published poems and simultaneous submissions. Accepts e-mail submissions (as attachment or pasted into body of message). "Prefer e-mail submission, but not required; if material is to be returned, please include a SASE." Time between acceptance and publication is 3 months. Guidelines available for SASE or by e-mail. Responds in 2 months. Pays 1 contributor's copy. Acquires one-time rights.

$ ☑ SHENANDOAH

Mattingly House, 2 Lee Ave., Washington and Lee University, Lexington VA 24450-0303. (540)458-8765. Fax: (540)458-8461. E-mail: lleech@wlu.edu. Website: http://shenandoah.wlu.edu. Established 1950. **Contact:** Lynn Leech, managing editor.

•Poetry published in *Shenandoah* has been included in *The Best American Poetry*.

Magazines Needs *Shenandoah*, published triannually at Washington and Lee University, is open to all styles and forms. Has published poetry by Mary Oliver, Andrew Hudgins, W.S. Merwin, and Rita Dove. *Shenandoah* is 224+ pages, digest-sized, professionally printed, perfect-bound, with full-color cover. Press run is 2,100. Subscription: $25/year, $45 for 2 years, $62 for 3 years. Sample: $12.

How to Contact Considers simultaneous submissions "only if we are immediately informed of acceptance elsewhere." No e-mail submissions. All submissions should be typed on 1 side of the paper only, with name and address clearly written on the upper right corner of the ms. Include SASE. Reads submissions September 1-May 15 only. Responds in 3 months. Pays $2.50/line, one-year subscription, and 1 contributor's copy. Acquires first publication rights. Staff reviews books of poetry in 7-10 pages, multi-book format. Send materials for review consideration. (Most reviews are solicited.)

Contest/Award Offerings Sponsors the annual James Boatwright III Prize for Poetry, a $1,000 prize awarded to the author of the best poem published in *Shenandoah* during a volume year. The Shenandoah/Glasgow Prize for Emerging Writers $2,500 awarded for poetry on alternate years (see separate entry in Contests/Awards section of this book).

☑ SHIP OF FOOLS

Ship of Fools Press, University of Rio Grande, Box 1028, Rio Grande OH 45674-9989. (740)992-3333. Website: http://meadhall.homestead.com/Ship.html. Established 1983. **Contact:** Jack Hart, editor.

Magazines Needs *Ship of Fools*, published "more or less quarterly," seeks "coherent, well-written, traditional or modern, myth, archetype, love—most types." Does not want "concrete, incoherent, or greeting card poetry." Considers poetry by children and teens. Has published poetry by Rhina Espaillat and Gale White. *Ship of Fools* is digest-sized, offset-printed, saddle-stapled, includes cover art and graphics. Press run is 200. Subscription: $8 for 4 issues. Sample: $2.

How to Contact No previously published poems or simultaneous submissions. Cover letter is preferred. Often comments on rejected poems. Guidelines available for SASE. Responds in one month. "If longer than six weeks, write and ask why." Pays 1-2 contributor's copies. Reviews books of poetry.

Additional Information Ship of Fools Press has "no plans to publish chapbooks in the next year due to time constraints."

Tips "Forget yourself; it is not you that matters, but the words."

◎ SHIRIM, A JEWISH POETRY JOURNAL

259 St. Joseph Ave., Long Beach CA 90803. (310)476-2861. Established 1982. **Contact:** Marc Dworkin, editor.

Magazines Needs *Shirim, A Jewish Poetry Journal*, published semiannually, prints "poetry that reflects Jewish living without limiting to specific symbols, images, or contents." Has published poetry by Robert Mezcy, Karl Shapiro, and Grace Schulmon. *Shirim* is 40 pages, 4x5, desktop-published, saddle-stapled, with cardstock cover. Press run is 200. Subscription: $7. Sample: $4.

How to Contact Submit 4 poems at a time. No previously published poems or simultaneous submissions. Cover letter is preferred. Seldom comments on rejected poems. Regularly publishes theme issues. Responds in 3 months. Acquires first rights.

☑ SIERRA NEVADA REVIEW

999 Tahoe Blvd., Incline Village NV 89451. E-mail: sncreview@sierranevada.edu. Website: www.sierranevada.edu/800. Established 1990. **Contact:** June Sylvester Saraceno, advisory editor.

Magazines Needs *Sierra Nevada Review*, published annually in May, features poetry and short fiction by new writers. Wants "image-oriented poems with a distinct, genuine voice. Although we don't tend to publish 'light verse,' we do appreciate, and often publish, poems that make us laugh. No limit on length, style, etc." Does not want "sentimental, clichéd, or obscure poetry." Has published poetry by Virgil Suárez, Simon Perchik, Carol Frith, and Marisella Veiga. *Sierra Nevada Review* is about 75 pages, with art on cover. Receives about 500 poems/year, accepts about 50. Press run is 500. Subscription: $10/year. Sample: $5.

How to Contact Submit up to 5 poems at a time. Considers simultaneous submissions; no previously published poems. Accepts e-mail submissions (pasted into body of message, no attachments). Reads submissions September 1-March 1 only. Sometimes comments on rejected poems. Guidelines available for SASE, by e-mail, or on Web site. Responds in about 3 months. Pays 2 contributor's copies.

Tips "We're looking for poetry that shows subtlety and skill."

☑ SKIDROW PENTHOUSE

68 East Third St., Suite 16, New York, NY 10003. (212)614-9505 or (212)286-2600. Website: http://skidrowpenthouse.com. Established 1998. **Contact:** Rob Cook and Stephanie Dickinson, co-editors.

Magazines Needs *Skidrow Penthouse* aims to "give emerging and idiosyncratic writers a new forum in which to publish their work. We are looking for deeply felt authentic voices, whether surreal, confessional, New York School, formal, or free verse. Work should be well crafted: attention to line-break and diction." Wants "poets who sound like themselves, not workshop professionals." Does not want "gutless posturing, technical precision with no subject matter, explicit sex and violence without craft, or abstract intellectualizing. We are not impressed by previous awards and publications." Has published poetry by Lisa Jarnot, Christopher Edgar, Aase Berg, Karl Tierney, James Grinwis, and Robyn Art. *Skidrow Penthouse* is 280 pages, 6 × 9, professionally printed, perfect-bound, with 4-color cover. Receives about 500 poems/year, accepts 3%. Press run is 300 (50 subscribers); 10% distributed free to journals for review consideration. Single copy: $12.50; subscription: $20. Make checks payable to Skidrow Penthouse.

How to Contact Submit 3-5 poems at a time. Considers previously published poems and simultaneous submissions. "Include a legal-sized SASE; name and address on every page of your submission. No handwritten submissions will be considered." Time between acceptance and publication is one year. Seldom comments on rejected poems. Responds in 2 months. Pays one contributor's copy. Acquires one-time rights. Reviews books and chapbooks of poetry and other magazines in 1,500 words, single-book format. Send materials for review consideration.

Additional Information "We're trying to showcase a poet in each issue by publishing up to 60-page collections within the magazine." Send query with SASE.

Tips "We get way too many anecdotal fragments posing as poetry; too much of what we receive feels like this morning's inspiration mailed this afternoon. The majority of those who submit do not seem to have put in the sweat a good poem demands. Also, the ratio of submissions to sample copy purchases is 50:1. Just because our name is *Skidrow Penthouse* does not mean we are a repository for genre work or 'eat, shit, shower, and shave' poetry."

☐ ◎ SKIPPING STONES: A MULTICULTURAL MAGAZINE

(Specialized: poetry by young writers under 18; bilingual; multicultural and social issues; nature/ecology), P.O. Box 3939, Eugene OR 97403. (541)342-4956. E-mail: editor@skippingstones.org. Website: www.skippingstones.org. Established 1988. **Contact:** Arun Toké, editor.

• *Skipping Stones,* now in its 21st year, has been the recipient of EdPress, NAME, and Parent's

Guide Awards, among others.

Magazines Needs *Skipping Stones: A Multicultural Magazine*, published bimonthly during the school year (5 issues), "encourages cooperation, creativity, and celebration of cultural and ecological richness." Wants "poetry by young writers under age 18, on multicultural and social issues, family, freedom—uplifting. No adult poetry, please." *Skipping Stones* is magazine-sized, saddle-stapled, printed on recycled paper. Receives about 500-1,000 poems/year, accepts 10%. Press run is 2,500. Subscription: $25. Sample: $6.

How to Contact Submit up to 5 poems at a time. Lines/poem: 30 maximum. Considers simultaneous submissions; no previously published poems. Accepts e-mail submissions. Cover letter is preferred. "Include your cultural background, experiences, and the inspiration behind your creation." Time between acceptance and publication is 6-9 months. "A piece is chosen for publication when all the editorial staff feel good about it." Seldom comments on rejected poems. Publishes multi-theme issues. Guidelines available for SASE. Responds in up to 4 months. Pays 1 contributor's copy, offers 25% discount for more. Acquires first serial rights and non-exclusive reprint rights.

Contest/Award Offerings Sponsors Annual Youth Honor Awards for 7- to 17-year-olds. Theme is "Multicultural, Social, International, and Nature Awareness." Guidelines available for SASE or on Web site. **Entry fee:** $3 (entitles entrant to a free issue featuring the 10 winners). **Deadline:** June 25.

☑ SLANT: A JOURNAL OF POETRY

Box 5063, University of Central Arkansas, 201 Donaghey Ave., Conway AR 72035-5000. (501)450-5107. Website: www.uca.edu/english/Slant/. Established 1987. **Contact:** James Fowler, editor.

Magazines Needs *Slant: A Journal of Poetry*, published annually in May, aims "to publish a journal of fine poetry from all regions of the United States and beyond." Wants "traditional and 'modern' poetry, even experimental; moderate length, any subject on approval of Board of Readers." Doesn't want "haiku, translations." Has published poetry by Hope Coulter, Paul Hostovsky, Louise Jaffe, Sandra Kohler, Eric Paul Shaffer, and Charles Harper Webb. *Slant* is 120 pages, professionally printed on quality stock, flat-spined, with matte card cover. Receives about 1,300 poems/year, accepts 70-75. Press run is 175 (70-100 subscribers). Sample: $10.

How to Contact Submit up to 5 poems at a time. Lines/poem: poems should be of moderate length. No previously published poems or simultaneous submissions. Submissions should be typed; include SASE. "Put name, address (including e-mail if available), and phone number at the top of each page." Accepts submissions September 1-November 15. Comments on rejected poems "on occasion." Guidelines available in magazine, for SASE, or on Web site. Responds in 3-4 months from November 15 deadline. Pays 1 contributor's copy. Poet retains rights.

Tips "We tend to publish those poems whose execution, line by line, does full justice to their conception. Often the decision to accept comes down to the matter of craft, language."

☐ ◎ SLATE & STYLE

(Specialized: by & for blind writers), 2704 Beach Dr., Merrick NY 11566. (516)868-8718. E-mail: LoriStay@aol.com. Website: www.nfb-writers-division.org. Established 1982. **Contact:** Loraine Stayer, editor.

Magazines Needs *Slate & Style*, published quarterly, is the magazine of the Writers' Division of the National Federation of the Blind. Published for blind writers, *Slate & Style* is available on cassette, in large print, in Braille, and by e-mail, and includes resources and articles of interest to blind writers. "We prefer contributors be blind writers, or at least writers by profession or inclination. New writers welcome. No obscenities. Will consider all forms of poetry including haiku. Interested in new talent." Considers poetry by children and teens, "but please specify age." Has published poetry by Kathy Nimmer, Katherine Barr, Sean Moore, Christopher Barnes, Richard Lighthouse, Anne J. Davidson, and Nancy Scott. *Slate & Style* (print format) is 28-32 pages, magazine-sized, stapled. Press run is 200 (160 subscribers, 4-5 libraries). Subscription/membership: $10/year (regardless of format). Sample: $3.

How to Contact Submit 3 poems at a time once or twice/year. Lines/poem: 5-36. No previously published poems or simultaneous submissions. Accepts submissions by e-mail (pasted into body of message). "On occasion we receive poems in Braille. I prefer print, since Braille slows me down. Typed is best." Cover letter is preferred. Reads submissions according to the following deadlines: February 16, May 15, August 15, November 15; "do not submit manuscripts in July." Comments on rejected poems "if requested." Guidelines available in magazine, for SASE, by e-mail, or on Web site. Responds in 2 weeks "if I like it." Pays 1 contributor's copy. Reviews books of poetry. Send materials for review consideration.

Contest/Award Offerings Sponsors an annual poetry contest, awarding 1st Prize: $100; 2nd Prize: $50; 3rd Prize: $25. Honorable mentions may also be awarded, and winning poems will be published in magazine. **Entry fee:** $5 for up to 3 poems. Make check or money order payable to NFB Writers' Division. "Include cover letter with title and your identifying information." Opens January 1st; **Deadline: June 1.** We are now sponsoring a poetry contest for blind students, K-12. Guidelines available for SASE, by e-mail, or on Web site.

Tips "Before you send us a poem, read it aloud. Does it sound good to you? We put our poetry into tape format, so we want it to sound and look good."

☑ SLIPSTREAM

Dept. W-1, P.O. Box 2071, Niagara Falls NY 14301-0071. (716)282-2616 (after 5 PM, EST). E-mail: editors@slipstreampress.org. Website: www.slipstreampress.org. Established 1980. **Contact:** Dan Sicoli, Robert Borgatti, and Livio Farallo, poetry editors.

Magazines Needs *Slipstream*, published annually in spring, is "about 95% poetry, with some artwork. We like new work with contemporary urban flavor. Writing must have a cutting edge to get our attention. Any length, subject, style. Best to see a sample to get a feel. Like city stuff as opposed to country." Wants "poetry that springs from the gut, screams from dark alleys, inspired by experience." Does not want "pastoral, religious, traditional, rhyming" poetry. Has published poetry by Terry Godbey, Gerald Locklin, David Chorlton, Martin Vest, Beth Royer, and Mofolasayo Ogundiran. *Slipstream* is 80-100 pages, 7x8½, professionally printed, perfect-bound. Receives more than 2,500 poetry submissions/year, accepts less than 10%. Press run is 500 (400 subscribers, 10 libraries). Subscription: $20 for 2 issues and 2 chapbooks. Sample: $10.

How to Contact No e-mail submissions. Sometimes comments on rejected poems. Publishes theme issues. Guidelines available for SASE or on Web site. Responds in up to 2 months "if SASE included." Pays 1-2 contributor's copies.

Contest/Award Offerings *Slipstream* Poetry Chapbook Contest (see separate listing in Contests & Awards).

Tips "Do not waste time submitting your work 'blindly.' Sample issues from the small press first to determine which ones would be most receptive to your work."

$ ☑ SLOPE

340 Richmond Ave., Buffalo NY 14222. E-mail: info@slope.org. Website: www.slope.org. Established 1999. **Contact:** Ethan Paquin, editor-in-chief. Member: CLMP.

- •At press time, *Slope* was not reading submissions. See Web site for updates. Poetry featured in *Slope* has been included in *The Best American Poetry*.

Magazines Needs *Slope*, published biannually online, features "work that is challenging, dynamic, and innovative. We encourage new writers while continuing to publish award-winning and established poets from around the world." Wants "no particular style. Interested in poetry in translation." Has published poetry by Forrest Gander, Paul Hoover, Eleni Sikelianos, James Tate, Bruce Beasley, and Charles Bernstein.

How to Contact Submit 3-6 poems at a time. No previously published poems or simultaneous submissions. Accepts e-mail submissions (as attachments) only. **"Please do not submit poems by postal mail.** Check Web site to see if we are currently reading." Time between acceptance and publication is 3-6 months. Seldom comments on rejected poems. Guidelines available by e-mail or on Web site. Acquires one-time rights.

Contest/Award Offerings Has sponsored the Heart + Express National American Sign Language Poetry Prize. See Web site for details.

☑ SMARTISH PACE

P.O. Box 22161, Baltimore MD 21203. E-mail: sreichert@smartishpace.com. Website: www. smartishpace.com and www.myspace.com/smartishpace. Established 1999. **Contact:** Stephen Reichert, editor.

Magazines Needs *Smartish Pace*, published in April, contains poetry and translations. "*Smartish Pace* is an independent poetry journal and is not affiliated with any institution." No restrictions on style or content of poetry. Has published poetry in the past year by Sherman Alexie, Michael Chitwood, Carol Frost, Vona Groarke, Brenda Hillman, David Rivard, Sappho and Chase Twichell. *Smartish Pace* is about 140 pages, digest-sized, professionally printed, perfect-bound, with full-color cover featuring contemporary artwork. Receives about 5,000 poems/year, accepts 1%. Press run is 1,100. Subscription: $20. Sample: $10.

How to Contact Submit no more than 6 poems at a time. Considers simultaneous submissions; no previously published poems. Responds in 1-5 months. Pays 1 contributor's copy. Acquires first rights. Encourages unsolicited reviews, essays, and interviews. Send materials for review consideration. All books received will also be listed in the Books Received section of each issue and on the Web site along with ordering information and a link to the publisher's Web site.

Contest/Award Offerings *Smartish Pace* hosts the annual Erskine J. Poetry Prize and the Beullah Rose Poetry Prize (for women) (see separate listings in Contests & Awards).

Also Offers Also available on **Poets Q&A, where readers can ask questions of poets and read their responses. Recent participants have included Robert Pinsky, Jorie Graham, Stephen Dunn, Carl Dennis, Eavan Boland, Campbell McGrath, and Robert Hass. "The Web site has constantly updated poetry news and ever expanding audio and video (poetry readings) section."**

Tips "Visit our Web site. Read a few issues."

$ ☑ ◎ SNOWY EGRET

(Specialized: nature-oriented poetry), P.O. Box 9265, Terre Haute IN 47808. Website: www. snowyegret.net. Established 1922 by Humphrey A. Olsen. **Contact:** the editors.

Magazines Needs *Snowy Egret*, published in spring and autumn, specializes in work that is "nature-oriented: poetry that celebrates the abundance and beauty of nature or explores the interconnections between nature and the human psyche." Has published poetry by Conrad Hilberry, Lyn Lifshin, Gayle Eleanor, James Armstrong, and Patricia Hooper. *Snowy Egret* is 60 pages, magazine-sized, offset-printed, saddle-stapled. Receives about 500 poems/year, accepts about 30. Press run is 400. Sample: $8; subscription: $15/year, $25 for 2 years.

How to Contact Guidelines available on Web site. Responds in 1 month. Always sends prepublication galleys. Pays $4/poem or $4/page plus 2 contributor's copies. Acquires first North American and one-time reprint rights.

Tips "First-hand, detailed observation gives poetry authenticity and immediacy."

☑ ◎ SONG OF THE SAN JOAQUIN

(Specialized: subjects pertinent to the San Joaquin Valley), P.O. Box 1161, Modesto CA 95353-1161. E-mail: SSJQ03psj@yahoo.com. Website: www.ChaparralPoets.org/SSJ.html. Established 2003. **Contact:** The Editor.

Magazines Needs *Song of the San Joaquin*, published quarterly, features "subjects about or pertinent to the San Joaquin Valley of Central California. This is defined geographically as the region from Fresno to Stockton, and from the foothills on the west to those on the east." Wants all forms and styles of poetry. "Keep subject in mind." Does not want "pornographic, demeaning, vague, or trite approaches." Considers poetry by children and teens. Has published poetry by Joyce Odam, Wilma Elizabeth McDaniel, Margarita Engle, Marnelle White, Frederick Zydek, and Nancy Haskett. *Song of the San Joaquin* is 60 pages, digest-sized, direct-copied, saddle-stapled, with cardstock cover with glossy color photo. Press run is 200 (25 copies to libraries); 40 distributed free to contributors.

How to Contact Submit up to 3 poems at a time. Lines/poem: open ("however, poems under 40 lines have the best chance"). Considers previously published poems; no simultaneous submissions. E-mail submissions are preferred; no disk submissions. Cover letter is preferred. "SASE required. All submissions must be typed on 1 side of the page only. Proofread submissions carefully. Name, address, phone number, and e-mail address should appear on all pages. Cover letter should include any awards, honors, and previous publications for each poem, and a biographical sketch of 75 words or less." Reads submissions "periodically throughout the year." Submit seasonal poems at least 3 months in advance. Time between acceptance and publication is 3-6 months. "Poems are circulated to an editorial board of 7 who then decide on the final selections." Seldom comments on rejected poems. Occasionally publishes theme issues. Upcoming themes available for SASE, by e-mail, or on Web site. Guidelines available in magazine, for SASE, by e-mail, or on Web site. Responds in up to 3 months. Pays 1 contributor's copy. Acquires one-time rights.

Additional Information "Poets of the San Joaquin, which sponsors this publication, is a chapter of California Federation of Chaparral Poets, Inc., and publishes an annual anthology of members' works. Information available for SASE or by e-mail."

Contest/Award Offerings Poets of the San Joaquin holds an annual local young poets' contest as well as regular poetry contests. Guidelines available for SASE or by e-mail.

Tips "Know the area about which you write. Poems do not need to be agricultural or nature-oriented but should reflect the lifestyles of the California Central Valley."

☑ ◎ SO TO SPEAK

A Feminist Journal of Language and Art (Specialized: women/feminism)George Mason University, 4400 University Dr., MSN 2C5, Fairfax VA 22030-4444. (703)993-3625. E-mail: sts@gmu.edu (inquiries only). Website: www.gmu.edu/org/sts. Established 1991. **Contact:** Megan Ronan, poetry editor.

Magazines Needs *So to Speak*, published semiannually, prints "high-quality work relating to feminism, including poetry, fiction, nonfiction (including book reviews and interviews), photography, artwork, collaborations, lyrical essays, and other genre-questioning texts." Wants "work that addresses issues of significance to women's lives and movements for women's equality and are especially interested in pieces that explore issues of race, class, and sexuality in relation to gender." *So to Speak* is 100-128 pages, digest-sized, photo-offset-printed, perfect-bound, with glossy cover, includes ads. Receives about 800 poems/year, accepts 10%. Press run is 1,000 (75 subscribers, 100 shelf sales); 500 distributed free to students/contributors. Subscription: $12. Sample: $7.

How to Contact Submit 3-5 poems at a time. Considers simultaneous submissions; no previously published poems. No e-mail submissions. "Please submit poems as you wish to see them in print. Be sure to include a cover letter with full contact info, publication credits, and awards received." Reads submissions August 15-October 15 and December 31-March 15. Time between acceptance and publication is 6-8 months. Seldom comments on rejected poems. Responds in 3 months if submissions are received during reading period. Pays 2 contributor's copies. Acquires one-time rights.

Contest/Award Offerings *So to Speak* holds an annual poetry contest that awards $500. Guidelines available for SASE, by e-mail, or on Web site.

☑ SOUL FOUNTAIN

90-21 Springfield Blvd., Queens Village NY 11428. (718)479-2594. E-mail: davault@aol.com. Website: www.TheVault.org. Established 1997. **Contact:** Tone Bellizzi, editor.

Magazines Needs *Soul Fountain*, published 3 times/year, is produced by The Vault, a not-for-profit arts project of the Hope for the Children Foundation, "committed to empowering young and emerging artists of all disciplines at all levels to develop and share their talents through performance, collaboration, and networking." Prints poetry, art, photography, short fiction, and essays. Open to all. "We publish quality submitted work, and specialize in emerging voices. We favor visionary, challenging, and consciousness-expanding material." Does not want "poems about pets, nature, romantic love, or the occult. Sex and violence themes not welcome." Welcomes poetry by teens. *Soul Fountain* is 28 pages, magazine-sized, offset-printed, saddle-stapled. Subscription: $24. Sample: $7. Make checks payable to Hope for the Children Foundation.

How to Contact Submit 2-3 poems at a time. Lines/poem: 1 page maximum. Considers previously published poems and simultaneous submissions. Accepts e-mail submissions (pasted into body of message). Poems should be camera-ready. "When e-mailing a submission, it is necessary to include your mailing address. Cover letter not needed. SASE with postal mail submissions is not necessary, but $2 in postage is appreciated." Time between acceptance and publication is up to 1 year. Guidelines available for SASE or on Web site. Pays 1 contributor's copy.

☑ THE SOUTH CAROLINA REVIEW

Center for Electronic & Digital Publishing, Strode Tower Room 611, Box 340522, Clemson SC 29634-0522. (864)656-3151 or 656-5399. Fax: (864)656-1345. Website: www.clemson.edu/caah/cedp/scrintro.htm. Established 1968. **Contact:** Wayne Chapman, editor.

Magazines Needs *The South Carolina Review*, published semiannually, is a literary magazine "recognized by the *New York Quarterly* as one of the top 20 of this type." Wants "any kind of poetry as long as it's good. Interested in seeing more traditional forms." Does not want "stale metaphors, uncertain rhythms, or lack of line integrity." Has published poetry by Stephen Cushman, Alberto Ríos, and Virgil Suárez. *The South Carolina Review* is 200 pages, digest-sized, professionally printed, flat-spined. Receives about 1,000 submissions of poetry/year, accepts about 100. Press run is 500 (350 subscribers, 250 libraries). Sample: $16.

How to Contact Submit 3-10 poems at a time. No previously published poems or simultaneous submissions. Cover letter is preferred. "Editor prefers a chatty, personal cover letter plus a list of publishing credits. Manuscript format should be according to new MLA Stylesheet." Submissions should be sent "in an 8x10 manila envelope so poems aren't creased." Do not submit during June, July, August, or December. Occasionally publishes theme issues. Responds in 2 months. Pays in contributor's copies. Staff reviews books of poetry.

☑ ◎ SOUTH DAKOTA REVIEW

(Specialized: American West subjects & work by Western authors), Dept. of English, University of South Dakota, 414 E. Clark St., Vermillion SD 57069. (605)677-5184 or 677-5966. Fax: (605)677-6409. E-mail: bbedard@usd.edu. Website: www.usd.edu/sdreview/. Established 1963. **Contact:** Brian Bedard, editor.

Magazines Needs *South Dakota Review*, published quarterly, prints "poetry, fiction, criticism, and scholarly and personal essays. When material warrants, emphasis is on the American West; writers from the West; Western places or subjects. There are frequent issues with no geographical emphasis; periodic special issues on one theme, one place, or one writer." Wants "originality, sophistication, significance, craft—i.e., professional work." Has published poetry by Allan Safarik, Joanna Gardner, Nathaniel Hansen, and Jeanine Stevens. Press run is 500-600 (450 subscribers, half libraries). Single copy: $10; subscription: $30/year, $45/2 years. Sample: $8.

How to Contact Submit 3-5 poems at a time. No e-mail submissions. Cover letter is required. Must include SASE. Reads submissions year round. Time between acceptance and publication is up to 6 months. Sometimes comments on rejected poems. Publishes theme issues. Guidelines available for SASE or on Web site. Responds in 2-3 months ("sometimes longer if still considering manuscript for possible use in a forthcoming issue"). Pays 1 contributor's copy and a one-year subscription. Acquires first North American serial rights and reprint rights.

Tips "We tend to favor the narrative poem, the concrete crafted lyric, the persona poem, and the meditative place poem. Yet we try to leave some room for poems outside those parameters to keep some fresh air in our selection process."

☐ THE SOUTHEAST REVIEW

Dept. of English, Florida State University, Tallahassee FL 32306. (850)644-2773. E-mail: serpoetry@gmail.com. Website: www.southeastreview.org. Established 1979. **Contact:** Rebecca Hazelton, poetry editor.

Magazines Needs *The Southeast Review*, published biannually, looks for "the very best poetry by new and established poets." *The Southeast Review* is 160 pages, digest-sized. Receives about 5,000 poems/year, accepts less than 4%. Press run is 1,000 (500 subscribers, 100 libraries, 200 shelf sales); 100 distributed free. Single copy: $8; subscription: $15/year. Sample: $6. Make checks payable to *The Southeast Review*.

How to Contact Submit 3-5 poems at a time. Considers simultaneous submissions; no previously published poems. Accepts submissions by postal mail only; SASE required. Cover letter is preferred ("very brief"). Reads submissions year round. Time between acceptance and publication is up to 1 year. Seldom comments on rejected poems. Guidelines available for SASE, by e-mail, or on Web site. Responds in up to 3 months. Pays 2 contributor's copies. Acquires first North American serial rights. Reviews books and chapbooks of poetry. "Please query the Book Review Editor (serbookreview@gmail.com) concerning reviews."

Contest/Award Offerings Sponsors an annual poetry contest. Winner receives $500 and publication; 9 finalists will also be published. **Entry fee:** $15 for 3 poems. **Deadline:** March. Guidelines available on Web site.

☑ SOUTHERN CALIFORNIA REVIEW

c/o Master of Professional Writing Program, 3501 Trousdale Parkway, Mark Taper Hall, THH 355J, University of Southern California, Los Angeles CA 90089-0355. (213)740-3252. E-mail:

scr@college.usc.edu. Website: www.usc.edu/scr. Established 1982. **Contact:** Poetry Editor.

Magazines Needs *Southern California Review (SCR)*, published semiannually in the fall and spring, "is the literary journal of the Master of Professional Writing program at the University of Southern California. It has been publishing fiction and poetry since 1982 and now also accepts submissions of creative nonfiction, plays, and screenplays." Features new, emerging, and established authors. Has published poetry by Yevgeny Yevtushenko, Philip Appleman, Tomaz Salamun, Joyce Carol Oates, Bei Ling, and Denise Levertov. *Southern California Review* is about 140 pages, digest-sized, perfect-bound, with a semi-glossy color cover with original artwork. Press run is 1,000. Sample: $10.

How to Contact Submit up to 3 poems at a time. Considers simultaneous submissions, "but please note this in the cover letter and notify us immediately if your submission is accepted for publication elsewhere." No previously published poems. Reads submissions year round. Guidelines available for SASE or on website. Responds in 3-6 months. Pays 2 contributor's copies. Rights revert to poets upon publication; "author is asked to cite appearance in *Southern California Review* when the work is published elsewhere."

Contest/Award Offerings The Ann Stanford Poetry Prize (see separate listing in Contests & Awards).

☑ SOUTHERN HUMANITIES REVIEW

9088 Haley Center, Auburn University, Auburn AL 36849-5202. E-mail: shrengl@auburn.edu. Website: www.auburn.edu/shr. Established 1967. **Contact:** Dan Latimer and Virginia M. Kouidis, co-editors.

Magazines Needs *Southern Humanities Review*, published quarterly, is "interested in poems of any length, subject, genre. Space is limited, and brief poems are more likely to be accepted. Translations welcome, but also send written permission from the copyright holder." Has published poetry by Donald Hall, Andrew Hudgins, Margaret Gibson, Stephen Dunn, Walt McDonald, and R.T. Smith. *Southern Humanities Review* is 100 pages, digest-sized. Press run is 800. Subscription: $15/year. Sample: $5.

How to Contact Submit 3-5 poems at a time. No previously published poems or simultaneous submissions. No e-mail submissions. "Send poems in a business-sized envelope. Include SASE. Avoid sending faint computer printout." Responds in 2 months, "possibly longer in summer." Always sends prepublication galleys. Pays 2 contributor's copies. Copyright reverts to author upon publication. Reviews books of poetry in approximately 750-1,000 words. Send materials for review consideration.

Contest/Award Offerings Sponsors the Theodore Christian Hoepfner Award, a $50 prize for the best poem published in a given volume of *Southern Humanities Review*.

Tips "For beginners, we recommend study and wide reading in English and classical literature, and, of course, American literature—the old works, not just the new. We also recommend study of or exposure to a foreign language and a foreign culture. Poets need the reactions of others to their work: criticism, suggestions, discussion. A good creative writing teacher would be desirable here, and perhaps some course work, too; and then submission of work, attendance at workshops. And again, the reading: history, biography, verse, essays—all of it. We want to see poems that have gone beyond the language of slippage and easy attitudes."

☑ SOUTHERN POETRY REVIEW

Dept. of Languages, Literature and Philosophy, Armstrong Atlantic State University, 11935 Abercorn St., Savannah GA 31419-1997. (912)344-3196. E-mail: rrparham@aug.edu. Website: www.spr.armstrong.edu. Established 1958. **Contact:** Robert Parham, editor. Member: CLMP.

•Work appearing in *Southern Poetry Review* received a 2005 Pushcart Prize.

Magazines Needs *Southern Poetry Review*, published semiannually, is the second oldest poetry journal in the region. Wants "poetry eclectically representative of the genre; no restrictions on form, style, or content." Does not want fiction, essays, or reviews. Has published poetry by Cathy Smith Bowers, Albert Goldbarth, Robert Morgan, Linda Pastan, Margaret Gibson, and R. T. Smith. *Southern Poetry Review* is 70-80 pages, digest-sized, perfect-bound, with 80 lb. matte cardstock cover with b&w photography, includes ads. Receives about 8,000 poems/year, accepts about 2%. Press run is 1,200. Single copy: $6; subscription: $12 individuals, $15 institutions. Make checks payable to *Southern Poetry Review*.

How to Contact Submit 5-7 poems at a time (10 pages maximum). Lines/poem: subject to limitations of space. Considers simultaneous submissions (with notification in cover letter); no previously published poems ("previously published" includes poems published or posted online). No e-mail or disk submissions. Cover letter is preferred. "Include SASE for reply; manuscript returned only if sufficient postage is included." Reads submissions year round. Time between acceptance and publication is 6 months. Poems are circulated to an editorial board ("multiple readers, lively discussion and decision-making"). Sometimes comments on rejected poems. Guidelines available in magazine, for SASE, by e-mail, or on Web site. Responds in 3 months. Always sends prepublication galleys. Pays 2 contributor's copies. Acquires one-time rights.

Tips "We suggest that before submitting, writers read a current issue to get a feel for our journal."

$ ☑ THE SOUTHERN REVIEW

Louisiana State University, Old President's House, Baton Rouge LA 70803. (225)578-5108. Fax: (225)578-5098. E-mail: southernreview@lsu.edu. Website: www.lsu.edu/thesouthernreview. Established 1935 (original series), 1965 (new series). **Contact:** The Editors.

•Work published in *The Southern Review* has been included frequently in *The Best American Poetry* and *The Pushcart Prize* as well as *The Beacon's Best of 1999*.

Magazines Needs *The Southern Review*, published quarterly, prints "fiction, poetry, critical essays, and book reviews, with emphasis on contemporary literature in the U.S. and abroad. Selections are made with careful attention to craftsmanship and technique and to the seriousness of the subject matter." Wants "any variety of poetry that is well crafted, though we cannot normally accommodate excessively long poems (i.e., 10 pages and over)." Has published poetry by Mary Oliver, Sydney Lea, Madeline DeFrees, Brendan Galvin, Claudia Emerson, and Jay Rogoff. *The Southern Review* is 240 pages, digest-sized, flat-spined, with matte card cover. Receives about 6,000 poetry submissions/year. Press run is 2,900 (2,100 subscribers, 70% libraries). Subscription: $25. Sample: $8.

How to Contact Submit up to 1-4 pages of poetry at a time. No previously published poems. No fax or e-mail submissions. "We do not require a cover letter, but we prefer one giving information about the author and previous publications." Reads submissions September-May. Guidelines available for SASE or on website. Responds in 1-2 months. Pays $30/printed page plus 2 contributor's copies. Acquires first North American serial rights. Staff reviews books of poetry in 3,000 words, multi-book format. Send materials for review consideration.

$ ☑ SOUTHWEST REVIEW

Southern Methodist University, P.O. Box 750374, Dallas TX 75275-0374. (214)768-1037. Fax: (214)768-1408. E-mail: swr@smu.edu. Website: www.smu.edu/southwestreview. Established 1915. **Contact:** Willard Spiegelman, editor. •Poetry published in Southwest Review has been included in The Best American Poetry and The Pushcart Prize.

Magazines Needs *Southwest Review*, published quarterly, prints fiction, essays, poetry, and occasional interviews. "We always suggest that potential contributors read several issues of the magazine to see for themselves what we like. We demand very high quality in our poems; we accept both traditional and experimental writing, but avoid unnecessary obscurity and private symbolism. We place no arbitrary limits on length but find shorter poems easier to fit into our format than longer ones. We have no specific limitations as to theme. Poems tend to be lyric and narrative free verse combining a strong voice with powerful topics or situations. Diction is accessible and content often conveys a strong sense of place." Has published poetry by Albert Goldbarth, John Hollander, Mary Jo Salter, James Hoggard, Dorothea Tanning, and Michael Rosen. *Southwest Review* is 144 pages, digest-sized, professionally printed, perfect-bound, with matte text stock cover. Receives about 1,000 poetry submissions/year, accepts about 32. Press run is 1,500. Subscription: $24. Sample: $6.

How to Contact No previously published poems or simultaneous submissions. Submit by mail or on Web site. Mailed manuscripts must be typed and should include SASE for a response. Guidelines available for SASE or on Web site. Responds within 1 month. Always sends prepublication galleys. Pays cash plus contributor's copies.

Contest/Award Offerings The Elizabeth Matchett Stover Memorial Award presents $250 to the author of the best poem or groups of poems (chosen by editors) published in the preceding year. Also offers The Morton Marr Poetry Prize (see separate listing in Contests & Awards).

☑ THE SOW'S EAR POETRY REVIEW

P.O. Box 127, Millwood VA 22646. E-mail: sowsearpoetry@yahoo.com. Website: www.sows-ear. kitenet.net. Established 1988. **Contact:** Kristin Zimet, submissions editor.

Magazines Needs *The Sow's Ear Poetry Review*, published quarterly, wants fine poetry of all styles and lengths. "Excellent art in black and white complements the poems. We often take more than 1 poem by an author we like. The 'Community of Poets' feature presents group submissions; define 'community' as broadly as you like. The 'Crossover' feature showcases works that marry the written word with another art form (for example, lyrics with music, word collages, or special calligraphy)." Has published poetry by Robert Morgan, Elizabeth Spires, Virgil Suárez, Susan Terris, and Franz Wright. *The Sow's Ear Poetry Review* is 32 pages, magazine-sized, professionally printed, saddle-stapled, with matte card cover. Receives about 3,000 poems/year, accepts about 75. Press run is 700 (600 subscribers, 15 libraries). Subscription: $20. Sample: $5. For subscriptions, contact Robert G Lesman, Managing Editor, P.O. Box 127 Millwood VA 22646.

How to Contact Submit up to 5 poems at a time. Considers simultaneous submissions "if you tell us promptly when work is accepted elsewhere"; no previously published poems, although will consider poems from chapbooks if they were never published in a magazine. Previously published poems may be included in 'Crossover' if rights are cleared. No e-mail submissions; postal submissions only. Include brief bio and SASE. Guidelines available for SASE, by e-mail, or on Web site. Responds in 3 months. Pays 2 contributor's copies. Acquires first publication rights. Inquire about reviews, interviews, and essays.

Contest/Award Offerings *The Sow's Ear* Poetry Competition and *The Sow's Ear* Chapbook Contest (see separate listings in Contests & Awards).

Tips "4 criteria help us judge the quality of submissions: 1) Does the poem make the strange familiar or the familiar strange, or both? 2) Is the form of the poem vital to its meaning? 3) Do the sounds of the poem make sense in relation to the theme? 4) Does the little story of the poem open a window on the Big Story of the human situation?"

▣ $ ☐ ◉ SPACEPORTS & SPIDERSILK

P.O. Box 782, Cedar Rapids IA 52406-0782. E-mail: spacesilk@yahoo.com. Website: www. samsdotpublishing.com. Established 2002. **Contact:** Marcie Lynn Tentchoff, editor. Member: The Speculative Literature Foundation.

Magazines Needs *Spaceports & Spidersilk*, published quarterly online, prints "fantasy, science fiction, sword and sorcery, alternate history, myths/folktales, spooky short stories, poems, illustrations, puzzles, nonfiction articles, and movie and book reviews, all for a reading audience of 9-18 years old." Wants "fantasy, science fiction, spooky horror, and speculative poetry" appropriate to age group. Does not want "horror with excessive blood and gore." Considers poetry by children and teens. Has published poetry by Bruce Boston, Karen A. Romanko, Guy Belleranti, Aurelio Rico Lopez III, and Kristine Ong Muslim. Receives about 180 poems/year, accepts about 30 (16%).

How to Contact Submit up to 5 poems at a time. Lines/poem: 25 maximum. Considers previously published poems; no simultaneous submissions. Accepts e-mail submissions only (pasted into body of message). "Submission should include snail mail address and a short (1-2 lines) bio." Reads submissions year round. Submit seasonal poems 6 months in advance. Time between acceptance and publication is 1-3 months. Often comments on rejected poems. Guidelines available on Web site. Responds in 4-6 weeks. Pays $2/original poem, $1/reprint. Acquires first, exclusive worldwide electronic rights for 90 days. Reviews books/chapbooks of poetry. Send materials for review consideration to Tyree Campbell.

Tips "We prefer to see material from younger writers whenever possible."

▦ ☐ SPEEDPOETS ZINE

86 Hawkwood St., Brisbane QLD 4122 Australia. (61)(7)3420-6092. E-mail: geenunn@yahoo. com.au. Website: www.speedpoets.org. Established 2002. **Contact:** Graham Nunn, editor.

Magazines Needs *SpeedPoets Zine*, published monthly, showcases "the community of poets that perform at the monthly SpeedPoets readings in Brisbane, as well as showcasing poets from all around the world." Wants "shorter, experimental pieces." Does not want long submissions. Has published poetry by Robert Smith, Steve Kilbey, Brentley Frazer, Jayne Fenton Keane, Graham Nunn, and Marie Kazalia. *SpeedPoets Zine* is 28 pages, digest-sized, photocopied, folded and stapled, with color cover. Press run is 100. Single copy: $5 for overseas/interstate contributors. Make checks payable to Graham Nunn (in AUD only, or send well-concealed cash).

How to Contact Submit 2 poems at a time. Lines/poem: 25 maximum. Considers previously published poems. Accepts e-mail submissions (pasted into body of message); no disk submissions. Cover letter is preferred. Reads submissions year round. Time between acceptance and publication is 2 weeks. Sometimes comments on rejected poems. Guidelines available by e-mail. Responds in 2 weeks. Rights revert to poet upon publication.

▣ SPILLWAY

P.O. Box 7887, Huntington Beach CA 92615-7887. (714)968-0905. E-mail: spillway2@tebotbach. org. Website: www.tebotbach.org. Established 1991. **Contact:** Mifanwy Kaiser, senior editor/ managing editor or J.D. Lloyd, editor.

Magazines Needs *Spillway*, published annually in August, celebrates "writing's diversity and power to affect our lives." Open to all voices, schools, and tendencies. "We publish poetry, translations, reviews, essays, black-and-white photography, and color artwork and photography for the cover." *Spillway* is about 176 pages, digest-sized, attractively printed, perfect-bound, with 2-color or 4-color card cover. Press run is 2,000. Single copy: $12; subscription: $21 for 2 issues, $33 for 4 issues. All prices include s&h. Make checks payable to *Spillway*. "We recommend ordering a sample copy before you submit, though acceptance does not depend upon purchasing a sample copy."

How to Contact Submit 3-6 poems at a time (6 pages maximum total). Considers previously published poems ("only in rare instances") and simultaneous submissions ("say where also submitted"). Email submissions only (Microsoft Word document attachment); no disk or fax submissions. Cover letter is required. Include brief bio. Responds in up to 6 months. Pays 1 contributor's copy. Acquires one-time rights. Reviews books of poetry in 500-2,500 words. Send materials for review consideration.

☑ SPINNING JENNY

c/o Black Dress Press, P.O. Box 1067, New York NY 10014. Website: www.spinning-jenny.com. Established 1994. **Contact:** C.E. Harrison, editor.

Magazines Needs *Spinning Jenny*, published once/year in the fall (usually September), has published poetry by Tina Cane, Michael Morse, Ryan Murphy, and Sheilah Coleman. *Spinning Jenny* is 96 pages, digest-sized, perfect-bound, with heavy card cover. "We accept less than 5% of unsolicited submissions." Press run is 1,000. Single copy: $8; subscription: $15 for 2 issues.

How to Contact Submit up to 6 poems at a time. No previously published poems or simultaneous submissions. Accepts submissions online (see Web site for guidelines). Reads submissions September 15-May 15 only. Seldom comments on rejected poems. Guidelines available for SASE, by e-mail, or on Web site. Responds within 4 months. Pays 3 contributor's copies. Authors retain rights.

☑ ◎ SPITBALL: THE LITERARY BASEBALL MAGAZINE

(Specialized: writing about baseball), 5560 Fox Rd., Cincinnati OH 45239. Website: www. angelfire.com/oh5/spitball. Established 1981. **Contact:** Mike Shannon, editor-in-chief.

Magazines Needs *Spitball: The Literary Baseball Magazine*, published semiannually, is "a unique magazine devoted to poetry, fiction, and book reviews exclusively about baseball. Newcomers are very welcome, but remember that you have to know the subject; we do, and our readers do. Perhaps a good place to start for beginners is one's personal reactions to the game, a game, a player, etc., and take it from there." **Writers submitting to *Spitball* for the first time must buy a sample copy (waived for subscribers). "This is a one-time-only fee, which we regret, but economic reality dictates that we insist those who wish to be published in *Spitball* help support it, at least at this minimum level." *Spitball* is 96 pages, digest-sized, computer-typeset, perfect-bound. Receives about 1,000 submissions/year, accepts about 40. Press run is 1,000. Subscription: $12. Sample: $6.**

How to Contact Submit a "batch" of poems at a time ("we prefer to use several of same poet in an issue rather than a single poem"). Lines/poem: open. No previously published poems or simultaneous submissions. Cover letter is required. Include brif bio and SASE. "Many times we are able to publish accepted work almost immediately." Pays 2 contributor's copies.

Additional Information "All material published in *Spitball* will be automatically considered for inclusion in the next *Best of Spitball* anthology."

Contest/Award Offerings 1) Poems submitted to *Spitball* will be considered automatically for Poem of the Month, to appear on the website. 2) "We sponsor the Casey Award (for best baseball book of the year) and hold the Casey Awards Banquet in late February or early March. Any chapbook of baseball poetry should be sent to us for consideration for the 'Casey' plaque that we award to the winner each year."

Tips "Take the subject seriously. We do. In other words, get a clue (if you don't already have one) about the subject and about the poetry that has already been done and published about base-ball. Learn from it—think about what you can add to the canon that is original and fresh—and don't assume that just anybody with the feeblest of efforts can write a baseball poem worthy of publication. And most importantly, stick with it. Genius seldom happens on the first try."

▣ ☐ SPLIZZ

4 St. Marys Rise, Burry Port, Carms SA16 0SH Wales. E-mail: splizzmag@yahoo.co.uk. Established 1993. **Contact:** Amanda Morgan, editor.

Magazines Needs *Splizz*, published quarterly, features poetry, prose, reviews of contemporary music, and background to poets. Wants "any kind of poetry. We have no restrictions regarding style, length, subjects." Does not want "anything racist or homophobic." Has published Colin Cross (UK), Anders Carson (Canada), Paul Truttman (U.S.), Jan Hansen (Portugal), and Gregory Arena (Italy). *Splizz* is 60-64 pages, A5, saddle-stapled, includes ads. Receives about 200-300 poems/year, accepts about 90%. Press run is 150 (35 subscribers). Single copy: £2 UK; subscription: £8 UK. Email for current rates. Payments accepted in cash or paypal to splizz@tiscali.co.uk. No checks please.

How to Contact Submit 5 poems at a time. No previously published poems or simultaneous submissions. Accepts e-mail submissions (as attachment). Cover letter is required. Include short bio. Typed submissions preferred. Name and address must be included on each page of submitted work. Include SAE with IRCs. Time between acceptance and publication is 4 months. Often comments on rejected poems. **Charges criticism fee.** "Just enclose SAE/IRC for response, and allow 1-2 months for delivery. For those sending IRCs, please ensure that they have been correctly stamped by your post office." Guidelines available in magazine, for SASE (or SAE and IRC), or by e-mail. Responds in 2 months. Sometimes sends prepublication galleys. Reviews books/chapbooks of poetry or other magazines in 50-300 words. Send materials for review consideration. E-mail for further enquiries.

Tips "Beginners seeking to have their work published, send your work to *Splizz*, as we specialize in giving new poets a chance to see their work published alongside more established writers."

☑ THE SPOON RIVER POETRY REVIEW

4241/Publications Unit, Illinois State University, Normal IL 61790-4241. Website: www.litline. org/spoon. Established 1976. **Contact:** Bruce Guernsey, editor and Tara Reeser, associate editor.

Magazines Needs *The Spoon River Poetry Review*, published semiannually, features "newer and well-known poets from around the country and world." Also features one Illinois poet per issue at length with an interview, biography, and several poems. Wants "compelling original poetry and translations that have a strong sense of the line." Also considers submissions for the journal's new feature, "Poets on Teaching," a 1,000 word practical essay written for, and by, teachers of poetry writing. *The Spoon River Poetry Review* is 128 pages, digest-sized, laser-set, with card cover. Receives about 3,000 poems/month, accepts 1%. Press run is 1,500. Subscription: $16. Sample: $10 (includes guidelines).

How to Contact Submit 3-5 poems at a time. No simultaneous submissions "unless we are notified immediately if a submission is accepted elsewhere. Include name and address, including e-mail address, on every poem." Do not submit mss April 15-September 15. Comments on rejected poems "many times, if a poet is promising." Guidelines available in magazine or on Web site. Responds in 3 months. Pays a year's subscription. Acquires first North American serial rights. Reviews books of poetry. Send materials for review consideration.

Contest/Award Offerings Sponsors *The Spoon River Poetry Review* Editor's Prize Contest (see separate listing in Contests & Awards).

Tips "Read and workshop with poets who are better than you. Subscribe to at least 5 literary magazines per year, especially those you'd like to be published in."

☑ SP QUILL MAGAZINE

Shadow Poetry, 1209 Milwaukee St., Excelsior Springs MO 64024. Phone/fax: (208)977-9114. E-mail: spquill@shadowpoetry.com. Website: www.shadowpoetry.com/magazine/spquill.html. Established 2000 (Shadow Poetry Web site), 2003 (SP Quill). **Contact:** Marie Summers, chief editor. Poetry Editor: Andrea Dietrich.

Magazines Needs *SP Quill Magazine* is "an interactive perfect-bound magazine for poets and writers, filled with poetry, flash fiction, book reviews, articles, contests, profiles/bios, artwork, quotes, and more." Wants high-quality poetry, flash fiction, and quotes. Does not want "anything in poor taste, or poorly crafted poetry." Considers poetry by children (parental permission required) and teens. *SP Quill Quarterly Magazine* is 60-150 pages, perfect-bound, glossy cover with artwork (cover design remains the same from issue to issue; artwork and photos are considered for the back cover). Receives about 500 poems/quarter, accepts less than 10%. Single copy: $15 U.S., $20 international. Make checks/money orders payable to Shadow Poetry.

How to Contact Submit up to 5 poems at a time. Lines/poem: 3 minimum, 30 maximum. No previously published poems or simultaneous submissions. Accepts fax, e-mail, disk, and postal submissions as well as submissions through online form. Cover letter is preferred. "Name of author, street address, and e-mail address must accompany all submissions, no exceptions. A small author bio may accompany submission. If work is accepted, participants will be contacted by mail or e-mail before magazine release date." Reads submissions by the following deadlines: February 28 (May issue) and August 31 (November issue). Welcomes seasonal poems for the appropriate issue. Time between acceptance and publication is 3 weeks or more. "Poems are decided upon and edited by the poetry editor and chief editor. Final drafts will be e-mailed or mailed to the accepted poet." Never comments on rejected poems. Publishes special issues; "submit up to eight cinquain for a special Spring issue and/or 3 etheree for a special Fall issue. For definitions of these poetry types, please visit the Shadow Poetry Web site." Guidelines available in magazine or on Web site. Acquires first rights. Reviews books/chapbooks of poetry.

Additional Information Shadow Poetry sponsors Shadows Ink Poetry Contest, Shadow Poetry's Annual Chapbook Competition, (see separate listings in Contests & Awards).

☑ ◎ SPRING: THE JOURNAL OF THE E.E. CUMMINGS SOCIETY

129 Lake Huron Hall, Grand Valley State University, Allendale MI 49401-9403. (616)331-3071. Fax: (616)331-3430. E-mail: websterm@gvsu.edu. Website: www.gvsu.edu/english/cummings/Index.html. **Contact:** Michael Webster, editor.

Magazines Needs *Spring: The Journal of the E.E. Cummings Society*, published annually (usually in the fall), is designed "to broaden the audience for E.E. Cummings, and to explore various facets of his life and art." **Contributors are required to subscribe.** Wants poems in the spirit of Cummings, primarily poems of one page or less. Does not want "amateurish" work. Has published poetry by John Tagliabue, Jacqueline Vaught Brogan, and Gerald Locklin. *Spring* is about 180 pages, digest-sized, offset-printed, perfect-bound, with light cardstock cover. Press run is 400 (200 subscribers, 25 libraries, 200 shelf sales). Subscription or sample: $17.50.

How to Contact No previously published poems or simultaneous submissions. Accepts fax and e-mail (as attachment) submissions. Cover letter is required. Reads submissions May-August only. Seldom comments on rejected poems. Guidelines available for SASE. Responds in 6 months. Pays 1 contributor's copy.

$ ☐ ◎ ST. ANTHONY MESSENGER

(Specialized: Catholic; spirituality/inspirational), 28 W. Liberty St., Cincinnati OH 45202-6498. Fax: (513)241-0399. Website: www.americancatholic.org. **Contact:** Christopher Heffron, poetry editor.

- •*St. Anthony Messenger* poetry occasionally receives awards from the Catholic Press Association Annual Competition.

Magazines Needs *St. Anthony Messenger*, published monthly, is a mgazine for Catholic families, mostly with children in grade school, high school, or college. Some issues feature a poetry page that uses poems appropriate for their readership. Poetry submissions are always welcome despite limited need. "We seek to publish accessible poetry of high quality. Spiritual/inspirational in nature a plus, but not required." Considers poetry by young writers, ages 14 and older. *St. Anthony Messenger* is 60 pages. Press run 280,000. Sample: free for 9x12 SASE.

How to Contact Submit "a few" poems at a time. Lines/poem: under 25. No previously published poems. Accepts fax and e-mail submissions. "Please include your phone number and a SASE with your submission. Do not send us your entire collection of poetry. Poems must be original." Submit seasonal poems several months in advance. Guidelines available for SASE, by fax, or on Web site. Pays $2/line on acceptance plus 2 contributor's copies. Acquires first worldwide serial rights.

▦ $ ☑ STAPLE

114-116 St. Stephen's Rd., Sneinton, Nottingham NG2 4FJ England. Established 1982 (redesigned 2001). **Contact:** Wayne Burrows, editor.

Magazines Needs *Staple*, published 3 times/year, accepts "poetry, short fiction, and articles about the writing process and general culture in relation to writing, plus some artwork and photography." *Staple* is about 150 pages, perfect-bound. Press run is 500 (350 subscribers). Single copy: £7.99; subscription: £20/year, £30/year overseas. Sample: £5.00 (back issue).

How to Contact Submit 6 poems or 1-2 stories/essays at a time. No previously published poems or simultaneous submissions. Cover letter with author bio note is preferred. Include SAE and 2 IRCs. Reads submissions by the following deadlines: end of March, July, and November. Sometimes comments on rejected poems. Responds in up to 3 months. Pays £25/poem, £25/story/essay.

$ ▨ STAR*LINE

(Specialized: science fiction, fantasy, horror), Science Fiction Poetry Association, 1412 NE 35th St., Ocala FL 34479. E-mail: SFPASL@aol.com. Website: www.sfpoetry.com. Established 1978. **Contact:** Marge Simon, editor.

Magazines Needs *Star*Line*, published bimonthly by the Science Fiction Poetry Association (see separate listing in Organizations), is a newsletter and poetry magazine. "Open to all forms—free verse, traditional forms, light verse—as long as your poetry shows skilled use of the language and makes a good use of science fiction, science, fantasy, horror, or speculative motifs." *Star*Line* is digest-sized, saddle-stapled. Receives about 300-400 submissions/year, accepts about 80. Has 250 subscribers. Subscription: $13 for 6 issues. Sample: $2. Send requests for copies/membership information to Samantha Henderson, SFPA Treasurer, P.O. Box 4846, Covina, CA 91723. Send submissions to *Star*Line* only.

How to Contact Submit 3-5 poems at a time. Lines/poem: preferably under 50. No simultaneous submissions. Accepts e-mail submissions (preferred; pasted into body of message, no attachments). Cover letter is preferred (brief). Submissions must be typed. Responds in 1 month. Pays $3 for 10 lines or less; $5 for 11-50 lines; 10¢ per line rounded to the next dollar for 51 + lines. Buys first North American serial rights. Reviews books of poetry "within the science fiction/fantasy field" in 50-500 words. Open to unsolicited reviews. Send materials for review consideration.

Also Offers The Association also publishes *The Rhysling Anthology*, a yearly collection of nominations from the membership "for the best science fiction/fantasy long and short poetry of the preceding year and *Dwarf Stars*, an annual collection of poetry ten lines or fewer."

☐ STEPPING STONES MAGAZINE: A LITERARY MAGAZINE FOR INNOVATIVE ART

First Step Press, P.O. Box 902, Norristown PA 19404-0902. E-mail: info@fspressonline.org. Website: www.fspressonline.org. Established 1996; reestablished 2009. **Contact:** Trinae A. Ross, publisher (editor@fspressonline.org).

Magazines Needs *Stepping Stones Magazine: A Literary Magazine for Innovative Art*, published 4 times/year online, delivered as a PDF document, seeks "poetry as diverse as are the authors themselves. Poems should have something to say other than, 'Hi, I'm a poem please publish me.'" Does not want "poems that promote intolerance for race, religion, gender, or sexual preference." Has published poetry by Clayton Vetter, Michael Hathaway, and Ivan Silverberg. Receives about 300 poems/year, accepts about 10-15%. Reviews chapbooks, Web sites, and other publications of interest to poets.

How to Contact Submit no more than 5 poems at a time. Considers previously published poems and simultaneous submissions. Prefers e-mail submissions; should include cover letter and formatted with a simple font and saved as .doc, .rtf, or .odf. Attach submissions and cover letter to e-mail and send to poetry@fspressonline.org. Read submissions year round. Guidelines available for SASE, by sending an e-mail to guidelines @fspressonline.org, or on Web site. Responds within 2 months. Pays one contributor's copy and free advertising space, though will implement a pay schedule when funding permits. Acquires one-time print and electronic rights.

Also Offers "Free advertising space is available for those wishing to promote their website, book, or other literary venture. The continuing goal of First Step Press is to provide sanctuary for new and established writers, to hone their skills and commune with one another within the comfort of our electronic pages."

Tips "The continued goal of *Stepping Stones Magazine: ALMIA* is to establish new poets with help from those more established in the poetry community. Your best chance of being published is to 1) read the guidelines, 2) follow the guidelines, and 3) be yourself. We are not looking for the next anyone...we are looking for the first you."

☑ ◎ THE WALLACE STEVENS JOURNAL

(Specialized: poems about/in the spirit of Wallace Stevens), Arts and Sciences, Clarkson University, Box 5750, Potsdam NY 13699-5750. (315)268-3987. Fax: (315)268-3983. E-mail: serio@clarkson.edu. Website: www.wallacestevens.com. Established 1977. **Contact:** Prof. Joseph Duemer, poetry editor (jduemer@clarkson.edu).

Magazines Needs *The Wallace Stevens Journal*, published semiannually by the Wallace Stevens Society, uses "poems about or in the spirit of Wallace Stevens or having some relation to his work. No bad parodies of Stevens's anthology pieces." Has published poetry by David Athey, Jacqueline Marcus, Charles Wright, X.J. Kennedy, A.M. Juster, and Robert Creeley. *The Wallace Stevens Journal* is 96-120 pages, digest-sized, typeset, flat-spined, with glossy cover with art. Receives 200-300 poems/year, accepts 15-20. Press run is 700. Subscription: $30 (includes membership in the Wallace Stevens Society). Sample: $10.

How to Contact Submit 1-4 poems at a time. No previously published poems, "though we have made a few exceptions to this rule." No fax or e-mail submissions, "though requests for information are fine." Cover letter is encouraged, but keep brief. Send clean, readable copy. Responds in up to 10 weeks. Always sends prepublication galleys. Pays 2 contributor's copies.

Acquires all rights. Returns rights with permission and acknowledgment. Staff reviews books of poetry. Send materials for review consideration "only if there is some clear connection to Stevens."

Tips "Please don't submit to *The Wallace Stevens Journal* if you have not read Stevens. We like parodies, but they must add a new angle of perception. Most of the poems we publish are not parodies but meditations on themes related to Wallace Stevens and those poets he has influenced. Those wishing to contribute might want to examine a previous issue."

◪ $ ☐ STICKMAN REVIEW

An Online Literary Journal721 Oakwater Lane, Port Orange FL 32128. E-mail: poetry@stickmanreview.com. Website: www.stickmanreview.com. Established 2001.

Magazines Needs *Stickman Review*, published semiannually online, is dedicated to printing great poetry, fiction, nonfiction, and artwork. Wants poetry "that is literary in intent; no restrictions on form, subject matter, or style." Does not typically want "rhyming poetry."

How to Contact Submit no more than 5 poems at a time. Considers simultaneous submissions; no previously published poems. Accepts e-mail submissions only (as attachment in Word, .rtf or .txt, or pasted into body of message); no postal submissions. Cover letter is preferred. Reads submissions year round. Time between acceptance and publication is 4-6 months. "Currently, the editors-in-chief review all submissions." Rarely comments on rejected poems. Guidelines available on Web site. Responds in up to 6 months. Pays $10/poem, up to $20/author. Acquires first rights.

Tips "Keep writing and submitting. A rejection is not necessarily a reflection upon the quality of your work. Be persistent, trust your instincts, and sooner or later, good things will come."

☐ ◎ STILL CRAZY

An Online Literary Journal721 Oakwater Lane, Port Orange FL 32128. E-mail: poetry@stickmanreview.com. Website: www.stickmanreview.com. Established 2001. (Specialized: writing by & about people over 50), E-mail: editor@crazylitmag.com. Website: www.crazylitmag.com. Established 2007. **Contact:** Barbara Kussow.

Magazines Needs *Still Crazy*, published biannually in January and July, publishes "poetry, short stories, and some short nonfiction pieces by and about people over fifty years of age." Wants "poems that tell a story." Does not want "rhyming poetry, or poetry that is too sentimental." *Still Crazy* is magazine-sized. Single copy, paper: $9; download: $3; subscription: $16/year. Use PayPal or contact editor if you wish to pay by check.

How to Contact Submit 3-5 poems at a time. Lines/poem: 30 maximum. Considers previously published poems and simultaneous submissions. Accepts e-mail submissions only (as attachment or cut and paste into body of e-mail). Cover letter is preferred; tell editor you are over fifty or writing about someone over fifty. Reads submissions year round. Time between acceptance and publication is up to one year. Sometimes comments on rejected poems. Sometimes publishes theme issues. Guidelines available on Web site. Responds in 6 months. Sometimes sends prepublication galleys. Pays one contributor's copy. Acquires one-time rights. Rights revert to poet upon publication.

$ ☐ ◎ STONE SOUP, THE MAGAZINE BY YOUNG WRITERS AND ARTISTS

Submissions Dept., P.O. Box 83, Santa Cruz CA 95063. (831)426-5557. Fax: (831)426-1161. E-mail: editor@stonesoup.com. Website: www.stonesoup.com. Established 1973. **Contact:** Ms. Gerry Mandel, editor.

•*Stone Soup* has received Parents' Choice and Edpress Golden Lamp Honor Awards.

Magazines Needs *Stone Soup*, published 6 times/year, showcases writing and art by children ages 13 and under. Wants free verse poetry. Does not want rhyming poetry, haiku, or cinquain. *Stone Soup* is 48 pages, 7x10, professionally printed in color on heavy stock, saddle-stapled, with coated cover with full-color illustration. Receives 5,000 poetry submissions/year, accepts about 12. Press run is 20,000 (14,000 subscribers, 5,000 shelf sales, 1,000 other). Subscription: membership in the Children's Art Foundation includes a subscription, $37/year. Sample: $5.

How to Contact No simultaneous submissions. No e-mail submissions. "Submissions can be any number of pages, any format. Include name, age, home address, and phone number. Don't include SASE; we respond only to those submissions under consideration and cannot return manuscripts." Guidelines available on website. Responds in up to 6 weeks. Pays $40, a certificate, and 2 contributor's copies plus discounts. Acquires all rights. Returns rights upon request. Open to reviews by children.

☐ THE STORYTELLER

2441 Washington Rd., Maynard AR 72444. (870)647-2137. E-mail: storyteller1@hightowercom. com. Website: www.thestorytellermagazine.com. Established 1996. **Contact:** Regina Williams, editor.

Magazines Needs *The Storyteller*, published quarterly, "is geared to, but not limited to, new writers and poets." Wants "any form, any subject, any style, but must have a meaning. Do not throw words together and call it a poem." Does not want "explicit sex, violence, horror, or explicit language. I would like it to be understood that I have young readers, ages 9-18." Considers poetry by children and teens. Has published poetry by Patrick Lobrutto, Bryan Byrd, and Gerald Zipper. *The Storyteller* is 72 pages, magazine-sized, desktop-published, with slick cover black and white photography, includes ads. Receives about 300 poems/year, accepts about 40%. Press run is 700 (more than 600 subscribers). Single copy: $6 U.S., $8 Canada and foreign; subscription: $20 U.S., $24 Canada & foreign.

How to Contact Submit 3 poems at a time, 1 poem per age. Lines/poem: up to 40. Considers previously published poems and simultaneous submissions, "but must state where and when poetry first appeared." No e-mail submissions; postal submissions only. "However, if accepted, you will be asked to send material by e-mail, if possible." Cover letter is preferred. Manuscripts must be typed and double-spaced. "Make sure name and address are on each page submitted. We are getting many submissions without names." Time between acceptance and publication is 9 months. "Poems are read and discussed by staff." Sometimes comments on rejected poems. Guidelines available for SASE or on Web site. Responds in 1 week. Pays $1 per poem; does not provide contributor's copies. Acquires first or one-time rights. Reviews books/chapbooks of poetry by subscribers only. Send materials for review consideration to Jamie Johnson, assistant editor.

Contest/Award Offerings Sponsors a quarterly contest. "Readers vote on their favorite poems. Winners receive a copy of the magazine and a certificate. We also nominate for the Pushcart Prize." See Web site for yearly contest announcements and winners.

Tips "Be professional. Do not send 4 or 5 poems on 1 page. Send us poetry written from the heart."

▣ ☑ STRAY BRANCH, THE

E-mail: thestraybranchlitmag@yahoo.com. Website: www.thestraybranch.org. Established 2008. Contact: D. Spencer-Berk, editor/publisher. **Magazine Needs** The Stray Branch, published twice per year, is an online journal " open to form and style but prefers free verse. Open to subject matter but prefers edgy, raw material written from the gut that reflects the heart and human experience. Wants poetry by real people that can be understood by all readers. The Stray Branch prefers works of a darker nature." Does not want " over-schooled, arrogant, self-righteous, religious, political, erotic poetry, or happy and light, pretty poetry. Not interested in rants, tantrums, and the use of profanity that is not fitting to the piece. Please, be tactful and respectful of the language." Has published poetry by Andy Robertson, Keith Estes, Kate Sjostrand, Lena Vanelslander, Michael Grover, and Justin Blackburn.

How to Contact Submit 6 poems at a time. "Maximum length for poems is no longer than 1 page, shorter poems are preferred and stand a better chance." Considers previously published poems; no simultaneous submissions. (Considers poetry posted on a public Web site/blog/forum and poetry posted on a private, password-protected forum as published.) Accepts e-mail submissions (pasted into body of message); no fax or disk submissions. Cover letter is unnecessary. Reads submissions October-July. Sometimes comments on rejected poems. Guidelines available on Web site. Responds in 3 weeks. Acquires one-time rights. Rights revert to poets upon publication.

☐ STRAYLIGHT

University of Wisconsin-Parkside, English Dept., 900 Wood Rd., P.O. Box 2000, Kenosha WI 53141. (262)595-2139. Fax: (262)595-2271. E-mail: straylight@litspot.net. Website: www.litspot.net/straylight. Established 2005. **Contact:** Poetry Editor.

Magazines Needs *Straylight*, published biannually, seeks "poetry of almost any style as long as it's inventive." *Straylight* is digest-sized. Single copy: $6; subscription: $10. Make checks payable to *Straylight*.

How to Contact Submit 3-6 poems at a time. No previously published poems or simultaneous submissions. Accepts e-mail submissions (preferred, as .rtf or .doc attachment); no fax or disk submissions. Cover letter is required. "Include contact information on all pages of submission." Reads submissions August 15-April 15. Submit seasonal poems 3 months in advance. Time between acceptance and publication is 6 months. Never comments on rejected poems. Sometimes publishes theme issues. Upcoming themes available on website. Guidelines available for SASE or on website. Responds in 2 months. Pays 2 contributor's copies. Additional payment when funding permits. Acquires first North American serial rights. Rights revert to poet upon publication.

Tips "We suggest you buy a sample copy to get a feel for what we publish."

▦ ▣ ☑ STRIDE MAGAZINE

Stride Publications, 4b Tremayne Close, Devoran, Cornwall TR3 6QE England. E-mail: submissions@stridemagazine.co.uk (submissions) or editor@stridemagazine.co.uk (inquiries). Website: www.stridemagazine.co.uk. Established 1982. **Contact:** Rupert Loydell, editor.

Magazines Needs *Stride Magazine*, published online, is "a gathering of new poetry, short prose, articles, news, reviews, and whatever takes our fancy. *Stride* is regularly updated with new contributions."

How to Contact Submit 4-5 poems at a time. Accepts e-mail submissions (pasted into body of message; no attachments). "Attachments or snail mail without SAEs will not be considered or replied to."

☐ ◎ STRUGGLE: A MAGAZINE OF PROLETARIAN REVOLUTIONARY LITERATURE

P.O. Box 13261, Detroit MI 48213-0261. (313)273-9039. E-mail: timhall11@yahoo.com. Website: www.strugglemagazine.net. Established 1985. **Contact:** Tim Hall, editor.

Magazines Needs *Struggle: A Magazine of Proletarian Revolutionary Literature*, published quarterly, focuses "on the struggle of the working people and all oppressed against the rich, dealing with such issues as racism, poverty, women's rights, aggressive wars, workers' struggle for jobs and job security, the overall struggle for a non-exploitative society, a genuine socialism." The poetry and songs printed are "generally short, any style; subject matter must criticize or fight—explicitly or implicitly—against the rule of the billionaires. We welcome experimentation devoted to furthering such content. We are open to both subtlety and direct statement." Has published poetry by Joseph Lampert, Shawn Crawford, ysabel Y. Gonzalez, Lisa Dawn Hilliker, Bob Vance, Louise Hammonds, Steve Moore, Traci Luker and Francee Bouvenire. *Struggle* is 36 pages, digest-sized, photocopied. Subscription: $10/year (4 issues); $12 for institutions, $15 for foreign, $5 for prisoners. Sample: $5 (for the now-customary double-sized issue of 72 pages). Make checks payable to "Tim Hall—Special Account (not to *Struggle*)."

How to Contact Submit up to 8 poems at a time. Accepts e-mail submissions (pasted into body of message, no attachments), but prefers postal mail. "Writers must include SASE. Name and address must appear on the opening page of each poem." Accepted work usually appears in the next or following issue. Comments on rejected poems "with every submission." Responds in 4 months, if possible, but often becomes backlogged. Pays one contributor's copy. "If you are unwilling to have your poetry published on our Web site, please inform us."

Tips "Show passion and fire. Humor also welcome. Prefer powerful, colloquial language over academic timidity. Look to Neruda, Lorca, Bly, Whitman, Braithwaite, Tupac Shakur, Muriel Rukeyser. Experimental, traditional forms both welcome. Especially favor: works reflecting rebellion by the working people against the rich; works against racism, sexism, militarism, imperialism; works critical of our exploitative culture; works showing a desire for—or fantasy of—a non-exploitative society; works attacking the Republican 'anti-terrorism' war frenzy and the Democrats' surrender to it."

⊞ ☑ ◎ STUDIO, A JOURNAL OF CHRISTIANS WRITING

727 Peel St., Albury NSW 2640 Australia. Phone/fax: (61)(2)6021-1135. E-mail: studio00@ bigpond.net.au. Established 1980. **Contact:** Paul Grover, publisher.

Magazines Needs *Studio, A Journal of Christians Writing*, published quarterly, prints "poetry and prose of literary merit, offering a venue for previously published, new, and aspiring writers, and seeking to create a sense of community among Christians writing." Also publishes occasional articles as well as news and reviews of writing, writers, and events of interest to members. Wants "shorter pieces [of poetry] but with no specification as to form or length (necessarily less than 200 lines), subject matter, style, or purpose. People who send material should be comfortable being published under this banner: *Studio, A Journal of Christians Writing*." Has published poetry by John Foulcher, Les Murray, and other Australian poets. *Studio* is 36 pages, digest-sized, professionally printed on high-quality recycled paper, saddle-stapled, with matte card cover. Press run is 300 (all subscriptions). Subscription: $60 AUD for overseas members. Sample: $10 AUD (airmail to U.S.).

How to Contact Lines/poem: less than 200. Considers simultaneous submissions. Cover letter is required. Include brief details of previous publishing history, if any. SAE with IRC required. "Submissions must be typed and double-spaced on one side of A4 white paper. Name and address must appear on the reverse side of each page submitted." Response time is 2 months. Time between acceptance and publication is 9 months. Pays 1 contributor's copy. Acquires first Australian rights. Reviews books of poetry in 250 words, single-book format. Send materials for review consideration.

Contest/Award Offerings Conducts a biannual poetry and short story contest.

Tips "The trend in Australia is for imagist poetry and poetry exploring the land and the self. Reading the magazine gives the best indication of style and standard, so send for a sample copy before sending your poetry. Keep writing, and we look forward to hearing from you."

☑ STUDIO ONE

Mary Commons, College of St. Benedict, St. Joseph MN 56374. E-mail: studio1@csbsju.edu. Website: http://clubs.csbsju.edu/studio1. Established 1976. **Contact:** Editor (changes yearly).

Magazines Needs *Studio One*, published annually in May, is a "literary and visual arts magazine designed as a forum for local, regional, and national poets/writers. No specifications regarding form, subject matter, or style of poetry submitted." Considers poetry by children and teens. Has published poetry by Bill Meissner, Eva Hooker, and Larry Schug. *Studio One* is 50-80 pages, typeset, with soft cover. Receives 600-800 submissions/year. No subscriptions, but a sample copy can be obtained by sending a self-addressed, stamped manila envelope and $6 for p&h. Make checks payable to *Studio One*.

How to Contact Submit no more than 5 poems at a time. Lines/poem: "poetry no more than 2 pages stands a better chance of publication." Considers simultaneous submissions; no previously published poems. Accepts e-mail submissions (pasted into body of message); "clearly show page breaks and indentations." Reads submissions by March 1 deadline for spring publication. Seldom comments on rejected poems.

$ ☑ THE SUN

107 N. Roberson St., Chapel Hill NC 27516. Website: www.thesunmagazine.org. Established 1974. **Contact:** Sy Safransky, editor.

Magazines Needs *The Sun*, published monthly, is "noted for honest, personal work that's not too obscure or academic. "We favor poetry that is accessible and emotionally evocative." We avoid traditional, rhyming poetry, as well as limericks and haiku. We're open to almost anything else: free verse, prose poems, short and long poems." Has published poetry by Ellen Bass, Christopher Bursk, Steve Kowit, Alison Luterman, Naomi Shihab Nye, Ellery Akers, and Tess Gallagher. *The Sun* is 48 pages, magazine-sized, offset-printed on 50 lb. paper, saddle-stapled. Press run is 80,000 (70,000 subscribers, 500 libraries). Receives 3,000 submissions of poetry/year, accepts about 30. Subscription: $36. Sample: $5.

How to Contact Submit up to 6 poems at a time. Considers previously published poems but strongly prefers unpublished work; no simultaneous submissions. "Poems should be typed and accompanied by a cover letter and SASE." Guidelines available for SASE or on Web site. Responds within 3-6 months. Pays $100-500 on publication plus contributor's copies and subscription. Acquires first serial or one-time rights.

▣ ▢ SUNKEN LINES

E-mail: dogger@sunkenlines.com. Website: www.sunkenlines.com. Established 2005. **Contact:** Dogger Banks, poetry editor.

Magazines Needs *Sunken Lines*, published quarterly online, is a magazine of poetry, fiction, essays, and artwork "intended as a forum for talented writers looking for more exposure, and as entertainment for our readers. We also publish an annual print edition." Wants "poems that evoke a strong response in the reader, whether it be laughter, empathy, the conjuring of a strong image, or admiration of a witty line. Formal or (accessible) free verse." Does not want "poems that are excessively religious, offensive, or miserable." Has published poetry by Larry Rapant, Tony Gruenewald, Suzanne Harvey, Anna Evans, Paul Lench, and Bruce Niedt. *Sunken Lines* (the print annual) is 24 pages, A4-sized, laser-printed, saddle-stapled. Receives about 500 poems/year, accepts about 20%. Press run is 150. Single copy: $5. Make checks payable to R. Grainger.

How to Contact Submit up to 5 poems at a time. Lines/poem: 40 maximum. Considers simultaneous submissions; no previously published poems. Accepts e-mail submissions (pasted into body of message or as attachment in MS Word or RTF format); no disk submissions. Cover letter is required. "Please be prepared to supply a short biography and optional photo upon notification of acceptance." Reads submissions year round. Time between acceptance and publication is up to 3 months. Poems are circulated to an editorial board. Sometimes comments on rejected poems. Guidelines available on Web site. Responds in one month. Acquires one-time rights. Rights revert to poet upon publication.

Tips "Check out current and back issues on Web site."

☑ SUNSTONE

343 N. Third W., Salt Lake City UT 84103-1215. (801)355-5926. Established 1974. **Contact:** Dixie Partridge, poetry editor.

Magazines Needs *Sunstone*, published 6 times/year, prints "scholarly articles of interest to an open, Mormon audience; personal essays; fiction and poetry." Wants "both lyric and narrative poetry that engages the reader with fresh, strong images, skillful use of language, and a strong sense of voice and/or place." Does not want "didactic poetry, sing-song rhymes, or in-process work." Has published poetry by Susan Howe, Anita Tanner, Robert Parham, Ryan G. Van Cleave, Robert Rees, and Virgil Suárez. *Sunstone* is 64 pages, magazine-sized, professionally printed, saddle-stapled, with semi-glossy paper cover. Receives more than 500 poems/year, accepts 40-50. Press run is 3,000. Subscription: $45 for 6 issues. Sample: $10 postpaid.

How to Contact Submit up to 5 poems at a time. Lines/poem: 40 maximum. No previously published poems or simultaneous submissions. Include name and address on each poem. Time between acceptance and publication is 2 years or less. Seldom comments on rejected poems. Guidelines available for SASE. Responds in 3 months. Pays 5 contributor's copies. Acquires first North American serial rights.

Tips "Poems should not sound like a rewording of something heard before. Be original; pay attention to language, sharp imagery. Contents should deepen as the poem progresses. We've published poems rooted strongly in place, narratives seeing life from another time or culture, poems on religious belief or doubt—a wide range of subject matter."

▣ ◎ SWELL

(Specialized: gay/lesbian/bisexual/transgendered), E-mail: swelleditor@yahoo.com. Website: www.swellzine.com. Established 1980. **Contact:** Jill Craig, editor.

Magazines Needs *Swell*, published quarterly online by NewTown Writers (see separate listing in Organizations), aims "to reach beyond the traditional boundaries of the printed word, exploring the limits of form, structure, and content, while giving a voice to emerging writers." Wants "work that reflects a spectrum of perspectives as diverse as the community from which it was born. Ideal publication candidates approach GLBT issues in a fresh way or present universal topics from a unique point of view."

How to Contact Lines/poem: no works over 3,000 words total. Welcomes multiple submissions as long as the total submitted is under the maximum word count. Accepts e-mail submissions only. Responds in 1-2 months. Rights revert to poet upon publication.

☑ SYCAMORE REVIEW

Dept. of English, Purdue University, 500 Oval Dr., West Lafayette IN 47907-2038. (765)494-3783. Fax: (765)494-3780. E-mail: sycamore@purdue.edu. Website: www.sycamorereview.com. Established 1988 (first issue May 1989). **Contact:** Poetry Editor (see website for current editor).

• Poetry published by *Sycamore Review* has appeared in *The Best American Poetry* and *The Pushcart Prize*.

Magazines Needs *Sycamore Review*, published semiannually in January and June, uses "personal essays, short fiction, short shorts, drama, translations, and quality poetry in any form. We aim to publish many diverse styles of poetry from formalist to prose poems, narrative, and lyric." Has published poetry by Denise Duhamel, Jonah Winter, Amy Gerstler, Mark Halliday, Dean Young, and Ed Hirsch. *Sycamore Review* is about 120 pages, 8x8, professionally printed, flat-spined, with matte color cover. Press run is 1,000 (200 subscribers, 50 libraries). Subscription: $12 ($14 outside U.S.). Sample: $7. Indiana residents add 5% sales tax. Make checks payable to Purdue University.

How to Contact Submit 3-6 poems at a time. with name and address on each page. Include SASE. Considers simultaneous submissions, if notified immediately of acceptance elsewhere; no previously published poems except translations. No fax or e-mail submissions. Cover letter is required. "Include phone number, short bio, and previous publications, if any, in cover letter." Put name and address on each page of ms, include SASE. Reads submissions August 1-March 1 only. Guidelines available for SASE or on website. Responds in 4-5 months. Pays 2 contributor's copies. Acquires first North American rights. After publication, all rights revert to author. Staff reviews books of poetry. Send materials for review consideration to editor-in-chief.

Tips "Poets who do not include a SASE do not receive a response."

$ ☐ ◎ TALES OF THE TALISMAN

(Specialized: science fiction; fantasy; horror), P.O. Box 2194, Mesilla Park NM 88047-2194. E-mail: hadrosaur@zianet.com. Website: www.talesofthetalisman.com. Established 1995. **Contact:** David Lee Summers, editor.

Magazines Needs *Tales of the Talisman*, published quarterly, prints "well-written, thought-provoking science fiction and fantasy." Wants "strong visual imagery. Strong emotion from a sense of fun to more melancholy is good." Does not want "graphic/gory violence or poetry that strays too far from the science fiction/fantasy genre." Has published poetry by Mike Allen, Ian Watson, David Kopaska-Merkel, Terrie Leigh Relf, and Deborah P. Kolodji. *Tales of the Talisman* is 86 pages, 814x1012, printed on 60 lb. white paper, perfect-bound, with full-color cardstock cover. Receives about 500 poems/year, accepts up to 5%. Press run is 200 (100 subscribers). Single copy: $8; subscription: $20/year. Make checks payable to Hadrosaur Productions.

How to Contact Submit 1-5 poems at a time. Considers previously published poems; no simultaneous submissions. Accepts e-mail submissions (pasted into body of message); no disk submissions. "For e-mail submissions, place the word 'Hadrosaur' in the subject line. Submissions that do not include this will be destroyed unread. Postal submissions will not be returned unless sufficient postage is provided." Accepts submissions from January 1-February 15 and July 1-August 15. Cover letter is preferred. Time between acceptance and publication is one year. Occasionally comments on rejected poems. Guidelines available for SASE or on Web site. Responds in 1 month. Sends prepublication galleys on request. Pays $4/poem plus 1 contributor's copy. Acquires one-time rights.

Tips "Read absolutely everything you can get your hands on, especially poetry outside your genre of choice, and ask 'What if?' This is a great source for original speculative poems."

☑ TAPROOT LITERARY REVIEW

P.O. Box 204, Ambridge PA 15003. (724)266-8476. E-mail: taproot10@aol.com. Established 1986. **Contact:** Tikvah Feinstein, editor.

Magazines Needs *Taproot Literary Review*, published annually, is "a very respected anthology with increasing distribution. We publish some of the best poets in the U.S. We enjoy all types and styles of poetry from emerging writers to established writers to those who have become valuable and old friends who share their new works with us." Has published poetry by Suzanne Richardson Harvey, Lyn Lifshin, Joe Kaldon, Ann Curran, Ellen Hyatt, Robert Michael O'Hearn, Michael Johnson, Miranda Coffey, Faith Romeo Cataffa, and Krikor N. Der Hohannesian. *Taproot Literary Review* is about 95 pages, offset-printed on white stock, with one-color glossy cover. Circulation is 500. Single copy: $8.95; subscription: $7.50. Sample: $5.

How to Contact Submit up to 5 poems at a time. Lines/poem: 35 maximum. No previously published poems or simultaneous submissions. Accepts submissions by e-mail (pasted into body of message), but "we would rather have a hard copy. Also, we cannot answer without a SASE." Cover letter is required (with general information). Reads submissions September 1-December 31 only. Guidelines available for SASE. Sometimes sends prepublication galleys. Pays 1 contributor's copy; additional copies are $6.50 each. Open to receiving books for review consideration. Send query first.

Contest/Award Offerings Sponsors the annual Taproot Writer's Workshop Annual Writing Contest. 1st Prize: $25 and publication in *Taproot Literary Review*; 2nd and 3rd Prizes: publication. Submit 5 poems of literary quality, in any form, on any subject except porn, religion, and politics. **Entry fee:** $12/5 poems (no longer than 35 lines each); fee includes copy of *Taproot*. **Deadline:** December 31. Winners announced the following March.

Tips "We publish the best poetry we can in a variety of styles and subjects, so long as it's literary quality and speaks to us. We love poetry that stuns, surprises, amuses, and disarms."

◫ ☑ TARPAULIN SKY

E-mail: editors@tarpaulinsky.com (inquiries) or submissions@tarpaulinsky.com (submissions). Website: www.tarpaulinsky.com. Established 2002. **Contact:** Poetry Editors. Editor: Christian Peet.

Magazines Needs *Tarpaulin Sky*, published biannually in print and online, features "highest-quality poetry, prose, cross-genre work, art, photography, interviews, and reviews. We are open to all styles and forms, providing the forms appear inevitable and/or inextricable from the poems. We are especially fond of inventive/experimental and cross-/trans-genre work. The best indication of our aesthetic is found in the journal we produce: Please read it before submitting your work. Also, hardcopy submissions may be received by different editors at different times; check guidelines before submitting." Has published poetry by Jenny Boully, Matthea Harvey, Bin Ramke, Eleni Sikelianos, Juliana Spahr, and Joshua Marie Wilkinson. Receives about 3,000 poems/year.

How to Contact Submit 4-6 poems at a time. Considers simultaneous submissions; no previously published poems. Accepts e-mail submissions ("best received as attachments in .rtf or .pdf formats"); no disk submissions. Cover letter is preferred. Reads submissions year round. Time between acceptance and publication is 2-6 months. "Poems are read by all editors. We aim for consensus." Rarely comments on rejected poems. Guidelines available for SASE, by e-mail, or on Web site. Responds in 1-4 months. Pays in contributor's copies and "by waiving readings fees for Tarpaulin Sky Press Open Reading Periods." Always sends prepublication galleys (electronic). Acquires first rights. Reviews books/chapbooks of poetry.

☑ TAR RIVER POETRY

Erwin Building Mailroom, East Carolina University, Greenville NC 27858-4353. (252)328-6783. E-mail: TarRiverPoetry@gmail.com. Website: http://core.ecu.edu/engl/trp. Established 1978. **Contact:** Luke Whisnant, editor; Carolyn Elkins, associate editor.

Magazines Needs *Tar River Poetry*, published twice/year, is an "'all-poetry' magazine that publishes 40-50 poems per issue, providing the talented beginner and experienced writer with a forum that features all styles and forms of verse." Wants "skillful use of figurative language; poems that appeal to the senses." Does not want "sentimental, flat-statement poetry." Has published poetry by William Stafford, Sharon Olds, Carolyn Kizer, A.R. Ammons, and Claudia Emerson. Has also published "many other well-known poets, as well as numerous new and emerging poets." *Tar River Poetry* is 64 pages, digest-sized, professionally printed on salmon stock, with matte card cover with photo. Receives 6,000-8,000 submissions/year, accepts 80-100. Press run is 900 (500 subscribers, 125 libraries). Subscription: $12. Sample: $6.50.

How to Contact Submit no more than 5 poems at a time. No previously published poems or simultaneous submissions. Accepts e-mail submissions only; no print submissions. "Detailed submission instructions appear on the Web site, along with writer's guidelines." Check Web site for reading periods: "we do not read manuscripts from May through August—submissions will be returned unread." Rarely comments on rejections "due to volume of submissions." Guidelines available for SASE or on Web site. Responds in 6 weeks. Pays 2 contributor's copies. Acquires first rights. Reviews books of poetry in 4,000 words maximum, single- or multi-book format. Query for reviews.

Tips "Writers of poetry should first be readers of poetry. Read and study traditional and contemporary poetry."

☐ ☑ TATTOO HIGHWAY

E-mail: submissions@tattoohighway.org. Website: www.tattoohighway.org. Established 1998. **Contact:** Sara McAulay, editor.

Magazines Needs *Tattoo Highway*, published biannually online, is a journal of poetry, literary prose, new media, and art. "We're open to most styles; only criterion is quality." Wants "language that is fresh, vivid, and original; writing that is smart and a little edgy, that engages with the world beyond the writer's own psyche. We like formal poetry if well handled." Does not want "self-pity, navel-contemplation, clichés, workshop hackery." Has published poetry by Oliver Rice, Carol Frith, Paul Hostovsky, Lyn Lifshin, Doug Ramspeck, Judith Skillman. Receives about 800 poems/year, accepts about 50.

How to Contact Submit up to 5 poems at a time. Considers previously published poems (if they've appeared in small-circulation print journals; unpublished work preferred) and simultaneous submissions ("but please let us know promptly if you place your piece elsewhere"). Accepts e-mail submissions (pasted into body of message) only. "For hypertext or New Media (Flash, etc.) submissions, please provide a URL where we may view the work." Reading periods vary; "typically last about three months. Blind readings by editorial board. Several rounds of 'triage' during the reading period, usually handled by e-mail. Face-to-face editorial meeting shortly after submission deadline, where final selections are made. Editor and poetry editor have final say." Sometimes comments on rejected poems. "If a poem has its moments, though it doesn't quite work, we try to acknowledge that. We encourage near-misses to try us again." Regularly publishes theme issues. Guidelines available on Web site. Responds in up to 3 months ("usually within 1 week of deadline"). Always sends prepublication galleys. No payment. Acquires first electronic rights; rights revert to author 90 days after online publication date.

Contest/Award Offerings "Picture Worth 500 Words" contest for poetry/prose. No entry fee; small prizes. See guidelines on Web site.

Tips "Read some past issues before submitting."

☒ ☑ THE TAYLOR TRUST: POETRY AND PROSE

P.O. Box 903456, Palmdale CA 93550-3456. E-mail: lavonne.taylor@sbcglobal.net. Website: thetaylortrust.wordpress.com. Established 2008 **Contact:** LaVonne Taylor, Editor and Publisher.

Magazines Needs *The Taylor Trust*, published quarterly, "considers ourselves egalitarian in that we accept most poetry forms. We also accept flash fiction, short stories, nonfiction. We publish more than one poem per author in each issue." Wants "all styles and forms. Prefers uplifting subject matter. Humorous poetry also accepted." Does not want "profanity or sexually explicit material. No age restrictions. Child must state age and give a short bio. Parental permission also required." Has published poetry by Mary L. Ports, Trisha Nelson, J.F. Connolly, Fredrick Zydek, John Fitzpatrick, Michael Lee Johnson. *The Taylor Trust* is 60-100 pages, digest-sized, press run, perfect bound with a heavy, clay-coated embossed stock full-bleed color photo background cover. Receives 800 poems/year; accepts 90%. Single copy: $8; subscription $24.

How to Contact Submit 6 poems at a time, between 4-100 lines. Considers previously published poems ("as long as the author owns the publication rights") and simultaneous submissions ("with the understanding that it is the author's duty to inform all concerned when a poem is accepted"). Accepts e-mail submissions pasted into body of e-mail message; disk submissions. Cover letter is required. "We require a bio of about 150-200 words with publication history adn any other information the author cares to provide. We prefer not to return declined hard copies, but if the author requests it, an SASE is required with postal submittals. SASEs are needed with requests for guidelines." Reads submissions year round. Submit seasonal poems 3 months in advance. Time between acceptance and publication is 3 months. Poems are circulated to an editorial board. Sometimes comments on rejected poems. Regularly published theme issues loosely based on the seasons. Upcoming themes available in magazine, by e-mail, and on Web site. Guidelines available for SASE, by e-mail, and on Web site. Responds in 1 week. Pays 1 contributor's copy. Acquires one-time rights, electronic rights, "selected poems from each print publication will be posted on the site." Rights revert to poet upon publication. Reviews poetry books, chapbooks, and other magazines and journals in 500-1,000 words.

Additional Information "Fee-based publishing on demand is available on a limited basis."

Tips "Follow the advice in *Poet's Market*. Behave professionally at all times. If your poetry is declined, try again with different subject matter or a different form."

☑ ◎ THE TEACHER'S VOICE

(Specialized: the American teacher experience, from pre-K to university professor), P.O. Box 150384, Kew Gardens NY 11415. E-mail: editor@the-teachers-voice.org. Website: www.the-teachers-voice.org. Established 2005. **Contact:** Andrés Castro, founder/managing editor.

Magazines Needs *The Teacher's Voice*, was founded as an experimental hardcopy literary magazine and is now free and online. "We publish poetry, short stories, creative nonfiction, and essays that reflect the many different American teacher experiences." Wants "all styles and forms. We ask to see critical creative writing that takes risks without being overly self-indulgent or inaccessible. We welcome work that ranges from 'art for art's sake' to radically social/political. Writing that illuminates the most pressing/urgent issues in American education and the lives of teachers gets special attention." Has published poetry by Edward Francisco, Sapphire, Hal Sirowitz, and Antler. Receives about 1,000 poems/year, accepts about 10%.

How to Contact Submit 3-5 poems at a time. Lines/poem: no limits. Considers previously published poems (if rights are held by the author) and simultaneous submissions (contact if submission has been accepted elsewhere). No e-mail or disk submissions. Send prose pieces under 2,000 words. Cover letter is preferred. "Are you a teacher, administrator, parent, student, librarian, custodian, coach, security officer, etc? We do not accept responsibility for submissions or queries not accompanied by a SASE with adequate postage." Reads submissions year round. Time between acceptance and publication is 4 months to 1 year. Poems are circulated to an editorial board. Guidelines available on Web site. Sometimes sends prepublication galleys "if requested." Acquires first rights and electronic reprint rights. Rights revert to poet "after work is first electronically published and archived on this site; no material on this site may be reproduced in any form without permission from their individual authors." No longer accepts online submissions.

Additional Information "Since we publish open as well as theme issues (that require enough thematic pieces to be compiled) and do rely on readership financial support, our publishing schedule and format may vary from year to year. We publish hardcopy limited press collections when funds allow. Our production goal is to showcase strong cohesive collections that support our mission and satisfy the needs of particular issues. For the moment, our new focus on electronic publishing is a matter of survival that offers many new possibilities and opportunities in keeping with the changing times."

Contest/Award Offerings Sponsors *The Teacher's Voice* Annual Chapbook Contest and *The Teacher's Voice* Annual Poetry Contest for Unpublished Poets. Guidelines for both contests available for SASE, by e-mail, or on Web site.

Tips "(1) Please, be daring. Take some personal risks in a few pieces. If you find it comfortable to write about your teaching experiences and students without ever making even subtle connections to history, current events, political and social institutions, and public policies, we may not be for you as we move ahead. (2) If you must, feel free to include a pseudonym in your cover letter. (3) If you are a teacher, become a poet. If you are a poet, become a teacher."

▣ ☑ TEARS IN THE FENCE

38 Hod View, Stourpaine, Nr. Blandford Forum, Dorset DT11 8TN England. (44)(1258)456803. Fax: (44)(1258)454026. E-mail: david@davidcaddy.wanadoo.co.uk. Website: www.myspace. com/tearsinthefence. Established 1984. **Contact:** David Caddy, general editor.

Magazines Needs *Tears in the Fence*, published 3 times/year, is a "small press magazine of poetry, fiction, interviews, essays, and reviews. We are open to a wide variety of poetic styles. Work that shows social and poetic awareness whilst prompting close and divergent readings. However, we like to publish a variety of work." Has published poetry by Nathaniel Tarn, Matina L. Stamatakis, Mary Maher, Ketaki Kushari Dyson, Donna Hilbert, Chris McCabe and Gary Metras. Regular columnists include Jennifer K. Dick, Sarah Hopkins, Tom Chivers, Rosie Jackson and David Caddy. *Tears in the Fence* is 144 pages, A5, docutech-printed on 110-gms. paper, perfect-bound, with matte card cover. Press run is 800 (522 subscribers). Subscription: $20/4 issues. Sample: $7.

How to Contact Submit 6 poems at a time. Accepts e-mail (pasted into body of message) and disk submissions. Cover letter with brief bio is required. Poems must be typed; include SASE. Time between acceptance and publication is 3 months. Pays one contributor's copy. Reviews books of poetry in 2,000-4,000 words, single- or multi-book format. Send materials for review consideration.

Also Offers The magazine runs a regular series of readings in London, and an annual international literary festival.

Tips "I think it helps to subscribe to several magazines in order to study the market and develop an understanding of what type of poetry is published. Use the review sections and send off to magazines that are new to you."

☑ ◎ TEXAS POETRY CALENDAR

(Specialized: poems with a TX connection), Dos Gatos Press, 1310 Crestwood Rd., Austin TX 78722. Phone/fax: (512)467-0678. E-mail: editors@dosgatospress.org. Website: www. dosgatospress.org. Established 2004 (under current editorship). **Contact:** Scott Wiggerman or David Meischen, co-editors.

Magazines Needs *Texas Poetry Calendar,* published annually in August, features a "week-by-week calendar side-by-side with poems with a Texas connection." Wants "a wide variety of styles, voices, and forms, including rhyme—though a Texas connection is preferred. Humor is welcome! Poetry *only!*" Does not want "children's poetry, erotic poetry, profanity, obscure poems, previously published work, or poems over 35 lines." *Texas Poetry Calendar* is about 144 pages, digest-sized, offset-printed, spiral-bound, with full-color cardstock cover. Receives about 600 poems/year, accepts about 70-75. Press run is 1,500; 70 distributed free to contributors. Single copy: $13.95 plus $3 shipping. Make checks payable to Dos Gatos Press.

How to Contact Submit 3 poems at a time. Lines/poem: 35 maximum, "including spaces and title." Considers simultaneous submissions; no previously published poems. No fax, e-mail, or disk submissions. Cover letter is required. "Include a short bio (100-200 words) and poem titles in cover letter. Also include e-mail address and phone number. Do not include poet's name on the poems themselves!" Reads submissions year round. Time between acceptance and publication is 3-4 months. Poems are circulated to an editorial board. Never comments on rejected poems. **"Entry fee for the** *Texas Poetry Calendar* **Awards ($5 for 3 poems) is required for all submissions—all poems submitted are eligible for cash awards."** (See Contest/Award Offerings below.) Guidelines available in magazine, by e-mail, or on Web site. Responds "only once a year, in spring." Sometimes sends prepublication galleys. Pays 1 contributor's copy. Acquires first, electronic, and reprint rights.

Contest/Award Offerings Sponsors the annual Texas Poetry Calendar Awards, offering 1st Prize: $250; 2nd Prize: $150; 3rd Prize: $75. "Award-winning poems receive special recognition in the calendar in which they are printed." Submit 3 poems. Guidelines available in magazine, by e-mail, or on Web site. **Entry fee:** $5 for 3 poems. **Deadline:** March 20 (postmark). "Judged by a nationally known poet—Robert McDowell, Naomi Shihab Nye, Kathleen Pierce, and Mark Doty."

$ ▨ ◎ THEMA

(Specialized: specific theme per issue), Thema Literary Society, P.O. Box 8747, Metairie LA 70011-8747. E-mail: thema@cox.net. Website: http://members.cox.net/thema. Established 1988. **Contact:** Gail Howard, poetry editor.

Magazines Needs *THEMA,* published triannually, uses poetry related to specific themes. "Each issue is based on an unusual premise. Please, please send SASE for guidelines before submitting poetry to find out the upcoming themes." Does not want "scatologic language, alternate lifestyle, explicit love poetry." Has published poetry by Virginia McGee Butler, Brent Fisk, Rose Hunter, and Jill Crammond Wickham. *THEMA* is 120 pages, digest-sized professionally printed, with glossy card cover. Receives about 400 poems/year, accepts about 8%. Press run is 400 (230 subscribers, 30 libraries). Subscription: $20 U.S./$30 foreign. Sample $10 U.S./$15 foreign.

How to Contact Submit up to 3 poems at a time. Include SASE. "All submissions should be typewritten on standard 8½x11 paper. Submissions are accepted all year, but evaluated after specified deadlines." Specify target theme. Editor comments on submissions. Upcoming themes and guidelines available in magazine, for SASE, by e-mail, or on Web site. Pays $10/poem and 1 contributor's copy. Acquires one-time rights.

Tips "Do not submit to *THEMA* unless you have one of *THEMA*'s upcoming themes in mind. And be sure to specify which one!"

▣ ◻ THICK WITH CONVICTION

E-mail: twczine@yahoo.com. Website: www.angelfire.com/poetry/thickwithconviction. Established 2005. **Contact:** Sara Blanton, Kristina Blanton, or Mandy Callen, editors.

Magazines Needs *Thick With Conviction*, published quarterly online, is "run by three quirky twenty-something women who are desperately searching for new and interesting ideas in poetry. We'd like to be moved to anger or tears." Wants all genres of poetry, "poems that make us exhale a deep sigh after reading them. Basically, if we can't feel the words in front of us, we're not going to be happy. We'd like to expose the world to poets who may not get the kind of exposure that more experienced poets do." Does not want "teen angst poems, religious poems, or greeting card tripe." Considers poetry by teens. Has published poetry by Taylor Corey Mesler, Kendall A. Bell, Paul Hostovsky, Melinda Blount, Bruce Niedt and Simon Perchik. Receives about 300 poems/year, accepts about 15%.

How to Contact Submit 3-5 poems at a time. Lines/poem: no limit. Considers previously published poems; no simultaneous submissions. Accepts e-mail submissions (pasted into body of message; "any attachments will be deleted"); no disk submissions. Cover letter is required. Reads submissions year round. Submit seasonal poems 3 months in advance. Time between acceptance and publication is 3 months. Never comments on rejected poems. Guidelines available on Web site. Responds in "roughly 1 to 2 weeks." Acquires one-time rights. Rights revert to poet upon publication.

Additional Information "We all accept photo submission. See our Web site for guidelines."

Tips "Take the time to read the poems on our Web site. If your style is similar, we'll most likely enjoy your work. The most important thing a writer can do is read, read, read. The more you read, the more your writing will grow and blossom. Be sure to have thick skin, and don't let rejections get you down."

⊠ ◻ THINK JOURNAL

P.O. Box 454, Downingtown PA 19335. E-mail: thinkjournal@yahoo.com. Established 2008. **Contact:** Christine Yurick, editor.

Magazines Needs *Think Journal*, published quarterly, is a "review of poetry, short stories, novel excerpts, and essays. The journal will serve as an outlet for writers who, paraphrasing Aristotle, represent things as they might be and as they ought to be. This journal is for the artist who struggles in the world of contemporary literature, for the artist who has asked themselves the question: Why write for a world that does not exist? Wants "content and meaning; words that are logically conceived and arranged; evidence of an active imagination; structure; as well as the integration of emotional and intellectual facts. Acceptance based on two criteria: content and literary artistry. The theme of the journal is a philosophical theme, an outlet for writers who live by a certain philosophy, in particular, the philosophy of Ayn Rand, and in general, a certain esthetic philosophy, one that focuses on form, structure, plot, reason and rationality. Open to different styles and forms as long as it has structure and thought behind it." Does not want contemporary literature/anti-art or profanity. Considers poetry by teens. *Think Journal* is 50 pages, digest-sized, desktop-printed, staple-bound with a cardstock cover containing original artwork. Single copy: $7; subscription: $20/year. Sample $6. Make checks payable to Christine Yurick.

How to Contact 3-6 poems at a time, no restrictions in length. Cover letter is preferred. "Always include a SASE with submissions. Cover letter and brief biography preferred. Please include your e-mail address on the cover page for further communications. Include your name and address on each page of your submission." Reads submissions year round. Does not accept previously published or simultaneous submissions. Time between acceptance and publication is 6-12 months. Sometimes comments on rejected poems. Guidelines in magazine or for SASE. Responds in 1-2 months. Pays 1 contributor's copy. Acquires one-time rights. Rights revert to poet upon publication.

☑ THIRD COAST

Dept. of English, Western Michigan University, Kalamazoo MI 49008-5331. (269)387-2675. Website: www.thirdcoastmagazine.com. Established 1995. **Contact:** Poetry Editors.

Magazines Needs *Third Coast*, published semiannually in March and September, is a national literary magazine of poetry, prose, creative nonfiction, translations, and drama. Wants "excellence of craft and originality of thought. Nothing trite." Has published poetry by Myronn Hardy, Sean Thomas Dougherty, Terrance Hayes, Margo Schlipp, Mark Halliday, Ted Kooser, and Philip Levine. *Third Coast* is 176 pages, digest-sized, professionally printed, perfect-bound, with 4-color cover with art. Receives about 2,000 poems/year, accepts about 1%. Press run is 1,000 (850 subscribers, 50 libraries, 100 shelf sales). Single copy: $9; subscription: $16/year, $28 for 2 years, $42 for 3 years. Sample: $6 (back issue).

How to Contact Submit up to 5 poems at a time via the Third Coast Submission Manager, found on Web site. Considers simultaneous submissions with notification; no previously published poems. Submissions by post will not be considered. Cover letter is preferred. "Poems should be typed single-spaced, with the author's name on each page. Stanza breaks should be double-spaced." Poems are circulated to assistant poetry editors and poetry editors; poetry editors make final decisions. Seldom comments on rejected poems. Guidelines available on Web site. Responds in 4 months. Pays 2 contributor's copies plus one-year subscription. Acquires first rights.

Contest/Award Offerings Sponsors an annual poetry contest. 1st Prize: $1,000 and publication; 4 finalists receive notification in prize-winning issue, possible publication, and a 3-year subscription. Guidelines available on Web site. **Entry fee:** $15, includes one-year subscription to *Third Coast*.

$ ☑ THE THREEPENNY REVIEW

P.O. Box 9131, Berkeley CA 94709. (510)849-4545. Website: www.threepennyreview.com. Established 1980. **Contact:** Wendy Lesser, editor.

- •Work published in *The Threepenny Review* has been included in *The Best American Poetry* and *The Pushcart Prize*.

Magazines Needs *The Threepenny Review*, published quarterly, is "a national review of literature, performing and visual arts, and social articles aimed at the intelligent, well-read (but not necessarily academic) reader." Wants "formal, narrative, short poems (and others). No bias against formal poetry; in fact, a slight bias in favor of it." Has published poetry by Anne Carson, Frank Bidart, Seamus Heaney, Robert Pinsky, and Louise Gluück. *The Threepenny Review* is a 36-page tabloid. Receives about 4,500 submissions of poetry/year, accepts about 40 poems. Press run is 10,000 (8,000 subscribers, 150 libraries). Subscription: $25. Sample: $12.

How to Contact Submit up to 5 poems at a time. Lines/poem: 100 maximum ("exceptions are possible"). No previously published poems or simultaneous submissions. No e-mail submissions accepted. **Do not submit mss September-December.** Guidelines available for SASE or on Web site. Responds in up to 2 months. Pays $200/poem plus one-year subscription. Acquires first serial rights. Guidelines available for SASE.

☒ $ ☑ TICKLED BY THUNDER

14076-86A Ave., Surrey BC V3W 0V9 Canada. E-mail: info@tickledbythunder.com. Website: www.tickledbythunder.com. Established 1990. **Contact:** Larry Lindner, editor/publisher.

Magazines Needs *Tickled by Thunder*, published up to 2 times/year, uses poems "about fantasy particularly; writing or whatever. Require original images and thoughts. Welcome humor and creative inspirational verse." Does not want "anything pornographic, childish, unimaginative."

Has published poetry by Laleh Dadpour Jackson and Helen Michiko Singh. *Tickled by Thunder* is 24 pages, digest-sized, published on Macintosh. Has 1,000 readers/subscribers. Subscription: $12 CAD/4 issues. Sample: $2.50 CAD.

How to Contact Submit 3-5 poems at a time. Lines/poem: up to 40 ("keep them short—not interested in long, long poems"). No e-mail submissions. Cover letter is required. Include "a few facts about yourself and brief list of publishing credits." Comments on rejected poems "80% of the time." Guidelines available for SASE or on Web site. Responds in up to 6 months. Pays 2¢/line, $2 CAD maximum. Acquires first rights. Reviews books of poetry in up to 300 words. Open to unsolicited reviews. Send materials for review consideration.

Additional Information Publishes **author-subsidized chapbooks**. "We are also interested in student poetry and publish it in our center spread: *Expressions*." Send SASE (or SAE and IRC) for details.

Contest/Award Offerings Offers a poetry contest 2 times/year. Prize: cash, publication, and subscription. **Entry fee:** $5 CAD for one poem; free for subscribers. **Deadlines:** the 15th of February, 15th of August.

☑ TIGER'S EYE

A JOURNAL OF POETRY, Tiger's Eye Press, P.O. Box 2935, Eugene OR 97402. E-mail: tigerseyepoet@yahoo.com. Website: www.tigerseyejournal.com. Established 2001. **Contact:** Colette Jonopulos and JoAn Osborne, editors.

Magazines Needs *Tiger's Eye: A Journal of Poetry*, published semiannually, features both established and undiscovered poets. "Besides publishing the work of several exceptional poets in each issue, we feature two poets in interviews, giving the reader insight into their lives and writing habits." Wants "both free verse and traditional forms; no restrictions on subject or length. We welcome sonnets, haibun, haiku, ghazals, villenelles, etc. We pay special attention to unusual forms and longer poems that may have difficulty being placed elsewhere. Poems with distinct imagery and viewpoint are read and re-read by the editors and considered for publication." Has published poetry by Shawn Fawson, Cheryl Loetscher, Patrick Carrington, Thomas Patterson, and Julie Marie Wade. *Tiger's Eye* is 64 pages, saddle-stitched. Receives 1,000 poems/year, accepts 100. Press run is 300. Single copy: $6; subscription: $11 for 2 issues. Make checks payable to Tiger's Eye Press.

How to Contact Submit 3-5 poems at a time, no multiple submissions. Considers simultaneous submissions with notification if a poem is accepted elsewhere; no previously published poems. No e-mail submissions. Cover letter is required. Include brief bio. SASE for notification only; no submissions are returned. Reads submissions year-round; deadlines are February 28 and August 31. Time between acceptance and publication is 3 months. "All poems are read by the editors, then filed as poems we definitely want to publish, those we are still considering, and those we aren't publishing. Our two featured poets are chosen, then letters and e-mails are sent out." Seldom comments on rejected poems. Guidelines available in magazine or on Web site. Responds in 6 months. Always sends prepublication galleys. Pays one contributor's copy to each poet, 2 to featured poets. Acquires one-time rights.

Additional Information *Tiger's Eye* nominates for *The Pushcart Prize*.

Contest/Award Offerings Tiger's Eye Annual Poetry Contest (see separate listing in Contests & Awards) and Editor's Choice Chapbook Contest. "The winner receives $100 and 25 copies of their chapbook. Do not send entire manuscript, but five pages of poetry, cover letter with poet's name and contact information; no identifying information on mss pages. $10 entry fee." Deadline: August 31, 2009.

Tips "We accept poems submitted by new poets with as much enthusiasm as those submitted by established poets. Poems with clean images, unique subjects, and strong voices have a good chance of being published in *Tiger's Eye*."

☑ TIMBER CREEK REVIEW

A JOURNAL OF POETRY, Tiger's Eye Press, P.O. Box 2935, Eugene OR 97402. E-mail: tigerseyepoet@yahoo.com. Website: www.tigerseyejournal.com. Established 2001. **Contact:** Colette Jonopulos and JoAn Osborne, editors.P.O. Box 16542, Greensboro NC 27416. E-mail: timber_creek_review@hoopsmail.com. Established 1994. **Contact:** John M. Freiermuth, editor.

Magazines Needs *Timber Creek Review*, published quarterly, prints short stories, literary nonfiction, and poetry. Wants all types of poetry. Does not want religious or pornographic poetry. Has published poetry by Jody Azzouni, Christine Graf, Jacqueline de Weever, Kathleen M. McCann, Patricia L. Hamilton, Frederick W. Bassett, Mitch LesCarbeau, Sheryl Nelms, and Ruth Holzer. *Timber Creek Review* is 80-84 pages, digest-sized, laser-printed, stapled, with colored paper cover. Receives about 1,000 poems/year, accepts about 8%. Press run is 150 (120 subscribers, 2 libraries, 30 shelf sales). Single copy: $4.75; subscription: $17; overseas mail add $8. Make checks payable to J.M. Freiermuth.

How to Contact Submit 3-6 poems at a time. Lines/poem: 3 minimum, "rarely over 30." Considers simultaneous submissions; no previously published poems. No e-mail or disk submissions. Cover letter is required. Reads submissions year round. Submit seasonal poems 10 months in advance. Time between acceptance and publication is 3-6 months. Never comments on rejected poems. Occasionally publishes theme issues. Guidelines available for SASE or by e-mail. Responds in up to 6 months. Pays one contributor's copy. Acquires first North American serial rights.

Tips "Turn off your TV and read that poety magazine that published your last poem, and maybe someone else will read your poem, too!"

☑ ◎ TIME OF SINGING, A MAGAZINE OF CHRISTIAN POETRY

P.O. Box 149, Conneaut Lake PA 16316. E-mail: timesing@zoominternet.net. Website: www.timeofsinging.bizland.com. Established 1958-1965, revived 1980. **Contact:** Lora H. Zill, editor.

Magazines Needs *Time of Singing, A Magazine of Christian Poetry*, published 4 times/year, seeks "poems that 'show' rather than 'tell.' The viewpoint is unblushingly Christian—but in its widest and most inclusive meaning." Wants free verse and well-crafted rhyme; would like to see more forms. Does not want "collections of uneven lines, sermons that rhyme, unstructured 'prayers,' and trite sing-song rhymes." Has published poetry by John Grey, Luci Shaw, Bob Hostetler, Frances P. Reid, Tony Cosier, Barbara Crooker, and Charles Waugaman. *Time of Singing* is 44 pages, digest-sized, offset from typescript. Receives more than 800 submissions/year, accepts about 175. Press run is 300 (150 subscribers). Subscription: $17 USD, $21 USD Canada, $30 USD overseas. Sample: $4, or 2 for $6 (postage paid).

How to Contact Submit up to 5 poems at a time. Lines/poem: prefers less than 40, "but will publish up to 60 lines if exceptional." Considers previously published poems (indicate when/where appeared) and simultaneous submissions. Accepts e-mail submissions (pasted into body of message or as attachment). Poems should be single-spaced. Time between acceptance and publication is up to one year. Comments "with suggestions for improvement if close to publication." Guidelines available for SASE, by e-mail, or on Web site. Responds in 4 months. Pays 1 contributor's copy.

Contest/Award Offerings Sponsors theme contests for specific issues. Guidelines available for SASE, by e-mail, or on Web site.

Tips "Study the craft. Be open to critique. A poet is often too close to his/her work and needs a critical, honest eye. *Time of Singing* publishes more literary-style verse, not greeting card style. Cover letters aren't needed, but if you do send one, it's unprofessional to use it to explain what your poem means. It shows me you don't have the confidence in your work, and you don't trust me, your first reader, to 'get it.' Poems that have to be explained in a cover letter are almost always rejected."

▣ ☑ ◎ TORCH: POETRY, PROSE AND SHORT STORIES BY AFRICAN AMERICAN WOMEN

E-mail: info@torchpoetry.org (inquiries); poetry@torchpoetry.org (submissions). Website: www.torchpoetry.org. Established 2006. **Contact:** Amanda Johnston, editor.

Magazines Needs *TORCH: Poetry, Prose, and Short Stories by African American Women*, published semiannually online, provides "a place to celebrate contemporary poetry, prose, and short stories by experienced and emerging writers alike. We prefer our contributors to take risks, and offer a diverse body of work that examines and challenges preconceived notions regarding race, ethnicity, gender roles, and identity." Has published poetry by Sharon Bridgforth, Patricia Smith, Shia Shabazz, Ana-Maurine Lara, and Remica L. Bingham. Receives about 250+ submissions/year, accepts about 20. Number of unique visitors: 300+/month.

How to Contact Submit 3 poems at a time. No previously published poems or simultaneous submissions. Accepts e-mail submissions only (as one attachment). Send to poetry@torchpoetry.org with "Poetry Submission" in subject line. Cover letter is preferred (in the body of the e-mail). Reads submissions April 1-August 31 only. Time between acceptance and publication is 2-7 months. Sometimes comments on rejected poems. Sometimes publishes theme issues. Guidelines available on Web site. Always sends prepublication galleys. No payment. Acquires rights to publish accepted work in online issue and in archives. Rights revert to poets upon publication.

Also Offers "Within *TORCH*, we offer a special section called Flame that features an interview, biography, and work sample by an established writer as well as an introduction to their Spark— an emerging writer who inspires them and adds to the boundless voice of creative writing by Black women." A free online newsletter is available; see Web site.

Tips "Black women, write freely. Know that your words are wanted, needed, and safe here. Read the previous issues online for examples of the type of writing *Torch* publishes."

☑ ◎ TO TOPOS: POETRY INTERNATIONAL

OSU Dept. of Foreign Languages & Literatures, 210 Kidder Hall, Corvallis OR 97331. (541)737-2146. Fax: (541)737-3563. E-mail: jkrause@oregonstate.edu. Website: http://oregonstate.edu/dept/foreign_lang/totopos/index.html. Established 1997. **Contact:** Joseph Krause, editor. Editors: Joseph Ohmann-Krause, Eric Dickey, and Roger Weaver. Founder: Roger Weaver.

•*To Topos* is funded through Poetry Enterprises, a nonprofit association.

Magazines Needs *To Topos: Poetry International*, published annually, is "committed to fostering social justice on an environmentally fragile planet. Its focus is Its focus is on human rights and poets often silenced by prevailing cultures, recognizing that the causes of poverty and injustice are often related to race, gender, nationality, and the effacement of earth-given resources. Most issues are thematically focused. Future themes include Turkish Poetry Today (2009) and Water (2010). Previous themes include Poverty and Poetry (with introduction by Michael Parenti), Indigenous American Poetry, Incarceration, Peace and the Sea, Forests, and North African Voices. Karen E. Holmberg, Allison Adelle Hedge Coke, Nabil Boudraa, Winon a LaDuke (White Earth Land Recovery Project) and Dr. William F. Schulz (Amnesty International) have served as guest editors or prefaced past issues. The journal is open to both aspiring and recognized poets. "The harmony of craft and message should be the primary consideration prior to submitting texts. The journal particularly invites submissions from refugees and the borderless. Black and white photography and imagery are particularly welcome to complement specific themes. The journal is primarily interested in living poets who believe words carry the gift of positive social change." Wants "poetry from all over the world and in any language, so long as it is accompanied by an English translation. The journal espouses a vision of pacifism and human rights but is not anchored in a political current." Does not want "self-serving poetry." Has published poetry by Louis Jenkins, Virgil Su a rez, Connie Wanek, Leonard Cirino, Khadija Al Mourabit, and Gé rard Bocholier. *To Topos* is 100-1 2 0 pages, digest-sized, docutech-printed, perfect-bound, with cardstock cover with graphics, includes ads (from Amnesty International usually). Receives between 100 and 300 poems per issue depending on the theme. Accepts 30-50%. Press run is 250-300, distributed to the international poetry community and to contributors. Single copy: $12 (+ $2.00 domestic postage; $3.50 international postage). Two-year subscription (includes postage): $25.

How to Contact Submit no more than 6 poems at a time. Submit poems that are theme-related. Accepts previously published poems (with the permission of the original copyright holder) and simultaneous submissions. Accepts e-mail (as attachment) and disk submissions; no fax submissions. "We prefer electronic submissions but accept hard copies by mail if SASE is included. All submissions should include a cover letter and a brief bio (2-4 lines)." Reads submissions year round. Time between acceptance and publication is 1-6 months. Poems are circulated to an editorial board. "Guest Editor makes initial selection, co-editors finalize, often seeking advice from consulting editors." Rarely comments on rejected poems. Regularly publishes theme issues. Deadline for Turkish Poetry Today issue: February 15, 2009; Water issue: February 15, 2010. Pays 1 contributor's copy. Acquires one-time rights. Rights revert to poet upon publication. Reviews books of poetry in 250 words, single-book format. "We review books relevant to theme. Books reviewed are selected by the editors. Contact editors to suggest titles."

Tips "The mission of this journal is to reveal the human face of poetry as a statement of urgency in today's world. *To Topos* is open to all aesthetic and stylistic orientations, but submissions should be a seed for social change along humanist principles without indulging in political or nationalist rhetoric."

▢ ◎ TRANSCENDENT VISIONS

(Specialized: psychiatric survivors & ex-mental patients)251 S. Olds Blvd., 84-E, Fairless Hills PA 19030-3426. (215)547-7159. Established 1992. **Contact:** David A. Kime, editor.

Magazines Needs *Transcendent Visions*, published annually, provides "a creative outlet for psychiatric survivors/ex-mental patients." Wants "experimental, confessional poems; strong poems dealing with issues we face. Any length or subject matter is OK, but shorter poems are more likely to be published." Does not want "rhyming poetry." Recently published work by White Elephant, Gabe Kaufman, Jamey Damert, Marc Pernaino, Teacup Mary, K.J. Kabza, and Arthur Longworth. *Transcendent Visions* is 50-60 pages, magazine-sized, photocopied, corner-stapled, with paper cover. Receives about 100 poems/year, accepts 20%. Press run is 200 (50 subscribers). Subscription: $6. Sample: $3. Make checks payable to David Kime.

How to Contact Submit 5 poems at a time. Considers previously published poems and simultaneous submissions. Cover letter is preferred. "Please tell me something unique about you, but I do not care about all the places you have been published." Time between acceptance and publication is 6 months. Guidelines available for SASE. Responds in 4 months. Pays one contributor's copy. Acquires first or one-time rights. Staff reviews books/chapbooks of poetry and other magazines in 20 words. Send materials for review consideration.

Tips "Find your own voice. Please send camera-ready poems, single-spaced. I don't like poems that go all over the page."

N ☑ TRIBECA POETRY REVIEW

25 Leonard Street, New York NY 10013.E-mail: editor@tribecareview.org. Website: www. tribecareview.org. Established 2009. **Contact:** Kenlynne Rini, editor.

Magazines Needs *Tribeca Poetry Review*, published annually in October, is "a new publication emerging out of the thick poetric history that is downtown New York. It seeks to expose its readers to the best smattering of poetry we can get our hands on. TPR will showcase new pieces by seasoned poets as well as illuminate the work of fresh voices." Wants "the kind of poetry that squirms in your head for days, hopefully longer, after reading it. Send us your best work. Will publish all forms (including traditional poesy, spoken word, or your experimental pieces) providing they translate well on the page, are intelligent, and well-crafted. New York City poets are always encouraged to submit their work, but this is NOT strictly a regional publication." Does not want "overly self-absorbed poems; pieces so abstract that all meaning and pleasure is lost on anyone but the poet; first drafts, goofy word play, trite nostalgia." Considers poetry by teens. "It's the poem itself that needs to resonate with readers, so the age of the poet means little. Occasionally, poetry by a 14 year old is more profound than the drivel generated by those adults who hang out unnecessarily in coffee shops and believe themselves 'poets.'" *Tribeca Poetry Review* is approximately 100 pages, digest-sized, professionally printed, flat-spine bound, with artwork cover. Press run is 500.

How to Contact Submit no more than 5 poems at a time up to 10 pages in total. No previously published poems or simultaneous submissions. Cover letter is required. "Please do not use your cover letter as a place to explain your poems. The letter is a place to introduce yourself and your work but not sell or explain either. Your name, address, contact phone and e-mail should be on each page submitted." Reads submissions year round. Time between acceptance and publication is up to 1 year. Sometimes comments on rejected poems. Guidelines on Web site. Responds in 2 months. Pays 2 contributor's copies. Acquires first North American serial rights.

☑ TULANE REVIEW

122 Norman Mayer, New Orleans LA 70118. (504)865-5160. Fax: (504)862-8958. E-mail: litsoc@ tulane.edu. Website: www.tulane.edu/~litsoc. Established 1988. **Contact:** Nathan Seltzer, editor-in-chief.

• *Tulane Review* is the recipient of an AWP Literary Magazine Design Award.

Magazines Needs *Tulane Review*, published biannually, is a national literary journal seeking quality submissions of prose, poetry, and art. "We consider all types of poetry." Wants "imaginative poems with bold, inventive images." Has published poetry by Virgil Suárez, Tom Chandler, Gaylord Brewer, and Ryan Van Cleave. *Tulane Review* is 80 pages, 7 × 9, perfect-bound, with 100# cover with full-color artwork. Receives about 1,200 poems/year, accepts about 30. Single copy: $5; subscription: $10. Make checks payable to *Tulane Review*.

How to Contact Submit up to 6 poems at a time. Lines/poem: 1-2 pages. Considers simultaneous submissions; no previously published poems. Accepts e-mail submissions; no fax or disk submissions. Cover letter is required. "Include brief biography." Reads submissions year round. Time between acceptance and publication is 3 months. "Poems are reviewed anonymously by a review board under a poetry editor's supervision. Recommendations are given to the editor, who makes final publication decisions." Often comments on rejected poems. Guidelines available in magazine, for SASE, by e-mail, or on Web site. Responds in 2 months. Pays 3 contributor's copies. Acquires first North American serial rights.

☑ ◎ THE TULE REVIEW

(Specialized: poets living in the greater Sacramento area), Sacramento Poetry Center, 1719 25th St., Sacramento CA 95816. (916)451-5569. E-mail: tulereview@sacramentopoetrycenter.org. Website: www.sacramentopoetrycenter.org. **Contact:** Brad Buchanan, managing editor.

Magazines Needs *The Tule Review*, published semiannually, uses "poetry, book reviews, and essays concerning contemporary poetry; occasionally includes an audio CD." Wants "all styles and forms of poetry." Primarily publishes poets living in the greater Sacramento area, but accepts work from anywhere. Has published poetry by Gary Snyder, Diane DiPrima, Jack Hirschman, Julia Connor, and Douglas Blazek. *The Tule Review* is 24-32 pages, digest-sized, saddle-stapled, with b&w cover artwork. Receives about 500 poems/year, accepts about 10-20%. Press run is 500; 80 distributed free to contributors and for review. Single copy: $6 ppd; subscription: $25/year (includes *Poetry Now*, a monthly publication). Make checks payable to Sacramento Poetry Center.

How to Contact Submit 3-6 poems at a time. Lines/poem: 96 maximum. Considers previously published poems; no simultaneous submissions. Accepts e-mail (pasted into body of message or as attachment) and disk submissions. "If you attach poems, put all poems into one attachment." Cover letter is required. Reads submissions year round. Submit seasonal poems 6 months in advance. Time between acceptance and publication is 1-6 months. Poems are circulated to an editorial board. Sometimes comments on rejected poems. Sometimes publishes theme issues. Upcoming themes available in magazine, by e-mail, or on website. Guidelines available in magazine, for SASE, by e-mail, or on website. Responds in 3-4 months. Pays 2 contributor's copies. Acquires first North American serial rights. Rights revert to poet upon publication. Reviews books/chapbooks of poetry and other magazines/journals.

Tips "Send us your best work!"

☑ ◎ TUNDRA: THE JOURNAL OF THE SHORT POEM

(Specialized: poems of 13 or fewer lines, including haiku and tanka), 22230 NE 28th Place, Sammamish WA 98074-6408. E-mail: WelchM@aol.com. Website: http://sites.google.com/site/tundrashortpoem/. Established 1999. **Contact:** Michael Dylan Welch, editor/publisher.

Magazines Needs *Tundra: The Journal of the Short Poem* showcases all short poetry, including haiku, tanka, and other genres. Wants "short poems of 13 or fewer lines rooted in immediate and objective imagery, including haiku and tanka." Does not want religious, topical, or confessional poetry. Has published poetry by Dana Gioia, X.J. Kennedy, Jane Hirshfield, Peter Pereira, Robert Bly, and Madeleine DeFrees. *Tundra* is 128 pages, digest-sized, offset-printed, perfect-bound, with glossy cover. Receives about 14,000 poems/year, accepts less than 1%. Press run is 1,200 (700 subscribers, 10 libraries, 50 shelf sales); 10 distributed free to such places as poetry centers. Single copy: $9; subscription: $21 for 3 issues. Make checks payable to Michael Dylan Welch.

How to Contact Submit 3-5 poems at a time ("up to 10 is okay if as short as haiku"). No previously published poems or simultaneous submissions. Accepts e-mail submissions (pasted into body of message; no attachments); no disk submissions. "Always include your full postal address with each e-mail submission." Cover letter is optional; "okay the first time you submit, but unnecessary thereafter unless you write something you are sure the editor needs to know. *Tundra* does not publish bios, so there's no need to include them except for the editor's information. Please include a #10 SASE with sufficient postage for return of the manuscript or for a response." Reads submissions year round. Time between acceptance and publication "varies, but is sometimes up to a year. The editor makes the sole decision, and may occasionally offer suggestions on poems whether accepted or returned. The editor will clearly indicate if he wants to see a revision." Recommends reading an issue before submitting, "but no purchase or subscription is required." Guidelines available for SASE, by e-mail, or on Web site. Responds in 3-4 months. Sometimes sends prepublication galleys. Pays 1 contributor's copy. Acquires first rights. "Rights revert to author after publication, but we may want to include selected poems on Web site in the future." Reviews books/chapbooks of poetry in 500-2,000 words, single- and multi-book format. Send materials for review consideration to Michael Dylan Welch.

Tips "If your work centers on immediate and objective imagery, *Tundra* is interested. All poems must be 13 or fewer lines, with only very rare exceptions (where each line is very short). If you think that a haiku is merely 5-7-5 syllables, then I do not want to see your work (see 'Becoming a Haiku Poet' online at www.haikuworld.org/begin/mdwelch.apr2003.html for reasons why). Due to the excessive volume of inappropriate submissions for *Tundra* in the past, I now encourage only well-established poets to submit."

$ ◎ TURTLE MAGAZINE FOR PRESCHOOL KIDS

(Specialized: ages 2-5), Children's Better Health Institute, 1100 Waterway Blvd., Indianapolis IN 46202. Website: www.cbhi.org or www.turtlemag.org.

Magazines Needs *Turtle Magazine for Preschool Kids*, published by Childen's Better Health Institute, is a magazine for children ages 2-5. "Colorful and entertaining...perfect for reading aloud." Wants light-hearted poetry appropriate for the age group. Reviews submissions for possible use in all Children's Better Health Institute publications.

How to Contact Manuscripts must be typewritten with poet's contact information in upper right-hand corner of each poem's page. SASE required. Submit seasonal material at least 8 months in advance. Guidelines available for SASE or on Web site. Responds in about 3 months. Pays $25 minimum for poetry. Acquires all rights.

Tips "We receive too many poetry submissions that are about kids, not for kids. Or, the subject matter is 1 that adults think children would or should like. Reading our guidelines is not enough. Careful study of current issues will acquaint writers with each title's 'personality.'"

Ⓝ ▣ $ ◪ T-ZERO QUARTERLY

727 Rapids St., Roanoke Rapids NC 27870. (757)477-3883. E-mail: t-zero@wvu.org. Website: http://writersvillage.com/tzero. Established 1998. **Contact:** Carolann Neilon Malley, poetry editor.

Magazines Needs *T-Zero*, published quarterly, "encourages occasional long, well-constructed sentences, artful adverbs, and image-evoking adjectives. Audience is primarily writers. We publish all forms of formal and free verse. All poems should be original." Does not want "greeting card verse." Sample copy is $6.99 (free online). *T-Zero* is 8x10, 56-110 pages, white book stock paper, glossy cover. Also provides .pdf version on web site.

How to Contact Submit up to five poems at a time, 60 lines maximum. No previously published poems or simultaneous submissions. Accepts submissions through website. "After your first contact, you will receive email instructions and a ticket number to attach your submission online." Reads submissions year round. Time between acceptance and publication is 6 months. Sometimes comments on rejected poems. Guidelines on Web site. "Payment starts at $15 for a single poem to $30 for a group of poems by a single writer appearing in the same issue." Acquires first North American serial rights, electronic rights, web archival rights. Publication is copyrighted.

▣ ▢ ◎ UGLY ACCENT: A LITERARY ADVERSARIA BROUGHT TO YOU BY THE MIDWEST

E-mail: poetry@uglyaccent.com. Website: www.uglyaccent.com. Established 2006. **Contact:**

Matt Friauf, poetry editors.

Magazine Needs UGLY ACCENT: A Literary Adversaria Brought to You by the Midwest, published quarterly online, seeks "to publish new talent, specifically those with some degree of separation to the Midwest. We wish to glorify the cesspool of talent that this part of the nation breeds." Has published poetry by Ron Czerwien, Eddie Kilowatt, Gene Tanta, Paul Gaszak, Karla Huston, and Bronwen Tate. Receives about 350 poems/year, accepts about 80 (22%).

How to Contact Submit 5 poems at a time. Lines/poem: open. Considers previously published poems and simultaneous submissions. Accepts e-mail submissions (as attachment); no disk submissions. Cover letter is preferred. Include 50-word bio with submission. Reads submissions from September 1-April 1. Time between acceptance and publication is 6-12 months. Poems are circulated to an editorial board. Often comments on rejected poems. Sometimes publishes theme issues. Guidelines available on Web site. Responds in 4-6 months. Does not pay. Acquires one-time rights and right to publish work in online archives. Rights revert to poets upon publication. Reviews books/chapbooks of poetry. Send materials for review consideration to the attention of Matt Friauf.

Tips "We are looking for writers with subtlety and a predilection for experimentation with language and form. We believe that poetry should test the elasticity of language and utilize the form for all its worth. Self-absorbed poems will not be tolerated; sure, all poems are autobiographical to some extent, but at least pretend to care about something else."

☐ UP AND UNDER: THE QND REVIEW

P.O. Box 115, Hainesport NJ 08036. E-mail: qndpoets@yahoo.com. Website: www. quickanddirtypoets.com. Established 2004. **Contact:** Kendall Bell, editor.

Magazines Needs *Up and Under: The QND Review*, published annually in March, is "a journal with an eclectic mix of poetry: sex, death, politics, IKEA, Mars, food, and jug handles alongside a smorgasbord of other topics covered in such diverse forms as the sonnet, villanelle, haiku, and free verse. We are interested in excellent poetry with no bias between free verse or traditional forms." Does not want "greeting card verse, graphic pornography." Has published poetry by Dan Maguire, Gina Larkin, Leonard Gontarek, Autumn Konopka, John Grey and Taylor Graham. *Up and Under* is 50-60 pages, digest-sized, laser-printed, saddle-stapled, with card cover with photograph, includes ads. Receives about 300 poems/year, accepts about 30 (or 10%). Press run is 100. Single copy: $7. Chapbooks are available online or through U.S. Mail. Make checks payable to Kendall Bell.

How to Contact Submit up to 5 poems at a time. Lines/poem: no limit. Considers simultaneous submissions (with notification); no previously published poems. Accepts e-mail submissions (pasted into body of message). Reads submissions September 1-December 30. Time between acceptance and publication is 3-6 months. Poems are circulated to an editorial board. Sometimes comments on rejected poems. Guidelines available in magazine, for SASE, or on Web site. Responds in 2-3 months. Pays 1 contributor's copy. Acquires one-time rights.

Tips "Take a moment to read the poems featured on our Web site before submitting. We prefer poetry that uses concrete imagery to engage all 5 senses."

▦ ☑ ◎ URTHONA MAGAZINE

(Specialized: Buddhism), Abbey House, Abbey Road, Cambridge CB5 8HQ England. +44(0)1223-362513. E-mail: urthonamag@onetel.com. Website: www.urthona.com. Established 1992. **Contact:** Poetry Editor.

Magazines Needs *Urthona*, published biannually, explores the arts and Western culture from a Buddhist perspective. Wants "poetry rousing the imagination." Does not want "undigested autobiography, political, or New Age-y poems." Has published poetry by Peter Abbs, Robert Bly, and Peter Redgrove. *Urthona* is 60 pages, A4, offset-printed, saddle-stapled, with 4-color glossy cover, includes ads. Receives about 300 poems/year, accepts about 40. Press run is 1,200 (200 subscribers, plus shelf sales in Australia and America). "See Web site for current subscription rates." Sample (including guidelines): $7.99 USD, $8.99 CAD.

How to Contact Submit 6 poems at a time. No previously published poems or simultaneous submissions. Accepts e-mail submissions (as attachment). Cover letter is preferred. Time between acceptance and publication is up to 8 months. Poems are circulated to an editorial board and are read and selected by poetry editor. Other editors have right of veto. Responds within 6 months. Pays 1 contributor's copy. Acquires one-time rights. Reviews books/chapbooks of poetry and other magazines in 600 words. Send materials for review consideration.

⟳ $ ☑ ◎ VALLUM

CONTEMPORARY POETRY, (Specialized: theme-driven issues), P.O. Box 326, Westmount Station, Montreal, Quebec H3Z 2T5 Canada. E-mail: info@vallummag.com. Website: www. vallummag.com. Established 2000. **Contact:** Joshua Auerbach and Helen Zisimatos, editors.

Magazines Needs *Vallum: Contemporary Poetry*, published annually, is "an international journal featuring high-quality, well-crafted contemporary poetry; open to most styles, and to new and established poets." Considers poetry by children and teens. Has published poetry by Franz Wright, A.F. Moritz, George Elliott Clarke, John Kinsella, and Medbh McGuckian. *Vallum* is 100 pages, 7x8½, digitally printed, perfect-bound, with color images on coated stock cover. Press run is 2,500. Single copy: $8.95; subscription: $17/year. Make checks payable to *Vallum*.

How to Contact Submit 4-7 poems at a time. No previously published poems or simultaneous submissions. No e-mail submissions. Cover letter is preferred. Include SASE (or SAE and IRC). Check Web site for submission deadlines. Sometimes comments on rejected poems. Always publishes theme issues. Guidelines available on website. Responds in 9-12 months. Pays honorarium and one contributor's copy. Acquires first North American serial rights. Reviews books/chapbooks of poetry in 500-700 words. Send materials for review consideration. Essays on poetics also considered. Query essays, interviews, and reviews by e-mail.

Tips "Hone your craft; read widely; be original."

▣ ☑ VALPARAISO POETRY REVIEW

CONTEMPORARY POETRY, (Specialized: theme-driven issues), P.O. Box 326, Westmount Station, Montreal, Quebec H3Z 2T5 Canada. E-mail: info@vallummag.com. Website: www. vallummag.com. Established 2000. **Contact:** Joshua Auerbach and Helen Zisimatos, editors.: Contemporary Poetry and PoeticsDept. of English, Valparaiso University, Valparaiso IN 46383-6493. (219)464-5278. Fax: (219)464-5511. E-mail: vpr@valpo.edu. Website: www.valpo.edu/english/vpr/. Established 1999. **Contact:** Edward Byrne, editor.

Magazines Needs *Valparaiso Poetry Review: Contemporary Poetry and Poetics*, published semiannually online, accepts "submissions of unpublished or previously published poetry, book reviews, author interviews, and essays on poetry or poetics that have not yet appeared online and for which the rights belong to the author. Query for anything else." Wants poetry of any length or style, free verse or traditional forms. Has published poetry by Charles Wright, Billy Collins, John Balaban, Stanley Plumly, and Annie Finch. Receives about 2,000 poems/year, accepts about 1%.

How to Contact Submit 3-5 poems at a time (no more than 5). Considers previously published poems ("original publication must be identified to ensure proper credit") and simultaneous submissions. Accepts e-mail submissions (pasted into body of message, no attachments); no fax or disk submissions. **Postal submissions preferred.** Cover letter is preferred. Include SASE. Reads submissions year round. Time between acceptance and publication is 6-12 months. Seldom comments on rejected poems. Guidelines available on Web site. Responds in up to 6 weeks. Acquires one-time rights. "All rights remain with author." Reviews books of poetry in single- and multi-book format. Send materials for review consideration.

▦ ☑ VAN GOGH'S EAR: BEST WORLD POETRY & PROSE

French Connection Press, 12 rue Lamartine, Paris 75009 France. (33)(1)4016-0535. Fax: (33) (1)4016-0701. E-mail: frenchcx@club-internet.fr. Website: www.frenchcx.com. Established 2002. **Contact:** Ian Ayres, founder/editor.

•Poetry published in *Van Gogh's Ear* has appeared in *The Best American Poetry*.

Magazines Needs *Van Gogh's Ear*, published annually in April, is an anthology series "devoted to publishing powerful poetry and prose in English and English translations by major voices and innovative new talents from around the globe." Has published poetry by Marilyn Monroe, Tony Curtis, Yoko Ono, James Dean, Xaviera Hollander, and Charles Manson. *Van Gogh's Ear* is 280 pages, digest-sized, offset-printed, perfect-bound, with 4-color matte cover with commissioned artwork. Receives about 1,000 poems/year, accepts about 30%. Press run is 2,000 (105 subscribers, 25 libraries, 1,750 shelf/online sales); 120 distributed free to contributors and reviewers. Single copy: $19; subscription: $36 for 2 years. "As a 501(c)(3) nonprofit enterprise, *Van Gogh's Ear* needs the support of individual poets, writers, and readers to survive. Any donation, large or small, will help *Van Gogh's Ear* continue to publish the best cross-section of contemporary poetry and prose. Because of being an anglophone publication based in France, *Van Gogh's Ear* is unable to get any grants or funding. Your contribution will be tax-deductible. Make donation checks payable to Committee on Poetry-*VGE*, and mail them (donations **only**) to the Allen Ginsberg Trust, P.O. Box 582, Stuyvesant Station, New York NY 10009. All U.S. checks/money orders for reading fees, subscriptions, and purchases must be made out to French Connection Press and sent to Michael Hathaway, 522 E. South Ave., St. John KS 67576-2212."

How to Contact Submit 6 poems or 2 prose pieces at a time. Lines/poem: 165 maximum (1,500 words maximum for prose). No previously published poems or simultaneous submissions. No fax, e-mail, or disk submissions. Cover letter is preferred. "**Send to the French Connection Press address only!** Please include SASE (or SAE with IRCs) or e-mail address along with a brief bio of up to 120 words." Reads submissions May 1-October 31. **Charges $10 (USD) reading fee for non-subscribers.** Time between acceptance and publication is one year. "Every submission is closely read by all members of the editorial board and voted upon." Seldom comments on rejections. "Our continued existence, and continued ability to read your work, depends mainly on subscriptions/donations. Therefore, we must ask that you at least purchase a sample copy before submitting work." Guidelines available in anthology or on Web site. Responds in 9 months. Always sends prepublication galleys. Pays 1 contributor's copy. Acquires one-time rights.

Tips "The goal of *Van Gogh's Ear* is for each volume to transport all who experience it into multifaceted realities that transcend color and culture through the uncensored pens of legendary and new talents from all walks of life. 'Intensity' is the key. And we are more than open to poets/writers who haven't been published before. Being published isn't as important as the work itself. Please note: Volume 7 will be the final volume of *Van Gogh's Ear*. We are currently accepting submissions for that volume."

▦ ☐ VERANDAH

c/o Faculty of Arts, Deakin University, 221 Burwood Hwy., Burwood, Victoria 3125 Australia. (61)(3)9251-7134. E-mail: verandah@deakin.edu.au. Website: www.deakin.edu.au/verandah.

Established 1986. **Contact:** Poetry Editor.

Magazines Needs *Verandah*, published annually in September, is "a high-quality literary journal edited by professional writing students. It aims to give voice to new and innovative writers and artists." Has published poetry by Christos Tsiolka, Dorothy Porter, Seamus Heaney, Les Murray, Ed Burger, and Joh Muk Muk Burke. *Verandah* is 120 pages, professionally printed on glossy stock, flat-spined, with full-color glossy card cover. Sample: $15 AUD.

How to Contact No e-mail submissions; postal submissions only. However, electronic version of work must be available if accepted by *Verandah*. **Do not submit work without the required submission form (available for download on Web site).** Reads submissions by May 31 deadline (postmark). Guidelines available on Web site. Pays one contributor's copy, "with prizes awarded accordingly." Acquires first Australian publishing rights.

Contest/Award Offerings Prizes awarded in each issue. Prize entry is automatic for Deakin students, no entry fee (student number is required). **Entry fee:** $5 AUD for first entry, $10 AUD for first 3, $5 AUD for each additional entry thereafter. Work submitted by non-Deakin students without an entry fee will be considered for publication, but will not be eligible for a prize. **Deadline:** May 31 (postmark). Guidelines available on Web site.

▦ ✐ VERSAL

Amsterdam, The Netherlands. E-mail: versal@wordsinhere.com. Website: www.wordsinhere.com. Established 2002. **Contact:** Megan M. Garr, editor.

Magazines Needs *Versal*, published annually by wordsinhere, is the only English-language literary magazine in the Netherlands and publishes new poetry, prose, and art from around the world. "We publish writers with an instinct for language and line break, content and form that is urgent, involved, and unexpected." Has published poetry by Naomi Shihab Nye, Ben Doller, Marilyn Hacker, Julie Marie Wade, Myronn Hardy, William Doreski, Dawn Lonsinger, and Sawako Nakayasu. *Versal* is 100 pages, 20cmx20cm, offset-printed, perfect-bound, with acid-free full-color cover. Receives about 1,000+ poems/year, accepts about 4%. Single copy: $15 USD. Ordering information available on Web site.

How to Contact Submit 3-5 poems at a time. Considers simultaneous submissions; no previously published poems. Accepts submissions online only (online submission system can be found on Web site. Cover letter is required (in body of e-mail). Reads submissions September 15-January 15. Time between acceptance and publication is 4-7 months. Poems are circulated to an editorial board. Sometimes comments on rejected poems. Guidelines available on Web site. Responds in 2 months. Sends prepublication PDF galleys. Pays 1 contributor's copy. Acquires one-time rights. Rights revert to poet upon publication.

Tips "Write as much as you can. Follow the guidelines. Resist the urge to send us poems about tulips, windmills, or sex and drug adventures. Support independent literary publishing: buy copies of *Versal* and any other lit mag you find."

✐ VERSE

Dept. of English, University of Richmond, Richmond VA 23173. Website: http://versemag.blogspot.com. Established 1984. **Contact:** Brian Henry and Andrew Zawacki, editors. Poetry published in Verse has also appeared in The Best American Poetry and The Pushcart Prize.

Magazines Needs *Verse*, published 3 times/year, is "an international poetry journal which also publishes interviews with poets, essays on poetry, and book reviews." Wants "no specific kind; we look for high-quality, innovative poetry. Our focus is not only on American poetry, but on all poetry written in English, as well as translations." Has published poetry by James Tate, John Ashbery, Barbara Guest, Gustaf Sobin, and Rae Armantrout. *Verse* is 128-416 pages, digest-sized, professionally printed, perfect-bound, with card cover. Receives about 5,000 poems/year, accepts 1%. Press run is 1,000. Single copy: $10; subscription: $18 for individuals, $39 for institutions. Sample: $6.

How to Contact *Verse* is closed to unsolicited submissions until further notice; check website for any updates. Unsolicited submissions will be recycled.

Tips "Read widely and deeply. Avoid inundating a magazine with submissions; constant exposure will not increase your chances of getting accepted."

$ ☑ THE VIRGINIA QUARTERLY REVIEW

P.O. Box 400223, Charlottesville VA 22904-4223. (434)924-3124. Fax: (434)924-1397. Website: www.vqronline.org. Established 1925.

Magazines Needs *The Virginia Quarterly Review* uses about 45-50 pages of poetry in each issue. No length or subject restrictions. Issues have largely included lyric and narrative free verse, most of which features a strong message or powerful voice. *The Virginia Quarterly Review* is 256 pages, digest-sized, flat-spined. Press run is 7,000.

How to Contact Submit up to 5 poems at a time. No simultaneous submissions. Accepts online submissions only at http://vqronline.org/submission/. Responds in 1-3 months. Guidelines available on website; do not request by fax. Pays $5/line.

Contest/Award Offerings Sponsors the Emily Clark Balch Prize for Poetry, an annual award of $1,000 given to the best poem or group of poems published in the *Review* during the year. 2007 winner was Peter Balakian.

▦ ☑ ◎ VOICES ISRAEL

P.O. Box 21, Metulla 10292, Israel. E-mail: hbarlev@netvision.net.il. Website: www.poetry-voices.8m.com. Established 1972. **Contact:** Helen Barlev, editor-in-chief.

Magazines Needs *Voices Israel*, published annually by The Voices Israel Group of Poets, is "an anthology of poetry in English, with worldwide contributions. We consider all kinds of poetry." Poems must be in English; translations must be accompanied by the original poem. *Voices Israel* is about 125 pages, digest-sized, offset from laser output on ordinary paper, flat-spined, with varying cover. Press run is 350. Single copy: $20 for nonmembers. Sample: $15 (back issue). "Members receive the anthology with annual dues ($35)." Visit Web site or e-mail millmanm@zahav.net.il for ordering information.

How to Contact Submit up to 4 poems/year. Lines/poem: 40 maximum. Considers previously published poems, "but please include details and assurance that copyright problems do not exist." Accepts e-mail submissions (preferred, as a single Word.doc or Word.rtf attachment). Send 7 hard copies, for distribution to the Editorial Board. Reads submissions June 1-October 7. No reading fee, but **a contribution of $10 for up to 4 poems is requested**. "This is not mandatory and will not affect acceptance or rejection of poems. We reply to all submissions but do not return poems. We do not guarantee publication of any poem. In poems that we publish, we reserve the right to correct obviously unintentional errors in spelling, punctuation, etc."

Contest/Award Offerings The annual International Reuben Rose Memorial Poetry Competition offers 1st Prize: $300; 2nd Prize $150; 3rd Prize: $100; 4th Prize: $50; and Honorable Mentions. Winning poems are published and distributed together with the *Voices Israel* anthology (as a separate booklet). Send poems of up to 40 lines each to John Dicks, P.O. Box 236, Kiriat Ata, 28101 Israel (john_d@netvision.net.il). Submit 2 copies of each poem: one with name and address; one with no identifying information. Enclose a cover letter providing the title(s) of the poem(s) submitted, your full name, address, and phone number. **Entry fee:** $5/poem (unlimited entries). Make checks payable to *Voices Israel*. **Deadline:** October 7th. Guidelines available on

Web site.

Also Offers *Monthly Poet's Voice*, edited by Ezra Ben-Meir, Herzl 45, Nahariya, 22406 Israel (ezrab@teacher.com), is a newsletter sent only to members of the Voices Israel Group of Poets in English.

☐ ◎ WATERWAYS: POETRY IN THE MAINSTREAM

(Specialized: thematic issues), Ten Penny Players, Inc., 393 Saint Pauls Ave., Staten Island NY 10304-2127. (718)442-7429. E-mail: tenpennyplayers@si.rr.com. Website: www.tenpennyplayers. org. Established 1977. **Contact:** Barbara Fisher and Richard Spiegel, poetry editors.

Magazines Needs *Waterways: Poetry in the Mainstream*, published 11 times/year, prints work by adult poets. "We publish theme issues and are trying to increase an audience for poetry and the printed and performed word. While we do 'themes,' sometimes an idea for a future magazine is inspired by a submission, so we try to remain open to poets' inspirations. Poets should be guided, however, by the fact that we are children's and animal rights advocates and are a NYC press. We are open to reading material from people we have never published, writing in traditional and experimental poetry forms." Does not want "haiku or rhyming poetry; never use material of an explicit sexual nature." Has published poetry by Ida Fasel, Will Inman, and Richard Kostelanetz. *Waterways* is 40 pages, 414x7, photocopied from various type styles, saddle-stapled, with matte card cover. Accepts 60% of poems submitted. Press run is 150. Subscription: $33. Sample: $4.

How to Contact Submit less than 10 poems at a time (for first submission). Considers simultaneous submissions. Accepts e-mail submissions (pasted into body of message). "Since we've taken the time to be very specific in our response, writers should take seriously our comments and not waste their emotional energy and our time sending material that isn't within our area of interest. Sending for our theme sheet and a sample issue and then objectively thinking about the writer's own work is practical and wise. Manuscripts that arrive without a return envelope are not sent back." Sometimes comments on rejected poems. Guidelines available for SASE or on Web site. Responds in less than 1 month. Pays 1 contributor's copy. Acquires one-time publication rights.

Additional Information Ten Penny Players publishes chapbooks "by children and young adults only—not by submission—they come through our workshops in the library and schools. Adult poets are published through our Bard Press imprint, **by invitation only**. Books evolve from the relationship we develop with writers we publish in *Waterways* and to whom we would like to give more exposure."

Tips "We suggest that poets attend book fairs and check our Web site. It's a fast way to find out what we're publishing. Without meaning to sound 'precious' or unfriendly, the writer should understand that small press publishers doing limited editions and all production work in-house are working from their personal artistic vision and know exactly what notes will harmonize, effectively counterpoint, and meld. Many excellent poems submitted to *Waterways* are sent back to the writers because they don't relate to what we are trying to create in a given month."

$ ◎ WEBER: THE CONTEMPORARY WEST

Weber State University, 1405 University Circle, Ogden UT 84408-1214. (801)626-6616. E-mail: weberjournal@weber.edu. Website: http://weberjournal.weber.edu. Established 1983. **Contact:** Michael Wutz, editor.

•Poetry published in *Weber* has appeared in *The Best American Poetry*.

Magazines Needs *Weber: The Contemporary West*, published 3 times/year, is "an interdisciplinary journal interested in relevant works covering a wide range of topics." Wants "three or four poems; we publish multiple poems from a poet." Does not want "poems that are flippant, prurient, sing-song, or preachy." Has published poetry by Naomi Shihab Nye, Carolyn Forche, Stephen Dunn, Billy Collins, William Kloefkorn, David Lee, Gary Gildner, and Robert Dana. *Weber* is 150 pages, offset-printed on acid-free paper, perfect-bound, with color cover. Receives about 250-300 poems/year, accepts 30-40. Press run is 1,000; 90% libraries. Subscription: $20 ($30 for institutions); $40 for outside the US. Sample: $10 (back issue).

How to Contact Submit 3-4 poems at a time, 2 copies of each (one without name). Considers simultaneous submissions; no previously published poems. Cover letter is preferred. Time between acceptance and publication is 15 months. Poems are selected by an anonymous (blind) evaluation. Themes and guidelines available in magazine, for SASE, by e-mail, or on Web site. Responds in up to 6 months. Always sends prepublication galleys. Pays 2 contributor's copies, a year's subscription, and a small honorarium ($100-300) depending on fluctuating grant monies. Acquires all rights. Copyright reverts to author after first printing.

Contest/Award Offerings The Dr. Sherwin W. Howard Poetry Award, a $500 cash prize, is awarded annually to the author of the best set of poems published in *Weber* during the previous year. The competition is announced each year in the Spring/Summer issue.

Tips "This journal is refereed by established poets—beginners not encouraged."

▨ $ ☑ WESTERLY

(Specialized: Australia, Asia, Indian Ocean region), English and Cultural Studies, University of Western Australia, Crawley 6009 Western Australia. (61)(8)6488-2101. Fax: (61)(8)6488-1030. E-mail: westerly@cyllene.uwa.edu.au. Website: http://westerly.uwa.edu.au. Established 1956. **Contact:** Natalia Lizama, administrator.

Magazines Needs *Westerly*, published annually in July and November, prints quality short fiction, poetry, literary critical, socio-historical articles, and book reviews with special attention given to Australia, Asia, and the Indian Ocean region. "We don't dictate to writers on rhyme, style, experimentation, or anything else. We are willing to publish short or long poems. We do assume a reasonably well-read, intelligent audience. Past issues of *Westerly* provide the best guides. Not consciously an academic magazine." *Westerly* is about 200 pages, digest-sized, "electronically printed." Press run is 1,200. Subscription information available at Web site.

How to Contact Submit up to three poems or one short story (two if quite short-suggested maximum length 5,000 words) at a time. No simultaneous submissions. Submit via post or e-mail. Cover letters should be brief and non-confessional. All manuscripts must show the name and address of the sender and should be single spaced in size 12 Times New Roman font. Deadline for July edition is 31st March and deadline for November edition is 31 July. Time between acceptance and publication may be up to one year depending on when work is submitted. Please wait for a response before forwarding any additional submissions for consideration. Contributors receive payment plus one complimentary copy. Acquires first publication rights; requests acknowledgment on reprints. Reviews books of poetry in multi-book format in an annual review essay. Send materials for review consideration. For further information on contributing, please see Web site.

Contest/Award Offerings The Patricia Hackett Prize (value approximately $750 AUD) is awarded annually for the best contribution published in the previous year's issue of *Westerly*.

Tips "Be sensible. Write what matters to you, but think about the reader. Don't spell out the meanings of the poems and the attitudes to be taken to the subject matter—i.e., trust the reader. Don't be swayed by literary fashion. Read the magazine, if possible, before sending submissions."

$ ☑ WESTERN HUMANITIES REVIEW

University of Utah, 255 S. Central Campus Dr., Room 3500, Salt Lake City UT 84112-0494. (801)581-6070. Fax: (801)585-5167. E-mail: whr@mail.hum.utah.edu. Website: www.hum.utah. edu/whr. Established 1947. **Contact:** Dawn Lonsinger, managing editor.

•Poetry published in *Western Humanities Review* has been selected for *The Best American Poetry* as well as the *Pushcart Prize* anthologies.

Magazines Needs *Western Humanities Review*, published semiannually in April and October, prints poetry, fiction, and a small selection of nonfiction. Wants "quality poetry of any form, including translations." Has published poetry by Charles Simic, Olena Kalytiak Davis, Ravi Shankar, Karen Volkman, Dan Beachy-Quick, Lucie Brock-Broido and Dan Chiasson. Innovative prose poems may be submitted as fiction, non-fiction to the appropriate editor. *Western Humanities Review* is 120-160 pages, digest-sized, professionally printed on quality stock, perfect-bound, with coated card cover. Receives about 1,500 submissions/year, accepts less than 10%. Press run is 1,000. Subscription: $16 to individuals in the U.S. Sample: $10.

How to Contact Considers simultaneous submissions but no more than 5 poems or 25 pages per reading period. No fax or e-mail submissions. Reads submissions October 1-May 1 only. Time between acceptance and publication is 1-3 issues. Managing editor makes an initial cut, then the poetry editor makes the final selections. Seldom comments on rejected poems. "We do not publish writer's guidelines because we think the magazine itself conveys an accurate picture of our requirements." Responds in up to 6 months. Pays 2 contributor's copies. Acquires first serial rights then rights revert to author.

Contest/Award Offerings Sponsors an annual contest for Utah writers.

☐ WESTWARD QUARTERLY: THE MAGAZINE OF FAMILY READING

Laudemont Press, P.O. Box 250, Kirkland IL 60146. (800)440-4043. E-mail: wwquarterly@ aol.com. Website: www.wwquarterly.com. Established 1999. **Contact:** Shirley Anne Leonard, editor.

Magazines Needs *WestWard Quarterly: The Magazine of Family Reading* prints poetry. Wants "all forms, including rhyme—we welcome inspirational, positive, reflective, humorous material promoting nobility, compassion, and courage." Does not want "experimental or avant-garde forms, offensive language, depressing or negative poetry." Considers poetry by children and teens. Has published poetry by Joseph Fecher, Brian Felder, Aaron Hillman, Leland Jamieson, Joyce I. Johnson, Michael Keshigian, Arlene Mandell, J. Alvin Speers, Charles Waugaman. *WestWard Quarterly* is 32 pages, digest-sized, laser-printed, saddle-stapled, with inkjet color cover with scenic photos, includes ads. Receives about 1,500 poems/year, accepts about 10%. Press run is 120 (60 subscribers). Single copy: $4; subscription: $15/year ($18 foreign). Make checks payable to Laudemont Press.

How to Contact Submit up to 5 poems at a time. Lines/poem: 40 maximum. Considers previously published poems and simultaneous submissions. Prefers e-mail submissions (pasted into body of message); no disk submissions. Reads submissions year round. Submit seasonal poems 3 months in advance. Time between acceptance and publication is "months." Often comments on rejected poems. Guidelines available for SASE, by e-mail, or on Web site. Responds in "weeks." Pays 1 contributor's copy. Acquires one-time rights.

Also Offers "Every issue includes a 'Featured Writer,' an article about 'Poets from the Past,' and a piece on improving writing skills or writing different forms of poetry."

☑ WHISKEY ISLAND MAGAZINE

English Dept., Cleveland State University, Cleveland OH 44115. (216)687-2056. Fax: (216)687-

6943. E-mail: whiskeyisland@csuohio.edu. Website: www.csuohio.edu/class/english/whiskeyisland/. Established 1977. **Contact:** Poetry Editor. (Student editors change yearly.)

Magazines Needs *Whiskey Island Magazine*, published semiannually, prints poetry, fiction, creative nonfiction, and art. Wants "writing that engages the reader immediately. It's always good to be interesting early." Has published poetry by Denise Duhamel, H.L. Hix, James Allen Hall, Jay Hopler, and Wayne Miller. *Whiskey Island Magazine* is about 100 pages, digest-sized, professionally printed, perfect-bound, with glossy stock cover. Receives 1,000-1,500 poetry mss/year, accepts 6%. Press run is 1,000. Subscription: $12 domestic, $20 overseas. Sample: $6. Make checks payable to *Whiskey Island Magazine*.

How to Contact Submit up to 5 poems at a time. No previously published poems. Cover letter is required. Include brief bio and SASE for reply only, with name, address, e-mail, and phone number on each page of ms. Accepts e-mail submissions. "Please put cover letter and contact information in body of e-mail, send poems as a Word or .rtf attachment. By postal mail: please include cover letter and SASE. Name, address, e-mail and phone number on each page of ms." Reads submissions year round. Poems are circulated to an editorial committee. Guidelines available in magazine, for SASE, by e-mail, or on Web site. Responds within 6 months. Pays 2 contributor's copies and one-year subscription.

Contest/Award Offerings Sponsors an annual poetry contest. $500 prize and publication to winning entry. **Entry fee:** $10. **Deadline:** entries accepted October 1-March 31. Guidelines available by e-mail or on Web site.

☑ ◎ WHITE LOTUS: A JOURNAL OF HAIKU & SENRYU POETRY

Shadow Poetry, 1209 Milwaukee St., Excelsior Springs MO 64024. Phone/fax: (208)977-9114. E-mail: whitelotus@shadowpoetry.com. Website: www.shadowpoetry.com/magazine/whitelotus.html. Established 2005 (Shadow Poetry Web site established 2000). **Contact:** Marie Summers, chief editor. Associate Editor: Kathy Lippard Cobb.

Magazines Needs *White Lotus*, published semiannually, is a "specialized journal of haiku, senryu, tanka, and haiga. Editors'/readers' choice awards are also featured. Articles, book reviews, and sumi-e are welcome." Wants "only haiku, senryu, tanka, haiga, and sumi-e of the highest quality from poets ages 13 and up." *White Lotus* is 32-60 pages, digest-sized, saddle-stapled, with glossy b&w cover; back cover reserved for a color-printed haiga. Receives about 500 haiku/senryu per issue, prints less than 10%. Single copy: $10 US/Int'l; subscription: $15/year US, $20/yr Int'l. Make checks/money orders payable to Shadow Poetry.

How to Contact Submit up to 10 haiku/senryu/tanka at a time. No previously published poems or simultaneous submissions. Accepts fax, e-mail, and disk submissions, as well as submissions through online form and by postal mail. Cover letter is preferred. "Name of author, street address, and e-mail address must accompany all submissions, no exceptions. If work is accepted, participants will be contacted by mail or e-mail within one month of submissions." Reads submissions according to the following deadlines: June 30 (Fall/Winter issue) and December 31 (Spring/Summer issue). Never comments on rejected poems. Guidelines available in magazine or on Web site. Sends prepublication galleys. "Final drafts will be e-mailed or mailed to the accepted poet." Acquires first rights.

Additional Information Shadow Poetry sponsors Shadows Ink Poetry Contest, Shadow Poetry's Annual Chapbook Competition, (see separate listings in Contests & Awards).

☒ ☑ WHITE WALL REVIEW

Dept. of English, Ryerson University, Jorgenson Hall, 10th Floor, 350 Victoria St., Toronto ON M5B 2K3 Canada. Website: http://www.ryerson.ca/wwr/. Established 1976. **Contact:** The

Editors (editors change every year).

Magazines Needs *White Wall Review*, published annually in August, focuses on printing "clearly expressed, innovative poetry and prose. No style is unacceptable." Has published poetry by Vernon Mooers and David Sidjak. *White Wall Review* is 90-144 pages, digest-sized, professionally printed, perfect-bound, with glossy card cover. Press run is 500. Subscription: $10 plus GST.

How to Contact Submit up to 5 poems at a time by mail only. Length: 5 pages/piece maximum. Cover letter is required. Include short bio. Guidelines available in magazine, for SASE. Responds "as soon as possible." Pays one contributor's copy.

Tips "Innovative work is especially appreciated."

⊟ ▢ WILD GOOSE POETRY REVIEW

Central Piedmont Community College, Levine Campus, P.O. Box 35009, Charlotte NC 28235-5009. (704)330-4397. E-mail: Patricia.Bostian@cpcc.edu. Website: www.wildgoosepoetryreview.com. Established 2005. **Contact:** Patricia Kennedy Bostian, editor.

Magazines Needs *Wild Goose Poetry Review*, published quarterly online, is a poetry journal with essays, reviews, and interviews. Wants "poetry that exudes a sense of place, that is well-crafted, with an eye to imagery and an ear to music." Does not want "erotica, abstract stream-of-consciousness, or gratuitous obscenities." Has published poetry by Anthony Abbott. Receives about 1,000 poems/year, accepts about 12%.

How to Contact Submit 3-5 poems at a time. Lines/poem: "no poems longer than two pages accepted." Considers simultaneous submissions; no previously published poems. Accepts e-mail submissions only (pasted into body of message); no disk submissions. Cover letter is preferred. Reads submissions year round. Time between acceptance and publication is up to 6 months. Poems are circulated to an editorial board. Comments on rejected poems. Guidelines available on Web site. Responds in 4-6 weeks. Rights revert to poet upon publication. Reviews books/chapbooks of poetry in 500 words. Send materials for review consideration to Patricia Bostian.

Tips "Read, read, read. Inspiration does not a poem make. Revise, revise, revise."

⊟ ▢ WILD VIOLET

P.O. Box 39706, Philadelphia PA 19106-9706. E-mail: wildvioletmagazine@yahoo.com. Website: www.wildviolet.net. Established 2001. **Contact:** Alyce Wilson, editor.

Magazines Needs *Wild Violet*, published quarterly online, aims "to make the arts more accessible, to make a place for the arts in modern life." Wants "poetry that is well crafted, that engages thought, that challenges or uplifts the reader. We have published free verse, haiku, blank verse, and other forms. If the form suits the poem, we will consider any form." Does not want "abstract, self-involved poetry; poorly managed form; excessive rhyming; self-referential poems that do not show why the speaker is sad, happy, or in love." Has published poetry by Lyn Lifshin, Andrew H. Oerke, Erik Kestler, Anselm Brocki, Carol Frith, Richard Fammerée, Joanna Weston and Graham Burchell. Accepts about 15% of work submitted.

How to Contact Submit 3-5 poems at a time. Considers simultaneous submissions (with notification); no previously published poems. Accepts e-mail submissions (pasted into body of message, or as text or Word attachment); no disk submissions. Cover letter is preferred. Reads submissions year round. Submit seasonal poems 3 months in advance. Time between acceptance and publication is 3 months. "Decisions on acceptance or rejection are made by the editor." Seldom comments on rejected poems, unless requested. Occasionally publishes theme issues. Guidelines available by e-mail or on Web site. Responds in up to 3 months. Pays by providing a bio and link on contributor's page. Requests electronic rights to publish and archive accepted works. Reviews books/chapbooks of poetry in 250 words, single-book format. Query for review consideration.

Contest/Award Offerings Sponsors an annual poetry contest, offering 1st Prize: $100 and publication in *Wild Violet*; 2 Honorable Mentions will also be published. Guidelines available by e-mail or on Web site. **Entry fee:** $5/poem. Judged by independent judges.

Tips "Read voraciously; experience life and share what you've learned. Write what is hardest to say; don't take any easy outs."

☑ WILLARD & MAPLE

163 S. Willard St., Box 34, Burlington VT 05401. E-mail: willardandmaple@champlain.edu. Established 1996. **Contact:** Poetry Editor.

Magazines Needs *Willard & Maple*, published annually in spring, is "a student-run literary magazine from Champlain College's Professional Writing Program that publishes a wide array of poems, short stories, creative essays, short plays, pen & ink drawings, photos, and computer graphics." Wants "creative work of the highest quality." Does not want any submissions over 5 typed pages in length; all submissions must be in English. Considers poetry by children and teens. Has published poetry by Geof hewitt, Rachel Orsini, Jason Briody, Suki Fredericks, and N.B. Smith. *Willard & Maple* is 200 pages, digest-sized, digitally printed, perfect-bound. Receives about 500 poems/year, accepts about 20%. Press run is 600 (80 subscribers, 4 libraries); 200 are distributed free to the Champlain College writing community. Single copy: $15. Contact Lulu Press for Contributor's Copy.

How to Contact Submit up to 5 poems at a time. Lines/poem: 100 maximum. Considers simultaneous submissions; no previously published poems. Accepts e-mail and disk submissions. Cover letter is required. "Please provide current contact information including an e-mail address. Single-space submissions, one poem/page." Reads submissions September 1 -March 31. Time between acceptance and publication is less than 1 year. "All editors receive a blind copy to review. They meet weekly throughout the academic year. These meetings consist of the submissions being read aloud, discussed, and voted upon." Seldom comments on rejected poems. Occasionally publishes theme issues. Upcoming themes available by e-mail. Responds in less than 6 months. Pays 2 contributor's copies. Acquires one-time rights. Reviews books/chapbooks of poetry and other magazines/journals in 1,200 words. Send materials for review consideration to the poetry editor.

Tips "The power of imagination makes us infinite."

▣ ☐ THE WILLOW

The Smithtown Poetry Society, P.O. Box 793, Nesconset NY 11767. (631)656-6690. Fax: (631)656-6690. E-mail: editor@thesmithtownpoetrysociety.com. Website: www.thesmithtownpoetrysociety.com. Established 1991. **Contact:** Sheryl Minter.

Magazines Needs *The Willow*, published quarterly online, features "new and upcoming poets alongside known poets. We also feature art, short stories, and poetry, regardless of length, that inspire intelligent thought and originality." Wants all forms of poetry. Does not want "poetry written without thought or in sing-song rhyme." Considers poetry by children and teens. Has published poetry by Marian Ford and Najwa Brax. Receives about 1,000 poems/year, accepts about 15%. Press run is 600; 300 distributed free to coffee shops. Single copy: $7; subscription: $20. Make checks payable to S. Minter.

How to Contact Submit up to 3 poems at a time. Lines/poem: 30 maximum (longer poems are considered but may take longer to publish, depending on magazine space; query before submitting). Considers previously published poems; no simultaneous submissions. Accepts disk submissions; no fax or e-mail submissions. Cover letter is preferred. "All submissions must be typed, double-spaced, with submitter's name and address clearly printed. Please include a SASE for all submissions if you would like your original work returned." Reads submissions year round. Submit seasonal poems 6 months in advance. **Charges $1 reading fee.** Time between acceptance and publication is up to one year. Poems are circulated to an editorial board. Sometimes comments on rejected poems. Guidelines available in magazine, for SASE, by e-mail, or on Web site. Responds in 1 month.

Contest/Award Offerings The Smithtown Poetry Society Yearly Contest is open to all poets and offers 50% of the contest proceeds as first prize; "the other half goes to the distribution of *The Willow.*" Submit up to 3 poems, 20 lines maximum each. **Entry fee:** $5. **Deadline:** June 1. Guidelines available in magazine, for SASE, or on Web site. "All submissions may be edited for grammar and punctuation."

☑ WILLOW REVIEW

College of Lake County, 19351 W. Washington St., Grayslake IL 60030-1198. (847)543-2956. E-mail: com426@clcillinois.edu. Website: www.clcillinois.edu/community/willowreview.asp. Established 1969. **Contact:** Michael F. Latza, editor.

- *Willow Review* is partially supported by a grant from the Illinois Arts Council, a state agency.

Magazines Needs *Willow Review*, published annually, is interested in poetry, creative nonfiction, and fiction of high quality. "We have no preferences as to form, style, or subject, as long as each poem stands on its own as art and communicates ideas." Has published poetry by Lisel Mueller, Lucien Stryk, David Ray, Louis Rodriguez, John Dickson, and Patricia Smith. *Willow Review* is 88-96 pages, digest-sized, professionally printed, flat-spined, with a 4-color cover featuring work by an Illinois artist. Press run is 1,000. Subscription: $18 for 3 issues, $30 for 5 issues. Sample: $5 (back issue).

How to Contact Submit up to 5 poems at a time. Considers simultaneous submissions "if indicated in the cover letter"; no previously published poems. No e-mail submissions; postal submissions only. Include SASE; **"manuscripts will not be returned unless requested."** Reads submissions September-May. Guidelines available on website. Pays 2 contributor's copies. All rights remain with the author.

Contest/Award Offerings Prizes totaling $400 are awarded to the best poetry and short fiction/creative nonfiction in each issue.

Also Offers The College of Lake County Reading Series (4-7 readings/academic year) has included Thomas Lux, Isabel Allende, Donald Justice, Galway Kinnell, Lisel Mueller, Amiri Baraka, and others. One reading is for contributors to *Willow Review*. Readings, usually held on Thursday evenings and widely publicized in Chicago and suburban newspapers, are presented to audiences of about 150 students and faculty of the College of Lake County and other area colleges, as well as residents of local communities.

☑ WISCONSIN REVIEW

Wisconsin Review Press, 800 Algoma Blvd., University of Wisconsin-Oshkosh, Oshkosh WI 54902. (920)424-2267. E-mail: wisconsinreview@uwosh.edu. Website: www.uwosh.edu/wisconsinreview. Established 1966.

Magazines Needs *Wisconsin Review*, published semiannually, is a "contemporary poetry, prose, and art magazine run by students at the University of Wisconsin OshKosh." Wants all forms and styles of poetry. Does not want " poetry that is racist, sexist, or unnecessarily vulgar." Considers poetry by children and teens. "Minors may submit material by including a written letter of permission from a parent or guardian." *Wisconsin Review* is 120 pages, digest-sized, perfect-bound, with 4-color glossy coverstock. Receives about 400 poetry submissions/year, accepts about 50; Press run is 2,000. Single copy: $5; subscription: $10 plus $3 extra per issue for shipments outside the U.S.

How to Contact Submit up to 5 poems at a time. Does not consider previously published poems or simultaneous submissions. Accepts e-mail submissions. "Online submissions are accepted only through manuscripthub.com." Type one poem/page, single-spaced, with name and address of writer on each page. Cover letter is required. Include 3-5 sentence bio and SASE if submitting by mail. Reads submissions September through May. Submit seasonal poems 6 months in advance. Time between acceptance and publication is 6-9 months. Sometimes comments on rejected poems. Guidelines available in magazine, for SASE, by e-mail, and on Web site. Responds in 4-6 months. Pays 2 contributor's copies. Reviews books and chapbooks of poetry, other magazines and journals. Send materials for review consideration to the editors.

Tips "We are open to any poetic form and style, and look for outstanding imagery, new themes, and fresh voices — poetry that induces emotions."

$ ☑ ◎ WISTERIA: A JOURNAL OF HAIKU, SENRYU, & TANKA

P.O. Box 150932, Lufkin TX 75915-0932. E-mail: wisteriajournal@gmail.com (inquiries and submissions). Website: www.wistaria.blogspot.com. Established 2006. **Contact:** T.A. Thompson, publisher and editor, editor staff: Gary Hotham.

Magazines Needs *Wisteria: A Journal of Haiku, Senryu, & Tanka*, published quarterly, is a small journal printing only haiku, senryu, and tanka forms. Published work by Sanford Goldstein, Stanford M. Forrester, Wanda D. Cook, Michael Dylan Welch, and Kirsty Karkow. *Wisteria* is 24 pages, 414x512, self-published, laser-printed, saddle-stapled, with cardstock cover with photo. Press run is 200; 25 distributed free to poetry publishers and small presses that publish haiku, senryu, and tanka. Accepts about 7% of poems submitted. Single copy: $3; subscription: $10/year. Make checks payable to T.A. Thompson (cash and money orders also accepted).

How to Contact Submit 5-7 poems at a time. No previously published poems or simultaneous submissions. No e-mail or disk submissions. E-mail and postal submissions only. "Please include name, address, e-mail in upper right corner of manuscript. SASE required for reply." Reads submissions year round. Time between acceptance and publication is 6 months. Sometimes comments on rejected poems. Guidelines available in magazine or on Web site. Responds in 1 month. Pays $1 maximum honorarium for postal submissions only. Acquires first rights. Rights revert to poet upon publication.

Contest/Award Offerings The Pinewood Haiku Contest (see separate listing in Contests & Awards).

Tips "Study the history of haiku and how contemporary English language has influenced this form today."

Ⓝ ▣ WOLF, THE

3, Holly Mansions, Fortune Green Rd., London NW6 1UB.E-mail: submissions@wolfmagazine.co.uk. Website: www.wolfmagazine.co.uk. Established 2002 **Contact:** James Byrne, editor.

Magazines Needs *The Wolf*, published 3 times per year, publishes "international translations, critical prose, and interviews with leading contemporary poets, which are frequently mentioned as distinguishing characteristics of the magazine. The poetry, however, comes purely through work submitted. There is no special treatment with regard to the consideration of any poet or poem. Since January 2008, *The Wolf* has benefited from Arts Council funding. Since receiving its grant the magazine has increased its content by a third and is perfect bound." $12 single issue, including postage and packing; $35 subscription. Accepts PayPal.

How to Contact Submit up to 5 poems by mail or e-mail. Reads submissions year round. Guidelines available on Web site. Responds in 6 months. Pays 1 contributor's copy. Accepts reviews of poetry books between 800-1,500 words.

Additional Information Also accepts critical essays on any poetry subject between 2,000-3,000 words. Welcomes artwork or photographs.

⬛ THE WORCESTER REVIEW

Worcester County Poetry Association, Inc., 1 Ekman St., Worcester MA 01607. (508)797-4770. E-mail: wcpaboard@yahoo.com. Website: www.geocities.com/wreview. Established 1973. **Contact:** Rodger Martin, managing editor.

Magazines Needs *The Worcester Review*, published annually by the Worcester County Poetry Association, encourages "critical work with a New England connection; no geographic limitation on poetry and fiction." Wants "work that is crafted, intuitively honest and empathetic." Has published poetry by Kurt Brown, Cleopatra Mathis, and Theodore Deppe. *The Worcester Review* is 160 pages, digest-sized, professionally printed in dark type on quality stock, perfect-bound, with matte card cover. Press run is 750. Subscription: $30 (includes membership in WCPA). Sample: $8.

How to Contact Submit up to 5 poems at a time (recommend 3 or less receive the most favorable readings). Considers previously published poems "if they do not conflict with our readership" and simultaneous submissions "if notified." Cover letter is required. Include brief bio. Poems should be typed on 8½x11 paper, with poet's name in upper left corner of each page. Include SASE for return of ms. Sometimes comments on rejected poems. Guidelines available for SASE or on Web site. Responds in up to 9 months. Pays 2 contributor's copies plus small honorarium. Acquires first rights.

Tips "Read some. Listen a lot."

⬛ WRITE ON!! POETRY MAGAZETTE

P.O. Box 901, Richfield UT 84701-0901. E-mail: jimnipoetry@yahoo.com. Established 1998. **Contact:** Jim Garman, editor.

Magazines Needs *Write On!! Poetry Magazette*, published monthly, features "poetry from poets around the world." Wants poetry of "any style; all submissions must be suitable for all ages to read." Does not want "adult or vulgar material." Considers poetry by children and teens. Has published poetry by Cathy Porter, B.Z. Niditch, Gerald Zipper, and Betty Shelley. *Write On!!* is 24 pages, digest-sized, photostat-copied, saddle-stapled. Receives about 500 poems/year, accepts about 50%. Press run is 50. Single copy: $4. Sample: $3. Make checks payable to Jim Garman.

How to Contact Submit 1-6 poems at a time. Lines/poem: 6 minimum, 28 maximum. Considers previously published poems and simultaneous submissions. Accepts e-mail submissions (pasted into body of message, no attachments). Reads submissions year round. Submit seasonal poems 2 months in advance. Time between acceptance and publication is one month. Never comments on rejected poems. Occasionally publishes theme issues. Guidelines available by e-mail. Responds in "approximately" 3 weeks. No payment or free copies provided. "*WRITE ON!!* contains no ads, no sponsors, all costs are out of pocket or from those desiring a copy." Acquires one-time rights, "which return to author upon publication."

Tips "Send only your best material after it has been refined."

⬛ WRITER'S BLOC

Dept. of Language & Literature, Texas A&M University-Kingsville, MSC 162, Kingsville TX 78363-8202. E-mail: c-downs@tamuk.edu (inquiries only). Website: www.tamuk.edu/langlit/writer's.

htm. Established 1980. **Contact:** C. Downs, faculty sponsor.

Magazines Needs *Writer's Bloc*, published annually in October, prints poetry, fiction, creative nonfiction, and graphic art. "About half of our pages are devoted to the works of Texas A&M University-Kingsville students and half to the works of writers and artists from all over the world." Wants quality poetry; no restrictions on content or form. *Writer's Bloc* is 96 pages, digest-sized. Press run is 300. Subscription: $7. Sample: $7.

How to Contact Submit no more than 3 pages of poetry at a time ("prose poems okay"). Lines/poem: 50 maximum. No previously published poems or simultaneous submissions. No e-mail submissions; postal submissions only. "Submissions should be typed, double-spaced; SASE required for reply." Reads submissions September-January only. "Manuscripts are published upon recommendation by a staff of students and faculty." Seldom comments on rejected poems. Guidelines available in magazine or for SASE. "Acceptance letters are sent out in October." Pays 1 contributor's copy.

$ ☑ ◎ WRITERS' JOURNAL

P.O. Box 394, Perham MN 56573. (218)346-7921. Fax: (218)346-7924. E-mail: writersjournal@writersjournal.com. Website: www.writersjournal.com. Established 1980. **Contact:** Esther M. Leiper, poetry editor.

Magazines Needs *WRITERS" Journal*, published bimonthly, offers "advice and guidance, motivation, and inspiration to the more serious and published writers and poets." Features 2 columns for poets: "Esther Comments" offers critiques of poems sent in by readers, and "Every Day with Poetry" discusses a wide range of poetry topics, often—but not always—including readers' work. Wants "a variety of poetry: free verse, strict forms, concrete, Oriental. Since we appeal to those of different skill levels, some poems are more sophisticated than others, but those accepted must move, intrigue, or otherwise positively capture me. 'Esther Comments' is never used as a negative force to put a poem or a poet down. Indeed, I focus on the best part of a given work and seek to suggest means of improvement on weaker aspects." Does not want anything "vulgar, preachy, or sloppily written." Considers poetry by children (school-age). Has published poetry by Lawrence Schug, Diana Sutliff, and Eugene E. Grollmes. *WRITERS' Journal* is 64 pages, magazine-sized, professionally printed, with paper cover. Receives about 900 submissions/year, accepts about 25 (including those used in columns). Press run is 20,000. Single copy: $5.99; subscription: $19.97/year U.S., add $15 for Canada/Mexico, $30 for Europe, all others add $35. Sample: $6.

How to Contact Submit 3-4 poems at a time. Lines/poem: 25 maximum. No e-mail submissions; postal submissions only. Responds in up to 5 months. Pays $5/poem plus 1 contributor's copy.

Contest/Award Offerings Sponsors poetry contests for previously unpublished poetry. Submit serious verse only, on any subject or in any form, 25 lines maximum. "Submit in duplicate: one with name and address, one without." Received 300 entries/contest. Winners announced in *The WRITERS' Journal*, for SASE, and on Web site. **Entry fee:** $3/poem for each contest. **Deadline:** April 30, August 30, and December 30. Guidelines available for SASE or on Web site.

☑ ◎ XAVIER REVIEW

(Specialized: focus on African American, Caribbean, Southern literature), Xavier University, 1 Drexel Dr., New Orleans LA 70125-1098. (504)520-7805. Fax: (504)520-7917. Website: www.xula.edu/review. Established 1980 (review), 1988 (press). **Contact:** Dr. Nicole P. Greene, editor (review) or Robert Skinner, interim executive editor (press).

Magazines Needs *Xavier Review*, published semiannually, is a journal of poetry, fiction, translations, essays, and reviews (contemporary literature) for professional writers, libraries, colleges, and universities. "Our content includes a focus on African American, Caribbean, and Southern literature, as well as works that touch on issues of religion and spirituality. We do, however, consider quality works on all themes." Has published poetry by Chris Waters, Lisa Sisk, Mark Taksa, Glenn Sheldon, Christine DeSimone, and Holly Pettit. Press run is 300. Subscription: $10/year for individuals, $15/year for institutions. Sample: $5.

How to Contact Submit 3-5 poems at a time. Include SASE. "Overseas authors only may submit by e-mail attachment." Pays 2 contributor's copies; offers 40% discount on additional copies.

Additional Information Xavier Review Press publishes book-length works of poetry and prose. Recent publications include *Turning Up the Volume* by Patrice Melnick and *Vespers at Mount Angel* by Stella Nesanovich. Books are available through website or by e-mailing rskinner@xula.edu. Query via e-mail: rskinner@xula.edu. **"Manuscripts should not be sent without permission of the editor."**

▣ ☑ YASOU EZINE

E-mail: joanneolivieri@sbcglobal.net. Website: http://yasouezine.tripod.com. Established 2000. **Contact:** Joanne Olivieri, editor.

Magazines Needs *Yasou Ezine*, published online 3 times/year in March, July, and November, is "an eclectic mix of poetry, short stories, art, photography and commentaries. We publish work which is geared towards celebrating life to it's fullest and accept work by beginning as well as seasoned writers. We also accept artwork and photography. All artists considered." Does not want "anything of a violent or sexually explicit nature." Considers poetry by children and teens. Has published poetry by Taylor Graham, B.Z. Niditch, Colleen Breuning, C. David Hay, Doug Draime, Corey Mesler, Lyn Lifshin, and Genny Harten-Borleis. Receives about 500 poems/year, accepts about 15%. Number of unique visitors: "hundreds per month." Sample: free online.

How to Contact Submit 3 poems at a time. Lines/poem: no limit. Considers previously published poems and simultaneous submissions. (Considers poetry posted on a public Web site/blog/forum and poetry posted on a private, password-protected forum as published.) Considers e-mail submissions (pasted into body of e-mail message); no disk submissions. Cover letter is unnecessary. "Read our guidelines page. Submissions not following the guidelines will be automatically deleted." Reads submissions year round. Time between acceptance and publication is 3 months. Never comments on rejected poems. Guidelines available on Web site. Responds in 1 week. Never sends prepublication galleys. Pays "for featured poet in each issue. We pay in cash, plus either a music CD or poetry chapbook." Rights revert to poets upon publication. Reviews chapbooks of poetry. **"For a modest fee of $5**, we will review chapbooks of poetry and publish the review in the following issue along with a link to the poet's Web site. Make checks payable to Joanne Olivieri."

Contest/Award Offerings Sponsors annual poetry contest. "The ezine sponsors a poetry contest annually at which time the rules and awards will be listed on our Web site. Please check Web site regularly for detailed information."

Tips "We encourage beginners to submit their work. We pride ourselves on recognizing the uniqueness of each poet and affording them the opportunity to be published. All styles and forms welcome."

☑ YEMASSEE

Dept. of English, University of South Carolina, Columbia SC 29208. (803)777-2085. E-mail: editor@yemasseejournal.org. Website: http://yemasseejournal.org. Established 1993. **Contact:** Darien Cavanaugh and Jonathan Maricle, co-editors.

Magazines Needs *Yemassee*, published semiannually, features "primarily fiction and poetry, but we are also interested in one-act plays, brief excerpts of novels, essays, reviews, and interviews with literary figures. Our essential consideration for acceptance is the quality of the work; we are open to a variety of subjects and writing styles." Does not want "poems of such a highly personal nature that their primary relevance is to the author; bad Ginsberg." Has published poetry by Nick Finney, Kwame Dawes, Pamela McClure, Rafael Campo, David Kirby, and Susan Ludvigson. *Yemassee* is 80-100 pages, perfect-bound. Receives about 3,500 poems/year, accepts about 90% unsolicited. Press run is 500. Subscription: $15 for 2 issues ($10 for students). Sample: $5. Make checks payable to Education Foundation/English Literary Magazine Fund.

How to Contact Submit up to 5 poems at a time. Lines/poem: less than 50, "but poems of exceptional quality are considered regardless of length." No previously published poems (in any form, print or electronic). Considers simultaneous submissions if identified as such and notified of acceptance elsewhere. No fax or e-mail submissions. Include SASE. Cover letter is required. "Each issue's contents are determined on the basis of blind selections. Therefore, we ask that all works be submitted without the author's name or address anywhere on the manuscript. Include this information along with the title(s) of the work(s) in a cover letter. For longer submissions, please include an approximate word count." Reads submissions August 15-May 15. Time between acceptance and publication is up to 4 months. "Staff reads and votes on 'blind' submissions." Guidelines available on Web site. Responds in up to 2 months after submission deadline. Pays 2 contributor's copies with the option to purchase additional copies at a reduced rate. Acquires first rights.

Contest/Award Offerings The Pocataligo Poetry Contest (see separate listing in Contests & Awards); William Richey Short Story Prize.

◼ ☑ ◎ ZEEK: A JEWISH JOURNAL OF THOUGHT AND CULTURE

(Specialized: Jewish writers/themes preferred), P.O. Box 1342, New York NY 10116. E-mail: zeek@zeek.net. Website: www.zeek.net. Established 2002. **Contact:** Richard Chess, poetry editor. Associate Editor: Dan Friedman.

Magazines Needs *Zeek: A Jewish Journal of Thought and Culture*, published monthly online and in print, seeks poetry that is "poetically daring, with shades of the numinous as it manifests in moments non-poets would ignore." Does not want "clichéd, 'inspirational,' or ethnocentric writing; something that could serve as a greeting card, political poster, etc.; cynicism." Has published poetry by Hal Sirowitz, Rodger Kamenetz, Linda Zisquit, Yerra Sugarman, Shirley Kaufman, others. *Zeek* (print version) is 96 pages, digest-sized, perfect-bound, includes photography. Receives about 500 poems/year, accepts about 20. Press run (print) is 2,000 (200 subscribers); online version gets 60,000 hits/month. Single copy: $7; subscription: $14/year. Make checks payable to Zeek Media Inc.

How to Contact Submit 3 poems at a time. Considers simultaneous submissions; no previously published poems. Accepts e-mail submissions only (pasted into body of message). Short cover letter is acceptable. Reads submissions year round. Time between acceptance and publication varies. "Poetry editor has final approval, but editorial board of four can propose or reject." Seldom comments on rejected poems. Occasionally publishes theme issues. Guidelines available on Web site. Responds anywhere from 1 month to 1 year. Pays 5 contributor's copies (to poets published in print edition). Acquires one-time rights. Reviews books of poetry.

Tips "If someone else can say it, let them. If no one else can say it, say *that*."

Book/Chapbook Publishers

Every poet dreams of publishing a collection of his or her work. However, it's surprising how many poets still envision putting out a thick, hardbound volume containing hundreds of poems. In reality, poetry books are usually slim, often paperback, with varying levels of production quality, depending on the publisher.

More common than full-length poetry books (i.e., 50-150 pages by modern standards) are poetry *chapbooks*, small editions of approximately 24-32 pages. They may be printed on quality paper with beautiful cover art on heavy stock; or they may be photocopied sheets of plain printer paper, folded and stapled or hand-sewn along the spine.

In this section you'll find a variety of presses and publishers of poetry books and chapbooks. However, it's a reflection of how poetry publishing works in the early 21st century that many book/chapbook publishing opportunities appear in the Contest & Awards section instead. To thoroughly search for a publisher/press, consult the Chapbook Publishers index (starting on page 498) and the Book Publishers index (starting on page 501) for a complete roundup of publishers that are listed in this edition of *Poet's Market*.

HOW LISTINGS ARE FORMATTED

Content of each listing was provided or verified by a representative of the press or publisher (poetry editor, managing editor, owner, etc.). Here is how that content is arranged in each listing:

Symbols. Icons at the beginning of each listing offer visual signposts to specific information about the publication: (**N**) this market is recently established and new to *Poet's Market*; (**⊠**) this market did not appear in the 2008 edition; (**■**) this market publishes primarily online (although it may also produce an annual print version or a "best of'" anthology); (**☑**) this market is located in Canada or (**⊕**) outside the U.S. and Canada; (**$**) this market pays a monetary amount (as opposed to contributor's copies); (**☐**) this market welcomes submissions from beginning poets; (**◪**) this market prefers submissions from skilled, experienced poets, will consider work from beginning poets; (**◨**) this market prefers submissions from poets with a high degree of skill and experience; (**◎**) this market has a specialized focus (listed in parentheses after magazine/journal title); (**⊘**) this market does not consider unsolicited submissions; and (**⊘**) this market is closed to *all* submissions. (Keys to these symbols are listed on the inside covers of this book and on page 3.)

Contact information. Next you'll find the information you need to contact the press or publisher, according to what was provided for each listing: name (in bold) of the publisher/press (with areas of specialization noted in parentheses where appropriate); regular mail address; telephone number; fax number; e-mail address; Web site address; year the publisher/press was established; the name of the person to contact (or an editorial title); and membership in small press/publishing organization(s). (**Note:** If a publisher or press wants electronic submissions exclusively, no street address may be given.)

Book/Chapbook Needs. This section provides an overview of the publisher/press, including such helpful information as editorial preferences; how manuscripts are considered; the number and kinds of books and/or chapbooks produced; a list of recently published titles; and production information about the titles (number of pages, printing/binding details, type of cover, press run).

How to Submit. This section states whether a poet should query with samples or send the complete manuscript; possible reading periods; reading fees, if applicable; response time; payment amount/terms; and how to order sample copies.

Additional Information. Editors/publishers may use this section to explain other types of publishing activities (such as broadsides, postcards or anthologies), elaborate on some aspect of production--anything beyond the basic details of the submission process that readers may find of interest.

Contest/Award Offerings. This section discusses prizes and competitions associated with the publisher, with either brief guidelines or a cross-reference to a separate listing in the Contests & Awards section.

Also Offers. Describes other offerings associated with this publisher (i.e., sponsored readings, Web site activities such as blogs and forums, related poetry groups, etc.).

Advice. Provides direct quotes from the editor/publisher about everything from pet peeves to tips on writing to views on the state of poetry today.

GETTING STARTED, FINDING A PUBLISHER

If you don't have a publisher in mind, read randomly through the listings, making notes as you go. (Don't hesitate to write in the margins, underline, use highlighters; it also helps to flag markets that interest you with Post-It Notes). Browsing the listings is an effective way to familiarize yourself with the kind of information presented and the publishing opportunities that are available at various skill levels.

If you're thinking of a specific publisher by name, however, begin with the General Index. Here all *Poet's Market* listings are alphabetized along with publishers from the 2007 edition that don't appear in this book (the latter are accompanied by a two-letter code explaining the publisher's absence; a key to these codes appears at the beginning of the General Index.) In addition, publishers/presses that have changed names since the 2007 edition are listed in the General Index, cross-referenced to the new names.

REFINE YOUR SEARCH

To supplement the General Index, we provide several more specific indexes to help you refine your marketing plan for your manuscript. Not every listing appears in one of these indexes, so use them only to reinforce your other research efforts. As mentioned earlier, the Chapbook Publishers Index and Book Publishers Index are good places to start when you have a poetry collection to submit. In addition, the following indexes may be helpful:

Openness to Submissions Index breaks out markets according to the symbols (◻ ◪ ◖ ◉) that appear at the beginning of each listing—signposts that indicate the level of writing an editor/publisher prefers to see. (For an explanation of these symbols, see page 3, the inside covers of this book, or the handy tear-out bookmark just inside the front cover.)

Geographical Index sorts publishers/presses by state and by countries outside the U.S. Some publishers are more open to poets from their region, so use this index when you're pinpointing local opportunities.

Subject Index groups all markets into categories according to areas of special focus. These include all specialized markets (appearing with the Y symbol) as well as broader categories such as online markets, poetry for children, markets that consider translations, and others. Save time when looking for a specific type of publisher/press by checking this index first.

THE NEXT STEP

Once you know how to interpret the listings in this section and identify markets for your work, the next step is to start submitting your poetry collection. See "Getting Started (and Using This Book)" on page 2 and "Frequently Asked Questions" on page 7 for advice, guidelines for preparing your manuscript and proper submissions procedures.

$ ☑ ADASTRA PRESS

(Specialized: letterpress-printed, hand-sewn chapbooks) 16 Reservation Rd., Easthampton MA 01027-1227. Established 1980. **Contact:** Gary Metras, publisher.

•Chosen Publisher of the Year 2006 by *Contemporary Poetry Review.*

Needs "Adastra is primarily a chapbook publisher using antique equipment and methods, i.e., hand-set type, letterpress printing, hand-sewn bindings. Any titles longer than chapbook length are by special arrangement and are from poets who have previously published a successful chapbook or two with Adastra. Editions are generally released with a flat-spine paper wrapper, and some titles have been bound in cloth. Editions are limited, ranging from 200- to 400-copy print runs. Some of the longer titles have gone into reprint, and these are photo-offset and perfect-bound. Letterpress chapbooks by themselves are not reprinted as single titles. Once they go out of print, they are gone. I am biased against poems that rhyme and/or are religious in theme. Sequences and longish poems are always nice to present in a chapbook format. Competition is keen. Less than 0.5% of submissions are accepted." Published chapbooks include *Poetic License* by Susan Terris, *Digger's Blues* by Jim Daniels, *Behind Our Memories* by Michael Hettich, and *Three* by Stephen Philbrick. Publishes 2-4 chapbooks/year. Sample hand-crafted chapbook: $8 postpaid.

How to Contact Chapbook mss should be 12-18 pages, double-spaced. No full-length mss will be considered. Submit in February of each year. Responds by April. Time between acceptance and publication can be as long as 2 years. Pays 10% of press run. "In the near future Adastra will change its reading period, so it would be best for any poets interested in submitting a chapbook manuscript to querie first with a 3-5 poem sample and an SASE."

Tips "Adastra Press is a one-man printer/publisher but releases more poetry titles per year than Random House, one of the largest trade book publishers in the world. I approach book-making as an art, and design each chapbook to fit the poetry. As *The Virginia Quarterly Review* wrote, Adastra is 'one of our most interesting smaller presses'; and Contemporary Poetry Review in 2007 selected Adastra as Publisher of the Year, beating literary and corporate giant Farrah, Straus & Giroux. Small, independent publishers, such as Adastra Press, are worthwhile and recognizable. Adastra is open to a wide range of poets. The criteria is moving and memorable poetry that speaks to the reader."

☑ AHSAHTA PRESS

MFA Program in Creative Writing, Boise State University, 1910 University Dr., Boise ID 83725-1525. (208)426-3134. Fax: (208)426-4373. E-mail: ahsahta@boisestate.edu. Website: http://ahsahtapress.boisestate.edu. Established 1976. **Contact:** Janet Holmes, editor.

Needs Ahsahta Press, which originally published contemporary poets of the American West, has since expanded its scope "to publish poets nationwide, seeking out and publishing the best new poetry from a wide range of aesthetics--poetry that is technically accomplished, distinctive in style, and thematically fresh." Has published *The True Keeps Calm Biding Its Story* by Rusty Morrison (James Laughlin Award, 2008), *Bone Pagoda* by Susan Tichy, *Case Sensitive* by Kate Greenstreet, *Quarantine* by Brian Henry, *Spell* by Dan Beachy-Quick, and *Saving the Appearances* by Liz Waldner.

How to Contact Considers multiple and simultaneous submissions. Reading period is temporarily suspended due to backlog, but the press publishes runners-up as well as winners of the Sawtooth Poetry Prize. Forthcoming, new, and backlist titles available on Web site. Most backlist titles: $9.95; most current titles: $17.50.

Contest/Award Offerings The Sawtooth Poetry Prize (see separate listing in Contests & Awards).

Tips "Ahsahta seeks distinctive, non-imitative, unpredictable, and innovatively crafted work. Please check our Web site for examples of what we publish."

$ ☐ AMSTERDAM PRESS

6199 State Hwy 43, Amsterdam OH 43903.Estab. 2007. 740-543-4333. E-mail: plainspoke@gmail.com. Website: www.amsterdampress.net. **Contact**: Cindy Kelly, editor.

Needs Amsterdam Press, publishes chapbooks and broadsides, wants "poetry of place, poetry grounded in sense images, poetry that leaps, and has a clear voice." Does not want "esoteric poetry that focuses on the universal." Manuscripts are selected through open submission. Chapbooks are 36 pages, laser-printed, saddle-stitched, with card cover and black and white art/graphics.

How to Contact Query first, with a few sample poems and a cover letter with brief bio and publication credits. Chapbook mss may include previously published poems. "Previously published poetry must be recognized on a separate page of mss." Responds to queries in 1-3 months; to mss in 1-3 months. Pays honorarium of $25-100 and 10 author's copies out of a press run of 100-300. Order sample books/chapbooks by sending $8 to Amsterdam Press, 6199 Steubenville Road SE, Amsterdam, OH 43903.

▦ ARC PUBLICATIONS

(Specialized: UK writers; world and overseas poets; translations), Nanholme Mill, Shaw Wood Rd., Todmorden, Lancashire OL14 6DA England. E-mail: arc.publications@btconnect.com. Website: www.arcpublications.co.uk. Established 1969. **Contact:** Tony Ward, managing editor, or Angela Jarman marketing and music editor.

Needs Publishes "contemporary poetry from new and established writers from the UK and abroad, specializing in the work of world poets writing in English, and the work of overseas poets in translation."

How to Contact *"At present we are not accepting submissions but keep updated by visiting the Web site."*

ARCTOS PRESS

P.O. Box 401, Sausalito CA 94966-0401. (415)331-2503. E-mail: runes@aol.com. Website: http://members.aol.com/RUNES. Established 1997. **Contact:** CB Follett, editor.

Needs Arctos Press, under the imprint HoBear Publications, publishes 1-2 paperbacks/year. "We publish quality, perfect-bound books and anthologies of poetry, usually theme-oriented, in runs of 1,500." Has published *GRRRRR, A Collection of Poems About BEARS* (anthology); *Prism*, poems by David St. John; *Fire Is Favorable to the Dreamer*, poems by Susan Terris; and others.

How to Contact "We do not accept unsolicited manuscripts unless a current call has been posted in *Poets & Writers* and/or elsewhere, at which time up to 5 poems related to the theme should be sent." Considers previously published poems (if author holds the rights) and simultaneous submissions ("if we are kept informed"). Accepts submissions by postal mail only. Upcoming themes and guidelines available for SASE or on Web site. Pays 1 author's copy; discounts available on additional copies.

☑ THE BACKWATERS PRESS

3502 N. 52nd St., Omaha NE 68104-3506. (402)451-4052. E-mail: thebackwaterspress@gmail.com. Website: www.thebackwaterspress.com. **Contact:** Greg Kosmicki, editor.

Needs "The Backwaters Press continues to accept manuscripts for consideration for publication through the Open Submissions category. We're looking for manuscripts between 65 and 80 pages in length. **There is a $25 reading fee.**"

How to Contact "Please see the Web site for complete details, or send a self-addressed, stamped envelope to 'Guidelines' at the above address, or e-mail with a subject line of 'Open Submission Guidelines.'" Books available through The Backwaters Press or Amazon.com.

Tips "The Backwaters Press is dedicated to publishing the best new literature we can find. Send your best work."

⦿ BARNWOOD PRESS

4604 47th Ave., S, Seattle WA 98118-1824. (206)225-6887. E-mail: barnwoodpress@earthlink.net. Website: www.barnwoodpress.org. Established 1975. **Contact:** Tom Koontz, editor.

Needs Barnwood Press publishes 1 paperback and 1 chapbook of poetry/year. Has recently published *New and Selected Poems* by Robert Ronnow, *Hitler's Mustache* by Peter Davis, *Sheer* by Martha Collins, and *Whatever You Can Carry: Poems of the Holocaust* by Stephen Herz. Chapbooks are usually 12-32 pages, offset-printed, saddle-stapled, with paper covers with art; size varies.

How to Contact Query first with a few sample poems and cover letter with brief bio and publication credits. Responds to queries and mss in 1 month. Order sample books/chapbooks through Web site.

BEAR STAR PRESS

185 Hollow Oak Dr, Cohasset CA 95973. Estab. 1996. Website: www.bearstarpress.com. Established 1996. **Contact:** Beth Spencer, editor/publisher. ;

How to Contact The Dorothy Brunsman Poetry Prize serves as their primary pool for finding new manuscripts. "You need not enter the contest to submit to us, but our first allegiance is to manuscripts that come with a reading fee since they help to keep the press going." See separate listing in Contests and Awards section of this book.

⦿ BELHUE PRESS

(Specialized: gay male poetry), 2501 Palisade Ave., Suite A1, Riverdale, Bronx NY 10463. E-mail: belhuepress@earthlink.net. Website: www.perrybrass.com. Established 1990. **Contact:** Tom Laine, editor.

Needs Belhue Press is a small press specializing in gay male poetry. "We are especially interested in books that get out of the stock poetry market." Wants "hard-edged, well-crafted, fun, and often sexy poetry. No mushy, self-pitying, confessional, boring, indulgent, teary, or unrequited love poems--yuck! Poet must be willing to promote book through readings, mailers, etc." Publishes 3 paperbacks/year; no chapbooks. **"We have a $10 sample and guideline fee.** Please send this before submitting any poetry. We have had to initiate this due to a deluge of bad, amateur, irrelevant submissions. After fee, we will give constructive criticism when necessary."

How to Contact Query first, with 6 pages of poetry and cover letter with brief bio and publication credits. Considers previously published poems and simultaneous submissions. Time between acceptance and publication is 1 year. Often comments on rejected poems. Will request criticism fees "if necessary." Responds "fast" to queries and submitted mss. No payment information provided.

Tips "The only things we find offensive are stupid, dashed off, 'fortune cookie' poems that show no depth or awareness of poetry. We like poetry that, like good journalism, tells a story."

$ ⦿ BIRCH BOOK PRESS

P.O. Box 81, Delhi NY 13753. Fax: (607)746-7453. E-mail: birchbrook@copper.net (inquiries only). Website: www.birchbrookpress.info. Established 1982. **Contact:** Barbara de la Cuesta, poetry editor. Member: American Academy of Poets, Small Press Center, Independent Book Publishers Association, American Typefounders Fellowship.

Needs Birch Brook Press began publishing in 1982 and "is a letterpress book printer/typesetter/ designer that uses monies from these activities to publish several titles of its own each year with cultural and literary interest." Specializes in literary work, flyfishing, baseball, outdoors, theme anthologies, translations of classics, and books about books. Has published *Woodstoves & Ravens*, by Robert Farmer, *Shadwell Hills*, by Rebecca Lilly, *Human/Nature* by Lance Lee, *Confessions of a Rational Lunatic* by Marcus Rome, *Jack's Beans* by Tom Smith, and *The Alchemy of Words* by Edward Francisco. Publishes 4 paperbacks and/or hardbacks/year. Specializes "mostly in anthologies with specific themes." Books are "handset letterpress editions printed in our own shop." **Offers occasional co-op contract.**

How to Contact Query first with sample poems, or send entire ms. No e-mail submissions; submissions by postal mail only. "Must include SASE with submissions." Occasionally comments on rejected poems. Guidelines available for SASE. Pays from $5-25 for publication in anthology. Royalty on co-op contracts. Order sample books by visiting our online catalog at: www.birchbookpress.info.

Tips "Send your best work, and see other Birch Brook Press books."

$ ☑ BLACK LAWRENCE PRESS

P.O. Box 327, Theresa NY 13691. E-mail: editors@blacklawrencepress.com. Website: www. blacklawrencepress.com. Established 2003. **Contact:** Colleen Ryor, editor.

Needs Black Lawrence Press seeks "to publish intriguing books of literature: novels, short story collections, poetry. Will also publish the occasional translation (from the German and French)." Has published poetry by D.C. Berry, James Reidel, and Stefi Weisburd. Publishes 10-12 books/year, mostly poetry and fiction. Manuscripts are selected through open submission and competition (see below). Books are 48-400 pages, offset-printed or high-quality POD, perfect-bound, with matte 4-color cover.

How to Contact "Regular submissions are considered on a year-round basis. Please check the general submissions page on our Web site for the most up-to-date guidelines information before submitting." Responds in up to 4 months for mss, "sometimes longer depending on backlog." Pays royalties. Sample books available through Web site.

Contest/Award Offerings The St. Lawrence Book Award, The Hudson Prize, and The Black River Chapbook Competition (see separate listings in Contests & Awards).

☑ BLUE LIGHT PRESS

1563-45th Avenue., San Francisco CA 94122. (415)665-7978 or (641)472-7882. E-mail: bluelightpress@aol.com. Established 1988. **Contact:** Diane Frank, chief editor.

Needs Blue Light Press publishes 3 paperbacks, 2 chapbooks/year. "We like poems that are imagistic, emotionally honest, and push the edge--where the writer pushes through the imagery to a deeper level of insight and understanding. No rhymed poetry." Has published poetry by Alice Rogoff, Tom Centolella, Stewart Florsheim, Nancy Berg, Michelle Demers, Stephen Schneider, Ken McCullough, Leah Shelleda, Becky Sakellariou, and Christopher Buckley. "Books are elegantly designed and artistic." Chapbooks are 30 pages, digest-sized, professionally printed, with original art on an elegant matte cover. Chapbooks available for $10 plus $2 p books for $15.95 plus $3 p&h.

How to Contact Submission guidelines available for SASE or by e-mail. Does not accept e-mail submissions. **Deadlines:** December 15, 2009 full-sized ms) and June 15, 2010 for chapbooks. "Read our guidelines before sending your ms."

Contest/Award Offerings The Blue Light Poetry Prize and Chapbook Contest (see separate listing in Contests & Awards).

Also Offers "We have an online poetry workshop with a wonderful group of American and international poets--open to new members 3 times per year. Send an e-mail for info. We work in person with local poets, and will edit/critique poems by mail; $40 for four poems."

Tips "Read some of the books we publish, including our new anthology. We like to publish poets with a unique vision and gorgeous or unusual language; poems that push the edge. Stay in the poem longer and see what emerges in your vision and language."

$ ☑ BOA EDITIONS, LTD.

250 N. Goodman Street, Suite 306, Rochester, NY 14607. (585)546-3410. Website: www. boaeditions.org. Established 1976. **Contact:** Thom Ward, poetry editor and Peter Conners, fiction editor.

Needs BOA Editions, a Pulitzer Prize-winning, not-for-profit publishing house acclaimed for its work, reads poetry mss for the American Poets Continuum Series (new poetry by distinguished poets in mid- and late career), the Lannan Translations Selection Series (publication of 2 new collections of contemporary international poetry annually, supported by The Lannan Foundation of Santa Fe, NM), and The A. Poulin, Jr. Poetry Prize (to honor a poet's first book; mss considered through competition--see separate listing in Contests & Awards). Has published poetry by W.D. Snodgrass, John Logan, Isabella Gardner, Richard Wilbur, and Lucille Clifton. Also publishes introductions by major poets of those less well-known (Gerald Stern wrote the foreword for Li-Young Lee's *Rose*, for example). BOA now also publishes fiction manuscripts for its American Reader Series. Check BOA's Web site for when the house is accepting fiction manuscripts.

How to Contact Check Web site for reading periods for the American Poets Continuum Series and The Lannan Translation Selection Series. "Please adhere to the general submission guidelines for each series." Guidelines available for SASE or on Web site. Pays advance plus 10 author's copies.

Contest/Award Offerings The A. Poulin, Jr. Poetry Prize (see separate listing in Contests & Awards).

Also Offers Available for download from Web site are reading and teaching guides for selected titles; and Season Sampler chapbooks, which provide introductions to BOA poets and their work.

☑ BOTTOM DOG PRESS, INC.

(Specialized: writing from the Midwest; working lives; Zen Buddhism), P.O. Box 425, Huron OH 44839. (419)433-5560, ext. 20784. E-mail: LsmithDog@smithdocs.net. Website: http://smithdocs. net. **Contact:** Larry Smith, director. Associate Editors: David Shevin and Laura Smith.

   •Imprint: Bird Dog Publishing

Needs Bottom Dog Press, Inc., "is a nonprofit literary and educational organization dedicated to publishing the best writing and art from the Midwest." Has published poetry by Jeff Gundy, Jim Daniels, Maj Ragain, Diane di Prima, and Sue Doro. Publishes the Midwest Series, Working Lives Series, and Harmony Series (105 books to date).

How to Contact Guidelines available on Web site.

Tips "Please read some of our books and send us a query before submitting anything."

☑ BRICKHOUSE BOOKS, INC.

306 Suffolk Rd., Baltimore MD 21218. (410)235-7690. E-mail: charriss@towson.edu. Website: www.towson.edu/~harriss/!bhbwebs.ite/bhb.htm. Established 1970. **Contact:** Clarinda Harriss, editor/director.

   •Imprints: New Poets Series, Chestnut Hills Press, and Stonewall.

Needs BrickHouse Books "is open to submissons of all kinds (poetry, novellas, plays, etc.), so long as they do not exceed 128 pages." New Poets Series brings out first books by promising new poets. Poets who have previously had book-length mss published are not eligible. Prior publication in journals and anthologies is strongly encouraged. Wants "excellent, fresh, nontrendy, literate, intelligent poems. Any form (including traditional), any style." BrickHouse Books and New Poets Series pay 20 author's copies (out of a press run of 500), the sales proceeds going back into the corporation to finance the next volume. "BrickHouse has been successful in its effort to provide writers with national distribution; in fact, The New Poets Series was named an Outstanding Small Press by the prestigious Pushcart Awards Committee, which judges some 5,000 small press publications annually." Chestnut Hills Press publishes **author-subsidized books**; "high-quality work only, however. Chestnut Hills Press has achieved a reputation for prestigious books, printing only the top 5% of manuscripts Chestnut Hills Press and New Poets Series receive." Chestnut Hills Press authors receive proceeds from sale of their books. The Stonewall series publishes work with a gay, lesbian, or bisexual perspective. BrickHouse Books and its subdivisions have published books by Joyce Brown, Mary Swann, A.M. Chaplin, and many others. Books are 42-200 pages. Chapbooks available for $10; full-length books for $15-25.

How to Contact Send a 50- to 55-page manuscript, **$10 reading fee**, and cover letter including bio and publication credits. "Do not query by phone or fax; e-mail or postal mail queries only. Do not send anything by certified mail; BHB is unable to sign for such deliveries." Considers simultaneous submissions. No e-mail submissions. "Cover letters should be very brief, businesslike, and include an accurate list of published work. Indicate if manuscript is to be considered for BrickHouse, New Poets Series, Chestnut Hills Press, or Stonewall." Manuscripts accepted for publication must be available on a CD provided by the author. Sometimes comments briefly on rejected poems. Responds in up to 1 year. Manuscripts "are circulated to an editorial board of professional, publishing poets. BrickHouse is backlogged, but the best 10% of the manuscripts it receives are automatically eligible for Chestnut Hills Press consideration," **a subsidy arrangement**. Send $5 and a 7x10 SASE for a sample volume.

☑ CAROLINA WREN PRESS

(Specialized: women; minorities; gay/lesbian), 120 Morris St., Durham NC 27701. (919)560-2738. Fax: (919)560-2759. E-mail: carolinawrenpress@earthlink.net. Website: www.carolinawrenpress. org. Established 1976. **Contact:** Andrea Selch, president.

Needs Publishes 1 poetry book/year, "usually through our poetry series. Primarily women and minorities, though men and majorities also welcome." Has published *Downriver* by Jeanne Leiby, as well as poetry by William Pitt Root, George Elliott Clarke, Jaki Shelton Green, Evie Shockley, and Erica Hunt.

How to Contact Query first, with 10 pages of sample poems and cover letter with brief bio and publication credits. Include SASE for reply only. Accepts e-mail queries, but send only letter and description of work; no large files. Reads unsolicited poetry submissions during the month of February. "Your best bet is to submit as part of our biennual poetry contest held in autumn of even-numbered years (e.g., 2008, 2010)." Guidelines available for SASE, by e-mail, or on Web site. Responds to queries in 3 months; to mss in 6 months. Payment varies.

Contest/Award Offerings Carolina Wren Press Poetry Contest for a First Book (see separate listing in Contests & Awards).

☑ $ ☑ COTEAU BOOKS

(Specialized: Canadian writers only), Thunder Creek Publishing Co-op, 2517 Victoria Ave., Regina SK S4P 0T2 Canada. (306)777-0170. Fax: (306)522-5152. E-mail: coteau@coteaubooks. com. Website: www.coteaubooks.com. Established 1975. **Contact:** Acquisitions Editor.

Needs Coteau Books is a "small literary press that publishes poetry, fiction, drama, anthologies, criticism, young adult novels--**by Canadian writers only**." Has published *The Crooked Good* by Louise Bernice Halfe, *Wolf Tree* by Randy Lundy, and *Predicting the Next Big Advertising Breakthrough Using a Potentially Dangerous Method* by Daniel Scott Tysdal.

How to Contact Submit mss (80-100 poems only) typed with at least 12-point font. No simultaneous or non-Canadian submissions. No e-mail or fax submissions. Cover letter is required. Include publishing credits and bio, and SASE for return of ms. Responds to queries and mss in 4 months. Always sends prepublication galleys. Author receives 10% royalties and 10 author's copies. Order samples by sending 9x12 SASE for catalog.

Additional Information Web site includes title and ordering information, author interviews, awards, news and events, submission guidelines, and links.

Tips "Generally, poets should have a number of publishing credits (single poems or series) in literary magazines and anthologies before submitting a manuscript."

☑ CROSS-CULTURAL COMMUNICATIONS

(Specialized: bilingual, translations, multicultural), 239 Wynsum Ave., Merrick NY 11566-4725. (516)868-5635. Fax: (516)379-1901. E-mail: cccpoetry@aol.com. Website: www.cross-culturalcommunications.com. Established 1971. **Contact:** Stanley H. or Bebe Barkan, or Mia Barkan Clarke.

Book/Chapbook Needs "Cross-Cultural Review began as a series of chapbooks (6-12 per year) of collections of poetry translated from various languages, and continues as the Holocaust, Women Writers, Latin American Writers, African Heritage, Italian Heritage, International Artists, Art & Poetry, Jewish, Israeli, Yiddish, Hebrew, Arabic, Armenian, American, Bengali, Brazilian (Portuguese), Bulgarian, Cajun, Catalan, Chicano, Chinese, Dutch & Flemish, Estonian, Finnish, Gypsy (Roma), Korean, Macedonian, Native American, Persian, Polish, Romanian, Russian, Serbian, Sicilian, Swedish, Scandinavian, Turkish, Ukrainian, Welsh, and Long Island and Brooklyn Writers Chapbook Series (with a number of other permutations in the offing)--issued simultaneously in palm-sized and regular paperback and cloth-binding editions, and boxed and canned editions, as well as audiocassette, CD, DVD, and videocassette. The Cross-Cultural International Writers Series, focusing on leading poets from various countries, includes titles by Leo Vroman (Holland) and Pablo Neruda (Chile). The Holocaust Series is for survivors. In addition to publications in these series, Cross-Cultural Communications has published anthologies and postcard and broadside portfolio collections by dozens of poets from many countries, a number in special bilingual limited editions, including such poets and translators as Sonja Akesson, Sven Alfons, Werner Aspenström, Vahé Baladouni, Jozo Boshkovski, August Bover, Sultan Catto, Rolando Certa, Herman de Coninck, Patrick Colnrad, Kristine Doll, Robert Dunn, Salvador Espriu, Kim Chi-ha, Ko Un, Frank Koenegracht, Naoshi Horiyama, Aaron Kramer, Sjoerd Kuyper, M.L. Liebler, Scott Rollins, Paul Snoek, Lynn Strongin, Peter Thabit, Aeronwy Thomas, Tomas Transtromer, and more." Sample chapbook: $10 postpaid.

   •See www.thedrunkenboat.com (Summer 2002 issue) for a profile and www.Poetryvlog.com for a video.

How to Contact Guidelines available for SASE. Pays 10% of print run.

Additional Information New: *Cross-Cultural Review Chapbook* (CCRCB), an occasional series of 16-48 page limited edition chapbooks (print runs of 100-150 copies) focusing on poetry (bilingual preferred). Sample: $15 postpaid. Pays 5-10 copies. The Seventh Quarry/CCC chapbook series, co-edited with Peter Thabit Jones, features a pairing of a British poet with a non-British poet. 64 pages (print run of 250-500 copies). $15 (Int'l Money Order for direct shipment from Swansea, Wales). Pays 10 copies.

Also Offers "Cross-Cultural Communications continues, on an occasional basis, to organize events for international poets and writers. In May 2009, CCC will host a spring Dylan Thomas walking tour of Greenwich Village, based on the *Guide* written by Welsh poets Peter Thabit Jones, editor of *The Seventh Quarry*, and Aeronwy Thomas (daughter of Dylan Thomas)."

$ ☑ JOHN DANIEL & COMPANY

Daniel & Daniel Publishers, Inc., P.O. Box 2790, McKinleyville CA 95519. (707)839-3495. Fax: (707)839-3242. E-mail: dandd@danielpublishing.com. Website: www.danielpublishing.com. Established 1980. **Contact:** John Daniel, editor.

Needs John Daniel & Company, an imprint of Daniel & Daniel Publishers, Inc., is a general small press publisher, specializing in literature, both prose and poetry. "Book-length manuscripts of any form or subject matter will be considered, but we do not want to see pornographic, libelous, illegal, or sloppily written poetry." Has published *Breathing Rice*, by Jean Lin, *Silently You Taught Me Much*, by Stella Zamvil, and *Dancing Fire*, by Marjorie Jackson. Publishes about 6 flat-spined poetry paperbacks/year. Books average 80 pages. Press runs average between 500-1,000. No longer issues a print catalog, but all books are shown and described on website.

How to Contact Query first, with 12 sample poems and cover letter with brief bio and publication credits. Considers simultaneous submissions. No fax or e-mail submissions. Responds to queries in 2 weeks; to mss in 2 months. Always sends prepublication galleys. Pays 10% royalties of net receipts. Acquires English-language book rights. Returns rights upon termination of contract.

Tips "Because we are downsizing our company, and therefore have less cash flow to work with, I'm sorry to say we are now publishing very little poetry. This doesn't mean we won't take a look at any manuscript we receive, but you should know that of late almost all poetry books we have published come out under our Fithian Press imprint, the imprint we use for copublishing."

☑ DOLPHIN-MOON PRESS

P.O. Box 22262, Baltimore MD 21203. Established 1973. **Contact:** James Taylor, president.

Needs Dolphin-Moon is "a limited-edition (500-1,000 copies) press that emphasizes quality work (regardless of style), often published in unusual/'radical' format." The writer is usually allowed a strong voice in the look/feel of the final piece. "We've published magazines, anthologies, chapbooks, pamphlets, perfect-bound paperbacks, records, audio cassettes, and comic books. All styles are read and considered, but the work should show a strong spirit and voice. Although we like the feel of 'well-crafted' work, craft for its own sake won't meet our standards either." Has published work by Teller, Michael Weaver, John Strausbaugh, Josephine Jacobsen, and William Burroughs.

How to Contact Query first, with 6-10 sample poems and a cover letter with brief bio and publication credits. "Please, no submission of complete manuscripts unless requested." No fax or e-mail submissions. Responds to queries and full-length submissions (if invited) in up to 1 month. Always sends prepublication galleys. Pays in author's copies (negotiable, usually 10% of the press run). Acquires first edition rights. Send SASE for catalog to purchase samples, or send $15 for a "sampler" (guaranteed to be up to $25 worth of publications).

Tips "Our future plans are to continue as we have since 1973, publishing the best work we can by local, up-and-coming, and nationally recognized writers--in a quality package."

☒ $ ☑ ÉCRITS DES FORGES

992 rue Royale # A, C.P. 335 Trois-Rivières QC G9A 5G4 Canada. (819)379-9813. Fax: (819)376-0774. E-mail: ecrits.desforges@tr.cgocable.ca. Website: www.ecritsdesforges.com. Established 1971. **Contact:** Stéphane Despatie, director. Directrice Générale: Maryse Baribeau.

Needs Écrits des Forges publishes poetry only that is "authentic and original as a signature. We have published poetry from more than 1,000 poets coming from most of the francophone countries: André Romus (Belgium), Amadou Lamine Sall (Sénégal), Nicole Brossard, Claude Beausoleil, Jean-Marc Desgent, and Jean-Paul Daoust (Québec)." Publishes 45-50 paperback books of poetry/year. Books are usually 80-88 pages, digest-sized, perfect-bound, with 2-color covers with art.

How to Contact Query first with a few sample poems and a cover letter with brief bio and publication credits. Responds to queries in up to 6 months. Pays royalties of 10-20%, advance of 50% maximum, and 25 author's copies. Order sample books by writing or faxing.

⌧ ◻ ETCHED PRESS

P.O. Box 3063, Wilmington NC 28406. Estab. 2008. (919)536-8258. E-mail: submit@etchedpress. com. Website: www.etchedpress.com. Contact Kevin Dublin, editor.

Needs *Etched Press* publishes poetry chapbooks and anthologies. "We're interested mostly in well-written collections of poetry that aren't pretentious and have universal themes." Does not want "poetry that will be forgotten." Has published Melanie Faith's *Bright Burning Fuse*. Publishes 3 chapbooks/year. Manuscripts are selected through open submission. Chapbooks are 12-40 pages, sheet-fed press printed, saddle-stitched, with cover stock designed in collaboration wtih the author. Anthologies are 40-70 pages, POD with art/graphics designed by a hired professional.

How to Contact "May submit via e-mail with the manuscript attached as a .doc or .pdf file complete with cover page that contains name, address, and e-mail. Any questions should be directed to inquiry@etchedpress.com." Responds to queries in 2 weeks; to mss in 2 months. Pays royalties of 25% and 25 author's copies (out of a press run of 200). Order sample books/ chapbooks by sending $5 to Etched Press Sample Chapbook, P.O. Box 3063, Wilmington NC 28406.

Tips "Please, please, please don't send submissions in the body of an e-mail. Even though copying and pasting it into a word document isn't that difficult, it's a little bothersome, affects presentation, and the editor dislikes it just a little from the start. Selling poetry today is difficult in book form for anyone whose name isn't recognized. I think chapbooks are perfect for the world of poetry. They're cheaper, meaning a person may be more inclined to buy one. They're also intimate, meaning a person may feel closer to the author."

✷ FINISHING LINE PRESS

P.O. Box 1626, Georgetown KY 40324. (859)514-8966. E-mail: FinishingBooks@aol.com. Website: www.finishinglinepress.com. Established 1998. **Contact:** Leah Maines, poetry editor.

　•Member of CLMP

Needs Finishing Line Press seeks to "discover new talent" and hopes to publish chapbooks by both men and women poets who have not previously published a book or chapbook of poetry. Has published *Parables and Revelations* by T. Crunk, *Family Business* by Paula Sergi, *Putting in a Window* by John Brantingham, and *Dusting the Piano* by Abigail Gramig. Publishes 50-60 poetry chapbooks/year. Chapbooks are usually 25-30 pages, digest-sized, laser-printed, saddle-stapled, with card covers with textured matte wrappers.

How to Contact Submit up to 26 pages of poetry with cover letter, bio, acknowledgments, and **$12 reading fee**. Responds to queries and mss in up to 1 month. Pay varies; pays in author's copies. "Sales profits, if any, go to publish the next new poet." Sample chapbooks available by sending $6 to Finishing Line Press or through Web site.

Contest/Award Offerings The Finishing Line Press Open Chapbook Competition and the New Women's Voices Chapbook Competition (see separate listings in Contests & Awards).

Tips "We are very open to new talent. If the poetry is great, we will consider it for a chapbook."

ⓝ ⓘ $ ☑ FLARESTACK POETS

P.O. Box 14779, Birmingham, West Midlands B13 3GU.Estab. 2008. E-mail: meria@binternet. com; jacquierowe@hotmail.co.uk. Website: www.flarestackpoets.co.uk. Contact: Meredith Andrea.

Needs Flarestack Poets wants "poems that dare outside current trends, even against the grain." Does not want "poems that fail to engage with either language or feeling." First chapbooks appearing in Autumn 2009. Publishes 8 chapbooks/year and 1 anthology. Manuscripts are selected through open submission and competition. "Our first chapbooks are winners of the 2009 Flarestack Poets Pamphlet competition. Thereafter we will consider open submissions." Chapbooks are 20-30 pages, professional photocopy, saddle-stitched, card cover.

How to Contact Quert first with a few sample poems and a cover letter with brief bio and publication credits. Manuscript may include previously published poems. Responds in 6 weeks. Pays royalties of 25% and 6 author's copies (out of a press run of 200). See Web site to order sample copies.

ⓘ ☑ FLARESTACK PUBLISHING

8 Abbot's Way, Pilton, Somerset BA4 4BN England. (44)(1749)890019. E-mail: cannula. dementia@virgin.net. Established 1995. **Contact:** Charles Johnson, editor.

• Flarestack Publishing is no longer accepting pamphlet submissions. Please see Web site for details.

Needs Flarestack Publishing ("talent to burn") aims to "find an audience for new poets, so beginners are welcome, but the work has to be strong and clear." Publishes 8 chapbooks/year. Chapbooks are usually 12-52 pages, A5, stapled, with card covers.

How to Contact Query first with a few sample poems (6 maximum) and a cover letter with brief bio and publication credits. "Normally we expect a few previous magazine acceptances, but no previous collection publication." Responds to queries in 6 weeks; to mss in 2 months. Pays royalties of 25% plus 6 author's copies (out of a press run of 50-100). Order sample chapbooks by sending £3.50.

☑ FLOATING BRIDGE PRESS

(Specialized: WA poets), PO Box 18814, Seattle, WA 98118. E-mail: floatingbridgepress@yahoo. com. Website: www.floatingbridgepress.org. Established 1994. **Contact:** The Editor.

Needs Floating Bridge Press publishes chapbooks and anthologies by Washington State poets, selected through an annual competition (see below). Has published *In the Convent We Become Clouds* by Annette Spaulding-Convy, *Toccata & Fugue* by Timothy Kelly, and *The Former St. Christopher* by Michael Bonacci, among others. The press also publishes *Floating Bridge Review*, an annual anthology featuring the work of Washington State poets. *Floating Bridge Review* is 86-144 pages, digest-sized, offset-printed, perfect-bound, with glossy cardstock cover. For a sample chapbook or anthology, send $13 postpaid.

Contest/Award Offerings For consideration, **Washington State poets only** should submit a chapbook ms of 20-24 pages of poetry. In addition to publication, the winner receives $500, 15 author's copies, and a reading in the Seattle area. All entrants receive a copy of the winning chapbook and will be considered for inclusion in *Floating Bridge Review*. Poet's name must not appear on the ms. Include a separate page with ms title, poet's name, address, phone number, and acknowledgments of any previous publications. Include SASE for results only; mss will not be returned. **Entry fee:** $12. **Deadline:** usual reading period is November 1-February 15 (postmark). Considers previously published individual poems and simultaneous submissions. Manuscripts are judged anonymously.

▦ ☑ **GALAXY PRESS**

(Specialized: experimental, Romantic, Neuromantic), 71 Recreation St., Tweed Heads NSW 2485 Australia. (61)(7)5536-1997. Established 1978. **Contact:** Lance Banbury, editor.

Needs Galaxy Press publishes "original avant-garde poetry and critical accounts as well as contemporary lyrics and prose poems." Latest guest imprint (November 2005) is a selection of the poetry of Wolf Larsen of Chicago. Latest in-house imprint (October 2009) is a laudatory poem on English soccers star David Beckham, titled "Beckham." Books are usually 16-20 pages, 15 × 21cm, offset/lithograph-printed, with glossy color card covers. Press run is 100. Obtain sample books or chapbooks by "written request."

How to Contact Considers simultaneous submissions. Cover letter is preferred. Often comments on rejected poems. Responds to queries in 2 weeks. Pays 5 author's copies.

Tips "Interests tend toward the Romantic and Neuromantic styles; a radical approach to imagery and emotions always welcome."

☑ **GERTRUDE PRESS**

(Specialized: gay, lesbian, bisexual, transgendered, queer-identified & allied), P.O. Box 83948, Portland OR 97283. E-mail: editor@gertrudepress.org. Website: www.gertrudepress.org. Established 1998. **Contact:** Eric Delehoy, founding editor.

Needs Gertrude Press, a nonprofit 501(c)(3) organization, showcases and develops "the creative talents of lesbian, gay, bisexual, trans, queer-identified, and allied individuals." Has published *Bone Knowing* by Kate Grant. Gertrude Press publishes 2 chapbooks/year (1 fiction, 1 poetry) as well as *Gertrude*, a semiannual literary journal (see separate listing in Magazines/Journals). Manuscripts are chosen through competition only (see below). Chapbooks are 20-24 pages, offset-printed, saddle-stapled, with cardstock cover with art.

How to Contact Refer to guidelines for Gertrude Press Poetry Chapbook Contest (see separate listing in Contests & Awards). Order sample chapbooks for $10.

Contest/Award Offerings The Gertrude Press Poetry Chapbook Contest (see separate listing in Contests & Awards).

☑ **GHOST PONY PRESS**

(Specialized: contemporary lyric; experimental), P.O. Box 260113, Madison WI 53726-0113. (608)238-0175. E-mail: ghostponypress@hotmail.com. Website: www.geocities.com/abraxaspress/. Established 1980. **Contact:** Ingrid Swanberg, editor/publisher.

Needs Ghost Pony Press has published 3 books of poetry by próspero saíz, including *the bird of nothing & other poems* (168 pages, 7x10, with sewn and wrapped binding; paperback available for $20, signed and numbered edition for $35). Also published *zen concrete & etc.* by d.a. levy (268 pages, magazine-sized, perfect-bound, illustrated; paperback available for $27.50).

How to Contact Query first, with a few sample poems (5-10) and cover letter with brief bio and publication credits. Include SASE. Considers previously published material for book publication. Accepts submissions by postal mail only; no e-mail submissions. Editor sometimes comments briefly on rejected poems. No promised response time. "We currently have a considerable backlog." Payment varies per project. Send SASE for catalog to buy samples.

▦ ☑ **GINNINDERRA PRESS**

(Specialized: Australian poets only), 79B Lipson Street, Port Adelaide SA 5015 Australia. E-mail: stephen@ginninderrapress.com.au. Website: www.ginninderrapress.com.au. Established 1996. **Contact:** Stephen Matthews, publisher.

•Please note: No longer accepting mss from writers residing outside of Australia.

Needs Ginninderra Press works "to give publishing opportunities to new writers." Has published poetry by Alan Gould and Geoff Page. Books are usually up to 72 pages, A5, laser-printed, saddle-stapled or thermal-bound, with board covers.

How to Contact Query first, with a few sample poems and a cover letter with brief bio and publication credits. Considers previously published poems; no simultaneous submissions. No fax or e-mail submisions. Time between acceptance and publication is 2 months. Seldom comments on rejected poems. Responds to queries in 1 week; to mss in 2 months.

☒ $ ☑ GOOSE LANE EDITIONS

(Specialized: Canadian poets only)500 Beaverbrook Court, Ste 300, Fredericton NB E3B 5X4 Canada. (506)450-4251. Fax: (506)459-4991. Website: www.gooselane.com. Established 1954. **Contact:** Ross Leckie, poetry editor.

Needs Goose Lane is a small literary press publishing Canadian fiction, poetry, and nonfiction. **Considers mss by Canadian poets only.** Receives about 400 mss/year, publishes 15-20 books/year, 4 of which are poetry collections. Has published *Beatitudes* by Herménégilde Chiasson and *Falsework* by Gary Geddes.

How to Contact "Call to inquire whether we are reading submissions." Accepts submissions by postal mail only. Guidelines available on Web site. Always sends prepublication galleys. Authors may receive royalties of up to 10% of retail price on all copies sold. Copies available to author at 40% discount.

Tips "Many of the poems in a manuscript accepted for publication will have been previously published in literary journals such as *The Fiddlehead*, *The Dalhousie Review*, or *The Malahat Review*."

GOTHIC PRESS

(Specialized: Gothic, Horror, Dark Fantasy)2272 Quail Oak, Baton Rouge LA 70808.Estab. 1979. 225-766-2906. E-mail: gothicpt12@aol.com. Website: www.gothicpress.com. **Contact:** Gary William Crawford, editor. Member, Science Fiction Poetry Association, Horror Writers Association.

Needs Gothic Press publishes gothic, horror, and dark fantasy poetry in their Gothic Chapbook series. Wants poetry in "any form or style as long as gothic or horror elements are present." Does not want science fiction. Has published Bruce Boston, Joey Froehlich, Scott C. Hocstad. Manuscripts are selected through open submission. Chapbooks are 10-80 pages, offset, saddle-stapled, with cardstock cover or interior illustration by commission. Send samples of art.

How to Contact Query first, with a few sample poems and a cover letter with brief bio and publication credits. Book/chapbook mss may include previously published poems. Responds to queries in 1 week; to mss in 4 weeks. Pays 10% advance against royalty. Order sample books/chapbooks by sending $6.

Tips "Know Gothic literature well."

☑ GRAYWOLF PRESS

2402 University Ave., Suite 203, Saint Paul MN 55114. Website: www.graywolfpress.org. Established 1974. **Contact:** Jeff Shotts, poetry editor.

•Poetry published in Graywolf Press collections has been included in *The Pushcart Prize*, and many books have won major awards.

Needs Graywolf Press is considered one of the nation's leading nonprofit literary publishers. "Graywolf introduces and promotes some of the most exciting and creative writers of our times." Considers only mss by poets widely published in magazines and journals of merit; **does not generally consider unsolicited mss by considers queries**. Has published poetry by Vijay Seshadri, Tess Gallagher, Tony Hoagland, Natasha Trethewey, Matthea Harvey, D.A. Powell, and many more. Publishes around 9 collections of poetry, 1-2 collections of poetry in translation, and 1-2 collections of essays on poetry/year.

How to Contact *No unsolicited mss. Query first, with 10 pages of poetry (as a sample from the ms) and cover letter with brief bio and publication credits. SASE required for reply. No e-mail queries. Reads queries postmarked January 15-December 1 only. Responds to queries in 3-6 months. Order sample books through Web site, or request catalog through online submission form.*

⬚ ⊘ GUERNICA EDITIONS INC.

(Specialized: pluriculturalism; international translation) P.O. Box 117, Station P, Toronto ON M5S 2S6 Canada. (416)658-9888. Fax: (416)657-8885. E-mail: guernicaeditions@cs.com. Website: www.guernicaeditions.com. Established 1978. **Contact:** Antonio D'Alfonso, poetry editor.

Needs "We wish to bring together the different and often divergent voices that exist in Canada and the U.S. We are interested in translations. We are mostly interested in poetry and essays on pluriculturalism." Has published poetry by Pier Paolo Pasolini, Pasquale Verdichio, Carole David, Jean-Marc Desgent, Gilles Cyr, Claudine Bertrand, Paul Bélanger, Denise Desaulets.

How to Contact Query with 1-2 pages of sample poems. Send SASE (Canadian stamps only) or SAE and IRCs for catalog.

Tips "We are interested in promoting a pluricultural view of literature by bridging languages and cultures. We specialize in international translation."

HELIKON PRESS

120 W. 71st St., New York NY 10023. Established 1972. **Contact:** William Leo Coakley, poetry editor.

Needs "We try to publish the best contemporary poetry in the tradition of English verse. We read (and listen to) poetry and ask poets to build a collection around particular poems. We print fine editions illustrated by good artists."

How to Contact *"Unfortunately, we cannot encourage submissions."*

HIGH LYRICAL EXPERIMENTS

(Specialized: experimental; paradoxism; outer-art), P.O. Box 141, Rehoboth NM 87322. E-mail: M_L_Perez@yahoo.com. Website: www.gallup.unm.edu ~ smarandache/ebooksliterature.htm. Established 1990. **Contact:** M. Lou, publisher.

Needs High Lyrical Experiments publishes 2-3 poetry paperbacks/year. Wants experimental poetry dealing with paradoxism. No classical poetry. See Web site for poetry samples. Has published poetry by Anatol Ciocanu, Nina Josu, and Al Bantos.

How to Contact Submit 3-4 poems at a time. No previously published poems or simultaneous submissions. Cover letter is preferred. Submit seasonal poems 1 month in advance. Time between acceptance and publication is 1 year. Seldom comments on rejected poems. Responds to queries in 1 month. Pays 100 author's copies. Order sample books by sending SASE.

Also Offers Free e-books available on Web site.

$ ⊘ HIGH PLAINS PRESS

(Specialized: WY and the American West), P.O. Box 123, Glendo WY 82213. (307)735-4370. Fax: (307)735-4590. E-mail: editor@highplainspress.com. Website: www.highplainspress.com. Established 1985. **Contact:** Nancy Curtis, poetry editor.

Needs High Plains Press considers books of poetry "about Wyoming and the American West, particularly poetry based on historical people/events or nature. We mainly publish historical nonfiction, but do publish 1 book of poetry every year." Has published *Bitter Creek Junction* by Linda Hasselstrom, *Small Talk* by Mary Lou Sanelli, and *The White Dove: A Celebration of Father*

Kino by Jane Candia Coleman.

How to Contact Query first with 3 sample poems (from a 50-poem ms). Accepts submissions by e-mail (as attachment); no fax or disk submissions. Time between acceptance and publication is up to 2 years. Guidelines available for SASE on Web site, by fax, or e-mail. Responds in 2 months. Sometimes sends prepublication galleys. Pays 10% of sales. Acquires first rights. Catalog available on request; sample books: $5.

Tips "Look at our previous titles."

▣ ⊘ HILLTOP PRESS

(Specialized: science fiction, dark fantasy), 4 Nowell Place, Almondbury, Huddersfield, West Yorkshire HD5 8PB England. Website: www.bbr-online.com/catalogue (online catalog). Established 1966. **Contact:** Steve Sneyd, editor.

Needs Hilltop Press publishes mainly science fiction poetry, plus some dark fantasy poetry. Publications in print include: a series of books on poetry in U.S. and UK SFanzines; collections, new and reprint, by individual science fiction poets including Andrew Darlington, Gavin Salisbury, Mary Ladd, Mark Sonnenfeld, John F. Haines, and Jimmie Dickie as well as Robert Cole, and Arthurian SF poetry by K.V. Bailey; dark fantasy, including Medusa poems anthology and work including family myth verse play by Frances Elizabeth Campbell, and ballad and Arthurian reprints. Orders from the U.S. can be placed through the Web site of BBR Solutions Ltd. (see above).

How to Contact *Does not accept unsolicited mss.Query (with SAE/IRC) with proposals for relevant projects.*

Tips "My advice for beginning poets is: a) Persist--don't let any 1 editor discourage you. 'In poetry's house are many mansions.' What 1 publication hates another may love; b) Be prepared for long delays between acceptance and appearance of work--the small press is mostly self-financed and part-time, so don't expect it to be more efficient than commercial publishers; c) Always keep a copy of everything you send out, put your name and address on everything you send, and always include adequately stamped SAE."

▣ $ ⊘ HIPPOPOTAMUS PRESS

(Specialized: Modernism), 22 Whitewell Rd., Frome, Somerset BA11 4EL England. Phone/fax: (44)(1373)466653. E-mail: rjhippopress@aol.com. Established 1974. **Contact:** Roland John, poetry editor.

Needs Hippopotamus Press publishes 6 books/year. "The Hippopotamus Press is specialized, with an affinity with Modernism. No Typewriter Poetry, Concrete Poetry, or Surrealism."

How to Contact Query first, with a few sample poems and cover letter with brief bio and publication credits. Considers simultaneous submissions and previously published poems. Responds in 6 weeks. Pays 712-10% royalties plus author's copies. Request book catalog to purchase sample books.

⊘ HOLIDAY HOUSE, INC.

(Specialized: poetry for children/teens), Editorial Dept., 425 Madison Ave., New York NY 10017. Website: www.holidayhouse.com. Established 1936.

Needs A trade children's book house. Has published hardcover books for children by John Updike and Walter Dean Myers. Publishes one poetry book/year, averaging 32 pages.

How to Contact *"The acceptance of complete book manuscripts of high-quality children's poetry is limited."* Send a query with SASE before submitting.

▨ $ ⊘ HOUSE OF ANANSI PRESS

(Specialized: work by Canadian authors), 110 Spadina Ave., Suite 801, Toronto ON M5V 2K4 Canada. (416)363-4343. Fax: (416)363-1017. Website: www.anansi.ca. Established 1967.

Needs House of Anansi publishes literary fiction and poetry by Canadian and international writers. "We seek to balance the list between well-known and emerging writers, with an interest in writing by Canadians of all backgrounds. We publish Canadian poetry only, and poets must have a substantial publication record--if not in books, then definitely in journals and magazines of repute." Does not want "children's poetry or poetry by previously unpublished poets." Has published *Power Politics* by Margaret Atwood and *Ruin & Beauty* by Patricia Young. Books are generally 96-144 pages, trade paperbacks with French sleeves, with matte covers.

How to Contact Canadian poets should query first with 10 sample poems (typed double-spaced) and a cover letter with brief bio and publication credits. Considers simultaneous submissions. Poems are circulated to an editorial board. Often comments on rejected poems. Responds to queries within 1 year, to mss (if invited) within 4 months. Pays 8-10% royalties, a $750 advance, and 10 author's copies (out of a press run of 1,000).

Tips "To learn more about our titles, check our Web site or write to us directly for a catalog. We strongly advise poets to build up a publishing résumé by submitting poems to reputable magazines and journals. This indicates 3 important things to us: 1, that he or she is becoming a part of the Canadian poetry community; 2, that he or she is building up a readership through magazine subscribers; and 3, it establishes credibility in his or her work. There is a great deal of competition for only 3 or 4 spots on our list each year--which always includes works by poets we have previously published."

⊘ ALICE JAMES BOOKS

University of Maine at Farmington, 238 Main St., Farmington ME 04938. Phone/fax: (207)778-7071. E-mail: ajb@umf.maine.edu. Website: www.alicejamesbooks.org. Established 1973. **Contact:** Contest Coordinator.

Needs "The mission of Alice James Books, a cooperative poetry press, is to seek out and publish the best contemporary poetry by both established and beginning poets, with particular emphasis on involving poets in the publishing process." Has published poetry by Jane Kenyon, Jean Valentine, B.H. Fairchild, and Matthea Harvey. Publishes flat-spined paperbacks of high quality, both in production and contents. Does not want children's poetry or light verse. Publishes 6 paperback books/year, 80 pages each, in editions of 1,500.

How to Contact Manuscripts are selected through competitions (see below).

Contest/Award Offerings The Kinereth Gensler Awards and The Beatrice Hawley Award (see separate listings in Contests & Awards).

⊘ THE JOHNS HOPKINS UNIVERSITY PRESS

2715 N. Charles St., Baltimore MD 21218. Fax: (410) 516-6968. Website: www.press.jhu.edu. Established 1878.

Needs "One of the largest American university presses, Johns Hopkins publishes primarily scholarly books and journals. We do, however, publish short fiction and poetry in the series Johns Hopkins: Poetry and Fiction, edited by John Irwin."

How to Contact *"Unsolicited submissions are not considered."*

KATYDID BOOKS

1 Balsa Rd., Santa Fe NM 87508. Website: http://katydidbooks.com. Established 1973. **Contact:** Karen Hargreaves-Fitzsimmons and Thomas Fitzsimmons, editors/publishers.

Needs Katydid Books publishes 1 paperback/year and 1 hardback/year. "We publish a series of

poetry: Asian Poetry in Translation (distributed by University of Hawaii Press)."
How to Contact *Currently not accepting submissions.*

LAPWING PUBLICATIONS

(Specialized: work by Irish poets),1 Ballysillan Dr., Belfast BT14 8HQ Northern Ireland. Phone/fax: (44)(2890)295800. E-mail: lapwing.poetry@ntlworld.com. Website: http://www.freewebs.com:80/lapwingpoetry/. Established 1989. **Contact:** Dennis Greig, editor.

•Lapwing will produce work only if and when resources to do so are available.

Needs Lapwing publishes "emerging Irish poets and poets domiciled in Ireland, plus the new work of a suitable size by established Irish writers. Non-Irish poets are also published. Emphasis on first collections preferrably not larger than 80 pages. Logistically, publishing beyond the British Isles is always difficult for 'hard copy' editions. From 2009 certain works are available in PDF format online. Prices will be £3, 3€, or $5 US." Publishes 6-10 chapbooks/year. Wants poetry of all kinds, but, "no crass political, racist, sexist propaganda, even of a positive or 'pc' tenor." Has published Zlatko Tomicic (*Croatia My Love*), Said (Iranian-German)-Goethe Medallion 2006-(*The Place I Die I Shall Not Belong*), Ilmar Lehtpere and Kristina Ehin (Estonian)-Popescue European Translation Award 2007-(*My Brother is Going Off to War*). Pamphlets up to 32 pages, chapbooks up to 44 pages, books 48-112 pages. Belfast binding (saddle-stitched signatures in a perfect binding 'look'), Belfast Japanese side stitch or Belfast square spined block binding.

How to Contact "Submit 6 poems in the first instance; depending on these, an invitation to submit more may follow." Considers simultaneous submissions. Accepts e-mail submissions (pasted into body of message). Cover letter is required. Poems are circulated to an editorial board. "All submissions receive a first reading. If these poems have minor errors or faults, the writer is advised. If poor quality, the poems are returned. Those 'passing' first reading are retained, and a letter of conditional offer is sent." Often comments on rejected poems. Responds to queries in 1 month; to mss in 2 months. Pays 20 author's copies; no royalties. "After initial publication, irrespective of the quantity, the work will be permanently available using 'print-on-demand' production; such publications will not always be printed exactly as the original, although the content will remain the same."

Tips "Clean; check spelling, grammar, punctuation, layout (i.e., will it fit a book page?); clear text. Due to limited resources, material will be processed well in advance of any estimated publishing date. All accepted material is strictly conditional on resources available, no favoritism. The Irish domestic market is small, the culture is hierarchical, poet/personality culture predominates, literary democracy is limited."

LETHE PRESS

NJ. Estab. 2003. (609)410-7391. E-mail: editor@lethepressbooks.com. Website: www.lethepressbooks.com. Contact: Steve Berman, publisher. Estab. 2001. "Named after the Greek river of memory and forgetfulness (and pronounced Lee-Thee), Lethe Press is a small press devoted to ideas that are often neglected or forgotten by mainstream, profit-oriented publishers." Distributes/promotes titles Lethe Books are distributed by Ingram Publications and Bookazine, and are available at all major bookstores, as well as the major online retailers.

How to Contact Send query letter. Accepts queries by e-mail.

LOONFEATHER PRESS

(Specialized: for MN-area writers), P.O. Box 1212, Bemidji MN 56619. E-mail: books@loonfeatherpress.com. Website: http://loonfeatherpress.com. Established 1979. **Contact:** Poetry Editors.

Needs Loonfeather Press publishes a limited number of quality poetry books. Has published

Imaginarium by Lynn Levin (a 2005 ForeWord Finalist); *The Rhubarb King* by Sharon Chmielarz; and *Traces in Blood, Bone, & Stone: Contemporary Ojibwe Poetry*, edited by Kimberly Blaeser.

How to Contact *Does not accept unsolicited mss.***Does accept query letters/e-mails. Check Web site for updates.**

☑ LOUISIANA STATE UNIVERSITY PRESS

3990 West Lakeshore Dr., Baton Rouge LA 70808. (225)578-6434. Fax: (225)578-6461. E-mail: jeaster@lsu.edu. Website: www.lsu.edu/lsupress. Established 1935. **Contact:** John Easterly, executive editor.

Needs A highly respected publisher of collections by poets such as Claudia Emerson, David Kirby, Brendan Galvin, Fred Chappell, Marilyn Nelson, and Henry Taylor. Publisher of the Southern Messenger Poets series edited by Dave Smith.

How to Contact *"Currently not accepting poetry submissions, since the lists are full through 2012."*

☑ LUNA BISONTE PRODS

(Specialized: experimental, avant-garde)137 Leland Ave., Columbus OH 43214-7505. Website: www.johnmbennett.net. Established 1974. **Contact:** John M. Bennett, editor/publisher.

Needs Luna Bisonte Prods considers book submissions. "Interested in avant-garde and highly experimental work only." Has published poetry by Jim Leftwich, Sheila E. Murphy, Al Ackerman, Richard Kostelanetz, Carla Bertola, Olchar Lindsann, and many others.

How to Contact Query first, with a few sample poems and cover letter with brief bio and publication credits. "Keep it brief. Chapbook publishing usually depends on grants or other subsidies, and is usually by solicitation. **Will also consider subsidy arrangements on negotiable terms.**" A sampling of various Luna Bisonte Prods products is available for $20.

Tips "Be blank."

☑ MAMMOTH BOOKS

MAMMOTH press, inc., 7 Juniata St., DuBois PA 15801. Established 1996. **Contact:** Antonio Vallone, publisher.

Needs MAMMOTH books, an imprint of MAMMOTH press inc., publishes 4 or more paperbacks/ year of creative nonfiction, fiction, and poetry. "We are open to all types of literary poetry." Has published *The House of Sages* by Philip Terman, *The Never Wife* by Cynthia Hogue, *These Happy Eyes* by Liz Rosenberg, and *Subjects for Other Conversations* by John Stigall. Books are usually 5 × 7 or 6 × 9, digitally printed, perfect-bound; covers vary (1- to 4-color).

How to Contact *Not currently reading unsolicited mss.*

Tips "Read big. Write big. Publish small. Join the heard."

☑ MARYMARK PRESS

(Specialized: experimental, avant-garde), 45-08 Old Millstone Dr., East Windsor NJ 08520. (609)443-0646. Established 1994. **Contact:** Mark Sonnenfeld, editor/publisher.

Needs Marymark Press's goal is "to feature and promote experimental writers. I will most likely be publishing broadsides, give-out sheets, and chapbooks this year. I want to see experimental writing of the outer fringe. Make up words, sounds, whatever, but say something you thought never could be explained. Disregard rules, if need be." No traditional, rhyming, or spiritual verse; no predictable styles. Has published poetry by Thaïs H. Miller, John M. Bennett, Sigismund Urban, Willi Melnikov, and Mel C. Thompson.

How to Contact Submit 3 poems at a time. Considers previously published poems and simultaneous submissions. Cover letter is preferred. "Copies should be clean, crisp, and camera-ready. I do not have the means to accept electronic submissions. A SASE should accompany all submissions, and include a telephone number if at all possible." Time between acceptance and publication is 1 month. Seldom comments on rejected poems. Guidelines available for SASE. Responds to queries and mss in up to 2 weeks. Pays at least 10 author's copies (out of a press run of 200-300). **May offer subsidy arrangements.** "It all depends upon my financial situation at the time. Yes, I might ask the author to subsidize the cost. It could be worth their while. I have good connections in the international small press." Order sample publications by sending a 6x9 SAE. "There is no charge for samples."

Tips "Experiment with thought, language, the printed word."

☑ MAVERICK DUCK PRESS

E-mail: maverickduckpress@yahoo.com. Website: www.maverickduckpress.com. Established 2005. **Contact:** Kendall A. Bell, editor.

Needs Maverick Duck Press is a "publisher of chapbooks from undiscovered talent. We are looking for fresh and powerful work that shows a sense of innovation or a new take on passion or emotion. Previous publication in print or online journals will increase your chances of us accepting your manuscript." Does not want "unedited work." Recently published *Romance* by Donora Hillard, *Selected Sonnets* by Anna Evans, *Pre-Elixir* by J. Michael Wahlgren, *The Forgotten* by Kendall A. Bell, and *Strange Gospels* by Kristina Marie Darling. Publishes 6-8 chapbooks/year. Manuscripts are selected through open submission. Chapbooks are 20-30 pages, photocopied, saddle-stapled, with cardstock covers (poet must provide desired cover art).

How to Contact Query first, with a few sample poems and a cover letter with brief bio and publication credits. Chapbook mss may include previously published poems. "Previous publication is always a plus, as we may be more familiar with your work. Chapbook manuscripts should have at least 20 poems." Pays 20 author's copies (out of a press run of 50).

Tips "Write and revise often. Read a lot of other poets. Your manuscript should be the strongest of your work."

MELLEN POETRY PRESS

P.O. Box 450, Lewiston NY 14092-8566. (716)754-2266. Fax: (716)754-4056. Website: www.mellenpress.com. Established 1973. **Contact:** Kelly Lang, poetry editor.

☑ MIDMARCH ARTS PRESS

300 Riverside Dr., New York NY 10025. Website: www.midmarchartspress.org.

Needs Midmarch Arts Press publishes 4-6 paperbacks/year, only one of which is poetry Has recently published *Rock Vein Sky* by Charlotte Mandel; *Luminations--art* by Oriole F. Feshbach.

How to Contact Query by letter or e-mail prior to submitting anything.

☑ MIDWEST VILLAGES & VOICES

(Specialized: Midwestern poetry), P.O. Box 40214, St. Paul MN 55104. (612)822-6878. Established 1979.

Needs Midwest Villages & Voices is a cultural organization and small press publisher of Midwestern poetry and prose.

How to Contact "We encourage and support Midwestern writers and artists. However, **at this time submissions are accepted by invitation only.** Unsolicited submissions are not accepted."

☑ MILKWEED EDITIONS

1011 Washington Ave. S., Suite 300, Minneapolis MN 55415-1246. (612)332-3192. Fax: (612)215-2550. E-mail: editor@milkweed.org. Website: www.milkweed.org. Established 1984. **Contact:** Poetry Reader.

Needs Milkweed Editions is "looking for poetry manuscripts of high quality that embody humane values and contribute to cultural understanding." Not limited in subject matter. Open to writers with previously published books of poetry or a minimum of 6 poems published in nationally distributed commercial or literary journals. Considers translations and bilingual mss. Has published *Hallelujah Blackout* by Alex Lemon, *Music for Landing Planes By* by Eireann Lorsung, *Atlas* by Katrina Vandenberg, and *Willow Room, Green Door* by Deborah Keenan.

How to Contact Submit 60 pages or more, typed on high-quality white paper. No fax or e-mail submissions. Do not send originals. Include SASE for reply. Accepts and reads unsolicited mss all year. "In the event that manuscripts are not accepted for publication, we prefer to recycle them. If you need your work returned, **please enclose a check for $5 rather than a stamped mailer**." Guidelines available for SASE or on Web site. Responds in up to 6 months. Order sample books through Web site.

☑ MOVING PARTS PRESS

(Specialized: translations; Latino/Chicano), 10699 Empire Grade, Santa Cruz CA 95060-9474. (831)427-2271. E-mail: frice@movingpartspress.com. Website: www.movingpartspress.com. Established 1977. **Contact:** Felicia Rice, poetry editor.

Needs Moving Part Press publishes handsome, innovative books, broadsides, and prints that "explore the relationship of word and image, typography and the visual arts, the fine arts and popular culture." Published *Codex Espangliensis: from Columbus to the Border Patrol* (1998) with performance texts by Guillermo Gómez-Peñña and collage imagery by Enrique Chagoya; *Cosmogonie Intime/An Intimate Cosmogony* (2005), a limited edition artists' book with poems by Yves Peyré, translated by Elizabeth R. Jackson, and drawings by Ray Rice.

How to Contact *Does not accept unsolicited mss.*

❖ ☑ MULTICULTURAL BOOKS

Suite 307, 6311 Gilbert Rd., Richmond BC V7C 3V7 Canada. (604)277-3864. E-mail: jrmbooks@ hotmail.com. Website: www.thehypertexts.com. Established 1985. **Contact:** Joe M. Ruggier, publisher.

Needs Multicultural Books publishes poetry and related literature as well as fiction and various forms of nonfiction. Publishes 1-6 books/year "depending on availability and quality." Manuscripts are selected through open submission. Books are 120 + pages, digitally photocopied, perfect-bound, with heavy color cardstock cover.

How to Contact Query first, with a few sample poems and a cover letter with brief bio and publication credits. Book mss may include previously published poems. "The only criteria is quality of work and excellence." Responds to queries in 2 months; to mss in 2 months. **Offers author-subsidy as well as publisher-subsidy options**; the selection process for the latter is extremely competitive and quality-conscious. "Authors who feel their work may be up to standard are welcome to query us with a sample or else submit an entire manuscript. All interested parties may consult our guidelines as well as our sample publication contract on Web site." Order sample books/chapbooks by contacting Joe M. Ruggier.

☑ NEW NATIVE PRESS

(Specialized: translations; marginalized & endangered languages), P.O. Box 661, Cullowhee NC 28723. (828)293-9237. E-mail: newnativepress@hotmail.com. Website: www.newnativepress. com. Established 1979. **Contact:** Thomas Rain Crowe, publisher.

Needs New Native Press has "selectively narrowed its range of contemporary 20th- and 21st-century literature to become an exclusive publisher of writers in marginalized and endangered languages. All books published are bilingual translations from original languages into English."

Publishes about 2 paperbacks/year. Has published *Kenneth Patchen: Rebel Poet in America* by Larry Smith; Gaelic, Welsh, Breton, Cornish, and Manx poets in an all-Celtic-language anthology of contemporary poets from Scotland, Ireland, Wales, Brittany, Cornwall, and Isle of Man, entitled *Writing The Wind: A Celtic Resurgence* (The New Celtic Poetry); and *Selected Poems* by Kusumagraj (poet from Bombay, India) in the Marathi language. Books are sold by distributors in 4 foreign countries, and in the U.S. by Baker & Taylor, Amazon.com, library vendors, and Small Press Distribution. Books are typically 80 pages, offset-printed on glossy 120 lb. stock, perfect-bound, with professionally designed color cover.

How to Contact Query first, with 10 sample poems and cover letter with brief bio and publication credits. Considers previously published poems and simultaneous submissions. Time between acceptance and publication is up to 1 year. Always comments on rejected poems. Responds in 2 weeks. Pays in author's copies ("amount varies with author and title").

Tips "We are looking for work indicative of rare and unique talent--and original voices--using language experimentally and symbolically, if not subversively."

NEW ORLEANS POETRY JOURNAL PRESS

2131 General Pershing St., New Orleans LA 70115. (504)891-3458. Established 1956. **Contact:** Maxine Cassin, publisher/editor. Co-Editor: Charles de Gravelles.

   •"For the present, due to Hurricane Katrina, all correspondence should be sent to Maxine Cassin at 140 Wylie Dr., #4, Baton Rouge LA 70808."

Needs "We prefer to publish relatively new and/or little-known poets of unusual promise or those inexplicably neglected." Does not want to see "cliché or doggerel, anything incomprehensible or too derivative, or workshop exercises. First-rate lyric poetry preferred (not necessarily in traditional forms)." Has published books by Everette Maddox, Charles Black, Malaika Favorite, Martha McFerren, Paul Petrie, Charles de Gravelles, and Ralph Adamo.

How to Contact *This market is currently closed to all submissions.*

Tips "Read as much as possible! Write only when you must, and don't rush into print! No poetry should be sent without querying first! Publishers are concerned about expenses unnecessarily incurred in mailing manuscripts. Telephoning is not encouraged."

☐ NEW RIVERS PRESS

MSU Moorhead, 1104 Seventh Ave. S., Moorhead MN 56563. E-mail: nrp@mnstate.edu. Website: www.newriverspress.com. Established 1968. **Contact:** Donna Carlson, managing editor.

Needs New Rivers Press publishes collections of poetry, novels or novellas, translations of contemporary literature, and collections of short fiction and nonfiction. "We will continue to publish books regularly by new and emerging writers, especially those with a connection to Minnesota or to New York City, but we also welcome the opportunity to read work of every character and to publish the best literature available by new and emerging authors nationwide. Each October and November, through the MVP competition (see below), we choose 3 books, 1 of them national (genre will vary by year) and 2 regional." Has published *The Pact* by Walter Roers, *Nice Girls* by Cezarija Abartis, *Mozart's Carriage* by Dan Bachhuber, *The Volunteer* by Candace Black, *The Hunger Bone* by Deb Marquart, and *Real Karaoke People* by Ed Bok-Lee, and *Terrain Tracks* by Purvi Shah.

How to Contact Book-length mss of poetry, short fiction, novellas, or creative nonfiction are all considered. No fax or e-mail submissions. Guidelines and catalog available on Web site.

Contest/Award Offerings The Minnesota Voices Project (MVP) awards $1,000, a standard book contract, and publication of a book-length ms by New Rivers Press. Every third year, the poetry competition is national, open to anyone residing in the U.S.; 2 additional annual prizes (1 prose, 1 in any genre) are open only to residents of Minnesota or New York City. All previously published poems must be acknowledged. Considers simultaneous submissions "if noted as such. If your manuscript is accepted elsewhere during the judging, you must notify New Rivers Press immediately. If you do not give such notification and your manuscript is selected, your signature on the entry form gives New Rivers Press permission to go ahead with publication." Submit 50-80 pages of poetry. Entry form (required) and guidelines available on Web site. **Entry fee:** $20. **Deadline:** submit September 15-November 1 (postmark). 2008 poetry winners were Elizabeth Oness (*Fallibility*) and Maya Pindyck (*Friend Among Stones*). 2008 judge: Michael Hettich.

$ ☑ OOLIGAN PRESS

(Specialized: gives preference to translated poetry, prose poetry, traditional verse, and works from local poets), Portland State University, P.O. Box 751, Portland OR 97207-0751. Website: www.ooligan.pdx.edu. Established 2001. **Contact:** Acquisitions Committee.

Needs Ooligan is a general trade press that "specializes in publishing authors from the Pacific Northwest and/or works that have specific value to that community. We are limited in the number of poetry titles that we publish as poetry represents only a small percentage of our overall acquisitions. We are open to all forms of style and verse; however, we give special preference to translated poetry, prose poetry, and traditional verse. Although spoken word, slam, and rap poetry are of interest to the press, we will not consider such work if it does not translate well to the written page. Ooligan does not publish chapbooks." Has published *Deer Drink the Moon*, edited by Liz Nakazawa and *American Scream* and *Palindrome Apocalypse* by the Croatian poet Durbravaka Oraic-Tolid, translated by Julienne Eden Busic. Manuscripts are selected through open submissions. Books are most often offset-printed and perfect-bound with soft covers.

How to Contact Query by postal mail, with 20 or more poems, a brief bio including poet's publication credits, and a SASE. May include previously published poems. Accepts simultaneous submissions. See Web site for explanation of acquisition process and complete submission guidelines. Responds to queries in 3 months. Payment varies, but generally 6-12% of retail price and 25 author's copies. Order sample books through Web site.

☑ ORCHISES PRESS

P.O. Box 320533, Alexandria VA 22320-4533. E-mail: lathbury@gmu.edu. Website: http://mason.gmu.edu/lathbury. Established 1983. **Contact:** Roger Lathbury, poetry editor.

•Orchises Press prefers not to receive unsolicited mss.

☑ OUTRIDER PRESS, INC.

2036 North Winds Drive, Dyer IN 46311. (219)322-7270. Fax: (219)322-7085. E-mail: outriderpress@sbcglobal.net. Website: www.outriderpress.com. **Contact:** Whitney Scott, editor. Estab. 1988. Small literary press and hand bindery; publishes many first-time authors. Publishes paperback originals. Books: 70 lb. paper; offset printing; perfect bound. Average print order: 2,000. **Published 25-30 debut authors within the last year.** Distributes titles through Baker & Taylor.

•Was a *Small Press Review* "Pick" for 2000.

How to Contact Accepts unsolicited mss. Query with SASE. Accepts queries by mail. Include estimated word count, brief bio, list of publishing credits. Agented fiction 10%. Responds in 6 weeks to queries; 4 months to mss. Accepts simultaneous submissions, electronic submissions, submissions on disk. Sometimes comments on rejected mss. In affiliation with Tallgrass Writers Guild, publishes an annual anthonlogy with cash prizes. The 2010 anthology theme is "The Changing Seasons," which can be directly Nature-centered, but also indirectly linked by including societal change experienced on a personal level as well as internal personal growth and change--as long as these somehow relate to our experience and connection with the natural world and its seasonal changes. Hard economic times can spur small-scale vegetable gardening, so the writer's experience of that garden's development through time could be appropriate. Another example: the changing geopolitical climate can signal a new direction to a personally "greener" lifestyle. As always, broadly interpreted with a variety of historic/geographic sttings welcomed. Deadline is February 27, 2010. For details and complete guidelines, e-mail.

Tips "It's always best to familiarize yourself with our publications. We're especially fond of humor/irony."

⊘ PATH PRESS, INC.

(Specialized: African American, Third World), P.O. Box 2925, Chicago IL 60690. (847)424-1620. Fax: (847)492-0177. Fax: (773)651-0210. E-mail: pathpressinc@aol.com. Established 1969. **Contact:** Bennett J. Johnson, president.

Needs Path Press is a small publisher of books and poetry primarily "by, for, and about African American and Third World people." Open to all types of poetic forms; emphasis is on high quality. Books are "hardback and quality paperbacks."

How to Contact Query first, with a few sample poems and cover letter with brief bio and publication credits. Submissions should be typewritten in ms format. Accepts submissions by e-mail (as attachment).

$ ⊘ PELICAN PUBLISHING COMPANY

(Specialized: regional/various; poetry books for children)1000 Burmaster St., Gretna LA 70053. E-mail: editorial@pelicanpub.com. Website: www.pelicanpub.com. Established 1926. **Contact:** Nina Kooij, editor-in-chief.

Needs Pelican Publishing Company is a medium-sized publisher of popular histories, cookbooks, regional books, children's books, and inspirational/motivational books. Considers poetry for "hardcover children's books only (1,100 words maximum), preferably with a regional focus. However, our needs for this are very limited; we publish 15 juvenile titles per year, and most of these are prose, not poetry." Has published *Alaskan Night Before Christmas* by Tricia Brown and *Hawaiian Night Before Christmas* by Carolyn Macy. Two of Pelican's popular series are prose books about Gaston the Green-Nosed Alligator by James Rice, and Clovis Crawfish by Mary Alice Fontenot. Books are 32 pages, magazine-sized, include illustrations.

How to Contact Printout of ms with a cover letter including "work and writing backgrounds and promotional connections." No previously published poems or simultaneous submissions. Guidelines available for SASE or on Web site. Responds to mss in 3 months. Always sends prepublication galleys. Pays royalties. Acquires all rights. Returns rights upon termination of contract. Typically, Pelican books sell for $15.95. Write for catalog or visit Web site to view catalog and/or buy samples.

Tips "Except for the rhyme in our *Night Before Christmas* series, we try to avoid rhyme altogether, especially predictable rhyme. Monotonous rhythm can also be a problem."

⊘ PERUGIA PRESS

(Specialized: first or second poetry book by a woman) P.O. Box 60364, Florence MA 01062. E-mail: info@perugiapress.com. Website: www.perugiapress.com. Established 1997. **Contact:** Susan Kan, director.

Needs Perugia Press publishes 1 collection of poetry each year, by a woman at the beginning of her publishing career (first or second books only). "Our books appeal to people who have been reading poetry for decades, as well as those who might be picking up a book of poetry for the first time. Slight preference for narrative poetry." Has published *Two Minutes of Light,* by Nancy K. Pearson, *Beg No Pardon,* by Lynne Thompson, *Kettle Bottom,* by Diane Gilliam Fisher, *Lamb,* by Frannie Lindsay, *The Disappearing Letters*, by Carol Edelstein. Books are an average of 88 pages, perfect-bound. First print run is 800-1,200. Order sample books through Web site.

How to Contact "We are not accepting general submissions at this time." *Manuscripts are selected through competition only.*

Contest/Award Offerings The Perugia Press Prize (see separate listing in Contests & Awards).

✅ PLAN B PRESS

(Specialized: experimental, concrete, visual poetry), P.O. Box 3242, Fairfax VA 22038. (215)732-2663. E-mail: planbpress@gmail.com. Website: www.planbpress.com. Established 1999. **Contact:** stevenallenmay, president.

Needs Plan B Press is a "small publishing company with an international feel. Our intention is to have Plan B Press be part of the conversation about the direction and depth of literary movements and genres. Plan B Press's new direction is to seek out authors rarely-to-never published, sharing new voices that might not otherwise be heard. Plan B Press is determined to merge text with image, writing with art." Publishes poetry and short fiction. Wants "experimental poetry, concrete/visual work." Does not want "sonnets, political or religious poems, work in the style of Ogden Nash." Has published poetry by Lamont B Steptoe, Michele Belluomini, Jim Mancinelli, Lyn Lifshin, Robert Miltner, and stevenallenmay. Publishes 1 poetry book/year and 5-10 chapbooks/year. Manuscripts are selected through open submission and through competition (see below). Books/chapbooks are 24-48 pages, with covers with art/graphics.

How to Contact Query first, with a few sample poems and a cover letter with brief bio and publication credits. Book/chapbook mss may include previously published poems. Guidelines available on Web site. Responds to queries in 1 month; to mss in 3 months. Author keeps royalties. Pays varying number of author's copies; press run varies per book. Order sample books/chapbooks by writing to Plan B Press or through Web site.

Contest/Award Offerings The annual Plan B Press Poetry Chapbook Contest (see separate listing in Contests & Awards).

Tips "Writing reveals the mirror to your soul. Don't think about words until you are in the editing phase, and then only look for errors. Whatever sense your work makes is for the reader to ascertain, not you. You are a beacon, a transmitter."

$ ✅ POETIC MATRIX PRESS

P.O. Box 1223, Madera CA 93639. (559)673-9402. E-mail: poeticmatrix@yahoo.com. Website: www.poeticmatrix.com. Established 1997. **Contact:** John Peterson, editor/publisher.

Needs Poetic Matrix Press publishes books (70-120 pages). "Poetic Matrix Press hosts a Slim Volume Series call for submissions of manuscripts every 2 years of between 70-80 pages. The manuscript selected will be published with full-color cover, perfect binding, and ISBN. The selected poet will receive 100 copies of the completed book and a $200 honorarium."

How to Contact Guidelines and submission dates available on our Web site. **Charges reading fee for Slim Volume Series submissions only.** For book information, contact the publisher. "Inquire about Author Assisted Financial Development publications for additional publishing options at Web site. Submit to our twice yearly online periodic letter via e-mail."

Tips "We seek writing of quality, with passion and intelligence."

🌐 ✅ POETRY SALZBURG

University of Salzburg, Dept. of English, Akademiestrasse 24, Salzburg A-5020 Austria. (43)(662)8044-4422. Fax: (43)(662)8044-167. E-mail: editor@poetrysalzburg.com. Website: www.poetrysalzburg.com. Established 1971 (as University of Salzburg Press). **Contact:** Dr. Wolfgang Goertschacher, Mag. Andreas Schachermayr, editors.

Needs Poetry Salzburg publishes "collections of at least 100 pages by mainly poets not taken up by big publishers." Publishes 6-8 paperbacks/year. Books are usually 100-350 pages, A5, professionally printed, perfect-bound, with card covers.

How to Contact Query first, with a few sample poems and a cover letter with brief bio and publication credits. Suggests authors publish in *Poetry Salzburg Review* (see separate listing in Magazines/Journals) first. Responds to queries in 4 weeks; to mss in about 3 months. Payment varies.

🅽 ☑ POOR MAN'S COPYRIGHT

P.O. Box 38720, Philadelphia PA 19104. Estab. 2009. E-mail: info@poormanscopyright.org. Website: www.poormanscopyright.org. **Contact**: Natacha Leonard, editor.

Needs *Poor Man's Copyright*, is an online chapbook publisher. "We also produce a limited number of hardcopies printed on 100% recycled paper as well as a book-length anthology of work from the site. all printed material will have ISBN numbers." Wants "long poems or long sequence poems on the urban cultural environment. The work is multicultural and all styles are welcome. For examples of writing in the tradition of the long poem, please consider Hughes' 'Montage of a Dream Deferred,' Stein's 'Tender Buttons,' and Rukeyser's 'The Book of the Dead.' We are particularly interested in how individual voice is supported or negated in an urban setting." Does not want "work that is overly sentimental, sexist, racist, or otherwise offensive to literary taste." Manuscripts are selected through open submission. Chapbooks are 16-24 pages, high-quality printed, saddle-stapled, with card stock cover.

How to Contact Submit work via e-mail to submissions@poormanscopyright.org. Considers simultaneous submissions. "Please notify *Poor Man's Copyright* should your work be accepted by another publisher. Manuscripts must be 10-15 typed pages in length and sent as an e-mail attachment in .rtf with cover letter." Pays 10 author's copies out of 100.

☑ PRESA :S: PRESS

PO Box 792, Rockford MI 49341.Estab. 2003. E-mail: presapress@aol.com. Website: www. presapress.com. **Contact**: Roseanne Ritzema, assistant editor.**Book/Chapbook Needs** Presa :S: Press publishes " perfect-bound paperbacks and saddle-stitched chapbooks of poetry." Wants " imagistic poetry where form is an extension of content, surreal, experimental, and personal poetry." Does not want " overtly political or didactic material." Has published poetry books by Kirby Congdon, Hugh Fox, Eric Greinke, Lyn Lifshin, Stanley Nelson, and A.D. Winans. Publishes 3-4 poetry books/year, 1-2 chapbooks/year, and an anthology. Manuscripts are selected through open submission. Books are 84-144 pages, laser-printed on 24 lb. paper, perfect-bound paperback with a laminated, color art cover. Chapbooks are 40-60 pages, laser-printed on 20-24 lb. paper, saddle-stitched with a color art cover. Anthologies are 250-325 pages, laser-printed, perfect-bound paperback with a laminated color art cover. Press runs 500-1,000 copies.

How to Contact Query first, with a few sample poems and a cover letter with brief bio and publication credits. Book/chapbook mss may include previously published poems. Responds to queries in 2-4 weeks; to mss in 8-12 weeks. Pays 25 author's copies.

☑ PRESS HERE

(Specialized: haiku, tanka), 22230 NE 28th Place, Sammamish WA 98074-6408. E-mail: WelchM@aol.com. Established 1989. **Contact:** Michael Dylan Welch, editor/publisher.

- Press Here publications have won the 1st-place Merit Book Award and other awards from the Haiku Society of America.

Needs Press Here publishes award-winning books of haiku, tanka, and related poetry by the leading poets of these genres, as well as essays, criticism, and interviews about these genres.

"We publish work only by those poets who are already frequently published in the leading haiku and tanka journals." Does not want any poetry other than haiku, tanka, and related genres. Has published poetry by Lee Gurga, paul m., Paul O. Williams, Pat Shelley, Cor van den Heuvel, and William J. Higginson. Publishes 2-3 poetry books/year, plus occasional books of essays or interviews. Manuscripts are selected through open submission. Books are 32-112 pages, offset-printed, perfect-bound, with glossy paperback covers.

How to Contact Query first, with a few sample poems and a cover letter with brief bio and publication credits. Book mss may include previously published poems ("previous publication strongly preferred"). "All proposals must be by well-established haiku or tanka poets, and must be for haiku or tanka poetry, or criticism/discussion of these genres. If the editor does not already know your work well from leading haiku and tanka publications, then he is not likely to be interested in your manuscript." Responds to queries in up to 1 month; to mss in up to 2 months. Pays a negotiated percentage of author's copies (out of a press run of 200-1,000). Catalog available for #10 SASE.

Tips "Press Here publishes only 2-3 titles per year by leading haiku and tanka poets. For Press Here to publish your book, you will likely already know other Press Here books and the work of their authors, and the editor would most likely already know you and your work. If not, then establish yourself in these genres first by publishing extensively in the leading haiku or tanka journals."

PRINCETON UNIVERSITY PRESS

(Specialized: poetry in translation only), 41 William St., Princeton NJ 08540. (609)258-4900. Fax: (609)258-6305. Website: www.press.princeton.edu. **Contact:** Hanne Winarsky, senior editor.

Needs "The Lockert Library of Poetry in Translation embraces a wide geographic and temporal range, from Scandinavia to Latin America to the subcontinent of India, from the Tang Dynasty to Europe of the modern day. It especially emphasizes poets who are established in their native lands and who are being introduced to an English-speaking audience. The series, nearly all of whose titles are bilingual editions, calls attention to some of the most widely-praised poetry available today. In the Lockert Library series, each book is given individual design treatment rather than stamped into a series mold. We have published a wide range of poets from other cultures, including well-known writers such as Hoölderlin and Cavafy, and those who have not yet had their due in English translation, such as Goöran Sonnevi. Manuscripts are judged with several criteria in mind: the ability of the translation to stand on its own as poetry in English; fidelity to the tone and spirit of the original, rather than literal accuracy; and the importance of the translated poet to the literature of his or her time and country."

How to Contact Submit hard copy of proposal with sample poems or full ms. Cover letter is required. Reads submissions year round. Manuscripts will not be returned. Comments on finalists only. Responds in 3-4 months.

☑ PUDDING HOUSE PUBLICATIONS

(Specialized: social issues; popular culture reflected in poetry arts)Shadymere Lane, Columbus OH 43213. (614)986-1881. E-mail: info@puddinghouse.com. Website: www.puddinghouse.com. Established 1979. **Contact:** Jennifer Bosveld, editor.

Needs Pudding House Publications prints chapbooks, anthologies, and broadsides. Has over 1,200 titles in print. Provides "a sociological looking glass through poems that speak to the pop culture, struggle in a consumer and guardian society, and more--through 'felt experience.' Speaks for the difficulties and the solutions." Pudding House is also the publisher of the respected national archive, POETS' GREATEST HITS--an invitational. Has recently published *The Allegories* by Dan Sicoli, *Barb Quill Down* by Bill Griffin, *Sonnets to Hamlet* by David Rigsbee, *Mischief* by

Charlene Fix, and over 700 others.

How to Contact Chapbooks considered outside of competitions, no query. Send complete ms and a cover letter with publication credits and bio. **Reading fee:** $12. Sometimes comments; "no more critiquing, too busy now." See main page at puddinghouse.com for chapbook guidelines.

Contest/Award Offerings Pudding House offers an annual chapbook competition. **Entry fee:** $15. **Deadline:** September 30. Guidelines available on website.

Also Offers "Our website is one of the greatest poetry websites in the country--calls, workshops, publication list/history, online essays, games, guest pages, calendars, poem of the month, poet of the week, much more." The website also links to the site for The Unitarian Universalist Poets Cooperative and American Poets Opposed to Executions, both national organizations.

Tips "Editors have pet peeves. I won't respond to or on postcards. I require SASEs. Love cover letters that are genuine, friendly, and don't state the obvious. Don't like poems with trite concepts or meaning dictated by rhyme. Thoroughly review our website; it will give you a good idea about our publication history and editorial tastes."

☑ THE PUDDIN'HEAD PRESS

P.O. Box 477889, Chicago IL 60647. (708)656-4900. E-mail: phbooks@compuserve.com. Website: www.puddinheadpress.com. Established 1985. **Contact:** David Gecic, editor-in-chief.

Needs The Puddin'head Press is interested in "well-rounded poets who can support their work with readings and appearances." Wants "quality poetry by active poets who read and lead interesting lives. We occasionally publish chapbook-style anthologies and let poets on our mailing lists know what type of work we're interested in for a particular project." Does not want experimental, overly political poetry, or poetry with overt sexual content; no shock or novelty poems. Has published poetry by Jared Smith, Carol Anderson, Larry Janowski, Sandy Goldsmith, and Norman Porter. Puddin'head Press publishes 2-3 books and 2-3 chapbooks per year. Books/chapbooks are 30-100 pages, perfect-bound or side-stapled ("we use various formats").

How to Contact "Please visit our Web site for submission guidelines." Poets must include SASE with submission. Responds to queries in 2 months. Pays various royalty rates "depending on the publication. We usually have a press run of 500 books." **About 10% of books are author subsidy-published.** Terms vary. Order sample books/chapbooks by sending $10 (price plus postage) to The Puddin'head Press (also available through Amazon). "Please visit our Web site and see what we publish."

Additional Information "In the last several years we have been increasingly active across the country. There are numerous readings and events that we sponsor. We do our own distribution, primarily in the Midwest, and also do distribution for other small presses. Please send a SASE for a list of our current publications and publication/distribution guidelines. We sell poetry books, not just print them. Submitted poetry is evaluated for its marketability and quality."

Also Offers "Extensive Web site with rare and used books, extensive links to who's who in poetry and online marketing."

Tips "It is difficult to find a quality publisher. Poets must have patience and find a press that will work with them. A good relationship between poet and publisher is important. Many good books will never be seen because the poet/publisher relationship is not healthy. If a poet is involved in the literary world, he will find a publisher, or a publisher will find him."

$ ☑ QED PRESS/CYPRESS HOUSE

155 Cypress St., Fort Bragg CA 95437. (800)773-7782. Fax: (707)964-7531. E-mail: joeshaw@cypresshouse.com. Website: www.cypresshouse.com. Established 1985. **Contact:** Joe Shaw, editor.

Needs QED Press publishes "clear, clean, intelligent, and moving work." Wants "concrete, personal, and spare writing. No florid rhymed verse." Has published poetry by Victoria Greenleaf, Luke Breit, Paula Tennant (Adams), and Cynthia Frank. Publishes 1 poetry book/year. Books are usually about 100 pages (75-80 poems), digest-sized, offset-printed, perfect-bound, with full-color cover.

How to Contact "We prefer to see six representative poems." Considers simultaneous submissions. Cover letter and SASE for return of materials are required. Time between acceptance and publication is up to 1 year. Poems are circulated to an editorial board. Responds to queries and mss in 1 month. Pays royalties of 7-12% and 25 author's copies (out of a press run of 500-1,000). Order sample books through Web site.

Also Offers Book packaging, and promotion and marketing services to start-up publishers.

$ ☒ RATTAPALLAX PRESS

(Specialized: the diversity of world cultures), 532 La Guardia Place, Suite 353, New York NY 10012. E-mail: info@rattapallax.com. Website: www.rattapallax.com. Established 1998. **Contact:** Poetry Editor.

Needs Rattapallax Press publishes "contemporary poets and writers with unique, powerful voices." Publishes 5 paperbacks and 3 chapbooks/year. Books are usually 64 pages, digest-sized, offset-printed, perfect-bound, with 12-pt. CS1 covers.

How to Contact Query first, with a few sample poems and cover letter with brief bio and publication credits. Include SASE. Requires authors to first be published in *Rattapallax* (see separate listing in Magazines/Journals). Responds to queries in 1 month; to mss in 2 months. Pays royalties of 10-25%. Order sample books from Web site.

☒ RED DRAGON PRESS

P.O. Box 320301, Alexandria VA 22320-0425. Website: www.reddragonpress.com. Established 1993. **Contact:** Laura Qa, editor/publisher.

Needs Red Dragon Press is a proponent "of works that represent the nature of man as androgynous, as in the fusing of male and female symbolism, and we support works that deal with psychological and parapsychological topics." Wants "innovative and experimental poetry and prose using literary symbolism and aspiring to the creation of meaningful new ideas, forms, and methods." Has published *The Distance of Ducks* by Louis Bourgeois, *Spectator Turns Witness* by George Karos, and *The Crown of Affinity* by Laura Qa. Publishes 3-4 chapbooks/year. Chapbooks are usually 64 pages, offset-printed on trade paper, perfect-bound.

How to Contact Submit up to 5 poems at a time with SASE. Considers previously published poems and simultaneous submissions. Cover letter with brief bio is preferred. **Reading fee: $5 for poetry and short fiction, $10 for novels.** Make checks or money orders payable to Red Dragon Press. Time between acceptance and publication is 8 months. "Poems are selected for consideration by the publisher, then circulated to senior editor and/or poets previously published for comment. Poems are returned to the publisher for further action, i.e., rejection or acceptance for publication in an anthology or book by a single author. Frequently, submission of additional works is required before final offer is made, especially in the process for a book by a single author." Often comments on rejected poems. Responds to queries in 10 weeks, to mss in one year. Purchase sample books at bookstores, or mail-order direct from Red Dragon Press at the above address.

☒ RED MOON PRESS

(Specialized: English-language haiku & related forms), P.O. Box 2461, Winchester VA 22604-1661. (540)722-2156. E-mail: jim.kacian@redmoonpress.com. Website: www.redmoonpress.com. Established 1993. **Contact:** Jim Kacian, editor/publisher.

Needs Red Moon Press "is the largest and most prestigious publisher of English-language haiku and related work in the world." Publishes 6-8 volumes/year, usually 3-5 anthologies and individual collections of English-language haiku, as well as 1-3 books of essays, translations, or criticism of haiku. Under other imprints, the press also publishes chapbooks of various sizes and formats.

How to Contact Query with book theme and information, and 30-40 poems or draft of first chapter. Responds to queries in 2 weeks, to mss (if invited) in 3 months. "Each contract separately negotiated."

Tips "Haiku is a burgeoning and truly international form. It is nothing like what your fourth-grade teacher taught you years ago, and so it is best if you familiarize yourself with what is happening in the genre (and its close relatives) today before submitting. We strive to give all the work we publish plenty of space in which to resonate, and to provide a forum where the best of today's practitioners can be published with dignity and prestige. All our books have either won awards or are awaiting notification. We intend to work hard to keep it that way."

$ ⊘ RONSDALE PRESS

(Specialized: Canadian poets only), 3350 W. 21st Ave., Vancouver BC V6S 1G7 Canada. (604)738-4688. Fax: (604)731-4548. E-mail: ronsdale@shaw.ca. Website: www.ronsdalepress. com. Established 1988. **Contact:** Ronald B. Hatch, director.

Needs Publishes 3 flat-spined paperbacks of poetry per year--**by Canadian poets only**--classical to experimental. "Ronsdale looks for poetry manuscripts that show the writer reads and is familiar with the work of some of the major contemporary poets. It's also essential that you have published some poems in literary magazines. We have never published a book of poetry when the author has not already published a goodly number in magazines." Has published *Return to Open Water* by Harold Rhenisch, *Mother Time* by Joanne Arnott, *Cobalt 3* by Kevin Roberts, *Poems for a New World* by Connie Fife, *Steveston* by Daphne Marlatt, and *After Ted & Sylvia* by Crystal Hurdle.

How to Contact Query first, with a few sample poems and cover letter with brief bio and publication credits. Considers previously published poems and simultaneous submissions. Often comments on rejected poems. Responds to queries in 2 weeks, to mss in 2 months. Pays 10% royalties and 10 author's copies. Write for catalog to purchase sample books.

Tips "Ronsdale looks for Canadian poetry with echoes from previous poets. To our mind, the contemporary poet must be well-read."

ROSE ALLEY PRESS

4203 Brooklyn Ave. NE, #103A, Seattle WA 98105-5911. (206)633-2725. E-mail: rosealleypress@juno.com. Website: www.rosealleypress.com. Established 1995. **Contact:** David D. Horowitz, editor/publisher.

• "Rose Alley Press does not consider unsolicited manuscripts."

$ ⊘ SAM'S DOT PUBLISHING

(Specialized: scifaiku, horror-ku, other minimalist poetry forms), P.O. Box 782, Cedar Rapids IA 52406-0782. E-mail: gatrix65@yahoo.com. Website: www.samsdotpublishing.com. Established 2003. **Contact:** Tyree Campbell, managing editor. Member: The Speculative Literature Foundation.

Needs Sam's Dot Publishing prints collections of scifaiku, horror-ku, and minimalist poetry. Publishes 2-3 chapbooks/year and one anthology/year. Manuscripts are selected through open submission. Chapbooks are 32 pages, offset-printed, saddle-stapled, with cardstock covers.

How to Contact Query first, with a few sample poems and a cover letter with brief bio and publication credits. Chapbook mss may include previously published poems. Responds to queries in 2 weeks; to mss in 4-6 weeks. Pays royalties of 12.5% minimum and 1-2 author's copies (out of a press run of 50-100). Order sample chapbooks by sending $8 to Tyree Campbell/Sam's Dot Publishing.

Tips "It's up to the writer to take the first step and submit work. Some of our best poems have come from poets who weren't sure if they were good enough. A basic knowledge of writing traditional haiku is helpful."

⊘ SARABANDE BOOKS, INC.

2234 Dundee Rd., Suite 200, Louisville KY 40205. (502)458-4028. Fax: (502)458-4065. E-mail: info@sarabandebooks.org. Website: www.SarabandeBooks.org. Established 1994. **Contact:** Sarah Gorham, editor-in-chief. Member: CLMP.

Needs Sarabande Books publishes books of poetry of 48 pages minimum. Wants "poetry that offers originality of voice and subject matter, uniqueness of vision, and a language that startles because of the careful attention paid to it--language that goes beyond the merely competent or functional. Has published poetry by Mark Jarman, Gerald Stern, Jean Valentine, Cate Marvin, Ralph Angel, Gabriel Fried, and Eleanor Lerman. Manuscripts are selected through our literary contests, invitation, and recommendation by a well-established writer. At least half of our list is drawn from contest submissions to the Kathryn A. Morton Prize in Poetry."

Contest/Award Offerings The Kathryn A. Morton Prize in Poetry (see separate listing).

Tips "We recommend that you request our catalog and familiarize yourself with our books. Our complete list shows a variety of style and subject matter."

⊘ SEAWEED SIDESHOW CIRCUS

P.O. Box 234, Jackson WI 53037. (414)791-1109. Fax: (262)644-0249. E-mail: sscircus@aol.com. Website: http://hometown.aol.com/SSCircus/sscweb.html. Established 1994. **Contact:** Andrew Wright Milam, editor.

Needs Seaweed Sideshow Circus is "a place for young or new poets to publish a chapbook." Has published *Main Street* by Steven Paul Lansky and *The Moon Incident* by Amy McDonald. Publishes one chapbook/year. Chapbooks are usually 30 pages, digest-sized, photocopied, saddle-stapled, with cardstock covers.

How to Contact Query first, with 5-10 sample poems and cover letter with brief bio and publications credits. Responds to queries in 3 weeks; to mss in 3 months. Pays 10 author's copies (out of a press run of 100). Order sample chapbooks by sending $6.

▦ ⊘ SECOND AEON PUBLICATIONS

19 Southminster Rd., Roath, Cardiff CF23 5AT Wales. Phone/fax: (44)(29)2049-3093. E-mail: peter@peterfinch.co.uk. Website: www.peterfinch.co.uk. Established 1966. **Contact:** Peter Finch, poetry editor.

•Does not accept unsolicited mss.

▦ ⊘ SOUTH PATTAYA PRESS

95/31 Moo 10 Classic Village, Nongphrue Banglamung, Chonburi 20150 Thailand. (661)7177 941. E-mail: nasomhong@yahoo.com. Established 2003. **Contact:** Jiraporn Sutta, editor.

Needs South Pattaya Press publishes 6 chapbooks/year. Manuscripts are selected through open submission. Chapbooks are 12 pages, stapled, with cardstock covers. "Series include (1) On Demand Series, and (2) a second series with partial subsidy, which provides payment of 3 copies."

How to Contact Query first, with a few sample poems and a cover letter with brief bio and publication credits. Submit by e-mail only. Chapbook mss may include previously published poems. Responds to queries in 3 months. Pays 3 author's copies. "**We publish chapbooks only by partial author subsidy.**" Order sample chapbooks by sending $16 to Jiraporn Sutta.

☑ STEEL TOE BOOKS

Western Kentucky University, 1906 College Heights Blvd. #11086, Bowling Green KY 42101-1086. (270)745-5769. E-mail: tom.hunley@wku.edu. Website: www.steeltoebooks.com. Established 2003. **Contact:** Dr. Tom C. Hunley, director.

Needs Steel Toe Books publishes "full-length, single-author poetry collections. Our books are professionally designed and printed. We look for workmanship (economical use of language, high-energy verbs, precise literal descriptions, original figurative language, poems carefully arranged as a book); a unique style and/or a distinctive voice; clarity; emotional impact; humor (word plays, hyperbole, comic timing); performability (a Steel Toe poet is at home on the stage as well as on the page)." Does not want "dry verse, purposely obscure language, poetry by people who are so wary of being called 'sentimental' they steer away from any recognizable human emotions, poetry that takes itself so seriously that it's unintentionally funny." Has published poetry by James Doyle, Jennifer Gresham, Ken Waldman, Martha Silano, Mary Biddinger, John Guzlowski, and Jeannine Hall Gailey. Publishes 1-3 poetry books/year. Manuscripts are selected through open submission. Books are 48-64 pages, perfect-bound, with full-color covers with art/graphics.

How to Contact "Check the Web site for news about our next open reading period." Book mss may include previously published poems. Responds to mss in 3 months. Pays $500 advance on 10% royalties and 10 author's copies. Order sample books by sending $12 to Steel Toe Books.

SWAN SCYTHE PRESS

2052 Calaveras Ave., Davis CA 95616-3021. E-mail: sandyjmc@mindspring.com. Website: www.swanscythe.com. Established 1999. **Contact:** Sandra McPherson, editor/publisher.

•Swan Scythe Press has been awarded a California Arts Council Multicultural Entry Grant and a Fideicomiso para la Cultura Mexico-EUA/US-Mexico Fund for Culture Grant.

Needs "After publishing 25 chapbooks, a few full-sized poetry collections, and 1 anthology, Swan Scythe Press is resting. **We cannot at this time consider manuscripts**, but our books are still for sale. A multi-ethnic press primarily publishing emerging writers, we have also published established poets such as Ted Joans and Jordan Smith." Has published poetry by Emmy Pérez, Maria Melendez, John Olivares Espinoza, Karen An-hwei Lee, Pos Moua, and Walter Pavlich. Order sample books/chapbooks by sending $11 to Swan Scythe Press or order through Web site.

How to Contact *Not considering mss at this time.*

$ ☑ SYNERGEBOOKS

11 Spruce Ct., Davenport FL 33837. (863)588-3770. Fax: (863)863-9021. E-mail: synergebooks@aol.com. Website: www.synergebooks.com. Established 1999. **Contact:** Deb Staples, acquisitions editor. Member: EPIC; PMA.

Needs SynergEbooks specializes in "quality works by talented new writers in every available digital format, including CD-ROMs and paperback. Poetry must have a very unique twist or theme and must be edited. We are looking specifically for poetry with religious overtones." Does not accept unedited work. Has published poetry by Theresa Jodray, Brenda Roberts, Vanyell Delacroix, Joel L. Young, and Chuck Kelly. SynergEbooks publishes up to 50 titles/year, less than 1% of them poetry. Books are usually 45-150 pages, print-on-demand, with paperback binding. "All of our titles are digital. There is no guarantee that a book will be put into print."

How to Contact Query by e-mail preferred, with a few sample poems and a cover letter with brief bio and publication credits. "We prefer no simultaneous submissions, but inform us if this is the case." Accepts e-mail submissions (as attachment) only. "Please do not send poetry via postal mail. Valid, working e-mail address is required." Guidelines available on Web site. Responds to queries in 1 month; to mss in up to 5 months. Pays royalties of 15-40% for electronic formats; up to 20% for paperbacks.

Tips "We are inundated with more poetry than prose every month; but we will accept the occasional anthology with a unique twist that is original and high quality. New poets welcome."

☑ TARPAULIN SKY PRESS

(Specialized: cross- & trans-genre work), P.O. Box 190, Saxtons River, VT 05154. E-mail: editors@ tarpaulinsky.com (inquiries). Website: www.tarpaulinsky.com. Established 2006. **Contact:** Elena Georgiou and Christian Peet, editors.

Needs Tarpaulin Sky Press publishes cross- and trans-genre works as well as innovative poetry and prose. Produces full-length books and chapbooks, hand-bound books and trade paperbacks, and offers both hand-bound and perfect-bound paperback editions of full-length books. "We're a small, author-centered press endeavoring to create books that, as objects, please our authors as much their texts please us." Has published books and chapbooks by Jenny Boully, Danielle Dutton, Joyelle McSweeney, Chad Sweeney, Andrew Michael Roberts, and Max Winter, as well as a collaborative book by Noah Eli Gordon as Joshua Marie Wilkinson.

How to Contact Writers whose work has appeared in or been accepted for publication in *Tarpaulin Sky* (see separate listing in Magazines/Journals) may submit chapbook or full-length manuscripts at any time, with no reading fee. Tarpaulin Sky Press also considers chapbook and full-length manuscripts from writers whose work has not appeared in the journal, but **asks for a $20 reading fee**. Make checks/money orders to Tarpaulin Sky Press. Cover letter is preferred. Reads periods may be found on the Web site.

☑ TEBOT BACH

P.O. Box 7887, Huntington Beach CA 92615-7887. (714)968-0905. E-mail: info@tebotbach.org. Website: www.tebotbach.org. **Contact:** Mifanwy Kaiser, editor/publisher.

Needs Tebot Bach (Welsh for "little teapot") publishes books of poetry. Has published *One Breath*, by Catharine Clark-Sayles, *Monkey Journal*, by Holly Prado; *Swagger and Remorse* by Richard Fox, *Dragon Ship* by Daniel F. Polikoff, and *A Café in Boca* by Sam Pereira.

How to Contact Query first, with a few sample poems and cover letter with brief bio and publication credits. Include SASE. Responds to queries and mss, if invited, in 3 months. Time between acceptance and publication is up to 2 years. Write to order sample books.

Contest/Award Offerings The Patricia Bibby First Book Award (see separate listing in Contests & Awards).

Also Offers An anthology of California poets. Must be current or former resident of California in order to submit, but no focus or theme required for poetry. Submit up to 6 poems with "California Anthology" written on lower left corner of envelope. Accepts submissions by e-mail (pasted into body of message or as attachment in Word). Deadline for submission is in August of the year call for submissions in announced. Please check the Web site for calls for submissions. Also publishes *Spillway: A Literary Journal* (see separate listing in Magazines/Journals).

$ ☑ TOKYO ROSE RECORDS/CHAPULTEPEC PRESS

4222 Chambers, Cincinnati OH 45223. E-mail: chapultepecpress@hotmail.com. Website: www. TokyoRoseRecords.com. Established 2001. **Contact:** David Garza.

Needs Chapultepec Press publishes books of poetry/literature, essays, social/political issues, art, music, film, history, popular science; library/archive issues, and bilingual works. Wants "poetry that works as a unit, that is caustic, fun, open-ended, worldly, mature, relevant, stirring, evocative. Bilingual. Looking for authors who have a publishing history. No poetry collections without a purpose, that are mere collections. Also looking for broadsides/posters/illuminations." Publishes 1-2 books/year. Books are usually 1-100 pages.

How to Contact Query first with a few sample poems, or a complete ms, and a cover letter with brief bio and publication credits. Pays 50% of profits and author's copies. Order sample books by sending $5 payable to David Garza.

☑ THE UNIVERSITY OF CHICAGO PRESS

1427 E. 60th St., Chicago IL 60637. (773)702-7700. Fax: (773)702-2705. Website: www.press. uchicago.edu. Established 1891. **Contact:** Randolph Petilos, poetry editor.

•Submissions by invitation only!

Needs "The University of Chicago Press has been publishing scholarly books and journals since 1891. Annually, we publish an average of four books in our Phoenix Poets series and four books of poetry in translation. Occasionally, we may publish a book of poetry outside Phoenix Poets, or as a paperback reprint from another publisher." Has published poetry by Colette LaBouff Atkinson, Don Bogen, Peter Campion, Gendun Chopel, David Gewanter, Guy Goffette, Fulke Greville, Vicki Hearne, Randall Mann, Greg Miller, Margeurite de Navarre, Robert Polito, Francisco de Quevedo, Susan Stewart, Sarra Copia Sulam, Elizabeth Tudor, Garcilaso de la Vega, and Jacint Verdaguer.

How to Contact *By invitation only.* No unsolicited mss.

☒ ☑ VEHICULE PRESS

(Specialized: work by Canadian poets only),P.O. Box 125 Station Place du Parc, Montreal QC H2X 4A3 Canada. (514)844-6073. Fax: (514)844-7543. E-mail: vp@vehiculepress.com. Website: www.vehiculepress.com. **Contact:** Carmine Starnino, poetry editor.

Needs Vehicule Press is a "literary press with a poetry series, Signal Editions, publishing the work of Canadian poets only." Publishes flat-spined paperbacks. Has published *The Empire's Missing Links* by Walid Bitar, *36 Cornelian Avenue* by Christopher Wiseman, and *Morning Gothic* by George Ellenbogen. Publishes Canadian poetry that is "first-rate, original, content-conscious."

How to Contact Query before submitting.

$ ☑ WASHINGTON WRITERS' PUBLISHING HOUSE

(Specialized: Washington, D.C.- and Baltimore-area poets only), PO Box 15271, Washington D.C., 20003. Website: www.washingtonwriters.org. Established 1973. **Contact:** Patric Pepper, president and managing editor. Member: CLMP.

•Individual books by WWPH authors have been nominated for and/or won many awards, e.g. the Towson University Prize.

Needs Washington Writers' Publishing House publishes books by Washington, D.C.- and Baltimore-area poets through its annual book competition. "No specific criteria, except literary excellence." Has published books by Brandel France de Bravo, Carly Sachs, Bruce MacKinnon, Piotr Gwiazda, Moira Egan, Jane Satterfield, Jean Nordhaus, and Gray Jacobik. Publishes 1-2 poetry books/year.

How to Contact Washington Writers' Publishing House considers book-length mss for publication by poets living within 60 driving miles of the U.S. Capitol (Baltimore area included) through competition only (see below).

Contest/Award Offerings Offers $500 and 50 copies of published book plus additional copies for publicity use. Manuscripts may include previously published poems. Submit 3 copies of a poetry ms of 50-60 pages, single-spaced (poet's name should not appear on ms pages). Include separate page of publication acknowledgments plus 2 cover sheets: one with ms title, poet's name, address, telephone number, and e-mail address, the other with ms title only. Include SASE for results only; mss will not be returned (will be recycled). Guidelines available for SASE or on Web site. "Author should indicate where they heard about WWPH." **Entry fee:** $20. **Deadline:** July 1-November 1 (postmark). Order sample books on Web site or by sending $12 plus $3 s&h to Washington Writers' Publishing House, P.O. Box 15271, Washington DC 20003.

Tips "Visit Web site. Washington Writers' Publishing House is a nonprofit cooperative poetry press reflecting the cultural and racial diversity of the Greater Washington-Baltimore area. The winning poet becomes a member of the organization and should be prepared to participate actively in the work of the press, including such areas as publicity, distribution, production, and fundraising. Our tradition of poets actively working on behalf of other poets is essential to the continued vitality and success of WWPH. Contest entrants should be willing to make this commitment should their work be selected for publication. Membership in WWPH is an opportunity to work together with many of the best writers in the region."

$ ☑ WEST END PRESS

(Specialized: social/political concerns; multicultural), P.O. Box 27334, Albuquerque NM 87125. (505)345-5729. Established 1976. **Contact:** John Crawford, publisher.

Needs West End Press publishes poetry, fiction, and drama with a social/cultural interest. Open as to form. Does not want "purely aesthetic, precious, self-involved poetry." Has published poetry by Laura Tohe, Joseph Bruchac, Charles Potts, and Michael Henson. Publishes 2 poetry books/year; occasional chapbooks and anthologies. Books/chapbooks are 48-96 pages, offset-printed, perfect-bound, with glossy 4-color covers.

How to Contact Query first, with a few sample poems and a cover letter with brief bio and publication credits. Book/chapbook mss may include previously published poems. Responds to queries in 6 weeks; to mss in 3 months. Pays royalties of 6%; 10% author's copies (out of a press run of 600-1,500). Order sample books/chapbooks postage-free by sending $8.95 to West End Press.

Tips "We prefer crude vigor to polished banality."

☑ WHITE EAGLE COFFEE STORE PRESS

P.O. Box 383, Fox River Grove IL 60021-0383. E-mail: WECSPress@aol.com. Website: whiteeaglecoffeestorepress.com. Established 1992.

Needs White Eagle is a small press publishing 2-3 chapbooks/year. "Alternate chapbooks are published by invitation and by competition. Author published by invitation becomes judge for next competition." Wants "any kind of poetry. No censorship at this press. Literary values are the only standard." Does not want "sentimental or didactic writing." Has published poetry by Timothy Russell, Connie Donovan, Scott Lumbard, Linda Lee Harper, Scott Beal, Katie Kingston, and Brian Brodeur. Sample: $6.95.

How to Contact *Regular submissions by invitation only.*

Contest/Award Offerings Winner receives $500 and 25 author's copies. All entrants will receive a copy of the winning chapbook. Considers previously published poems and simultaneous submissions, with notice. Submit complete chapbook ms (20-24 pages), paginated, with table of contents. Poet's name should not appear on ms pages. Include 2 cover sheets: 1 with ms title, poet's name, address, phone number, and brief biography; second with ms title and 125-word statement about poet's work to be included in chapbook (poet's name should not appear on second cover sheet). Include list of credits for previously published poems. No e-mail submissions. Include SASE for results only; mss will not be returned. Guidelines available for SASE or on Web site. **Entry fee:** $15. **Deadline:** October 31 (postmark) for 2008. "Each competition is judged by either the author of the most recent chapbook published by invitation or by previous competition winners." Responds 3 months after deadline.

Tips "Poetry is about a passion for language. That's what we're about. We'd like to provide an opportunity for poets of any age who are fairly early in their careers to publish something substantial. We're excited by the enthusiasm shown for this press and by the extraordinary quality of the writing we've received."

☑ WOODLEY MEMORIAL PRESS

(Specialized: work by KS poets), English Dept., Washburn University, 1700 SW College Ave., Topeka KS 66621. E-mail: karen.barron@washburn.edu. Website: www.washburn.edu/reference/woodley-press. Established 1980. **Contact:** Paul Fecteau, managing editor; Kevin Rabas, Acquisitions editor.

Needs Woodley Memorial Press publishes 1-4 perfect-bound paperbacks/year, "most being collections from Kansas or with Kansas connections. Terms are individually arranged with author on acceptance of manuscript." Has published *Sunflower Sinner* by Cynthia Dennis, *Thailand Journal* by Denise Low, and *Kansas Poems of William Stafford*. Sample books may be ordered from Woodley Memorial Press.

How to Contact Guidelines available on Web site. Responds to queries in 2 weeks; to mss in 6 months. Time between acceptance and publication is 1 year.

Tips "We look for experienced writers who are part of their writing and reading communities."

Contests & Awards

This section contains a wide array of poetry competitions and literary awards. These range from state poetry society contests (with a number of modest monetary prizes) to prestigious honors bestowed by private foundations, elite publishers and renowned university programs. Because these listings reflect such a variety of skill levels and degrees of competitiveness, it's important to read each carefully and note its unique requirements. Never enter a contest without consulting the guidelines and following directions to the letter (including manuscript formatting, number of lines or pages of poetry accepted, amount of entry fee, entry forms needed and other details).

Important note: As we gathered information for this edition of *Poet's Market*, we found that some competitions hadn't yet established their 2009 fees and deadlines. In such cases, we list the most recent information available as a general guide. Always consult current guidelines for updates before entering any competition.

WHERE TO ENTER?

While it's perfectly okay to "think big," being realistic may improve your chances of winning a prize for your poetry. Many of the listings in the Contests & Awards section begin with symbols that reflect their level of difficulty:

Contests ideal for beginners and unpublished poets are coded with the (☐) symbol. That's not to say these contests won't be highly competitive—there may be a large number of entries. However, you may find these entries are more on a level with your own, increasing your chances of being "in the running" for a prize. Don't assume these contests reward low quality, though. If you submit less than your best work, you're wasting your time and money (in postage and entry fees).

Contests for poets with more experience are coded with the (◨) symbol. Beginner/unpublished poets are usually still welcome to enter, but the competition is keener here. Your work may be judged against that of widely published, prize-winning poets, so consider carefully whether you're ready for this level of competition. (Of course, nothing ventured, nothing gained—but those entry fees *do* add up.)

Contests for accomplished poets are coded with the (◓) symbol. These may have stricter entry requirements, higher entry fees and other conditions that signal these programs are not intended to be "wide open" to all poets.

Specialized contests are coded with the (◎) symbol. These may include regional contests; awards for poetry written in a certain form or in the style of a certain poet; contests for women, gay/lesbian, ethnic, or age-specific poets (for instance, children or older adults); contests for translated poetry only; and many others.

There are also symbols that give additional information about contests. The (🆕) symbol indicates the contest is newly established and new to *Poet's Market*; the (✖) symbol indicates this contest did not appear in the 2008 edition; the (✚) symbol identifies a Canadian contest or award and the (🌐) symbol an international listing. Sometimes Canadian and international contests require that entrants live in certain countries, so pay attention when you see these symbols.

ADDITIONAL CONTESTS & AWARDS

Contest information also appears in listings in other sections of the book (Magazines/Journals, Book/Chapbook Publishers, Conferences, Workshops & Festivals and Organizations). To make sure you don't overlook these opportunities, we've cross-referenced them under Additional Contests & Awards at the back of this section. For details about a contest associated with a market in this list, go to that market's page number.

WHAT ABOUT ENTRY FEES?

Most contests charge entry fees, and these are usually quite legitimate. The funds are used to cover expenses such as paying the judges, putting up prize monies, printing prize editions of magazines and journals, and promoting the contest through mailings and ads. If you're concerned about a poetry contest or other publishing opportunity, see "Is It a 'Con'?" on page 56 for advice on some of the more questionable practices in the poetry world.

OTHER RESOURCES

Widen your search for contests beyond those listed in Poet's Market. Many Internet writer's sites have late-breaking announcements about competitions old and new. Often these sites offer free electronic newsletter subscriptions, sending valuable information right to your e-mail inbox.

The writer's magazines at your local bookstore regularly include listings for upcoming contests, as well as deadlines for artist's grants at the state and national level. (See Grants on page 443.) The Association of Writers & Writing Programs (AWP) is a valuable resource, including its publication, Writer's Chronicle. (See Organizations, page 471.) State poetry societies are listed throughout this book; they offer many contests, as well as helpful information for poets (and mutual support). To find a specific group, search the General Index for listings under your state's name or look under "poetry society" or "society."

Don't overlook your local connections. City and community newspapers, radio and TV announcements, bookstore newsletters and bulletin boards, and your public library can be terrific resources for competition news, especially regarding regional contests.

$ ☑ "DISCOVERY" POETRY CONTEST

THE JOAN LEIMAN JACOBSON POETRY PRIZES Unterberg Poetry Center, 92nd Street Y, 1395 Lexington Ave., New York NY 10128. (212)415-5759 (voicemail). Website: www.92y.org/poetry. **Contact:** Contest Coordinator. The "Discovery" Poetry Contest is designed to attract large audiences to poets who have not yet published a book. Awards a cash prize to 4 winners, plus a reading at The Unterberg Poetry Center and publication in a literary journal of national distribution, to be announced. New guidelines available on Web site. Endowed by Joan L. and Dr. Julius H. Jacobson, II.

$ ☑ THE 46ER PRIZE FOR POETRY

8405 Bay Parkway, C8, Brooklyn NY 11214. E-mail: diane@blacklawrencepress.com. Website: www.adirondackreview.homestead.com. Established 2000. **Contact:** Diane Goettel, editor. With Black Lawrence Press, The Adirondack Review (see separate listing in Magazines/Journals) offers the 46er Prize for Poetry, to be awarded once each year for a previously unpublished poem. Winner receives $400 and publication in The Adirondack Review. Honorable Mention poems will also be published and receive an honorarium of $30. Considers simultaneous submissions if notified immediately of acceptance elsewhere. Submit up to 3 original poems, unpublished in either print or on-line publications. Submissions should be sent to diane@blacklawrencepress.com with poet's name, address, phone number, and e-mail address included. E-mail should be titled 46er PRIZE SUBMISSION in subject line; poems must be pasted into body of message. Guidelines available by e-mail (from diane@blacklawrencepress.com) or on Web site. **Entry fee:** $5 for 1 poem, $8 for 2 poems, $10 for 3 poems. Make payment through Web site via PayPal. **Deadline:** May 1. Winners announced during the summer. Judges: The Adirondack Review editors.

$ ☑ THE 49TH PARALLEL POETRY AWARD

Bellingham Review, Western Washington University, Mail Stop 9053, Bellingham WA 98225. (360)650-4863. E-mail: bhreview@cc.wwu.edu. Website: www.wwu.edu/~bhreview. **Contact:** Contest Director. The annual 49th Parallel Poetry Award offers 1st Prize of $1,000, plus publication in and a year's subscription to Bellingham Review (see separate listing in Magazines/Journals). Runners-up and finalists may be considered for publication. Submissions must be unpublished and not accepted for publication elsewhere. Considers simultaneous submissions, but work must be withdrawn from the competition if accepted for publication elsewhere. Submit up to 3 poems. "Poems within a series will each be treated as a separate entry." For each entry, include a 3x5 index card stating the title of the work, the category (poetry), the poet's name, phone number, address, and e-mail. "Make sure writing is legible on this card. Author's name must not appear anywhere on the manuscript." Include SASE for results only; mss will not be returned. Guidelines available for SASE or on Web site. **Entry fee:** $18 for first entry (up to 3 poems); $10 each additional poem. Make checks payable to Bellingham Review. "Everyone entering the competition will receive a complimentary two-issue subscription to Bellingham Review." **Deadline:** entries must be postmarked December 1-March 15. 2008 winner was Kaveh Bassiri ("Invention of God"). 2008 judge: Aimee Nezhukumatathil. Winners will be announced by July 2009.

☒ ABZ PRESS FIRST BOOK POETRY PRIZE

P.O. Box 2746, Huntington WV 25727-2746. E-mail: editorial@abzpress.com. Website: http://abzpress.com. Wants poetry manuscripts between 48-80 pages. "Each manuscript must be bound only with a binder clip. Include a table of contents, acknowledgements, and two title pages.

One title page should have only the title. The second title page should have the author's name, address, phone number with area code, and e-mail address. Please indicate any poetry books or chapbooks (with fewer than 48 pages) you may have published. Simultaneous Submissions are OK with us. Include SASE to receive notice of contest winner. Let us know if you win another prize." Guidelines available on Web site. **Entry fee:** $25; includes one copy of winning book "if you send a 7x10 SASE with $3 in US postage. **Deadline:** "We read entries submitted between May 1-June 30."

$ ☑ AKRON POETRY PRIZE

The University of Akron Press, Akron OH 44325-1703. (330)972-5342. Fax: (330)972-8364. E-mail: uapress@uakron.edu. Website: www3.uakron.edu/uapress/poetryprize. **Contact:** Mary Biddinger, editor and award director. Offers annual award of $1,000 plus publication of a book-length ms. Submissions must be unpublished. Considers simultaneous submissions (with notification of acceptance elsewhere). Submit 48 or more pages, typed, single-spaced; optional self-addressed postcard for confirmation. Mss will not be returned. Do not send mss bound or enclosed in covers. See Web site for complete guidelines. **Entry fee:** $25. **Deadline:** entries accepted May 1-June 15 only. Competition receives 500+ entries. 2008 winner was Rachel Dilworth for The Wild Rose Asylum : Poems of the Magdalen Laundries of Ireland. 2009 judge: Martin Espada. Winner posted on Web site by September 30. Intimate friends, relatives, current and former students of the final judge (students in an academic, degree-conferring program or its equivalent) were not eligible to enter the 2009 Akron Poetry Prize competition.

$ ☑ AGHA SHAHID ALI PRIZE IN POETRY

The University of Utah Press, J. Willard Marriott Library, Suite 5400, University of Utah, 295 South 1500 East Salt Lake City UT 84112. (801)581-6771. Fax: (801)581-3365. Website: www.uofupress. com/Agha-Shahid-Ali. Established 2003. The University of Utah Press and the University of Utah Department of English offer an annual award of $1,000, publication of a book-length poetry ms, and a reading in the Guest Writers Series. Poems must be unpublished as a collection, but individual poems may have been previously published elsewhere. Considers simultaneous submissions; "however, entrants must notify the Press immediately if the collection submitted is accepted for publication elsewhere during the competition." Submit 48-64 typed pages of poetry, with no names or other identifying information appearing on title page or within ms. Include cover sheet with complete contact information (name, address, telephone, e-mail address). Submissions must be in English. Mss will not be returned. Guidelines available on Web site. **Entry fee:** $25/book submission. **Deadline:** 2009: February 1-April 15. Competition receives over 300 mss/year. 2008 winner was Jessica Garratt. 2008 judge: Medbh McGuckian. Winner announced on press Web site after September 1; series editor contacts winning poet. Copies of winning books are available for $14.95 from University of Utah Press ((800)621-2736 for order fulfillment) or through Web site.

$ ALLIGATOR JUNIPER'S NATIONAL WRITING CONTEST

Prescott College, 220 Grove Ave., Prescott AZ 86301. E-mail: aj@prescott.edu. Website: www. prescott.edu/highlights/alligator_juniper/index.html. Established 1995. Alligator Juniper, published annually in June, awards $500 each and publication to first and prize winners in poetry, fiction, and creative nonfiction. Finalists are selected for publication and paid 4 contributor's copies. Submissions must be unpublished. Considers simultaneous submissions ("inform us in your cover letter and contact us immediately if your work is accepted elsewhere"). Submit up to 5 poems at a time with reading fee (separate fee for each additional entry). Submissions must be typed with numbered pages; single-spaced okay for poetry entries. "Writers agree that by entering the contest they allow Alligator Juniper to select their work for publication even if it does not place first." Cover letter is required with the following statement: "I have read and understand the guidelines for Alligator Juniper 's national writing contest." Include SASE for results only; mss are not returned. "All entrants receive a personal letter from one of our staff regarding the status of their submissions." No e-mail submissions. Guidelines available for SASE, by e-mail, or on Web site. **Entry fee:** $15/entry (5 poems or 5 pages of poetry). Each entrant receives a copy of Alligator Juniper, a $10 value. **Deadline:** submit May 1-October 1 (postmark). 2009 winner was Zach Savich. Winner announced in late January. Alligator Juniper is available for $10.

$ ☑ THE AMERICAN POET PRIZE FOR POETRY

The American Poetry Journal, P.O. Box 2080, Aptos CA 95001-2080. E-mail: editor@americanpoetryjournal.com. Website: www.americanpoetryjournal.com. Established 2004. **Contact:** J.P. Dancing Bear, editor. The American Poet Prize for Poetry offers $500 and publication in The American Poetry Journal (see separate listing in Magazines/Journals). All entries will be considered for publication, and all entrants receive a year's subscription. Submissions must be unpublished. Considers simultaneous submissions with notification. Accepts multiple submissions with separate fee for each entry (3 poems). Submit up to 3 original poems (10 pages maximum total). Include cover with poem titles, poet's name, contact information (including e-mail address), and bio. Include SASP for confirmation of delivery of ms and SASE for results only. Guidelines available on Web site. **Entry fee:** $16; all entrants receive a year's subscription to The American Poetry Journal. Make checks payable to Dream Horse Press. **Deadline:** June 30. Judge: all selections and winners made by the editor. Personal friends, relatives, and/or students of the editor are NOT eligible for the contest (their entry fees will be refunded).

$ ☑ THE AMERICAN POETRY JOURNAL BOOK PRIZE

P.O. Box 2080, Aptos CA 95001-2080. E-mail: editor@americanpoetryjournal.com. Website: www.americanpoetryjournal.com. Established 2004. **Contact:** J.P. Dancing Bear, editor. The American Poetry Journal Book Prize awards $1,000 and book publication. Submit 50-65 paginated pages of poetry, table of contents, acknowledgments, bio, and e-mail address (for results). No SASE required; mss will be recycled. Guidelines available on Web site. **Entry fee:** $20. Make checks payable to Dream Horse Press. **Deadline:** February 28 (check Web site for updates). Winners of previous contests were Theodore Worozbyt, Matthew Guenette, and Lisa Lewis.

$ ☑ THE AMERICAN POETRY REVIEW/HONICKMAN FIRST BOOK PRIZE

1700 Sansom St., Suite 800, Philadelphia PA 19103. (215)496-0439. Fax: (215)569-0808. Website: www.aprweb.org. Established 1972. Annual award to encourage excellence in poetry, and to provide a wide readership for a deserving first book of poems. Offers $3,000, publication of a book-length ms, and distribution by Copper Canyon Press through Consortium. Open to U.S. citizens writing in English and who have not yet published a book-length collection of poems which was assigned an ISBN. Guidelines available on Web site. **Entry fee:** $25/book ms. **Deadline:** October 31. 2008 winner was Matthew Dickman (All American Poem).

$ ☑ ANABIOSIS PRESS CHAPBOOK CONTEST

2 South New St., Bradford MA 01835. (978)469-7085. E-mail: rsmyth@anabiosispress.org. Website: www.anabiosispress.org. **Contact:** Richard Smyth, editor. The Anabiosis Press Chapbook Contest offers $100 plus publication of the winning chapbook and 75 copies of the first run.

Submit 16-20 pages of poetry on any subject. Include separate pages with a biography, table of contents, and acknowledgments for any previous publications. Include SASE with correct postage for return of ms. **Entry fee:** $11 (all entrants receive a copy of the winning chapbook). Make checks payable to The Anabiosis Press. **Deadline:** June 30 (postmark). Winners announced by September 30. 2008 winner was William Keener (Gold Leaf on Granite).

$ ☑ THE ANHINGA PRIZE FOR POETRY

Anhinga Press, Tallahassee FL 32302. (850)442-1408. Fax: (850)442-6323. E-mail: info@anhinga. org. Website: www.anhinga.org. Established 1973. **Contact:** Rick Campbell, poetry editor. The annual Anhinga Prize awards $2,000 and publication to a book-length poetry ms. Guidelines available for SASE or on website. **Entry fee:** $25. **Deadline:** submit February 15-May 1. Past judges include Donald Hall, Joy Harjo, Robert Dana, Reginald Shepherd, and Sidney Wade. Past winners include Frank X. Gaspar, Julia Levine, Keith Ratzlaff, and Lynn Aarti Chandhok.

$ ARIZONA LITERARY CONTEST & BOOK AWARDS

Arizona Authors Association, 6145 W. Echo Lane, Glendale, AZ 85302. (623)847-9343. E-mail: info@azauthors.com. Website: www.azauthors.com. **Contact:** Toby Heathcotte, president. Arizona Authors Association sponsors annual literary contest in poetry, short story, essay, unpublished novels, and published books (fiction, nonfiction, and children's literature). Awards publication in Arizona Literary Magazine, publication of novel by and other prizes by Five Star Publications, Inc. and $100 1st Prize, $50 2nd Prize, and $25 3rd Prize in each category. Poetry submissions must be unpublished. Considers simultaneous submissions. Submit any number of poems on any subject up to 42 lines. Entry form and guidelines available for SASE. **Entry fee:** $10/poem. **Deadline:** reads submissions January 1-July 1. Competition receives 1,000 entries/ year. Recent poetry winners include Cappy Love Hanson and Margaret C Weber. Judges: Arizona authors, editors, and reviewers. Winners announced at an award banquet by November 8.

$ ☐ ARIZONA STATE POETRY SOCIETY ANNUAL CONTEST

14030 North 64th Street, Scottsdale AZ 85254. (480)368-7935. Website: www.azpoetry.org. Offers a variety of cash prizes in several categories ranging from $10-125; 1st, 2nd, and 3rd Prize winners are published in Sandcutters, ASPS's quarterly publication, which also lists names of Honorable Mention winners. See guidelines for detailed submission information (available for SASE or on website). **Entry fee:** varies according to category; see guidelines. **Deadline:** approximately September 15 (postmark). Competition receives over 1,000 entries/year. "ASPS sponsors a variety of monthly contests for members. Membership is available to anyone anywhere."

$ ☐ ART AFFAIR POETRY CONTEST

P.O. Box 54302, Oklahoma City OK 73154. Website: www.shadetreecreations.com. **Contact:** Barbara Shepherd. The annual Art Affair Poetry Contest offers 1st Prize: $40 and certificate; 2nd Prize: $25 and certificate; and 3rd Prize: $15 and certificate. Honorable Mention certificates will be awarded at the discretion of the judges. Open to any poet. Poems must be unpublished. Multiple entries accepted with entry fee for each and may be mailed in the same packet. Submit original poems on any subject, in any style, no more than 60 lines (put line count in the upper right-hand corner of first page). Include cover page with poet's name, address, phone number, and title of poem. Do not include SASE; poems will not be returned. Guidelines available on Web site. **Deadline:** October 1, 2009 (postmark). **Entry Fee:** $3/poem. Make check payable to Art Affair. Winners' list will be published on the Art Affair Web site in December. 2008 winners were Marcia Molay, Carol Matos, and Maria Rachel Hooley.

$ ☐ ARTIST TRUST

(Specialized: WA resident artists)1835 12th Ave., Seattle WA 98122. (206)467-8734. Fax: (206)467-9633. E-mail: info@artisttrust.org. Website: www.artisttrust.org. **Contact:** Heather Helbach-Olds, Director of Programs. Artist Trust is a nonprofit arts organization that provides grants to artists (including poets) who are residents of the state. Applications for Grants for Artist Projects (GAP) are accepted each year in February; awards grants of up to $1,500. Applications for Fellowship Program are accepted in June of odd-numbered years; awards $7,500 merit-based awards. **Deadline:** GAP, last Friday of February annually; Fellowship, second Friday of June in odd-numbered years. Each competition receives 200-300 literary entries/year. Most recent winners include Stacey Levine, Ann Pancake, and Brenda Miller. Also publishes a newsletter (4 times/year) full of information on arts-related topics and cultural issues; and Artists' Assets (published annually) full of resources for artists of all disciplines.

$ ☐ THE ART OF MUSIC ANNUAL WRITING CONTEST

(Specialized: music-related writing)The Art of Music, Inc., P.O. Box 85, Del Mar CA 92014-0085. (619)884-1401. Fax: (858)755-1104. E-mail: info@theartofmusicinc.org. Website: www.theartofmusic.org. Established 1998. **Contact:** Elizabeth C. Axford, M.A., director. The Art of Music Annual Writing Contest offers cash prizes and publication in The Art of Music: A Collection of Writings. 1st Prize: $150; 2nd Prize: $100; 3rd Prize: $50; also presents winners with a copy of each anthology, and a certificate. In addition, the top entries are published in the anthology. Open to all writers ages 4 and up; signature of a parent or guardian is required for entrants under 18 years old. Entry may consist of an original music-related poem, short story, essay, song lyric, or cover illustration. Manuscripts must be titled and typed, with no identifying information on any page. No entries will be returned. Each entry must be accompanied by an official entry form. Guidelines and entry form available on website. **Entry fee:** $20. Make checks/money orders payable to The Art of Music, Inc. All entrants receive a copy of The Art of Music: A Collection of Writings, Volume 1 or Volume 2 (designate preference on entry form). **Deadline:** June 30 (postmark). Judges: published poets, authors, and songwriters. Winners announced by e-mail by October 31. Copies of anthologies available through website.

$ ☑ ARTS & LETTERS/RUMI PRIZE FOR POETS

Campus Box 89, Georgia College & State University, Milledgeville GA 31061. (478)445-1289. E-mail: al@gcsu.edu. Website: http://al.gcsu.edu. Established 1999. **Contact:** Contest Director. The Arts & Letters Prizes competition offers $1,000 and publication in Arts & Letters Journal (see separate listing in Magazines/Journals) to the winner of the Rumi Prize for Poets. All submissions will be considered for publication. Submissions must be unpublished. Considers simultaneous submissions if notified immediately of acceptance elsewhere. Accepts multiple submissions with separate fee for each. Submit up to 8 pages of poetry, typed, single-spaced, one poem (or part of a poem) per page. Include cover sheet with ms title, poet's name, address ("where you want your subscription(s) to be sent"), phone number, and e-mail address. Poet's name must not appear anywhere on ms. Mail submission unfolded and unstapled in large-size manila envelope with "Poetry" marked on outside. Include #10 SASE for results only; mss will not be returned. Guidelines available on website. **Entry fee:** $15 USD; includes a 2-issue subscription to Arts & Letters. For multiple submissions, a gift subscription may be designated; indicate recipient's name and address. Make checks/money orders payable to GCSU (note " Arts & Letters" in the memo section). **Deadline:** submit January 1-March 17 (postmark). 2006 winner was Margaret Rabb. 2007 judge: A. Van Jordan. "We strongly urge writers who have close personal ties to judges not to submit to our competition. Please do not write to or contact final judges in any way. If you have any questions, contact the journal's editorial staff." Winners announced in July by SASE or on Web site.

▦ $ ☐ AUSTRALIAN-IRISH HERITAGE WRITER'S PRIZE

Australian-Irish Heritage Association, P.O. Box 1583, Subiaco WA 6904 Australia. (61)(8)9384-1368. E-mail: aiha@irishheritage.net. Website: www.irishheritage.net. Established 1997. **Contact:** Pavla Walsh, coordinator. Offers annual awards. See Web site for current year's entry details.

$ ☑ AUTUMN HOUSE POETRY PRIZE

Autumn House Press, P.O. Box 60100, Pittsburgh PA 15211. (412)381-4261. E-mail: msimms@autumnhouse.org. Website: http://autumnhouse.org. Established 1999. **Contact:** Michael Simms, editor. Offers annual prize of $2,500 and publication of book-length ms with national promotion. Submission must be unpublished as a collection, but individual poems may have been previously published elsewhere. Considers simultaneous submissions. Submit 50-80 pages of poetry ("blind judging--2 cover sheets requested"). Guidelines available for SASE, by e-mail, or on website. **Entry fee:** $25/ms. **Deadline:** June 30 annually. Competition receives 700 entries/year. 2007 winner was Miriam Levine. 2008 judge: Naomi Shihab Nye. Winners announced through mailings and through ads in Poets & Writers, American Poetry Review, and Writer's Chronicle (extensive publicity for winner). Copies of winning books available from Amazon. com, Barnes & Noble, Borders, and other retailers. "Autumn House is a nonprofit corporation with the mission of publishing and promoting poetry. We have published books by Gerald Stern, Ruth L. Schwartz, Ed Ochester, Andrea Hollander Budy, Jo McDougall, and others." Advice: "Include only your best poems."

$ ☑ THE MURIEL CRAFT BAILEY MEMORIAL AWARD

4956 St. John Dr., Syracuse NY 13215. (315)488-8077. E-mail: poetry@comstockreview.org. Website: www.comstockreview.org. Contact: John M. Bellinger, managing editor. The annual Muriel Craft Bailey Memorial Award offers 1st Prize: $1,000; 2nd Prize: $250; 3rd Prize: $100; Honorable Mentions; plus publication of winners and selected finalists in The Comstock Review (see separate listing in Magazines/Journals). Submissions must be unpublished in any media, print or electronic. No simultaneous submissions. Submit poems of 40 lines each, beginning wtih the first line of text below the title (do not count blank lines). Put poet's name, address, phone number, and e-mail address on reverse side of each page. "We read each poem 'blind,' so we do not want to see your name on the front of the poem." Poems with identification visible to judges on the front side of page will be disqualified. Include SASE for results only; no poems will be returned. See our Web site for full guidelines. **Entry fee:** $5/poem. Make checks payable to The Comstock Review (combine fees on a single check for multiple entries). **Deadline:** reads May 1-July 1 (postmark). 2008 judge: Marie Howe; 2009 Judge: Maxine Kumin.

☐ THE BAILEY PRIZE

(Specialized: open to upper-level undergraduate & graduate-level writing students)The Chrysalis Reader, 1745 Gravel Hill Rd., Dillwyn VA 23936. (434)983-3021. Fax: (434)983-1074. E-mail: chrysalis@hovac.com. Website: www.swedenborg.com/chrysalis. **Contact:** The Editor. Celebrating more than 20 years of publishing established and emerging writers, The Chrysalis Reader offers The Bailey Prize, an annual publishing prize for undergraduate and graduate-level students. The Chrysalis Reader, published yearly in the fall, is an anthology of poetry, fiction, and non-fiction. Winners will be published in CR (see separate listing in Magazines/Journals), receive 3 copies of the issue, and have their work available online after print publication. The Bailey Prize is open to nominations by instructors of undergraduate and graduate-level courses. Instructors may submit a maximum of 3 nominations from their students' output within one academic year. Nominations may be any combination of previously unpublished poetry (100 lines maximum) or fiction or nonfiction (3,100 words maximum). "We welcome both traditional and experimental writing with an emphasis on insightful writing related to the Chrysalis Reader's annual theme. The 2010 theme is "bridges." Submit one copy of each entry with writer's contact information. Include a cover letter and SASE. No email or disk submissions. No nominated entries will be returned. Guidelines available on website. **Entry fee:** none. **Deadline:** All entries must be dated on or before May 31 to be considered for that year's publishing cycle.

$ ☑ BAKELESS LITERARY PUBLICATION PRIZES

Break Loaf Writers' Conference, Middlebury College, Middlebury VT 05753. (802)443-2018. E-mail: bakelessprize@middlebury.edu. Website:www.bakelessprize.org. **Contact:** Ms. Jennifer Bates, contest coordinator. The Bread Loaf Writers' Conference (see separate listing in Conferences, Workshops & Festivals) sponsors the Bakeless Literary Publication Prizes for new authors of literary works in poetry, fiction, and creative nonfiction. Awards publication by Graywolf Press of a book-length ms, and a fellowship to attend the Bread Loaf Writers' Conference. Submissions must be unpublished as a collection, but individual poems may have been previously published elsewhere. Considers simultaneous submissions, "but contestants are asked to notify the contest coordinator immediately if a manuscript has been accepted for publication elsewhere." Submit at least 50 pages of poetry, typed double- or single-spaced on letter-size paper. Good-quality photocopies or letter-quality printed mss acceptable. Include 2 cover pages: one with poet's name, address, phone number, ms title, and genre (poetry) indicated; one with only ms title and genre. Poet's name must not appear on any ms page. Do not include author's note, bio, or acknowledgments page. Include SASP for confirmation of ms receipt and SASE for results only; mss will not be returned. Guidelines available on website. **Entry Fee:** $10/submission. Make checks payable to Middlebury College. **Deadline:** Submissions accepted between September 15 and November 1. Winners announced in May.

$ ☑ THE WILLIS BARNSTONE TRANSLATION PRIZE

(Specialized: translations from any language)1800 Lincoln Ave., Evansville IN 47722. Phone/fax: (812)488-1042. E-mail: evansvillereview@evansville.edu. Website: http://english.evansville.edu/EvansvilleReview.htm. Established 1989. **Contact:** Dominic Huether, poetry editor. The annual Willis Barnstone Translation Prize offers an annual award of $1,000 and publication in The Evansville Review for translated poems from any language and any time period, ancient to contemporary. Submissions must be unpublished. Each translated poem must not exceed 200 lines. "Please staple the translation to a copy of the original (which identifies the original poet) and put the name, address, and phone number of the translator(s) on the back of the translation page." Accepts multiple entries (up to 10/translator). Include SASE for results; mss will not be returned. Guidelines available for SASE or on website. **Entry fee:** $5 for the first poem, $3 for each subsequent poem. Make checks payable to The University of Evansville. **Deadline:** December 1. Competition receives 400 entries/year. Winner will be announced in April in The Evansville Review and to entrants who provided SASEs.

$ ☑ BARROW STREET PRESS BOOK CONTEST

P.O. Box 1558, Kingston RI 02881. E-mail: info@barrowstreet.org. Website: www.barrowstreet.

org. Established 2002. **Contact:** Contest Coordinator. Barrow Street Press publishes one poetry book/year through the annual Barrow Street Press Book Contest. Winner receives $1,000 and publication. Submit a 50- to 70-page ms of original, previously unpublished poetry in English. Manuscript should be typed, single-spaced on white 8½x11 paper. Clear photocopies acceptable. Include 2 title pages and an acknowledgments page listing any poems previously published in journals or anthologies. Author's name, address, and daytime phone number should appear on first title page only, and nowhere else in ms. Include SASE for results only; no mss will be returned. Guidelines available on website. **Entry fee:** $25; include mailer with $2.13 postage for copy of winning book. Make checks payable to Barrow Street. **Deadline:** June 30. 2009 judge: David Wojahn.

$ ☐ BELLEVUE LITERARY REVIEW PRIZE FOR POETRY

(Specialized: humanity, health, and healing) Bellevue Literary Review, New York University School of Medicine, OBV-A612, 550 First Ave., New York NY 10016. (212)263-3973. E-mail: info@BLReview.org. Website: www.BLReview.org. Established 2005. **Contact:** Stacy Bodziak. The annual Bellevue Literary Review Prize for Poetry recognizes outstanding writing related to themes of health, healing, illness, the mind, and the body. Offers $1,000 for best poem and publication in Bellevue Literary Review (see separate listing in Magazines/Journals). All entries will be considered for publication. No previously published poems (including Internet publication) or simultaneous submissions. Submit up to 3 poems (5 pages maximum). Electronic (online) submissions only (as Word document with *.doc extension); combine all poems into one document and use first poem as document title. See guidelines for additional submission details. Guidelines available for SASE or on website. **Entry fee:** $15/submission, limit of 2 submissions per person (one-year subscription available for additional $5). **Deadline:** August 1. Winner announced in December. 2009 judge: Naomi Shihab Nye. Previous judges include Edward Hirsch (2006), Rafael Campo (2007), and Marie Howe (2008).

$ ☑ GEORGE BENNETT FELLOWSHIP

Phillips Exeter Academy, 20 Main St., Exeter NH 03833-2460. Website: http://www.exeter.edu/about_us/about_us_537.aspx. Established 1968. **Contact:** Charles Pratt, selection committee coordinator. Provides an annual $10,000 fellowship plus residency (room and board) to a writer with a ms in progress. The Fellow's only official duties are to be in residence while the academy is in session and to be available to students interested in writing. The committee favors writers who have not yet published a book-length work with a major publisher. Application materials and guidelines available for SASE or on website. **Entry fee:** $5. **Deadline:** December 1. Competition receives 190 entries. Recent award winners were Maggie Dietz (2002-2003), Nia Stephens (2003-2004), and Erin Soros (2004-2005). Winners will be announced by mail in March. "Please, no telephone calls or e-mail inquiries."

$ ☑ THE PATRICIA BIBBY FIRST BOOK AWARD

Tebot Bach, P.O. Box 7887, Huntington Beach CA 92615-7887. E-mail: info@tebotbach.org. Website: www.tebotbach.org. Established 2005. **Contact:** Mifanwy Kaiser. The Patricia Bibby First Book Award offers $1,000 and publication of a book-length poetry manuscript by Tebot Bach (see separate listing in Book/Chapbook Publishers). Open to "all poets writing in English who have not committed to publishing collections of poetry of 36 poems or more in editions of over 400 copies." Submissions must be unpublished as a collection, but individual poems may have been previously published elsewhere. Considers simultaneous submissions, but Tebot Bach must be notified immediately by e-mail if the collection is accepted for publication.

Partial guidelines: Submit 50-84 pages of poetry, letter-quality, single-spaced; clear photocopies acceptable. Use binder clip; no staples, folders, or printer-bound copies. Include 2 title pages: 1 (not fastened to ms) with ms title, poet's name, address, phone number, and e-mail address; the second (fastened to ms) with ms title only. Also include table of contents. Include SASP for notification of receipt of entry and SASE for results only; mss will not be returned. Complete guidelines available by e-mail or on Web site. **Reading fee:** $25. Make checks/money orders payable to Tebot Bach with reading fee and title of ms. on the notation line. **Deadline:** October 31 (postmark) annually. Winner announced each year in April. Judges are selected annually.

$ ☑ BINGHAMTON UNIVERSITY MILT KESSLER POETRY BOOK AWARD

(Specialized: poets over 40)Binghamton University Creative Writing Program, P.O. Box 6000, Binghamton NY 13902. (607)777-2713. Fax: (607)777-2408. E-mail: cwpro@binghamton.edu. Website: http://english.binghamton.edu/cwpro. Established 2001. **Contact:** Maria Mazziotti Gillan, award director. Offers annual award of $1,000 for a book of poetry judged best of those published that year by a poet over the age of 40. "Submit books published that year; do not submit manuscripts." Entry form and guidelines available for SASE, by e-mail, or on Web site. **Entry fee:** none; "just submit 3 copies of book." **Deadline:** March 1. Competition receives 500 books/year. 2007 winner was Albert Goldbarth. Winner will be announced in June in Poets & Writers and on Web site, or by SASE if provided. (**NOTE:** Not to be confused with the Milton Kessler Memorial Prize for Poetry sponsored by Harpur Palate).

$ ☑ THE BLACK RIVER CHAPBOOK COMPETITION

Black Lawrence Press, P.O. Box 327, Theresa NY 13691. E-mail: info@blacklawrencepress.com. Website: www.blacklawrencepress.com. Established 2003. **Contact:** Colleen Ryor, editor. The semiannual Black River Chapbook Competition awards $300, publication by Black Lawrence Press (see separate listing in Book/Chapbook Publishers), and 25 copies to the winner. Considers simultaneous submissions, but notify immediately if ms is accepted elsewhere. Submit 16-40 pages of poetry, paginated, with cover letter with brief bio and contact information (include valid e-mail address), acknowledgments page (if applicable), and table of contents. No e-mail submissions. Include SASE or e-mail address for results only; mss will not be returned. Guidelines available on Web site. **Entry fee:** $15/entry; multiple submissions accepted with entry fee for each. Make checks/money orders payable to Black Lawrence Press. **Deadline:** October 31 (fall) and May 31 (spring) (postmark). Spring 2008 winner was T.J. Beitelman (Pilgrims: A Love Story).

$ ☑ BLUE LIGHT POETRY PRIZE AND CHAPBOOK CONTEST

1563-45th Ave., San Francisco CA 94123. (415)440-8668 or (641)472-7882. E-mail: bluelightpress@ aol.com. Established 1988. **Contact:** Diane Frank, chief editor. The Blue Light Poetry Prize and Chapbook Contest offers a cash prize and publication by Blue Light Press (see separate listing in Book/Chapbook Publishers). "The winner will receive a $100 honorarium and 50 copies of his or her book, which can be sold for $10 each, for a total of $600." Submit ms of 10-24 pages, typed or printed with a laser or inkjet printer. No e-mail submissions. Include SASE and postcard for notification of receipt of ms, SASE for contest results only; no mss will be returned. Guidelines available with SASE or by e-mail. **Entry fee:** $20. Make checks payable to Blue Light Press. **Deadline:** June 1 for chapbook contest. Winner announced in November. Deadline is January 31 for full-length ms contest, 50-80 pages. Send e-mail for guidelines. Winner announced May 1.

$ ☑ BLUE LYNX PRIZE FOR POETRY

Eastern Washington University Press, 534 E Spokane Falls Blvd, Ste 203., Spokane WA 99202. 1-800-508-9095. Fax: (509)368-6596. E-mail: ewupress2@mail.ewu.edu. Website: http://ewupress.ewu.edu. **Contact:** Chris Howell, senior editor. Offers annual award of $2,000 and publication by EWU Press. For U.S. authors only. Must be unpublished as a collection, but individual poems may have been previously published elsewhere. Submit 48 pages of poetry for the Blue Lynx Prize. Include table of contents and SASE for notification. Please visit our Web site for complete guidelines. **Entry fee:** $25. Make checks payable to EWU Press. **Deadline:** May 15 annually. Competition receives 400 entries/year. 2008 winner was Jorn Ake (Boys Whistling Like Canaries). Final judge: David Wojahn. Winner announced in fall of contest year. Copies of winning books available from EWU Press.

$ ☑ THE BOSTON REVIEW ANNUAL POETRY CONTEST

Boston Review, 35 Medford St., Suite 302, Somerville MA 02143. (617)591-0505. Fax: (617)591-0440. E-mail: review@bostonreview.net (inquiries only). Website: www.bostonreview.net. Established 1975. **Contact:** Poetry Contest Coordinator. Offers $1,500 and publication in Boston Review (see separate listing in Magazines/Journals). "Any poet writing in English is eligible, unless he or she is a current student, former student, or close personal friend of the judge." Submissions must be unpublished. Submit up to 5 poems, no more than 10 pages total, in duplicate. Include cover sheet with poet's name, address, and phone number; no identifying information on the poems themselves. No mss will be returned. Guidelines available for SASE or on Web site. **Entry fee:** $20 ($30 for international submissions); all entrants receive a one-year subscription to Boston Review. Make checks payable to Boston Review. **Deadline:** June 1 (postmark). Winner announced in early November on Web site. 2008 winner was Sarah Arvio. 2009 Judge: Rae Armantrout.

☒ $ BPNICHOL CHAPBOOK AWARD

(Specialized: works published in Canada)344 Bloor Street West, Suite 505 Toronto ON Canada M5S 3A7. (416)964-7919. Fax: (416)964-6941. Website: www.pcwf.ca. **Contact:** Rocco de Giacomo, committee chairman. Established 1985. Sponsored by the Phoenix Community Works Foundation. The bpNichol Chapbook Award offers $1,000 CAD for the best poetry chapbook (10-48 pages) in English published in Canada. Poet or publisher may submit 3 copies (not returnable) and a brief curriculum vitae of the author with address, telephone number, and e-mail. Guidelines available on Web site. **Deadline:** March 31. Competition receives between 40-60 entries on average. 2008 winners were Jay Millar and Clara Benson.

$ ☑ THE BRIAR CLIFF REVIEW FICTION, POETRY AND CREATIVE NONFICTION CONTEST

3303 Rebecca St., Sioux City IA 51104-2100. Website: www.briarcliff.edu/bcreview. **Contact:** Jeanne Emmons, poetry editor. The Briar Cliff Review (see separate listing in Magazines/Journals) sponsors an annual contest offering $1,000 and publication to each First Prize winner in fiction, poetry, and creative nonfiction. Previous year's winner and former students of editors ineligible. Winning pieces accepted for publication on the basis of First-Time Rights. Considers simultaneous submissions, "but notify us immediately upon acceptance elsewhere." Submit 3 poems, single-spaced on 812x11 paper, no more than 1 poem/page. Include separate cover sheet with author's name, address, e-mail, and poem title(s); no name on ms. Include SASE for results only; mss will not be returned. Guidelines available on Web site. **Entry fee:** $20 for 3 poems. "All entrants receive a copy of the magazine (a $15 value) containing the winning entries." **Deadline:**

November 1. Judge: the editors of The Briar Cliff Review.

$ ☑ BRIGHT HILL PRESS POETRY BOOK AWARD

P.O. Box 193, 94 Church St., Treadwell NY 13846-0193. (607)829-5055. Fax: (607)829-5054. E-mail: wordthur@stny.rr.com. Website: www.brighthillpress.org. Established 1992. **Contact:** Bertha Rogers, editor-in-chief/founding director. Member: Council of Literary Magazines and Presses, NYC. The annual Bright Hill Press Poetry Book Award offers $1,000, publication of a book-length ms, and 25 author's copies. Submissions must be unpublished as a collection, but individual poems may have been previously published elsewhere. Considers simultaneous submissions if Bright Hill Press is notified of acceptance elsewhere. Submit 48-65 pages of poetry, paginated and secured with bulldog or spring clip. Include bio, table of contents, and acknowledgments page. Include 2 title pages: 1 with ms title, poet's name, address, and phone number; 1 with ms title only. Include SASE for results only; mss will not be returned. Guidelines available for SASE, by e-mail, or on Web site. **Entry fee:** $25 for Word Thursdays/Bright Hill Press members; $17 for nonmembers. **Deadline:** was November 30 (postmark) for 2009. Competition receives over 300 entries/year. Winners will be announced in summer of the year following the contest. Copies of winning books available from Bright Hill Press (see Web site); include **with entry only** a sturdy 6x8 or 9x12 envelope with $1.65 postage affixed to receive a free copy of an award-winning Bright Hill Press poetry book (affix $2 postage for padded envelope). "Publish your poems in literary magazines before trying to get a whole manuscript published. Publishing individual poems is the best way to hone your complete manuscript."

$ ☑ BRIGHT HILL PRESS POETRY CHAPBOOK AWARD

P.O. Box 193, 94 Church St., Treadwell NY 13846-0193. (607)829-5055. Fax: (607)829-5054. E-mail: wordthur@stny.rr.com. Website: www.brighthillpress.org. Established 1992. **Contact:** Bertha Rogers, editor-in-chief/founding director. Member: Council of Literary Magazines and Presses, NYC. The annual Bright Hill Press Chapbook Award offers $300, publication of a chapbook-length ms, and 25 author's copies. Submissions must be unpublished as a collection, but individual poems may have been previously published elsewhere. Considers simultaneous submissions if Bright Hill Press is notified of acceptance elsewhere. Submit 16-24 pages of poetry, paginated and secured with bulldog or spring clip. Include bio, table of contents, and acknowledgments page. Include 2 title pages: 1 with ms title, poet's name, address, and phone number; 1 with ms title only. Include SASE for results only; mss will not be returned. Guidelines available for SASE, by e-mail, or on Web site. **Entry fee:** $10 for Word Thursdays/Bright Hill Press members; $12 for nonmembers. Multiple entries accepted with separate fee for each. **Deadline:** July 31 (postmark). Competition receives over 300 entries/year. Copies of winning chapbooks available from Bright Hill Press (see Web site); include **with entry only** a 5x7 SASE with $1.31 postage affixed and receive a free copy of a recent winning Bright Hill Press poetry chapbook. "Publish your poems in literary magazines before trying to get a whole manuscript published. Publishing individual poems is the best way to hone your complete manuscript."

$ ☑ BRITTINGHAM PRIZE IN POETRY

University of Wisconsin Press, Dept. of English, 600 N. Park St., University of Wisconsin, Madison WI 53706. E-mail: rwallace@wisc.edu. Website: www.wisc.edu/wisconsinpress/index.html. Established 1985. **Contact:** Ronald Wallace, poetry series editor. The annual Brittingham Prize in Poetry is one of 2 prizes awarded by The University of Wisconsin Press (see separate listing for the Felix Pollak Prize in Poetry in this section). Offers $1,000 plus publication, with an additional $1,500 honorarium to cover expenses of a reading in Madison. Submissions must be unpublished as a collection, but individual poems may have been published elsewhere (publication must be acknowledged). Considers simultaneous submissions if notified of selection elsewhere. Submit 50-80 unbound ms pages, typed single-spaced (with double spaces between stanzas) or double-spaced. Clean photocopies are acceptable. Include title page with poet's name, address, and telephone number. No translations. Include SASE for results only; mss will not be returned. Guidelines available for SASE or on Web site. **Entry fee: $25. NOTE:** $25 fee applies to consideration of same entry for the Felix Pollak Prize in Poetry--1 fee for 2 contest entries. Make checks/money orders payable to University of Wisconsin Press. **Deadline:** submit September 1-27 (postmark). 2008 Brittingham Prize winner was Philip Pardi (Meditations on Rising and Falling). Qualified readers will screen all mss. Judge: "a distinguished poet who will remain anonymous until the winners are announced in mid-February."

$ ☑ DOROTHY BRUNSMAN POETRY PRIZE

(Specialized: poets living west of the central time zone) Bear Star Press, 185 Hollow Oak Dr., Cohasset CA 95973. (530)891-0360. E-mail: online form. Website: www.bearstarpress.com. Established 1996. **Contact:** Beth Spencer, editor/publisher. The annual Dorothy Brunsman Poetry Prize awards $1,000 and publication by Bear Star Press to the best book-length ms by a poet who resides in the Western states (within Mountain or Pacific time zones, plus Alaska and Hawaii). "The contest also serves as our best pool for finding new voices." Submission must be unpublished as a collection, but individual poems may have been previously published elsewhere (as long as poet retains copyright). Considers simultaneous submissions (contact immediately if ms status changes). Submit ms of 50-65 pages of original poetry, in any form, on any subject. Use a plain 10-12 point font. Include separate cover sheet with poet's name, address, and phone number; no identifying information on mss pages. Include SASP for notification of receipt (do not send by Registered Mail) and SASE for results; mss will not be returned. Guidelines available for SASE or on Web site. **Entry fee: $20. Deadline:** November 30 (postmark); reads mss in September, October, and November. 2008 winner was Kathryn Cowles (Eleanor, Eleanor, Not Your Real Name). Judge: mss judged in house. Winner notified on or before February 1; winner information posted on Web site. Copies of winning books available through Web site. "Send your best work; consider its arrangement. A 'wow' poem early on keeps me reading."

$ BURNING BUSH POETRY PRIZE

(Specialized: community-centered values, democratic processes) Burning Bush Publications, P.O. Box 4658, Santa Rosa CA 95402. Website: www.bbbooks.com. Offers annual award of $200 plus publication in online e-zine, In Our Own Words (see separate listing in Magazines/Journals), to a poet whose writing "inspires others to value human life and the natural world instead of short-term economic advantage; speaks for community-centered values and democratic processes, especially those whose voices are seldom heard; demonstrates poetic excellence; and educates readers of the relevance of the past to the present and future." Prefers unpublished work, "but published poems may be submitted. If published before, please include where, when, and any acknowledgment information we may need." Submit 3 poems maximum, any style or form. Include index card with name, address, e-mail, phone, and title of each poem submitted. Also include SASE with sufficient postage for return of work. "Submissions without SASE will not be returned. If your poem is selected for the Poetry Prize, we will need a brief (50 words) biographical statement from you." Guidelines available on Web site. **Entry fee: $10. Deadline:** June 1. Competition receives 100 entries/year. 2008 winner was Anthony Russell White. Winner announced in late August.

$ ☑ BURNSIDE REVIEW CHAPBOOK COMPETITION

P.O. Box 1782, Portland OR 97207. E-mail: sid@burnsidereview.org. Website: www. burnsidereview.org. Established 2004. **Contact:** Sid Miller, editor. The annual Burnside Review Chapbook Competition awards $200, publication, and 25 author's copies to winning poet. Guidelines available for SASE or on Web site. **Entry fee:** $15. **Deadline:** March 15-June 30. 2009 winner was Steve Price (*Journal of Lovesickness*, Vol. 11). (See separate listing for Burnside Review in Magazines/Journals.)

$ THE WITTER BYNNER FOUNDATION FOR POETRY, INC.

P.O. Box 10169, Santa Fe NM 87504. (505)988-3251. Fax: (505)986-8222. E-mail: bynnerfoundation@ aol.com. Website: www.bynnerfoundation.org. **Contact:** Steven Schwartz, executive director. Awards grants, ranging from $1,000 to $10,000, exclusively to nonprofit organizations for the support of poetry-related projects in the area of: 1) support of individual poets through existing nonprofit institutions; 2) developing the poetry audience; 3) poetry translation and the process of poetry translation; and 4) uses of poetry. "May consider the support of other creative and innovative projects in poetry." Letters of intent accepted annually August 1-December 31; requests for application forms should be submitted to Steven Schwartz, executive director. Additional information available by fax, e-mail, or on Web site. **Deadline:** Applications, if approved, must be returned to the Foundation postmarked by February 1.

☑ $ CAA POETRY AWARD

(Specialized: Canadian poets)Canadian Authors Association, Box 419, Campbellford ON K0L 1L0 Canada. (705)653-0323. Fax: (705)653-0593. E-mail: admin@CanAuthors.org. Website: www.CanAuthors.org. **Contact:** Alec McEachern, national director. The CAA Poetry Award offers $1,000 CAD and a silver medal to Canadian writers for a poetry collection (by a single poet) published during the year. Guidelines available on Web site. **Entry fee:** $35 CAD/title. **Deadline:** December 15; except for works published after December 1, in which case the postmark deadline is January 15. Competition receives 100 entries/year. 2006 winner was Barry Dempster (*The Burning Alphabet*); 2007 winner was Sarah Klassen (*A Curious Beatitute*); 2008 winner was Asa Boxer (*The Mechanical Bird*). All awards are given at the CAA Awards Banquet at the annual conference.

$ ☑ GERALD CABLE BOOK AWARD

Silverfish Review Press, P.O. Box 3541, Eugene OR 97403. (541)344-5060. E-mail: sfrpress@ earthlink.net. Website: www.silverfishreviewpress.com. Established 1979. **Contact:** Rodger Moody, editor. Offers annual award of $1,000, publication by Silverfish Review Press, and 100 author copies to the best book-length ms of original poetry by an author who has not yet published a full-length collection. No restrictions on the kind of poetry or subject matter; no translations. Individual poems may have been previously published elsewhere, but must be acknowledged. Considers simultaneous submissions (notify immediately of acceptance elsewhere). Submit at least 48 pages of poetry, no names or identification on ms pages. Include separate title sheet with poet's name, address, and phone number. Include SASP for notification of receipt and SASE for results; no mss will be returned. Accepts e-mail submissions in Word, plain text, or rich text; send entry fee and SASE by regular mail. Guidelines available for SASE, by e-mail, or on Web site. **Entry fee:** $20. Make checks payable to Silverfish Review Press. **Deadline:** October 15 (postmark). 2007 winner was Joel Friederich (*Blue to Fill the Empty Heaven*). Winner announced in March. Copies of winning books available through Web site. "All entrants who enclose a booksize envelope and $2.23 in postage will receive a free copy of a recent winner of the book award."

⊠ CAKETRAIN CHAPBOOK COMPETITION

P.O. Box 82588, Pittsburgh PA 15218.E-mail: caketrainjournal@hotmail.com. Website: http://www.caketrain.org/competitions.html.Annual chapbook contest sponsored by Cake Train literary journal. Can submit by mail with SASE or by e-mail.See Web site for guidelines. Winner receives a $250 cash prize and 25 copies of their chapbook. **Entry fee:** $15 for reading fee only or $20 for entry fee and copy of winning chapbook. **Deadline:** October 1. Past winners include Elizabeth Skurnick's Check-In (2005); Tom Whalen's Dolls (2007); and Claire Hero's afterpastures (2008).

$ ⊠ CAROLLINA WREN PRESS POETRY CONTEST FOR A FIRST BOOK

120 Morris St., Durham NC 27701. (919) 560-2738. Fax: (919) 560-2759. E-mail: carolinawrenpress@earthlink.net. Website: www.carolinawrenpress.org. Established 1976. **Contact:** Contest Director. The biennial Carolina Wren Press Poetry Contest for a First Book offers $1,000 and publication by Carolina Wren Press (see separate listing in Book/Chapbook Publishers). Open only to poets who have published no more than 1 full-length collection (48 pages or more). Submissions must be unpublished as a collection, but individual poems may have been previously published elsewhere. Manuscripts that have been previously self-published or that are available online in their entirety are not eligible. Considers simultaneous submissions (notify immediately of acceptance elsewhere). Submit 2 copies of a poetry ms of 48-60 pages. Page count should include title page, table of contents, and optional dedication page. See guidelines for complete formatting and submission details. Include SASE for results only; mss will not be returned. Guidelines available for SASE, by e-mail, or on Web site (in July). **Entry fee:** $20. **Deadline:** December 1, 2010 (postmark). 2010 judge: TBA. Copies of winning books available through Web site, Amazon, or local bookstore.

$ ⊠ CAVE CANEM POETRY PRIZE

(Specialized: African American) Cave Canem Foundation, Inc., 584 Broadway, Suite 508, New York NY 10012. E-mail: dantemicheaux@ccpoets.org. Website: www.cavecanempoets.org. Established 1999 (prize) and 1996 (foundation). **Contact:** Alison Meyers, Cave Canem director. Offers "annual first book award dedicated to presenting the work of African American poets who have not been published by a professional press. The winner will receive $500 cash, publication, and 50 copies of the book." **U.S. poets only.** Considers simultaneous submissions, but they should be noted. "If the manuscript is accepted for publication elsewhere during the judging, immediate notification is requested." Send 2 copies of manuscript of 50-75 pages. The author's name should not appear on the manuscript. 2 title pages should be attached to each copy. The first must include the poet's name, address, telephone number, and the title of the manuscript; the second should list the title only. Number the pages." Include SASE for notification of receipt of ms; mss will not be returned. Guidelines available for SASE or on Web site. **Entry fee:** $15. **Deadline:** April 30. 2007 winner was Ronaldo V. Wilson (The Narrative of the Brown Boy and the White Man, The University of Pittsburgh Press). 2009 judge: Yusef Komunyakaa. Winners will be announced by press release in October of year of contest. Copies of winning books are available from "any bookseller, because the publishers are Graywolf Press, University of Georgia Press, and University of Pittsburgh Press. Cave Canem sponsors a weeklong retreat each summer and a regional workshop in New York. It sponsors readings in various parts of the country. The winner of the prize and the judge are featured in an annual reading." Recommends "being at a stage in your development where some of your poems have already been published in literary journals. Manuscripts not adhering to guidelines will not be forwarded to judge nor returned to applicant."

$ ☑ THE CENTER FOR BOOK ARTS' ANNUAL POETRY CHAPBOOK COMPETITION

28 W. 27th St., 3rd Floor, New York NY 10001. (212)481-0295. E-mail: info@centerforbookarts. org. Website: www.centerforbookarts.org. Established 1995. **Contact:** Alexander Campos, executive director. Offers $500 cash prize, a $500 reading honorarium, and publication of winning manuscript in a limited edition letterpress-printed and handbound chapbook (10 copies reserved for poet). Must be unpublished as a collection, but individual poems may have been published elsewhere. Submit no more than 500 lines or 24 pages on any subject, in any form; may be collection or sequence of poems or a single long poem. Bind with a simple spring clip. Include table of contests and acknowledgments page. Include 2 cover pages: 1 with ms title, poet's name, address, phone number, and e-mail; 1 without poet's identification. (Page count does not include table contents, acknowledgments page, titles pages, or cover sheet.) Include #10 SASE for results; mss will not be returned. Guidelines and entry form available for SASE, by e-mail, or on Web site. **Entry fee:** $25. Make checks payable to The Center for the Book Arts. **Deadline:** December 1 (postmark). Competition receives 500-1,000 entries/year. 2008 winner was Robert Ostrom (To Show the Living). 2009 judges: Kim Addonizio and Sharon Dolin. Winner announced in April. Copies of winning chapbooks available through Web site. "Center for Book Arts is a nonprofit organization dedicated to the traditional crafts of bookmaking and contemporary interpretations of the book as an art object. Through the Center's Education, Exhibition, and Workspace Programs, we ensure that the ancient craft of the book remains a viable and vital part of our civilization."

$ ☑ CIDER PRESS REVIEW BOOK AWARD

777 Braddock Lane, Halifax PA 17032. E-mail: editor@ciderpressreview.com (inquiries only). Website: http://ciderpressreview.com/bookaward. Established 1999. **Contact:** Contest Director. The annual Cider Press Review Book Award offers $1,000, publication, and 25 author's copies. CPR acquires first publication rights. Initial print run is not less than 1,000 copies. Submissions must be unpublished as a collection, but individual poems may have been previously published elsewhere. Submit book-length ms of 48-80 pages. "Submissions can be made online using the submission form on the Web site or by mail. If sending by mail, include 2 cover sheets--1 with title, author's name, and complete contact information; and 1 with title only, all bound with a spring clip. Include SASE for results; manuscripts cannot be returned. Online submissions must be in Word for PC or PDF format, and should not include title page with author's name. The editors strongly urge contestants to use online delivery if possible." **Entry fee:** $25. All entrants will receive a copy of the winning book. **Deadline:** submit September 1-November 30 (postmark). 2007 winner was Robin Chapman (Abundance). 2009 judge: David St. John.

$ ☐ CNW/FFWA FLORIDA STATE WRITING COMPETITION

(formerly CNW/FFWA Florida State Writing Competition), Florida Freelance Writers Association, P.O. Box A, North Stratford NH 03590-0167. (603)922-8338. E-mail: contest@writers-editors. com. Website: www.writers-editors.com. Established 1978. **Contact:** Dana K. Cassell, award director. Offers annual awards for nonfiction, fiction, children's literature, and poetry. Awards for each category are 1st Prize: $100 plus certificate; 2nd Prize: $75 plus certificate; 3rd Prize: $50 plus certificate; plus Honorable Mention certificates. Poetry submissions must be unpublished. Submit any number of poems on any subject in traditional forms, free verse, or children's. Entry form and guidelines available for SASE or on Web site. **Entry fee:** $3/poem (members), $5/poem (nonmembers). **Deadline:** March 15. Competition receives 350-400 entries/year. Competition is judged by writers, librarians, and teachers. Winners will be announced on May 31 by mail and on Web site.

$ ☑ COLORADO PRIZE FOR POETRY

Center for Literary Publishing, Dept. of English, Colorado State University, Fort Collins CO 80523. (970)491-5449. E-mail: creview@colostate.edu. Website: http://coloradoprise.colostate. edu. Estab. 1995. **Contact:** Stephanie G'Schwind, editor. The annual Colorado Prize for Poetry awards an honorarium of $1,500 and publication of a book-length ms. Submission must be unpublished as a collection, but individual poems may have been published elsewhere. Submit approximately 40-100 pages of poetry (no set minimum or maximum) on any subject, in any form, double- or single-spaced. Include 2 titles pages: one with ms title only, the other with ms title and poet's name, address, and phone number. Enclosed SASP for notification of receipt and SASE for results; mss will not be returned. Guidelines available for SASE or by e-mail. **Entry fee:** $25; includes one-year subscription to Colorado Review (see separate listing in Magazines/ Journals). **Deadline:** submission period was October 1-January 12 for 2009. Winner announced in May. 2008 winner was Endi Bogue Hartigan (One Sun Storm), selected by Martha Ronk. 2009 judge was James Longenbach.

ℕ THE CONNECTICUT RIVER REVIEW POETRY CONTEST

c/o CRR Contest, CPS, P.O. Box 270554, West Hartford, CT 06127. E-mail: connpoetry@comcast. net. Website: http://ct-poetry-society.org/publications.htm. Prizes of $400, $200, and $100 will be awarded and winning poems will be published in Connecticut River Review. Send up to 3 unpublished poems, any form, 80 line limit. Include two copies of each poem: one with complete contact information in the upper right hand corner and one with NO contact information.Include SASE for results only (no poems will be returned). Winning poems must be submitted by disc or email following notification. **Entry fee:** Entry fee: $15 for up to 3 poems. Please make out check to Connecticut Poetry Society. See separate entries in Magazines and Organizations sections of this book.

$ ☑ CRAB ORCHARD SERIES IN POETRY FIRST BOOK AWARD

Dept. of English, Mail Code 4503, Faner Hall 2380, Southern Illinois University Carbondale, 1000 Faner Dr., Carbondale IL 62901. Website: www.siu.edu/~crborchd. Established 1995. **Contact:** John Tribble, series editor. The Crab Orchard Series in Poetry First Book Award offers $2,500 ($1,000 prize plus $1,500 honorarium for a reading at Southern Illinois University Carbondale) and publication. "Manuscripts should be 50-75 pages of original poetry, in English, by a U.S. citizen or permanent resident who has neither published, nor committed to publish, a volume of poetry 40 pages or more in length (individual poems may have been previously published). Current students and employees of Southern Illinois University and authors published by Southern Illinois University Press are not eligible." See guidelines for complete formatting instructions. Guidelines available for SASE or on Web site. **Entry fee:** $25/submission; includes a copy of the summer/fall Crab Orchard Review (see separate listing in Magazines/Journals). Make checks payable to Crab Orchard Series in Poetry. **Deadline:** see guidelines or check Web site. 2007 winner was Sean Nevin (Oblivio Gate).

$ ☒ CRAB ORCHARD SERIES IN POETRY OPEN COMPETITION AWARDS

Dept. of English, Mail Code 4503, Faner Hall 2380, Southern Illinois University Carbondale, 1000 Faner Dr., Carbondale IL 62901. Website: www.siu.edu/~crborchd. Established 1995. **Contact:**

Jon Tribble, series editor. The Crab Orchard Series in Poetry Open Competition Awards offer 1st Prize: $3,500 and publication of a book-length ms; and 2nd Prize: $1,500 and publication of a book-length ms. "Cash prize totals reflect a $1,500 honorarium for each winner for a reading at Southern Illinois University Carbondale. Publication contract is with Southern Illinois University Press. Entrants must be U.S. citizens or permanent residents." Submissions must be unpublished as a collection, but individual poems may have been previously published elsewhere. Considers simultaneous submissions, but series editor must be informed immediately upon acceptance. Manuscripts should be typewritten or computer-generated (letter quality only, no dot matrix), single-spaced; clean photocopy is recommended as mss are not returned. See guidelines for complete formatting instructions. Guidelines available for SASE or on Web site. **Entry fee:** $25/submission; includes a copy of the winning Crab Orchard Review (see separate listing in Magazines/Journals). Make checks payable to Crab Orchard Series in Poetry. **Deadline:** see guidelines or check Web site. 2007 winners were Ciaran Berry (1st prize, Sphere of Birds) and Jake Adam York (2nd prize, A Murmuration of Starlings).

$ ☑ LOIS CRANSTON MEMORIAL POETRY PRIZE

Calyx, Inc., P.O. Box B, Corvallis OR 97339. E-mail: calyx@proaxis.com. Website: www. calyxpress.org. Established 2002. CALYX (see separate listing in Magazines/Journals) offers the annual Lois Cranston Memorial Poetry Prize of $300, publication in CALYX, and a one-volume subscription. Finalists will be published on the CALYX Web site and receive a one-volume subscription. No previously published poems or simultaneous submissions. Submit up to 3 poems/entry (6 pages total maximum). Include separate cover letter with poet's name, address, phone number, e-mail address, and title(s) of poem(s). No names on poems. No mss will be returned. Guidelines available for SASE, by e-mail, or on Web site. **Entry fee:** $15 for up to 3 poems. Make checks payable to CALYX. **Deadline:** submit March 1-May 31 (inclusive postmark dates). Winners notified by October 30 and announced on Calyx' s website. 2008 winner was Hilde Weisert ("Finding Wilfred Owen Again"). 2008 judge Ursula K. Le Guin.

☐ CREATIVITY UNLIMITED PRESS® ANNUAL POETRY COMPETITION

30819 Casilina Dr., Rancho Palos Verdes CA 90275. E-mail: ihf@cox.net. Established 1978. **Contact:** Shelley Stockwell-Nicholas, PhD, editor. Annual invitation to submit offers possible widespread publication, with full credit to the author--Creativity Unlimited Press® uses poetry submitted in published texts and newsletters. "We often use poems as chapter introductions in self-help books. Short, clever, quippy, humorous, and delightful language encouraged. No inaccessible, verbose, esoteric, obscure poetry." Enter no more than 2 pages/poem, double-spaced, 1 side of page. Submissions may be previously published "provided writer has maintained copyright and notifies us." Accepts e-mail submissions. **Deadline:** December 31.

$ ☑ DANA AWARD IN POETRY

200 Fosseway Dr., Greensboro NC 27455. (336)644-8028 (for emergency questions only). E-mail: danaawards@pipeline.com. Website: www.danaawards.com. Established 1996. **Contact:** Mary Elizabeth Parker, award chair. Offers annual award of $1,000 for the best group of 5 poems. Submissions must be unpublished and not under promise of publication when submitted. Considers simultaneous submissions. Submit 5 poems on any subject, in any form; no light verse. Include separate cover sheet with name, address, phone, e-mail address, and titles of poems. Entries by regular mail only. Include SASE for winners list only; no mss will be returned. Guidelines available for SASE, by e-mail, or on Web site. **Entry fee:** $15 for 5 poems. **Deadline:** October 31 (postmark). Winner will be announced in early spring by phone, letter, and e-mail.

$ ☐ DANCING POETRY CONTEST

Artists Embassy International, 704 Brigham Ave., Santa Rosa CA 95404-5245. (707)528-0912. E-mail: jhcheung@comcast.net. Website: www.DANCINGPOETRY.com. Established 1993. **Contact:** Judy Cheung, contest chair. Annual contest offers 3 Grand Prizes of $100, five 1st Prizes of $50, ten 2nd Prizes of $25, and twenty 3rd Prizes of $10. The 3 Grand Prize-winning poems will be choreographed, costumed, premiered, and videotaped at the annual Dancing Poetry Festival at Palace of the Legion of Honor, San Francisco; Natica Angilly's Poetic Dance Theater Company will perform the 3 Grand Prize-winning poems. In addition, "all prizes include an invitation to read your prize poem at the festival, and a certificate suitable for framing." Submissions must be unpublished or poet must own rights. Submit 2 copies of any number of poems, 40 lines maximum (each), with name, address, phone number on 1 copy only. Foreign language poems must include English translations. Include SASE for winners list. No inquiries or entries by fax or e-mail. Entry form available for SASE. **Entry fee:** $5/poem or $10 for 3 poems. **Deadline:** May 15 annually. Competition receives about 500-800 entries. Winners will be announced by mail; Grand Prize winners will be contacted by phone. Ticket to festival will be given to all winners. Artist Embassy International has been a nonprofit educational arts organization since 1951, "Furthering intercultural understanding and peace through the universal language of the arts."

$ ☐ LYNN DECARO POETRY COMPETITION FOR HIGH SCHOOL STUDENTS

(Specialized: student poets in grades 9-12) Connecticut Poetry Society, P.O. Box 270554, West Hartford CT 06127-0554. E-mail: connpoetry@comcast.net. Website: www.ct-poetry-society.org. **Contact:** Contest Director. The Lynn DeCaro Poetry Competition honors the memory of Lynn DeCaro, a promising young member of Connecticut Poetry Society who died of leukemia in 1986. Offers prizes of $75, $50, and $25; prize poems will be published in Long River Run II. Open to high school students (grades 9-12). Send up to 3 unpublished poems, any form, 40 line limit. Include 2 copies of each poem: one with complete contact information and one with NO contact information. Both copies must be marked: Lynn DeCaro Competition. Include SASE for results only (no poems will be returned). Winning poems must be submitted by disk or e-mail following notification. **Entry fee:** none. **Deadline:** submit December 1-March 15. 2008 judge: Stephen Campiglio.

Ⓝ DELAWARE DIVISION OF THE ARTS

820 N. French St., Wilmington DE 19801. (302)577-8278. Fax: (302)577-6561. Website: www. artsdel.org. **Contact:** Kristin Pleasanton, art & artist services coordinator. Award "to help further careers of emerging and established professional artists." For Delaware residents only. Prize: $10,000 for masters; $5,000 for established professionals; $3,000 for emerging professionals. Judged by out-of-state, nationally recognized professionals in each artistic discipline. No entry fee. Guidelines available after January 1 on Web site. Accepts inquiries by e-mail, phone. Expects to receive 25 fiction entries. **Deadline: August 1**. Open to any writer. Results announced in December. Winners notified by mail. Results available on Web site. "Follow all instructions and choose your best work sample."

$ ☑ DEL SOL PRESS ANNUAL POETRY PRIZE

89 Elm Ridge Rd., Stow MA 01775. E-mail: editor@webdelsol.com. Website: http://webdelsol. com/DelSolPress. Established 2003. **Contact:** Michael Neff, publisher. Offers annual award of a $1,200 honorarium, book publication, and 20 author copies. Submissions may include previously published poems and may be entered in other contests. Submit 50-100 typed ms pages; start each

poem on new page. Type or word-process on standard white paper, 1 side of page only. Paginate consecutively with a table of contents. Bind with a binder clip (no paperclips). Include 2 cover pages: 1 with poet's contact information (phone, e-mail, address), 1 with the ms title only. Poet's name should not appear on the manuscript itself. Attach publications acknowledgments, if any. Include SASP for notification of receipt of ms; no mss will be returned. Guidelines available on Web site. **Entry fee:** $24 (includes copy of winning book if 8x10 SASE with sufficient postage is sent with entry). Make checks payable to Web del Sol. **Deadline:** see Web site for current deadline. Winners will be announced on Web site and at WebdelSol.com. Copies of winning books available from Del Sol Press. Advice: "Send only your best. Our standards are high. Check the poetry we publish on WebdelSol.com."

$ ☑ DIAGRAM/NEW MICHIGAN PRESS CHAPBOOK CONTEST

c/o Ander Monson, Dept of English, PO Box 210067, University of Arizona, Tucson, AZ 85721-0067. E-mail: nmp@thediagram.com. Website: www.newmichiganpress.com/nmp. Established 2000. **Contact:** Ander Monson, editor. The annual DIAGRAM /New Michigan Press Chapbook Contest offers $1,000 plus publication and author's copies, with discount on additional copies. Also publishes 2-4 finalist chapbooks each year. Submit 18-44 pages of poetry, fiction, mixed-genre, or genre-bending work (images okay if b/w). Include SASE. Guidelines available on Web site. **Entry fee:** $15. **Deadline:** April 1.

$ ☐ JAMES DICKEY PRIZE FOR POETRY

Georgia State University, P.O. Box 3999, Atlanta GA 30302-3999. (404)413-5833. Fax: (404)413-5877. Website: www.webdelsol.com/Five_Points. Established 1996. **Contact:** Megan Sexton, editor. The annual James Dickey Prize for Poetry awards $1,000 and publication in Five Points. Submissions must be unpublished. Submit up to 3 typed poems, no more than 50 lines each. Include name and address on cover sheet. Enclose 2 SASEs: 1 to acknowledge receipt of ms, 1 for results. Guidelines available for SASE or on Web site. **Entry fee:** $20 domestic, $30 foreign (includes one-year subscription). Make checks payable to Georgia State University. **Deadline:** December 1. Winner announced in spring.

$ ☑ DREAM HORSE PRESS NATIONAL POETRY CHAPBOOK PRIZE

P.O. Box 2080, Aptos CA 95001-2080. E-mail: dreamhorsepress@yahoo.com. Website: www.dreamhorsepress.com. Established 1999. **Contact:** J.P. Dancing Bear, editor/publisher. The Dream Horse Press National Poetry Chapbook Prize offers an annual cash prize and multiple copies of a handsomely printed chapbook (prize amounts change yearly, check Web site for current information; 2008 prize was $500 and 25 copies). All entries will be considered for publication. Submissions may be previously published in magazines/journals but not in books or chapbooks. Considers simultaneous submissions with notification. "Submit 18-24 double-spaced pages of poetry in a readable font with acknowledgments, bio, e-mail address for results, and entry fee. Poet's name should not appear anywhere on the manuscript." Accepts multiple submissions (with separate fee for each entry). Manuscripts will be recycled after judging. Guidelines available on Web site. **Entry fee:** changes annually; check Web site (2008 fee was $15). Make checks/money orders made payable to Dream Horse Press. **Deadline:** check Web site (2008 deadline was May 31). Recent previous winners include Amy Holman, Cyntha Arrieu-King, and Charles Sweetman. 2008 judge: C.J. Sage.

▦ $ ☑ T.S. ELIOT PRIZE

(Specialized: collections published in the UK & Ireland)The Poetry Book Society, 4th Floor,

2 Tavistock Place, London WC1H 9RA England. (44)(207)833-9247. Fax: (44)(207)833-2990. E-mail: info@poetrybooks.co.uk. Website: www.poetrybooks.co.uk. Established 1993. **Contact:** Chris Holifield, award director. Offers annual award for the best poetry collection published in the UK/Republic of Ireland each year. Prize: $29,500 to winner and $1,960 to shortlisted poets (donated by Mrs. Valerie Eliot). Submissions must be previously published and may be entered in other contests. Book/manuscript must be submitted by publisher and have been published (or scheduled to be published) the year of the contest. Entry form and guidelines available for SASE or by fax or e-mail. **Deadline:** early August. Competition receives 100 entries/year. 2007 winner was Sean O'Brien (The Drowned Book). Recent judges: Andrew Motin (chair), Lavinia Greenlaw, and Tobias Hill. Also runs a Shadowing Scheme for schools. The 2008 winner will be announced in January 2009.

$ ☑ T.S. ELIOT PRIZE FOR POETRY

Truman State University Press, 100 E. Normal, Kirksville MO 63501-4221. (660)785-7336. Fax: (660)785-4480. E-mail: tsup@truman.edu. Website: http://tsup.truman.edu. Press established 1986. **Contact:** Nancy Rediger. Offers annual award of $2,000 and publication. "The manuscript may include individual poems previously published in journals or anthologies, but may not include a significant number of poems from a published chapbook or self-published book." Submit 60-100 pages. Include 2 title pages: 1 with poet's name, address, phone number, and ms title; the other with ms title only. Include SASE for acknowledgment of ms receipt only; mss will not be returned. Guidelines available for SASE or on Web site. **Entry fee:** $25. **Deadline:** October 31. Competition receives more than 500 entries/year. 2008 winner was Victoria Brockmeier (My Maiden Cowboy Names). 2008 judge: Grace Schulman.

$ ☑ EMERGING VOICES

PEN USA, c/o Antioch University, 400 Corporate Pointe, Culver City CA 90230. (310)862-1555, ext. 357. Fax: (310)862-1556. E-mail: ev@penusa.org. Website: www.penusa.org. **Contact:** Adam Somers, executive director. Annual program offering $1,000 stipend and 8-month fellowship to writers in the early stages of their literary careers. Program includes one-on-one sessions with mentors, seminars on topics such as editing or working with agents, courses in the Writers' Program at UCLA Extension, and literary readings. Participants selected according to potential and lack of access to traditional publishing and/or educational opportunities. No age restrictions; selection is not based solely on economic need. Participants need not be published, but "the program is directed toward poets and writers of fiction and creative nonfiction with clear ideas of what they hope to accomplish through their writing. Mentors are chosen from PEN's comprehensive membership of professional writers and beyond. Participants are paired with established writers sharing similar writing interests and often with those of the same ethnic and cultural backgrounds." Program gets underway in January. See Web site for brochure and complete guidelines. **Deadline:** September 5, 2009 (for 2010 cycle). "Materials must arrive in the PEN offices by the submission deadline--no exceptions."

$ ☑ ERSKINE J. POETRY PRIZE

P.O. Box 22161, Baltimore MD 21203. E-mail: sreichert@smartishpace.com. Website: www. smartishpace.com. Established 1999. **Contact:** Stephen Reichert, editor. The annual Erskine J. Poetry Prize offers 1st Prize: $200 and publication of the winning poem in Smartish Pace (see separate listing in Magazines/Journals); 2nd and 3rd Prizes: winning poems will be published in Smartish Pace. Winners also receive additional Internet and advertising exposure. Honorable mention (usually 5 to 12) also published in Smartish Pace. All entries will be considered for publication in Smartish Pace. Submit 3 poems, with poet's name, address, e-mail, telephone number (preferred), and "Erskine J." at the top of each page of poetry submitted. Include bio. Entries may be submitted online or by e-mail (as attachment) or regular mail. Include SASE with postal entries. Guidelines available on Web site. **Entry fee:** $5/3 poems; additional poems may be submitted for $1/poem (limit of 12 poems). Make checks/money orders payable to Smartish Pace. **Deadline:** August 15, 2009. 2008 winners were Chris Hays (1st prize), Andrew Kozma (2nd prize), and Haines Eason (3rd prize). There were 7 Finalists also published in Issue 16 of Smartish Pace. Judge: Stephen Reichert (editor).

▣ $ ☑ FAR HORIZONS AWARD FOR POETRY

The Malahat Review, University of Victoria, P.O. Box 1700, Stn CSC, Victoria BC V8W 2Y2 Canada. (250)721-8524. Fax: (250)472-5051. E-mail: malahat@uvic.ca. Website: www.malahatreview.ca. **Contact:** Awards Coordinator. The biennial Far Horizons Award for Poetry offers $500 CAD, publication in The Malahat Review (see separate listing in Magazines/Journals), and payment at the rate of $40 CAD per printed page upon publication. Open to "emerging poets from Canada, the United States, and elsewhere" who have not yet published a full-length book (48 pages or more). Submissions must be unpublished. No simultaneous submissions. Submit up to 3 poems per entry, each poem not to exceed 60 lines; no restrictions on subject matter or aesthetic approach. Include separate page with poet's name, address, e-mail, and poem title(s); no identifying information on mss pages. No e-mail submissions. Do not include SASE for results; mss will not be returned. Guidelines available on Web site. **Entry fee:** $25 CAD, $30 USD ($35 USD for entries from Mexico and outside North America); includes a one-year subscription to The Malahat Review. **Deadline:** May 1 (postmark) of alternate years (2010, 2012, etc.). 2008 winner: Tadzio Richards. Winner and finalists contacted by e-mail. Winner announced in fall in The Malahat Review, on Web site, and in quarterly e-newsletter, Malahat lite.

$ ☑ THE FIELD POETRY PRIZE

Oberlin College Press, Oberlin College, 50 N. Professor St., Oberlin OH 44074. (440)775-8408. E-mail: oc.press@oberlin.edu (inquiries only). Website: www.oberlin.edu/ocpress. Established 1969. **Contact:** Linda Slocum, managing editor. The annual FIELD Poetry Prize for a book-length collection of poems offers $1,000 and publication in the FIELD Poetry Series. Submit non-returnable ms of 50-80 pages. Guidelines available for SASE or on Web site. **Entry fee:** $22; includes one-year subscription to FIELD (see separate listing in Magazines/Journals). Make checks payable to Oberlin College Press. **Deadline:** submit during May only (postmark). 2008 winner was Dennis Hinrichsen (Kurosawa's Dog).

$ ☑ THE FINISHING LINE PRESS OPEN CHAPBOOK COMPETITION

Finishing Line Press, P.O. Box 1626, Georgetown KY 40324. (859)514-8966. E-mail: FinishingBooks@aol.com. Website: www.finishinglinepress.com. Established 1998. **Contact:** Leah Maines, poetry editor. The Finishing Line Press Open Chapbook Competition offers a $1,000 cash award and publication. All entries will be considered for publication. Open to all poets regardless of past publications. Submit up to 26 pages of poetry. Include bio, acknowledgments, and cover letter. Guidelines available by e-mail or on Web site. **Entry fee:** $15. **Deadline:** July 15 (postmark) for 2010.

$ ☐ FLIP KELLY POETRY PRIZE, THE

6199 Steubenville Road SE, Amsterdam OH 43903.740-543-4333. E-mail: plainspoke@gmail.com. Website: www.plainspoke.net. Established 2007. **Contact:** Cindy Kelly, editor. The Flip Kelly

Poetry Prize offers a $100 honorarium for best chapbook and publication in Gob Pile Chapbook series. Two runners-up receive publication of chapbook in Gob Pile chapbook series. Chapbook submissions may include previously published works, with acknowledgment. Poems may be entered in other contests and/or under consideration elsewhere. Submit cover letter and copy of manuscript with poet's name, address, phone number. Guidelines and entry forms available for SASE, by e-mail, and on Web site. Entry fee: $15. **Deadline: December 31, 2009.** 2009 judge: TBA. Winners will be announced January 15, 2010 (or sooner). Copies of winning chapbooks will be available from www.plainspoke.net for $6. " Amsterdam Press was founded in 2007." **Advice** " We favor the plain-spoken over the esoteric. We like specific, not universal."

$ ☑ FLUME PRESS CHAPBOOK COMPETITION

California State University at Chico, 400 W. First St., Chico CA 95929-0830. (530)898-5983. E-mail: flumepress@csuchico.edu. Website: www.csuchico.edu/engl/flumepress. Established 1984. **Contact:** Casey Huff, poetry editor. Flume Press selects chapbooks for publication through its biennial competition (alternates between poetry and fiction). Winner receives $500 and 25 author's copies. Submission must be unpublished as a collection, but individual poems may have been previously published. Considers simultaneous submissions if poet agrees to withdraw ms from other competitions if chosen as a winner by Flume. Submit 24-30 pages, including title, table of contents, and acknowledgments page. Include cover sheet with poet's name and address; poet's name should not appear on ms pages. Include SASE for return of ms and comments. Guidelines available on Web site. **Entry fee:** $20 (each entrant receives a copy of the winning chapbook). **Deadline:** December 1 (postmark), even numbered years. Chapbooks available for $10 from Flume Press.

$ ☑ THE ROBERT FROST FOUNDATION ANNUAL POETRY AWARD

(Specialized: poems written in the spirit of Robert Frost)The Robert Frost Foundation, Lawrence Library, 51 Lawrence St., Lawrence MA 01841. (978)725-8828. E-mail: frostfoundation@comcast. net. Website: www.frostfoundation.org. Established 1997. Offers annual award of $1,000. Submissions may be entered in other contests. Submit up to 3 poems of not more than 3 pages each (2 copies of each poem, 1 with name, address, and phone number), written in the spirit of Robert Frost. Guidelines available for SASE and on Web site. **Entry fee:** $10/poem. **Deadline:** September 15. Competition receives over 600 entries/year. 2008 winner was Elizabeth Klise von Zerneck. Winners will be announced at the annual Frost Festival and by SASE following the Festival (late October). Winning poem can be viewed on Web site.

$ ☑ KINERETH GENSLER AWARD

(Specialized: New England, NY, NJ residents)Alice James Books, 238 Main St., Farmington ME 04938. Phone/fax: (207)778-7071. E-mail: ajb@umf.maine.ed. Website: www.alicejamesbooks. org. Established 1973. **Contact:** Contest Coordinator. The Kinereth Gensler Award offers $2,000 and publication by Alice James Books (see separate listing in Book/Chapbook Publishers); winners become members of the Alice James Books cooperative, with a 3-year commitment to the editorial board. **Entrants must reside in New England, New York, or New Jersey.** Submissions must be unpublished as a collection, but individual poems may have been previously published elsewhere (in publications of less than 48 pages). Submit 2 copies of ms of 50-70 pages, typed single-spaced and paginated, with table of contents and acknowledgments page; bio is optional. Use binder clips; no staples, folders, or printer-bound copies. Title page of each ms copy must include poet's name, address, and phone number. Enclose SASP for acknowledgment of receipt of ms, #10 SASE for results; mss will not be returned. Guidelines available for SASE or on Web site. **Entry fee:** $25/ms. Make checks/money orders payable to Alice James Books. For a free book (does not apply to books not yet published), include an additional 6x9 envelope with $2 in postage attached; write title of selection on back of envelope. **Deadline:** October 2008. 2007 winners were Idra Novey (The Next Country) and Carey Salerno (Shelter). Judges: members of the Alice James Books Editorial Board. Winners announced in December. Copies of winning books available through Web site.

$ ☑ GERTRUDE PRESS POETRY CHAPBOOK CONTEST

(Specialized: gay, lesbian, bisexual, transgendered, queer-identified & allied) P.O. Box 83948, Portland OR 97283. E-mail: editor@gertrudepress.org (inquiries only). Website: www. gertrudepress.org. Established 1998. **Contact:** Eric Delehoy, founding editor. Gertrude Press (see separate listing in Books/Chapbooks) sponsors an annual chapbook competition. Offers $50, publication, and 50 author copies (out of a press run of 200) to the winning poet. Individual poems may have been previously published; unpublished poems are welcome. Submit 16-20 pages of poetry (postal submissions only). "Poetry may be of any subject matter, and writers from all backgrounds are encouraged to submit." Include list of acknowledgments and cover letter indicating how poet learned of the contest. Guidelines available in Gertrude (see separate listing in Magazines/Journals), for SASE, by e-mail, or on Web site. **Entry fee:** $15; includes copy of the winning chapbook. **Deadline:** submit September 1-January 15 (postmark) annually. 2007 winner was Michael Montlack.

$ ☑ ALLEN GINSBERG POETRY AWARDS

Poetry Center, Passaic County Community College, One College Blvd., Paterson NJ 07505-1179. (973)684-6555. E-mail: mgillan@pccc.edu. Website: www.pccc.edu/poetry. Established 1979. **Contact:** Maria Mazziotti Gillan, editor/executive director. The Allen Ginsberg Poetry Awards offer annual prizes of 1st Prize: $1,000, 2nd Prize: $200, and 3rd Prize: $100. All winning poems, honorable mentions, and editor's choice poems will be published in Paterson Literary Review (see separate listing in Magazines/Journals). Winners will be asked to participate in a reading that will be held in the Paterson Historic District. Submissions must be unpublished. Submit up to 5 poems (no poem more than 2 pages long). Send 4 copies of each poem entered. Include cover sheet with poet's name, address, phone number, and poem titles. Poet's name should not appear on poems. Include SASE for results only; poems will not be returned. Guidelines available for SASE or on Web site. **Entry fee:** $15 (includes subscription to Paterson Literary Review). Write "poetry contest" in memo section of check and make payable to PCCC. **Deadline:** April 1 (postmark). Winners will be announced the following summer by mail and in newspaper announcements. 2007 winners were Kenneth Hart and Glenn Morazzini (1st), R.G. Evans and Linda Radice (2nd), and Patti Conroy (3rd).

☑ $ GOVERNOR GENERAL'S LITERARY AWARDS

(Specialized: Canadian citizens/permanent residents; English- and French-language works) The Canada Council for the Arts, P.O. Box 1047, 350 Albert St., Ottawa ON K1P 5V8 Canada. (613)566-4414, ext. 5573. Fax: (613)566-4410. E-mail: bianca.spence@canadacouncil.ca. Website: www.canadacouncil.ca/prizes/GGLA. Established 1957. **Contact:** Lori Knoll, program assistant. Established by Parliament, the Canada Council for the Arts "provides a wide range of grants and services to professional Canadian artists and art organizations in dance, media arts, music, theater, writing, publishing, and the visual arts." The Governor General's Literary Awards, valued at $25,000 CAD each, are given annually for the best English-language and best French-language work in each of 7 categories, including poetry. Non-winning finalists each receive $1,000 CAD. Books must be first edition trade books written, translated, or illustrated by Canadian citizens or permanent residents of Canada and published in Canada or abroad during the previous year (September 1 through the following September 30). Collections of poetry must be at least 48 pages long, and at least half the book must contain work not published previously in book form. In the case of translation, the original work must also be a Canadian-authored title. Books must be submitted by publishers with a Publisher's Submission Form, which is available on request from the Writing and Publishing Section of the Canada Council for the Arts. Guidelines and current deadlines on the Web site and available by mail, telephone, fax, or e-mail.

$ ☑ GRANDMOTHER EARTH NATIONAL AWARD

Grandmother Earth Creations, P.O. Box 2018, Cordova TN 38088. (901)309-3692 or (901)216-4496 (cell). E-mail: Gmoearth@aol.com. Website: www.grandmotherearth.org. Established 1994. **Contact:** Frances Cowden, award director. Offers annual award of $1,250 with varying distributions each year; $1,250 minimum in awards for poetry and prose; $100 first, etc., plus publication in anthology; non-winning finalists considered for anthology if permission is given. Submissions may be published or unpublished. Considers simultaneous submissions. Submit at least 3 poems, any subject, in any form. Include SASE for winners list. Guidelines available for SASE or on Web site. **Entry fee:** $10 for 3 works, $2 each additional work. Entry fee includes a copy of the anthology. **Deadline:** July 15. 2008 winners were Lynn Veach Sadler, Miriam Doege, Heather Halderman, Timothy Russell, and others. 2008 judge: Daniel Dalquist. Winners will be announced in October at the Mid-South Poetry Festival in Memphis. Copies of winning poems or books available from Grandmother Earth Creations.

$ ☑ GREAT LAKES COLLEGES ASSOCIATION NEW WRITERS AWARD

GLCA, 535 W. William, Ste. 301, Ann Arbor MI 48103. (734)661-2350. Fax: (734)661-2340. E-mail: shackelford@glca.org. Website: www.glca.org. **Contact:** Deanna Shackelford, program coordinator. Director of Program Development: Gregory Wegner. Offers annual award to the best first book of poetry, fiction, and creative non-fiction among those submitted by publishers. The winning authors tour several of the 13 GLCA-member colleges (as invited) reading, lecturing, visiting classes, doing workshops, and publicizing their books. Each writer receives an honorarium of at least $500 from each college visited, as well as travel expenses, hotel accommodations, and hospitality. Tours are schedules during the academic year. Submissions must be previously published. Publishers should submit 4 copies of galleys or the printed book plus a statement of the author's agreement to commit to the college tour. Guidelines available for SASE, by e-mail, or on Web site. **Deadline:** July 25th, 2009 for 2010 award. Additional details will be available on the GLCA Web site. 2008 poetry winner was Lynne Thompson, Beg No Pardon (Perugia Press); fiction winner was Andy Mozina, The Women Were Leaving the Men (Wayne State University Press); creative nonfiction winner was Ander Monson, Neck Deep and Other Predicaments (Graywolf Press). 2009 winners were: Can Waters, Desert Gothic (University of Iowa Press) for fiction; Aracelis Girmay, Teeth (Curbstone Press) for poetry; and Melissa J. Delbridge, Family Bible (University of Iowa Press) for creative nonfiction.

$ ☑ GREG GRUMMER POETRY AWARD

MSN 2D6, George Mason University, 4400 University Dr., Fairfax VA 22030-4444. (703)993-2915. E-mail: phoebe@gmu.edu (inquiries only). Website: http://phoebejournal.com/. Established 1970. **Contact:** Contest Coordinator. The Greg Grummer Poetry Award offers $1,000 and publication in Phoebe: A Journal of Literature and Art (see separate listing in Magazines/

Journals) for winner, possible publication for finalists, and a copy of awards issue to all entrants. Submissions must be unpublished. Submit up to 4 poems (not to exceed 20 pages total), any subject, any form, with name on cover page only. Include SASE for results only; mss will not be returned. Guidelines available for SASE or on Web site. **Entry fee:** $15/entry. Make checks/money orders payable to Phoebe /GMU. **Deadline:** December 1 (postmark). Contest receives 300-400 submissions. Back copy of awards issue available for $6.

$ ☑ GUGGENHEIM FELLOWSHIPS

John Simon Guggenheim Memorial Foundation, Writing Fellowships, 90 Park Ave., New York NY 10016. (212)687-4470. E-mail: fellowships@jsgmf.org. Website: www.gf.org. Established 1925. Guggenheim Fellowships are awarded each year to poets, as well as fiction and creative nonfiction writers, "on the basis of unusually distinguished achievement in the past and exceptional promise for future accomplishment." 2007 Fellowships were awarded to 25 writers; amounts averaged $40,211 each. Submit career summary, statement of intent, and no more than 3 published books. Guidelines, application form (required), and additional information available for SASE, by e-mail, or on Web site. **Deadline:** was September 15 for 2008 awards. **Entry fee:** none. 2007 Fellowship recipients in poetry were Christopher Buckley, Greg Delanty, Erica Funkhouser, A. Van Jordan, Dana Levin, Malena Mörling, D. Nurkse, Kathleen Peirce, and Lawrence Raab.

$ ☑ THE DONALD HALL PRIZE IN POETRY

AWP Award Series in Poetry, The Association of Writers & Writing Programs, Carty House, Mail Stop 1E3, George Mason University, Fairfax VA 22030-4444. E-mail: chronicle@awpwriter.org (inquiries only). Website: www.awpwriter.org. Established 2003. The Association of Writers & Writing Programs (AWP) sponsors an annual competition for the publication of excellent new book-length works, the AWP Award Series, which includes The Donald Hall Prize in Poetry. Offers annual award of $4,000 and publication for the best book-length ms of poetry (book-length defined for poetry as 48 pages minimum of text). Open to published and unpublished poets alike. "Poems previously published in periodicals are eligible for inclusion in submissions, but manuscripts previously published in their entirety, including self-published, are not eligible. As the series is judged anonymously, no list of acknowledgments should accompany your manuscript. You may submit your manuscript to other publishers while it is under consideration by the Award Series, but you must notify AWP immediately in writing if your manuscript is accepted elsewhere. Your manuscript must be submitted in accordance with the eligibility requirements, format guidelines, and entry requirements or it will be disqualified." Complete guidelines, including important formatting information, eligibility requirements, and required entry form available on Web site. **Entry fee:** $10 (AWP members) or $25 (nonmembers). Make checks/money orders payable in U.S. dollars only to AWP. **Deadline:** mss must be postmarked between January 1-February 28. 2008 winner was Beth Bachmann (Temper). 2009 judge: Jean Valentine.

$ ☑ J.C. AND RUTH HALLS, AND DIANE MIDDLEBROOK FELLOWSHIPS IN POETRY

(Specialized: MFA or PhD in creative writing required)Wisconsin Institute for Creative Writing, English Dept., 600 North Park St., Madison WI 53706. Website: http://creativewriting.wisc.edu. Established 1986. **Contact:** Jesse Lee Kercheval, director. Offers annual fellowships, will pay $27,000 for one academic year. Applicants will teach one creative writing class/semester at University of Wisconsin and give a public reading at the end of their stay. Considers simultaneous submissions. Submit 10 poems maximum on any subject, in any form. Applicants must have a MFA or PhD in creative writing. Applicants cannot have published a book (chapbooks will not disqualify an applicant). Guidelines available on website. **Reading fee:** $45. **Deadline:** applications must be received in the month of February. Competitions receive 300 entries/year. Judges: faculty of the creative writing program. Results will be sent to applicants by May 1. "The fellowships are administered by the Program in Creative Writing at the University of Wisconsin-Madison. Funding is provided by the Jay C. and Ruth Halls Writing Fund and the Carl Djerassi and Diane Middlebrook Fund through the University of Wisconsin Foundation."

$ BEATRICE HAWLEY AWARD

Alice James Books, 238 Main St., Farmington ME 04938. Phone/fax: (207)778-7071. E-mail: ajb@umf.maine.ed. Website: www.alicejamesbooks.org. Established 1973. **Contact:** Contest Coordinator. The Beatrice Hawley Award offers $2,000 and publication by Alice James Books (see separate listing in Book/Chapbook Publishers). Winners have no cooperative membership commitment. "In addition to the winning manuscript, one or more additional manuscripts may be chosen for publication." Entrants must reside in the U.S. Submissions must be unpublished as a collection, but individual poems may have been previously published elsewhere (in publications of less than 48 pages). Submit 2 copies of ms of 50-70 pages, typed single-spaced and paginated, with table of contents and acknowledgments page; bio is optional. Use binder clips; no staples, folders, or printer-bound copies. Title page of each ms copy must include poet's name, address, and phone number. Include SASP for acknowledgment of receipt of ms, #10 SASE for results only; mss will not be returned. Guidelines available for SASE or on Web site. **Entry fee:** $25/ ms. Make checks/money orders payable to Alice James Books (write "Beatrice Hawley Award" on memo line). **Deadline:** December 1 (postmark) for 2008. 2007 winner was Lia Purpura (King Baby). Judges: members of the Alice James Books Editorial Board. Winners announced in April. Copies of winning books available through Web site.

$ ☑ JAMES HEARST POETRY PRIZE

North American Review, University of Northern Iowa, 1222 West 27th St., Cedar Falls IA 50614-0516. (319)273-6455. Fax: (319)273-4326. E-mail: nar@uni.edu. Website: http://webdelsol.com/ NorthAmReview/NAR. **Contact:** Vince Gotera, poetry editor. The James Hearst Poetry Prize offers 1st Prize: $1,000; 2nd Prize: $100; and 3rd Prize: $50. All winners and finalists will be published in North American Review (see separate listing in Magazines/Journals). Submissions must be unpublished. No simultaneous submissions. Submit up to 5 poems, 2 copies each; **NO NAMES** on ms pages. Cover sheet is required (MS Word or PDF). Include SASP for acknowledgment of receipt of ms and #10 SASE for results (or provide e-mail address on cover sheet); mss will not be returned. Guidelines available for SASE, by fax, e-mail, or on Web site. **Entry fee:** $18 (includes one-year subscription). Make checks/money orders payable to North American Review. **Deadline:** October 31 (postmark).

▦ $ FELICIA HEMANS PRIZE FOR LYRICAL POETRY

(Specialized: University of Liverpool members & students)The University of Liverpool, Foundation Building, Brownlow Hill, Liverpool L69 72X England. (44)(151)794-2428. E-mail: sarah.okeeffe@liverpool.ac.uk. Established 1899. **Contact:** Faculties Support Office, University of Liverpool. Offers annual award of £30. Open to past or present members and students of the University of Liverpool. Considers simultaneous submissions. Submit 1 poem. Guidelines available for SASE only. **Deadline:** May 1. Competition receives 12-15 entries. Judges are the Professors of English Literature in the University. The winner and all other competitors will be notified by mail in June.

$ ☑ THE HODDER FELLOWSHIP

Princeton University, Lewis Center for the Arts, 185 Nassau St., Princeton NJ 08542. (609)258-4096. Fax: (609)258-2230. E-mail: jbraude@princeton.edu. Website: www.princeton.edu/arts/lewis_center/society_of_fellows/. **Contact:** Janine Braude. "Stipends of $62,000 will be given to writers of exceptional promise to pursue independent projects at Princeton University during the 2010-2011 academic year. Typically the fellows are poets, playwrights, novelists, creative nonfiction writers, and translators who have published 1 highly acclaimed work and are undertaking a significant new project that might not be possible without the 'studious leisure' afforded by the fellowship." Preference is given to applicants outside academia. Candidates for the Ph.D. are not eligible. Submit a résumé, sample of previous work (10 pages maximum, not returnable), a project proposal of 2-3 pages. Guidelines available on Web site. **Deadline:** November 1, 2009 (postmark). Announcement of the Hodder Fellow is posted on the Web site in March.

$ ☑ TOM HOWARD/JOHN H. REID POETRY CONTEST

Tom Howard Books, c/o Winning Writers, 351 Pleasant St., PMB 222, Northampton MA 01060-3961. (866)946-9748. Fax: (413)280-0539. E-mail: johnreid@mail.qango.com. Website: www.winningwriters.com/tompoetry. Established 2003. **Contact:** John H. Reid, award director. Offers annual award of 1st Prize: $2,000; 2nd Prize: $1,000; 3rd Prize: $500; 4th Prize: $250; 5 High Distinction Awards of $200 each; and 6 Most Highly Commended Awards of $100 each. The top 15 entries will be published on the Winning Writers Web site. Submissions may be published or unpublished and may have won prizes elsewhere. Considers simultaneous submissions. Submit poems in any form, style, or genre. "There is no limit on the number of lines or poems you may submit." No name on ms pages; type or computer-print on letter-size white paper, single-sided. Submit online or by regular mail. Guidelines available for SASE or on Web site. **Entry fee:** $7 USD for every 25 lines (exclude poem titles and any blank lines from line count). **Deadline:** December 15-September 30. Competition receives about 1,000 entries/year. 2007 winner was Zoe Krasney("Another Country"). 2007 judges: John H. Reid and Dee C. Konrad. Winners announced in February at WinningWriters.com. Entrants who provide valid e-mail addresses will also receive notification.

$ ☑ THE HUDSON PRIZE

(Formerly the Ontario Prize) Black Lawrence Press, P.O. Box 327, Theresa, NY 13691. E-mail: editors@blacklawrencepress.com. Website: www.blacklawrencepress.com. Established 2003. **Contact:** Colleen Ryor, editor. The Hudson Prize is awarded annually for an unpublished collection of poetry or short stories. Winner receives $1,000, publication by Black Lawrence Press (see separate listing in Book/Chapbook Publishers), 10 author copies, and an interview in The Adirondack Review (see separate listing in Magazines/Journals). Finalists will receive a copy of the winning book. All finalists will be considered for standard publication. Accepts simultaneous submissions, but notify immediately if ms is accepted elsewhere. Submit book-length ms, paginated, with cover letter with brief bio and contact information (including valid e-mail), table of contents, and an acknowledgments page (if applicable). "Finalists will be notified and asked to submit another copy of the manuscript for final judging." Include 2 cover pages: 1 with ms title, brief bio, and poet's contact information (including e-mail); the second with ms title only. Clip together the cover letter, cover pages, acknowledgments, and entry fee. No e-mail submissions. Include SASE or e-mail address for results only; mss will not be returned. Guidelines available on Web site. **Entry fee:** $25. Make checks/money orders payable to Dzanc Books. **Deadline:** March 31 annually. 2008 winner was Abayomi Animashaun (The

Giving of Pears).

$ ☑ THE LYNDA HULL MEMORIAL POETRY PRIZE

Crazyhorse, Dept. of English, College of Charleston, 66 George St., Charleston SC 29424. (843)953-7740. E-mail: crazyhorse@cofc.edu. Website: http://crazyhorse.cofc.edu. Established 1960. **Contact:** Prize Director. The annual Lynda Hull Memorial Poetry Prize offers $2,000 and publication in Crazyhorse (see separate listing in Contests & Awards). All entries will be considered for publication. Submissions must be unpublished. Submit online or by mail up to 3 original poems (no more than 10 pages). Include cover page (placed on top of ms) with poet's name, address, e-mail, and telephone number; no identifying information on mss (blind judging). Accepts multiple submissions with separate fee for each. Include SASP for notification of receipt of ms and SASE for results only; mss will not be returned. Guidelines available for SASE or on Web site. **Entry fee:** $16/ms for new entrants; $14/ms for poets who have entered the Crazyhorse prizes before (indicate on ms cover page). Fee includes a one-year/2 issue subscription to Crazyhorse ; for each poetry ms entered and fee paid, subscription is extended by 1 year. Make checks payable to Crazyhorse ; credit card payments also accepted (see Web site for details). **Deadline:** September 1-December 15 (postmark). Winners announced by April. 2008 winner: Jeff Walker ("Itchy Is As Scratchy Does"). 2008 judge: Billy Collins. 2007 winner: Jude Nutter ("O'Hara in Paradise"). 2007 judge: Marvin Bell.

$ ☐ INKWELL ANNUAL POETRY CONTEST

Inkwell, Manhattanville College, 2900 Purchase St., Purchase NY 10577. (914)323-7239. Fax: (914)323-3122. E-mail: inkwell@mville.edu. Website: www.inkwelljournal.org. Established 1995. **Contact:** Contest Coordinator. The Inkwell Annual Poetry Competition awards $1,000 grand prize and publication in Inkwell (see separate listing in Magazines/Journals) for best poem. Submissions must be unpublished. Submit up to 5 poems at a time, no more than 40 lines/poem, typed in 12 pt. font. Include cover sheet with poet's name, address, phone number, e-mail, and poems titles and line counts. No name or address should appear on mss. Also include Submission Checklist (download from Web site). Indicate "Poetry Competition" on envelope. Include SASE for results only; mss will not be returned. Guidelines available on Web site. **Entry fee:** $10 for first poem, $5 for each additional poem (USD only). Make checks payable to Manhattanville--Inkwell. **Deadline:** August 1-October 30 (postmark). 2008 judge: Major Jackson.

$ ☑ THE IOWA POETRY PRIZES

The University of Iowa Press, 100 Kuhl House, 119 West Park Rd., Iowa City IA 52242-1000. (319)335-2000. E-mail: uipress@uiowa.edu. Website: www.uiowapress.org. The University of Iowa Press offers the annual Iowa Poetry Prizes for book-length mss (50-150 pages) originally in English by new or established poets. Winners will be published by the Press under a standard royalty contract. Poems from previously published books may be included only in mss of selected or collected poems, submissions of which are encouraged. Considers simultaneous submissions if Press is immediately notified if the book is accepted by another publisher. Guidelines available on Web site. **Entry fee:** $20. **Deadline:** postmarked during April only. 2008 winners were Full Catastrophe Living by Zach Savich and something has to happen next by Andrew Michael Roberts.

$ ☑ THE IOWA REVIEW AWARD IN POETRY

308 EPB, University of Iowa, Iowa City IA 52242. (319)335-0462. E-mail: iowa-review@uiowa.

edu. Website: www.iowareview.org. Established 1970. **Contact:** Contest Coordinator. The Iowa Review Award in Poetry, Fiction, and Nonfiction presents $1,000 to each winner in each genre, $500 to runners-up. Winners published in The Iowa Review (see separate listing in Magazines/Journals). Submissions must be unpublished. Considers simultaneous submissions (with notification of acceptance elsewhere). Submit up to 10 pages of poetry, double- or single-spaced; one poem or several. Include cover page with poet's name, address, e-mail and/or phone number, and title of each work submitted. Personal identification must not appear on ms pages. Label mailing envelope "Contest: Poetry." Include SASP for confirmation of receipt of entry, SASE for results. Guidelines available on website. **Entry Fee:** $20 for entry and yearlong subscription. Make checks payable to The Iowa Review. **Deadline:** submit January 1-31 (postmark). 2008 winners were Dave Snyder (1st Prize) and Mary Austin Speaker (runners-up). 2009 judge: Li-Young Lee.

$ JOSEPH HENRY JACKSON AWARD

(Specialized: northern CA or NV residents ages 20-35)c/o Intersection for the Arts, 446 Valencia St., San Francisco CA 94103. (415)626-2787. Fax: (415)626-1636. Website: www.theintersection. org. Established 1955. **Contact:** Awards Coordinator. The Joseph Henry Jackson Award offers $2,000 to the author of an unpublished work-in-progress of fiction (novel or short stories), nonfictional prose, or poetry. Applicants must be residents of northern California or Nevada for 3 consecutive years immediately prior to the March 31 deadline and must be between the ages of 20 and 35 as of the deadline. Guidelines and entry form (required) available on Web site. **Entry fee:** none. **Deadline:** March 31. Competition receives 150-180 entries. 2008 winner was Kelly Luce (fiction, "Ms. Yamada's Toaster").

$ ☑ JAPANESE LITERARY TRANSLATION PRIZE

(Specialized: Japanese into English)Donald Keene Center of Japanese Culture, Columbia University, 507 Kent Hall, New York NY 10027. (212)854-5036. Fax: (212)854-4019. E-mail: donald-keene-center@columbia.edu. Website: www.donaldkeenecenter.org. **Contact:** Miho Walsh, associate director. Established 1981. The Donald Keene Center of Japanese Culture at Columbia University annually awards $6,000 for the Japan-U.S. Friendship Commission Prize for the Translation of Japanese Literature. A prize is given for the best translation of a modern work of literature or for the best classical literary translation, or the prize is divided between a classical and a modern work. Submissions may be previously published. Considers simultaneous submissions. Translated works submitted for consideration may include: a) unpublished mss; b) works in press; c) translations published after January 1, 2007. Submit 7 hard copies of book-length ms or published book. Entry form and guidelines available for SASE, by fax, e-mail, or on Web site. **Deadline:** March 1, 2009. Competition receives 20-25 entries/year. 2007 award winners were Anthony H. Chambers for his translation of Tales of Moonlight and Rain by Akinari Ueda, and Kozue Uzawa and Amelia Fielden for their translation of tanka poems in Ferris Wheel: 101 Modern and Contemporary Tanka.Winners are announced through press releases and on Web site.

$ ☐ JOHN WOOD COMMUNITY COLLEGE CREATIVE WRITING CONTEST

Business Office/Writing Contest, John Wood Community College, 1301 S. 48th St., Quincy IL 62305. (217)641-4940. Fax: (217)641-4900. E-mail: klangston@jwcc.edu. Website: www. jwcc.edu. Established 1990. **Contact:** Kelli Langston, contest coordinator, or Janet McGovern ((217)641-4905; jmcgovern@jwcc.edu). Offers annual award for original, unpublished poetry, fiction, and nonfiction. Categories include non-rhyming poetry, traditional rhyming poetry, plus a category for all other poetry forms (i.e., haiku, limerick, etc.). 1st, 2nd, and 3rd Prizes awarded in each category, plus Honorable Mention certificates. Cash prizes based on dollar total of entry fees. Guidelines available for SASE, by fax, e-mail, or on Web site. **Entry fee:** $5/poem; $7/ nonfiction or fiction piece. **Deadline:** entries accepted January 2-April 3. Competition receives 50-100 entries. "We are offering a new critiquing service of works submitted to the contest. **If you wish a written critique, you must include an additional $5 per poem and/or $15 per story (include up to 3 pages).** Critiques will be sent as soon as possible after judging."

$ ☑ JUNIPER PRIZE FOR POETRY

University of Massachusetts Press, Amherst MA 01003. (413)545-2217. Fax: (413)545-1226. E-mail: info@umpress.umass.edu. Website: www.umass.edu/umpress. Established 1964. **Contact:** Carla Potts. The University of Massachusetts Press offers the annual Juniper Prize for Poetry, awarded in alternate years for first and subsequent books. Prize includes publication and $1,500 in addition to royalties. In even-numbered years (2008, 2010, etc.), only "subsequent" books will be considered: mss whose authors have had at least 1 full-length book or chapbook (of at least 30 pages) of poetry published or accepted for publication. Self-published work is not considered to lie within this "books and chapbooks" category. In odd-numbered years (2009, 2011, etc.), only "first books" will be considered: mss by writers whose poems may have appeared in literary journals and/or anthologies but have not been published or accepted for publication in book form. Considers simultaneous submissions, "but if accepted for publication elsewhere, please notify us immediately. A separate check is required for each submission. Manuscripts by more than 1 author, entries of more than 1 manuscript simultaneously or within the same year, and translations are not eligible." Submit paginated ms of 50-70 pages of poetry, with paginated contents page, credits page, and information about previously published books. Include 2 cover sheets: 1 with contact information, one without. Manuscripts will not be returned. Guidelines available for SASE or on Web site. **Entry fee:** $20. **Deadline:** submit August 1-September 29 (postmark). 2008 winner was L.S. Klatt (Interloper). Winners announced online in April on the press Web site.

$ ☑ HAROLD MORTON LANDON TRANSLATION AWARD

(Specialized: any language into English)The Academy of American Poets, 584 Broadway, Suite 604, New York NY 10012-3210. (212)274-0343. Fax: (212)274-9427. E-mail: awards@poets.org. Website: www.poets.org. Established 1934. **Contact:** awards coordinator. Offers one $1,000 award each year to recognize a published translation of poetry from any language into English. Guidelines available for SASE or on Web site. **Deadline:** December 31 (postmark) of year in which book was published.

$ ☑ THE JAMES LAUGHLIN AWARD

The Academy of American Poets, 584 Broadway, Suite 604, New York NY 10012. (212)274-0343. Fax: (212)274-9427. E-mail: awards@poets.org. Website: www.poets.org. Offered since 1954. **Contact:** awards coordinator. Offers $5,000 prize to recognize and support a poet's second book (ms must be under contract to a publisher). Submissions must be made by a publisher in ms form. The Academy of American Poets purchases copies of the Laughlin Award-winning book for distribution to its members. Poets must be U.S. citizens. Entry form, signed by the publisher, required. Entry form and guidelines available for SASE (in January) or on Web site. **Deadline:** submissions accepted between January 1 and May 15. Winners announced in August.

$ ☑ THE LAUREATE PRIZE FOR POETRY

The National Poetry Review, P.O. Box 2080, Aptos CA 95001-2080. E-mail: editor@ natonalpoetryreview.com. Website: www.nationalpoetryreview.com. **Contact:** C.J. Sage, editor. The Laureate Prize for Poetry, an annual award of $300 and publication in The National Poetry Review (see separate listing in Magazines Journals), "will honor 1 new poem that TNPR believes has the greatest chance of standing the test of time and becoming part of the literary canon." Submissions must be unpublished and uncommitted (not promised for first publication elsewhere). Considers simultaneous submissions, "but if the work is selected by TNPR for the prize or for publication, it must be withdrawn from elsewhere unless you have withdrawn it from us 2 weeks before our acceptance." Submit up to 3 poems (10 page maximum per group of 3). Include a brief bio, contact information, and poet's e-mail address for results. Guidelines available on Web site. **Entry fee:** $15/entry; accepts multiple submissions with separate entry fee for each 3-poem group. "If you include a small book-sized SASE with $1.60 postage with your entry, we will provide you a copy of the winner's issue." Make checks payable to The National Poetry Review. **Deadline:** December 31 (postmark).

$ ☐ THE LEAGUE OF MINNESOTA POETS CONTEST

Website: www.mnpoets.org (see Web site for current contact information). **Contact:** Christina Flaugher, contest chair. Annual contest offers 18 different categories, with 3 prizes in each category ranging from $10-125. See guidelines for poem lengths, forms, and subjects. Guidelines available for #10 SASE, by e-mail, or on Web site. **Entry fee:** (nonmembers) $1/poem per category; $2/poem (limit 6) for Grand Prize category; (members) $5 for 17 categories; $1/poem (limit 6) for Grand Prize category. Make checks payable to LOMP Contest. **Deadline:** July 31. Nationally known, non-Minnesota judges. Winners will be announced at the October LOMP Conference and by mail. Additional information regarding LOMP membership available on Web site.

$ ☑ THE LEDGE POETRY AWARDS COMPETITION

40 Maple Ave., Bellport NY 11713. Website: www.theledgemagazine.com. **Contact:** Contest Director. Offers annual awards of 1st Prize: $1,000; 2nd Prize: $250; 3rd Prize: $100; and all 3 winners will be published in The Ledge (see separate listing in Magazines/Journals). All entries will be considered for publication. Submissions must be unpublished. Considers simultaneous submissions. "No restrictions on form or content. Excellence is the only criterion." Submit 3 poems. Include SASE for results or return of ms. Guidelines available on Web site. **Entry fee:** $10 for the first 3 poems, $3 for each additional poem; $20 subscription to The Ledge gains free entry for the first 3 poems. **Deadline:** April 30 (postmark). Winners announced in September.

$ ☑ THE LEDGE POETRY CHAPBOOK CONTEST

The Ledge Press, 40 Maple Ave., Bellport NY 11713. Website: www.theledgemagazine.com. **Contact:** Contest Director. The Ledge Poetry Chapbook Contest offers an annual prize of $1,000, publication by The Ledge Press, and 25 chapbook copies. Considers simultaneous submissions. Accepts multiple submissions with separate entry fee for each. " No restrictions on form or content. Excellence is the only criterion." Submit 16-28 pages of poetry with bio and acknowledgements, if any. Include title page with poet's name, address, phone number, and e-mail address (if applicable). Include SASE for results or return of ms. Guidelines available on Web site. **Entry fee:** $18; all entrants will receive a copy of the winning chapbook upon publication. **Deadline:** October 31. Sample chapbooks available for $8 postpaid. Winner announced in March.

$ ☑ THE LEVIS POETRY PRIZE

Four Way Books, Box 535, Village Station, New York NY 10014. (212)334-5430. Fax: (212)334-5435. E-mail: editors@fourwaybooks.com. Website: www.fourwaybooks.com. Established 1993. **Contact:** Martha Rhodes, director. The Levis Poetry Prize, offered biennially in odd-numbered years, offers publication by Four Way Books (see separate listing in Book/Chapbook Publishers), honorarium ($1,000), and a reading at one or more participating series. Open to any poet writing in English. Entry form and guidelines available on website. **Entry fee:** $25. **Deadline:** March 31 (postmark). Winner announced by mail and on website. Copies of winning books available through Four Way Books online and at bookstores (to the trade through University Press of New England).

▣ $ ☑ LITERAL LATTE FOOD VERSE AWARDS

200 East 10th St., Suite 240, New York NY 10003. Website: www.literal-latte.com. **Contact:** Contest Director. The annual Literary Latté Food for Verse Awards offers 1st Prize: $500 for best poem with food as an ingredient. All entries considered for publication in Literal Latte (see separate listing in Magazines/Journals). Submissions must be unpublished. Include cover page with poet's name, address, phone number, and poem titles/first lines; no identifying information on mss pages. Include SASE or e-mail for results. Guidelines available for SASE, by e-mail, or on website. **Entry fee:** $10 for up to 6 poems, $15 for 12 poems. Make checks/money orders payable to Literal Latté. **Deadline:** January 15 (postmark).

▣ $ ☑ LITERAL LATTE POETRY AWARDS

200 East 10th St., Suite 240, New York NY 10003. Website: www.literal-latte.com. **Contact:** Contest Director. The annual Literal Latté Poetry Awards offer 1st Prize: $1,000; 2nd Prize: $300; 3rd Prize: $200. All entries considered for publication in Literal Latté (see separate listing in Magazines/Journals). Submissions must be unpublished. All styles welcome, 2,000 words maximum. Include cover page with poet's name, address, and telephone number; no identifying information on ms pages. Include SASE or e-mail for results. Guidelines available for SASE, by e-mail, or on Web site. **Entry fee:** $10 for up to 6 poems, $15 for 12 poems. Make checks/money orders payable to Literal Latté. **Deadline:** July 15 (postmark).

$ ☑ FRANCES LOCKE MEMORIAL POETRY AWARD

The Bitter Oleander Press, 4983 Tall Oaks Dr., Fayetteville NY 13066-9776. (315)637-3047. Fax: (315)637-5056. E-mail: info@bitteroleander.com. Website: www.bitteroleander.com. Established 1974. **Contact:** Paul B Roth. The Frances Locke Memorial Poetry Award offers $1,000, publication in The Bitter Oleander (see separate listing in Magazines/Journals), and 5 contributor's copies. Submit up to 5 poems, each no more than 2 pages in length, legibly typed or computer generated. Include poet's name, address, and phone number or e-mail on each poem. Include a short biography with submission. No e-mail submissions. Include SASE for results only; mss will not be returned. Guidelines available on Web site. **Entry fee:** $10 for up to 5 poems, $2 each additional poem. **Deadline:** June 15 (postmark). 2008 winner: Samantha Stiers.

▣ $ ☑ LONG POEM PRIZE

(Specialized: long poem or poem cycle)The Malahat Review, University of Victoria, P.O. Box 1700, Stn CSC, Victoria BC V8W 2Y2 Canada. (250)721-8524. Fax: (250)472-5051. E-mail: malahat@uvic.ca. Website: www.malahatreview.ca. **Contact:** Awards Coordinator. The biennial Long Poem Prize offers 2 awards of $500 CAD each for a long poem or cycle (10-20 printed pages). Includes publication in The Malahat Review (see separate listing in Magazines/Journals) and payment at $40 CAD per printed page upon publication. Open to "entries from Canadian, American, and overseas authors." Submissions must be unpublished. No simultaneous submissions. Submit a single poem or cycle of poems, 10-20 published pages (a published page equals 32 lines or less, including breaks between stanzas); no restrictions on subject matter or aesthetic approach. Include separate page with poet's name, address, e-mail, and title; no identifying information on mss pages. No e-mail submissions. Do not include SASE for results; mss will not be returned. Guidelines available on Web site. **Entry fee:** $35 CAD, $40 USD ($45 USD for entries from Mexico and outside North America); includes one-year subscription to The Malahat Review. **Deadline:** February 1 (postmark) of alternate years (2009, 2011, etc.). 2007 winners: Aurian Haller, Harold Rhenisch. 2007 Judges: Margo Button, Brian Bartlett, and John Pass. Winners and finalists notified by e-mail. Winners announced in summer in The Malahat Review, on Web site, and in quarterly e-newsletter, Malahat lite.

$ ☑ NAOMI LONG MADGETT POETRY AWARD

(Specialized: African American)Lotus Press, P.O. Box 21607, Detroit MI 48221. (313)861-1280. Fax: (313)861-4740. E-mail: lotuspress@aol.com. Website: www.lotuspress.org. Established 1972. **Contact:** Constance Withers. Offers annual award of $500 and publication by Lotus Press, Inc. for a book-length ms by an African American poet. "Individual poems may be previously published, but poems published in a collection of your own work, self-published or not, will not be considered. Please do not submit a manuscript which you have submitted, or which you plan to submit during the period of consideration, to another publisher. However, you may enter another competition as long as you notify us that you have done or plan to do so. If you are notified that your manuscript has won another award or prize, you must inform us of this immediately. If you have already had a book published by Lotus Press, you are ineligible. However, inclusion in a Lotus Press anthology does not disqualify you." Submit 2 complete copies of approximately 60-90 page ms, exclusive of table of contents or other optional introductory material. **See guidelines for special formatting instructions.** Enclose stamped, self-addressed postcard to confirm receipt of material; no SASE as mss will not be returned. Mail by First Class Priority; no Certified, Federal Express, or other mail requiring a signature. **Deadline:** entries must be received between January 2 and March 31. Guidelines available for SASE, by e-mail, or on Web site. Winner and judges announced no later than June 1. Copies of winning books available for sale from Lotus Press at the address above. Advice: "Read some of the books we have published, especially award winners. Read a lot of good contemporary poetry. Those who have worked over a period of years at developing their craft will have the best chance for consideration. The work of novices is not likely to be selected."

$ ☑ MAIN STREET RAG'S ANNUAL CHAPBOOK CONTEST

P.O. Box 690100, Charlotte NC 28227-7001. (704)573-2516. E-mail: editor@mainstreetrag.com. web site: www.MainStreetRag.com. Established 1996. **Contact:** M. Scott Douglass, editor/publisher. Annual chapbook contest by Main Street Rag (see separate listing in Magazines/Journals) offers 1st Prize: $500 and 50 copies of chapbook. "As many as 19 runners-up have been published in previous contests, and every manuscript entered is considered for publication." All entrants receive a copy of the winning chapbook. Submit 24-32 pages of poetry, no more than 1 poem/page. Guidelines available for SASE, by e-mail, or on Web site. **Entry fee:** $15. **Deadline:** May 31. 2008 winner was Kim Triedman (bathe in it or sleep).

$ ☑ MAIN STREET RAG'S ANNUAL POETRY BOOK AWARD

P.O. Box 690100, Charlotte NC 28227-7001. (704)573-2516. E-mail: editor@mainstreetrag.com.

Website: www.MainStreetRag.com. Established 1996. **Contact:** M. Scott Douglass, editor/publisher. Main Street Rag' s Annual Poetry Book Award offers 1st Prize: $1,000 and 50 copies of book; runners-up may also be offered publication. Submit 48-84 pages of poetry, no more than 1 poem/page (individual poems may be longer than 1 page). Guidelines available for SASE, by e-mail, or on Web site. **Entry fee:** $20 (or $25 to include a copy of the winning book). **Deadline:** January 31. 2008 winner was Roy Seeger (The Boy Whose Hands Were Birds).

$ ☑ MANY MOUNTAINS MOVING POETRY BOOK CONTEST

Many Mountains Moving Press,1705 Lombard St., Philadelphia PA 19146. E-mail: editors@mmminc.org. Website: http://mmminc.org. The Many Mountains Moving Poetry Book Contest offers $1000 and publication of a book-length poetry ms by Many Mountains Moving Press. Open to all poets writing in English. More than half of ms may not have been published as a collection, but individual poems and chapbook-length sections may have been previously published if publisher gives permission to reprint. Accepts email submissions (as an attachment, without any identification in the mss. itself). Considers simultaneous submissions "if the poet agrees to notify MMM Press of acceptance elsewhere." Submit 50-100 typed pages of poetry, single- or double-spaced. Include cover letter with ms title, brief bio, poet's name, address, phone number, and e-mail address(es). Poet's name must not appear anywhere on ms. Acknowledgments may be sent but are not required. Include SASE for results only; no mss will be returned. Guidelines available on Web site. **Entry fee:** $25; entitles entrant to discount on a subscription and discounts on any selected Many Mountains Moving Press books (use order form, available on Web site). Make checks/money orders payable to Many Mountains Moving Press. **Deadline:** August 1 (postmark). 2009 judge TBA.

$ ☑ THE MORTON MARR POETRY PRIZE

(Specialized: traditional poetry forms)Southern Methodist University, P.O. Box 750374, Dallas TX 75275-0374. (214)768-1037. Fax: (214)768-1408. E-mail: swr@smu.edu. Website: www.smu.edu/southwestreview. Established 1915. **Contact:** Prize Coordinator. The annual Morton Marr Poetry Prize awards 1st Prize: $1,000 and 2nd Prize: $500 to a poet who has not yet published a first book of poetry. Winners will be published in Southwest Review (see separate listing in Magazines/Journals). Submit 6 poems in a "traditional" form (e.g., sonnet, sestina, villanelle, rhymed stanzas, blank verse, et al). Include cover letter with poet's name, address, and other relevant information; no identifying information on entry pages. Manuscripts will not be returned. Guidelines available on Web site. **Entry fee:** $5/poem. **Deadline:** September 30 (postmark). 2007 winners: Gretchen Steele Pratt (1st Place), Bradford Gray Telford (2nd Place), Elizabeth Rosen (HM), and Chloë Joan López (HM).

$ ☑ THE LENORE MARSHALL POETRY PRIZE

The Academy of American Poets, 584 Broadway, Suite 604, New York NY 10012. (212)274-0343. Fax: (212)274-9427. E-mail: awards@poets.org. Website: www.poets.org. Established 1975. **Contact:** awards coordinator. Offers $25,000 for the most outstanding book of poems published in the U.S. in the previous year. Contest is open to books by living American poets published in a standard edition (40 pages or more in length with 500 or more copies printed). Self-published books are not eligible. Publishers may enter as many books as they wish (books must be submitted in the year after their publication). Four copies of each book must be submitted and none will be returned. Guidelines, required entry form available for SASE or on website. **Entry fee:** $25/title. **Deadline:** entries must be submitted between April 1 and June 15.

$ ☑ MARSH HAWK PRESS POETRY PRIZE

P.O. Box 206, East Rockaway NY 11518-0206. E-mail: marshhawkpress1@aol.com. Website: www. MarshHawkPress.org. Established 2001. **Contact:** Prize Director. The Marsh Hawk Press Poetry Prize offers $1,000 plus publication of a book-length ms. Submissions must be unpublished as a collection, but individual poems may have been previously published elsewhere. Submit 48-70 pages of original poetry in any style in English, typed single-spaced, and paginated. Contest manuscripts may be submitted by electronic upload. See Web site for more information. If submitting via Post Office mail, the manuscript must be bound with a spring clip. Include 2 title pages: 1 with ms title, poet's name, and contact information only; 1 with ms title only (poet's name must not appear anywhere in the ms). Also include table of contents and acknowledgments page. Include SASE for results only; manuscript will not be returned. Guidelines available on Web site. **Entry fee:** $20. Make check/money order payable to Marsh Hawk Press. **Deadline:** April 30, 2009. 2008 winner was Michael Rerick (In Ways Impossible to Fold). 2009 Judge: Forrest Gander.

▦ $ ☐ MELBOURNE POETS UNION NATIONAL POETRY COMPETITION

Melbourne Poets Union, P.O. Box 266, Flinders Lane VIC 8009 Australia. E-mail: shann3056@ optusnet.com.au. Website: http://home.vicnet.net.au/~mpuinc/MPU/home.htm/. Established 1977. **Contact:** Leon Shann. Offers annual prizes of $1,500 AUD plus book vouchers, book prizes. Submissions must be unpublished. Submit unlimited number of poems on any subject, in any form, up to 50 lines. "Open to Australian residents living in Australia or overseas." Entry form and guidelines available for SASE (or SAE and IRC). **Entry fee:** $6 AUD/poem; $15 AUD/3 poems. Under 18s (3) Aus 50c postage stamps or equivalent. **Deadline:** October 31. Competition receives over 500 entries/year. Winners announced on the last Friday of November by newsletter, mail, phone, and on Web site. "The $1,500 prize money comes directly from entry money, the rest going to paying the judge and costs of running the competition."

$ ☑ MIDNIGHT SUN POETRY CHAPBOOK CONTEST

(formerly Susan Blalock Poetry Chapbook Contest) Permafrost, Chapbook Division, c/o English Dept., University of Alaska Fairbanks, P.O. Box 755720, Fairbanks AK 99775. E-mail: fbpfrost@ uaf.edu. Website: www.uaf.edu/english/permafrost. Established 1977. **Contact:** Poetry Editor. The Midnight Sun Poetry Chapbook Contest offers $100, publication, and 30 author's copies. Submit a ms of no more than 36 pages. Include SASE. Guidelines available on Web site. **Entry fee:** $10, includes a one-issue subscription to Permafrost (see separate listing in Magazines/ Journals). **Deadline:** March 31.

$ ☐ MILFORD FINE ARTS COUNCIL NATIONAL POETRY CONTEST

Milford Fine Arts Council, 40 Railroad Ave., South, Milford CT 06460. Website: www.milfordarts. org. Established 1976. **Contact:** Tom Bouton, Writer's Group chairperson. Offers annual award of 1st Prize: $100; 2nd Prize: $50; 3rd Prize: $25; plus winners will be published in Milford Fine Arts Council's annual publication, High Tide. Submissions must be unpublished. No simultaneous submissions. Poems entered may not have won any other prizes or honorable mentions. Poets must be 18 years and older. "Poems must be typed single-spaced on white standard paper, 10-30 lines (including title), no more than 48 characters/line, on any subject, in any style, rhymed or unrhymed. Use standard font, clear and legible, 1 poem/page, no script or fax. NO foul language. No bio or date, only the words 'Unpublished Original' typed above the poem." Include poet's name, address, ZIP code, and phone number or e-mail address in the middle back of the submitted poem, no identifying information on the front of the page. Poems will be judged on form, clarity, originality, and universal appeal. "Entries may be considered for publication in High Tide. If you do not want your poems considered for publication, then you must print on the back of the poem (below your name, address, and ZIP code) 'For National Poetry Contest Only.'" Include SASE for results only, with NOTIFICATION printed on bottom left corner of envelope; no poems will be returned. Guidelines available for SASE or on Web site. **Entry fee:** $3 for one poem, $6 for 3 poems, $2 for each additional poem after 3. Contestants may enter an unlimited number of poems (will be judged individually, not as a group). Check or money order accepted, no cash. **Deadline:** February 26, 2010.

$ ☑ MISSISSIPPI REVIEW PRIZE

118 College Dr. #5144, Hattiesburg MS 39406-0001. (601)266-4321. Fax: (601)266-5757. E-mail: rief@mississippireview.com. Website: www.mississippireview.com. The Mississippi Review Prize offers an annual award of $1,000 each in poetry and fiction. Winners and finalists comprise one issue of Mississippi Review. Submissions must be unpublished. Submit up to 3 poems/entry (totaling 10 pages or less). No limit on number of entries. Put "MR Prize" plus poet's name, address, phone number, e-mail address, and title(s) on page 1 of entry. Manuscripts will not be returned. **Entry fee:** $15/entry. Make checks payable to Mississippi Review. Each entrant receives a copy of the prize issue. **Deadline:** submit April 1-October 1 (postmark). Winners announced in January.

$ ☑ MONEY FOR WOMEN

(Specialized: women's concerns, feminism)Barbara Deming Memorial Fund, Inc., P.O. Box 309, Wilton NH 03085-0309. **Contact:** Susan Pliner, executive director. Offers biannual small grants of up to $1,500 to feminists in the arts "whose work addresses women's concerns and/or speaks for peace and justice from a feminist perspective." Submissions may be previously published and entered in other contests. Application form available for SASE. Entrants must use application form with correct deadline date. Applicants must be citizens of U.S. or Canada. **Application fee:** $20. **Deadline:** June 30. Receives 400 applications/year. 2008 grantees in poetry were Latash N. Nevada Diggs, Pilar Gómez Ibañez, Catherine Jagoe, and Crystal A. Williams. Winners announced in November.

$ ☑ JENNY MCKEAN MOORE WRITER IN WASHINGTON

Dept. of English, George Washington University, Washington DC 20052. (202)994-6515. Fax: (202)994-7915. E-mail: dmca@gwu.edu. Website: www.gwu.edu/~english. Offers fellowship for a visiting lecturer in creative writing, currently about $55,000 for 2 semesters. Stipend varies slightly from year to year, depending on endowment payout. Teaching duties involve 2 workshops per semester--one for undergraduate students, the other free to the community. Apply with résumé and writing sample of 25 pages or less. Books may be submitted but will not be returned without SASE. Awarded to writers in different genres each year, typically alternating between poets and fiction writers. Check Web site for specific genre each year. **Deadline:** November 15.

$ ☑ SAMUEL FRENCH MORSE POETRY PRIZE

Dept. of English, 406 Holmes, Northeastern University, Boston MA 02115. (617)373-4546. Fax: (617)373-2509. E-mail: g.rotella@neu.edu. Website: www.english.neu.edu. **Contact:** Prof. Guy Rotella, editor. Offers annual prize of book publication (ms 50-70 pages) by NU/UPNE and $1,000. Open to U.S. poets who have published no more than 1 book of poetry. Entry must be unpublished in book form but may include poems previously published elsewhere. Manuscripts will not be returned. Guidelines available on Web site (under "Publications"). **Entry fee:** $20.

Deadline: August 1 for inquiries; September 15 for single copy of ms. Competition receives approximately 400 entries/year. Recent winners include Jennifer Atkinson, Ted Genoways, and Dana Roeser. Previous judges: Marilyn Hacker, Rosanna Warren, Robert Cording, and Ellen Bryant Voigt.

$ ☑ THE KATHRYN A. MORTON PRIZE IN POETRY

Sarabande Books, Inc., P.O. Box 4456, Louisville KY 40205. E-mail: info@sarabandebooks.org. Website: www.SarabandeBooks.org. Established 1994. **Contact:** Sarah Gorham, editor-in-chief. Member: CLMP. The Kathryn A. Morton Prize in Poetry is awarded annually to a book-length ms (at least 48 pages). Winner receives $2,000, publication, and a standard royalty contract. All finalists are considered for publication. Entry form and SASE are required. Guidelines available for SASE, by e-mail, or on Web site. **Entry fee:** $25. **Deadline:** submit January 1-February 15 (postmark) only. Competition receives approximately 1,400 entries. 2008 winner was Karyna McGlynn for her manuscript I Have to Go Back to 1994 and Kill a Girl. 2009 will be judged by Dan Chiasson. "To avoid conflict of interest, students in a degree-granting program or close friends of a judge are ineligible to enter the contest in the genre for which their friend or teacher is serving as judge. Sarabande, as a member of CLMP, complies with its Contest Code of Ethics."

$ ☑ NATIONAL BOOK AWARD

The National Book Foundation, 95 Madison Ave., Suite 709, New York NY 10016. (212)685-0261. E-mail: nationalbook@nationalbook.org. Website: www.nationalbook.org. Presents $10,000 in each of 4 categories (fiction, nonfiction, poetry, and young people's literature), plus 16 short-list prizes of $1,000 each to Finalists. Submissions must be previously published and **must be entered by the publisher**. General guidelines available on Web site; interested publishers should phone or e-mail the Foundation. **Entry fee:** $125/title. **Deadline:** see Web site for current year's deadline. 2008 poetry winner was Mark Doty.

$ ☑ THE NATIONAL POET HUNT CONTEST

Schoolcraft College, 18600 Haggerty Rd., Livonia MI 48152-2696. (734)462-4400, ext. 5327. Fax: (734)462-4679. E-mail: macguffin@schoolcraft.edu. Website: www.schoolcraft.edu/macguffin. Established 1996. **Contact:** Carol Was, poetry editor. The National Poet Hunt Contest offers 1st Prize: $500 and publication in a future issue of The MacGuffin ; may also award 2 Honorable Mentions and publication. Open to all writers. Submissions must be unpublished and may be entered in other contests. Submit 5 typed poems on any subject, in any form. Put name and address on separate 3x5 index card only. Include SASE for winners' list only; entries will not be returned. Guidelines available for SASE, by fax, e-mail, or on Web site. **Entry fee:** $15/entry (5 poems). Make checks payable to Schoolcraft College. **Deadline:** check Web site for current deadline. 2008 judge: Vivian Shipley.

🌐 $ ☑ NATIONAL POETRY COMPETITION

Poetry Society, 22 Betterton Street, London WC2H 9BX United Kingdom. E-mail: info@poetrysociety.org.uk. Website: www.poetrysociety.org.uk. Established 1978. **Contact:** Competition Organiser. The National Poetry Competition offers 1st Prize: £5,000; 2nd Prize: £1,000; 3rd Prize: £500; plus 10 commendations of £50 each. Winners will be published in Poetry Review (see separate listing in Magazines/Journals), and on the Poetry Society Web site and will receive a year's free membership in the Poetry Society (see separate listing in Organizations). Open to anyone aged 17 or over. Entries "received from all around the world.

All entries are judged anonymously and past winners include both published and previously unknown poets." Submissions must be unpublished (poems posted on Web sites are considered published). Submit original poems in English, on any subject, no more than 40 lines/poem, typed on 1 side only of A4 paper, double- or single-spaced. Each poem must be titled. No identifying information on poems. Do not staple ms pages. Accepts online submissions; full details available on the National Poetry Competition pages on the Poetry Society Web site. Entry form (required) available for A5 SAE (1 entry form covers multiple entries, may be photocopied). Include SAE or SAP for notification of receipt of postal entries (confirmation of online entries will be e-mailed at time of submission); mss will not be returned. Guidelines available on Web site. **Entry fee:** £5 for first poem, £3 for each subsequent entry (Poetry Society members can enter a second poem free of charge). "Only sterling (checks, postal orders, money orders, or credit cards) will be accepted. All other payments will be returned. Checks must be drawn from UK banks." Make checks payable to the Poetry Society. **Deadline:** October 31.

$ ☑ THE NATIONAL POETRY REVIEW BOOK PRIZE

E-mail: nationalpoetryreview@yahoo.com. Website: www.nationalpoetryreview.com. The National Poetry Review Book Prize offers $1,000, publication of a book-length ms, and 15 author copies. All entries will be considered for publication. Submit 45-80 pages of poetry. Include cover letter with bio and acknowledgments page. **See Web site for entry address and details.** Include e-mail address for results (no SASEs; mss will not be returned). Guidelines available on Web site. **Fee:** $25. Make checks payable to The National Poetry Review. **Deadline:** September 30 (postmark).

$ ☑ THE PABLO NERUDA PRIZE FOR POETRY

Nimrod, Literary Contest--Poetry, The University of Tulsa, 800 S. College, Tulsa OK 74104. Website: www.utulsa.edu/nimrod. **Contact:** Contest Coordinator. The annual Nimrod Literary Awards include The Pablo Neruda Prize for Poetry, which offers 1st Prize: $2,000 and publication in Nimrod: International Journal of Poetry and Prose (see separate listing in Magazines/Journals); and 2nd Prize: $1,000 and publication. Nimrod retains the right to publish any submission. Submissions must be unpublished. Work must be in English or translated by original author. Submit 3-10 pages of poetry (1 long poem or several short poems). Poet's name must not appear on ms. Include cover sheet with poem title(s), poet's name, address, phone and fax numbers, and e-mail address (poet must have a U.S. address by October of contest year to enter). Mark "Contest Entry" on submission envelope and cover sheet. Include SASE for results only; mss will not be returned. Guidelines available for #10 SASE or on Web site. **Entry fee:** $20; includes one-year subscription (2 issues) to Nimrod. Make checks payable to Nimrod. **Deadline:** entries accepted January 1-April 30 (postmark). 200 winners were Natalie Diaz (1st Prize, "When My Brother Was an Aztec" and Others) and Keet Je Kuipers (2nd Prize, "Barn Elegy" and Others). Winners will be announced on Nimrod's Web site.

$ ☑ NERVE COWBOY CHAPBOOK CONTEST

P.O. Box 4973, Austin TX 78765. Website: www.jwhagins.com/ChapContest.html. Established 1995. **Contact:** Joseph Shields and Jerry Hagins, co-editors. The Nerve Cowboy Chapbook Contest offers 1st Prize: $200, publication, and 50 author's copies; 2nd Prize: $100, publication, and 30 author's copies. Submit 24-40 pages of poetry and/or short fiction. Include SASE for return of ms. Guidelines available on Web site. **Entry fee:** $10 (all entrants receive a copy of the winning chapbook and a discount on the 2nd Prize chapbook). Make checks payable to Nerve Cowboy. **Deadline:** January 31st of each year. 2008 winners included Michael Flanagan, 1st

Prize, A Million Years Gone and Nicholas Benca, 2nd Prize, Heirloom.

$ ☑ NEW LETTERS PRIZE FOR POETRY

University of Missouri-Kansas City, University House, 5101 Rockhill Rd., Kansas City MO 64110-2499. E-mail: newletters@umkc.edu. Website: www.newletters.org. Established 1986. **Contact:** Contest Coordinator. The annual New Letters Poetry Prize awards $1,500 and publication in New Letters (see separate listing in Magazines/Journals) to the best group of 3-6 poems. All entries will be considered for publication in New Letters. Submissions must be unpublished. Considers simultaneous submissions with notification upon acceptance elsewhere. Accepts multiple entries with separate fee for each. Submit up to 6 poems (need not be related). Include 2 cover sheets: 1 with poet's name, address, e-mail, phone number, prize category (poetry), and poem title(s); the second with category and poem title(s) only. No identifying information on ms pages. Accepts electronic submissions. Include SASE for notification of receipt of ms and entry number, and SASE for results only (send only 1 envelope if submitting multiple entries); mss will not be returned. Guidelines available for SASE or on Web site. **Entry fee:** $15 for first entry, $10 for each subsequent entry; includes cost of a one-year subscription, renewal, or gift subscription to New Letters (shipped to any address within the U.S.). Make checks payable to New Letters. **Deadline:** May 18 (postmark). 2008 winner was Laurie Zimmerman. 2008 judge: Christopher Buckley. "Current students and employees of the University of Missouri-Kansas City, and current volunteer members of the New Letters and BkMk Press staffs, are not eligible."

$ ☐ NEW MILLENNIUM AWARD FOR POETRY

New Millennium Writings, Room EM, P.O. Box 2463, Knoxville TN 37901. Website: www.newmillenniumwritings.com. **Contact:** Don Williams, editor. Offers 2 annual awards of $1,000 each. Submissions must be unpublished and may be entered in other contests. Submit up to 3 poems, 5 pages maximum. No restrictions on style, form, or content. Include name, address, phone number, and a #10 SASE for notification. All contestants receive the next issue at no additional charge. Entry form available on Web site. Include SASE or e-mail address for results; mss will not be returned. Guidelines available for SASE or on Web site. **Entry fee:** $17. Make checks payable to New Millennium Writings. **Deadline:** June 17 and November 17 (each deadline may be extended once; check Web site for updates). Competition receives 2,000 entries/year. "2 winners and all finalists will be published." Most recent award winner was Patricia Jaggers. Enter online at www.WritingAwards.com.

$ ☑ NEW WOMEN'S VOICES CHAPBOOK COMPETITION

Finishing Line Press, P.O. Box 1626, Georgetown KY 40324. (859)514-8966. E-mail: FinishingBooks@aol.com. Website: www.finishinglinepress.com. Established 1998. **Contact:** Leah Maines, poetry editor. The New Women's Voices Chapbook Competition offers $1,000 and publication by Finishing Line Press for a chapbook-length ms by a woman poet who has not yet published a full-length collection (previous chapbook publication is okay). All entries will be considered for publication; up to 10 entries will be selected for the New Women's Voices series. Submit up to 26 pages of poetry. Include bio, acknowledgments, and SASE. Guidelines available on Web site. **Entry fee:** $15. **Deadline:** February 15 (postmark). Judge: Varies.

$ ☐ NFSPS COLLEGE/UNIVERSITY LEVEL POETRY AWARDS

(Specialized: student writing)P.O. Box 520698, Salt Lake City UT 84152-0698. (801)484-3113. Fax: (801)606-3444. E-mail: SBSenior@juno.com. Website: www.nfsps.org. **Contact:** N. Colwell Snell, chairman. Offers 2 annual awards of $500 each; 1 as the Edna Meudt Memorial Award, the second as the Florence Kahn Memorial Award. Each prize includes publication of winning ms, with 75 copies awarded to the respective poet. Recipients will be invited to read at the annual NFSPS (National Federation of State Poetry Societies) convention; NFSPS will provide an additional travel stipend to be presented at the convention to recipients in attendance (winners are responsible for the balance of convention costs). Open to all freshmen, sophomores, juniors, and seniors of an accredited university or college. Submit a ms of 10 original poems, 1 poem to each page, single-spaced, each poem titled. Each poem must be no more than 46 lines (including spaces between stanzas) and have no more than 50 characters/line (including spaces between words and punctuation). Manuscript must be titled and must include cover page with name, address, phone number in upper left-hand corner; ms title centered on page. May include dedication page. No other identification on any page other than cover page. **NOTE:** A current, official NFSPS application, completed and duly notarized, must accompany ms at time of submission. No e-mail submissions or special deliveries; First Class Mail only. Entry form and guidelines available for SASE or on Web site. Send 4 copies of the manuscript. **Entry fee:** none. **Deadline:** notarized applications and mss received on or before February 1 (no entry mailed before January 1). Winners will be selected on or before March 31 and announced after April 15. Each recipient's state poetry society is also notified. Copies of winning books available on NFSPS Web site.

$ ☐ NFSPS COMPETITIONS

90 High Farms Road, West Hartford, CT 06107-1509. (860)655-3263. E-mail: connpoetry@comcast.net. Website: www.nfsps.org. **Contact:** Christine Beck, contest chair. NFSPS sponsors a national contest with 50 different categories each year, including the NFSPS Founders Award of 1st Prize: $1,500; 2nd Prize: $500; 3rd Prize: $250. Rules for all contests are given in a brochure available from Caroline Walton, editor of Strophes newsletter, at 6176 West Pinedale Circle, Crystal River, FL 34429 (e-mail: carowaltonb@embarqmail.com); or from Christine Beck at the address above; or on the NFSPS Web site. **Entry fee:** (for members) $1/poem or $8 total for 8 or more categories, plus $5/poem for NFSPS Founders Award (limit 4 entries in this category alone). Some categories are for members only. All poems winning over $15 are published in the ENCORE Prize Poem Anthology. NFSPS also sponsors the annual Stevens Poetry Manuscript Competition and the NFSPS College/University Level Poetry Awards (see separate listings this section).

$ ☑ JESSE BRYCE NILES MEMORIAL CHAPBOOK AWARD

4956 St. John Dr., Syracuse NY 13215. (315)488-8077. E-mail: poetry@comstockreview.org. Website: www.comstockreview.org. The Jesse Bryce Niles Memorial Chapbook Award runs every other year, next in 2009, and offers $1,000 plus publication and 50 author's copies; each entrant also receives a copy. Submissions must be unpublished as a collection, but individual poems may have been previously published in journals. Considers simultaneous submissions "as long as the poet notifies us immediately upon acceptance elsewhere." Submit 25-34 pages of poetry, single-spaced (1 page = 38 lines maximum, including spacing between lines; poems may run longer than 1 page). **Manuscripts either too short or too long will be disqualified.** "Do not count title page, acknowledgments, dedication, or bio in the page length. Do not send illustrations, photos, or any other graphics attached to the poems. You may submit a table of contents, which may list the manuscript name only, not the poet's name (not counted in page total for manuscript)." Manuscripts should be paginated and secured with a binder clip; no staples or plastic covers. Include 2 cover pages: 1 with ms title, poet's name, address, phone number, and e-mail address; second with ms title only. List acknowledgments on a separate, removable page with same identifying information. Poet's name should not appear on poems.

Include SASE for results only; mss will not be returned. Guidelines available for SASE or on Web site. **Entry fee:** $25/chapbook. **Deadline:** submit August 1-September 30 (postmark). **Offered every other year.** 2007 winner was Jennifer Key (The Manifest Destiny of Desire). 2009 judge: Kathleen Bryce Niles; all entries are screened by the editors of The Comstock Review (see separate listing in Magazines/Journals). Winner is notified in December. Copies of winning chapbooks are available for $12 saddle-stitched, $14 if perfect-bound. E-mail for ordering details.

$ OHIOANA POETRY AWARD

(Helen and Laura Krout Memorial) (Specialized: native & resident OH authors)Ohioana Library Association, 274 E. First Ave., Suite 300, Columbus OH 43201. (614)466-3831. Fax: (614)728-6974. E-mail: ohioana@ohioana.org. Website: www.ohioana.org. **Contact:** Linda Hengst, executive director. Offers annual Ohioana Book Awards. Up to 6 awards may be given for books (including books of poetry) by authors born in Ohio or who have lived in Ohio for at least 5 years. The Ohioana Poetry Award of $1,000 (with the same residence requirements), made possible by a bequest of Helen Krout, is given yearly "to an individual whose body of published work has made, and continues to make, a significant contribution to poetry, and through whose work as a writer, teacher, administrator, or in community service, interest in poetry has been developed." **Deadline:** nominations to be received by December 31. Competition receives several hundred entries. 2008 award winners were Paul Zimmer for Crossing to Sunlight Revisited ; 2008 Ohioana Poetry Award winner was Philip Brady. Ohioana Quarterly regularly reviews books by Ohio authors and is available through membership in Ohioana Library Association ($25/year).

$ ◘ OHIO POETRY DAY CONTESTS

Ohio Poetry Day Association, Dept. of English, Heidelberg College, 310 East Market, Tiffin OH 44883. Website: www.ohiopoetryassn.com. Established 1937. **Contact:** Bill Reyer, contest chair. Offers annual slate of 30-40 contest categories. Prizes range from $75 down; all money-winning award poems are published in an annual anthology (runs over 100 pages). Submissions must be unpublished. Submit 1 poem/category on topic and in form specified. Some contests open to everyone, but others open only to Ohio poets. "Each contest has its own specifications. Entry must be for a specified category, so entrants need rules." Entry form and guidelines available for SASE. **Entry fee:** $10 inclusive, unlimited number of categories. **Deadline:** usually end of May; see guidelines for each year's deadline. Competition receives over 4,000 entries/ year. Winners and judges for most recent contest listed in winners' anthology. Judges are never announced in advance. Winners list available in August for SASE (enclose with poem entries); prizes given in October. Copies of annual prize anthologies available from Amy Jo Zook, contest treasurer (3520 State Route 56, Mechanicsburg OH 43044) for $9 plus postage (prices can differ from year to year). "Ohio Poetry Day is the umbrella. Individual contests are sponsored by poetry organizations and/or individuals across the state. OPD sponsors several and selects the Poet of the Year; have four memorial funds." Join mailing list at any time by sending contact information by postcard or letter. Advice: "Revise, follow rules, look at individual categories for a good match."

$ ◙ THE ORPHIC PRIZE FOR POETRY

Dream Horse Press, P.O. Box 2080, Aptos CA 95001-2080. E-mail: dreamhorsepress@yahoo. com. Website: www.dreamhorsepress.com. Established 1999. **Contact:** J.P. Dancing Bear, editor/ publisher. The Orphic Prize for Poetry offers an annual award of $1,000 and publication of a book-length ms by Dream Horse Press. All entries will be considered for publication. Both free and formal verse styles are welcome. Submissions may be entered in other contests, "but if your manuscript is accepted for publication elsewhere, you must notify Dream Horse Press immediately." Submit 48-80 pages of poetry, paginated, with table of contents, acknowledgments, and bio. Include separate cover letter with poet's name, biographical information, and e-mail address (when available). Poet's name should not appear anywhere on the ms. Manuscripts will be recycled after judging. Guidelines available on Web site. **Entry fee:** $25/ms entered. Entry fees are non-refundable. Make checks/money orders payable to Dream Horse Press. **Deadline:** December 1 for 2008; check Web site for deadlines and details for subsequent years. Recent winners include: S.D. Lishan, Gaylord Brewer, and Bruce Cohen. Judging will be anonymous.

$ ☑ GUY OWEN PRIZE

Southern Poetry Review, Dept. of Languages, Literature and Philosophy, Armstrong Atlantic State University, 11935 Abercorn St., Savannah GA 31419-1997. (912)921-5633. E-mail: rrparham@aug.edu (inquiries only). Website: www.spr.armstrong.edu. Established 1958. **Contact:** Robert Parham, editor. The annual Guy Owen Prize offers $1,000 and publication in Southern Poetry Review (see separate listing in Magazines/Journals) to the winning poem selected by a distinguished poet. All entries will be considered for publication. Submissions must be unpublished. "We consider work published online or posted there as previously published." Considers simultaneous submissions if indicated as such. Submit 3-5 poems (10 pages maximum). Include cover sheet with poet's name and contact information; no identifying information on ms pages. No e-mail or disk submissions. Include SASE for results only; mss will not be returned. Guidelines available in magazine, for SASE, by e-mail, or on website. **Entry fee:** $15; includes one-year subscription to Southern Poetry Review. Make checks payable to Southern Poetry Review. **Deadline:** submit March 1-June 15 (postmarked). 2007 winner was Marianna Busching.

$ ☐ PACIFIC NORTHWEST WRITERS ASSOCIATION (PNWA) LITERARY CONTEST

PMB 2717 - 1420 NW Gilman Blvd, Ste 2, Issaquah, WA 98027. (425)673-2665. Fax: (206) 824-4559. E-mail: pnwa@pnwa.org. Website: www.pnwa.org. Established 1956. **Contact:** Kelli Liddane. "Calling all writers. Submit your writing to 12 categories for our annual literary contest." **Entry fee:** $35 for PNWA members, $50 for non-PNWA members per category. **Deadline:** February. Check Web site for specific date. Over $12,000 in prize monies. Winners will be announced at awards banquet at annual PWNA Summer Writers Conference in Seattle, WA. "The Pacific Northwest Writers Association, a nonprofit organization, is dedicated to Northwest writers and the development of writing talent from pen to publication through education, accessibility to the publishing industry, and participation in an interactive vital writer community. In addition to the annual literary contest, PNWA hosts an annual conference each summer in the Seattle area. See Web site for further membership and conference details."

$ ☑ THE PATERSON POETRY PRIZE

Poetry Center, Passaic County Community College, One College Blvd., Paterson NJ 07505-1179. (973)684-6555. E-mail: mgillan@pccc.edu. Website: www.pccc.edu/poetry. Established 1979. **Contact:** Maria Mazziotti Gillan, editor/executive director. The Paterson Poetry Prize offers an annual award of $1,000 for the strongest book of poems (48 or more pages) published in the previous year. The winner will be asked to participate in an awards ceremony and to give a reading at The Poetry Center. Minimum press run: 500 copies. Publishers may submit more than 1 title for prize consideration; 3 copies of each book must be submitted. Include SASE for results; books will not be returned (all entries will be donated to the Poetry Center Library). Guidelines and application form (required) available for SASE or on Web site. **Entry fee:** none.

Deadline: February 1 (postmark). Winners will be announced in Poets & Writers Magazine and on Web site. 2007 winners were Christopher Bursk (The First Inhabitants of Arcadia) and Patricia Smith (Teahouse of the Almighty). The award splits between 2 winners.

$ ☑ PAUMANOK POETRY AWARD

English Dept., Knapp Hall, Farmingdale State University of New York, 2350 Broadhollow Rd., Farmingdale NY 11735. E-mail: brownml@farmingdale.edu. Website: www.farmingdale.edu. Established 1990. **Contact:** Dr. Margery Brown, director. Offers 1st Prize of $1,000 plus an all-expense-paid feature reading in their 2009-2010 visiting writers series. **(Please note: travel expenses within the continental U.S. only.)** Also awards two 2nd Prizes of $500 plus expenses for a reading in the series. Submit cover letter, 1 paragraph literary bio, and 3-5 poems (no more than 10 pages total), published or unpublished. Include cover page with name, address, and phone number. Guidelines available for SASE or on Web site. **Entry fee:** $25. Make checks payable to Farmingdale State University of New York, VWP. **Deadline:** by September 15 (postmark). Include SASE for results (to be mailed by late December); results also posted on Web site. Competition receives over 600 entries. 2007 winners were Yvonne Jackson (1st Prize) and Lynn Aarti Chandhok and Maurice Riordan (runners-up).

$ ☑ PAVEMENT SAW PRESS CHAPBOOK AWARD

321 Empire Street, Montpelier, OH 43543-1301. E-mail: info@pavementsaw.org. Website: www. pavementsaw.org. Established 1992. **Contact:** David Baratier, editor. Pavement Saw Press Chapbook Award offers $500, publication, and 50 author copies. Open to all poets regardless of previous publication history. Submit up to 32 pages of poetry. Include signed cover letter with poet's name, address, phone number, e-mail, publication credits, a brief biography, and ms title. Also include 2 cover sheets: 1 with poet's contact information and ms title, 1 with the ms title only. Do not put poet's name on mss pages except for first title page. No mss will be returned. Guidelines available for SASE or on Web site. **Entry fee:** $15. "Every entrant will receive the equivalent cost of the entry fee in Pavement Saw Press titles." Make checks payable to Pavement Saw Press. **Deadline:** December 30 (entries must be postmarked by this date to be eligible). 2007 winner was Susan Terris (Marriage License).

$ ☑ PEARL POETRY PRIZE

Pearl Editions, 3030 E. Second St., Long Beach CA 90803-5163. (562)434-4523 or (714)968-7530. E-mail: pearlmag@aol.com. Website: www.pearlmag.com. Established 1974. **Contact:** Joan Jobe Smith, Marilyn Johnson, and Barbara Hauk, poetry editors. The annual Pearl Poetry Prize awards $1,000, publication, and 25 author's copies for a book-length ms. Guidelines available for SASE or on Web site. **Entry fee:** $20 (includes a copy of the winning book). **Deadline:** submit May 1-July 15 only. 2007 winner was Lavonne J. Adams (Through the Glorieta Pass). 2008 judge: Gerald Locklin.

$ ☐ JUDITH SIEGEL PEARSON AWARD

(Specialized: subject concerning women)Wayne State University/Family of Judith Siegel Pearson, 5057 Woodward Ave., Suite 9408, Detroit MI 48202. (313)577-2450. Fax: (313)577-8618. E-mail: rhonda@wayne.edu. **Contact:** Rhonda Agnew, competition coordinator. Offers an annual award of up to $500 for the best creative or scholarly work on a subject concerning women. The type of work accepted rotates each year: drama and nonfictional prose in 2008; poetry in 2009; essays in 2010, fiction in 2011, drama in 2012. Open to all interested writers and scholars. Submissions must be unpublished. Submit 4-10 poems (20 pages maximum). Guidelines available for SASE or by fax or e-mail. **Deadline:** March 2.

$ PEN CENTER USA LITERARY AWARD IN POETRY

(Specialized: writers living west of the Mississippi)PEN Center USA, c/o Antioch University Los Angeles, 400 Corporate Pointe, Culver City CA 90230. (310)862-1555, ext. 361. Fax: (310)862-1556. E-mail: awards@penusa.org. Website: www.penusa.org. **Contact:** Awards Coordinator. Literary Award winners are granted PEN USA membership and given a cash prize of $1,000 at the gala Literary Awards Festival in Los Angeles. Open to writers living west of the Mississippi. Submit 4 copies of the entry. Entry form and guidelines available for SASE, by fax, e-mail, or on Web site. **Entry fee:** $35. **Deadline:** December 13, 2008 for 2009. Winner will be announced in fall of 2009 and honored at the Awards Festival in Los Angeles in Winter 2009.

$ ☑ PERUGIA PRESS PRIZE

(Specialized: first or second poetry book by a woman)P.O. Box 60364, Florence MA 01062. E-mail: info@perugiapress.com. Website: www.perugiapress.com. Established 1997. **Contact:** Susan Kan, director. The Perugia Press Prize for a first or second poetry book by a woman offers $1,000 and publication. Poet must be a living U.S. resident with no more than 1 previously published book of poems (chapbooks don't count). Submissions must be unpublished as a collection, but individual poems may have been previously published in journals, chapbooks, and anthologies. Considers simultaneous submissions if notified of acceptance elsewhere. Submit 48-72 pages (white paper) "with legible typeface, pagination, and fastened with a removable clip. No more than 1 poem per page." Two cover pages required: 1 with ms title, poet's name, address, telephone number, and e-mail address; and 1 with ms title only. Include table of contents and acknowledgments page. No e-mail submissions. No translations or self-published books. Multiple submissions accepted if accompanied by separate entry fee for each. Include SASE for winner notification only; mss will be recycled. Guidelines available on Web site. **Entry fee:** $25. Make checks payable to Perugia Press. **Deadline:** submit August 1-November 15 (postmark). "Use USPS only, not FedEx or UPS." Winner announced by April 1 by e-mail or SASE (if included with entry). Judges: panel of Perugia authors, booksellers, scholars, etc.

$ ☑ THE RICHARD PETERSON POETRY PRIZE

Dept. of English, Mail Code 4503, Faner Hall 2380, Southern Illinois University Carbondale, 1000 Faner Dr., Carbondale IL 62901. Website: www.siu.edu/~crborchd. Established 1995. **Contact:** Jon Tribble, managing editor. The Richard Peterson Poetry Prize offers $1,500 plus publication in the Winter/Spring issue of Crab Orchard Review (see separate listing in Magazines/Journals). "Submissions must be unpublished original work not under consideration elsewhere, written in English by a U.S. citizen or permanent resident. Name, address, telephone number, and/or e-mail address should appear only on the title page of manuscript; author's name should not appear on any subsequent pages. Mark 'poetry' on outside of envelope. Include #10 SASE for notification of winners." See guidelines for complete formatting instructions. Guidelines available for SASE or on Web site. **Entry fee:** $10/entry (3 poems, 100 line limit per poem, no more than 1 poem per page; poet may submit up to 3 separate entries if not entering the fiction or nonfiction categories of the contest). Each fee entitles entrant to a copy of the winter/spring Crab Orchard Review featuring the prize winner; include complete address. Make checks payable to Crab Orchard Review. **Deadline:** see guidelines or check Web site.

$ PEW FELLOWSHIPS IN THE ARTS

(Specialized: PA resident of Bucks, Chester, Delaware, Montgomery, or Philadelphia County; 25

or older)230 S. Broad St., Suite 1003, Philadelphia PA 19102. (215)875-2285. Fax: (215)875-2276. Website: www.pewarts.org. Established 1991. **Contact:** Melissa Franklin, award director. "The Pew Fellowships in the Arts provide financial support directly to artists so they may have the opportunity to dedicate themselves wholly to the development of their artwork for up to 2 years. Up to 12 fellowships of $60,000 each (in 3 different categories) awarded each year." Must be a Pennsylvania resident of Bucks, Chester, Delaware, Montgomery, or Philadelphia County for at least 2 years. Matriculated students, full or part-time, are not eligible. Application and guidelines available mid-August. **Deadline:** December of the preceding year. Judges: panel of artists and art professionals. Winner will be announced by letter.

$ ☑ JAMES D. PHELAN AWARD

(Specialized: CA-born writers ages 20-35)c/o Intersection for the Arts, 446 Valencia St., San Francisco CA 94103. (415)626-2787. Fax: (415)626-1636. Website: www.theintersection.org. Established 1935. **Contact:** Awards Coordinator. The James D. Phelan Award offers $3,000 to the author of an unpublished work-in-progress of fiction (novel or short stories), nonfictional prose, poetry, or drama. Applicants must be California-born (although they may now reside outside of the state), and must be between the ages of 20 and 35 as of the March 31 deadline. Guidelines and entry form (required) available on Web site. **Entry fee:** none. **Deadline:** March 31. Competition receives 150-180 entries. 2008 winner was Allison Benis White (poetry, "Small Porcelain Head").

$ ☑ PINEWOOD HAIKU CONTEST

Wisteria, P.O. Box 150932, Lufkin TX 75915-0932. E-mail: wisteriajournal@gmail.com (inquiries only). Website: www.wistaria.blogspot.com. Established 2006. **Contact:** T.A. Thompson, founder. The annual Pinewood Haiku Contest offers 1st Prize: $100; 2nd Prize: $50; 3rd Prize: $25. Winners will be published in the April issue of Wisteria: A Journal of Haiku, Senryu, and Tanka. For contemporary English-language haiku; no rules as to syllable or line count. Submissions must be unpublished. Submit 2 copies of each haiku, typed, on a 3x5 index card. 1 card only should include the poet's name, address, and e-mail for contact purposes. Only 1 haiku/card. No e-mail submissions. Guidelines available for SASE or on Web site. **Entry fee:** $2/ poem or 3 poems for $5; 3 poems maximum, cash or money order only, no checks. Make money orders payable to T.A. Thompson. **Deadline:** accepts entries November 1-February 14. Winners will be notified by e-mail and postal mail; no SASE required.

$ ☑ PLAN B PRESS POETRY CHAPBOOK CONTEST

P.O. Box 3242, Fairfax VA 22038. (215)732-2663. E-mail: planbpress@gmail.com. Website: www.planbpress.com. Established 1999. **Contact:** Contest Coordinator. The annual Plan B Press Poetry Chapbook Contest offers $225, publication by Plan B Press (see separate listing in Book/ Chapbook Publishers), and 50 author's copies. Poems may be previously published individually. Accepts multiple submissions with separate fee for each. Submit up to 24 poems (48 pages total maximum) in English. Include table of contents and list of acknowledgments. Include e-mail address or SASE for notification of winner; mss will not be returned. Author retains copyright of poems, but Plan B reserves rights to layout and/or cover art and design. Guidelines available on Web site. **Entry fee:** $15. **Deadline:** was March 1 for 2009. 2008 winner was Will Hastings (Stones Rounded by Years of Conversation). 2009 final judge: Deborah Ager.

$ ☑ THE POCATALIGO POETRY CONTEST

Yemassee, Dept. of English, University of South Carolina, Columbia SC 29208. (803)777-2085.

E-mail: editor@yemasseejournal.org. Website: http://yemasseejournal.org. Established 1993. Contact: Contest Coordinator. The annual Pocataligo Poetry Contest offers a $500 prize and publication in Yemassee (see separate listing in Magazines/Journals). Submissions must be unpublished. Considers simultaneous submissions with notice of acceptance elsewhere. Accepts multiple entries with separate $10 fee and SASE for each. Submit 3-5 poems (15 pages total), typed. Include cover letter with poet's name, contact information, and poem title(s); no identifying information on ms pages except poem title (which should appear on every page). Include SASE for results only; mss will not be returned. Guidelines available on Web site. **Entry fee:** $10. Make checks payable to Educational Foundation/English Literary Magazine Fund. **Deadline:** February 15 (postmark) annually.

$ ☑ POETIC LICENSE CONTEST

Mkashef Enterprises, P.O. Box 688, Yucca Valley CA 92286-0688. E-mail: alayne@inetworld. net. Website: www.asidozines.com. Established 1998. **Contact:** Alayne Gelfand, poetry editor. Offers an annual poetry contest with awards of 1st Prize: $500; 2nd Prize: $100; 3rd Prize: $40; plus publication in anthology and 1 copy. 5 honorable mentions receive 1 copy; other poems of exceptional interest will also be included in the anthology. Themes and deadlines available for SASE or e-mail. Submissions may be previously published. Submit any number of poems, any style, of up to 50 lines/poem. Include name, address, phone number, and e-mail (if available) on each poem. Enclose a SASE for notification of winners. Accepts e-mail (as attachment or pasted into body of message), disk, or postal submissions. "Judges prefer original, accessible, and unforced works." Guidelines available for SASE or by e-mail. **Entry fee:** $1/poem. **Deadline:** available for SASE or by e-mail. "We're looking for fresh word usage and surprising imagery. Please keep in mind that our judges automatically give attention to non-rhyming or exceptional rhyming poetry. Each contest seeks to explode established definitions of the theme being spotlighted. Be sure to send SASE or e-mail for current theme and deadline before submission. If you contact us during a period in which we aren't publishing, your contact information will be saved and you will be contacted with information on any new contest(s) as they begin accepting submissions."

$ ☑ POETR 2010 INTERNATIONAL POETRY COMPETITION

Atlanta Review, P.O. Box 8248, Atlanta GA 31106. E-mail: atlrev@yahoo.com (inquiries only). Website: www.atlantareview.com. Established 1994. **Contact:** Dan Veach, editor/publisher. Atlanta Review (see separate listing in Magazines/Journals) sponsors an annual international poetry competition, offering $2,010 Grand Prize, 20 International Publication Awards (winners will be published in Atlanta Review), and 30 International Merit Awards (includes certificate, Honorable Mention in Atlanta Review, and free issue). Poems must not have been published in a nationally distributed print publication. Put your name and address on each page (e-mail and phone optional). Include SASE for results only (outside of U.S., SAE only, no IRC required); no entries will be returned. Guidelines available on Web site. **Entry fee:** $5 for the first poem, $3 for each additional poem. Make checks payable to Atlanta Review. "Checks in your national currency are acceptable at the current exchange rate. We also accept uncancelled stamps from your country." **Deadline:** March 1, 2010. Winners will be announced in August; Contest Issue published in October. Contest Issue available for $4, or free with $10 subscription to Atlanta Review.

$ ☑ THE POETRY CENTER BOOK AWARD

1600 Holloway Ave., San Francisco CA 94132. (415)338-2227. Fax: (415)338-0966. E-mail:

poetry@sfsu.edu. Website: www.sfsu.edu/~poetry. Established 1980. **Contact:** Elise Ficarra, associate director. Offers award to an outstanding book of poems published by an individual author in the current year. Awards one prize of $500 and an invitation to read at The Poetry Center. Books by a single author; no collaborative works, anthologies, or translations. Must be published and copyrighted during year of contest. Publisher, author, or reader may submit entries. **Entry fee:** $10. **Deadline:** July 1-January 31 annually (e.g., entries published during 2009 will be accepted up until January 31, 2010). Competition receives 200-250 entries annually. 2007 winner, selected by Sesshu Foster, was Noah Eli Gordon (Novel Pictorial Noise, Harper Books). Winner will be announced on website and through press release. "The Poetry Center and American Poetry Archives at San Francisco State University were established in 1954. Its archives include the largest circulating tape collection of writers reading their own work in the United States."

$ ☑ THE POETRY COUNCIL OF NORTH CAROLINA ANNUAL POETRY CONTEST

(Specialized: NC residents or anyone with NC connection) E-mail: edcockrelll@hotmail.com. Website: www.oldmp.com/poetrycouncilofnc/. **Contact:** Ed Cockrell. The Poetry Council of North Carolina is "an organization whose sole purpose is to sponsor annual adult and student poetry contests and to publish the winning poems in our book, Bay Leaves. There is no membership fee. All winners are invited to read their poems at Poetry Day in the fall of each year, either late September or early October." Open to residents and anyone with a "North Carolina connection" (persons born in NC, transients from other states who either attend school or work in NC, and NC residents temporarily out of state). Offers 4 adult and 2 student contests with prizes ranging from $10 to $25; all winning poems plus Honorable Mentions will be published in Bay Leaves (50+ pages, perfect-bound). Guidelines available for SASE or on Web site. **Entry fee:** $3/poem, 1 poem/contest. **Deadline:** see Web site. Competition receives 200+ entries/year. Winners list available for SASE, also appears in Bay Leaves and on Web site. Copies of Bay Leaves available from Poetry Council of North Carolina. "Please read the guidelines carefully. Send only your best work. You can enter only 1 poem in each contest."

$ ☑ POETRY SOCIETY OF AMERICA AWARDS

Poetry Society of America, 15 Gramercy Park, New York NY 10003. (212)254-9628. E-mail: brett@poetrysociety.org. Website: www.poetrysociety.org. Offers the following awards **open to PSA members only**: **The Writer Magazine/Emily Dickinson Award** ($250, for a poem inspired by Dickinson though not necessarily in her style); **Cecil Hemley Memorial Award** ($500, for a lyric poem that addresses a philosophical or epistemological concern); **Lyric Poetry Award** ($500, for a lyric poem on any subject); **Lucille Medwick Memorial Award** ($500, for an original poem in any form on a humanitarian theme); **Alice Fay Di Castagnola Award** ($1,000 for a manuscript-in-progress of poetry or verse-drama). The following awards are **open to both PSA members and nonmembers**: **Louise Louis/Emily F. Bourne Student Poetry Award** ($250, for the best unpublished poem by a student in grades 9-12 from the U.S.); **George Bogin Memorial Award** ($500, for a selection of 4-5 poems that use language in an original way to reflect the encounter of the ordinary and the extraordinary and to take a stand against oppression in any of its forms); **Robert H. Winner Memorial Award** ($2,500, to acknowledge original work being done in mid-career by a poet who has not had substantial recognition, open to poets over 40 who have published no more than one book). Entries for the **Norma Farber First Book Award** ($500) and the **William Carlos Williams Award** (purchase prize between $500 and $1,000, for a book of poetry published by a small press, nonprofit, or university press) **must be submitted directly by publishers**. Complete submission guidelines for all awards are available on website.

Entry fee: all of the above contests are free to PSA members; nonmembers pay $15 to enter any or all of contests 6-8; $5 for high school students to enter single entries in the student poetry competition; high school teachers/administrators may submit unlimited number of students' poems (one entry/student) to student poetry award for $20. **Deadline:** submissions accepted October 1-December 22 (postmark). Additional information available on website.

$ ❏ THE POETRY SOCIETY OF VIRGINIA ADULT AND STUDENT CONTESTS

24 Skipwith Green Circle, Richmond VA 23294. E-mail: contest@poetrysocietyofvirginia.org (for information only). Website: www.PoetrySocietyOfVirginia.org (for rules and guidelines). **Contact:** Contest Chair. Adult contest offers many categories for original, unpublished poems--both specified and unspecified forms and topics. Student contest is school grade-specific. Offers numerous cash prizes (varies by year). Guidelines available for SASE or on website (guidelines must be followed). **Entry fee:** $4/poem for adults; no fee for students and PSV members. ("Membership fee of $25 covers entries in all categories and can be sent with entry and membership form, available on website or for SASE.") Designate entries as "adult" or "student" and send to Contest Chair at the above address. **Deadline:** January 19 (postmark) annually (Edgar Allan Poe's birthday). Winning entries may be published in a booklet or on the PSV website unless author indicates otherwise on each poem entered. "Follow guidelines to ensure inclusion of poem in contest. Always include SASE for any return information."

$ ❏ POETS' DINNER CONTEST

2214 Derby St., Berkeley CA 94705-1018. (510)841-1217. **Contact:** Dorothy V. Benson. Contestant must be present to win. Submit 3 anonymous typed copies of original, unpublished poems in not more than 3 of the 8 categories (Humor, Love, Nature, Beginnings & Endings, Spaces & Places, People, Theme [Earth], and Poet's Choice). Winning poems (Grand Prize, 1st, 2nd, 3rd) are read at an awards banquet and Honorable Mentions are presented. Cash prizes awarded; Honorable Mention receives books. The event is nonprofit. "Since 1927 there has been an annual awards banquet sponsored by the ad hoc Poets' Dinner Committee, currently at Francesco's in Oakland." Guidelines available for SASE. **Entry fee:** none. **Deadline:** January 15. Competition receives about 300 entries. Recent contest winners include Stephen Sadler (Grand Prize), Linda Prather, Amy Miller, Joyce Odam, Gregory DeHart, Tom Odegard, Laverne Frith, Joan Gelfand (1st Prizes). 2007 Judges: Kathleen Norris, Jonah Bornstein, Andrea Hollander Budy, Patricia Clark, Suzanne C. Smith, Vincent Nixon. Remembering, an anthology of winning poems from the Poets' Dinner over the last 25 years, is available by mail for $6 plus tax from Dorothy V. Benson at the contest address.

$ ☑ FELIX POLLAK PRIZE IN POETRY

University of Wisconsin Press, Dept. of English, 600 N. Park St., University of Wisconsin, Madison WI 53706. E-mail: rwallace@wisc.edu. Website: www.wisc.edu/wisconsinpress/index.html. Established 1994. **Contact:** Ronald Wallace, poetry series editor. The annual Felix Pollack Prize in Poetry is one of 2 prizes awarded by the University of Wisconsin Press (see separate listing for the Brittingham Prize in Poetry). Offers $1,000 plus publication, with an additional $1,500 honorarium to cover expenses of a reading in Madison. Submissions must be unpublished as a collection, but individual poems may have been published elsewhere (publication must be acknowledged). Considers simultaneous submissions if notified of selection elsewhere. Submit 50-80 unbound ms pages, typed single-spaced (with double spaces between stanzas) or double-spaced. Clean photocopies are acceptable. Include title page with poet's name, address, and telephone number. No translations. Include SASE for results only; mss will not be returned. Guidelines available for SASE or on Web site. **Entry fee:** $25. **NOTE:** $25 fee applies to consideration of same entry for the Brittingham Prize in Poetry--1 fee for 2 contest awards. Make checks/money orders payable to University of Wisconsin Press. **Deadline:** submit September 1-27 (postmark). 2007 Pollak Prize winner was Barbara Goldberg (The Royal Baker's Daughter). Qualified readers will screen all mss. Judge: "a distinguished poet who will remain anonymous until the winners are announced in mid-February."

$ ☑ PORTLANDIA CHAPBOOK CONTEST

The Portlandia Group, PMB 225, 6663 SW Beaverton-Hillsdale Hwy., Portland OR 97225. E-mail: braucher@portlandia.com. Established 1999. **Contact:** Karen Braucher, award director. Offers biennial prize of $200, publication of chapbook, and 30 copies. Submissions must be unpublished as a collection, but individual poems may have been previously published in journals. Considers simultaneous submissions. Submit 24 pages of poetry with table of contents, acknowledgments, and bio. Include 2 title pages: 1 with ms title and personal info, the other with ms title only. Include SASE for results only; no mss will be returned. "See guidelines for the year you are submitting." Guidelines available for SASE or by e-mail. **Entry fee:** $15/entry, includes copy of winning chapbook. **Deadline:** March 1 for 2008 (check biennial guidelines). Competition receives about 200 entries/year. Past winners include Judith Taylor, Kurt S. Olsson, Elisa A. Garza, John Surowiecki, Ron Drummond, John Pursley III, and Jen Karetnick. Copies of winning chapbooks ($8, includes shipping) are available from The Portlandia Group.

$ ☑ THE JACKLYN POTTER YOUNG POETS COMPETITION

(Specialized: Washington, DC-area high school students)The Word Works, 1200 North Quaker Lane, Alexandria VA 22302. (703)931-5177. Website: www.worksdc.com. **Contact:** W. Perry Epes, director. The annual Jacklyn Potter Young Poets Competition is open to Washington, DC-are high school students. 2 winners receive an honorarium and read their original work at the Joaquin Miller Cabin in Rock Creek Park in an appearance with an established poet. The winners and other notable entrants will be recommended for a reading at the Nora School Poetry Series held in Silver Spring, MD. Submit 5-6 poems with poet's name, address, and phone number in the upper right corner of every ms page. Include a separate cover page with poet's name, address, phone number, e-mail address, name of school, grade, expected graduation date, and listed titles of poems submitted. Include SASE for results. **Deadline:** submit January 1-March 31.

$ ☑ A. POULIN, JR. POETRY PRIZE

BOA Editions, Ltd., 250 N. Goodman St., Suite 306, Rochester NY 14607. (585)546-3410. Website: www.boaeditions.org. Established 1976. **Contact:** Thom Ward, poetry editor. BOA Editions, Ltd. (see separate listing in Book/Chapbook Publishers) sponsors the annual A. Poulin, Jr. Poetry Prize for a poet's first book. Awards $1,500 and publication. Individual poems may have been previously published. Considers simultaneous submissions. Submit 48-100 pages of poetry, paginated consecutively, typed or computer-generated in 11 pt. font. Bind with spring clip (no paperclips). Include cover/title page with poet's name, address, and telephone number. Also include table of contents; list of acknowledgments; and entry form (available for download on Web site). Multiple entries accepted with separate entry fee for each. No e-mail submissions. Include SASP for notification of receipt and SASE for results. Mss will not be returned. Guidelines available on Web site in May. **Entry fee:** $25. **Deadline:** submit August 1-November 30 annually. 2009 judge: Thomas Lux. Winner announced in March.

$ ☑ THE PRAIRIE SCHOONER BOOK PRIZE SERIES

University of Nebraska Press, 201 Andrews Hall, P.O. Box 880334, University of Nebraska, Lincoln NE 68588-0334. (402)472-0911. Fax: (402)472-9771. E-mail: jengelhardt2@unl.edu. Website: http://prairieschooner.unl.edu. Established 1926. **Contact:** Contest Director. The annual Prairie Schooner Book Prize Series offers $3,000 and publication of a book-length collection of poetry by the University of Nebraska Press; one runner-up receives $1,000. Individual poems may have been previously published elsehwere. Considers simultaneous submissions if notified immediately of acceptance elsewhere. Submit at least 50 pages of poetry with acknowledgments page (if applicable). Poet's name should not appear on ms pages. Xeroxed copies are acceptable. Bind with rubber band or binder clip only. Include 2 cover pages: one with poet's name, address, phone number, and e-mail address; the other with ms title only. Include SASP for acknowledgment of receipt of ms and #10 SASE for results only; mss will not be returned. Guidelines available for SASE, by e-mail, or on Web site. **Entry fee:** $25. Make checks payable to Prairie Schooner. **Deadline:** January 15-March 15 annually. 2008 winner was Kara Candito (*Taste of Cherry*). Winners announced on website in early July, with results mailed shortly thereafter. (See separate listing for Prairie Schooner in Magazines/Journals.)

$ ☑ THE PSA NATIONAL CHAPBOOK FELLOWSHIPS

Poetry Society of America, 15 Gramercy Park, New York NY 10003. (212)254-9628. E-mail: brett@poetrysociety.org. Website: www.poetrysociety.org. Established 2002. The PSA National Chapbook Fellowships offer 2 prizes of $1,000 and publication of winning chapbook mss, with distribution by the Poetry Society of America. Open to any U.S. resident who has not published a full-length poetry collection. **(Poets who apply to this contest may not apply to The PSA New York Chapbook Fellowships.)** Does not accept entries by fax or e-mail. Guidelines available for SASE or on Web site. **Entry fee:** $12 for both PSA members and nonmembers. Make checks/ money orders payable to Poetry Society of America. **Deadline:** submit October 1-December 22 (postmarked). Most recent judges: Mary Doty and Cole Swenson. Additional information available on Web site.

$ ☑ THE PSA NEW YORK CHAPBOOK FELLOWSHIPS

(Specialized: open to NYC residents only)Poetry Society of America, 15 Gramercy Park, New York NY 10003. (212)254-9628. E-mail: brett@poetrysociety.org. Website: www.poetrysociety. org. Established 2002. The PSA New York Chapbook Fellowships offer 2 prizes of $1,000 and publication of each of winning chapbook mss, with distribution by the Poetry Society of America. Open to any New York City resident (in the 5 boroughs) who is 30 or under and has not published a full-length poetry collection. **(Poets who apply to this contest may not apply to The PSA National Chapbook Fellowships.)** Does not accept entries by fax or e-mail. Guidelines available for SASE or on Web site. **Entry fee:** $12 for both PSA members and nonmembers. Make checks/money orders payble to Poetry Society of America. **Deadline:** submit October 1-December 22 (postmarked). Most recent judges: Arthur Sze and Linda Gregg. Additional information available on Web site.

$ ☑ THE PULITZER PRIZE IN LETTERS

The Pulitzer Prize Office, 709 Journalism, Columbia University, New York NY 10027. (212)854-3841. Fax: (212)854-3342. E-mail: pulitzer@www.pulitzer.org. Website: www.pulitzer.org. **Contact:** the Pulitzer Prize Board. The Pulitzer Prize for Letters annually awards 2 prizes of $10,000 each and a certificate for the most distinguished books of poetry and fiction published during the preceding year (U.S. authors only). Anyone, including the author, may submit a book that's eligible. Submit 4 copies of published books (or galley proofs if book is being published after October 15), completed entry form, 1 photograph, and 1 biography. Entry form and guidelines available for SASE, by fax, or on Web site. **Entry fee:** $50. **Deadline:** October 15. Competition receives about 150 entries/year. 2007 poetry winner was Natasha Trethewey for *Native Guard* (Houghton Mifflin). 2007 judges: Cynthia Huntington, Rafael Campo, and Claudia Emerson.

$ ☑ QUERCUS REVIEW PRESS POETRY SERIES BOOK AWARD

Quercus Review Press, Modesto Junior College, Div. of Literature & Language Arts, 435 College Ave., Modesto CA 95350. (209)575-6183. E-mail: pierstorffs@mjc.edu. Website: www. quercusreview.com. Established 1999. **Contact:** Contest Coordinator. Quercus Review Press publishes 1 poetry book/year selected through the Poetry Series Book Award. Offers $1,000, publication, and 50 author's copies. Book mss may include previously published poems. Submit 46-96 pages in ms format. Include cover letter and SASE. Guidelines available on Web site. **Entry fee:** $20 ($25 to receive a copy of winning book). **Deadline:** June - October 16 (postmark). 2007 winner was *Recycle Suburbia*, by Dan Nowack.

☑ $ QWF A.M. KLEIN PRIZE FOR POETRY

(Specialized: books by Quebec authors) Quebec Writers' Federation, 1200 Atwater Ave., Westmount QC H3Z 1X4 Canada. Phone: (514)933-0878. E-mail: admin@qwf.org. Website: www.qwf.org. **Contact:** Lori Schubert, executive director. Offers annual awards of $2,000 CAD each for poetry, fiction, nonfiction, first book, and translation. Submissions must be previously published. Open to authors "who have lived in Quebec for at least 3 of the past 5 years." Submit 5 copies of a book of at least 48 pages. Entry forms and instructions available at qwf. org in April. **Entry fee:** $20 CAD/submission. **Deadline:** May 31 for books published between October 1 and May 15; August 1 for books published between May 15 and September 30 (bound proofs are acceptable; the finished book must be received by September 30). Poetry competition receives approximately 10 entries. 2007 winner was David Solway (*Reaching for Clear*). Winners announced in November. "QWF was formed in 1988 to honor and promote literature written in English by Quebec authors." QWF also publishes QWRITE, "a newsletter offering information and articles of interest to membership and the broader community and has an online literary journal, carte blanche, at http://www.carte-blanche.org/."

$ ☑ THE RAIZISS/DE PALCHI TRANSLATION AWARDS

(Specialized: Italian poetry translated into English)The Academy of American Poets, 584 Broadway, Suite 604, New York NY 10012. (212)274-0343. Fax: (212)274-9427. E-mail: awards@ poets.org. Website: www.poets.org. Established 1934. **Contact:** awards coordinator. Awarded for outstanding translations of modern Italian poetry into English. A $5,000 book prize and a $20,000 fellowship are awarded in alternate years. Guidelines and entry form available for SASE or on Web site. **Deadline:** see Web site for current deadlines for book and fellowship awards. Winner announced in January.

$ ☑ RATTLE POETRY PRIZE

RATTLE, 12411 Ventura Blvd., Studio City CA 91604. (818) 505-6777. E-mail: timgreen@rattle. com. Website: www.rattle.com. Established 2006. The RATTLE Poetry Prize awards 1st Prize of $5,000, plus ten $100 Honorable Mentions. Additional entries may be offered publication as well. Open to writers worldwide (see Web site for special international guidelines). Poems must be written in English (no translations). No previously published poems or works accepted for publication elsewhere. No simultaneous submissions. Submit no more than 4 poems/entry. Multiple entries by a single poet accepted; however, each 4-poem group must be treated as a separate entry with its own cover sheet and entry fee. Include cover sheet with poet's name, address, e-mail address, phone number, and poem titles. No contact information should appear on poems. Include SASE for results only; no poems will be returned. **Note:** Poems also may be entered through online submission on Web site. Guidelines available by e-mail or on Web site. **Entry fee:** $18; includes one-year subscription to RATTLE (see separate listing in Magazines/Journals). Make checks/money orders payable to RATTLE (for credit card entries, see Web site). **Deadline:** August 1 (postmark). 2008 winner was Joseph Fasano ("Mahler in New York"). Judge: editors of RATTLE in blind review. Winners announced in September.

$ MARGARET REID POETRY CONTEST FOR TRADITIONAL VERSE

Tom Howard Books, c/o Winning Writers, 351 Pleasant St., PMB 222, Northampton MA 01060-3961. (866)946-9748. Fax: (413)280-0539. E-mail: johnreid@mail.qango.com. Website: www.winningwriters.com/margaret. Established 2004. **Contact:** John Reid, award director. Offers annual award of 1st Prize: $2,000; 2nd Prize: $1,000; 3rd Prize: $500; 4th Prize: $250; 5 High Distinction Awards of $200 each; and 6 Most Highly Commended Awards of $100 each. The top 15 entries will be published on the Winning Writers Web site. Submissions may be published or unpublished, may have won prizes elsewhere, and may be entered in other contests. Submit poems in traditional verse forms, such as sonnets, ballads, odes, blank verse, and haiku. No limit on number of lines or number of poems submitted. No name on ms pages; type or computer-print on letter-size white paper, single-sided. Guidelines available for SASE or on Web site. Submit online or by mail. **Entry fee:** $7 USD for every 25 lines (exclude poem title and any blank lines from count). **Deadline:** November 15-June 30. 2008 winner was Reena Ribalow ("Jerusalem of Heaven, Jerusalem of Earth"). 2008 judges: John H. Reid and Dee C. Konrad. Winners announced in October at WinningWriters.com; entrants who provide valid e-mail addresses also receive notification.

$ ☑ RIVERSTONE POETRY CHAPBOOK AWARD

Riverstone, A Press for Poetry, P.O. Box 1421, Carefree AZ 85377. Established 1992. Website: www.riverstonepress.org. The Riverstone Poetry Chapbook Award offers $100, publication, and 50 copies to the winner. Submissions may include previously published poems. Considers simultaneous submissions. Submit chapbook ms of 16-24 pages of poetry; include "poems in their proposed arrangement, title page, table of contents, and acknowledgments. All styles welcome." Accepts multiple entries with separate entry fees. Include SASE for contest results; no mss will be returned. Guidelines available for SASE or on Web site. **Entry fee:** $10. "All entrants will receive a copy of the most recent winning chapbook." **Deadline:** check Web site for when Riverstone starts reading mss again. Order sample chapbooks by sending $5 plus $1 shipping.
   •**Will not be reading mss in 2008-2009.**

ROANOKE-CHOWAN POETRY AWARD

(Specialized: NC resident authors) The North Carolina Literary & Historical Association, 4610 Mail Service Center, Raleigh NC 27699-4610. (919)807-7290. Fax: (919)733-8807. E-mail: michael.hill@ncmail.net. Website: www.ah.dcr.state.nc.us/affiliates/lit-hist/awards/awards.htm. **Contact:** Michael Hill, awards coordinator. Offers annual award for "an original volume of poetry published during the 12 months ending June 30 of the year for which the award is given." Open to "authors who have maintained legal or physical residence, or a combination of both, in North Carolina for the 3 years preceding the close of the contest period." Submit 3 copies of each entry. Guidelines available for SASE or by fax or e-mail. **Deadline:** July 15. Competition receives about 15 entries. 2006 winner was James Applewhite (Selected Poems). Winner announced by mail October 15.

$ ☑ ANNA DAVIDSON ROSENBERG AWARDS FOR POEMS ON THE JEWISH EXPERIENCE

Jewish Community Center of San Francisco, 3200 California St., San Francisco CA 94118. (415)292-1200. Fax: (415)276-1550. E-mail: taubecenter@jccsf.org. Website: www.jccsf.org. Established 1987 by Judah L. Magnus Museum and the children of Anna Davidson Rosenberg. Offers prizes of $1,000, $500, and Honorable Mentions for original, unpublished poems (in English) on the Jewish Experience. Open to all interested writers. Submit up to 3 poems (no more than 10 pages total). "Manuscripts should be submitted in quadruplicate, with a cover note listing the author's name, address, phone number, and e-mail address." No names on poems; entries judged anonymously. "Submissions will not be returned; please do not send your only copies." No fax or e-mail submissions. Guidelines available on Web site. **Entry fee:** none. **Deadline:** was December 1 (postmark) for 2008. 2008 judges: Jennifer Barber, Joshua Rivkin, and Susan Terris. Winners announced no later than March 1 at www.jccsf.org and at www. dorothyprizes.org. Reception, award ceremony, and poetry reading in April.

•• There was no award given in 2002 or in 2003; poets should query regarding the status of the award for 2004 before submitting. (Note: The Judah L. Ma

$ ☑ BEULLAH ROSE POETRY PRIZE

(Specialized: poetry by women)P.O. Box 22161, Baltimore MD 21203. E-mail: cbanks@ smartishpace.com. Website: www.smartishpace.com. Established 1999. **Contact:** Clare Banks, associate editor. The annual Beullah Rose Poetry Prize for exceptional poetry by women offers 1st Prize: $200 and publication of the winning poem in Smartish Pace (see separate listing in Magazines/Journals); 2nd and 3rd Prizes: winning poems will be published in Smartish Pace. Winners also receive additional Internet and advertising exposure. Submit 3 poems, with poet's name, address, e-mail, telephone number (preferred), and "Beulah Rose Poetry Prize" at the top of each page of poetry submitted. Include bio. Entries may be submitted online or by e-mail (as attachment) or regular mail. Include SASE with postal entries. Guidelines available on Web site. **Entry fee:** $5 for 3 poems; additional poems may be submitted for $1/poem (12 poem maximum). Make checks/money orders payable to Smartish Pace. **Deadline:** November 1. Judges: Clare Banks and Traci O'Dea, associate editors.

☑ THE SACRAMENTIO POETRY CENTER BOOK PRIZE

(formerly the Cathy Washington Prize) The Sacramento Poetry Center. P.O. Box 160406, Sacramento CA 95816.916-451-5569. E-mail: buchanan@csus.edu. Website: www. sacramentopoetrycenter.org. Established: 2008. **Contact:** Brad Buchanan. The Sacramento Poetry Center Book Prize offers an annual prize of book publication, $1000, and 50 free copies of the winning book. Submissions must be unpublished as a collection, but individual poems may have been previously published elsewhere. Considers simultaneous submissions, with notification. Submit 48-70 pages of poetry. Include 2 title pages: name and contact information (including email address, if possible) should appear on first title page only. Staff, volunteers, or board members of the Sacramento Poetry Center, or their relations, may not submit manuscripts for consideration in this contest. Guidelines available for SASE, on Web site, or by e-mail. **Entry fee:** $20. Check should be made out to The Sacramento Poetry Center. **Deadline:** April 1, 2010. Winner announced in June by email. Copies of winning books available for $12 from The Sacramento Poetry Center. " The Sacramento Poetry Center is a non-profit organization dedicated to furthering the cause of poetry in the Sacramento area and nationwide. We welcome work from anyone, anywhere." **Advice**: " Never lose heart. SPC supports the CLMP Code of Ethics and will adhere to its precepts regarding contests, so we're as fair as it gets."

$ ☑ ERNEST SANDEEN PRIZE IN POETRY

Dept. of English, University of Notre Dame, Notre Dame IN 46556-5639. (574)631-7526. Fax: (574)631-4795. E-mail: creativewriting@nd.edu. Website: http://www.nd.edu/~alcwp/ sandeen.html. Established 1994. **Contact:** Director of Creative Writing. The Sandeen Prize in Poetry offers $1,000 (a $500 award and a $500 advance against royalties from the Notre Dame Press) and publication of a book-length ms. Open to poets who have published at least 1 volume of poetry. "Please include a photocopy of the copyright and the title page of your previous volume. Vanity press publications do not fulfill this requirement. We will pay special attention to second volumes. Please include a vita and/or a biographical statement that includes your publishing history. We will be glad to see a selection of reviews of the earlier collection." Submit 2 copies of ms (inform if ms is available on computer disk). Include SASE for acknowledgment of receipt of ms and SASE for return of ms. **Entry fee:** $15; includes one-year subscription to Notre Dame Review (see separate listing in Magazines/Journals). Make checks payable to University of Notre Dame. **Deadline:** submit May 1- September 1, 2012. 2009 winner was Luisa Igloria (Juan Luna's Revolver). Winners announced by the end of January.

$ ☑ SAWTOOTH POETRY PRIZE

Ahsahta Press, MS1525, 1910 University Dr., Boise State University, Boise ID 83725-1525. (208)426-2195. Fax: (208)426-4373. E-mail: ahsahta@boisestate.ed. Website: http://ahsahtapress. boisestate.edu. The Sawtooth Poetry Prize, sponsored by Ahsahta Press (see separate listing in Books/Chapbooks), honors a book of original poetry in English by a single author. Offers a $1,500 honorarium upon publication and 25 author's copies. Translations are not eligible for this award. "Students and former students of Boise State University and of this year's judge may not enter; close friends of the judge are also not considered eligible." Considers simultaneous submissions, "but entrants are asked to notify Ahsahta Press immediately if a manuscript becomes committed elsewhere." Submit 48-100 pages of poetry, single-spaced, printed on 1 side of 8½x11 or A4 page only. Number pages consecutively. Include acknowledgments page and biographical note, which will be removed before judging. Include 2 title pages: 1 with poet's name, address, phone number, and e-mail address (if available); and 1 without. Poet's name should not appear anywhere else on ms; only the anonymous title page will be sent to the readers and judge. Contain pages in a plain manila folder or bind manuscript with a secure clip; do not bind ms in a notebook. Include SASP for notification of receipt of ms and SASE (#10 business) for results; mss will not be returned. Guidelines available on Web site. **Entry fee:** $25/ms. Make checks payable to Ahsahta Press. (See Web site for payment options outside the U.S.) "Entrants will receive a copy of the winning book when it is printed if they include a 7x10 self-addressed mailer with $3.95 postage. Our books measure 6x8 and will not fit in smaller-sized mailers." **Deadline:** submit January 1-March 1 (postmark). "In addition to announcements in national publications, the winning book and author will be featured on the Ahsahta Web site, as will lists of finalists and semi-finalists." 2008 winner was Barbara Maloutas with The Whole Marie. 2009 judge: Rae Armantrout. "Ahsahta Press, a member of the Council of Literary Magazines and Presses, conforms to the CLMP Code of Ethics and participated in its drafting." Winner will be announced in May 2009.

$ ☑ HELEN SCHAIBLE SHAKESPEAREAN/PETRARCHAN SONNET CONTEST

Poets and Patron of Chicago, Illinois, 416 Gierz St., Downers Grove IL 60515. Website: www. poetsandpatrons.net. **Contact:** Barbara Eaton, contest chair. The annual Helen Schaible Shakespearean/Petrarchan Sonnet Contest is open to anyone. **For sonnets only!** Offers 1st Prize: $50; 2nd Prize: $35; 3rd Prize: $15; plus 3 Honorable Mentions and 3 Special Recognitions (non-cash). **Submit only 1 entry** (2 copies) of either a Shakespearean or a Petrarchan sonnet, which must be original and unpublished. Entry must be typed on 8½x11 paper, double-spaced. Name and address in the upper right-hand corner on only 1 copy. All necessary guidelines appear in this listing. Include SASE with entry to receive winners' list. **Entry fee:** none. **Deadline:** September 1 annually (postmark). Competition receives 150 entries/year. 2008 contest winners were (1st) Teresa Coe, (2nd) Robert Klein Engler, (3rd) Julianna McCarthy. Winners will be notified by mail by November 1, 2009. Poets and Patrons runs 4 workshops a year and Chicagoland Poety Contest. Open membership, $10. offer workshops in Chicago Public Library $10 each. "Read the guidelines--1 sonnet only!"

$ ☐ MONA SCHREIBER PRIZE FOR HUMOR

OUS FICTION & NONFICTION15442 Vista Haven Place, Sherman Oaks CA 91403. E-mail: brad. schreiber@att.net. Website: www.brashcyber.com. Established 2000. **Contact:** Brad Schreiber. Offers annual awards of 1st Prize: $500; 2nd Prize: $250; 3rd Prize: $100. All winners are posted on Web site. Submissions must be unpublished and may be entered in other contests. Submit any number of poems, 750 words maximum/poem. Include contact information on each poem submitted, including e-mail. No SASEs. Guidelines available on Web site. **Entry fee:** $5/ poem. **Deadline:** December 1 annually. Competition receives 340-350 entries/year. Judge: Brad Schreiber. Winners announced December 24 by phone (if U.S.) or by e-mail. "Take risks in form, content, theme, and language."

$ ☐ CLAUDIA ANN SEAMAN POETRY AWARD

(Specialized: students grades 9-12)The Community Foundation of Dutchess County, 80 Washington St., Suite 201, Poughkeepsie NY 12601. (845)452-3077. Fax: (845)452-3083. Website: www.CFDCNY.org. **Contact:** Nevill Smythe, Vice President/Programs. Established 1983. Annual national contest offering award of $500 (1st Prize). Open to U.S. students grades 9-12. Submissions must be unpublished. Considers simultaneous submissions. Submit 1-2 unpublished poems on any subject, in any form. "Entry must contain student and school names, addresses, and phone numbers and the name of the English or writing teacher." Entry guidelines available on Web site. **Entry fee:** none. **Deadline:** June 1. Winner contacted by phone or in writing. Copies of last year's winning poem may be obtained by contacting the Community Foundation by phone, in writing, or on Web site. "The Community Foundation is a nonprofit organization serving Dutchess and Ulster County, New York, and the surrounding area; it administers numerous grant programs, scholarship funds, and endowment funds for the benefit of the community. This is an excellent opportunity for young, previously unpublished poets to earn recognition for their work. Since there's no fee, there is little to lose; realize, however, that a national contest will have more entries than a regional competition."

$ ☐ SHADOW POETRY'S ANNUAL CHAPBOOK COMPETITION

Shadows Ink Publications, 1209 Milwaukee St., Excelsior Springs MO 64024. Fax: (208)977-9114. E-mail: shadowpoetry@shadowpoetry.com. Website: www.shadowpoetry.com. Established 2000. **Contact:** James Summers, award director. Offers biannual award of $250, 50 copies of published chapbook, and 25% royalties paid on each copy sold through Shadow Poetry (retail only). Submissions must be unpublished as a whole (collection). No simultaneous submissions. (Winning poet retains copyrights and may publish individual poems elsewhere later.) Submit ms of 16-40 pages, acknowledgments, table of contents, poet bio, etc., in addition to the poetry. Poetry to be submitted on any subject, in any form, in good taste. "Cover letter required with name, address, phone, age, and e-mail address. Enclose cover letter, manuscript, and cover ideas/art, if applicable, in #90 (9x12) envelope. Include #10 SASE for winner notification and SASP for entry receipt (optional)." Guidelines available for SASE or on Web site. **Entry fee:** $18/ms. Make checks/money orders payable to Shadow Poetry. **Deadline:** December 31. "Notification of winner on April 10 by e-mail and SASE." Copies of winning or sample chapbooks available from Shadow Poetry for $12 US; $12.50 CAN; $15 INT (see Web site for titles).

$ ☐ SHADOWS INK POETRY CONTEST

Shadows Ink Publications, 1209 Milwaukee St., Excelsior Springs MO 64024. Fax: (208)977-9114. E-mail: shadowpoetry@shadowpoetry.com. Website: www.shadowpoetry.com. Established 2000. **Contact:** James Summers, award director. Offers annual award of 1st Prize: $100 and publication in chapbook (plus 20 copies of published work); 2nd Prize: $75; 3rd Prize: $35; top 3 winners also receive a certificate, printed copy of winning poem, and a ribbon. The top 40 placing poems will be published in a Shadows Ink Poetry Chapbook, and all poets appearing in this publication will receive 1 free copy (additional copies available for $8 each plus shipping). Submissions must be unpublished. No simultaneous submissions. (Winning poets retain copyrights and may publish poems elsewhere later.) Submit maximum of 10 poems, 24 line limit each, on any subject, in any form. "Entry form must be present with mail-in entries. Submit entries in duplicate with name, address, phone number, and e-mail address (when available) on upper left-hand corner of one sheet. Enclose #10 SASE for winners list. Include an additional SASE for entry receipt (optional). If no SASE is included for receipt, Shadow Poetry will e-mail an entry confirmation to the contestant, if applicable." Entry form and guidelines available for SASE or on Web site. **Entry fee:** $5/poem. Make checks/money orders payable to Shadow Poetry. **Deadline:** December 31. Competition receives 150 entries/year. "Winners will be announced February 1 by e-mail and to those who requested a winners list. Results will also be posted on the Shadow Poetry Web site."

THE SHENANDOAH/GLASGOW PRIZE FOR EMERGING POETS

Washington and Lee University, Mattingly House, Lexington VA 24450-2116. (540)458-8765. Fax: (540)458-8461. E-mail: lleech@wlu.edu. Website: shenandoah.wlu.edu. **Contact:** Lynn Leech, managing editor. Award for poet with only one published book. Prize: $2,500, publication of new work in Shenandoah. Judged by anonymous writer/editor, announced after prize winner is selected. Entry fee: $25 (includes 1-yr subscription to Shenandoah ; send credit card information or make checks payable to Shenandoah). To apply send first book, 5 poems, SASE, and vita, along with check for $25 (from either author or publisher). Cover letter should include name, address, phone and e-mail. Books submitted for consideration will not be returned and will be donated to the University library after the contest. Guidelines available on Web site. Accepts inquiries by e-mail. Results announced on Web site and winners notified by mail or e-mail in May. Deadline: post-marked between March 15-31. Open to any poet.

☒ $ ☑ SHORT GRAIN CONTEST

Box 67, Saskatoon, SK S7K 3K1 Canada. (306)244-2828. Fax: (306)244-0255. E-mail: grainmag@sasktel.net (inquiries only). Website: www.grainmagazine.ca. **Contact:** Mike Thompson, business administrator (inquiries only). The annual Short Grain Contest includes a category for poetry of any style, including prose poetry up to 100 lines), offering 4 prizes with a first prize of $1,250 plus publication in Grain Magazine (see separate listing in Magazines/Journals). Each entry must be original, unpublished, not submitted elsewhere for publication or broadcast, nor accepted elsewhere for publication or broadcast, nor entered simultaneously in any other contest or competition for which it is also eligible to win a prize. Entries must be typed on 8½x 11 paper. It must be legible. Faxed and/or electronic entries not accepted. No simultaneous submissions. A separate covering page must be attached to the text of your entry, and must provide the following information: poet's name, complete mailing address, telephone number, e-mail address, entry title, category name, and line count. An absolutely accurate word or line count is required. No identifying information on the text pages. Entries will not be returned. Include SASE for results only. **Entry fee:** $30 CAD; $36 US and international entrants; includes 1 year subscription to Grain Magazine. **Deadline:** April 1 for 2009. Winning entries will be posted on the Grain Magazine website in late April/early May.

$ ☑ SLIPSTREAM POETRY CHAPBOOK CONTEST

Dept. W-1, P.O. Box 2071, Niagara Falls NY 14301-0071. (716)282-2616 (after 5 PM, EST). E-mail: editors@slipstreampress.org. Website: www.slipstreampress.org. Established 1980. **Contact:** Contest Director. The annual Slipstream Poetry Chapbook Contest awards $1,000, publication of a chapbook ms, and 50 author's copies. All entrants receive copy of winning chapbook and an issue of Slipstream (see separate listing in Magazines/Journals). Considers simultaneous submissions if informed of status. Accepts previously published work with acknowledgments. Submit up to 40 pages of poetry, any style, format, or theme. Manuscripts will not be returned. Guidelines available for SASE or on Web site. **Entry fee:** $20. **Deadline:** December 1. Latest winner is Carrie Shipers (Rescue Conditions). Winner announced late spring/early summer.

$ ☐ KAY SNOW WRITING AWARDS

Willamette Writers, 9045 SW Barbur Blvd., Suite 5A, Portland OR 97219-4027. (503)452-1592. Fax: (503)452-0372. E-mail: wilwrite@willamettewriters.com. Website: www.willamettewriters. com. Established 1986. **Contact:** Pat Macaodha, award director. Offers annual awards of 1st Prize: $300; 2nd Prize: $150; 3rd Prize: $50 in several genres, including poetry. Submissions must be unpublished. Submit up to 2 poems (1 entry fee), maximum 5 pages total, on any subject, in any style or form, single-spaced, 1 side of paper only. Entry form and guidelines available for SASE or on Web site. **Entry fee:** $10 for members of Willamette Writers; $15 for nonmembers. **Deadline:** January 15-April 23 (postmarked) for 2008. Competition receives 150 entries. 2008 poetry winners were Morgan Songi, Karen Kelta, and Carla Moberg. Winners will be announced July 20th. "Write and send in your very best poem. Read it aloud. If it still sounds like the best poem you've ever heard, send it in."

$ ☑ THE RICHARD SNYDER MEMORIAL PUBLICATION PRIZE

Ashland Poetry Press, 401 College Ave., Ashland University, Ashland OH 44805. (419)289-5957 or (419)289-5110. Website: www.ashland.edu/aupoetry. Established 1969. **Contact:** Sarah Wells, managing editor. Offers annual award of $1,000 plus book publication in a paper-only edition of 1,000 copies. Submissions must be unpublished in book form. Considers simultaneous submissions. Submit 50-80 pages of poetry. **Entry fee:** $25. **Deadline:** April 30 annually. Competition receives 350 entries/year. 2008 Winner was Marc J. Sheehan (Vengeful Hymns). Annual judge: Robert Phillips. Winners will be announced in Writer's Chronicle and Poets & Writers. Copies of winning books available from Small Press Distribution, Baker & Taylor, and directly from the Ashland University Bookstore online. The Ashland Poetry Press publishes 2-4 books of poetry/year.

$ ☐ SOCIETY OF SOUTHWESTERN AUTHORS WRITING CONTEST

P.O. Box 35484, Tucson AZ 85740. (520)293-6373. Fax: (520)293-6363. E-mail: ashleen@comcast.net. Website: www.ssa-az.org. Established 1972. **Contact:** Ashleen O'Gaea, contest coordinator. Society of Southwestern Authors Writing Contest offers annual awards for: short story, personal essay/memoirs, poetry, short stories appropriate for ages 6-12. Cash prizes: 1st-$300; 2nd- $150; 3rd- $75; honorable mention- $25; award certificates; first through honorable mention printed in the Society's annual anthology magazine, The Story Teller. All winners receive copies of The Story Teller. Open to beginners. Submissions must be unpublished. No simultaneous submissions. Submit 40 lines maximum on any subject. All forms welcome. Entry forms and guidelines available on Web site or may be requested by email or send SASE to post office address. **Entry fee:** $10 per poem. **Deadline:** June 1, 2009. Competition receives 95 poems on average each year. 2008 winners: Mary Jo Maguire, Barbara Peabody, Corrine Rawlin, Jean Gietzen, Jay Krenz-Lichtsinn. 2008 judges: Steve Cox, Ken Kennon, Cassius Sargent. Winner notified by mail within a month of being selected. Awards presented at awards luncheon held on the 3rd Sunday of October or sent by mail if winner cannot be present. Copies of winning anthologies available for $10 per copy from SSA. " SSA is a non-profit association of writers and other publishing professionals, founded in 1972. Its objective is to conduct a program of activities designed to promote mutually-supportive friendship among writers, provide recognition of members' achievements, and encourage and assist persons seeking to become published writers. In addition to the writing contest, it sponsors an annual conference in September." Advice: " All contest entrants are asked to read all the requirements thoroughly, and then reread them, to avoid disqualification. However, SSA is writer friendly and encouraging new writers is high on our list."

$ ☑ SOUL-MAKING LITERARY COMPETITION

National League of American Pen Women, Nob Hill, San Francisco Bay Area Branch, 1544 Sweetwood Dr., Broadmoor Vlg. CA 94015-2029. Phone/fax: (650)756-5279. E-mail: PenNobHill@aol.com. Website: www.soulmakingcontest.us. Established 1993. **Contact:** Eileen Malone, award director. Annual open contest offers cash prizes in each of 11 literary categories, including poetry and prose poem. 1st Prize: $100; 2nd Prize: $50; 3rd Prize: $25. Submissions in some categories may be previously published. Submit 3 one-page poems on soul-making theme; any form for open poetry category. No names or other identifying information on mss; include 3x5 card with poet's name, address, phone, fax, e-mail, title(s) of work, and category entered. Include SASE for results only; mss will not be returned. Guidelines available on Web site. **Entry fee:** $5/entry. **Deadline:** November 30. Competition receives 300 entries/year. Names of winners and judges are posted on Web site. Winners announced in January by SASE and on Web site. Winners are invited to read at the Koret Auditorium, San Francisco. Event is televised.

$ ☑ THE SOW'S EAR CHAPBOOK COMPETITION

P.O. Box 127, Millwood VA 22646. E-mail: rglesman@gmail.com. Website: www.sows-ear.kitenet.net. Established 1988. **Contact:** Robert Lesman, managing editor. The Sow's Ear Poetry Review (see separate listing in Magazines/Journals) sponsors an annual chapbook competition. Offers $1,000, publication as the Spring issue of the magazine, and 25 author's copies. Open to adults. Submissions may be previously published individually if poet holds publication rights. Considers simultaneous submissions, "but if your chapbook is accepted elsewhere, you must withdraw promptly from our competition." Submit 22-26 pages of poetry; no length limit on poems, but no more than 1 poem on a page. Include title page and table of contents. Poet's name should not appear on poems, title page, or table of contents. Include separate sheet with chapbook title, poet's name, address, phone number, e-mail address (if available), and publication credits for submitted poems, if any. Include SASE or e-mail address for results only; entries will not be returned. Guidelines available for SASE, by e-mail, or on Web site. **Entry fee:** $20; includes subscription. Make checks payable to The Sow's Ear Poetry Review. Submit in March and April. **Deadline:** May 1 (postmark).

$ ☑ THE SOW'S EAR POERY COMPETITION

P.O. Box 127, Millwood, VA 22646. E-mail: rglesman@gmail.com. Website: www.sows-ear. kitenet.net. Established 1988. **Contact:** Errol Hess, managing editor. The Sow's Ear Poetry Review (see separate listing in Magazines/Journals) sponsors an annual contest for unpublished poems. Offers $1,000 and publication in The Sow's Ear Poetry Review ; also offers the option of publication for top finalists. Submit up to 5 unpublished poems. Include separate sheet with poem titles, poet's name, address, phone number, and e-mail address (if available). "We will check with finalists before sending to final judge." Poet's name should not appear on poems. Include SASE for results only; entries will not be returned. Guidelines available for SASE, by e-mail, or on Web site. **Entry fee:** $20 for up to 5 poems. Contestants receive a year's subscription. Make checks payable to The Sow's Ear Poetry Review. Subit in September orOctober. **Deadline:** November 1 (postmark). Past judges include Gregory Orr and Marge Piercy. "4 criteria help us judge the quality of submissions: 1) Does the poem make the strange familiar or the familiar strange, or both? 2) Is the form of the poem vital to its meaning? 3) Do the sounds of the poem make sense in relation to the theme? 4) Does the little story of the poem open a window on the Big Story of the human situation?"

$ ☐ SPIRE PRESS POETRY CONTEST

532 LaGuardia Place, Suite 298, New York NY 10012. E-mail: editor@spirepress.org. Website: www.spirepress.org. Established 2002. **Contact:** Shelly Reed, award director. Offers annual award of publication with royalty contract and promotion; cash prizes (see guidelines for each year). Submissions must be unpublished. Considers simultaneous submissions as long as Spire Press is informed. Submit a chapbook ms of 18-40 pages of poetry in any form (shorter poems preferred). Include SASE. **Entry fee:** $18/ms. **Deadline:** May 1. Competition receives 400 entries/year. Past winners include Elizabeth Rees (Now That We're Here), Christina Olson (Before I Came Home Naked), Lori Romero (The Emptiness That Makes Other Things Possible), and Anthony Russell White (Faith of Leaping). Winners will be announced on Web site after contest deadline. Copies of winning chapbooks available through Web site, Amazon, selected bookstores, and Spire Press.

$ ☑ THE SPOON RIVER POETRY REVIEW EDITORS' PRIZE

4241 Dept. of English, Publications Unit, Illinois State University, Normal IL 61790-4241. Website: www.litline.org/spoon. Established 1976. **Contact:** Prize Director. The Spoon River Poetry Review Editors' Prize awards $1,000 to 1 winning poem; 2 runners-up will receive $100 each. Winning poem, runners-up, and honorable mentions will be published in the fall issue of The Spoon River Poetry Review (see separate listing in Magazines/Journals). Submissions must be unpublished. Submit 2 copies of 3 poems, maximum 10 pages total. On each page of 1 copy only include poet's name, address, and phone number. No fax or e-mail submissions. Include SASE for results only; mss will not be returned. Guidelines available for SASE or on Web site. **Entry fee:** $16; includes one-year subscription or gift subscription. (Indicate preference and include recipient's name and address.) **Deadline:** April 15 (postmark). 2008 winner was Alexis Quinlan, judged by Paul Zimmer.

$ ☐ SPS STUDIOS BIANNUAL POETRY CARD CONTEST

Blue Mountain Arts, Inc., P.O. Box 1007, Dept. E, Boulder CO 80306. Website: www.sps. com. SPS Studios offers a biannual poetry contest with prizes of $300, $150, and $50 for each competition (winning poems are also published on the SPS Web site). "Poems can be rhyming or non-rhyming, although we find that non-rhyming poetry reads better. We suggest you write about real emotions and feelings and that you have some special person or occasion in mind as you write. Poems are judged on the basis of originality and uniqueness. English-language entries only, please. Enter as often as you like." All entries must be the original creation of the submitting poet, who must own all rights to the entries. Poet gives permission to SPS Studios, Inc. to publish and display the entry on the Web (in electronic form only) if the entry is selected as a winner or finalist. Contest is open to everyone except employees of SPS Studios and their families. Submit entries through online form or by postal mail. "If submitting by regular mail, please do not send us the only copy of your work. If you'd like your entry material returned, enclose a SASE. Label each submission with your name, snail mail address, phone number, and e-mail address (if you have 1)." Guidelines available on Web site. **Entry fee:** none. **Deadline:** June 30 and December 31. Winners will be contacted within 45 days of the deadline date.

▥ ☑ THE ANN STANFORD POETRY PRIZE

c/o Master of Professional Writing Program, 3501 Trousdale Parkway, Mark Taper Hall, THH 355J, University of Southern California, Los Angeles CA 90089-0355. (213)740-3253. E-mail: scr@ college.usc.edu. Website: www.usc.edu/scr. Established 1982. **Contact:** Contest Coordinator. The Ann Stanford Poetry Prize offers 1st Prize: $1,000; 2nd Prize: $200; 3rd Prize: $100. Winners will be published in the Fall edition of Southern California Review (see separate listing in Magazines/Journals). Submissions must be unpublished. Submit up to 5 poems. Include cover sheet with poem titles, poet's name, address, phone number, and e-mail. No identification on submission pages. Incomplete submissions will not be accepted. Include SASE for results. Guidelines available on Web site. **Entry fee:** $10 for up to 5 poems. All entrants receive a free issue of Southern California Review. **Deadline:** December 31.

$ ☑ WALLACE E. STEGNER FELLOWSHIPS

Creative Writing Program, Stanford University, Stanford CA 94305-2087. (650)725-1208. Fax: (650)723-3679. E-mail: mpopek@stanford.edu. Website: www.stanford.edu/dept/english/cw. **Contact:** Mary Popek, program administrator. Offers 5 fellowships in poetry of $26,000 plus tuition of over $7,000/year for promising writers who can benefit from 2 years of instruction and criticism at the Writing Center. "We do not require a degree for admission. No school of writing is favored over any other. Chronological age is not a consideration." **Deadline:** December 1 (postmark). Competition receives about 600 entries/year for poetry. 2008/2009 fellows in poetry were John Evans, Chanda Feldman, Jennifer Foerster, Dina Hardy, and Peter Kline.

$ THE WALLACE STEVENS AWARD

The Academy of American Poets, 584 Broadway, Suite 604, New York NY 10012-3210. (212)274-0343. Fax: (212)274-9427. Website: www.poets.org. Award established 1994. Awards $100,000 annually to recognize outstanding and proven mastery in the art of poetry. **No applications are accepted.** 2006 winner was Michael Palmer. 2006 judges: Robert Hass, Fanny Howe, Susan Stewart, Arthur Sze, and Dean Young.

$ ☐ STEVENS POETRY MANUSCRIPT CONTEST

22614 N. Santiam Hwy., Lyons OR 97358. E-mail: eberry@wvi.com. Website: www.nfsps.com. **Contact:** Eleanor Berry, contest chair. National Federation of State Poetry Societies (NFSPS) offers annual award of $1,000, publication of ms, and 50 author's copies. Individual poems may have been previously published in magazines, anthologies, or chapbooks, but not the entire ms as a collection. Simultaneous submissions allowed. Submit 48-70 pages of poetry by a single author, typewritten, or computer printed, 1 poem or column of poetry to a page. Pages numbered, with table of contents, but no author identification anywhere in ms. Include 2 title pages; 1 with no author identification, the other with name of poet, address, phone number, email address and state poetry society member affiliation, if applicable. No staples or binders; plain manila folder and/or manuscript clip permitted. No illustrations. No disk submissions; no certified or registered mail. Optional: Include SASE for results only; mss will not be returned. Guidelines available for SASE or on Web site. **Entry fee:** $20 for NFSPS members; $25 for nonmembers. Make checks/money orders payable to NFSPS. **Deadline:** October 15 (postmark). Winners announced in January following deadline; entrants who include an email address or SASE will be notified of winner. Book will be published by June and sold at annual NFSPS convention and winning poet (if present) will read from it. Copies of books available through NFSPS Web site.

$ ☑ THE ST. LAWRENCE BOOK AWARD

Black Lawrence Press, P.O. Box 327, Theresa NY 13691. E-mail: editors@blacklawrencepress. com. Website: www.blacklawrencepress.com. Established 2003. **Contact:** Colleen Ryor, editor. The St. Lawrence Book Award is awarded annually for a first collection of poetry or short stories. Prize includes $1,000, publication, 10 author copies, and an interview with the winner in The Adirondack Review (see separate listing in Magazines/Journals). Prizes awarded on publication. Finalists will receive a copy of the winning book. All finalists will be considered for standard publication. "Entrants must not have had a full-length book published. Chapbooks do not count as full-length books." Considers simultaneous submissions, but notify immediately if ms is accepted elsewhere. Submit book-length ms, paginated, with cover letter with brief bio and contact information (including valid e-mail), table of contents, and an acknowledgments page (if applicable). "Finalists will be notified and asked to submit another copy of the manuscript for final judging." Include 2 cover pages: 1 with ms title, brief bio, and poet's contact information (including e-mail); the second with ms title only. Clip together the cover letter, cover pages, acknowledgments, and entry fee. No e-mail submissions. Include SASE or e-mail address for results only; mss will not be returned. Guidelines available on Web site. **Entry fee:** $25. Make checks/money orders payable to Black Lawrence Press. **Deadline:** August 31 annually. 2008 winner was Yelizaveta Renfro (A Catalogue of Everything in the World).

$ ☑ THE RUTH STONE PRIZE IN POETRY

Vermont College, 36 College St., Montpelier VT 05602. (802)828-8633. Fax: (802)828-8649. E-mail: hungermtn@vermontcollege.edu. Website: www.hungermtn.org. Established 2002. **Contact:** Miciah Bay Gault, managing editor. The annual Ruth Stone Prize in Poetry offers $1,000 and publication in Hunger Mountain: The VCFA Journal of the Arts (see separate listing in Magazines/Journals); 2 Honorable Mentions also published. Submit up to 3 poems, not to exceed 6 pages. **Entry fee:** $20. **Deadline:** December 10. Guidelines available for SASE or on Web site. "Include SASE and index card with poem titles and address; do not put name on poems."

$ ☑ MAY SWENSON POETRY AWARD

Utah State University Press, 7800 Old Main Hill, Logan UT 84322-7800. (435)797-1362. Fax:

(435)797-0313. E-mail: michael.spooner@usu.edu. Website: www.usu.edu/usupress. Established 1996. **Contact:** Michael Spooner, director. The annual May Swenson Poetry Award offers $1,000 and publication by Utah State University Press for a full-length poetry collection. No restrictions on form or subject. Submit 50-100 pages of original poetry. Include cover sheet with poet's name and address. Include SASE for results; mss will not be returned. Guidelines available on Web site. **Entry fee:** $25; includes copy of winning book. **Deadline:** September 30 (postmark). 2008 winner was Idris Anderson (Mrs. Ramsay's Knee). 2009 Judge: Billy Collins. See Web site for latest winners and more information.

$ ☑ TANKA SOCIETY OF AMERICA INTERNATIONAL ENGLISH-LANGUAGE TANKA COMPETITION

Website: www.tankasocietyofamerica.com. Offers cash awards and publication of winning poems in Ribbons (see separate listing in Magazines/Journals), the journal of the Tanka Society of America (see separate listing in Organizations). All rights revert to poets after publication. Open to all except TSA officers and judges. Submissions must be unpublished. No simultaneous submissions. Submit any number of original tanka, in English. Guidelines and details available in March issue of Ribbons or on Web site. Written inquiries may be sent to Michael McClintock, president, Tanka Society of America, 9230 N. Stoneridge Lane, Fresno CA 93720.

$ THE TEXAS INSTITUTE OF LETTERS POETRY AWARD

Website: http://texasinstituteofletters.org. Established 1936. The Texas Institute of Letters gives annual awards for books by Texas authors, including the Helen C. Smith Memorial Award for Best Book of Poetry, a $1,200 award. Books must have been first published in the year in question, and entries may be made by authors or by their publishers. Complete guidelines and award information available on Web site. **Deadline:** see Web site. Receives about 30 entries/year. 2007 winner was Cate Marvin (Fragment of the Head of a Queen).

$ ☑ TIGER'S EYE POETRY CONTEST

P.O. Box 2935, Eugene OR 97402. E-mail: tigerseyepoet@yahoo.com. Website: www. tigerseyejournal.com. The Tiger's Eye Poetry Contest offers $500, $100, and $50 to the top 3 poems submitted; in addition, 1 contest entrant will be awarded an editors' choice chapbook contract, with winner receiving 50 copies and publication in the Mid-Spring issue of Tiger's Eye (see separate listing in Magazines/Journals). No previously published poems. Considers simultaneous submissions. Submit 3 poems that represent your best work. No restrictions on form, subject, or length. "We welcome sonnets, haibun, haiku, ghazals, villenelles, etc., as well as free verse and experimental poetry." Include cover page with poet's name and contact information; no identifying information on mss pages. Guidelines available on Web site. **Entry fee:** $10 for 3 poems. **Deadline:** February 28 (postmark). 2009 judge: Thomas Patterson.

$ ☑ LENA-MILES WEVER TODD POETRY SERIES BOOK COMPETITION

Pleiades Press, Dept. of English, University of Central Missouri, Warrensburg MO 64093. (660)543-8106. E-mail: pleiades@ucmo.edu. Website: www.ucmo.edu/englphil/pleiades. Established 1990. **Contact:** Kevin Prufer, editor. The annual Lena-Miles Wever Todd Poetry Series Book Competition offers $1,000 and publication of a book-length ms. Open to all American writers, regardless of previous publication. Submission must be unpublished as a collection, but individual poems may have been previously published elsewhere. Submit at least 48 pages of poetry (one copy). Include 2 cover sheets: one with ms title, poet's name, address, and phone number; the second with ms title only. Also include acknowledgments page for previously published poems. Include SASE for results; for an additional large SASE with $1.24 postage affixed, entrant will receive a copy of the winning book. Guidelines available for SASE or on website. **Entry fee:** $15. Make checks/money orders payable to Pleiades Press. **Deadline:** September 30 (postmark). 2008 winner was Susan Parr for Pacific Shooter. 2009 Final Judge: Martha Collins.

$ ☑ TOWSON UNIVERSITY PRIZE FOR LITERATURE

(Specialized: book MD writer)Towson University, College of Liberal Arts, Towson MD 21252. (410)704-2128. Fax: (410)704-6392. E-mail: eduncan@towson.edu. Website: www.towson.edu. **Contact:** Chair of the English Dept. Offers annual prize of $1,000 "for a single book or book-length manuscript of fiction, poetry, drama, or imaginative nonfiction by a Maryland writer. The prize is granted on the basis of literary and aesthetic excellence as determined by a panel of distinguished judges appointed by the university. The first award, made in the fall of 1980, went to novelist Anne Tyler." Work must have been published within the 3 years prior to the year of nomination or must be scheduled for publication within the year in which nominated. Submit 5 copies of work in bound form or in typewritten, double-spaced ms form. Entry form and guidelines available on Web site (search "Towson Prize for Literature"). **Deadline:** June 15. Competition receives 8-10 entries. 2007 winner was Ron Tanner (A Bed of Nails, Bkmk Press).

$ ☑ TRANSCONTINENTAL POETRY AWARD

Pavement Saw Press,321 Empire Street, Montpelier, OH 43543. E-mail: info@pavementsaw. org. Website: www.pavementsaw.org. Established 1992. **Contact:** David Baratier, editor. The Transcontinental Poetry Award offers $1,000, publication, and a percentage of the print run for a first book. "Each year, Pavement Saw Press will seek to publish at least 1 book of poetry and/or prose poems from manuscripts received during this competition, which is open to anyone who has not previously published a volume of poetry or prose. Writers who have had volumes of poetry and/or prose under 40 pages printed, or printed in limited editions of no more than 500 copies, are eligible." Submit 48-70 pages of poetry (1 poem/page), paginated and bound with a single clip. Include 2 cover sheets: 1 with ms title, poet's name, address, phone number, and e-mail, if available, the second with ms title only (this sheet should be clipped to ms). Also include one-page cover letter (a brief biography, ms title, poet's name, address, and telephone number, e-mail, and poet's signature) and acknowledgments page (journal, anthology, chapbook, etc., and poem published). Include SASP for acknowledgment of receipt; SASE unnecessary as result will be sent with free book and no mss will be returned. Guidelines available for SASE or on Web site. **Entry fee:** $20; electronic submissions $27. "All U.S entrants will receive books, chapbooks, and journals equal to, or more than, the entry fee. Add $3 (USD) for other countries to cover the extra postal charge if sending by mail." Make checks payable to Pavement Saw Press. **Deadline:** reads submissions in June, July, and until August 15 (must have August 15 or earlier postmark).

$ ☑ TUFTS POETRY AWARDS

(Specialized: for emerging poet & for first book)The Center for the Arts and Humanities at Claremont Graduate University, 160 E. 10th St., Harper East B7, Claremont CA 91711-6165. (909)621-8974. Website: www.cgu.edu/tufts. Established 1992. **Contact:** Susan Hampson, special events coordinator. The annual Kingsley Tufts Poetry Award offers $100,000 for a work by an emerging poet, "one who is past the very beginning but has not yet reached the acknowledged pinnacle of his/her career." The Kate Tufts Discovery Award ($10,000) is for a first book. Books considered for the 2010 awards must have been published between September 15, 2008 and

September 15, 2009. Entry form and guidelines available for SASE or on Web site. **Deadline:** September 15, 2009. 2008 winners are Tom Sleigh (Space Walk) and Jannice Harrington (Even the Hollow My Body Made is Gone). Winners announced in February. Check Web site for updated deadlines and award information.

$ ☑ WAR POETRY CONTEST

(Specialized: war-themed poetry)Winning Writers, 351 Pleasant St., PMB 222, Northampton MA 01060-3961. (866)946-9748. Fax: (413)280-0539. E-mail: adam@winningwriters.com. Website: www.winningwriters.com/war. Established 2002. **Contact:** Adam Cohen, award director. Offers annual award of 1st Prize: $2,000; 2nd Prize: $1,200; 3rd Prize: $600; 12 Honorable Mentions of $100 each. All prizewinners receive online publication at WinningWriters.com; selected finalists may also receive online publication. Submissions must be unpublished. Considers simultaneous submissions. Submit 1-3 poems of up to 500 lines total on the theme of war, any form, style, or genre. No name on ms pages, typed or computer-printed on letter-size white paper, single-sided. Submit online or by regular mail. Guidelines available for SASE or on Web site. **Entry fee:** $15 for group of 1-3 poems. **Deadline:** November 15-May 31. Competition receives about 650 entries/ year. 2007 winner was Kyle McDonald for "The Rose of Ilium." 2007 judge: Jendi Reiter. Winners announced on November 15 at WinningWriters.com and in free e-mail newsletter. Entrants who provided valid e-mail addresses will also receive notification. (See separate listing for the Wergle Flomp Humor Poetry Contest in this section and for Winning Writers in the Additional Resources section.)

$ ☑ WASHINGTON POETS ASSOCIATION ANNUAL POETRY CONTEST

Website: www.washingtonpoets.org. Established 1971. Sponsored annually by the Washington Poets Association (see separate listing in Organizations), offers over $1,000 total in cash awards. Entries accepted in 4 categories: William Stafford Award (any form), Carlin Aden Award (traditional rhyme/meter), Charlie Proctor Award (humorous, any form), and Francine Porad Award (haiku). Submissions must be made online only. Previously published poems, poems that have won awards, and poems awarded money frmo any previous WPA contest are not eligible. There is a 50-line maximum limit to any poem submitted. Submit up to 10 poems per contest. See guidelines for complete instructions. Include SASE for notification; poems will not be returned. Entry form and guidelines available on Web site. **Entry fee:** $5 general fee, plus $1/ poem entered. **Deadline:** 2009's submission period was January 21-May 15. "Washington Poets Association reserves the right to publish winning poems in its newsletter and Web site and is granted permission to print Award and Honorable Mention poems in future anthologies."

$ ☑ THE WASHINGTON PRIZE

The Word Works, P.O. Box 42164, Washington DC 20015. E-mail: editor@wordworksdc.com (inquiries only). Website: www.wordworksdc.com. Established 1981. **Contact:** Miles Moore, prize administrator. The Washington Prize offers $1,500 and publication of a book-length ms of original poetry in English by a living American poet (U.S. or Canadian citizen or resident). Submit a ms of 48-64 pages. Include title page with poet's name, address, phone number, e-mail address, and signature. Poet's name and contact information should appear on the title page only. Also include table of contents (with ms title) and a cover letter containing acknowledgments and a brief bio.Attach acknowledgments and bio to title page with a staple. Use a binder clip to secure the ms. No scripts will be returned. Indicate the information source where you learned about the Washington Prize (for example, AWP newsletter, Poets & Writers Magazine, the Word Works Web site). Send entries to this address only by First Class Mail: Nancy White, administrator,

Word Works Washington Prize, Dearlove Hall, Adirondack Community College, 640 Bay Road, Queensbury NY 12804. **Entry fee:** $25 (includes copy of winning book). Make checks payable to The Word Works and should be drawn from a US Bank only. **Deadline:** submit January 15-March 1 (postmark). Winners announced in 2009. Book publication planned for January 2010.

$ ☑ ROBERT WATSON LITERARY PRIZES

The Greensboro Review, MFA Writing Program, 3302 HHRA Building, University of North Carolina at Greensboro, Greensboro NC 27402-6170. Website: www.greensbororeview.org. Established 1966. **Contact:** Contest Coordinator. The annual Robert Watson Literary Prizes include a $500 award for poetry. All entries meeting guidelines will be considered for publication in The Greensboro Review (see separate listing in Magazines/Journals). Submissions must be unpublished. No simultaneous submissions. Submit poems of any length, typed. No e-mail submissions. Include SASE for results or (with additional postage) for return of ms (mss will not be returned unless specifically requested by author). Guidelines available in magazine, for SASE, or on Web site. **Entry fee:** none. **Deadline:** December 31 (postmark) annually.

$ ☑ WERGLE FLOMP HUMOR POETRY CONTEST

(Specialized: parody of vanity contest entries)Winning Writers, 351 Pleasant St., PMB 222, Northampton MA 01060-3961. (866)946-9748. Fax: (413)280-0539. E-mail: adam@ winningwriters.com. Website: www.winningwriters.com/wergle. Established 2002. **Contact:** Adam Cohen, award director. Offers annual award of 1st Prize: $1,359; 2nd Prize: $764; 3rd Prize: $338; plus 12 Honorable Mentions of $72.95 each. All prizewinners receive online publication at WinningWriters.com. Submissions may be previously published. Considers simultaneous submissions. Submit 1 poem of any length, in any form, but must be "a humor poem that has been submitted to a 'vanity poetry contest' as a joke. See Web site for examples." Entries accepted only through Web site; no entries by regular mail. Guidelines available on Web site. **Entry fee:** none. **Deadline:** August 15-April 1. Competition receives about 800 entries/year. 2008 winner was Benjamin Taylor Lilly for "First Edition, 2008." 2008 judge: Jendi Reiter. Winners announced on August 15 at WinningWriters.com and in free e-mail newsletter. "Please read the past winning entries and the judge's comments published at WinningWriters.com. Guidelines are a little unusual--please follow them closely. See separate listing for the War Poetry Contest in this section and for Winning Writers in the Additional Resources section.

▣ $ WESTERN AUSTRALIAN PREMIER'S BOOK AWARDS

(Specialized: native & resident poets of Western Australia) State Library of Western Australia, Alexander Library Bldg., Perth Cultural Centre, Perth WA 6000 Australia. (61)(8)9427-3111. Fax: (61)(8)9427-3256. E-mail: doug.george@slwa.wa.gov.au. Website: www.slwa.wa.gov.au/pba. html. Established 1982. **Contact:** Doug George, awards manager. Offers annual poetry prize of $7,500 AUD for a published book of poetry. Winner also eligible for Premier's Prize of $20,000 AUD. Submissions must be previously published. Open to poets born in Western Australia, current residents of Western Australia, or poets who have resided in Western Australia for at least 10 years at some stage. Entry form and guidelines available for SASE or on Web site. **Entry fee:** none. **Deadline:** March, 2009. Competition receives about 10-15 entries in poetry category per year (175 overall). 2006 poetry winner was Dennis Haskell for All the Time in the World. Judges: Mr. Andrew Taylor, Ms. Chloe Mauger, Prof. John Tonkin, and Ms. Margot Lang. Winners announced in November each year (i.e., June 2008 for 2007 awards) at a presentation dinner given by the Premier of Western Australia. "The contest is organized by the State Library of Western Australia, with money provided by the Western Australian State Government to support literature."

$ ☑ THE WHITE PINE PRESS POETRY PRIZE

White Pine Press, P.O. Box 236, Buffalo NY 14201. E-mail: wpine@whitepine.org. Website: www.whitepine.org. Established 1973. **Contact:** Dennis Maloney, editor. The White Pine Press Poetry Prize offers $1,000 plus publication for a book-length collection of poems by a U.S. author. Submissions must be unpublished as a collection, but individual poems may have been previously published elsewhere. Submit 60-80 pages of poetry, typed, with table of contents. Include cover sheet with poet's name, address, e-mail address, and phone number. No e-mail submissions. Include SASP for notification of receipt of ms and SASE for results only; mss will not be returned. Guidelines available for SASE or on Web site. **Entry fee:** $20. Make checks payable to White Pine Press. **Deadline:** submit July 1-November 30 (postmark). 2008 winner was Al Maginnes (Ghost Alphabet). Judge: poet of national reputation. Winning books available from local booksellers and White Pine Press.

$ WHITING WRITERS' AWARDS

Mrs. Giles Whiting Foundation, 1133 Avenue of the Americas, 22nd Floor, New York NY 10036-6710. Website: www.whitingfoundation.org. **Contact:** Barbara K. Bristol, director. The Foundation makes awards of $50,000 each to up to 10 writers of fiction, nonfiction, poetry, and plays. Winners are chosen by a selection committee drawn from a list of recognized writers, literary scholars, and editors. Recipients of the award are selected from nominations made by writers, educators, and editors from communities across the country whose experience and vocations bring them in contact with individuals of unusual talent. The nominators and selectors are appointed by the foundation and serve anonymously. **Direct applications and informal nominations are not accepted by the foundation.**

$ ☑ THE WALT WHITMAN AWARD

The Academy of American Poets, 584 Broadway, Suite 604, New York NY 10012. (212)274-0343. Fax: (212)274-9427. E-mail: awards@poets.org. Website: www.poets.org. Award established 1975. **Contact:** awards coordinator. Offers $5,000, publication of a poet's first book by Louisiana State University Press, and a one month residency at the Vermont Studio Center. The Academy of American Poets purchases copies of the Whitman Award-winning book for distribution to its members. Submit mss of 50-100 pages. Poets must be American citizens. Entry form required; entry form and guidelines available for SASE (in August) or on Web site. **Entry fee:** $25. **Deadline:** November 30. 2008 winner was Jonathan Thirkield (The Waker's Corridor). Winner announced in May.

$ ☑ STAN AND TOM WICK POETRY PRIZE

Wick Poetry Center, 301 Satterfield Hall, Kent State University, P.O. Box 5190, Kent OH 44242-0001. (330)672-2067. Fax: (330)672-3333. E-mail: wickpoet@kent.edu. Website: http://dept.kent.edu/wick. Established 1994. **Contact:** Maggie Anderson, director. Offers annual award of $2,000 and publication by Kent State University Press. Open to poets writing in English who have not yet published a full-length collection. Submissions must be unpublished as a collection, but individual poems may have been previously published elsewhere. Considers simultaneous submissions as long as the Wick Poetry Center receives notice upon acceptance elsewhere. Submit 50-70 pages of poetry. Include cover sheet with poet's name, address, telephone number, e-mail address, and title of ms. Guidelines available for SASE or on Web site. **Entry fee:** $20. **Deadline:** submit February 1-May 1. Competition receives 700-800 entries.

$ THE RICHARD WILBUR AWARD

(Specialized: American poets only) Dept. of English, University of Evansville, 1800 Lincoln Ave., Evansville IN 47722. (812)488-2963. Website: http://english.evansville.edu/english/WilburAwardGuidelines.htm. **Contact:** William Baer, series director. Offers a biennial award (even-numbered years) of $1,000 and book publication to "recognize a quality book-length manuscript of poetry." Submissions must be unpublished original poetry collections ("although individual poems may have had previous journal publications") and "public domain or permission-secured translations may comprise up to 1/3 of the manuscript." Considers simultaneous submissions. Open to all American poets. Submit ms of 50-100 typed pages, unbound, bound, or clipped. Manuscripts should be accompanied by 2 title pages: 1 with ms title, author's name, address, e-mail, and phone number; 1 with ms title only. Include SASE for results only; mss are not returned. Guidelines available for SASE or on Web site. **Entry fee:** $25/ms. **Deadline:** December 1. Competition receives 300-500 entries. Winning ms is published and copyrighted by the University of Evansville Press.

N WISCONSIN INSTITUTE FOR CREATIVE WRITING FELLOWSHIP

University of Wisconsin-Madison, Creative Writing, Madison WI 53706. (608)263-3374. E-mail: rfkuka@wisc.edu. Website: www.creativewriting.wisc.edu. **Contact :** Ron Kuka, program coordinator. Fellowship provides time, space and an intellectual community for writers working on first books. Receives approximately 300 applicants a year for each genre. Prize: $17,000 for a 9-month appointment. Judged by English Department faculty and current fellows. **Entry fee**: $40, payable to the Department of English. Applicants should submit up to 10 pages of poetry or one story of up to 30 pages and a résumé or vita directly to the program during the month of February. An applicant's name must not appear on the writing sample (which must be in ms form) but rather on a separate sheet along with address, social security number, phone number, e-mail address and title(s) of submission(s). Candidates should also supply the names and phone numbers of two references. Accepts inquiries by e-mail and phone. **Deadline: February**. "Candidates must not yet have published, or had accepted for publication, a book by application deadline." Open to any writer with either an M.F.A. or Ph.D. in creative writing. Please enclose a SASE for notification of results. Results announced by May 1. "Send your best work. Stories seem to have a small advantage over novel excerpts."

$ ☑ WORKING PEOPLE'S POETRY COMPETITION

Blue Collar Review, P.O. Box 11417, Norfolk VA 23517. E-mail: red-ink@earthlink.net (inquiries only). Website: www.partisanpress.org. The Working People's Poetry Competition offers $100 and a one-year subscription to Blue Collar Review (see separate listing in Magazines/Journals) and "one year posting on of winning poem on our Web site. Poetry should be typed as you would like to see it published, with your name and address on each page. Include cover letter with entry." Guidelines available on Web site. **Entry fee:** $15. Make checks payable to Partisan Press. **Deadline:** May 1. Previous winner was Kent Newkirk.

$ ☑ THE YALE SERIES OF YOUNGER POETS

(Specialized: U.S. poets under age 40)Yale University Press, P.O. Box 209040, New Haven CT 06520-9040. Website: http://yalepress.yale.edu/yupbooks/youngerpoets.asp. **Contact:** Contest Coordinator. Established 1919. The Yale Series of Younger Poets offers publication and royalties to 1 winning book-length ms. Open to U.S. citizens under age 40 at the time of entry who have not published a volume of poetry; poets may have published a limited edition chapbook of 300 copies or less. Poems may have been previously published in newspapers and periodicals and used in the book ms if so identified. No translations. Submit 48-64 pages of poetry, paginated, printed single-sided, with each new poem starting on a new page. Do not bind or staple ms; loose sheets may be placed in an envelope of appropriate size. Include 2 cover sheets: 1 showing ms title, poet's name, address, telephone number, e-mail address, and page count; the second with manuscript title only. Also include table of contents and acknowledgments page, as well as a brief bio at the end of ms (optional). Include SASP for notification of receipt of ms and SASE for results; mss will not be returned. No e-mail submissions. Guidelines (with additional submission details) available on Web site. **Entry fee:** $15. Make checks/money orders payable to Yale University Press. **Deadline:** submit October 1-November 15 (postmark). 2008 winner was Arda Collins (It is Daylight).

$ ☑ THE W.B. YEATS SOCIETY ANNUAL POETRY COMPETITION

W.B. Yeats Society of New York, National Arts Club, 15 Gramercy Park S, New York NY 10003. (212)780-0605. Website: www.YeatsSociety.org. Established 1990. **Contact:** Andrew McGowan, president. Offers annual $250 cash prize for 1st Place, $100 cash prize for 2nd Place, and optional Honorable Mentions. Open to beginner as well as established poets. Winners are invited to read their poems at an awards event held each spring in New York; also inducted as Honorary Members of the W.B. Yeats Society, a 501(c)(3) charitable organization (see separate listing in Organizations). Submissions must be unpublished. Considers simultaneous submissions. Submit any number of unpublished poems in any style or form, up to 60 lines each, typed on letter-size paper without poet's name. Guidelines available for SASE or on Web site; no entry form required. **Entry fee:** $8 for first poem, $7 for each additional poem. Attach a 3x5 card to each entry containing the poem's title along with the poet's name, address, and phone/fax/e-mail. **Deadline:** February 1 annually. Receives 100-200 entries/year. 2008 winners were Steve Lautermilch, Char Sundust, Michael Colonnese, and Margot Zucker Mindich. 2008 judge: Alice Quinn. Winners selected by March 31 and announced in April. Winning entries and judge's report are posted on the Society's Web site. Printed report available for SASE.

ADDITIONAL CONTESTS & AWARDS

The following listings also contain information about contests and awards. Turn to the page numbers indicated for details about their offerings.

Grants

State & Provincial

Arts councils in the United States and Canada provide assistance to artists (including poets) in the form of fellowships or grants. These grants can be substantial and confer prestige upon recipients; however, **only state or province residents are eligible**. Because deadlines and available support vary annually, query first (with a SASE) or check Web sites for guidelines.

UNITED STATES ARTS AGENCIES

Alabama State Council on the Arts, 201 Monroe St., Montgomery AL 36130-1800. (334)242-4076. E-mail: staff@arts.alabama.gov. Web site: www.arts.state.al.us.

Alaska State Council on the Arts, 411 W. Fourth Ave., Suite 1-E, Anchorage AK 99501-2343. (907)269-6610 or (888)278-7424. E-mail: aksca_info@eed.state.ak.us. Web site: www.eed.state.ak.us/aksca.

Arizona Commission on the Arts, 417 W. Roosevelt St., Phoenix AZ 85003-1326. (602)771-6501. E-mail: info@azarts.gov. Web site: www.azarts.gov.

Arkansas Arts Council, 1500 Tower Bldg., 323 Center St., Little Rock AR 72201. (501)324-9766. E-mail: info@arkansasarts.com. Web site: www.arkansasarts.com.

California Arts Council, 1300 I St., Suite 930, Sacramento CA 95814. (916)322-6555. E-mail: info@caartscouncil.com. Web site: www.cac.ca.gov.

Colorado Council on the Arts, 1625 Broadway, Suite 2700, Denver CO 80202. (303)892-3802. E-mail: online form. Web site: www.coloarts.state.co.us.

Commonwealth Council for Arts and Culture (Northern Mariana Islands), P.O. Box 5553, CHRB, Saipan MP 96950. (670)322-9982 or (670)322-9983. E-mail: galaidi@vzpacifica.net. Web site: www.geocities.com/ccacarts/ccacwebsite.html.

Connecticut Commission on Culture & Tourism, Arts Division, One Financial Plaza, 755 Main St., Hartford CT 06103. (860)256-2800. Web site: www.cultureandtourism.org.

Delaware Division of the Arts, Carvel State Office Bldg., 4th Floor, 820 N. French St., Wilmington DE 19801. (302)577-8278 (New Castle Co.) or (302)739-5304 (Kent or Sussex Counties). E-mail: delarts@state.de.us. Web site: www.artsdel.org.

District of Columbia Commission on the Arts & Humanities, 410 Eighth St. NW, 5th Floor, Washington DC 20004. (202)724-5613. E-mail: cah@dc.gov. Web site: http://dcarts.dc.gov.

Florida Arts Council, Division of Cultural Affairs, R.A. Gray Building, Third Floor, 500 S.

Bronough St., Tallahassee FL 32399-0250. (850)245-6470. E-mail: info@florida-arts.org. Web site: http://dcarts.dc.gov.

Georgia Council for the Arts, 260 14th St., Suite 401, Atlanta GA 30318. (404)685-2787. E-mail: gaarts@gaarts.org. Web site: www.gaarts.org.

Guam Council on the Arts & Humanities Agency, P.O. Box 2950, Hagatna GU 96932. (671)646-2781. Web site: www.guam.net.

Hawaii State Foundation on Culture & the Arts, 2500 S. Hotel St., 2nd Floor, Honolulu HI 96813. (808)586-0300. E-mail: ken.hamilton@hawaii.gov. Web site: http.state.hi.us/sfca.

Idaho Commission on the Arts, 2410 N. Old Penitentiary Rd., Boise ID 83712. (208)334-2119 or (800)278-3863. E-mail: info@arts.idaho.gov. Web site: www.arts.idaho.gov.

Illinois Arts Council, James R. Thompson Center, 100 W. Randolph, Suite 10-500, Chicago IL 60601. (312)814-6750. E-mail: iac.info@illinois.gov. Web site: www.state.il.us/agency/iac.

Indiana Arts Commission, 150 W. Market St., Suite 618, Indianapolis IN 46204. (317)232-1268. E-mail: IndianaArtsCommission@iac.in.gov. Web site: www.in.gov/arts.

Institute of Puerto Rican Culture, P.O. Box 9024184, San Juan PR 00902-4184. (787)724-0**700.** **E-mail: www@icp.gobierno.pr. Web site: www.icp.gobierno.pr.**

Iowa Arts Council, 600 E. Locust, Des Moines IA 50319-0290. (515)281-6412. Web site: www.iowaartscouncil.org.

Kansas Arts Commission, 700 SW Jackson, Suite 1004, Topeka KS 66603-3761. (785)296-3335. E-mail: KAC@arts.state.ks.us. Web site: http://arts.state.ks.us.

Kentucky Arts Council, 21st Floor, Capital Plaza Tower, 500 Mero St., Frankfort KY 40601-1987. (502)564-3757 or (888)833-2787. E-mail: kyarts@ky.gov. Web site: http://artscouncil.ky.gov.

Louisiana Division of the Arts, Capitol Annex Bldg., 1051 N. 3rd St., 4th Floor, Room #420, Baton Rouge LA 70804. (225)342-8180. Web site: www.crt.state.la.us/arts.

Maine Arts Commission, 193 State St., 25 State House Station, Augusta ME 04333-0025.

(207)287-2724. E-mail: MaineArts.info@maine.gov. Web site: www.mainearts.com.

Maryland State Arts Council, 175 W. Ostend St., Suite E, Baltimore MD 21230. (410)767-6555. E-mail: msac@msac.org. Web site: www.msac.org.

Massachusetts Cultural Council, 10 St. James Ave., 3rd Floor, Boston MA 02116-3803. (617)727-3668. E-mail: mcc@art.state.ma.us. Web site: www.massculturalcouncil.org.

Michigan Council of History, Arts, and Libraries, 702 W. Kalamazoo St., P.O. Box 30705, Lansing MI 48909-8205. (517)241-4011. E-mail: artsinfo@michigan.gov. Web site: www.michigan.gov/hal/0,1607,7-160-17445_19272---,00.html.

Minnesota State Arts Board, Park Square Court, 400 Sibley St., Suite 200, St. Paul MN 55101-1928. (651)215-1600 or (800)866-2787. E-mail: msab@arts.state.mn.us. Web site: www.arts.state.mn.us.

Mississippi Arts Commission, 501 N. West St., Suite 701B, Woolfolk Bldg., Jackson MS 39201. (601)359-6030. Web site: www.arts.state.ms.us.

Missouri Arts Council, 815 Olive St., Suite 16, St. Louis MO 63101-1503. (314)340-6845 or (866)407-4752. E-mail: moarts@ded.mo.gov. Web site: www.missouriartscouncil.org.

Montana Arts Council, 316 N. Park Ave., Suite 252, Helena MT 59620-2201. (406)444-6430. E-mail:

Grants

mac@mt.gov. Web site: www.art.state.mt.us.

National Assembly of State Arts Agencies, 1029 Vermont Ave. NW, 2nd Floor, Washington DC 20005. (202)347-6352. E-mail: nasaa@nasaa-arts.org. Web site: www.nasaa-arts.org.

Nebraska Arts Council, 1004 Farnam St., Plaza Level, Omaha NE 68102. (402)595-2122 or (800)341-4067. Web site: www.nebraskaartscouncil.org.

Nevada Arts Council, 716 N. Carson St., Suite A, Carson City NV 89701. (775)687-6680. E-mail: online form. Web site: http://dmla.clan.lib.nv.us/docs/arts.

New Hampshire State Council on the Arts, 21/2 Beacon St., 2nd Floor, Concord NH 03301-4974. (603)271-2789. Web site: www.nh.gov/nharts.

New Jersey State Council on the Arts, 225 W. State St., P.O. Box 306, Trenton NJ 08625. (609)292-6130. Web site: www.njartscouncil.org.

New Mexico Arts, Dept. of Cultural Affairs, P.O. Box 1450, Santa Fe NM 87504-1450. (505)827-6490 or (800)879-4278. Web site: www.nmarts.org.

New York State Council on the Arts, 175 Varick St., New York NY 10014. (212)627-4455. Web site: www.nysca.org.

North Carolina Arts Council, 109 East Jones St., Cultural Resources Building, Raleigh NC 27601. (919)807-6500. E-mail: ncarts@ncmail.net. Web site: www.ncarts.org.

North Dakota Council on the Arts, 1600 E. Century Ave., Suite 6, Bismarck ND 58503. (701)328-7590. E-mail: comserv@state.nd.us. Web site: www.state.nd.us/arts.

Ohio Arts Council, 727 E. Main St., Columbus OH 43205-1796. (614)466-2613. Web site: www.oac.state.oh.us.

Oklahoma Arts Council, Jim Thorpe Building, 2101 N. Lincoln Blvd., Suite 640, Oklahoma City OK 73105. (405)521-2931. E-mail: okarts@arts.ok.gov. Web site: www.arts.state.ok.us.

Oregon Arts Commission, 775 Summer St. NE, Suite 200, Salem OR 97301-1280. (503)986-0082. E-mail: oregon.artscomm@state.or.us. Web site: www.oregonartscommission.org.

Pennsylvania Council on the Arts, 216 Finance Bldg., Harrisburg PA 17120. (717)787-6883. Web site: www.pacouncilonthearts.org.

Rhode Island State Council on the Arts, One Capitol Hill, Third Floor, Providence RI 02908. (401)222-3880. E-mail: info@arts.ri.gov. Web site: www.arts.ri.gov.

South Carolina Arts Commission, 1800 Gervais St., Columbia SC 29201. (803)734-8696. E-mail: info@arts.state.sc.us. Web site: www.southcarolinaarts.com.

South Dakota Arts Council, 711 E. Wells Ave., Pierre SD 57501-3369. (605)773-3301. E-mail: sdac@state.sd.us. Web site: www.artscouncil.sd.gov.

Tennessee Arts Commission, 401 Charlotte Ave., Nashville TN 37243-0780. (615)741-1701. Web site: www.arts.state.tn.us.

Texas Commission on the Arts, E.O. Thompson Office Building, 920 Colorado, Suite 501, Austin TX 78701. (512)463-5535. E-mail: front.desk@arts.state.tx.us. Web site: www.arts.state.tx.us.

Utah Arts Council, 617 E. South Temple, Salt Lake City UT 84102-1177. (801)236-7555. Web site: http://arts.utah.gov.

Vermont Arts Council, 136 State St., Drawer 33, Montpelier VT 05633-6001. (802)828-3291. E-mail: online form. Web site: www.vermontartscouncil.org.

Virgin Islands Council on the Arts, 5070 Norre Gade, St. Thomas VI 00802-6872. (340)774-5984. Web site: http://vicouncilonarts.org.

Virginia Commission for the Arts, Lewis House, 223 Governor St., 2nd Floor, Richmond VA 23219. (804)225-3132. E-mail: arts@arts.virginia.gov. Web site: www.arts.state.va.us.

Washington State Arts Commission, 711 Capitol Way S., Suite 600, P.O. Box 42675, Olympia WA 98504-2675. (360)753-3860. E-mail: info@arts.wa.gov. Web site: www.arts.wa.gov.

West Virginia Commission on the Arts, The Cultural Center, Capitol Complex, 1900 Kanawha Blvd. E., Charleston WV 25305-0300. (304)558-0220. Web site: www.wvculture.org/arts.

Wisconsin Arts Board, 101 E. Wilson St., 1st Floor, Madison WI 53702. (608)266-0190. E-mail: artsboard@arts.state.wi.us. Web site: www.arts.state.wi.us.

Wyoming Arts Council, 2320 Capitol Ave., Cheyenne WY 82002. (307)777-7742. E-mail: ebratt@state.wy.us. Web site: http://wyoarts.state.wy.us.

CANADIAN PROVINCES ARTS AGENCIES

Alberta Foundation for the Arts, 10708-105 Ave., Edmonton AB T5H 0A1. (780)427-9968. Web site: www.affta.ab.ca/index.shtml.

British Columbia Arts Council, P.O. Box 9819, Stn. Prov. Govt., Victoria BC V8W 9W3. (250)356-1718. E-mail: BCArtsCouncil@gov.bc.ca. Web site: www.bcartscouncil.ca.

The Canada Council for the Arts, 350 Albert St., P.O. Box 1047, Ottawa ON K1P 5V8. (613)566-4414 or (800)263-5588 (within Canada). Web site: www.canadacouncil.ca.

Manitoba Arts Council, 525-93 Lombard Ave., Winnipeg MB R3B 3B1. (204)945-2237 or (866)994-2787 (in Manitoba). E-mail: info@artscouncil.mb.ca. Web site: www.artscouncil.mb.ca.

New Brunswick Arts Board (NBAB), 634 Queen St., Suite 300, Fredericton NB E3B 1C2. (506)444-4444 or (866)460-2787. Web site: www.artsnb.ca.

Newfoundland & Labrador Arts Council, P.O. Box 98, St. John's NL A1C 5H5. (709)726-2212 or (866)726-2212. E-mail: nlacmail@nfld.net. Web site: www.nlac.nf.ca.

Nova Scotia Department of Tourism, Culture, and Heritage, Culture Division, 1800 Argyle St., Suite 601, P.O. Box 456, Halifax NS B3J 2R5. (902)424-4510. E-mail: cultaffs@gov.ns.ca. Web site: www.gov.ns.ca/dtc/culture.

Ontario Arts Council, 151 Bloor St. W., 5th Floor, Toronto ON M5S 1T6. (416)961-1660 or (800)387-0058 (in Ontario). E-mail: info@arts.on.ca. Web site: www.arts.on.ca.

Prince Edward Island Council of the Arts, 115 Richmond St., Charlottetown PE C1A 1H7. (902)368-4410 or (888)734-2784. E-mail: info@peiartscouncil.com. Web site: www.peiartscouncil.com.

Québec Council for Arts & Literature, 79 boul. René-Lévesque Est, 3e étage, Quebec QC G1R 5N5. (418)643-1707 or (800)897-1707. E-mail: info@calq.gouv.qc.ca. Web site: www.calq.gouv.qc.ca.

The Saskatchewan Arts Board, 2135 Broad St., Regina SK S4P 1Y6. (306)787-4056 or (800)667-7526 (Saskatchewan only). E-mail: sab@artsboard.sk.ca. Web site: www.artsboard.sk.ca.

Yukon Arts Funding Program, Cultural Services Branch, Dept. of Tourism & Culture, Government of Yukon, Box 2703 (L-3), Whitehorse YT Y1A 2C6. (867)667-8589 or (800)661-0408 (in Yukon). E-mail: arts@gov.yk.ca. Web site: www.tc.gov.yk.ca/216.html.

Conferences, Workshops & Festivals

There are times when we want to immerse ourselves in learning. Or perhaps we crave a change of scenery, the creative stimulation of being around other artists, or the uninterrupted productivity of time alone to work.

That's what this section of *Poet's Market* is all about, providing a selection of writing conferences and workshops, artist colonies and retreats, poetry festivals, and even a few opportunities to go traveling with your muse. These listings give the basics: contact information, a brief description of the event, lists of past presenters, and offerings of special interest to poets. Contact an event that interests you for additional information, including up-to-date costs and housing details. **(Please note that most directors had not finalized their 2009 plans when we contacted them for this edition of *Poet's Market*. However, where possible, they provided us with their 2008 dates, costs, faculty names or themes to give you a better idea of what each event has to offer.)**

Before you seriously consider a conference, workshop or other event, determine what you hope to get out of the experience. Would a general conference with one or two poetry workshops among many other types of sessions be acceptable? Or are you looking for something exclusively focused on poetry? Do you want to hear poets speak about poetry writing, or are you looking for a more participatory experience, such as a one-on-one critiquing session or a group workshop? Do you mind being one of hundreds of attendees, or do you prefer a more intimate setting? Are you willing to invest in the expense of traveling to a conference, or would something local better suit your budget? Keep these questions and others in mind as you read these listings, view Web sites and study conference brochures.

Some listings are coded with symbols to provide certain "information at a glance." The (N) symbol indicates a recently established conference/workshop; the (✗) symbol indicates this conference/workshop did not appear in the 2008 edition; the (☑) symbol denotes a Canadian event and the (⊞) symbol one located outside the U.S. and Canada.

The Additional Conferences, Workshops & Festivals list at the end of this section cross-references conference, workshop and festival information in other sections of this book. To find out more, go to the page number indicated for each listing.

AMERICAN CHRISTIAN WRITERS CONFERENCES

P.O. Box 110390, Nashville TN 37222. (800)21-WRITE. E-mail: ACWriters@aol.com. Website: www.ACWriters.com. Established 1981. **Contact:** Reg Forder, director. Annual 2-day events. Holds 30 conferences/year in cities including Houston, Boston, Minneapolis, Chicago, St. Louis, Detroit, Atlanta, Miami, Phoenix, and Los Angeles. Location: usually a major hotel chain like Holiday Inn. Average attendance: 40-80.

Purpose/Features Open to anyone. Conferences cover fiction, poetry, writing for children. Offers poets ms critiques.

Costs/Accommodations Cost: $99-169. Participants responsible for all meals. Accommodations available on site.

Additional Information Also sponsors an annual Caribbean Christian Writers Conference Cruise each November. Additional information available for SASE, by e-mail, or on Web site.

▦ ANAM CARA WRITER'S AND ARTIST'S RETREAT

Eyeries, Beara, Co. Cork, Ireland. +353 (0)27 74441. Fax: +353 (0)27 74448. E-mail: anamcararetreat@gmail.com. Website: www.anamcararetreat.com. **Contact:** Sue Booth-Forbes, director. Offers up to one-month individual retreats as well as workshops for writers and artists. Length of workshops varies with subject and leader/facilitator. Location: "Beara is a rural and hauntingly beautiful part of Ireland that is kept temperate by the Gulf Stream. The retreat sits on a hill overlooking Coulagh Bay, the mountains of the Ring of Kerry, and the Slieve Mishkish Mountains of Beara. The village of Eyeries is a short walk away." Average attendance: 5 residents at the retreat when working individually; 12-18 workshop participants.

Purpose/Features "Anam Cara is open to novice as well as professional writers and artists. Applicants are asked to provide a written description on the focus of their work while on retreat. Residencies are on a first-come, first-deposit-in basis." 2007 workshops included sessions on poetry, painting, haiku, creative nonfiction, and fiction.

Costs/Accommodations 2009 cost: residency fee ranges from & #8364;600-700/week for individual retreats, depending on room, and includes full room and board; editorial consulting; laundry; sauna; hot tub overlooking Coulagh Bay; 5 acres of gardens, meadows, riverbank and cascades, river island, swimming hole, and several unique working spots, such as the ruin of a stone mill and a sod-roofed beehive hut. Overflow from workshops stay in nearby B& Bs, a 10-minute walk or 2-minute drive away. Transportation provided if needed. Details regarding transporation to Anam Cara available on Web site.

Additional Information Requests for specific information about rates and availability can be made through the Web site; also available by fax or e-mail.

ⓝ ARTIST-IN-RESIDENCE NATIONAL PARKS

E-mail: Acadia_Information@nps.gov. Website: http://www.nps.gov/archive/volunteer/air. htm. **Contact:** Artist-In-Residence Coordinator. 29 National Parks offer residency programs open to two-dimensional visual artists, photographers, sculptors, performers, writers, composers, video/filmmakers, and others. See Web site for individual park and contact information.

▦ ART WORKSHOPS IN GUATEMALA

4758 Lyndale Ave. S., Minneapolis MN 55419-5403. (612)825-0747. E-mail: info@artguat.org. Website: www.artguat.org. Established 1995. **Contact:** Liza Fourre, director. Annual 10-day creative writing courses, held in February, March, July, and October. Location: workshops held in Antigua, the old colonial capital of Guatemala. Average attendance: limit 10 students.

Purpose/Features Art Workshops in Guatemala provides "the perfect getaway for creative writers of all skill levels looking for a memorable and inspiring writing/travel experience."

Workshops include "Journey of the Soul" (with Sharon Doubiago) and "Snapshots in Words" (with Roseann Lloyd).

Costs/Accommodations 2009 cost: $1,745. Includes "tuition, lodging in a beautiful old colonial home, a hearty breakfast, ground transportation, and some pretty interesting cultural field trips."

Additional Information Individual poetry critiques included. Call, write, e-mail, or check Web site.

ASPEN SUMMER WORDS WRITING RETREAT & LITERARY FESTIVAL

110 E. Hallam St., Suite 116, Aspen CO 81611. (970)925-3122. Fax: (970)920-5700. E-mail: info@ aspenwriters.org. Website: www.aspenwriters.org. Established 1976. Annual 5-day writing retreat and concurrent 5-day literary festival. 2009 dates: June 21-26. Location: Aspen, Colorado. Average attendance: 120 for the retreat, 300 for the festival.

Purpose/Features Offers a celebration of words and ideas featuring 30 top authors, agents, and editors in up to 5 daily literary events for readers and writers. Offers poetry workshops, readings, publishing panels, interviews, Q& As, and agent/editor meetings. 2009 poetry faculty included Ron Carlson, Hallie Ephron, Gary Ferguson, William Loizeaux, Christopher Merrill, Nic Pizzolatto, and Pamela Painter.

Costs/Accommodations 2008 cost: $475 for 4-day workshop and a $25 reading fee for juried workshops; $250 for 2-day symposium; $175 for 2-day reader's retreat; $200 for literary festival (5-day pass). Offers $50 discount for workshop participants and Aspen Writers' Foundation members. Participants responsible for dinner only; lunch and a continental breakfast are included in the tuition. "We offer two wine and hors d'oeuvres receptions for ASW registrants." Information on overnight accommodations available on website.

Additional Information 2009: Deadline for admission was April 6; deadline for discount housing was May 9. Writing sample required for some courses. A limited number of partial-tuition scholarships available. Brochure and application available by phone, fax, e-mail (include regular mailing address with all e-mail inquiries), or can be downloaded from website.

ᴺ ATLANTIC CENTER FOR THE ARTS

1414 Art Center Ave, New Smyrna Beach FL 32618. (386)427-6975. Website: http:// atlanticcenterforthearts.org. Three week long residency offered several times a year.

Purpose/Features "Associates selected will get one-on-one experience with a Master Artist. The Master Artist selects Associate Residents from the applications."

Costs/Accommodations $850; $25 non-refundable application fee. Financial aid is availableParticipants responsible for all meals.Accommodations available on site. See Web site for application schedule and materials.

AUSTIN INTERNATIONAL POETRY FESTIVAL

P.O. Box 41224, Austin TX 78704. (512)731-5907. E-mail: aipfdirector@gmail.com. Website: www.aipf.org. **Contact**: Ashley S. Kim, festival director. Established 1993. Annual 4-day event. 2010 dates: April 15-18. Location: Austin, TX. Average attendance: 250.

Purpose/Features Open to all poets. Offers poets workshops, faculty readings, participant readings, and slams. Adult and youth yearly anthologies and anthology readings. 2008 featured poets included Afaa Weaver, Eran Tzelgov, Olga Samples Davis, John Row, Jericho Brown, Agnes Meadows, Bob Mudd, plus many U.S. and Austin area poets.

Costs/Accommodations 2010 cost: $35; includes anthology submission fee, program bio, scheduled reading at one of AIPF's 15 venues, participation in all events, two catered meals, workshop participation, and more.

Additional Information Offers poetry contest as part of festival. Guidelines available on Web site. Registration form available on Web site. "Largest non-juried poetry festival in the U.S.!"

BREAD LOAF WRITERS' CONFERENCE

; Middlebury College, Middlebury VT 05753. (802)443-5286. Fax: (802)443-2087. Email: blwc@middlebury.edu. Website: www.middlebury.edu/blwc. **Contact:** Noreen Cargill, administrative manager. Director: Michael Collier. Established 1926. Annual 11-day event. 2009 dates: August 12-23. Location: mountain campus of Middlebury College. Average attendance: 230.

Purpose/Features Conference is designed to promote dialogue among writers and provide professional critiques for students. Offers poets workshops, lectures, faculty readings, and ms critiques. 2009 poetry presenters included Edward Hirsch, Brigit Pegeen Kelly, Alan Shapiro, Tom Sleigh, Arthur Sze, Natasha Trethewey, Ellen Bryan Voight.

Costs/Accommodations 2009 cost: $2,469 (general applicant) or $2,365 (auditor), including tuition, room, and board. Conference fellowships and scholarships available. See website for eligibility guidelines, application deadlines, and other important information.

Additional Information Sponsors the Bakeless Literary Publication Prizes, an annual book series competition for new authors of literary works in poetry, fiction, and creative nonfiction (see separate listing in Contests & Awards).

CAVE CANEM

(Specialized: African American poets)584 Broadway, Suite 508, New York NY 10012. (212)941-5720. Fax: (212)941-5724. E-mail: alisonmeyers@ccpoets.org. Website: www.cavecanempoets.org. Established 1996. **Contact:** Alison Myers, executive director. Three-year fellowship, completed in five years. Successful candidates participate in an annual residency. Usually held last week in June. Location: University of Pittsburgh at Greensburg, PA. Average attendance: 54.

Purpose/Features Open to African American poets. Participants selected based on a sample of 6-8 poems. Offerings include workshops by fellows and faculty, evening readings. 2008 faculty included co-founders Toi Derricotte, Cornelius Eady, Colleen J. McElroy, Carl Phillips, Claudia Rankine, and Reginald Shepherd. Guest poet: Ntozake Shange.

Costs/Accommodations 2008 cost: $500, including room and board. Tuition is free. For complete information, contact Cave Canem.

Additional Information Poets should submit 6-8 poems with cover letter. 2009 deadline: March 17, 2009, receipt with accepted poets notified by April 30. Cave Canem Foundation also sponsors the Cave Canem Poetry Prize (see separate listing in Contests & Awards section).

CHAUTAUQUA WRITERS' CENTER

P.O. Box 28, Chautauqua NY 14722. (617)447-0503. E-mail: csilver230@aol.com. Website: http://writers.ciweb.org. Established 1988. **Contact:** Clara Silverstein, program director. Annual season of 9 separate weeklong workshops held late June to late August. Participants may attend one week or more. Location: Victorian lakeside village in western New York; most Writers' Center programs offered in the Literary Arts Center at Alumni Hall. Average attendance: no more than 12 workshop participants and 5 non-participating auditors may enroll in each workshop to assure individual attention.

Purpose/Features Provides "a lively community of writers at all levels of development who cultivate the courage, craft, and vision necessary to grow as artists" under the tutelage of nationally recognized poets-in-residence. Poetry workshops meet 2 hours daily, 8:30-10:30 a.m. 2008 poetry faculty includes Susan Grimm, Margaret Gibson, Philip Terman, Geraldine Connolly, Todd Davis, Philip Brady, Jim Daniels, Terrance Hayes, and Laura Kasischke. Other features include prose workshops, free Sunday afternoon readings by writers-in-residence,

Brown Bag lunches and lectures every Tuesday and Friday at 12:15 p.m,, and open mic events every Sunday.

Costs/Accommodations 2008 cost: $100/weeklong workshop. Participants responsible for gate fees ($325/week), housing, and meals. See Web site for accommodations options, which range from the Athenaeum Hotel to local rooming houses and condos.

Additional Information Most workshop leaders offer private half hour conferences. Fee: $25, payable directly to leader. Additional information available by phone, e-mail, or on Web site. Also sponsors The Chautauqua Writers' Festival (see separate listing in this section). Publishes the literary journal *Chautauqua* (see separate listing in Magazines/Journals).

COLGATE WRITERS' CONFERENCE

Office of Summer Programs, Colgate University, 13 Oak Dr., Hamilton NY 13346. (315)228-7770. Fax: (315)228-6543. E-mail: info@cvwc.net. Website: www.cvwc.net. **Contact:** Matthew Leone, conference director. Established 1996. Annual weeklong event. 2009 dates: June 21-27. Location: Colgate University, "an expansive campus, with classrooms, dormitories, libraries, and recreational facilities all in close proximity to each other." Average attendance: 75.

Purpose/Features Open to "all serious writers or aspirants." Offers poets workshops, lectures, readings, and ms critiques. 2009 poetry staff included Peter Balakian, Jennifer Brice, Jon Clinch, Paul Cody, Justin Cronin, Ryan Fischer-Harbage, Alice Fulton.

Costs/Accommodations 2009 cost: for poetry workshop, $995 (tuition, room, and board); $750 for day students. Meal plan available for day students. Accommodations available on site.

Additional Information Each applicant must submit a ms with his/her application. Brochure and registration form available for SASE or on Web site.

THE COLRAIN POETRY MANUSCRIPT CONFERENCE

Concord Poetry Center, 40 Stow. St., Concord MA 01742. (978)897-0054. E-mail: conferences@ colrainpoetry.com. Website: www.colrainpoetry.com. Established 2004. **Contact:** Joan Houlihan, founding director. Usually held 10 times/year in 3-day, weekend sessions. Location: Colrain, MA, Greenfield, MA, and others. Average attendance: 12 poets.

Purpose/Features "The first poetry conference realistically designed to set poets who have a completed manuscript or a manuscript-in-progress on a path toward book publication. Three-day intensive conference includes a manuscript preparation workshop and in-depth meetings with poetry press editors." Also offers evening poetry readings, an editorial panel Q& A, and an after-conference strategy session. 2009 faculty include Joan Houlihan (Concord Poetry Center), Frederick Marchant (Suffolk University), Jeffrey Levine (Tupelo Press), Martha Rhodes (Four Way Books), Jeffrey Shotts (Graywolf Press), Ellen Dore Watson (Smith College Poetry Center), and others.

Costs/Accommodations 2009 cost: $995-$1395, includes lodging, meals, and tuition.

Additional Information Details, application, and registration form available on Web site.

THE CONFERENCE ON POETRY AND TEACHING

(Specialized: for high school & middle school teachers)The Frost Place, P.O. Box 74, Franconia NH 03580. (603)823-5510. E-mail: rfrost@ncia.net. Website: www.frostplace.org. **Contact:** Jim Schley and Baron Wormser, co-directors. Annual event. 2009 dates: June 28-July 2.

Purpose/Features Designed for high school and middle school classroom teachers to work closely with their peers. Brings together poets and teachers to address "how poetry can be shared with young people, not as a fossilized system of literary tropes but as a living art."

Costs/Accommodations 2009 cost: $625 plus $97 for five lunches and 2 dinners (optional but recommended). Additional cost of $546 ($495 for NH residents) for 3 graduate credits through

Plymouth State University. Overnight accommodations available locally.

Additional Information To apply, send letter describing current teaching situation and literary interests. Additional information available on Web site.

GERALDINE R. DODGE POETRY FESTIVAL

Geraldine R. Dodge Poetry Program, P.O. Box 1239, Morristown NJ 07962-1239. (973)540-8442 ext. 5. Website: www.dodgepoetry.org. Established 1986. Biennial 4-day event usually held in early fall. 2008 dates: September 25-28; check Web site for 2010 dates. Location: Waterloo Village in Stanhope, NJ. Average attendance: nearly 17,000 in 2006.

Purpose/Features Biennial celebration of poetry for poets, students, teachers, and the general public. Presents panels, talks, and workshops covering a range of topics and issues related to poetry; offers an ambitious schedule of poetry readings featuring the cream of contemporary poets. 2008 featured poets included Billy Collins, Lucille Clifton, Martin Espada, Edward Hirsch, Ted Kooser, and many more.

Costs/Accommodations Check Web site for latest information. Passes can be purchased at a discount for multiple days. Audience members responsible for own lodging and meals. Information on overnight accommodations available on Web site.

Additional Information Sign up online for mailing list.

⌖ FESTIVAL INTERNATIONAL DE LA POÉSIE

Maison de la Po& #233;sie, 1497 Laviolette, C.P. 335, Trois-Rivi& #232;res QC G9A 5G4 Canada. (819)379-9813. Fax: (819)376-0774. E-mail: info@fiptr.com. Website: www.fiptr.com. Established 1985. President/Founder: Gaston Bellemare. Annual 10-day poetry festival. 2008 dates: 3-12 October 08. Location: Trois Rivi& #232;res, Quebec, Canada. Average attendance: 35,000-40,000.

Purpose/Features The International Poetry Festival/Festival international de la poe& #233;sie has become "a veritable literary Happening." Showcases 125 poets from 30 countries spanning 5 continents. Poets participate in over 350 events in more than 90 different venues, including cafes, bars, restaurants, art galleries, theatres, and museums. Readings are all in French. Program and list of participating poets available on Web site.

Costs/Accommodations Dinner and lunch reservations recommended at restaurants where poetry readings take place. Accommodations available at local inns, pensions, motels, and hotels. Information on travel and overnight accommodations available from the Tourism Bureau (Office de Tourisme et des Congrès de Trois-Rivie& #232;res) at www.tourismetroisrivieres. com. **Additional Information** Offers several festival prizes for published and unpublished poets. Guidelines available on Web site.

FINE ARTS WORK CENTER

24 Pearl St., Provincetown MA 02657. (508)487-9960, ext. 103. Fax: (508)487-8873. E-mail: workshops@fawc.org. Website: www.fawc.org. Established 1968. **Contact:** Dorothy Antczak, summer program director. Offers more than 70 weeklong and weekend workshops in poetry, fiction, and creative nonfiction. Location: The Fine Arts Work Center in Provincetown.

Purpose/Features The Fine Arts Work Center in Provincetown is "a nonprofit organization dedicated to providing emerging writers and visual artists with time and space in which to pursue independent work in a community of peers." Seven-month fellowships are awarded to poets and fiction writers in the emerging stages of their careers; professional juries make admissions decisions. The 2009 Summer Workshop program runs from June 13 through August 21, 2009.

Costs/Accommodations 2009 cost: Summer Workshop Program fees range $600-725.

Accommodations available at the Work Center for $675 for 6 nights. Additional accommodations available locally.

Additional Information See Web site for details and an application form.

FISHTRAP

P.O. Box 38, Enterprise OR 97828. (541)426-3623. E-mail: rich@fishtrap.org. Website: www.fishtrap.org. **Contact:** Rick Bombaci, director. Established 1988. Holds annual summer workshops. 2009 dates: July 5-12. Location: "The old Methodist Camp at the edge of the Eagle Cap Wilderness." Average attendance: 12/workshop; 8 workshops offered, not all in poetry. Workshops followed by weekend "gathering" with readings, discussions, live music.

Purpose/Features Open to anyone. "Fishtrap's mission is to "promote good writing and clear thinking in and about the West; also to encourage and promote new writers." Offers poetry workshops, open mics, friendly and egalitarian atmosphere.

Costs/Accommodations 2009 cost: $400 for 5-day workshop; $75-200/person for cabin lodging; $50-175 for meals. Other accommodations available locally. Information on overnight accommodations available on Web site.

Additional Information Awards up to 5 fellowships. Covers room and board and workshop registration. Additional information available on Web site.

▧ ☑ FOOTHILL COLLEGE WRITERS' CONFERENCE

12345 El Monte Rd., Los Altos Hills CA 94022. (650)949-7924. Fax: (650)949-7695. E-mail: svetichkella@foothill.edu. Website: www.foothill.edu/la/conference. Established 1976. **Contact:** Kella de Castro Svetich, PhD/Director. Annually in July. Location: Los Altos, California. Average attendance: 150-250.

Purpose/Features Open to any writers. Offers poets workshops, lectures, faculty readings, participant readings, ms critiques. panels. 2009 presenters included: Alan Cheuse, Lesley Dauer, Sharon Doubiago, Danielle Haysbert, Scott Inguito, Linda Janakos, Avotcja Jiltonilro, Carol Lem, and more.

Costs/Accommodations $53. Participants responsible for all meals. Accommodations available at area hotels. Information on overnight accommodations available in brochure, by e-mail, on Web site.

THE FROST PLACE ADVANCED SEMINAR

The Frost Place, P.O. Box 74, Franconia NH 03580. (603)823-5510. E-mail: rfrost@ncia.net. Website: www.frostplace.org. **Contact:** Jeanne Marie Beaumont, seminar director. Held annually in early August following the Frost Place Annual Festival of Poetry. 2009 dates: August 2-7. Average attendance: limited to 16 participants.

Purpose/Features Priority given to those who have participated in A Frost Place Seminar at least once before as well as talented first-time participants. Offers daily lecture on poetry of the past, workshop focusing on participant poems, and evening reading. 2009 poetry staff: Jeanne Marie Beaumont, Martha Collins, Jeffrey Harrison, and guest presenter Susan Thomas.

Costs/Accommodations 2009 cost: $975 tuition includes six dinners and four lunches.

Additional Information available on Web site.

THE FROST PLACE SEMINAR ON POETRY AND TEACHING

The Frost Place, P.O. Box 74, Franconia NH 03580. (603)823-5510. E-mail: rfrost@ncia.net. Website: www.frostplace.org. **Contact:** Baron Wormser, seminar director; Dawn Potter, Associate Director. 2009 dates: June 28-July 2.

Purpose/Features "A unique opportunity for teachers to work closely with their peers and with a team of illustrious, enthusiastic poets. Biographies of the guest poets and information about applications, tuition, financial aid, and accommodations are available on the Web site."

Costs/Accommodations 2009: $625 tuition plus $97 for five lunches and two dinners. For an additional $546 ($495) for New Hampshire Residents, this conference can be taken as a credit-level course, earning three credits through Plymouth State University.

GREEN LAKE WRITERS CONFERENCE

Green Lake Conference Center, W2511 State Highway 23, Green Lake WI 54941-9599. 920-294-7327 or 920-294-3323. E-mail: janwhite@glcc.org. Website: www.glcc.org. Established 1948. **Contact:** Jan White. Annual weeklong event. 2009 dates: August 23-28. Location: Green Lake, WI.

Purpose/Features "Attendees may be well-published or beginners, may write for secular and/or Christian markets. Leaders are experienced writing teachers. Spend 11½ contact hours in the workshop of your choice: fiction, nonfiction, poetry, inspirational/devotional. Also take in as many seminars as you wish to enhance specific skills: marketing, humor, songwriting, writing for children, self-publishing, writing for churches, interviewing, memoir writing, the magazine market. Evening: panels of experts will answer your questions. Social and leisure activities."

Costs/Accommodations Brochure and scholarship info from Web site or contact Jan White.

Additional Information GLCC is in South Central Wisconsin, has 1000 acres, 212 miles of shoreline on Wisconsin's deepest lake, and offers a beautiful resort setting. Hotels, lodges, and all meeting rooms are a/c. Affordable rates, excellent meals. Party and writers' showcase.

▨ HAIKU NORTH AMERICA CONFERENCE

1275 Fourth St. PMB #365, Santa Rosa CA 95404. E-mail: welchm@aol.com. Website: www.haikunorthamerica.com. Established 1991. **Contact:** Michael Dylan Welch Five days, held every two years at varying locations throughout North America. 2009 dates: August 5-9, 2009 (tenth biennial conference), National Library of Canada, 395 Wellington Street, Ottawa, Ontario, Canada. 2011 dates to be determined.

Purpose/Features Haiku North America (HNA) is the largest gathering of haiku poets and scholars in the United States and Canada. It is an extended weekend full of workshops, papers, panels, readings, performances, book sales, and socialization with fellow poets, translators, scholars, editors, and publishers. Both established and aspiring haiku poets are welcome. HNA conferences take place every two years, usually in the summer, in changing locations around the continent. Conference events include readings that highlight various geographical regions, a banquet, a conference haiku anthology, and a rich variety of workshops and presentations by the leading haiku aficionados currently exploring haiku as a literary art. Past featured presenters have included William J. Higginson, Sonia Sanchez, Haruo Shirane, Jane Hirshfield, Hiroaki Sato, James W. Hackett, Cor van den Heuvel, Steven Carter, Sam Hamill, Lucien Stryk, Kazuo Sato, Janine Beichman, Gerald Vizenor, Regina Weinreich, Lee Gurga, Jim Kacian, Richard Gilbert, Michael Dylan Welch, and many more.

Costs/Accommodations Typically around $200, including a banquet and some additional meals. Accommodations at discounted hotels nearby are an additional cost. Information available on Web site as details are finalized closer to the conference date.

Additional Information Past conferences have been held in San Francisco (twice), Toronto, Portland (Oregon), Chicago, Boston, New York City, Port Townsend (Washington), Winston-Salem (North Carolina), and Ottawa (Ontario). In the words of Jim Kacian, founder of the Haiku Foundation, "Haiku North America . . . is intellectually diverse, socially expansive, emotionally gratifying," and "provides more than any other single experience the sense that haiku is a literary force to be reckoned with and capable of work that matters in the rest of the world."

HIGHLAND SUMMER CONFERENCE

P.O. Box 7014, Radford University, Radford VA 24142. (540)831-5366. Fax: (540)831-5951. E-mail: rbderrick@radford.edu. Website: www.radford.edu/~arsc. Established 1977. **Contact:** Dr. Grace Toney Edwards, director. Annual 2-week event. Dates: Two weeks in early June. Location: Radford University campus. Average attendance: 25.

Purpose/Features Open to everyone. "The conference, a lecture/seminar/workshop combination, is conducted by well-known guest writers and offers the opportunity to study and practice creative and expository writing within the context of regional culture." Poetry, fiction, and essays (prose) are generally covered each year, as are various topics. Recent workshops led by Ron Rash, Bill Brown, Frank X Walker, and Darnell Arnoult.

Costs/Accommodations 2007 cost: $816-1944; daily meal plans are available and individual meals may also be purchased. On-site housing costs range from $29-40/night. On-site accommodations available at one of the university dormitories. Accommodations also available at local motels.

Additional Information Brochure and registration form available for SASE.

INDIANA UNIVERSITY WRITERS' CONFERENCE

464 Ballantine Hall, Indiana University, Bloomington IN 47405. (812)855-1877. Fax: (812)855-9535. E-mail: writecon@indiana.edu. Website: www.indiana.edu/~writecon. Established 1940. **Contact:** Bob Bledsoe, director. Annual week-long event. 2009 dates: June 14-19. Location: Bloomington campus of Indiana University. Average attendance: 100.

Purpose/Features Open to all. Offers poets workshops, classes, readings, and ms critiques. 2009 poetry faculty included Thomas Lux, Arcelis Girmay, and David Trinidad.

Costs/Accommodations 2009 cost: $500 for workshop (including all classes); $250 for classes only. $50 application fee. Information on overnight accommodations available on Web site.

Additional Information Poetry workshop applicants must submit up to 10 pages of poetry with application. Registration form available for SASE, by e-mail, or on Web site.

IOWA SUMMER WRITING FESTIVAL

C215 Seashore Hall, University of Iowa, Iowa City IA 52242. (319)335-4160. Fax: (319)335-4039. E-mail: iswfestival@uiowa.edu. Website: www.uiowa.edu/~iswfest. Established 1987. **Contact:** Amy Margolis, director. Annual 6-week event. See Web site for dates. Includes one-week and weekend workshops at the University of Iowa campus. Average attendance: 150/week.

Purpose/Features "Open to all adults 21 and over who have a desire to write." Offers poets workshops, lectures, discussions, and participant readings in either weeklong or weekend formats. Participants in weeklong workshops have private conference/critique with workshop leader. 2008 poetry staff included Michael Dennis Browne, Katie Ford, Douglas Goetsch, Richard Jackson, Michael Morse, and Juliet Patterson.

Costs/Accommodations 2007 cost: $250 for a weekend course and $500-525 for a one-week course. Participants responsible for most meals. Accommodations available at area hotels. Information on overnight accommodations available by phone or on Web site.

Additional Information Brochure and registration form available upon request or on Web site.

THE IWWG SUMMER CONFERENCE

The International Women's Writing Guild, P.O. Box 810, Gracie Station, New York NY 10028. (212)737-7536. Fax: (212)737-9469. E-mail: iwwg@iwwg.org. Website: www.iwwg.org. Established 1978. **Contact:** Hannelore Hahn, executive director. 2009 dates: June 12-19. Location: Skidmore College in Saratoga Springs, NY. Average attendance: 450.

Purpose/Features Open to all women. Around 65 workshops offered each day. 2008 poetry staff included Barbara Garro, Marj Hahne, D.H. Melhem, Myra Shapiro, and Susan Baugh.

Costs/Accommodations 2008 cost: $1,085 (single), $945 (double) for IWWG members; $1,130 (single), $990 (double) for nonmembers. Includes program and room and board for 7 nights, 21 meals at Skidmore College. Shorter conference stays available, such as 5 days or weekend. Commuters welcome.

Additional Information Post-conference retreat weekend also available. Additional information available for SASE, by e-mail, or on Web site.

ⓝ JACKSON HOLE WRITERS CONFERENCE

P.O. Box 1974, Jackson WY 83001. (307)413-3331. E-mail: tim@jacksonholewritersconference.com. Website: http://jacksonholewritersconference.com. Established 1990. **Contact**: Tim Sandlin. Annual four day event held in Jackson, Wyoming. Dates for 2009: Jan. 25-28. Average attendance: 110.

Purpose/Features Open to "all writers, fiction, poetry nonfiction, adventure/travel magazine, and young adult." Offers poets workshops, lectures, participant readings, and ms critiques. Poetry presenters for 2009 were: Ravi Shankar, Katharine Coles.

Costs/Accommodations 2008 cost was $360-390. Participants responsible for some meals. Accommodations available at area hotels. Information on overnight accommodations available in brochure, by e-mail, and on Web site.

Additional Information Brochure and registration form available by e-mail and on Web site.

JENTEL ARTIST RESIDENCY PROGRAM

Jentel Foundation, 130 Lower Piney Creek Rd., Banner WY 82832. (307)737-2311. Fax: (307)737-2305. E-mail: jentel@jentelarts.org. Website: www.jentelarts.org. Established 2000. One-month residencies throughout the year, scheduled the 15th of 1 month through the 13th of the following month. Application deadlines are September 15 and January 15 annually. Location: Banner, WY. Average attendance: 2 writers in any genre (also 4 visual artists in any media).

Purpose/Features Residency program for writers and visual artists who are U.S. citizens or from the international community currently residing in the U.S., are 25 years and older, and are not matriculated students. "Set in a rural ranch setting in the foothills of the Big Horn Mountains of North Central Wyoming, Jentel offers unfettered time and space to focus on the creative process, experience of Wyoming landscape, and interact as desired with a small community of writers and artists." Special features include Jentel Presents, a monthly evening of slide presentations and readings by residents in 1 of the surrounding communities.

Costs/Accommodations Residents are responsible for travel expenses and personal items. "Jentel provides a private accommodation in a shared living space, a comfortable private studio, and a stipend to help defray the cost of food and personal expenses. Staff takes residents grocery shopping weekly after the stipend is distributed. Staff will pick up and drop off residents at the airport and bus station in Sheridan, 20 miles from the ranch setting of Jentel." Accommodation provided in a large house with common living and dining areas; fully equipped kitchen; library with computer, printer, and Wireless Internet access; media room with television, DVD/video player, and CD player; spacious private bedroom; and separate private studio.

Additional Information Brochure and application form available for self-addressed mailing label and 58 cents postage, or on Web site.

KENYON REVIEW WRITERS WORKSHOP, THE

Kenyon College, Gambier OH 43022. (740)427-5207. E-mail: reacha@kenyon.edu. Website: www.kenyonreview.org/workshops. **Contact:** Anna Duke Reach, director of summer programs and special events. Annual 8-day event. 2009 dates: June 21-27. Location: the Kenyon College campus. Average attendance: 10/class.

Resources

Purpose/Features Offers the time, setting, and community for writers to practice and develop their art. Focuses on the generation and revision of new work, although participants may bring works-in-progress. Offers poets one-on-one meetings with instructors, exercises and discussions, and public readings by distinguished visiting writers and workshop participants. 2009 poetry instructors were David Baker, Carl Phillips, Deborah Digges.

Costs/Accommodations 2008 cost: $1,995 (includes tuition, room, and meals). A $200 discount is offered to returning participants. Participants are housed in modern campus apartments with computer access.

Additional Information College and non-degree graduate credit available. Online application form and writing sample submission available on Web site. Early application is encouraged as space is limited.

□ NELSON CENTER FOR THE ARTS RESIDENCY, KIMMEL HARDING

801 3rd Corso, Nebraska City NE 68410.402-874-9600. Fax: 402-874-9600. E-mail: pfriedli@ khncenterforthearts.org. Website: www.khncenterforthearts.org. Established 2001. **Contact:** Pat Friedli, assistant director. Annual event consisting of 2, 4, 6, or 8 week stays.

Purpose/Features Open to all skill levels. See Web site for details.

Costs/Accommodations $25 application fee, participant responsible for all meals. Accommodations available on site.

KUNDIMAN POETRY RETREAT

(Specialized: Asian American) 245 Eighth Ave #151, New York NY 10011. E-mail: info@kundiman. org. Website: www.kundiman.org. Established 2002. **Contact:** Sarah Gambito, executive director. Annual 5 day retreat in the last week of June. 2008 dates were June 25-29. Location: The University of Virginia, Charlottesville, VA. Average attendance: 18.

Purpose/Features Open to Asian American poets. Offers poets workshops, lectures, faculty readings, fellow readings, and mentorship sessions with fellows. 2008 poetry presenters include Bei Dao, Tan Lin, and Aimee Nezhukumatathil. **Costs/Accommodations** $325 - includes all housing and meal costs. Tuition is free to accepted fellows. Accommodations available on site.

Additional Information Guidelines available on Web site. Brochure and registration form available on Web site. "Open to Asian American poets. Renowned faculty will conduct workshops and provide one-on-one mentorship sessions with fellows. Readings and informal social gatherings will also be scheduled. Fellows selected based on sample of 6-8 poems and short essay answer. Applications should be received between February 1-March 1."

ℕ ☑ LEDIG HOUSE INTERNATIONAL WRITERS RESIDENCY

55 Fifth Ave., 15th Floor, New York NY 10003.Fax: (212)206-6114. E-mail: writers@artomi.org. Website: www.artomi.org. Residency duration: 2 weeks to 2 months. Average attendance: Up to 20 writers per session. Residency. Site: "Up to 20 writers per session--10 at a given time-- live and write on the stunning 300 acre grounds and sculpture park that overlooks the Catskill Mountains."

Costs/Accommodations Residents provide their own transportation. Offers overnight accommodations.

Additional Information "Agents and editors from the New York publishing community are invited for dinner and discussion. Bicycles, a swimming pool, and nearby tennis court are available for use."

LIFE PRESS CHRISTIAN WRITERS' CONFERENCE

P.O. Box 2018, Cordova TN 38088. (901)309-3692. E-mail: gmoearth@aol.com. Website: www.

grandmotherearth.org. Established 1998. **Contact:** Frances Cowden. Annual one-day event. 2008 date: August 2. Location: Cordova, TN. Average attendance: 45.

Purpose/Features Open to all writers. Offers poets workshops, lectures, readings, and ms critiques. 2007 staff included Robert Hall, Florence Bruce, Cindy Beebe, and Sarah Hull Gurley.

Costs/Accommodations 2008 cost: $35 registration fee (includes one contest entry, critique of all entries, continental breakfast and lunch); $30 (includes registration with entries plus food, but no critique); or $25 (includes food, no entries); $20 fee for spouses. Information on overnight accommodations available in brochure.

Additional Information Individual poetry critiques available. Poets should submit a limit of 6 works/category and $10 fee. "One payment for all entries--send with entries." Sponsors contest for "poetry and prose in general, open to all writers. Other contests require attendance." National Awards for poetry (open to everyone, 50-line limit) are $50, $25, $15, and $10. Conference Awards for poetry (open to those who register for the conference, 30-line limit) are $50, $15, and $10. **Entry fee:** "$5 entitles you to one entry; $2 for each additional entry." **Deadline:** July 6 for 2008. Critique from the judges is available for $10 for all entries. Guidelines available for SASE.

MONTEREY COWBOY POETRY & MUSIC FESTIVAL

1120 Forest Ave., #319, Pacific Grove CA 93950. (800)722-9652. E-mail: info@ montereycowboy.com. Website: www.montereycowboy.com. Established 1998. **Contact:** Frank Pinney, president or Gerry Montgomery, show clerk/treasurer. Annual 2-day, 3-night event. 2009 dates: December 11-13. Location: Monterey Conference Center. Average attendance: 2,000.

Purpose/Features Open to the general public. Celebrates cowboy poetry and music. Offerings include 7 separate shows of varying theme, all featuring poets and musicians. Other special features include an open mic at noon on Saturday and Sunday, and a Western art and gear show.

Costs/Accommodations 2009 cost: admission either $30 or $35; an All-Event Pass, $200. Covers admission costs only; participants responsible for own housing and meals. Information on overnight accommodations available on Web site. Accommodations include special rates at area hotels.

Additional Information Brochure available on Web site.

MONTEVALLO LITERARY FESTIVAL

Sta. 6420, University of Montevallo, Montevallo AL 35115. (205)665-6420. Fax: (205)665-6422. E-mail: murphyj@montevallo.edu. Website: www.montevallo.edu/english. Established 2003. **Contact:** Dr. Jim Murphy, director. Annual 2-day event. 2008 dates: April 18-19. Location: several sites on the bucolic University of Montevallo campus. Average attendance: 60-100.

Purpose/Features Presents "a unique opportunity for participants to interact with some of the top writers in the country. Participants attend workshops in poetry, prose, or drama, working closely on their own writing with some of the country's most distinguished poets, fiction writers, playwrights, and writers of nonfiction." Offers poets readings, panels, workshops, and ms critiques. 2008 poetry workshop leader: Claudia Emerson. Prior poetry workshop leaders have included Angela Ball, Don Bogen, Andrew Hudgins, Rodney Jones, Jeff Thomson, Natasha Trethewey, Catherine Bowman, and Frank X Walker.

Costs/Accommodations 2007 cost: $45 for festival, including meals; $95 for festival, including meals and workshop. Offers overnight accommodations at Ramsay Conference

Center on campus; rooms $40/night. Call (205)665-6280 for reservations. Free on-campus parking. Additional information available at www.montevallo.edu/cont_ed/ramsay.shtm.
Additional Information Poetry workshop participants submit up to 5 pages of poetry; e-mail as Word doc to Jim Murphy (murphyj@montevallo.edu) at least 2 weeks prior to festival. Brochure available on website. Information on upcoming festival available in February.

MOUNT HERMON CHRISTIAN WRITERS CONFERENCE

P.O. Box 413, Mount Hermon CA 95041. (831)335-4466. Fax: (831)335-9413. E-mail: rachel. williams@mounthermon.org. Website: www.mounthermon.org/writers. Established 1970. **Contact:** David R.Talbott, director of adult ministries. Annual 5-day event held over Palm Sunday weekend. 2010 dates: March 26-30. Location: In heart of California redwoods near Santa Cruz, Mount Hermon Conference Center. Average attendance: 425-475.
Purpose/Features Open to "anyone interested in the craft of writing for the Christian market (though not limited to CBA)." Covers poetry, fiction, nonfiction, article writing, greeting card writing, writing for children, plus three mentoring tracks, a teen writing track, and professional career track for published authors. Twelve major morning tracks, 70 optional afternoon workshops. 70 teaching faculty made up of publishing reps of leading Christian book and magazine publishers, seven agents and selected freelancers. Residential conference with meals buffet style with faculty and registrants. Private appointments with faculty available at no fee; Other special features: FREE pre-conference critique service for fully-paid registrants; High spiritual impact.
Costs/Accommodations See Web site for specifics. "We no longer publish a brochure. All information and registration procedures are online annually by December 1."

NAPA VALLEY WRITERS' CONFERENCE

Napa Valley College, 1088 College Ave., St. Helena CA 94574. (707)967-2900 ext 1611. E-mail: writecon@napavalley.edu. Website: www.napawritersconf.org. **Contact:** Anne Evans, managing director; or Nan Cohen, poetry director. Established 1981. Annual weeklong event. 2008 dates: July 27-August 1. Location: Upper Valley Campus in the historic town of St. Helena, 25 miles north of Napa in the heart of the valley's wine growing community. Excellent cuisine provided by Napa Valley Cooking School. Average attendance: 48 in poetry and 48 in fiction.
Purpose/Features "Serious writers of all backgrounds and experience are welcome to apply." Offers poets workshops, lectures, faculty readings, ms critiques, and meetings with editors. "Poetry session provides the opportunity to work both on generating new poems and on revising previously written ones." 2009 poetry faculty includes Elizabeth Alexander, Carl Dennis, Jane Hirschfield, and David St. John in poetry, with Robert Boswell, Peter Ho Davies, Antonya Nelson, and ZZ Packer in fiction.
Costs/Accommodations 2008 cost: $750, including breakfast, lunch, 2 dinners, and attendance at all conference events. Scholarships are available. Information on overnight accommodations available. Limited accommodations in local homes available on a first-come, first-served basis; $30 one-time placement fee.
Additional Information All applicants are asked to submit a qualifying ms with their registration (no more than 5 poems) as well as a brief description of their writing background. Participants who have been admitted in the past do not need to submit a qualifying manuscript. Include $10 reading fee and $100 tuition deposit with application. Rolling admissions begin March 15. Scholarship deadline April 15. Application form and all information available on Web site.

⊠ PALM BEACH POETRY FESTIVAL

3199 B-3 Lake Worth Road, Lake Worth FL 33480. (561)868-2063. Fax: (561)582-2635. E-mail:

palmbeachpoefest@aol.com. Website: www.palmbeachpoetryfestival.org. Established: 2005. **Contact**: Miles Coon, founder and director. Annual weeklong event held in January. Location: Old School Square Cultural Arts Center, 51 North Swinton Ave., Delray Beach FL 33444. Average attendance: 96 workshop participants; 250-300 at readings, craft lectures, and panel discussion.

Purpose/Features Designed for "advanced and intermediate poets, who must apply for admission." Offers workshops, lectures, panels, faculty readings, participant readings, and individual conferences with workshop leaders. 2009 faculty included Denise Duhamel, Martin Espada, Kelle Groom, Kimiko Hahn, Michael Hettich, Laura Kasischke, Thomas Lux, Ann Marie Macari, Taylor Mali, Gregory Orr, Lynne Procope, and Gerald Stern.

Costs/Accommodations 2009: $150-200 per night, includes continental breakfast. Participants responsible for all meals except Gala Dinner. Accommodations available at area hotels. Information available by e-mail or on Web site.

Additional Information Offers Palm Beach County High School students poetry contest as part of the Festival. Guidelines available by e-mail. Brochure and registration forms available by fax, e-mail, and on Web site. "Our deadline for workshop applications is October 31, but we encourage poets to apply after that date as openings may exist."

PIMA WRITERS' WORKSHOP

Pima College, 2202 W. Anklam Rd., Tucson AZ 85709-0170. (520)206-6084. E-mail: mfiles@ pima.edu. Established 1987. **Contact:** Meg Files, director. Annual 3-day event. 2008 dates: May 30-June 1. Location: Pima College's Center for the Arts, "includes a proscenium theater, a black box theater, a recital hall, and conference rooms, as well as a courtyard with amphitheater." Average attendance: 300.

Purpose/Features Open to all writers, beginning and experienced. Offers poets workshops, ms critiques, writing exercises, and workshop's atmosphere--"friendly and supportive, practical and inspirational." Past poetry staff has included Peter Meinke, Steve Kowit, David Citino, and others.

Costs/Accommodations 2008 cost: $80, can include individual consultation. Participants responsible for own meals. Information on overnight accommodations available.

Additional Information Brochure and registration form available for SASE or by fax or e-mail.

POETRY WEEKEND INTENSIVES

40 Post Ave., Hawthorne NJ 07506. (973)423-2921. Fax: (973)523-6088. E-mail: mariagillan@ msn.com. Website: www.pccc.cc.nj.us/poetry. Established 1997. **Contact:** Maria Mazziotti Gillan, executive director. Usually held 4 times/year in March, June, October, and December. Location: generally at St. Marguerite's Retreat House, an English manor house at the Convent of St. John the Baptist in Mendhan, NJ; also several other convents and monasteries. Average attendance: 26.

Purpose/Features Open to all writers. "The purpose of this retreat is to give writers the space and time to focus totally on their own work in a serene and beautiful setting away from the pressures and distractions of daily life." Sample theme: "Writing Your Way Home--Poetry of Memory and Place." "Writing weekend poets will find support and encouragement, stimulating activities leading to the creation of new work, workshop leaders who are actively engaged in the writing life, opportunities to read their work aloud to the group, a circle of writer friends, and networking opportunities." Poetry Weekend Intensives are led by Maria Mazziotti Gillan and Laura Boss. Other special features include one-on-one conferences with lead poet faculty.

Costs/Accommodations 2005 cost: $375, including meals. Offers a $25 early bird discount. Housing in on-site facilities included in the $375 price.

Additional Information Individual poetry critiques available. Poets should bring poems to weekend. Registration form available for SASE or by fax or e-mail. Maria Mazziotti Gillan is the director of the Creative Writing Program of Binghamton University--State University of New York, executive director of the Poetry Center at Passaic County Community College, and edits *Paterson Literary Review*. Laura Boss is the editor of *Lips* magazine. Fifteen professional development credits are available for each weekend.

◪ SAGE HILL SUMMER WRITING EXPERIENCE

P.O. Box 1731, Saskatoon SK S7K 3S1 Canada. Phone: (306)652-7395. Fax: (306)244-0255. E-mail: sage.hill@sasktel.net. Website: www.sagehillwriting.ca. Established 1990. **Contact:** Steven Ross Smith, executive director. Annual 10-day adult summer program. 2009 dates: July 20-31. Location: St. Michael's Retreat, Lumsden, Saskatchewan. Average attendance: varies according to specific workshop (usually 5-11 participants).Spring Poetry Colloquium, a 14-day program for 8 writers working with 2 instructors, Erin Mour& #233; and John Pass. 2009: May 13-26.

Purpose/Features Open to writers, 19 years of age and older, who are working in English. No geographic restrictions. Offers poets workshops, labs, colloquia, and readings. 2007 poetry staff included Jeanette Lynes, John Steffler, and Nicole Brossard.

Costs/Accommodations 2009 summer program cost: $1,195 CAD, including instruction, accommodations, meals, and all facilities. Accommodations available on site.

Additional Information Writing sample and $50 CAD deposit required with application. Additional information available for SASE, by phone, e-mail, or on Web site.

THE SANDHILLS WRITERS CONFERENCE

Augusta State University, Augusta GA 30904. (706)729-2417. Fax: (706)729-2247. E-mail: akellman@aug.edu. Website: www.sandhills.aug.edu. Established 1975. **Contact:** Anthony Kellman, conference director. Annual 3-day event usually held the third weekend in March. 2009 dates: March 19-21. Location: campus of Augusta State University. Facilities are handicapped accessible. Average attendance: 100.

Purpose/Features Designed to "hone the creative writing skills of participants and provide networking opportunities." Open to all aspiring writers. Offers poets craft lectures, ms evaluations, and readings. 2009 poetry presenters included Martin Lammon.

Costs/Accommodations 2007 cost: $156 full conference registration; $110 conference-only registration (no ms critique); $76 full conference student registration. All registrations include 2 lunches. Accommodations available at area hotels. Information on overnight accommodations available on Web site.

Additional Information Offers poetry contest as part of conference; also offers scholarships to college students. Guidelines available by e-mail or on Web site. Brochure and registration form available for SASE or on Web site.

SAN DIEGO STATE UNIVERSITY WRITERS' CONFERENCE

5250 Campanile Dr., San Diego CA 92182-1920. (619)594-2517. Fax: (619)594-8566. E-mail: rbrown2@mail.sdsu.edu. Website: www.ces.sdsu.edu. Established 1984. **Contact:** Rose Brown, program coordinator. Annual 3-day event. 2009 dates: February 6-8th. Location: Doubletree Hotel (Mission Valley), 7450 Hazard Center Dr., San Diego. Average attendance: 400.

Purpose/Features Open to writers of fiction, nonfiction, children's books, poetry, and screenwriting. "We have participants from across North America." Offers poets workshops, networking lunch, and editor appointments and consultations.

Costs/Accommodations 2009 cost: $365-485 (through January 4), including one meal. Accommodations available on site. Information on overnight accommodations available.

Additional Information "Editors and agents give awards for favorite submissions." Information and registration form available on website.

SANTA BARBARA WRITERS CONFERENCE

P.O. Box 6627, Santa Barbara CA 93160. (805)964-0367. E-mail: info@sbwritersconference.com. Website: www.sbwritersconference.com. Established 1973. **Contact:** Marcia Meier, executive director. Annual event. 2009 dates: June 20-25. Location: Fess Parker's Doubletree Resort in Santa Barbara. Average attendance: 450.

Purpose/Features Open to everyone. Covers all genres of writing. Offers poets workshops, lectures, faculty readings, participant readings, ms critiques, master classes, young writers program, and meetings with agents and editors. 2009 poetry presenters included Christopher Buckley and Perie J. Longo.

Costs/Accommodations 2009 cost: $675 before March 1, $875 after (including all workshops, speakers, and lectures, and closing awards breakfast). Accommodations available on site or nearby. Information on overnight accommodations available by e-mail or on Web site.

Additional Information Offers poetry contest as part of conference. Guidelines available on Web site. Brochure and registration form available on Web site.

◪ SASKATCHEWAN FESTIVAL OF WORDS

Moose Jaw Cultural Centre, 217 Main St. N., Moose Jaw SK S6H 0W1. (306)691-0557. Fax: (306)693-2994. E-mail: word.festival@sasktel.net. Website: www.festivalofwords.com. Established 1997. **Contact:** Donna Lee Howes, artistic director. Annual 4-day event. 2009 dates: July 16-19. Location: Moose Jaw Library/Art Museum complex in Crescent Park. Average attendance: about 4,000 admissions.

Purpose/Features "The Saskatchewan Festival of Words celebrates the imaginative uses of language, and features fiction and nonfiction writers, screenwriters, poets, children's authors, songwriters, dramatists, and film makers. Our festival is an ideal place for people who love words to mingle, promote their books, get acquainted, share ideas, conduct impromptu readings, and meet their fans." Offers poets workshops, readings, and open mics. 2008 poetry program presenters included Molly Peacock, Ken Babstock, Don Domanski, Daphne Marlatt, Gerald Hill, and Dave Margoshes.

Costs/Accommodations Accommodations available at local mineral spa, inns, campgrounds, and bed & breakfast establishments. Information on overnight accommodations available for SASE or by phone or e-mail.

Additional Information Complete information about festival presenters, events, costs, and schedule available on Web site. Festival presented by Living Skies Festival of Words, Inc.

SBWC MARCH POETRY CONFERENCE

PO Box 6627, Santa Barbara CA 93160. (805) 964-0367. E-mail: info@sbwritersconference.com. Website: www.sbwritersconference.com. Established 2007. **Contact:** Marcia Meier, executive director. Annual event. 2009 dates: March 15-17. Average attendance: 75.

Purpose/Features Open to everyone. Offers poets workshops, faculty readings, ms critiques. seminars, and a master class with a featured poet. 2008: Philip Levine; 2009: Cornelius Eady; 2010: Dorianne Laux.

Costs/Accommodations $325 for commuter students. This includes all workshops and lunches and dinners from Friday dinner through Sunday lunch. Cost including lodging at retreat center is $495 for a double-occupancy room and all meals. Accommodations available on site.

Additional Information Brochure and registration form available on Web site.

SEWANEE WRITERS' CONFERENCE

735 University Ave., Sewanee TN 37383-1000. (931)598-1141. E-mail: cpeters@sewanee.edu. Website: www.sewaneewriters.org. Established 1990. **Contact:** Cheri B. Peters, creative writing programs manager. Annual 12-day event held the last 2 weeks in July. Location: the University of the South ("dormitories for housing, Women's Center for public events, classrooms for workshops, Sewanee Inn for dining, etc."). Attendance: about 120.

Purpose/Features Open to poets, fiction writers, and playwrights who submit their work for review in a competitive admissions process. "Participants belong to a workshop devoted to constructive critique of members' manuscripts; in addition, each participant has an individual, private manuscript conference with a faculty member. Readings, craft lectures, panels, and Q& A sessions round out the formal offerings; numerous social functions offer opportunities for informal exchange and networking. Workshops are genre-based rather than theme-based." 2008 poetry faculty featured Daniel Anderson, Claudia Emerson, Andrew Hudgins, Mark Jarman, Brad Leithauser, Mary Jo Salter, Mark Strand, and Greg Williamson. Guest poets Leigh Anne Couch, Charles Martin, and Nigel Thompson will give readings, as will conference director Wayatt Prunty; Martin and Thompson will lead a short workshop on poetry translation.

Costs/Accommodations 2008 cost: $1,700, inclusive of single rooms with shared bathroom facilities. Each year scholarships and fellowships based on merit are available on a competitive basis.

Additional Information A ms should be sent in advance after admission to the conference. Write for brochure and application forms; no SASE necessary. Additional information available on Web site.

Ⓝ SOAPSTONE: A WRITING RETREAT FOR WOMEN

622 S.E. 29th Ave., Portland OR 97214. (503)233-3936. E-mail: retreats@soapstone.org. Website: www.soapstone.org. Duration: 1-4 weeks. Average attendance: 30 writers/year. Retreat/ residency. "Soapstone provides women writers with a stretch of uninterrupted time for their work and the opportunity to live in semi-solitude close to the natural world. In addition to that rare but essential commodity for a writer-a quiet space away from jobs, children, and other responsibilities-Soapstone provides something less tangible but also invaluable: the validation and encouragement necessary to embark upon or sustain a long or difficult writing project." Located in Oregon's Coast Range, nine miles from the ocean, the retreat stands on twenty-two acres of densely forested land along the banks of Soapstone Creek and is home to much wildlife. The writers in residence enjoy a unique opportunity to learn about the natural world and join us in conscious stewardship of the land.

Costs/Accommodations Residents must provide all of their own transportation. See Web site for more information. Offers overnight accommodations.

Additional Information Application materials required include 3 copies of the completed application, a writing sample (no more than 3 pages of poetry or 5 pages, double-spaced, of prose), and application fee. Applications must be postmarked between July 1-August 1 each year. For brochure, visit Web site.

S.O.M.O.S., SOCIETY OF THE MUSE OF THE SOUTHWEST

P.O. Box 3225, 233B Paseo del Pueblo Sur, Taos NM 87571. (575)758-0081. Fax: (575)758-4802. E-mail: somos@laplaza.com. Website: www.somostaos.org. Established 1983. **Contact:** Dori Vinella, executive director. "We offer readings, special events, and workshops at different times during the year." Length of workshops varies. Location: various sites in Taos. Average attendance: 10-50.

Purpose/Features Open to anyone. "We offer workshops in various genres--fiction, poetry, nature writing, etc." Past workshop presenters have included Denise Chavez, Marjorie Agosin, Judyth Hill, Robin Becker, Sawnie Morris, and Lise Goett. Other special features include the 2-day Annual Taos Storytelling Festival in October, a Winter Writers Series (January-February), and Summer Writer's Series (July-August).

Costs/Accommodations See website for current information.

Additional Information Additional information available by fax, e-mail, or on website. "Taos has a wonderful community of dedicated and talented writers who make S.O.M.O.S. workshops rigorous, supportive, and exciting." Also publishes *Chokecherries*, an annual anthology.

SOUTHAMPTON WRITERS CONFERENCE

Stony Brook Southampton, 239 Montauk Hwy., Southampton NY 11968. (631)632-5030. E-mail: southamptonwriters@notes.cc.sunysb.edu. Website: www.stonybrook.edu/writers. **Contact:** Adrienne Unger, coordinator. Established 1976. Annual 11-day event. 2009 dates: July 15-26. Location: Stony Brook Southampton's seaside campus "in the heart of the Hamptons." Average attendance: 12/workshop.

Purpose/Features Open to new and established writers, graduate students, and upper-level undergraduate students. Offers poetry workshops and readings. 2007 poetry staff included Billy Collins and Derek Walcott.

Costs/Accommodations 2007 cost: $25 application fee; $2,100 for workshop, room and board; $1,500 workshop only (includes breakfast and lunch). Accommodations available on site.

Additional Information "Evening events will feature regular faculty and award-winning visiting authors. Participants will also enjoy a rich schedule of formal and informal social gatherings--author receptions, open mic nights, and special literary events. Early application is encouraged." Brochure and registration form available by e-mail or on website.

ⓝ ⊡ SPLIT ROCK ARTS PROGRAM ONLINE MENTORING FOR WRITERS

University of Minnesota, 360 Coffey Hall, St. Paul MN 55108-6084. (612)625-8100. Fax: (612)624-6210. E-mail: onlinementor@umn.edu. Website: www.cce.umn.edu/mentoring. Established 2003 **Contact:** Anastasia Faunce, program director. Program connects writers with outstanding mentors to provide individually tailored, constructive assistance with literary fiction, nonfiction, and poetry projects of any size or scope. The primary goal is for experienced mentors to enable poets to strengthen and sustain their writing as they work one-on-one with an experienced writer and teacher of writing, toward self-defined goals. **Purpose/Features** Open to All writers-beginning, intermediate, or advanced-who would like constructive criticism on work in progress, whether it's getting through a first draft or readying a manuscript for publication. Current mentors include: Wesley Brown, Sharon Doubiago, Patricia Weaver Francisco, Rigoberto Gonz& #225;lez, Linda Hasselstrom, Susan Hubbard, Pablo Medina, Valerie Miner, Jim Moore, Ruth L. Schwartz, Sylvia Watanabe, and Catherine Watson. **Costs/Accommodations** 2009 cost: $150, Introductory Groundwork; $405-$900, three-, six-, or nine-hour mentorships. All mentorships are noncredit. Mentorships held online. **Additional Information** Registration is ongoing. Additional information available on Web site.

Costs/Accommodations 2007 cost: $25 application fee; $2,100 for workshop, room and board; $1,500 workshop only (includes breakfast and lunch). Accommodations available on site.

Additional Information "Evening events will feature regular faculty and award-winning visiting authors. Participants will also enjoy a rich schedule of formal and informal social gatherings--author receptions, open mic nights, and special literary events. Early application is encouraged." Brochure and registration form available by e-mail or on website.

SPLIT ROCK ARTS PROGRAM SUMMER WORKSHOPS

University of Minnesota, 360 Coffey Hall, 1420 Eckles Ave., St. Paul MN 55108-6084. (612)625-8100. Fax: (612)624-6210. E-mail: splitrockarts@umn.edu. Website: www.cce.umn.edu/splitrockarts. Established 1983. **Contact:** Anastasia Faunce, program director. Summer series of weeklong and 3-day workshops in creative writing, visual art, and design. 2010 dates: June 15-July 30. Locations: University's Twin Cities campus and Cloquet Forestry Center in Northern MN. Average attendance: 500.

Purpose/Features Open to anyone over 18 years old interested in writing and literature. Offers writers a variety of workshops in all genres and with renowned faculty. 2010 faculty to be determined. 2009 writing faculty included Joseph Duemer, Candace Fleming, Jacqueline Kolosov, Josip Novakovich, Eric Rohmann, Scott Russell Sanders, Ruth Schwartz, Matthew Specktor, William Wenthe, and others.

Costs/Accommodations 2009 cost: $555 tuition (noncredit); undergraduate/graduate credit available for additional fee. Scholarships available. Participants responsible for most meals. Accommodations available on site or at area hotels.

Additional Information Print catalogs available in February. Registration opens in late February. Additional information available on Web site.

SQUAW VALLEY COMMUNITY OF WRITERS POETRY WORKSHOP

P.O. Box 1416, Nevada City CA 95959. (530)470-8440. E-mail: info@squawvalleywriters.org. Website: www.squawvalleywriters.org. Established 1969. **Contact:** Brett Hall Jones, executive director. Annual 7-day event. 2008 dates: July 19-26. Location: The Squaw Valley USA's Lodge in the Sierras near Lake Tahoe. Average attendance: 60 for poetry.

Purpose/Features The Poetry Program is founded "on the belief that when poets gather in a community to write new poems, each poet may well break through old habits and write something stronger and truer than before. To help this happen we work together to create an atmosphere in which everyone might feel free to try anything. In the mornings we meet in workshops to read to each other the work of the previous 24 hours; each participant also has an opportunity to work with each staff poet. In the late afternoons we gather for a conversation about some aspect of craft. On several late afternoons staff poets hold brief individual conferences." 2009 poetry presenters include Robert Hass, Brenda Hillman, and Sharon Olds.

Costs/Accommodations 2008 cost: $750 for poetry tuition (includes 6 evening meals), $25 reading/application fee. Accommodations extra. "We arrange housing for participants in local houses and condominiums at a variety of rates." Information on overnight accommodations available on Web site.

Additional Information A limited amount of financial aid is available. Brochure available by e-mail (include mailing address for response) or on Web site. Also publishes the annual *Squaw Valley Community of Writers Omnium Gatherum and Newsletter* containing "news and profiles on our past participants and staff, craft articles, and book advertising."

STEAMBOAT SPRINGS WRITERS CONFERENCE

P.O. Box 774284, Steamboat Springs CO 80477. (970)879-8138. E-mail: info@steamboatwriters.com. Website: www.steamboatwriters.com. Established 1982. **Contact:** Susan de Wardt, director. Annual one-day event usually held in mid-July. Location: a "renovated train station, the Depot is home of the Steamboat Springs Arts Council--friendly, relaxed atmosphere." Average attendance: 35-40 (registration limited).

Purpose/Features Open to anyone. Conference is "designed for writers who have limited time. Instructors vary from year to year, offering maximum instruction during a weekend at a nominal cost." Previous poetry instructors include David Mason, Renate Wood, Jim Tipton, and Donald

Revell.

Costs/Accommodations 2008 cost: $50 before May 19; then $60. Includes seminar and catered luncheon. "A variety of lodgings available."

Additional Information Brochure and registration form available for SASE, by e-mail, or on Web site. Optional: Friday evening dinner (cost not included in registration fee); readings by participants (no cost).

TAOS SUMMER WRITERS' CONFERENCE

University of New Mexico, Dept. of English Language and Literature, MSC03 2170, 1 University of New Mexico, Albuquerque NM 87131-0001. (505)277-5572. Fax: (505)277-2950. E-mail: taosconf@unm.edu. Website: www.unm.edu/~taosconf. Established 1999. **Contact:** Sharon Oard Warner, director. Annual 5-day (weeklong) and 2-day (weekend) workshops usually held mid-July. Location: Sagebrush Inn in Taos. Average attendance: 180 total; 100 places available in each weekend, 180 places available in weeklong workshops. Class size limited to 12/class, usually smaller.

Purpose/Features Open to everyone, beginners to experienced. Minimum age is 18. Friendly, relaxed atmosphere with supportive staff and instructors. Offers both weekend and weeklong workshops in such areas as fiction, poetry, memoir, publishing, screenwriting, and craft, with master classes in novel, poetry, and memoir. One-on-one consultations with agents and editors available. Workshop presenters have included Pam Houston, Antonya Nelson, Dana Levin, Jonis Agee, and John Dufresne. Special features include evening readings and panels, open mic sessions, and tours of the D.H. Lawrence Ranch.

Costs/Accommodations 2009 cost: $325 for weekend, $625 for weeklong sessions, discounted tuition rate of $275 per weekend workshop with weeklong workshop or master class, including workshop registration and special events. Nearest airport is Albuquerque International Sunport. Taos is about 170 miles north of Albuquerque. Information on overnight accommodations available. Sagebrush Inn, Comfort Suites, and Quality Inn offer special rates.

Additional Information Brochure and registration form available by e-mail or on Web site. "Taos is a unique experience of a lifetime. The setting and scenery are spectacular; historical and natural beauty abound. Our previous attendees say they have been inspired by the place and by the friendly, personal attention of our instructors."

▦ TY NEWYDD WRITERS' CENTRE

Llanystumdwy, Criccieth, Gwynedd LL52 0LW Wales. (44)(1766)522 811. Fax: (44)(1766)523095. E-mail: post@tynewydd.org. Website: www.tynewydd.org. Established 1990. **Contact:** Executive Director. Runs courses throughout the year, as well as writers' retreats. Location: Ty Newydd, The National Writers' Centre for Wales. Average attendance: maximum of 16 on any course.

Purpose/Features Open to anyone over 16 years of age. Courses are designed to "promote the writing and understanding of literature by providing creative writing courses at all levels for all ages. Courses at Ty Newydd provide the opportunity of working intimately and informally with two professional writers." Courses specifically for poets of all levels of experience and ability are offered throughout the year.

Costs/Accommodations 2009 cost: 5 nights' stay & #163;495 (single room) and & #163;435 (shared room). Please refer to Web site for costs in respect to shorter courses and further information about accommodation.

Additional Information Brochure and registration form available for SASE, or request by e-mail.

UNIVERSITY OF NORTH DAKOTA WRITERS CONFERENCE

Dept. of English, Box 7209, University of North Dakota, Grand Forks ND 58202. (701)777-

3321. E-mail: writersconference@und.nodak.edu. Website: www.writersconference.und.edu. **Contact:** Kathy King, administrative director. Established 1970. Annual 4- to 5-day event. 2006 dates: March 31-April 4. Location: the University of North Dakota Memorial Union. Average attendance: 3,000-5,000. "Some individual events have as few as 20, some over 1,000."
Purpose/Features Offers poets panel discussions, readings, and book signings. 2009 poetry staff included Jacqueline Osherow and Greg Williamson.
Costs/Accommodations All events are free and open to the public. Accommodations available at area hotels. Information on overnight accommodations available on website.
Additional Information Schedule and other information available on website.

UNIVERSITY OF WISCONSIN-MADISON'S SCHOOL OF THE ARTS AT RHINELANDER

715 Lowell Center, 610 Langdon St., Madison WI 53703. (608)263-3494. Fax: (608)262-1694. E-mail: mmcclenaghan@dcs.wisc.edu. Website: www.dcs.wisc.edu/lsa/writing/index.html. Established 1964. **Contact:** Miranda McClenaghan, director. Annual 5-day event. 2009 dates: July 19-24. Location: James Williams Middle School in Rhinelander. Average attendance: 300.
Purpose/Features Open to all levels and ages. Offers poets workshops and related workshops in creativity. 2008 poetry staff included Mary Sue Koeppel, Richard Terrill, and Laurel Yourke.
Costs/Accommodations 2009 cost: registration costs ranged from $199-349; university credit fees are additional. Information on overnight accommodations available.
Additional Information Catalog available in mid-March. Additional information available by phone, e-mail, or on Web site.

▨ VERMONT STUDIO CENTER

P.O. Box 613, Johnson VT 05656. (802)635-2727. Fax: (802)635-2730. E-mail: writing@vermontstudiocenter.org. Website: www.vermontstudiocenter.org. Established 1984. **Contact:** Gary Clark, writing program director. From 2-12 weeks, year-round; most residents stay for 4 weeks. Community size: 50+ writers and visual artists/month.
Purpose/Features "The Vermont Studio Center is an international creative community located in Johnson, Vermont, and serving more than 600 American and international artists and writers each year (50 per month). A Studio Center Residency features secluded, uninterrupted writing time, the companionship of dedicated and talented peers, and access to a roster of two distinguished Visiting Writers each month. All VSC Residents receive three meals a day, private, comfortable housing and the company of an international community of painters, sculptors, poets, printmakers and writers. Writers attending residencies at the Studio Center may work on whatever they choose--no matter what month of the year they attend." Offers poets participant readings.
Costs/Accommodations "The cost of a 4-week residency is $3,750. Generous fellowship and grant assistance available. "Accommodations available on site. "Residents live in single rooms in ten modest, comfortable houses adjacent to the Red Mill Building. Rooms are simply furnished and have shared baths. Complete linen service is provided. The Studio Center is unable to accommodate guests at meals, overnight guests, spouses, children or pets."
Additional Information Fellowships application deadlines are February 15, June 15 and October 1. Writers encouraged to visit Web site for more information. May also e-mail, call, fax.

WESLEYAN WRITERS CONFERENCE

Wesleyan University, Middletown CT 06457. (860)685-3604. Fax: (860)685-2441. E-mail: agreene@wesleyan.edu. Website: www.wesleyan.edu/writers. Established 1956. **Contact:** Anne Greene, director. Annual 5-day event. 2009 dates: June 14-19. Location: the campus of Wesleyan University "in the hills overlooking the Connecticut River, a brief drive from the Connecticut shore. Wesleyan's outstanding library, poetry reading room, and other university facilities are open to participants." Average attendance: 100.

Purpose/Features "The conference welcomes everyone interested in the writer's craft, and participants are a diverse, international group. Both new and experienced writers are welcome. You may attend all of the seminars, including poetry, the novel, short story, fiction techniques, literary journalism, memoir, and multi-media work." Offers poets workshops, seminars, lectures, readings, ms critiques, meetings with editors and agents, and special panel presentations. Recent poetry presenters include Honor Moore, Mark Doty, Peter Gizzi, Elizabeth Willis, Sherwin Bitsui, Laura Cronk, Ravi Shankar.

Costs/Accommodations See Web site for current rates. 2008 cost: $850 day student rate (includes tuition only); $1,125 day student rate with meals; $1,298 boarding student rate (includes tuition, meals, room for 5 nights). Accommodations available on site or at area hotels. Information on overnight accommodations available on Web site.

Additional Information Scholarships/teaching fellowships offered. Additional information available by phone, fax, or on Web site.

WHIDBEY ISLAND WRITERS' CONFERENCES

The Whidbey Island Writers' Association, P.O. Box 1289, Langley WA 98260. (360)331-6714. E-mail: writers@writeonwhidbey.org. Website: www.writeonwhidbey.org. Established 1997. Annual event. 2009 dates: February 27-28. Location: South Whidbey High School and various sites in the Whidbey Island area. Average attendance: 250.

Purpose/Features Open to writers of every genre and skill level. Offers poets workshops, lectures, readings, author critiques, and "Author Fireside Chats." 2008 poetry presenters included Lorraine Healy, Gloria Burgess, Nancy Pagh, and Molly Larson Cook.

Costs/Accommodations 2008 cost: $375 WIWA members, $395 nonmembers. Participants responsible for most meals. Accommodations available at area hotels. Information on overnight accommodations available on Web site.

Additional Information Offers Benefactor's Award Writing Contest as part of conference. Open to conference attendeees only. Guidelines available on Web site. Program and registration form available on Web site. Brochure available by calling (360)331-6714.

WINTER POETRY & PROSE GETAWAY IN CAPE MAY

18 North Richards Ave., Ventnor NJ 08406. (609)823-5076. E-mail: info@wintergetaway.com. Website: www.wintergetaway.com. Established 1994. **Contact:** Peter E. Murphy, founder/director. Annual 4-day event. 2010 dates: January 15-18. Location: The Grand Hotel on the Oceanfront in Historic Cape May, NJ. Average attendance: 200 (10 or fewer participants in each poetry workshop).

Purpose/Features Open to all writers, beginners and experienced, over the age of 18. "Now in its 17th year, the Winter Poetry and Prose Getaway is well known for its challenging and supportive workshops featuring small classes led by award-winning writers, including Stephen Dunn, recipient of the 2001 Pulitzer Prize in poetry. The poetry workshop meets for an hour or so each morning before sending you off with an assignment that will encourage and inspire you to produce exciting new work. After lunch, you will read your new drafts in a feedback session led by experienced poet-teachers who help identify the poem's virtues and offer suggestions to strengthen its weaknesses. The groups are small, and you receive positive attention to help your poem mature. Late afternoons allow you to choose from tutorials, panels, talks, walking on the beach, or you may continue working." Previous faculty has included Renee Ashley, Laure-Anne Bosselaar, Kurt Brown, Catherine Doty, Stephen Dunn, Douglas Goetsch, James Richardson, and many more.

Costs/Accommodations 2009 cost: $385 registration, including 2 lunchs, 2 receptions, and a poetry tutorial with one of the poets on staff. Room packages start at $225. A $25 Early Bard Discount is available if paid in full by November 15.

Additional Information Brochure and registration form available on web site. "The Getaway is a conference where you will write! You will receive feedback but the workshops emphasize creating new material or revising works in progress. It is open to all writers, beginners and experienced, over the age of 18. Teachers can earn 17 hours of professional development credit as well as graduate credit from Rutgers University."

▧ THE WRITING SALON

P.O. Box 2454, Taos NM 87571. (877)994-8267. E-mail: info@thewritingsalon.net. Website: www. thewritingsalon.net. **Contact:** James Nave. Estab. 2004. See Web site for scheduled workshops. Duration: 2 days. Average attendance: 20. Workshop. "At the Writing Salon we believe that, while we often write alone, we are part of a community of writers that spans the globe, and that by coming together we can serve each other by offering new perspectives, ideas, and inspiration. Whenever a writer lifts a pen - to invent or reinvent, to speak truth or tell a story, to collaborate, to dream, to make it messy then clean it up, to communicate - the world is a better place. The Writing Salon was born from the Artist's Way creativity camps, workshops, and retreats that poet James Nav& #233; produced with Julia Cameron from 1995 to 2003. In 2004, Nav& #233;, along with writer/editor Allegra Huston, held the first Writing Salon in the legendary artists' colony of Taos, New Mexico. The Taos Writing Salon is now a yearly event, and we're constantly adding international Salons in places of secret beauty around the world."

ADDITIONAL CONFERENCES/WORKSHOPS/FESTIVALS

Resources

Organizations

There are many organizations of value to poets. These groups may sponsor workshops and contests, stage readings, publish anthologies and chapbooks or spread the word about publishing opportunities. A few provide economic assistance or legal advice. The best thing organizations offer, though, is a support system to which poets can turn for a pep talk, a hard-nosed (but sympathetic) critique of a manuscript or simply the comfort of talking and sharing with others who understand the challenges, and joys, of writing poetry.

Whether national, regional or as local as your library or community center, each organization has something special to offer. The listings in this section reflect the membership opportunities available to poets with a variety of organizations. Some groups provide certain services to both members and nonmembers.

These symbols may appear at the beginning of some listings: The (N) symbol indicates a recently established organization new to *Poet's Market*; the ( ) symbol indicates this organization did not appear in the 2008 edition; the ( ) symbol denotes a Canadian organization and the ( ) symbol one headquartered outside the U.S. and Canada.

Since some organizations are included in listings in the other sections of this book, we've cross-referenced these listings under Additional Organizations at the end of this section. For further details about an organization associated with a market in this list, go to that market's page number.

To find out more about groups in your area (including those that may not be listed in *Poet's Market*), contact your YMCA, community center, local colleges and universities, public library and bookstores (and don't forget newspapers and the Internet). If you can't find a group that suits your needs, consider starting one yourself. You might be surprised to discover there are others in your locality who would welcome the encouragement, feedback and moral support of a writer's group.

92ND STREET Y UNTERBERG POETRY CENTER

1395 Lexington Ave., New York NY 10128. (212)415-5759. E-mail: unterberg@92y.org. Website: www.92y.org/poetry. Established 1939. The Unterberg Poetry Center offers "students of all ages the opportunity to hone their skills as writers and deepen their appreciation as readers." Offers annual series of readings by major literary figures (weekly readings late September through May), writing workshops, master classes in fiction and poetry, and lectures and literary seminars. Also co-sponsors the "Discovery"/Boston Review Poetry Contest (see separate listing in Contests & Awards).

⊕ ACADEMI–YR ACADEMI GYMREIG/THE WELSH ACADEMY

Mount Stuart House, 3rd Floor, Cardiff CF10 5FQ Wales. (44)(29)2047-2266. Fax: (44)(29)2049-2930. E-mail: post@academi.org. Website: www.academi.org. Established 1959. **Contact:** Peter Finch, chief executive. Academi is the Welsh National Literature Promotion Agency and Society of Writers and is open to "the population of Wales and those outside Wales with an interest in Welsh writing." Currently has 2,000 members. Levels of membership/dues: associate, full, and fellow; £15/year (waged) or £7.50/year (unwaged). Offerings include promotion of readings, events, conferences, exchanges, tours; employment of literature-development workers; publication of a quarterly events magazine; publication of a literary magazine in Welsh (Taliesin). Sponsors conferences/workshops and contests/awards. Publishes A470: What's On In Literary Wales, a magazine appearing quarterly containing information on literary events in Wales. Available to nonmembers for £15 (annual subscription). Academi is also a resident company of the Wales Millenium Centre, where it runs the Glyn Jones Center, a resource centre for writers and the public. Additional information available for SASE (or SAE and IRC), by fax, e-mail, or on Web site.

THE ACADEMY OF AMERICAN POETS

584 Broadway, Suite 604, New York NY 10012-5243. (212)274-0343. Fax: (212)274-9427. E-mail: academy@poets.org. Website: www.poets.org. Executive Director: Tree Swenson. Established 1934. The Academy of American Poets was founded to support the nation's poets at all stages of their careers and to foster the appreciation of contemporary poetry. Levels of membership/dues: begin at $35/year (contributing member). Administers The Walt Whitman Award; The James Laughlin Award; The Harold Morton Landon Translation Award; The Lenore Marshall Poetry Prize; The Raiziss/de Palchi Translation Award; and The Wallace Stevens Award. (For further details, see individual listings in the Contests & Awards section.) Also awards The Fellowship of the Academy of American Poets ($25,000 to honor distinguished poetic achievement, no applications accepted) and The University & College Poetry Prizes. Publishes American Poet, an informative semiannual journal sent to all Academy members. The Academy's other programs include National Poetry Month (April), the largest literary celebration in the world; the Poetry Audio Archive, a 700-volume audio library capturing the voices of contemporary American poets for generations to come; an annual series of poetry readings and special events; and Poets. org, which includes thousands of poems, hundreds of essays and interviews, lesson plans for teachers, a National Poetry Almanac, a national Calendar of Events, and the National Poetry Map.

ADIRONDACK LAKES CENTER FOR THE ARTS

P.O. Box 205, Rte. 28, Blue Mountain Lake NY 12812. (518)352-7715. Fax: (518)352-7333. E-mail: alca@frontiernet.net. Website: www.adk-arts.org. Established 1967. **Contact:** Susan Sessions, program director. Promotes "visual and performing arts through programs and services, serves established professional and aspiring artists and the region through educational programs and activities of general interest." An independent, private, nonprofit educational organization open to everyone. Currently has 1,300 members. Levels of membership/dues: individual, family, and business ("there is no set fee for membership, a gift of any size makes you a member"). Offerings include workshops for adults and children, reading performances, discussions, and lectures. Offers a "comfortable, cozy performance space--coffeehouse setting with tables, candles, etc." Computers available for members and artists. Publishes a triannual newsletter/schedule containing news, articles, photos, and a schedule of events. "All members are automatically sent the schedule and others may request a copy." Sponsors a few readings each year. "These are usually given by the instructor of our writing workshops." Members meet each July. Additional information available for SASE, by e-mail, or on website.

⊠ AMERICAN BOOKSELLERS FOUNDATION FOR FREE EXPRESSION

275 7th Ave., Suite 1504, New York NY 10001. (212)587-4025. Fax: (212)587-2436. E-mail: chris@abffe.com. Website: www.abffe.com. Established 1990. **Contact:** Chris Finan, president. "The American Booksellers Foundation for Free Expression is the bookseller's voice in the fight against censorship. Founded by the American Booksellers Association, ABFFE's mission is to promote and protect the free exchange of ideas, particularly those contained in books, by opposing restrictions on the freedom of speech; issuing statements on significant free expression controversies; participating in legal cases involving First Amendment rights; collaborating with other groups with an interest in free speech; and providing education about the importance of free expression to booksellers, other members of the book industry, politicians, the press and the public." Levels of membership/dues: $50. "ABFFE is the bookseller's voice in all free speech controversies involving books and other written material. We alerted booksellers to the dangers posed by the USA Patriot Act and helped them communicate their concerns to Congress. We are also active on the local level. ABFFE opposes efforts to ban books in public schools and libraries and files amicus briefs in cases challenging school censorship." Additional information available on Web site.

⊠ AMERICAN HAIKU ARCHIVES

California State Library, Library & Courts II Bldg, Sacramento CA 95814. E-mail: WelchM@aol. com. Website: www.americanhaikuarchives.org. The American Haiku Archives, founded in 1996, is the world's largest public collection of haiku and related poetry books and papers outside Japan. This repository is housed at the California State Library in Sacramento, California, and is dedicated to preserving the history of North American haiku. Materials are publicly available for research purposes through the library's California History Room. The American Haiku Archives actively seeks donations of books, journals, recordings, letters, ephemera, and personal papers relating to haiku poetry in all languages, but especially North American languages. The American Haiku Archives also appoints an honorary curator every July for a one-year term. The intent of this appointment is to honor leading haiku poets, translators, or scholars for their accomplishments or service in support of haiku poetry as a literary art. Past honorary curators have been George Swede, H. F. Noyes, Hiroaki Sato, Francine Porad, Makoto Ueda, William J. Higginson, Leroy Kanterman, Lorraine Ellis Harr, Robert Spiess, Cor van den Heuvel, Jerry Kilbride, and Elizabeth Searle Lamb. Additional information about the archives is available on the Web site.

ARIZONA AUTHORS ASSOCIATION

6145 W Echo Lane, Glendale, AZ 85302. (623)847-9343. E-mail: info@azauthors.com. Website: www.azauthors.com. Established 1978. **Contact:** Toby Heathcote, president. Provides education and referral for writers and others in publishing. Statewide organization. Currently has 200 members. Levels of membership/dues: Published, Unpublished (seeking publication), Professional (printers, agents, and publishers), and Student; $45/year for authors, $30/year students, $60/year professionals. Sponsors conferences, workshops, contests, awards. Sponsors annual literary contest in poetry, short story, essay, unpublished novels, and published books (fiction, children's, and nonfiction). Publishes Arizona Literary Magazine and Arizona Authors Newsletter. Members meet monthly. Additional information available on Web site.

THE ASSOCIATION OF WRITERS & WRITING PROGRAMS (AWP)

Mail Stop 1E3, George Mason University, Fairfax VA 22030-4444. (703)993-4301. E-mail: services@awpwriter.org (membership contact). Website: www.awpwriter.org. Established 1967. Offers a variety of services for writers, teachers, and writing programs, including networking and resources, job placement assistance (helps writers find jobs in teaching, editing, and other related fields), writing contests, literary arts advocacy, and forums. Levels of membership/dues: annual individual membership is $65/year; $110 for 2 years; students who provide photocopy of valid student ID pay $40/year (all prices apply to U.S. residents only). Membership includes 6 issues of The Writer's Chronicle (containing information about grants and awards, publishing opportunities, fellowships, and writing programs); access to the online AWP Job List (employment opportunity listings for writers); access to AWP eLink, a members-only Web site; a 50% discount on AWP Award Series entry fees; discount on registration for annual conference; and more. The Writer's Chronicle is available by subscription only for $20/year (6 issues). The AWP Award Series for novel, poetry, fiction, and creative nonfiction includes the Donald Hall Prize for Poetry (see separate listing in Contests & Awards). Additional information available on Web site.

THE BEATLICKS

1300 El Paseo Road, Suite G #308, Las Cruces NM 88001. E-mail: beatlickjoe@yahoo.com. Website: www.beatlick.com. Established 1988. **Contact:** Joe Speer, editor. International organization open to "anyone interested in literature." Currently has 200 members. "There is no official distinction between members, but there is a core group that does the work, writes reviews, organizes readings, etc." Offerings include publication of work (have published poets from Australia, Egypt, India, and Holland) and reviews of books and venues. Publishes Beatlick News 4 times/year, a networking tool designed to inform poets of local events and to bring awareness of the national scene. "We include poems, short fiction, art, photos, and articles about poets and venues." Submit short pieces, no vulgar language. "We try to elevate the creative spirit. We publish new voices plus well-established talents." Subscription: $15/year. Additional information available for SASE or by e-mail. "We promote all the arts."

ⓃN BOWERY POETRY CLUB

308 Bowery Street, New York NY 10012. (212)614-0505. Fax: (212)614-8539. E-mail: mail@bowerypoetry.com. Website: www.bowerypoetry.com. Established 2002. **Contact**: Gary Glazner. The Bowery Poetry Club and Cafe hosts regional open mic and poetry events. "Hosting between 20 and 30 shows a week, the Bowery Poetry Club (BPC) is proud of our place in the lineage of populist art: The Yiddish theater, burlesque, vaudeville, beat poetry, jazz, and punk that gave the Bowery its name." Offers workshops for adults and young poets. "Each Tuesday night at 6:30 pm touring Slam poets give a craft talk as part of our WordShop series." Nationally known writers give readings that are open to the public. Sponsors open mic readings for the public each Tuesday night at 7 pm as part of the Urbana Poetry Slam; format: open mic, featured poet, poetry slam. See Web site for more information and schedule.

BRIGHT HILL LITERARY CENTER

P.O. Box 193, 94 Church St., Treadwell NY 13846-0193. (607)829-5055. Fax: (607)829-5054. E-mail: wordthur@stny.rr.com. Website: www.brighthillpress.org. Established 1992. **Contact:** Bertha Rogers, founding director. Bright Hill Literary Center serves residents in the Catskill Mountain region, greater New York, and throughout the U.S. Includes the Bright Hill Library & Internet Center, with "thousands of volumes of literary journals, literary prose and poetry, literary criticism and biography, theater, reference, art, and children's books available for reading and research (noncirculating, for the time being). Wireless Internet access is available." Sponsors workshops for children and adults. Sponsors contests/awards (Bright Hill Press book and chapbook competitions; see separate listings in Contests & Awards). Publishes 5-7 books of poetry each year.

⚡ BURNABY WRITERS' SOCIETY

6584 Deer Lake Ave., Burnaby BC V5G 3T7 Canada. E-mail: info@bws.bc.ca. Website: www. bws.bc.ca. Established 1967. **Contact:** Eileen Kernaghan. Corresponding membership in the society, including a newsletter subscription, is open to anyone, anywhere. Currently has 100 members. Levels of membership/dues: regular ($30 CAD); students/seniors ($20 CAD/year). Sample newsletter in return for SASE with Canadian stamp. Holds monthly meetings at The Burnaby Arts Centre (located at 6450 Deer Lake Ave.), with a business meeting at 7:30 followed by a writing workshop or speaker. Members of the society stage regular public readings of their own work. Sponsors open mic readings for the public. Sponsors a poetry contest open to British Columbia residents. Competition receives about 100-200 entries/year. Past contest winners include Mildred Tremblay, Irene Livingston, and Kate Braid. Additional information available on Web site.

CALIFORNIA STATE POETRY SOCIETY

CSPS/CQ, P.O. Box 7126, Orange CA 92683. Website: www.californiaquarterly.blogspot.com. **Contact:** Membership Chair. The California State Poetry Society "is dedicated to the adventure of poetry and its dissemination. Although located in California, its members are from all over the U.S. and abroad." Levels of membership/dues: $30/year. Benefits include membership in the National Federation of State Poetry Societies (NFSPS); 4 issues of California Quarterly (see separate listing in Magazines/Journals), Newsbriefs, and The Poetry Letter. Sponsors monthly and annual contests. Additional information available for SASE or on website.

⚡ CANADIAN POETRY ASSOCIATION

331 Elmwood Dr., Suite 4-212, Moncton NB E1A 1X6 Canada. Phone/fax: (506)204-1732. E-mail: info@canadianpoetryassoc.com. Website: www.canadianpoetryassoc.com. Established 1985. "We promote all aspects of the reading, writing, publishing, purchasing, and preservation of poetry in Canada. The CPA promotes the creation of local chapters to organize readings, workshops, publishing projects, and other poetry-related events in their area." Membership is open to anyone with an interest in poetry, including publishers, schools, libraries, booksellers, and other literary organizations. Levels of membership/dues: $30 CAD/year; seniors, students, and fixed income, $20 CAD; International, $40 USD. Publishes a magazine, Poemata, featuring news articles, chapter reports, poetry by new members, book reviews, markets information, announcements, and more. Membership form available for SASE or on Web site. Also sponsors The CPA Annual Poetry Contest, with 3 cash prizes plus up to 5 Honorable Mentions. **Open to the public.** Winning poems published in Poemata and on CPA Web site. **Deadline:** January 30, 2008. Guidelines available for SASE or on Web site.

COLUMBINE POETS OF COLORADO

P.O. Box 6245, Westminster CO 80021. (303)431-6774. E-mail: anitajg5@aol.com. Website: www. Nazcaresources.com/columbine. Established 1978. **Contact:** Anita Jepson-Gilbert, secretary/ treasurer. Statewide organization open to anyone interested in poetry. Currently has around 100 members. An affiliate of the National Federation of State Poetry Societies (NFSPS). Levels of membership/dues: $15 for Members-at-Large, (includes membership in the national and state societies), and $35 (includes membership in the national, state, and local Foothills Chapter in Denver). Offerings for the Denver Foothills Chapter include weekly workshops and monthly critiques. Sponsors contests, awards for students and adults, an Annual Poetry Fest and some publications. Additional information available with SASE, by phone, e-mail, or on Web site.

CONNECTICUT POETRY SOCIETY

P.O. Box 702, Manchester CT 06040. E-mail: connpoetry@comcast.net. Website: www.ct-poetry-society.org/. Established 1978. **Contact:** Christine Beck, president. The Connecticut Poetry Society is a nonprofit organization dedicated to the promotion and enjoyment of poetry through chapter meetings, contests, and poetry-related events. Statewide organization open to non-Connecticut residents. Currently has about 150 members. Levels of membership/dues: full, $25/year; student, $10/year. Membership benefits include automatic membership in The National Federation of State Poetry Societies (NFSPS); a free copy of The Connecticut River Review, a national poetry journal published by CPS (see separate listing in Magazines/Journals); opportunity to publish in Long River Run II, a members-only poetry journal; quarterly CPS and NFSPS newsletters; annual April poetry celebration; and membership in any of 10 state chapters. Sponsors conferences and workshops. Sponsors The Connecticut River Review Annual Poetry Contest, The Brodinsky-Brodine Contest, The Winchell Contest, The Lynn Decaro High School Competition, and The Dehn Poetry Competition (see separate listings in Contests & Awards). Members and nationally known writers give readings that are open to the public. Members meet monthly. Additional information available by SASE or on Web site.

COUNCIL OF LITERARY MAGAZINES AND PRESSES (CLMP)

154 Christopher St., Suite 3C, New York NY 10014. (212)741-9110. E-mail: info@clmp.org. Website: www.clmp.org. Established 1967. "Dedicated to supporting and actively promoting the field of independent literary publishing." Open to publishers who are primarily literary in nature, have published at least one issue/title prior to applying for membership, publish at least one issue/title annually on an ongoing basis, have a minimum print run of 500 per issue or title, do not charge authors a fee, are not primarily self-publishing, and do not primarily publish children's/students' work. Currently has over 500 members. Levels of membership/dues: based on publishing organization's annual budget. See Web site for complete member application process. Benefits include free and discounted monographs, subscription to email listserves and online databases, annual copy of The Literary Press and Magazine Directory, plus many valuable services. Additional information available by e-mail or on Web site.

FURIOUS FLOWER POETRY CENTER

(Specialized: African American poetry)MSC 3802, James Madison University, Harrisonburg VA 22807. (540)568-8883. Fax: (540)568-8888. E-mail: gabbinjv@jmu.edu. Website: www.jmu. edu/furiousflower. Established 1999. **Contact:** Joanne Gabbin, PhD, Executive Director. A non-membership-based organization. "The mission of the Furious Flower Poetry Center is to advance the genre of African American poetry by providing opportunities for education, research, and publication." Sponsors workshops and conferences related to African American poetry, including an annual poetry camp for children of the community. Sponsored national conferences in 1994 and 2004. Nationally known writers give readings that are open to the public. Sponsors open mic readings for the public; also sponsors the Central Shenandoah Valley Slam Team. Additional information available by e-mail or on website.

GEORGIA POETRY SOCIETY

P.O. Box 2184, Columbia GA 31902. (334)448-4715. E-mail: georgiapoetrysociety@yahoo.com. Website: www.georgiapoetrysociety.org. Established 1979. **Contact:** Steven Owen Shields, president. Statewide organization open to any person who is in accord with the objectives to secure fuller public recognition of the art of poetry, stimulate an appreciation of poetry, and enhance the writing and reading of poetry. Currently has 200 members. Levels of membership/ dues: Active, $30 ($40 family), fully eligible for all aspects of membership; Student, $15, does not vote or hold office, and must be full-time enrolled student through college level; Lifetime, same as Active but pays a one-time membership fee of $500, receives free anthologies each year, and pays no contest entry fees. Membership includes affiliation with NFSPS. Holds at least one workshop annually. Contests are sponsored throughout the year, some for members only. "Our contests have specific general rules, which should be followed to avoid the disappointment of disqualification. See the website for details." Publishes Georgia Poetry Society Newsletter, a quarterly, and The Reach of Song, an annual anthology devoted to contest-winning poems and member works. Each quarterly meeting (open to the public) features at least one poet of regional prominence. Also sponsors a monthly open mic at the Columbus Library (Macon Rd) in Columbus, GA (open to the public). Sponsors Poetry in the Schools project. Additional information available on website.

HAIKU SOCIETY OF AMERICA

P.O. Box 31, Nassau NY 12123. E-mail: lstparker@cs.com. Website: www.hsa-haiku.org. Established 1968. **Contact:** Lane Parker, secretary. The Haiku Society of America is composed of haiku poets, editors, critics, publishers, and enthusiasts dedicated to "promoting the creation and appreciation of haiku and related forms (haibun, haiga, renku, senryu, sequences, and tanka) among its members and the public." Currently has over 800 members. Levels of membership/ dues: $33 U.S.; $30 seniors or full-time students (in North America); $35 USD in Canada and Mexico; $45 USD for all other areas. Membership benefits include a year's subscription (3 issues in 2007) to the Society's journal, Frogpond (see separate listing in Magazines/Journals), and to the quarterly HSA Newsletter ; the annual information sheet; an annual address/e-mail list of HSA members; and eligibility to submit work to the members' anthology. Administers the following annual awards: The Harold G. Henderson Awards for haiku, The Gerald Brady Awards for senryu, The Bernard Lionel Einbond Awards for renku, The Merit Book Awards, and The Nicholas Virgilio Haiku Awards for youth. Guidelines available in the newsletter or on website. Meets quarterly at various locations throughout the U.S. Additional information available for SASE or on website.

THE HUDSON VALLEY WRITERS' CENTER

300 Riverside Dr., Sleepy Hollow NY 10591. (914)332-5953. Fax: (914)332-4825. E-mail: info@ writerscenter.org. Website: www.writerscenter.org. Established 1988. **Contact:** Jerri Lynn Fields, executive director. "The Hudson Valley Writers' Center is a nonprofit organization devoted to furthering the literary arts in our region. Its mission is to promote the appreciation of literary excellence, to stimulate and nurture the creation of literary works in all sectors of the population, and to bring the diverse works of gifted poets and prose artists to the attention of the public." Open to all. Currently has 350 members. Levels of membership/dues: individual ($35/year), family ($50/year), senior/student ($25/year), and friend ($100/year and up). Offerings include public

readings by established and emerging poets/writers, workshops and classes, monthly open mic nights, paid and volunteer outreach opportunities, and an annual chapbook competition with Slapering Hol Press (see separate listing in Contests & Awards). Additional information available for SASE, by fax, e-mail, or on Web site.

INTERNATIONAL READING ASSOCIATION

800 Barksdale Rd., Newark DE 19714-8139. (800)336-7323. Fax: (302)731-1057. E-mail: pubinfo@ reading.org. Website: www.reading.org. "For 50 years, the International Reading Association has been a professional home for those who help others learn to read. Today, our network and resources reach hundreds of thousands of teachers, researchers, students, administrators, tutors, parents, and others-in every part of the world."

INTERNATIONAL WOMEN'S WRITING GUILD

P.O. Box 810, Gracie Station, New York NY 10028. (212)737-7536. Fax: (212)737-9469. E-mail: iwwg@iwwg.org. Website: www.iwwg.org. Established 1976. **Contact:** Hannelore Hahn, founder/executive editor. A network for the personal and professional empowerment of women through writing. Levels of membership/dues: $45/year (domestic and overseas). The Guild publishes a bimonthly 32-page journal, Network, which includes members' achievements, contests, calendar, and extensive publishing opportunities. Other benefits include regional/ local writing groups and kitchen tables, agent list, and dental and vision insurance, health insurance in New York City. "We offer approximately 8 writing workshops throughout the U.S., including the weeklong summer conference held at Skidmore College in Saratoga Springs, New York. Poetry workshops are interspersed in the conference programs." Additional information available by fax, e-mail, or on Web site.

IOWA POETRY ASSOCIATION

(Specialized: IA residents only)2325 61st St., Des Moines IA 50322. (515)279-1106. Website: www.iowapoetry.com. Established 1945. **Contact:** Lucille Morgan Wilson, editor. Statewide organization open to "anyone interested in poetry, with a residence or valid address in the state of Iowa." Currently has about 425 members. Levels of membership/dues: Regular ($8/ year) and Patron ($15 or more/year; "same services, but patron members contribute to cost of running the association"). Offerings include "semiannual workshops to which a poem may be sent in advance for critique; annual contest--also open to nonmembers--with no entry fee; IPA Newsletter, published 5 or 6 times/year, including a quarterly national publication listing of contest opportunities; and an annual poetry anthology, Lyrical Iowa, containing prize-winning and high-ranking poems from contest entries, available for $10 postpaid. No requirement for purchase to ensure publication." Semiannual workshops "are the only 'meetings' of the association." Additional information available for SASE or on Web site.

THE KENTUCKY STATE POETRY SOCIETY

E-mail: www.tcscott@cebridge.com. Website: www.kystatepoetrysociety.org. Established 1966. **Contact:** A. Carol Scott, president. Regional organization open to all. Member of The National Federation of State Poetry Societies (NFSPS). Currently has about 230 members. Levels of membership/dues: students ($5); adults ($20); senior adults ($15); other categories: Life; Patron; Benefactor. Offerings include association with other poets; information on contests and poetry happenings across the state and nation; annual state and national contests; national and state annual conventions with workshops, selected speakers, and open poetry readings. Sponsors workshops, contests, awards. Membership includes the quarterly KSPS Newsletter. Also includes a quarterly newsletter, Strophes, of the NFSPS; and the KSPS journal, Pegasus, published 3 times/year: a Spring/ Summer and Fall/Winter issue which solicits good poetry for publication (need not be a member to submit), and a Prize Poems issue of 1st Place contest winners in over 30 categories. Members or nationally known writers give readings that are open to the public. Members meet annually. Membership information available by e-mail or on Web site.

THE LEAGUE OF CANADIAN POETS

920 Yonge St., Suite 608, Toronto ON M4W 3C7 Canada. (416)504-1657. E-mail: readings@poets. ca. Website: www.poets.ca. Established 1966. **Contact:** Ingrel Madrus, Readings/Membership Coordinator. A nonprofit national association of professional publishing and performing poets in Canada. Its purpose is "to enhance the status of poets and nurture a professional poetic community to facilitate the teaching of Canadian poetry at all levels of education and to develop the audience for poetry by encouraging publication, performance, and recognition of Canadian poetry nationally and internationally. As well as providing members and the public with many benefits and services, the League speaks for poets on many issues such as freedom of expression, Public Lending Right, CanCopy, contract advice, and grievance." Open to all Canadian citizens and landed immigrants; applications are assessed by a membership committee. Currently has 600 members. Levels of membership/dues: Full ($175 CAD); Associate ($60 CAD); Student ($20 CAD); and Supporting ($100 CAD). Membership benefits include a one-year subscription to monthly e-newsletter, discount on Gift Shop purchases, listing in online members' catalog, and more (benefits increase with membership level). Sponsors The Pat Lowther Memorial Award (for a book of poetry by a Canadian woman published in the preceding year; $1,000 CAD prize) and The Gerald Lampert Memorial Award (recognizes the best first book of poetry published by a Canadian in the preceding year; $1,000 CAD). Additional information available on Web site.

THE LIT

2570 Superior Ave., Suite 203, Cleveland, OH 44114. E-mail: info@the-lit.org. Website: www. the-lit.org. Established 1974. **Contact:** Judith Mansour-Thomas, executive director. Founded "to foster a supportive community for poets and writers throughout Northern Ohio and to expand the audience for creative writing among the general public." Currently has 300 members. Levels of membership/dues are regular: $35/year; students and seniors $25. Membership benefits include subscription to Muse Magazine and discounts on services and facilities at the Literary Center. The Literary Center offers classes and an event space for writers and readers. The Lit conducts a monthly workshop where poets can bring their work for discussion. Publishes a monthly calendar of literary events in NE Ohio; a quarterly magazine, Muse, which includes articles on the writing life, news, markets, and an annual writing contest in all genres; and 2 chapbooks/year featuring an anthology of work by area poets. "The Lit also sponsors a dramatic reading series, 'Poetry: Mirror of the Arts,' which unites poetry and other art forms performed in cultural settings; and 'Writers & Their Friends,' a biennial literary showcase of new writing (all genres), performed dramatically by area actors, media personalities, and performance poets." Additional information available for SASE, by e-mail, or on website.

THE LOFT LITERARY CENTER

Suite 200, Open Book, 1011 Washington Ave. S, Minneapolis MN 55414. (612)215-2575. E-mail: loft@loft.org. Website: www.loft.org. Established 1974. "The Loft is the largest and most comprehensive literary center in the country, serving both writers and readers with a variety of readings, Spoken Word performances, educational programs, contests and grants, and writing facilities." Supporting members (starting at $60/year - $25 for students/low income) receive benefits including discounted tuition, admission charges, and contest fees; check-out privileges at The Loft's Rachel Anne Gaschott Resource Library; rental access to the Book Club Meeting Room and writers' studios; a year's subscription to A View from the Loft ; and more. Information on additional benefit leves, classes/workshops, contests and grants, and readings by local and national writers available at the Web site.

MAINE POETS SOCIETY

E-mail: ahammond5@verizon.net. Established 1936. **Contact:** Anne Hammond. Maine Poets Society is an organization "committed to fostering poetry in Maine and beyond. Membership open to all poets who reside at least part-time in Maine." Levels of membership/dues: $15. Make checks payable to Anne Hammond, Treasurer. Email Anne for mailing address. Membership benefits include access to writing groups and round robins as well as a subscription to Stanza, a newsletter published 3 times/year containing contest-winning poems. Sponsors 3 contests/ year with cash prizes for 1st, 2nd, and 3rd Prize; open to members only. Meets third Saturday of February, May, and September. "Our locations change to allow Mainers from across the state to easily join us." Additional information available by e-mail.

MASSACHUSETTS STATE POETRY SOCIETY

, INC. 64 Harrison Ave., Lynn MA 01905. E-mail: msps.jcmaes@comcast.net. Website: http:// mastatepoetrysociety.tripod.com/. Established 1959. **Contact:** Jeanette C. Maes, president. Dedicated to the writing and appreciation of poetry and promoting the art form. Statewide organization open to anyone with an interest in poetry. Currently has 200 members. Levels of membership/dues: $15/year. Member benefits include subscription to Bay State Echo, published 5 times/year with members' news and announcements; members-only contests; round-robin critique groups; members-only annual anthology; workshops at society meetings; and automatic membership in National Federation of State Poetry Societies (NFSPS). Sponsors contests open to all poets. Guidelines available for SASE or on Web site. Members or nationally known writers give readings that are open to the public. Sponsors open mic readings for members and the public for National Poetry Day. Members meet 5 times/year. Additional information available for SASE or on Web site.

MOUNTAIN WRITERS SERIES

Mountain Writers Center, 2804 S.E. 27th Ave., #2, Portland OR 97202. (503)232-4517. E-mail: pdxmws@mountainwriters.org. Website: www.mountainwriters.org. **Contact:** Bob Kreider, program associate. Established 1973. "Mountain Writers Series is an independent nonprofit organization dedicated to supporting writers, audiences, and other sponsors by promoting literature and literacy through artistic and educational literary arts events in the Pacific Northwest." Currently has about 150 members. Levels of membership/dues: Basic ($50); Student/Retired ($25); Family ($75); Contributing ($100); Supporting ($500); and Patron ($1,000). Mountain Writers Series offers intensive one-day and 2-day workshops, weekend master classes, 5-week, 8-week, and 10-week courses about writing." Authors who have participated recently include David James Duncan, Linda Gregg, C.K. Williams, Li-Young Lee, Kim Addonizio, and David St. John. Sponsors readings that are open to the public. Nationally and internationally known writers are sponsored by the Mountain Writers Series Northwest Regional Residencies Program (reading tours) and the campus readings program (Pulitzer Prize winners, Nobel Prize winners, MacArthur Fellows, etc.). Additional information available for SASE, by fax, e-mail, or on Web site.

NATIONAL FEDERATION OF STATE POETRY SOCIETIES (NFSPS)

Website: www.nfsps.org. Established 1959. "NFSPS is a nonprofit organization exclusively educational and literary. Its purpose is to recognize the importance of poetry with respect to national cultural heritage. It is dedicated solely to the furtherance of poetry on the national level and serves to unite poets in the bonds of fellowship and understanding." Currently has 7,000 members. Any poetry group located in a state not already affiliated, but interested in affiliating, with NFSPS may contact the membership chairman (see Web site). In a state where no valid group exists, help may also be obtained by individuals interested in organizing a poetry group for affiliation. Most reputable state poetry societies are members of the National Federation and advertise their various poetry contests through the NFSPS quarterly newsletter Strophes (sample copy available for SASE and $1), edited by Caroline Walton, 6176 W. Pinedale Circle, Crystal River, FL 34429 (e-mail: carowalton@tampabay.rr.com). **Beware of organizations calling themselves state poetry societies (however named) that are not members of NFSPS, as such labels are sometimes used by vanity schemes trying to sound respectable.** NFSPS holds an annual 3-day convention in a different state each year with workshops, an awards banquet, and addresses by nationally known poets. Sponsors an annual 50-category national contest (see separate listing for NFSPS Competitions in Contests & Awards). Additional information available by e-mail or on Web site.

NATIONAL WRITERS ASSOCIATION

10940 S. Parker Rd., #508, Parker CO 80134. (303)841-0246. Fax: (303)841-2607. E-mail: natlwritersassn@hotmail.com. Website: www.nationalwriters.com. Established 1937. **Contact:** Sandy Whelchel, executive director. National organization with regional affiliations open to writers. Currently has 2,000 members. Levels of membership/dues: Professional ($85); Regular ($65) and Student ($30). Hosts an annual Summer Conference where workshops, panels, etc., are available to all attendees, including poets. Also offers a yearly poetry writing contest with cash awards of $100, $50, and $25. **Entry fee:** $10/poem. **Deadline:** October 1. Send SASE for judging sheet copies. Publishes Authorship, an annual magazine. Sample copy available for 9x12 envelope with $1.21 postage. Available to nonmembers for $20. Additional information available for SASE, by fax, e-mail, or on Web site.

NATIONAL WRITERS UNION

113 University Place, 6th Floor, New York NY 10003. (212)254-0279. Fax: (212)254-0673. E-mail: nwu@nwu.org. Website: www.nwu.org. Poets eligible for membership if they've published at least 5 poems, or if they've written 5 poems and are actively writing and trying to publish their work. Other standards apply for various forms of writing (see website). Offers members such services as a grievance committee, contract guidelines, health insurance, press credentials, and caucuses and trade groups for exchange of information about special markets. Levels of membership/dues: $95 for those earning less than $5,000/year; $155 for those earning $5,000-25,000; $210 for those earning $25,000-50,000; and $260 for those whose writing income is more than $50,000/year. Membership form available online. Members receive The American Writer, the organization's newsletter. See website for complete information.

NEVADA POETRY SOCIETY

P.O. Box 7014, Reno NV 89510. (775)322-3619. Established 1976. **Contact:** Sam Wood, president. Statewide organization. Currently has 30 members. Levels of membership/dues: Active and Emeritus ($10). Offerings include membership in the National Federation of State Poetry Societies (NFSPS), which includes a subscription to their publication, Strophes ; monthly challenges followed by critiquing of all new poems; lessons on types of poetry. Members of the society are occasionally called upon to read to organizations or in public meetings. Members meet monthly. Additional information available for SASE. "We advise poets to enter their poems in contests before thinking about publication."

NEW HAMPSHIRE WRITERS' PROJECT

2500 North River Rd., Manchester NH 03106. (603)314-7980. Fax: (603)314-7981. E-mail: info@ nhwritersproject.org. Website: www.nhwritersproject.org. Established 1988. **Contact:** Kathy Wurtz, executive director. Statewide organization open to writers at all levels in all genres. Currently has 700+ members. Levels of membership/dues: $45/year; $25/year for seniors and students. Offerings include workshops, seminars, an annual conference, and a literary calendar. Sponsors daylong workshops and 4- to 6-week intensive courses. Also sponsors the biennial New Hampshire Literary Awards for outstanding literary achievement (including The Jane Kenyon Award for Outstanding Book of Poetry). Publishes NH Writer, a bimonthly newsletter for and about New Hampshire writers. Members and nationally known writers give readings that are open to the public. Additional information available for SASE, by fax, e-mail, or on Web site.

NEWTOWN WRITERS

(Specialized: gay/lesbian/bisexual/transgendered)E-mail: frauman8@aol.com. Website: www. newtownwriters.org. Established 1980. **Contact:** Director. NewTown Writers, a gay and lesbian writers' workshop based in Chicago, IL, is dedicated to advancing GLBTQ literary expression. "NewTown Writers' mission is to foster and give voice to literature--plays, novels, poetry, short stories, essays--which springs from our experiences." Open to anyone. In addition to bi-weekly workshops, NewTown Writers sponsors weekly workshop-style meetings, a performance series, and publishes Off the Rocks (anthology) and Swell (see separate listing in Magazines/Journals). Additional information available by e-mail or on website.

NEW YORK CENTER FOR INDEPENDENT PUBLISHING

The General Society of Mechanics & Tradesmen, 20 W. 44th, New York NY 10036. (212)764-7021. Fax: (212)840-2046. E-mail: info@smallpress.org. Website: http://nycip.org. Established 1984. "The Small Press Center is a nonprofit educational program and resource center for independent publishing, as well as a membership organization of independent and small press publishers and their enthusiasts." National organization open to "any person, company, or organization that supports the small press." Levels of membership/dues: Friends Membership ($50 Individual, $75 Dual/Family, $100 Contributing Friends, $250 Literary Benefactors, $300 Corporate Sponsors, $500 Patrons); Publisher Membership ($75 for one year; $100 for 2 years). Membership benefits include the quarterly Small Press Center Newsletter ; discounts on workshops, lectures, and audiotapes; invitations to readings and special events; and discount on Books on Writing & Publishing: A Bibliography in Progress, with 1,700 listings (additional or unique benefits available according to membership type and level). Sponsors the Small Press Book Fair in March and the New York Round Table Writers' Conference (www.writersconferencenyc.org) in April. Offers "a place in which the public may examine and order the books of independent publishers, free from commercial pressures. The Center is open five days a week." Additional information available for SASE, by fax, e-mail, or on website.

THE NORTH CAROLINA POETRY SOCIETY

(Specialized: NC poets) Officers change annually; please contact through Web site at www. ncpoetrysociety.org. Established 1932. Purpose is "to foster the writing of poetry; to bring together in meetings of mutual interest and fellowship the poets of North Carolina; to encourage the study, writing, and publication of poetry; and to develop a public taste for the reading and appreciation of poetry." Statewide and out-of-state organization open to "all interested persons." Currently has about 320 members. Levels of membership/dues: Adult ($25/year) and Student

($10/year). NCPS conducts 6 general meetings and numerous statewide workshops each year; sponsors annual poetry contests with categories for adults and students (open to anyone, with small fee for nonmembers; December/January deadline; cash prizes); publishes the contest-winning poems in the annual anthology Pinesong ; publishes a newsletter; and supports other poetry activities. Also sponsors the annual Brockman/Campbell Book Award for a book of poetry (over 20 pages) by a North Carolina poet (native-born or current resident for 3 years). Prize: $200. **Entry fee:** $10 for nonmembers. **Deadline:** May 1. Competitions receive 300 entries/year. Nationally known writers give readings that are open to the public. Sponsors open mic readings that are open to the public. Additional information available on Web site.

NORTH CAROLINA WRITERS' NETWORK

P.O. Box 78002, Charlotte NC 28271. (704)246-6314. E-mail: mail@ncwriters.org. Website: www.ncwriters.org. Established 1985. Supports the work of writers, writers' organizations, independent bookstores, little magazines and small presses, and literary programming statewide. Currently has 1,100 members. Levels of membership/dues: $75/year; seniors/students, $55/year. Membership benefits include The Writers' Network News, a 24-page bimonthly newsletter containing organizational news, national market information, and other literary material of interest to writers; and access to the NCWN Library & Resource Center, other writers, workshops, writer's residencies, conferences, readings and competitions, and NCWN's critiquing and editing service. Annual fall conference features nationally known writers, publishers, and editors, held in a different North Carolina location each November. Sponsors competitions in short fiction, nonfiction, and poetry for North Carolina residents and NCWN members. Guidelines available for SASE or on Web site.

OHIO POETRY ASSOCIATION

5580 Beverly Hills Dr., Apt B, Columbus OH 43213. (740)694-5013. E-mail: david@ohiopoetryassn. org. Website: www.ohiopoetryassn.com. Established in 1929 as Verse Writers' Guild of Ohio. **Contact:** Bob Casey, president. Promotes the art of poetry, and furthers the support of poets and others who support poetry. Statewide membership with additional members in several other states, Japan, and England. Affiliated with the National Federation of State Poetry Societies (NFSPS). Open to poets and writers of all ages and ability, as well as to non-writing lovers of poetry. Currently has about 215 members. Levels of membership/dues: Regular ($18); Student (including college undergrads, $8); Associate ($8); Senior ($15); Life; and Honorary. Member benefits include regular contests; meeting/workshop participation; assistance with writing projects; networking; twice-yearly magazine, Common Threads (see separate listing in Magazines/Journals), publishing only poems by members; quarterly Ohio Poetry Association Newsletter ; quarterly NFSPS newsletters (Strophes); automatic NFSPS membership; and contest information and lower entry fees for NFSPS contests. Members are automatically on the mailing list for Ohio Poetry Day contest guidelines (OPA financially supports Ohio Poetry Day; see separate listing in Contests & Awards). Individual chapters regularly host workshops and seminars. Members and nationally known writers give readings that are open to the public (at quarterly meetings; public is invited). Sponsors open mic readings for members and the public. Past readers have included Lisa Martinovic, David Shevin, Michael Bugeja, David Citino, and Danika Dinsmore. Members meet quarterly (September, December, March, May). Additional information available by e-mail or on Web site. "In short, OPA provides poets with opportunities to share info, critique, publish, sponsor contests, and just socialize."

PEN AMERICAN CENTER

588 Broadway, Suite 303, New York NY 10012. (212)334-1660. E-mail: pen@pen.org. Website:

www.pen.org. Established 1922. PEN American Center "is the largest of the 141 centers of International PEN, the world's oldest human rights organization and the oldest international literary association. PEN American Center works to advance literature, to defend free expression, and to foster international literary fellowship." The 2,900 members of the PEN American Center include poets, playwrights, essayists, editors, novelists (for the original letters in the acronym PEN), as well as translators and those editors and agents who have made a substantial contribution to the literary community. Levels of membership/dues: $75 Member (must meet standard qualifications to become a Member; see Web site); $40 Associate Member and $20 Student (both open to everyone). Membership benefits include subscription to PEN America Journal, discounts on admission to public programs, discounted access to Grants and Awards Available to American Writers (an online database), access to online bulletin board, and more (additional benefits at Member level, including reciprocal privileges in PEN American Center branches and in foreign centers for those traveling abroad). Sponsors public literary programs, forums on current issues, visits by prominent authors to inner-city schools, the promotion of international literature to U.S. readers, and grants and loans to writers with emergency financial need. Publishes PEN America Journal (available through Web site and selected bookstores, or by subscription at $18/year); and Grants and Awards Available to American Writers online (access available through membership or nonmember subscription of $12/year). Administers the PEN/ Joyce Osterwell Award for Poetry for a new and emerging American poet of literary character ($5,000), and the PEN Award for Poetry in Translation ($3,000) for book-length translations of poetry into English from any language. Also sponsors the annual PEN World Voices: The New York Festival of International Literature. Additional information on membership and all programs and activities available on Web site.

PITTSBURGH POETRY EXCHANGE

P.O. Box 4279, Pittsburgh PA 15203. (412)481-POEM. Website: http://pghpoetryexchange. pghfree.net. **Contact:** Michael Wurster, coordinator. Established 1974. A community-based volunteer organization for local poets, it functions as a service organization and information exchange, conducting ongoing workshops, readings, forums, and other special events to promote poets and poetry. No dues or fees. "Any monetary contributions are voluntary, often from outside sources. We've managed not to let our reach exceed our grasp." Currently has about 30 members (with a mailing list of 400). Reading programs are primarily committed to local and area poets, with honorariums of $25-85. Sponsors a minimum of 3 major events each year in addition to a monthly workshop (first Monday, 8 p.m, City Books); these include reading programs in conjunction with community arts festivals, such as South Side Poetry in October- -a series of readings throughout the evening at various shops, galleries, and bookstores. Poets from out of town may contact the Exchange for assistance in setting up readings at bookstores to help sell their books. "We have been partnering with Autumn House Press in co-sponsoring events and bringing some of its authors to town." Members meet on an ongoing basis, at least twice monthly. Additional information available for SASE or on Web site. "Pittsburgh is a very exciting literary town."

POETRY BOOK SOCIETY

4th Floor, 2 Tavistock Place, London WC1H 9RA England. (44)20 7833 9247. Fax: (44)20 7833 5990. E-mail: info@poetrybooks.co.uk. Website: www.poetrybooks.co.uk. **Contact:** Ms. Chris Holifield. Established 1953. A book club that promotes "the best newly published contemporary poetry to as wide an audience as possible." Membership: 2,200. Levels of membership/dues: £40/year Full Member; £12/year Associate Member; £50/year Full International Member. All members receive a subscription to the quarterly PBS Bulletin, 25% discount on almost all poetry books published in the UK, and advance notice of poetry events; Full Members also receive 4 PBS Choice selections free. New members receive a welcome gift. The PBS selectors also recommend other books of special merit each quarter. Sponsors the T.S. Eliot Prize for the best new single author collection published in the UK and Ireland in the calendar year. The Poetry Book Society is subsidized by the Arts Council of England. Additional information available by e-mail or on Web site.

THE POETRY FOUNDATION

444 N. Michigan Ave., Suite 1850, Chicago IL 60611-4034. (312)787-7070. Fax: (312)787-6650. E-mail: mail@poetryfoundation.org. Website: http://poetryfoundation.org. Established 2003. President: John Barr. The Poetry Foundation is an independent literary organization committed to a vigorous presence for poetry in our culture. It exists to discover and celebrate the best poetry and to place it before the largest possible audience. Initiatives include publishing Poetry magazine (see separate listing in Magazines/Journals); distributing Ted Kooser's American Life in Poetry newspaper project; funding and promotion of Poetry Out Loud: National Recitation Contest (in partnership with the National Endowment for the Arts and state arts associations); Poetry Everywhere, a series of short poetry films airing on public television and on transportation systems across the country; The Essential American Poets podcast series featuring seminal recordings of major American Poets reading from their work, as selected by former Poet Laureate Donald Hall; and www.poetryfoundation.org, an award-winning comprehensive online resource for poetry featuring an archive of more than 6,500 poems by more than 600 classic and contemporary poets. The site also includes the poetry blog "Harriet," poetry-related articles, a bestseller list, video programming, a series of poetry podcasts, and reading guides about poets and poetry. The Poetry Foundation annually awards the Ruth Lilly Poetry Prize, of $100,000, and the Ruth Lilly Poetry Fellowships, 5 annual awards of $15,000 to young poets to support their further studies in poetry. In 2004 the Foundation established a family of prizes called the Pegasus Awards to honor under-recognized poets and types of poetry (The Neglected Masters Award, The Emily Dickinson First Book Award, The Mark Twain Poetry Award, The Randall Jarrell Award in Criticism, The Children's Poet Laureate, and The Verse Drama Award). Additional information available on Web site.

POETRY LIBRARY

The Saison Poetry Library, Royal Festival Hall, London SE1 8XX UK. (44)(207)921-0943/0664. Fax: (44)(207)921-0939. E-mail: info@poetrylibrary.org.uk. Website: www.poetrylibrary.org.uk; www.poetrymagazines.org.uk. Established 1953. **Contact:** Chris McCabe and Miriam Valencia, assistant librarians. A "free public library of modern poetry. It contains a comprehensive collection of all British poetry published since 1912 and an international collection of poetry from all over the world, either written in or translated into English. As the United Kingdom's national library for poetry, it offers loan and information services and a large collection of poetry magazines, cassettes, compact discs, videos, records, poem posters, and cards; also press cuttings and photographs of poets."

THE POETRY SOCIETY

22 Betterton St., London WC2H 9BX United Kingdom. (44)(207)420-9880. Fax: (44)(207)240-4818. E-mail: info@poetrysociety.org.uk. Website: www.poetrysociety.org.uk. Established 1909. One of Britain's most dynamic arts organizations, with membership open to all. "The Poetry Society exists to help poets and poetry thrive in Britain today. Our members come from all over the world, and their support enables us to promote poetry on a global scale." Publishes Poetry Review (see separate listing in Magazines/Journals), Britain's most prominent poetry

magazine, and Poetry News, the Society's newsletter, as well as books and posters to support poetry in the classroom. Runs the National Poetry Competition (see separate listing in Contests & Awards) and The Foyle Young Poets of the Year Award (for poets aged 11-17), as well as many other competitions, services, and education projects for readers and writers of poetry. "Visit the website for a full idea of the range of activities The Poetry Society is engaged with."

POETRY SOCIETY OF NEW HAMPSHIRE

31 Reservoir, Farmington NH 03835. (603)332-0732. E-mail: poetrysocietyofnh@gmail. com. Established 1964. **Contact:** Patricia L. Frisella, president. A statewide organization for anyone interested in poetry. Currently has 200 members. Levels of membership/dues: Junior ($10); Regular ($20). Offerings include annual subscription to quarterly magazine, The Poet's Touchstone ; critiques, contests, and workshops; public readings; and quarterly meetings with featured poets. The Poet's Touchstone is available to nonmembers for $6 (single issue). Members and nationally known writers give readings that are open to the public. Sponsors open mic readings for members and the public. Additional information available for SASE or by e-mail. "We do sponsor a national contest four times a year with $100, $50, and $25 prizes paid out in each one. People from all over the country enter and win."

THE POETRY SOCIETY OF SOUTH CAROLINA

(PSSC)P.O. Box 1090, Charleston SC 29402. E-mail: FlatBlueSky@hotmail.com. Website: www. poetrysocietysc.org. Established 1920. **Contact:** James J. Lundy, Jr., president. The Poetry Society of South Carolina supports "the reading, writing, study, and enjoyment of poetry." Statewide organization open to anyone interested in poetry. Offers programs in Charleston that are free and open to the public September-May (except for members-only holiday party in December). Currently has 150 members. Levels of membership/dues: $15 student, $25 individual, $35 family, $50 patron, and $100 business or sponsor. Membership year runs July 1-June 30. Membership benefits include discounts to PSSC-sponsored seminars and workshops held in various SC locations; a copy of the annual Yearbook of contest-winning poems; eligibility to read at the open mic and to enter contests without a fee; and an invitation to the annual holiday party. Sponsors a monthly Writers' Group, a January open mic reading featuring PSSC members, a Charleston Poetry Walk during Piccolo Spoleto in June, and a May Forum leading to an audience-selected poetry prize. Sponsors two yearly contests, totaling 20-25 contest categories, some with themes; some are open to all poets, others open only to SC residents or PSSC members. Guidelines available on website. **Deadline:** November 15 (Fall round) and February 15 (Spring round). Also offers the Skylark Prize, a competition for SC high school students. Sometimes offers a chapbook competition. Members and nationally known writers give readings that are open to the public. Poets have included Billy Collins, Henry Taylor, Cathy Smith Bowers, and Richard Garcia, as well as emerging poets from the region. Additional information available by e-mail or on website.

POETRY SOCIETY OF TENNESSEE

18 S. Rembert, Memphis TN 38104. E-mail: RSTRpoet@cs.com. Website: www.tpstn.org. Established in 1953. **Contact:** Russell H. Strauss, president. Purpose is "to promote writing, reading, and appreciation of poetry among members of the society and the community; to improve poetry writing skills of members and local students. State poetry society, with some out-of-state members. Affiliate of National Federation of State Poetry Societies (NFSPS). Current membership about 70. Dues $20 a year for adults, $25 to include the yearbook (Tennessee Voices); $8 for students, including yearbook. Yearbook contains names, addresses, e-mail addresses of officers and members; winning poems by members and student members; and more. Society activities include programs with speakers; poetry contests, readings, and workshops; one

meeting a year dedicated to students; plus Mid-South Poetry Festival first Saturday in October with workshop and prizes. Poetry readings about four times a year in local restaurants and bookstores. Regular meetings at 2 p.m. on first Saturday of each month (September-May) in basement of Evergreen Presbyterian Church across from Rhodes College (Parkway at College St.). No meetings in summer months. Newsletter Tennessee Voices Bulletin) every 2 months to members or for SASE.

THE POETRY SOCIETY OF TEXAS

610 Circle View Dr. (817)477-1754. E-mail: jlstrother@sbcglobal.net Website: www. poetrysocietyoftexas.org. **Contact**: Jeannette L. Strother. Established 1921. "The purpose of the society shall be to secure fuller public recognition of the art of poetry, to encourage the writing of poetry by Texans, and to kindle a finer and more intelligent appreciation of poetry, especially the work of living poets who interpret the spirit and heritage of Texas." Poetry Society of Texas is a member of the National Federation of State Poetry Societies (NFSPS). Has 25 chapters in cities throughout the state. Currently has 300 members. Levels of membership/dues: Active ($25) for native Texans, Citizens of Texas, or former Citizens of Texas who were active members; Associate ($25) for all who desire to affiliate; also Student ($12.50); Sustaining; Benefactors; and Patrons of the Poets. Offerings include annual contests with prizes in excess of $5,000 as well as monthly contests (general and humorous); 8 monthly meetings; annual awards banquet; annual summer conference in a different location each year; round-robin critiquing opportunities sponsored at the state level; and Poetry in Schools with contests at state and local chapter levels. "Our monthly state meetings are held at the Preston Royal Branch of the Dallas Public Library. Our annual awards banquet is held at the Crown Plaza Suites in Dallas. Our summer conference is held at a site chosen by the hosting chapter. Chapters determine their meeting sites." PST publishes A Book of the Year, which presents annual and monthly award-winning poems, coming contest descriptions, minutes of meetings, by-laws of the society, history, and information. Also publishes the Poetry Society of Texas Bulletin, a monthly newsletter that features statewide news documenting contest winners, state meeting information, chapter and individual infor! mation, news from the NFSPS, and announcements of coming activities and offerings for poets. "A Book of the Year is available to nonmembers for $8." Members and nationally known writers give readings. "All of our meetings are open to the public." Additional information available for SASE, by e-mail, or on Web site.

POETS & WRITERS, INC.

90 Broad St., Suite 2100, New York NY 10004. (212)226-3586. Website: www.pw.org. Established 1970. Poets & Writers' mission is "to foster the professional development of poets and writers, to promote communication throughout the U.S. literary community, and to help create an environment in which literature can be appreciated by the widest possible public." The largest nonprofit literary organization in the nation, P&W offers information, support, resources, and exposure to poets, fiction writers, and nonfiction writers at all stages in their careers. Sponsors the Readings/Workshops Program, through which P&W sponsors more than 1,700 literary events in New York, California, and other cities in the U.S. Publishes the online Directory of American Poets and Writers with a searchable database of over 7,000 writers; Poets & Writers Magazine (print); and Poets & Writers Online, which offers topical information, the Speakeasy Message Forum (a central meeting place for writers), and links to over 1,500 websites of interest to writers. Sponsors the Writers Exchange Contest (emerging poets and fiction writers are introduced to literary communities outside their home states); the Jacobson Poetry Prize ($50,000 award for an early to mid-career poet; no nominations accepted); the Barnes & Noble Writers for Writers Award; and the Amy Award (see separate listing in Contests & Awards).

POETS HOUSE

594 Broadway, Ste 510, New York NY 10012. (212)431-7920. Fax: (212)431-8131. E-mail: info@ poetshouse.org. Website: www.poetshouse.org. Established 1985. Poets House, a national poetry library and literary center, is a "home for all who read and write poetry." Levels of membership/ dues: begin at $40/year; along with other graduated benefits, each new or renewing member receives free admission to all regularly scheduled programs. Resources include the 50,000-volume poetry collection, conference room, exhibition space, and a Children's Room. Over 200 annual public programs include panel discussions and lectures, readings, seminars and workshops, and The People's Poetry Gathering. In addition, Poets House continues its collaboration with public library systems, Poetry in The Branches, a multi-faceted program model to help libraries nationwide create a complete environment for poetry locally (see website for information). Finally, each April Poets House hosts the Poets House Showcase, a comprehensive exhibit of the year's new poetry releases from commercial, university, and independent presses across the country. (**Note: Poets House is not a publisher.**) Copies of new titles become part of the library collection, and comprehensive listings for each of the books are added to Directory of American Poetry Books, a free, searchable online database featuring over 20,000 poetry titles published 1996-2007. "Poets House depends, in part, on tax-deductible contributions of its nationwide members." Additional information available by fax, e-mail, or on website.

QUINCY WRITERS GUILD

(217)885-3327. E-mail: chillebr@adams.net. Established 1989. **Contact:** Carol Hillebrenner, treasurer. Purpose is "to encourage writers to write and, if they wish, get published." Regional organization open to all those who love to write and want mutual support in their passion. Currently has 18 members. Levels of membership/dues: $15/year. Offers "support, encouragement, whatever information we can gather for each other, and special speakers on the writing craft." Meets at Bickford Cottage the first Monday of most months. Sponsors conferences/ workshops. Publishes a newsletter about upcoming meetings and "anything the editor thinks might interest others." E-mail newsletter is free for one year. Additional information available by e-mail.

SCIENCE FICTION POETRY ASSOCIATION

(Specialized: science fiction, fantasy, horror) PO Box 4846, Covina, CA 91723. E-mail: SFPATreasurer@gmail.com. Website: www.sfpoetry.com. Established 1978. **Contact:** Samantha Henderson, treasurer. The Science Fiction Poetry Association was founded "to bring together poets and readers interested in science fiction poetry (poetry with some element of speculation, usually science fiction, fantasy, or horror)." Levels of membership/dues: $21 USD (U.S., Canada, Mexico) for one-year memberships/renewals; $25 USD for overseas. Membership benefits include 6 issues/year of Star*Line (see separate listing in Magazines/Journals), a journal filled with poetry, reviews, articles, and more; one issue of the annual Rhysling Anthology of the best science fiction poetry of the previous year; opportunity to nominate one short poem and one long poem to be printed in the anthology, and to vote for which poems should receive that year's Rhysling award; half-priced advertising on the SFPA website, with greater subject matter leeway than non-members; eligibility to vote for SFPA officers (or run for officer); mailings with the latest news. Additional information available on website.

⊕ SCOTTISH POETRY LIBRARY

5 Crichton's Close, Edinburgh EH8 8DT Scotland. (44)(131)557-2876. Fax: (44)(131)557-8393. E-mail: inquiries@apl.org.uk. Website: www.spl.org.uk. **Contact:** Julie Johnstone, librarian. Director: Robyn Marsack. A reference information source and free lending library; also lends

by post and from its 13 outreach collections. Arranges poetry-writing workshops throughout Scotland, mainly for young people. The library has a web-based catalog available at www.spl. org.uk, which allows searches of all the library's resources, including books, magazines, and audio material--over 30,000 items of Scottish and international poetry. Need not be a member to borrow material; memberships available strictly to support the library's work. Levels of membership/dues: £25 individual; £15 concessionary/low-waged;; £40 organizational. Benefits include semiannual newsletter, annual report, new publications listings, and book offers. The School of Poets is open to anyone; "at meetings, members divide into small groups in which each participatn reads a poem, which is then analyzed and discussed." Meetings normally take place at 7:30 p.m. on the second Tuesday of each month at the library. Also offers a Critical Service in which groups of up to 6 poems, not exceeding 200 lines in all, are given critical comment by members of the School: 15 for each critique (with SAE). Publishes the Scottish Poetry Index, a multi-volume indexing series, photocopied, spiral-bound, that indexes poetry and poetry-related material in selected Scottish literary magazines from 1952 to present; an audio CD of contemporary Scottish poems, The Jewel Box (January 2000); and various anthologies available from www.spl.org.uk. A wide range of poetry events takes place throughout the year. Additional information available by e-mail or on website.

SMALL PUBLISHERS ASSOCIATION OF NORTH AMERICA

(SPAN)1618 W. Colorado Ave., Colorado Springs CO 80904. (719)475-1726. Fax: (719)471-2182. E-mail: info1@spannet.org. Website: www.spannet.org. **Contact:** Scott Flora, executive director. Established 1996. Founded to "advance the image and profits of independent publishers and authors through education and marketing opportunities." Open to "authors, small- to medium-sized publishers, and the vendors who serve them." Currently has 1,300 members. Levels of membership /dues: Regular ($95/year); Associate Vendor ($120/year). Offers marketing ideas, sponsors annual conference. Publishes SPAN Connection, "a 24-page monthly newsletter jam-packed with informative, money-making articles." Available to nonmembers for $8/issue. Additional information available for SASE, by fax, or on website.

TANKA SOCIETY OF AMERICA

1636 Edward's Dr., Point Roberts WA 98281. E-mail: Jemrich@aol.com. Website: www. tankasocietyofamerica.com. Established 2000. **Contact:** Carole MacRury, secretary. The Tanka Society of America, a nonprofit volunteer organization, aims to further the writing, reading, study, and appreciation of tanka poetry in English. Open to anyone interested in tanka. Membership dues for USA, Canada, and International are available on website. Membership offerings include the quarterly Ribbons: Tanka Society of America Journal (see separate listing in Magazines/Journals) and eligibility to submit poems to annual members' anthology. The Tanka Society of American also conducts an annual international tanka competition with cash awards and publication of winning poems. Additional information available by e-mail or on website.

UNIVERSITY OF ARIZONA POETRY CENTER

1508 E. Helen St., P.O. Box 210150, Tucson AZ 85721. (520)626-3765. Fax: (520)621-5566. E-mail: poetry@u.arizona.edu. Website: www.poetrycenter.arizona.edu. **Contact:** Gail Browne, executive director. Established 1960. Open to the public, the University of Arizona Poetry Center is a contemporary poetry archive and a nationally acclaimed poetry collection that includes over 60,000 items. Programs and services include a library with a noncirculating poetry collection and space for small classes; poetry-related meetings and activities; facilities, research support, and referral information about poetry and poets for local and national communities; Reading Series; community creative writing classes and workshops; bilingual Poets-in-Preschools program; high school poet-in-residence; a one-month summer residency offered each year to an emerging writer selected by jury; and poetry awards, readings, and special events for high school, undergraduate, and graduate students. Additional information available for SASE, by fax, e-mail, or on website. "One can become a 'Friend of the Poetry Center' by making an annual contribution."

WASHINGTON POETS ASSOCIATION

Website: www.washingtonpoets.org. Established 1971. **Contact:** president. The Washington Poets Association seeks to "serve and inspire individuals and communities across the state by supporting the creation, presentation, and appreciation of poetry through events, publications, recognition, and education." Regional organization open to poets and fans of poetry. Currently has 380 members. Levels of membership/dues: $20/year. Membership benefits include e-newsletter; discounted admission to events; ability to submit to Cascade Journal (plus one free copy and discounts on the purchase of additional copies); and advance notification of contests, events, readings, and publishing opportunities. Sponsors conferences/workshops and poetry festivals. Also sponsors On the Road poetry workshops for underserved areas in Washington state. Sponsors the Washington Poets Association Annual Poetry Contest (see separate listing in Contests & Awards). Publishes quarterly newsletter, Word! ; available to nonmembers free on Web site. Members and nationally known writers give readings that are open to the public. Sponsors open mic readings for the public "scheduled weekly, monthly, and quarterly at venues across the state." Additional information available on Web site.

WISCONSIN FELLOWSHIP OF POETS

E-mail: nevers@wisc.edu. Website: www.wfop.org. Established 1950. **Contact:** Gillian Nevers, Membership Chair, 2022 Jefferson Street, Madison WI 53711. President: Lester Smith. Statewide organization open to residents and former residents of Wisconsin who are interested in the aims and endeavors of the organization. Currently has 485 members. Levels of membership/ dues: Active ($25); Student ($12.50). Sponsors biannual conferences, workshops, contests and awards. Publishes Wisconsin Poets' Calendar, poems of Wisconsin (resident) poets. Also publishes Museletter, a quarterly newsletter. Members or nationally known writers give readings that are open to the public. Sponsors open mic readings. Additional information available for SASE to WFOP membership chair at the above address, by e-mail, or on website.

WORCESTER COUNTY POETRY ASSOCIATION

1 Ekman St., Worcester MA 01607. (508)797-4770. E-mail: wcpaboard@yahoo.com. Website: http://wcpa.homestead.com. Established 1971. **Contact:** Membership Chair. The Worcester County Poetry Association is "open to all who appreciate poetry and wish to support the vibrant Worcester poetry community." Levels of membership/dues: $30 (Individual); $12 (Student, Senior, or Low Income); $50 (WCPA Friend); $75 (WCPA Patron); $150 (WCPA Benefactor); $250 (Poetry Reading Sponsor); $1,000 (Permanent Endowment). Membership benefits include annual subscription to The Worcester Review (see separate listing in Magazines/Journals); all WCPA mailings, including broadsides, calendars, and The Issue ; and fee-free submission to the WCPA Annual Poetry Contest. Additional information available for SASE, by e-mail, or on website.

ℕ 🌐 WORDS WITHOUT BORDERS

P.O. Box 1658, New York NY 10276.E-mail: wordswithoutborders@gmail.com. Website: www. wordswithoutborders.org. "Words Without Borders opens doors to international exchange through translation, publications, and promotion of the world's best writing. Our ultimate aim is to introduce exciting international writing to the general public--travelers, teachers, students, publishers, and a new generation of eclectic readers-- by presenting international literature not as a static, elite phenomenon, but a portal through which to explore the world. The heart of WWB's work is www.wordswithoutborders.org, its online magazine. Monthly issues feature new selections of contemporary world literature, most of which would never have been accessible to English-speaking readers without WWB." Members and international writers give readings that are open to the public. See Web site for additional information.

☑ THE WORD WORKS

P.O. Box 42164, Washington DC 20015. E-mail: editor@wordworksdc.com. Website: www. wordworksdc.com. Established 1974. **Contact:** Karren L. Alenier, president. Word Works is "a nonprofit literary organization publishing contemporary poetry in single-author editions, usually in collaboration with a visual artist." Levels of membership/dues: $35 (basic), $50 (sustaining). Membership benefits at the basic level include choice of 2 books from The Word Works book list, newsletter, and 20% discount on additional book orders; in addition to these benefits, sustaining members are eligible for on-line critique of several poems (member needs access to an e-mail account). Sponsors an ongoing poetry reading series, educational programs, and the Hilary Tham Capital Collection (publishing mostly poets from metropolitan Washington, DC). Sponsors The Washington Prize and The Jacklyn Potter Young Poets Competition (see separate listings in Contests & Awards). Additional information available on website.

THE WRITER'S CENTER

4508 Walsh St., Bethesda MD 20815. (301)654-8664. Fax: (801)730-6233. E-mail: postmaster@ writer.org. Website: www.writer.org. Established 1976. **Contact:** Gregory Robison, executive director. Voluntary, membership organization open to all skill levels. "The Writer's Center is a nonprofit community of writers supporting each other in the creation and marketing of literary texts." Levels of membership/dues: $40/year individual; $25/year full-time student; $50/year family. Annually conducts hundreds of workshops; hosts literary events, readings, and conferences; publishes Writer's Carousel, a quarterly magazine of articles and writing news for members. Also publishes Poet Lore, America's oldest poetry journal (see separate listing in Magazines/Journals). Additional information available by e-mail or on website.

☑ WRITERS' FEDERATION OF NOVA SCOTIA

1113 Marginal Rd., Halifax NS B3H 4P7 Canada. (902)423-8116. Fax: (902)422-0881. E-mail: talk@writers.ns.ca. Website: www.writers.ns.ca. Established 1975. **Contact:** Jane Buss, executive director. Purpose is "to foster creative writing and the profession of writing in Nova Scotia; to provide advice and assistance to writers at all stages of their careers; and to encourage greater public recognition of Nova Scotian writers and their achievements." Regional organization open to anybody who writes. Currently has 800 members. Levels of membership/dues: $40 CAD annually ($20 CAD students). Offerings include resource library with over 2,500 titles, promotional services, workshop series, annual festivals, manuscript reading service, and contract advice. Sponsors the Atlantic Writing Competition for unpublished works by beginning writers, and the annual Atlantic Poetry Prize for the best book of poetry by an Atlantic Canadian. Publishes Eastword, a bimonthly newsletter containing "a plethora of information on who's doing what; markets and contests; and current writing events and issues." Members and nationally known writers give readings that are open to the public. Additional information available on Web site.

☑ WRITERS GUILD OF ALBERTA

11759 Groat Rd., Edmonton AB T5M 3K6 Canada. (780)422-8174. Fax: (780)422-2663. E-mail:

mail@writersguild.ab.ca. Website: www.writersguild.ab.ca. Established 1980. Founded to "provide a community of writers which exists to support, encourage, and promote writers and writing; to safeguard the freedom to write and read; and to advocate for the well-being of writers." Provincial organization open to emerging and professional writers. Currently has over 1,000 members. Offerings include retreats/conferences; monthly events; bimonthly magazine that includes articles on writing and a market section; weekly electronic bulletin with markets and event listings; and the Stephan G. Stephansson Award for Poetry (Alberta residents only). Additional information available by phone, e-mail, or on website.

THE WRITERS ROOM

740 Broadway, 12th Floor, New York NY 10003. (212)254-6995. Fax: (212)533-6059. E-mail: writersroom@writersroom.org. Website: www.writersroom.org. Established 1978. Provides a "home away from home" for any writer who needs space to work. Open 24 hours a day, 7 days a week, **for members only**. Currently has about 350 members. Emerging and established writers may apply. Levels of membership/dues: vary from $400 to $600/half year, plus one-time initiation fee of $75. Large loft provides desk space, Internet access, storage, and more. Call for application or download from website.

⚃ THE WRITERS' UNION OF CANADA

(Specialized: Canadian citizens or landed immigrants only)90 Richmond St. East, Suite 200, Toronto ON M5C 1P1 Canada. (416)703-8982. Fax: (416)504-9090. E-mail: info@writersunion. ca. Website: www.writersunion.ca. Established 1973. Dedicated to advancing the status of Canadian writers by protecting the rights of published authors, defending the freedom to write and publish, and serving its members. National organization open to poets who have had a trade book published by a commercial or university press; must be a Canadian citizen or landed immigrant. Currently has over 1,600 members. Levels of membership/dues: $185 CAD/year. Offerings include contact with peers, contract advice/negotiation, grievance support, and electronic communication. Sponsors conferences/workshops. Sponsors Annual General Meeting, usually held in May, where members debate and determine Union policy, elect representatives, attend workshops, socialize, and renew friendships with their colleagues from across the country. Publishes The Writers' Union of Canada Newsletter 4 times/year. Regional reps meet with members when possible. For writers not eligible for membership, the Union offers, for a fee, publications on publishing, contracts, and more; a Manuscript Evaluation Service for any level writer; Contract Services, including a Self-Help Package; and 3 annual writing competitions for developing writers. Additional information available for SASE (or SAE and IRC), by fax, e-mail, or on website.

YEATS SOCIETY OF NEW YORK, W. B.

National Arts Club, 15 Gramercy Park S, New York NY 10003. Website: www.YeatsSociety.org. Established 1990. **Contact:** Andrew McGowan, president. Founded "to promote the legacy of Irish poet and Nobel Laureate William Butler Yeats through an annual program of lectures, readings, poetry competition, and special events." National organization open to anyone. Currently has 450 members. Levels of membership/dues: $25/year; $15/year students. Sponsors The W.B. Yeats Society Annual Poetry Competition (see separate listing in Contests & Awards). Also sponsors conferences/workshops. Each April, presents an all-day Saturday program, "A Taste of Yeats Summer School in Ireland." Nationally known writers give readings that are open to the public. Members meet approximately monthly, September to June. Additional information available on website.

Resources

ADDITIONAL ORGANIZATIONS

Resources

RESOURCES

Poets in Education

Whether known as PITS (Poets in the Schools), WITS (Writers in the Schools), or similar names, programs exist nationwide that coordinate residencies, classroom visits and other opportunities for experienced poets to share their craft with students. Many state arts agencies include such "arts in education" programs in their activities (see Grants on page 424 for contact information). Another good source is the National Assembly of State Arts Agencies (see below), which offers an online directory of contact names and addresses for arts education programs state-by-state. The following list is a mere sampling of programs and organizations that link poets with schools. Contact them for information about their requirements (some may insist poets have a strong publication history, others may prefer classroom experience) or check their Web sites where available.

The Academy of American Poets, 584 Broadway, Suite 604, New York NY 10012-5243. (212)274-0343. E-mail: academy@poets.org. Web site: www.poets.org (includes links to state arts in education programs).

Arkansas Writers in the Schools, WITS Director, 333 Kimpel Hall, University of Arkansas, Fayetteville AR 72701. (479)575-5991. E-mail: wits@cavern.uark.edu. Web site: www. uark.edu/ ~ wits.

California Poets in the Schools, 1333 Balboa St. #3, San Francisco CA 94118. (415)221-4201. E-mail: info@cpits.org. Web site: www.cpits.org.

e-poets.network, a collective online cultural center that promotes education through videoconferencing (i.e., "distance learning"); also includes the *Voces y Lugares* project. Web site: http://learning.e-poets.net (includes online contact form).

Idaho Writers in the Schools, Log Cabin Literary Center, 801 S. Capitol Blvd., Boise ID 83702. (208)331-8000. E-mail: info@thecabinidaho.org. Web site: www.thecabinidaho. org.

Indiana Writers in the Schools, University of Evansville, Dept. of English, 1800 Lincoln Ave., Evansville IN 47722. (812)488-2962. E-mail: rg37@evansville.edu. Web site: http://english.evansville.edu/WritersintheSchools.htm.

Michigan Creative Writers in the Schools, ArtServe Michigan, 17515 W. Nine Mile Rd., Suite 1025, Southfield MI 48075. (248)557-8288 **OR** 1310 Turner St., Suite B, Lansing MI 48906. (517)371-1720 (toll free at (800)203-9633). E-mail: online form. Web site: www. artservemichigan.org.

National Assembly of State Arts Agencies, 1029 Vermont Ave. NW, 2nd Floor, Washington DC 20005. (202)347-6352. E-mail: nasaa@nasaa-arts.org. Web site: www.nasaa-arts.org.

National Association of Writers in Education (NAWE), P.O. Box 1, Sheriff Hutton, York YO60 7YU England. (44)(1653)618429. Web site: www.nawe.co.uk.

Oregon Writers in the Schools, Literary Arts, 224 NW 13th Ave., Suite 306, Portland OR 97209. (503)227-2583. E-mail: john@literary-arts.org. Web site: www.literary-arts.org/wits.

PEN in the Classroom (PITC), Pen Center USA, Þco Antioch University, 400 Corporate Pointe, Culver City CA 90230. (310)862-1555. E-mail: pitc@penusa.org. Web site: www.penusa.org/go/classroom.

"Pick-a-Poet," The Humanities Project, Arlington Public Schools, 1439 N. Quincy St., Arlington VA 22207. (703)228-6299. E-mail: online form. Web site: www.humanitiesproject.org.

Potato Hill Poetry, 6 Pleasant St., Suite 2, South Natick MA 01760. (888)5-POETRY. E-mail: info@potatohill.com. Web site: www.potatohill.com (includes online contact form).

Seattle Writers in the Schools (WITS), Seattle Arts & Lectures, 105 S. Main St., Suite 201, Seattle WA 98104. (206)621-2230. Web site: www.lectures.org/wits.html.

Teachers & Writers Collaborative, 520 Eighth Ave., Suite 2020, New York NY 10018. (212)691-6590 or (888)BOOKS-TW (book orders). E-mail: info@twc.org. Web site: www.twc.org. "A catalog of T&W books is available online, or call toll-free to request a print copy.

Texas Writers in the Schools, 1523 W. Main, Houston TX 77006. (713)523-3877. E-mail: mail@witshouston.org. Web site: www.writersintheschools.org.

Writers & Artists in the Schools (WAITS), COMPAS, Landmark Center, Suite 304, 75 Fifth St. West, St. Paul MN 55102-1496. (651)292-3254. E-mail: daniel@compas.org. Web site: www.compas.org.

Youth Voices in Ink, Badgerdog Literary Publishing, Inc., P.O. Box 301209, Austin TX 78703-0021. (512)538-1305. E-mail: info@badgerdog.org. Web site: www.badgerdog.org.

Resources

Glossary of Listing Terms

A3, A4, A5. Metric equivalents of 11¾ × 16½, 8¼ × 11¾, and 5⅞ × 8¼ respectively.

Acknowledgments page. A page in a poetry book or chapbook that lists the publications where the poems in the collection were originally published; may be presented as part of the copyright page or as a separate page on its own.

Anthology. A collection of selected writings by various authors.

Attachment. A computer file electronically "attached" to an e-mail message.

AUD. Abbreviation for Australian Dollar.

b&w. Black & white (photo or illustration).

Bio. A short biographical statement often requested with a submission.

CAD. Abbreviation for Canadian Dollar.

Camera-ready. Poems ready for copy camera platemaking; camera-ready poems usually appear in print exactly as submitted.

Chapbook. A small book of about 24-50 pages.Circulation. The number of subscribers to a magazine/journal.

CLMP. Council of Literary Magazines and Presses; service organization for independent publishers of fiction, poetry, and prose.

Contributor's copy. Copy of book or magazine containing a poet's work, sometimes given as payment.

Cover letter. Brief introductory letter accompanying a poetry submission.

Coverstock. Heavier paper used as the cover for a publication.

Digest-sized. About 5½ × 8½, the size of a folded sheet of conventional printer paper.

Download. To "copy" a file, such as a registration form, from a Web site.

Electronic magazine. See *online magazine*.E-mail. Mail sent electronically using computer and modem or similar means.

Euro. Currency unit for the 27 member countries of the European Union; designated by EUR or the INSERT EURO symbol.

FAQ. Frequently Asked Questions.

Font. The style/design of type used in a publication; typeface.

Galleys. First typeset version of a poem, magazine, or book/chapbook.

GLBT. Gay/lesbian/bisexual/transgender (as in "GLBT themes").

Honorarium. A token payment for published work.Internet. A worldwide network of computers offering access to a variety of electronic resources.

IRC. International Reply Coupon; a publisher can exchange IRCs for postage to return a manuscript to another country.

JPEG. Short for *Joint Photographic Experts Group*; an image compression format that allows digital images to be stored in relatively small files for electronic mailing and viewing on the Internet.

Magazine-sized. About 8½ × 11, the size of an unfolded sheet of conventional printer paper.

ms. Manuscript.

mss. Manuscripts.

Multi-book review. Several books by the same author or by several authors reviewed in one piece.

Offset-printed. Printing method in which ink is transferred from an image-bearing plate to a "blanket" and then from blanket to paper.

Online magazine. Publication circulated through the Internet or e-mail.

p&h. Postage & handling.

p&p. Postage & packing.

"Pays in copies." See *contributor's copy*.

PDF. Short for *Portable Document Format*, developed by Adobe Systems, that captures all elements of a printed document as an electronic image, allowing it to be sent by e-mail, viewed online, and printed in its original format.

Perfect-bound. Publication with glued, flat spine; also called "flat-spined."

POD. See *print-on-demand*.

Press run. The total number of copies of a publication printed at one time.

Previously published. Work that has appeared before in print, in any form, for public consumption.

Print-on-demand. Publishing method that allows copies of books to be published as they're requested, rather than all at once in a single press run.

Publishing credits. A poet's magazine publications and book/chapbook titles.

Query letter. Letter written to an editor to raise interest in a proposed project.

Reading fee. A monetary amount charged by an editor or publisher to consider a poetry submission without any obligation to accept the work.

Rich Text Format. Carries the.rtf filename extension. A file format that allows an exchange of text files between different word processor operating systems with most of the formatting preserved.

Rights. A poet's legal property interest in his/her literary work; an editor or publisher may acquire certain rights from the poet to reproduce that work.

ROW. "Rest of world."

Royalties. A percentage of the retail price paid to the author for each copy of a book sold.

Saddle-stapled. A publication folded, then stapled along that fold; also called "saddle-stitched."

SAE. Self-addressed envelope.

SASE. Self-addressed, stamped envelope.

SASP. Self-addressed, stamped postcard.Simultaneous submission. Submission of the same manuscript to more than one publisher at the same time.

Subsidy press. Publisher who requires the poet to pay all costs, including typesetting, production, and printing; sometimes called a "vanity publisher."

Tabloid-sized. 11 × 15 or larger, the size of an ordinary newspaper folded and turned sideways.

Text file. A file containing only textual characters (i.e., no graphics or special formats).

Unsolicited manuscript. A manuscript an editor did not ask specifically to receive.

URL. Stands for "Uniform Resource Locator," the address of an Internet resource (i.e., file).

USD. Abbreviation for United States Dollar.Web site. A specific address on the Internet that provides access to a set of documents (or "pages").

Glossary of Poetry Terms

This glossary is provided as a quick-reference only, briefly covering poetic styles and terms that may turn up in articles and listings in *Poet's Market*. For a full understanding of the terms, forms, and styles listed here, as well as common literary terms not included, consult a solid textbook or handbook, such as John Drury's *The Poetry Dictionary* (Writer's Digest Books). (Ask your librarian or bookseller for recommendations).

Abstract poem: conveys emotion through sound, textures, and rhythm and rhyme rather than through the meanings of words.

Acrostic: initial letters of each line, read downward, form a word, phrase, or sentence.

Alliteration: close repetition of consonant sounds, especially initial consonant sounds. (Also known as *consonance*.)

Alphabet poem: arranges lines alphabetically according to initial letter.

American cinquain: derived from Japanese haiku and tanka by Adelaide Crapsey; counted syllabic poem of 5 lines of 2-4-6-8-2 syllables, frequently in iambic feet.

Anapest: foot consisting of 2 unstressed syllables followed by a stress (- - ´).

Assonance: close repetition of vowel sounds. Avant-garde: work at the forefront--cutting edge, unconventional, risk-taking.

Ballad: narrative poem often in ballad stanza (4-line stanza with 4 stresses in lines 1 and 3, 3 stresses in lines 2 and 4, which also rhyme).

Ballade: 3 stanzas rhymed *ababbcbC* (*C* indicates a refrain) with envoi rhymed *bcbC*.

Beat poetry: anti-academic school of poetry born in '50s San Francisco; fast-paced free verse resembling jazz.

Blank verse: unrhymed iambic pentameter.

Caesura: a deliberate rhetorical, grammatical, or rhythmic pause, break, cut, turn, division, or pivot in poetry.

Chant: poem in which one or more lines are repeated over and over.

Cinquain: any 5-line poem or stanza; also called "quintain" or "quintet." (See also *American cinquain*.)

Concrete poetry: see *emblematic poem*.

Confessional poetry: work that uses personal and private details from the poet's own life.

Consonance: see *alliteration*.

Couplet: stanza of 2 lines; pair of rhymed lines.

Dactyl: foot consisting of a stress followed by 2 unstressed syllables (´ - -).

Didactic poetry: poetry written with the intention to instruct.

Eclectic: open to a variety of poetic styles (as in "eclectic taste").

Ekphrastic poem: verbally presents something originally represented in visual art, though more than mere description.

Elegy: lament in verse for someone who has died, or a reflection on the tragic nature of life.

Emblematic poem: words or letters arranged to imitate a shape, often the subject of the poem.

Enjambment: continuation of sense and rhythmic movement from one line to the next; also called a "run-on" line.

Envoi: a brief ending (usually to a ballade or sestina) no more than 4 lines long; summary.

Epic poetry: long narrative poem telling a story central to a society, culture, or nation.

Epigram: short, witty, satirical poem or saying written to be remembered easily, like a punchline.

Epigraph: a short verse, note, or quotation that appears at the beginning of a poem or section; usually presents an idea or theme on which the poem elaborates, or contributes background information not reflected in the poem itself.

Epitaph: brief verse commemorating a person/group of people who died.

Experimental poetry: work that challenges conventional ideas of poetry by exploring new techniques, form, language, and visual presentation.

Fibs: short form based on the mathematical progression known as the Fibonacci sequence; syllable counts for each line are 1/1/2/3/5/8/13 (count for each line is derived by adding the counts for the previous two lines).

Flarf: a malleable term that may refer to 1) poetic and creative text pieces by the Flarflist Collective; any poetry created from search engine (such as Google) results; any intentionally bad, zany, or trivial poetry.

Foot: unit of measure in a metrical line of poetry.Found poem: text lifted from a non-poetic source such as an ad and presented as a poem.

Free verse: unmetrical verse (lines not counted for accents, syllables, etc.).

Ghazal: Persian poetic form of 5-15 unconnected, independent couplets; associative jumps may be made from couplet to couplet.

Greeting card poetry: resembles verses in greeting cards; sing-song meter and rhyme.

Haibun: originally, a Japanese form in which elliptical, often autobiographical prose is interspersed with haiku.

Haikai no renga: see *renku*.

Hay(na)ky: a 3-line form, with 1 word in line 1, 2 words in line 2, and 3 words in line 3.

Haiku: originally, a Japanese form of a single vertical line with 17 sound symbols in a 5-7-5 pattern. In English, typically a 3-line poem with fewer than 17 syllables in no set pattern, but exhibiting a 2-part juxtapositional structure, seasonal reference, imagistic immediacy, and a moment of keen perception of nature or human nature. The term is both singular and plural.

Hokku: the starting verse of a renga or renku, in 5, 7, and then 5 sound symbols in Japanese; or in three lines, usually totaling fewer than 17 syllables, in English; the precursor for what is now called haiku. (See also *haiku*).

Iamb: foot consisting of an unstressed syllable followed by a stress (- ´).Iambic pentameter: consists of 5 iambic feet per line.

Imagist poetry: short, free verse lines that present images without comment or explanation; strongly influenced by haiku and other Oriental forms.

Kyrielle: French form; 4-line stanza with 8-syllable lines, the final line a refrain.

Language poetry: attempts to detach words from traditional meanings to produce something new and unprecedented.Limerick: 5-line stanza rhyming *aabba*; pattern of stresses/line is traditionally 3-3-2-2-3; often bawdy or scatalogical.

Line: basic compositional unit of a poem; measured in feet if metrical.

Linked poetry: written through the collaboration of 2 or more poets creating a single poetic work.Long poem: exceeds length and scope of short lyric or narrative poem; defined arbitrarily, often as more than 2 pages or 100 lines.

Lyric poetry: expresses personal emotion; music predominates over narrative or drama.

Metaphor: 2 different things are likened by identifying one as the other (A = B).Meter: the rhythmic measure of a line.

Minute: a 12-line poem consisting of 60 syllables, with a syllabic line count of 8,4,4,4,8,4,4,4, 8,4,4,4; often consists of rhyming couplets.

Modernist poetry: work of the early 20th century literary movement that sought to break with the past, rejecting outmoded literary traditions, diction, and form while encouraging innovation and reinvention.

Narrative poetry: poem that tells a story.

New Formalism: contemporary literary movement to revive formal verse.

Nonsense verse: playful, with language and/or logic that defies ordinary understanding.

Octave: stanza of 8 lines.

Ode: a songlike, or lyric, poem; can be passionate, rhapsodic, and mystical, or a formal address to a person on a public or state occasion.

Pantoum: Malayan poetic form of any length; consists of 4-line stanzas, with lines 2 and 4 of one quatrain repeated as lines 1 and 3 of the next; final stanza reverses lines 1 and 3 of the previous quatrain and uses them as lines 2 and 4; traditionally each stanza rhymes *abab*.Petrarchan sonnet: octave rhymes *abbaabba*; sestet may rhyme *cdcdcd*, *cdedce*, *ccdccd*, *cddcdd*, *edecde*, or *cddcee*.

Prose poem: brief prose work with intensity, condensed language, poetic devices, and other poetic elements.

Quatrain: stanza of 4 lines.

Refrain: a repeated line within a poem, similar to the chorus of a song.

Regional poetry: work set in a particular locale, imbued with the look, feel, and culture of that place.

Renga: originally, a Japanese collaborative form in which 2 or more poets alternate writing 3 lines, then 2 lines for a set number of verses (such as 12, 18, 36, 100, and 1,000). There are specific rules for seasonal progression, placement of moon and flower verses, and other requirements. (See also *linked poetry*.)

Rengay: an American collaborative 6-verse, thematic linked poetry form, with 3-line and 2-line verses in the following set pattern for 2 or 3 writers (letters represent poets, numbers indicate the lines in each verse): A3-B2-A3-B3-A2-B3 or A3-B2-C3-A2-B3-C2. All verses, unlike renga or renku, must develop at least one common theme.

Renku: the modern term for renga, and a more popular version of the traditionally more aristocratic renga. (See also *linked poetry*.)

Rhyme: words that sound alike, especially words that end in the same sound.

Rhythm: the beat and movement of language (rise and fall, repetition and variation, change of pitch, mix of syllables, melody of words).

Rondeau: French form of usually 15 lines in 3 parts, rhyming *aabba aabR aabbaR* (*R* indicates a refrain repeating the first word or phrase of the opening line).

Senryu: originally, a Japanese form, like haiku in form, but chiefly humorous, satirical, or ironic, and typically aimed at human foibles. (See also *haiku* and *zappai*.)

Sequence: a group or progression of poems, often numbered as a series.

Sestet: stanza of 6 lines.

Sestina: fixed form of 39 lines (6 unrhymed stanzas of 6 lines each, then an ending 3-line stanza), each stanza repeating the same 6 non-rhyming end-words in a different order; all 6 end-words appear in the final 3-line stanza.

Shakespearean sonnet: rhymes *abab cdcd efef gg*.Sijo: originally a Korean narrative or thematic lyric form. The first line introduces a situation or problem that is countered or developed in line 2, and concluded with a twist in line 3. Lines average 14-16 syllables in length.

Simile: comparison that uses a linking word (*like, as, such as, how*) to clarify the similarities.

Sonnet: 14-line poem (traditionally an octave and sestet) rhymed in iambic pentameter; often presents an argument but may also present a description, story, or meditation.Spondee: foot consisting of 2 stressed syllables (´ ´).

Stanza: group of lines making up a single unit; like a paragraph in prose.

Strophe: often used to mean "stanza"; also a stanza of irregular line lengths.

Surrealistic poetry: of the artistic movement stressing the importance of dreams and the subconscious, nonrational thought, free associations, and startling imagery/juxtapositions.

Tanka: originally, a Japanese form in one or 2 vertical lines with 31 sound symbols in a 5-7-5-7-7 pattern. In English, typically a 5-line lyrical poem with fewer than 31 syllables in no set syllable pattern, but exhibiting a caesura, turn, or pivot, and often more emotional and conversational than haiku.

Tercet: stanza or poem of 3 lines.

Terza rima: series of 3-line stanzas with interwoven rhyme scheme (*aba, bcb, cdc...*).

Trochee: foot consisting of a stress followed by an unstressed syllable (´ -).

Villanelle: French form of 19 lines (5 tercets and a quatrain); line 1 serves as one refrain (repeated in lines 6, 12, 18), line 3 as a second refrain (repeated in lines 9, 15, 19); traditionally, refrains rhyme with each other and with the opening line of each stanza.

Visual poem: see *emblematic poem*.

Waka: literally, "Japanese poem," the precursor for what is now called tanka. (See also *tanka*.)

War poetry: poems written about warfare and military life; often written by past and current soldiers; may glorify war, recount exploits, or demonstrate the horrors of war.

Zappai: originally Japanese; an unliterary, often superficial witticism masquerading as haiku or senryu; formal term for joke haiku or other pseudo-haiko.

Zeugma: a figure of speech in which a single word (or, occasionally, a phrase) is related in one way to words that precede it, and in another way to words that follow it.

Chapbook Publishers Index

A poetry chapbook is a slim volume of 24-50 pages (although chapbook lengths can vary; some are even published as inserts in magazines). Many publishers and journals solicit chapbook manuscripts through competitions. Read listings carefully, check Web sites where available, and request guidelines before submitting. See Frequently Asked Questions on page xx for further information about chapbooks and submission formats.

Special Indexes

Book Publishers Index

The following are magazines and publishers that consider full-length book manuscripts (over 50 pages, often much longer). See Frequently Asked Questions on page xx for further information about book manuscript submission.

Special Indexes

Openness to Submissions Index

In this section, all magazines, publishers, and contests/awards with primary listings in *Poet's Market* are categorized according to their openness to submissions (as indicated by the symbols that appear at the beginning of each listing). Note that some markets are listed in more than one category.

☐WELCOMES SUBMISSIONS FROM BEGINNING POETS

☑OPEN TO BEGINNERS AND SKILLED POETS

☑PREFERS SKILLED AND EXPERIENCED POETS

◎ SPECIALIZED FOCUS

Geographical Index

This section offers a breakdown of U.S. publishers and conferences/workshops arranged alphabetically by state or territory, followed by listings for Canada, Australia, France, Ireland, Japan, the United Kingdom, and other countries–a real help when trying to locate publishers in your region as well as conferences and workshops convenient to your area.

ALABAMA
Conferences, Workshops & Festivals
Montevallo Literary Festival 458

Magazines/Journals
Black Warrior Review 99
Poem 240
Southern Humanities Review 286

ALASKA
Book/Chapbook Publishers
Midnight Sun Poetry Chapbook Contest 406

Magazines/Journals
Alaska Quarterly Review 70
Permafrost 235

ARIZONA
Book/Chapbook Publishers
Riverstone Poetry Chapbook Award 423

Magazines/Journals
Alligator Juniper's National Writing Contest 373
Heart 165
Roadrunner Haiku Journal 270

ARKANSAS
Magazines/Journals
Arkansas Review 80
Foliate Oak Online, The 151
Poesia 242
Slant 280
Storyteller, The 296

AUSTRALIA
Book/Chapbook Publishers
Ginninderra Press 346

Magazines/Journals
FreeXpresSion 154
Galaxy Press 346
SpeedPoets Zine 289

NORTH CAROLINA
Book/Chapbook Publishers

Subject Index

This index focuses on markets indicating a specialized area of interest, whether regional, poetic style, or specific topic (these markets show a ◎ symbol at the beginning of their listings). It also includes markets we felt offered special opportunities in certain subject areas. Subject categories are listed alphabetically, with additional subcategories indicated under the "Specialized" heading (in parentheses behind the market's name). Pease Note: 1) This index only partially reflects the total markets in this book; many do not identify themselves as having specialized interests and so are not included here. 2) Many specialized markets have more than one area of interest and will be found under multiple categories. 3) When a market appears under a heading in this index, it does not necessarily mean it considers only poetry associated with that subject, poetry only from that region, etc. It's still best to read all listings carefully as part of a thorough marketing plan.

Bilingual/Foreign Language

Buddhism

Christian

Form/Style Asian

Gay/Lesbian/Bisexual/ Transgendered

Poetry by Children

Poetry by Teens

Poetry for Children

Poetry for Teens

Religious Poetry

Science Fiction

Senior Citizen/Aging

Social Issues

Specialized various

Spirituality/Inspirational

Sports/Recreation

Students

Themes

Translations

Women various

Working Class Issues

Writing

General Index

B

Special Indexes

N

Special Indexes

X

Y

Z